www.wadsworth.com

www.wadsworth.com is the World Wide Web site for Thomson Wadsworth and is your direct source to dozens of online resources.

At *www.wadsworth.com* you can find out about supplements, demonstration software, and student resources. You can also send e-mail to many of our authors and preview new publications and exciting new technologies.

www.wadsworth.com
Changing the way the world learns®

RACE, CLASS, & GENDER

AN ANTHOLOGY SIXTH EDITION

Margaret L. Andersen
University of Delaware

Patricia Hill Collins
University of Maryland

THOMSON
WADSWORTH

Australia • Brazil • Canada • Mexico • Singapore
Spain • United Kingdom • United States

THOMSON
™
WADSWORTH

Race, Class, and Gender, Sixth Edition
Margaret L. Andersen and Patricia Hill Collins

Senior Acquisitions Editor, Sociology:
Robert Jucha
Assistant Editor: Kristin Marrs
Editorial Assistant: Katia Krukowski
Technology Project Manager: Dee Dee Zobian
Marketing Manager: Michelle Williams
Marketing Assistant: Jaren Boland
Marketing Communications Manager:
Linda Yip
Project Manager, Editorial Production:
Cheri Palmer
Creative Director: Rob Hugel

Print Buyer: Judy Inouye
Permissions Editor: Roberta Broyer
Production Service: Dusty Friedman, The Book Company
Copy Editor: Jane E. Loftus
Cover Designer: Yvo Riezebos
Cover Image: Copyright © Jones Collection at the Museum of Delaware/ Alvin Smith
Cover Printer: Phoenix Color Corp
Compositor: Interactive Composition Corporation
Printer: Courier Corporation/Stoughton

The cover art, "Untitled" by Alvin Smith (1985), is part of the Paul Jones Collection of African-American Art at the University of Delaware—a collection of over 1500 pieces of art. You can get more information about the Jones Collection at **www.museums.udel.edu/jones**.

Library of Congress Control Number: 2006922153

ISBN 0-495-00689-0

Thomson Higher Education
10 Davis Drive
Belmont, CA 94002-3098
USA

For more information about our products, contact us at:
Thomson Learning Academic Resource Center
1-800-423-0563

For permission to use material from this text, or product, submit a request online at
http://www.thomsonrights.com.

Any additional questions about permissions can be submitted by e-mail to
thomsonrights@thomson.com.

CONTENTS

PREFACE   xi

ABOUT THE EDITORS   xix

ABOUT THE CONTRIBUTORS   xxi

I WHY RACE, CLASS, AND GENDER STILL MATTER   1
Margaret L. Andersen and Patricia Hill Collins

1 *Missing People and Others: Joining Together
   to Expand the Circle*   17
   Arturo Madrid

2 *La Güera*   22
   Cherríe Moraga

3 *Oppression*   29
   Marilyn Frye

4 *A Different Mirror*   32
   Ronald T. Takaki

5 *From a Native Daughter*   45
   Haunani-Kay Trask

6 *Age, Race, Class, and Sex: Women
   Redefining Difference*   52
   Audre Lorde

Suggested Readings for Part I   60

InfoTrac College Edition: Search Terms   60

InfoTrac College Edition: Bonus Reading   60

Companion Website   60

II SYSTEMS OF POWER AND INEQUALITY   61
Margaret L. Andersen and Patricia Hill Collins

RACE AND RACISM   91

7   *Racism without "Racists"*   91
Eduardo Bonilla-Silva

8   *White Privilege: Unpacking the Invisible Knapsack*   98
Peggy McIntosh

9   *Of Race and Risk*   103
Patricia J. Williams

10   *Seeing More than Black and White*   105
Elizabeth Martinez

11   *What White Supremacists Taught a Jewish Scholar
about Identity*   111
Abby L. Ferber

CLASS AND INEQUALITY   116

12   *Growing Gulf between Rich and Rest of Us*   116
Holly Sklar

13   *Tired of Playing Monopoly?*   118
Donna Langston

14   *The Hidden Cost of Being African American*   127
Thomas M. Shapiro

15   *Black Picket Fences: Privilege and Peril among
the Black Middle Class*   136
Mary Pattillo-McCoy

16   *Broken Levees, Unbroken Barriers*   143
Jason De Parle

GENDER AND SEXISM   147

17   *Sex and Gender through the Prism of Difference*   147
Maxine Baca Zinn, Pierrette Hondagneu-Sotelo, and
Michael Messner

18   *Ideological Racism and Cultural Resistance:
Constructing Our Own Images*   156
Yen Le Espiritu

19   *A White Woman of Color*   166
Julia Álvarez

20 *Masculinities and Athletic Careers*   172
    Michael Messner

21 *Toward a Theory of Disability and Gender*   185
    Thomas J. Gerschick

ETHNICITY AND NATIONALITY   190

22 *Is This a White Country, or What?*   190
    Lillian Rubin

23 *Optional Ethnicities: For Whites Only?*   198
    Mary C. Waters

24 *Salsa and Ketchup: Transnational Migrants Straddle Two Worlds* 207
    Peggy Levitt

25 *"Mexicanness" in New York: Migrants Seek New
    Place in Old Racial Order*   214
    Robert Smith

26 *Migration and Vietnamese American Women:
    Remaking Ethnicity*   220
    Nazli Kibria

SEXUALITY AND HETEROSEXISM   228

27 *"You Talkin' to Me?"*   228
    Jean Kilbourne

28 *Where Has Gay Liberation Gone?: An Interview with
    Barbara Smith*   234
    Amy Gluckman and Betsy Reed

29 *Globalizing Sex Workers' Rights*   238
    Kamala Kempadoo

30 *Black Sexuality: The Taboo Subject*   247
    Cornel West

31 *The Invention of Heterosexuality*   252
    Jonathan Ned Katz

Suggested Readings for Part II   265

InfoTrac College Edition: Search Terms   265

InfoTrac College Edition: Bonus Reading   265

Companion Website   265

III THE STRUCTURE OF SOCIAL INSTITUTIONS 267
Margaret L. Andersen and Patricia Hill Collins

WORK AND ECONOMIC TRANSFORMATION 283

32 *Race, Class, Gender, and Women's Works* 283
Teresa Amott and Julie Matthaei

33 *The Indignities of Unemployment* 292
Kenneth W. Brown

34 *"Soft" Skills and Race* 294
Philip Moss and Chris Tilly

35 *The Invisible Poor* 303
Katherine S. Newman

36 *Doméstica* 312
Pierrette Hondagneu-Sotelo

FAMILIES 321

37 *Our Mothers' Grief: Racial-Ethnic Women and the Maintenance of Families* 321
Bonnie Thornton Dill

38 *Navigating Interracial Borders: Black-White Couples and Their Social Worlds* 335
Erica Chito Childs

39 *Straight Is to Gay As Family Is to No Family* 343
Kath Weston

40 *Unequal Childhoods* 348
Annette Lareau

41 *Chappals and Gym Shorts: An Indian Muslim Woman in the Land of Oz* 358
Almas Sayeed

MEDIA AND CULTURE 365

42 *Racist Stereotyping in the English Language* 365
Robert B. Moore

43 *Crimes against Humanity* 376
Ward Churchill

44 *Media Magic: Making Class Invisible* 384
Gregory Mantsios

45 *The Myth of the Latin Woman: I Just Met a Girl Named María* 393
Judith Ortiz Cofer

46 *Gladiators, Gazelles, and Groupies: Basketball
     Love and Loathing*   398
     Julianne Malveaux

HEALTH AND SOCIAL WELFARE   404

47 *Can Education Eliminate Race, Class, and
     Gender Inequality?*   404
     Roslyn Arlin Mickelson and Stephen Samuel Smith

48 *Welfare Reform, Family Hardship, and Women of Color*   413
     Linda Burnham

49 *Aid to Dependent Corporations: Exposing Federal
     Handouts to the Wealthy*   422
     Chuck Collins

50 *Race, Poverty and Disability: Three Strikes and
     You're Out! or Are You?*   426
     Pamela Block, Fabricio E. Balcazar, and Christopher B. Keys

51 *Just Choices: Women of Color, Reproductive
     Health, and Human Rights*   433
     Loretta J. Ross, Sarah L. Brownlee, Dazon Dixon Diallo,
     Luz Rodriquez, and SisterSong Women of Color
     Reproductive Health Project

STATE INSTITUTIONS AND VIOLENCE   442

52 *The First Americans: American Indians*   442
     C. Matthew Snipp

53 *Policing the National Body: Sex, Race, and
     Criminalization*   450
     Jael Silliman

54 *Military Mirrors a Working-Class America*   459
     David M. Halbfinger and Steven A. Holmes

55 *Rape, Racism, and the Law*   468
     Jennifer Wriggins

56 *How Safe Is America?*   475
     Desiree Taylor

Suggested Readings for Part III   479

InfoTrac College Edition: Search Terms   479

InfoTrac College Edition: Bonus Reading   479

Companion Website   480

IV SOCIAL CHANGE AND SITES OF CHANGE   481

Margaret L. Andersen and Patricia Hill Collins

SITES OF CHANGE   493

57 *The Starbucks Paradox*   493
Kim Fellner

58 *Interrupting Historical Patterns: Bridging Race and Gender Gaps between Senior White Men and Other Organizational Groups*   499
Nancie Zane

59 *Women of Color on the Front Line*   511
Celene Krauss

60 *"Whosoever" Is Welcome Here: An Interview with Reverend Edwin C. Sanders II*   522
Gary David Comstock

61 *Silent Covenants*   530
Derrick Bell

PROCESSES OF CHANGE   535

62 *How the New Working Class Can Transform Urban America*   535
Robin D. G. Kelley

63 *From the Ground Up*   543
Charon Asetoyer

64 *Manifesta*   547
Jennifer Baumgardner and Amy Richards

65 *What Does an Ally Do?*   550
Paul Kivel

66 *Can I Get a Witness?: Testimony from a Hip Hop Feminist*   557
Shani Jamila

Suggested Readings for Part IV   565

InfoTrac College Edition: Search Terms   565

InfoTrac College Edition: Bonus Reading   565

Companion Website   566

INDEX   567

Race, Class, and Gender is an anthology that introduces students to how race, class, and gender shape the experiences of diverse groups in the United States. We want the book to help students see how the lives of different groups develop in the context of their race, class, and gender location in society. Central to the book is the idea that race, class, and gender are interconnected. As a result, the particular configuration of these factors in a given life is critical to understanding a person's or group's experience.

Since the publication of the first edition of this book, the study of race, class, and gender has become much more present in people's thinking and teaching. Yet, as our introductory essay will argue, not all of the work on race, class, and gender is centered in the intersectional framework that is central to this book. Often, people continue to treat one or the other of these social factors in isolation. Many studies of race, class, and gender also treat these factors as if they are equivalent. And, with the growth of race, class, and gender studies, many have added other social factors, such as sexuality, nationality, or disability—to name a few—to the list of social differences that are sources of oppression and inequality. We are glad to see such a profusion of work, although we continue to think that a framework that emphasizes the structural intersections of race, class, and gender is critical.

We see our anthology as more than a collection of readings—it is strongly centered in an analytical framework about the interconnections among race, class, and gender. Thus, in this edition we have expanded the analysis of race, class, and gender to further develop the framework of intersectionality, or as Patricia Hill Collins has labeled it, the *matrix of domination*. We have done this by re-organizing the book in a way to feature this framework, and we have re-written the introductory essays in a way that better distinguishes what we mean by this from other models of studying "difference." (See especially the introduction to Part I in this regard.) You will quickly see that we have re-organized the book from five into four major parts and have done so both to expand our inclusion of the topics of ethnicity and sexuality in Part II and to avoid having the section of social change seem tacked on at the very end.

The four major parts of the book thus include an opening section, "Why Race, Class, and Gender Still Matter." We continue to include essays in the opening section that engage students in personal narratives, as a way of helping them step beyond their own social location and to see how race, class, gender, sexuality, and other social factors shape people's lives differently. But we have changed this section from a focus on shifting one's point of view, although that it still important, to addressing the persistent realities of race, class, and gender—even in an age when the dominant modes of thinking claim that they no longer matter.

The new organization also allows us to link ethnicity, nationality, and sexuality to the study of the intersections of race, class, and gender in an expanded way. Although we caution readers against thinking that all forms of difference are the same, we know that race, class, and gender are interconnected with other systems of power and inequality. We have, therefore, retitled the second section of this book from one that originally was just about conceptualizing race, class, and gender to a title (Part II, "Systems of Power and Inequality") that now reflects how we conceptualize race, class, gender, ethnicity, and sexuality as linked through systems of power and inequality.

Part III ("The Structure of Social Institutions") continues with a focus on how race, class, and gender structure social institutions—now and historically. This part now includes the original focus on work, families, culture, and the state, but we have developed it to include more attention to the media and culture, as well as to include more material on violence, health, and disability.

Finally, we have made a major revision in the final part of the book ("Social Change and Sites of Change"). We noted that many instructors rarely commented on the original final section ("Making a Difference"), and we thought about how students typically seemed overwhelmed by the possibility of making a difference once they understood the structural basis of race, class, and gender. We did not want to leave students with the false impression that change is easy or that it can always be accomplished. Particularly in an age when there is more resistance to change, we wanted students to think about various ways that change occurs, as well as some of the different sites where change can take place. Primarily, we wanted students and faculty to know that change is not just a matter of individual action. Rather, change can sometimes be gradual— sometimes more radical, sometimes a matter of small changes—in different realms of social life (attitudes, behaviors, and large-scale changes). We have organized the last section to reflect both the different ways that change takes place (or not) and the different sites where we can think about change taking place.

Throughout, our book is grounded in a sociological perspective; several articles also provide a historical foundation for understanding how race, class, and gender have emerged. We include materials that bring a global dimension to the study of race, class, and gender—not just by looking comparatively at other cultures but also by analyzing how the process of globalization is shaping life in the United States.

As in earlier editions, we have selected articles based primarily on two criteria: (1) accessibility to undergraduate readers and the general public, not just highly trained specialists; and, (2) articles that are grounded in race *and* class *and* gender—in other words, intersectionality. Not all articles accomplish this as much as we would like, but we try not to select articles that focus exclusively on one while ignoring the others. In this regard, our book differs significantly from other anthologies on race, class, and gender that include a lot of articles on each, but do less to show how they are connected. We also distinguish our book from those that are centered in a multicultural perspective. Although multiculturalism is important, we do not think that the appreciation of cultural differences is the only thing that race, class, and gender are about. Rather, we see race, class, and gender as embedded in the structure of society and significantly influencing group cultures. But race, class, and gender are also structures of group opportunity, power, and privilege. We searched for articles that are conceptually and theoretically informed and at the same time accessible to undergraduate readers. Although it is important to think of race, class, and gender as analytical categories, we do not want to lose sight of how they affect human experiences and feelings; thus, we have included personal narratives that are reflective and analytical. We think that personal accounts generate empathy and also help us connect personal experiences to social structural conditions.

Organization of the Book

As noted above, we have significantly re-organized the book to reflect how we approach the study of race, class, and gender. The first part establishes the framework with which we approach the study of race, class, and gender. We introduce each of the four parts with an essay by us that analyzes the issues raised by the reading selections. These essays are an important part of this book, because they establish the framework that we use to think about race, class, and gender.

Part I, "Why Race, Class, and Gender Still Matter," contains several narrative pieces that reflect on how race, class, and gender shape individual and collective experiences. These different accounts are not meant to represent everyone who has been excluded, but to ground readers in the practice of thinking about the lives of people who rarely occupy the center of dominant group thinking. When excluded groups are placed in the forefront of thought, they are typically stereotyped and distorted. When you look at society through the different perspectives of persons reflecting on their location within systems of race, class, and gender oppression, you begin to see just how much race, class, and gender really matter—and continue to matter, despite claims to the contrary. Because the essays in this part are grounded in personal experiences, they capture student interest, but we also use them analytically to think beyond any one person's life.

Part II, "Systems of Power and Inequality," provides the conceptual foundation for understanding how race, class, and gender are linked together and how they link with other systems of power and inequality, especially ethnicity and sexuality. We treat each of these separately here, not because we think they stand alone, but to show students how each operates so they can better see their interlocking nature. The introductory essay provides working definitions for these major concepts and presents some of the contemporary data through which students can see how race, class, and gender stratify contemporary society.

In Part III, "The Structure of Social Institutions," we examine how intersecting systems of race, class, and gender shape the organization of social institutions and how, as a result, these institutions affect group experience. Social scientists routinely document how Latinos, African Americans, women, workers, and other distinctive groups are affected by institutional structures. We know this is true but want to go beyond these analyses to scrutinize how institutions are constructed through race, class, and gender relations. The articles in Part III show how we should not relegate the study of racial-ethnic groups, the working class, and women only to subjects marked explicitly as race, class, or gender studies. As categories of social experience, race, class, and gender shape all social institutions and systems of meaning; thus, it is important to think about people of color, different class experiences, and women in analyzing all social institutions and belief systems.

Finally, in Part IV, "Social Change and Sites of Change," we look at social change. Throughout the book, we have avoided a "social problems" approach, as if race, class, and gender are solely about victimization. People are not just victims; they are creative and visionary. As a result, people organize to resist oppression and to work for social justice. But they do so (or not) in particular social contexts when sometimes change is more difficult than at other times. In this part of the book, we want students to think about the conditions in which change can occur, as well as resistance to change. Change can also occur on several levels—the level of individual change, but also the levels of organizational and/or broad-scale societal change. Not all are possible at every point in time. Thus, we focus on social change as a process, as well as look at particular social locations where change can take place.

Developing a complex understanding of the interrelationships among race, class, and gender is not easy and involves a long-term process that involves personal, intellectual, and political change. We do not claim to be models of perfection in this regard. We have been pleased by the strong response to the first five editions of this book, and we are fascinated by how race, class, and gender studies have developed in the short period of time since the publication of the first edition. We know further work is needed. Our own teaching and thinking has been transformed by developing this book. We imagine many changes still to come.

New Additions to the Sixth Edition

We have made several changes in the sixth edition that strengthen and refresh *Race, Class, and Gender.* These include the following:

- Nineteen new readings.
- Reorganization of the book into four parts, allowing us to focus more on the connections among race, class, gender, ethnicity, and sexuality, as well as developing a stronger section on social change.
- Four revised introductions by us. These introductions articulate the analytical model we use to understand the intersections among race, class, and gender. See especially the comparison of "the matrix of domination" and "difference, additive, and multicultural models" elaborated in the first introductory essay for Part I.
- A new section on ethnicity and nationality. This section includes some of the readings from the original section, but by moving it into the part titled "Systems of Power and Inequality" we are better able to link the renewed interest in ethnicity and nationality to the study of race, class, and gender.
- A revised section on sexuality and heterosexism, including a reading that shows students the historical evolution of heterosexism as a concept.
- A stronger presentation of material on social change. We have substantially revised the fourth part of the book (originally Part V) to focus on how social change occurs. This also brings a strong focus on social movements, as well as other forms of collective and individual action, to the material in the book.
- New material on race, class, and the military. Given the context of contemporary world and national affairs, we thought it important to have students ask questions about how race, class, and gender are engaged in current affairs. Although more work needs to be done in this area, we have included a piece on the military that raises important questions about the relationship between systems of inequality and who most likely carries the burden of warfare.

Pedagogical Features

We realize that the context in which you teach matters. If you teach in an institution where students are more likely to be working class, perhaps how the class system works will be more obvious to them than it is for students in a more privileged college environment. Many of those who use this book will be teaching in segregated environments, given the high degree of race and class—and even gender—segregation in education. Thus, how one teaches this book should reflect the different environments in which faculty work. Ideally, the material in this book should be discussed in a multiracial, multicultural atmosphere, but we realize that is not always the case. We hope that the content of the book and the pedagogical features that enhance it will help bring a more inclusive analysis to educational settings than might be there to start with. We see this book as more than just a collection of readings. The book has an analytical logic to its organization and content, and we think it can be used to format a course. Of course, some faculty will use it in an order different from the way we imagine it, but we hope the four part introductions will help people develop the presentation of their course. We also hope that the various pedagogical tools will help people expand their teaching and learning beyond the pages of the book.

We have included features with this edition that provide faculty with additional teaching tools. They include the following:

- *Bonus Reading:* Wadsworth's InfoTrac® College Edition feature enables us to provide an additional recommended reading at the end of every section of the book. These are articles that we have selected because they further examine the issues in each major section. Through the InfoTrac College Edition, students and faculty can retrieve an online, full-text copy of articles not included in the text per se.
- *Suggested Readings:* In addition, we have included lists of suggested readings at the conclusion of each section for students and faculty who want to explore these topics further. We have selected these books based on their currency and their accessibility to undergraduate students.
- *Search Terms:* Students who purchase the book are given a password to Wadsworth's InfoTrac College Edition feature. We have included terms at the end of each section that students can use on InfoTrac College Edition to find additional information on subjects that interest them. These terms can also be used as the basis for in-class discussion, exercises, exams, or research projects.
- *Instructor's Manual:* This edition includes an instructor's manual with suggestions for class exercises, discussion and examination questions, and course assignments.
- *Index:* This index will help students and faculty locate particular topics in the book quickly and easily.
- *Website:* Online support is available through the Wadsworth Sociology Resource Center. We encourage people to browse the *Race, Class, and Gender* page at the Wadsworth Website or related resources. The address is www.thomsonedu.com/sociology.

A Note on Language

Reconstructing existing ways of thinking to be more inclusive requires many transformations. One transformation needed involves the language we use when referring to different groups. Language reflects many assumptions about race, class, and gender; and for that reason, language changes and evolves as knowledge changes. The term *minority*, for example, marginalizes groups, making them seem somehow outside the mainstream or dominant culture. Even worse, the term *non-White*, routinely used by social scientists, defines groups in terms of what they are not and assumes that Whites have the universal experiences against which the experiences of all other groups are measured. We have consciously avoided using both of these terms throughout this book, although this is sometimes unavoidable.

We have capitalized Black in our writing because of the specific historical experience, varied as it is, of African Americans in the United States. We also capitalize White when referring to a particular group experience; however, we recognize that White American is no more a uniform experience than is African American. We realize that these are arguable points, but we want to make our decision apparent and explicit. For the benefit of purists who like to follow the rules, we note that the *Chicago Manual of Style* recognizes that these grammatical questions are also political ones; this edition suggests that writers might want to capitalize Black and White to reflect the fact that they are referring to proper names of groups. We use *Hispanic* and *Latina/o* interchangeably, though we recognize that is not how groups necessarily define themselves. When citing data from other sources (typically government documents), we use "Hispanic," because that is usually how such data are reported.

Language becomes especially problematic when we want to talk about features of experience that different groups share. Using shortcut terms like Hispanic, Latina/o, Native American, and women of color homogenizes distinct historical experiences. Even the term *White* falsely unifies experiences across such factors as ethnicity, region, class, and gender, to name a few. At times, though, we want to talk of common experiences across different groups, so we have used labels such as Latina/o, Asian American, Native American, and women of color to do so. Unfortunately, describing groups in this way reinforces basic categories of oppression. We do not know how to resolve this problem but want readers to be aware of the limitations and significance of language as they try to think more inclusively about diverse group experiences.

ACKNOWLEDGMENTS

An anthology rests on the efforts of more people than the editors alone. This book has been inspired by our work with scholars and teachers from around the country who are working to make their teaching and writing more inclusive and sensitive to the experiences of all groups. Over the years of our own collaboration, we have each been enriched by the work of those trying to make higher education a more equitable and fair institution. In that time, our work has grown from many networks that have generated new race, class, and gender scholars. These associations continue to sustain us.

Many people contributed to the development of this book. We especially thank Dana Hysock at the University of Delaware for her research assistance and for developing the new instructor's manual. We appreciate the support given by our institutions, with special thanks to Joel Best, chair of the Department of Sociology (University of Delaware); William Falk, Chair of the Department of Sociology (University of Maryland). We also thank Victoria Becker, Linda Keen, and Judy Watson (University of Delaware) for their invaluable secretarial support. And we thank Tammy Anderson, Maxine Baca Zinn, Elizabeth Higginbotham, Valerie Hans, and Susan Miller for offering suggestions for particular readings and always encouraging and supporting this project. Bob Jucha and Kristin Marrs have joined this project with enthusiasm, fresh ideas, and expert advice. We sincerely appreciate their hard work and vision for the book and look forward to continuing our collaboration with them. We also thank the reviewers, who provided valuable commentary on the prior edition and thus helped enormously in the development of the sixth edition:

Susan Rose, Dickinson College
Barbara Perry, University of Ontario
Kathleen Ja Sook Bergquist, University of Nevada
Barbara Gurr, Southern Connecticut State University
C.N. Lee, University of Massachusetts–Amherst
Ralph Pyle, Michigan State University
Scott Youngstedt, Saginaw Valley State University
Mona Scott, Mesa Community College

Developing this book has been an experience based on friendship, hard work, travel, and fun. We especially thank Valerie, Roger, and Richard for giving us the support, love, and time we needed to do this work well. This book has deepened our friendship, as we have grown more committed to transformed ways of thinking and being. We are lucky to be working on a project that continues to enrich our work and our friendship.

Margaret L. Andersen (B.A., Georgia State University; M.A., Ph.D., University of Massachusetts, Amherst) is Edward F. and Elizabeth Goodman Rosenberg Professor of Sociology (and Women's Studies) at the University of Delaware. She is the author of *Thinking about Women: Sociological Perspectives on Sex and Gender*, 7th ed. (Allyn and Bacon, 2006); *Sociology: Understanding a Diverse Society*, 4th ed. (Wadsworth, 2006; co-authored with Howard F. Taylor); *Sociology: The Essentials*, 4th ed. (Wadsworth, 2007; also co-authored with Howard F. Taylor); and *Understanding Society: An Introductory Reader* (Wadsworth, 2004; co-edited with Kim Logio and Howard F. Taylor). She is the recipient of the 2006 American Sociological Association Jessie Bernard Award, given annually to a sociologist whose work has enriched the study of women in sociology. She is a recipient of the University of Delaware's Excellence-in-Teaching Award and the College of Arts and Science Outstanding Teaching Award. She currently chairs the National Advisory Board for the Center for Comparative Studies in Race and Ethnicity at Stanford University, where she has been a Visiting Professor.

Patricia Hill Collins (B.A., Brandeis University; M.A.T., Harvard University; Ph.D., Brandeis University) is Wilson Elkins Professor of Sociology at the University of Maryland, College Park, and Charles Phelps Taft Emeritus Professor of African American Studies and Sociology at the University of Cincinnati. She is the author of numerous articles and books including *Black Sexual Politics: African Americans, Gender and the New Racism* (Routledge, 2004); *Fighting Words: Black Women and the Search for Justice* (University of Minnesota, 1998); and *Black Feminist Thought: Knowledge, Consciousness, and the Politics of Empowerment* (Unwin Hyman 1990; Routledge 2000), which won the Jessie Bernard Award of the American Sociological Association and the C. Wright Mills Award of the Society for the Study of Social Problems. Her latest book is *From Black Power to Hip Hop: Racism, Nationalism, and Feminism* (Temple University Press, 2005).

Julia Álvarez is the author of several books including, *How the Garcia Girls Lost Their Accents, In the Time of Butterflies, A Cafecito Story,* and *In the Name of Salomé*. She is originally from the Dominican Republic but migrated to the United States when she was ten years old.

Teresa Amott is Provost and dean of faculty at Hobart and William Smith Colleges. She is the author of *Race, Gender, and Work: A Multicultural Economic History of Women in the United States* (with Julie Matthaei) and *Caught in Crisis: Women in the U.S. Economy Today*.

Charon Asetoyer is the founder and executive director of the Native American Women's Health Education Resource Center, based on the Yankton Sioux Reservation in Lake Andes, South Dakota. She has been involved in community organizing and activism on women's health issues for the past twenty years.

Maxine Baca Zinn is professor of sociology at Michigan State University and senior research associate with the Julian Samora Research Institute. She is co-author of *Diversity in Families, In Conflict and Order,* and *Social Problems* (with D. Stanley Eitzen), and the co-editor of *Gender through the Prism of Difference: A Sex and Gender Reader* (with Pierrette Hondagneu-Sotelo and Michael A. Messner).

Fabricio Balcazar is associate professor in the Department of Psychology at the University of Illinois at Chicago (UIC). He is also the director of the Center for Capacity Building on Minorities with Disabilities Research at UIC.

Jennifer Baumgardner is a writer, speaker and activist. She is the co-author (with Amy Richards) of two books: *Manifesta: Young Women, Feminism, and the Future* (2000) (included in this anthology) and *Grassroots: A Field Guide for Feminist Activism* (2005).

Derrick Bell is Visiting Professor of Law at New York University Law School. During the 1960s, he counseled on hundreds of school desegregation cases.

Pamela Block is associate professor at the State University of New York at Stony Brook. She is also an adjunct faculty member at the Center for Alcohol and Addiction Studies at Brown University.

Eduardo Bonilla-Silva is research professor at Duke University. He is the author of *White Supremacy and Racism in the Post-Civil Rights Era; White Out: The Continuing Significance of Racism;* and *Racism Without Racists: Color-Blind Racism and the Persistence of Racial Inequality in the United States.*

Kenneth W. Brown is a contributor to Essence magazine. While unemployed, he completed an associate's degree; later, he worked in financial services while pursuing a bachelor's degree.

Sarah L. Brownlee is an expert in community organizing and gay and lesbian issues. She is the former director of the National Center for Human Rights Education and a massage therapist.

Linda Burnham is cofounder and executive director of the Women of Color Resource Center. She is the author of Women's Education in the Global Economy and co-author of *Working Hard, Staying Poor.*

Erica Chito Childs is assistant professor of sociology at Eastern Connecticut State University. She is a council member for the American Sociological Association section on Racial and Ethnic Minorities.

Ward Churchill (enrolled Keetoowah Band Cherokee) is a long-time native rights activist and professor of ethnic studies and coordinator of American Indian studies for the University of Colorado. His books include *Agents of Repression, Fantasies of the Master Race, From a Native Son,* and *A Little Matter of Genocide: Holocaust and Denial in the Americas.*

Judith Ortiz Cofer is the Franklin Professor of English and Creative Writing at the University of Georgia. She is the author of numerous books of poetry and essays, and a novel, *The Line of the Sun.* She has won the PEN/Martha Albrand Special Citation in nonfiction for her book *Silent Dancing.*

Chuck Collins is the cofounder and director of United for a Fair Economy—an organization that draws attention to the income and wealth inequality in the United States. He is the author of several books, including

Economic Apartheid in America: A Primer on Economic Inequality and Insecurity, and he writes regularly for Dollars and Sense.

Gary David Comstock is University protestant chaplain and visiting associate Professor at Wesleyan University. He has published numerous books, including *Gay Theology Without Apology; Unrepentant, Self-Affirming, Practicing: Lesbian/Bisexual/Gay People Within Organized Religion; Que(e)rying Religion: A Critical Anthology;* and *Violence against Lesbians and Gay Men.*

Jason DeParle is a senior writer at *The New York Times.* He is the author of the book *American Dream: Three Women, Ten Kids, and a Nation's Drive to End Welfare.*

Dazon Dixon Diallo is the founder and president of SisterLove Women's AIDS project and a public health expert and human rights activist.

Bonnie Thornton Dill is professor of women's studies and director of the Research Consortium on Gender, Race, and Ethnicity at the University of Maryland, College Park. Her books include *Women of Color in U.S. Society*, co-edited with Maxine Baca Zinn, and *Across the Boundaries of Race and Class: Work and Family among Black Female Domestic Servants.*

Yen Le Espiritu is professor in the Department of Ethnic Studies at the University of California, San Diego. She is the author of *Asian American Panethnicity, Filipino American Lives,* and *Asian American Women and Men: Labor, Laws, and Love,* which received a book award from the American Sociological Association.

Kim Fellner is one of the founders of the National Organizers Alliance. She was an anti-war activist during the Vietnam War era and became involved in community organization during graduate school.

Abby I. Ferber is associate professor and director of women's studies at the University of Colorado at Colorado Springs. She is the author of *White Man Falling: Race, Gender and White Supremacy* and *Hate Crime in America: What Do We Know?* She is co-author of *Making a Difference: University Students of Color Speak Out* and co-editor of the anthology, *Privilege: A Reader* with Michael Kimmel.

Marilyn Frye is professor and associate chair of the Department of Philosophy at Michigan State University. She is the author of numerous books and essays, including *The Politics of Reality* and *Willful Virgin.* With her partner, Carolyn Shafer, she created and manages Bare Bones Studios for Women's Art—space and facilities for art making in a wide range of media.

Thomas J. Gerschick is associate professor at Illinois State University. He is the Illinois State University faculty advisor for Habitat for Humanity.

Amy Gluckman is a social studies teacher in an alternative high school in Lowell, Massachusetts. She is part of an editorial collective that publishes the progressive economics magazine *Dollars and* Sense and, with Betsy Reed, is the editor of a book, *Homo Economics: Capitalism, Community, and Lesbian and Gay Life*.

David M. Halbfinger is a writer for *The New York Times*.

Steven A. Holmes is an editor in the Washington Bureau of *The New York Times*.

Pierrette Hondagneu-Sotelo is professor of sociology, American Studies, and ethnicity at the University of Southern California. She is author of *Gendered Transitions: Mexican Experiences of Immigration* and *Doméstica: Immigrant Workers Cleaning and Caring in the Shadow of Affluence*, which won the Society for Social Problems C. Wright Mills Award.

Shani Jamila is a poet and activist. She is a Fulbright Scholar who has a master's degree in African diaspora cultural studies from the University of California, Los Angeles. She has traveled extensively throughout Africa and the Caribbean and is known for her work on hip-hop and feminism. Shani is a producer and co-host of Blackademics—a weekly talk radio show on the Washington DC bureau of the Pacifica network.

Jonathan Ned Katz was the first tenured lesbian and gay studies professor in the United States (Department of Lesbian and Gay Studies, City College of San Francisco). He is the founder of the Queer Caucus of the College Art Association. He is also the co-founder of the activist group Queer Nation.

Robin D. G. Kelley is a professor of history and Africana studies at New York University. He is the author of numerous books, including *Freedom Dreams: The Black Radical Imagination; Three Strikes: The Fighting Spirit of Labor's Last Century; Race Rebels: Culture Politics and the Black Working Class*; and *Yo' Mama's DisFunktional!*

Kamala Kempadoo is professor of social science at York University, Canada. She is the author of *Sexing the Caribbean: Gender, Race and Sexual Labor* and *Global Sex Workers: Rights, Resistance, and Redefinition*.

Christopher Keys is department chair and professor of community psychology at DePaul University.

Nazli Kibria is associate professor of sociology at Boston University. She is the author of *Becoming Asian American: Identities of Second Generation Chinese and Korean Americans* and *Family Tightrope: The Changing Lives of Vietnamese Americans.*

Jean Kilbourne has twice received the Lecturer of the Year award from the National Association for Campus Activities. She has lectured on numerous college and university campuses across the United States and Canada. She has made several award-winning documentary films, including the *Killing Us Softly* series.

Paul Kivel is co-founder of the Oakland Men's Project. He has appeared on numerous national radio and television programs speaking on male violence, racism and diversity, and raising boys into healthy and productive men.

Celene Krauss is professor of sociology and women's studies at Kean University. She has written extensively on women's issues and toxic waste protests, with a focus on race, ethnicity, and class. Her work has appeared in *Sociological Forum, Qualitative Sociology*, and other journals and books.

Donna Langston is the director of ethnic studies at the University of Colorado, Denver, and the author of several books, including *A to Z of American Women and Activists, Changing Our Power: An Introduction to Women's Studies*, and *The Native American World.*

Annette Lareau is professor of sociology at the University of Maryland. Her first book was entitled *Home Advantage: Social Class and Parental Intervention in Elementary Education.*

Peggy Levitt is associate professor of sociology at Wellesley College and research fellow at the Hauser Center for Nonprofit Organizations at Harvard University. She is co-director of the *Emerging Transnational Dynamics Initiative.*

Audre Lorde, who passed away in 1992, grew up in the West Indian community of Harlem in the 1930s, the daughter of immigrants from Grenada. She was professor of English at Hunter College and a major figure in the lesbian and feminist movements. Among her works are *Sister Outsider; Zami: A New Spelling of My Name; Uses of the Erotic;* and numerous other books and essays.

Arturo Madrid is Murchison Distinguished Professor of the Humanities at Trinity University and the recipient of the Charles Frankel Prize in the Humanities, National Endowment for the Humanities, in 1996. From 1984 until 1993 he served as founding president of The Tomás Rivera Center, a national institute for policy studies on Latino issues.

Julianne Malveaux holds a Ph.D. in economics and is a syndicated columnist who writes regularly for *Essence* and also appears regularly on CNN, BET, Fox News, MSNBC, and other television news shows. She is the author of *Wall Street, Main Street, and the Side Street: A Mad Economist Takes a Stroll.* She is president and CEO of her own multimedia company.

Gregory Mantsios is the director of worker education at Queens College, the City University of New York.

Elizabeth Martinez is a Chicana scholar and activist. She is the cofounder of the Institute for MultiRacial Justice. Her latest book is *De Colores Means All of Us: Latina Views for a Multi-Colored Century.*

Julie Matthaei is a professor of economics at Wellesley College. Her books include *An Economic History of Women in America: Women's Work, The Sexual Division of Labor, and the Development of Capitalism* and (with Teresa Amott) *Race, Gender, and Work: A Multicultural Economic History of Women in the United States.*

Peggy McIntosh is associate director of the Wellesley College Center for Research on Women. She is founder and codirector of the National SEED Project on Inclusive Curriculum—a project that helps teachers make school climates fair and equitable. She is cofounder of the Rocky Mountain Women's Institute.

Michael A. Messner is chair of the Department of Sociology at the University of Southern California. His latest book is *Taking the Field: Women, Men, and Sports.* His other books include *Masculinities, Gender Relations, and Sport, Power at Play: Sports and the Problem of Masculinity*, and *The Politics of Masculinities: Men in Movements.*

Roslyn Arlin Mickelson is professor of sociology and women's studies at the University of North Carolina at Charlotte. She is the author of *Children on the Streets of the Americas: Globalization, Homelessness, and Education in the United States, Brazil, and Cuba.*

Robert B. Moore writes frequently on feminist issues and is the author of the classic "Racist Stereotyping in the English Language" included in this volume.

Cherríe Moraga is artist-in-residence in the Departments of Drama and Portuguese at Stanford University. She is the co-editor of *This Bridge Called*

My Back: Writing by Radical Women of Color and the author of numerous plays including *Shadow of a Man* and *Heroes and Saints*.

Philip Moss is a professor in the Department of Regional Economic and Social Development at the University of Massachusetts, Lowell. He studies the impacts of structural change on economic opportunity. With Chris Tilly he has published *Stories Employers Tell: Race, Skill, and Hiring in America*.

Katherine S. Newman is Malcolm Wiener Professor of Urban Studies at the John F. Kennedy School of Government, Harvard University, and dean of social science at the Radcliffe Institute for Advanced Study. She is the author of *Rampage; The Social Roots of School Shootings; No Shame in My Game: The Working Poor in the Inner City;* and *Falling from Grace: Downward Mobility in the Age of Affluence*.

Mary E. Pattillo is associate professor of sociology and African American studies at Northwestern University. She is the author of *Black Picket Fences: Privilege and Peril among the Black Middle Class* and a forthcoming book (with William Julius Wilson and Richard Taub), *The Roots of Racial Tensions: Urban Ethnic Neighborhoods*.

Betsy Reed, a former editor of *Dollars and Sense*, is a senior editor at *The Nation*. She is co-editor with Amy Gluckman of the anthology *Homo Economics: Capitalism, Community, and Lesbian and Gay Life*.

Amy Richards is co-founder of the Third Wave Foundation. She was chosen by the American Association of University Women as a Woman of Distinction. She works as a consultant, lecturer, and writer.

Luz Rodriquez is an expert on Latina health. She is the former executive director of Casa Atabex Ache, a health organization for women of color.

Loretta J. Ross is the executive director of the National Center for Human Rights Education, which focuses on domestic human rights violations.

Lillian Rubin lives and works in San Francisco. She is an internationally known lecturer and writer. Some of her books include *The Man with the Beautiful Voice, Tangled Lives, The Transcendent Child,* and *Intimate Strangers*.

Almas Sayeed is the Child Welfare Policy Coordinator at the Kansas Coalition Against Sexual and Domestic Violence.

Thomas M. Shapiro is Pokross Chair of Law and Social Policy at Brandeis University. His latest book is *The Hidden Cost of Being African American*. His earlier work with Melvin L. Oliver, *Black Wealth/White Wealth*, has won several awards including the American Sociological Association Distinguished Scholarly Award.

Jael Silliman is associate professor of women's studies at the University of Iowa. She is the co-editor of *Dangerous Intersections: Feminist Perspective on Population, Environment, and Development* and the author of *Jewish Portraits, Indian Frames: Women's Narratives from a Diaspora of Hope*.

Holly Sklar is a journalist who writes regularly for numerous publications, including *Z Magazine*, *The Nation*, the *Philadelphia Inquirer*, and *USA Today*. She is also the author of *The Perils of the Growing American Wealth Gap*; *Chaos or Community*; *Streets of Hope: The Fall and Rise of an Urban Neighborhood*; and *Trilateralism: The Trilateral Commission and Elite Planning for World Management*.

Robert Smith is assistant professor of sociology at Barnard College. He is the author of *Migration, Settlement, and Transnational Life*, as well as numerous articles on migration and transnational communities.

Stephen Samuel Smith is professor of political science at Winthrop University. His interests include the politics of education, urban political economy, social movements, and program evaluation.

C. Matthew Snipp is a professor of sociology at Stanford University. He is the author of *American Indians: The First of This Land and Public Policy Impacts on American Indian Economic Development*. His tribal heritage is Oklahoma Cherokee and Choctaw.

Ronald T. Takaki is professor of ethnic studies at the University of California, Berkeley. He is the author of several books, including *Iron Cages: Race and Culture in 19th Century America*; *Strangers from a Different Shore: A History of Asian Americans*; and *A Different Mirror: A History of Multicultural America*.

Desiree Taylor is a mixed-race woman whose work has been published in *Reconstructing Gender: A Multicultural Anthology*.

Chris Tilly is university professor in the Department of Regional Economic and Social Development at the University of Massachusetts, Lowell. He is the author of *Half a Job: Bad and Good Part-Time Jobs in a Changing Labor Market*; *Glass Ceilings and Bottomless Pits: Women's Work, Women's Poverty* (with Randy Albelda); and *Stories Employers Tell: Race, Skill, and Hiring in America* (with Philip Moss).

Haunami-Kay Trask is a Hawaiian scholar and poet and has been an activist in the Native Hawaiian community for over 20 years. She is professor and former director of the Center for Hawaiian Studies at the University of Hawaii at Manoa.

Mary C. Waters is professor of sociology and Harvard College Professor at Harvard University. She is the author of *Black Identities: West Indian Immigrant Dreams* and *American Realities; Ethnic Options: Choosing Identities in America;* and numerous articles on race, ethnicity, and immigration.

Cornel West is Class of 1943 University Professor of Religion at Princeton University. He is the author of numerous articles and books including *The American Evasion of Philosophy: A Genealogy of Pragmatism, The Cornel West Reader, Race Matters*, and *Democracy Matters.*

Kath Weston is a sociocultural anthropologist who has written several books, including *Families We Choose: Lesbians, Gays, and Kinship; Render Me, Gender Me; Long Slow Burn;* and *Gender in Real Time.*

Patricia J. Williams is the James L. Dohr professor of law at Columbia University and the author of *The Alchemy of Race and Rights* and *The Diary of a Law Professor.* She is a regular contributor to The *Nation.*

Jennifer Wriggins is associate professor of law at the University of Southern Maine. She specializes in the practice of civil litigation.

Nancie Zane is affiliated faculty for the Center for Organizational Dynamics at the University of Pennsylvania. She is also a partner with Praxis Consulting Group, a consulting firm that specializes in organizational development.

WHY RACE, CLASS, AND GENDER STILL MATTER

Margaret L. Andersen
and Patricia Hill Collins

The United States is a nation where people are supposed to be able to rise above their origins. Those who want to succeed, it is believed, can do so with hard enough work and good enough effort. Furthermore, the nation is founded on the principle of equality. Although equality has historically been denied to many, there is now a legal framework in place that guarantees protection from discrimination and equality of treatment for all citizens before the law. Historic social movements, such as the civil rights movement and the feminist movement, have also raised people's consciousness about the rights of minority groups and women. Moreover, these movements have generated new opportunities for multiple groups—African Americans, Latinos, White women, disabled people, gays and lesbians, and older people, to name some of the groups who have been beneficiaries of civil rights action and legislation. And, if you ask Americans if they support non-discrimination policies, the overwhelming number will say yes. Why, then, do race, class, and gender still matter?

Race, class, and gender still matter because they continue to structure society in ways that value some lives more than others. They matter because they structure the opportunities, resources, and power of some, even while other groups struggle. They matter because they remain the foundations for systems of power and inequality that, despite our nation's diversity, continue to be among the most significant social facts of people's lives. Thus, despite having removed the formal barriers of opportunity, the United States is still highly stratified along lines of race, class, and gender.

The persistent reality of race, class, and gender inequality was made apparent to the U.S. public when Hurricane Katrina struck New Orleans and the Gulf Coast in the fall of 2005. Many were surprised by the televised images of poor, African American people—abandoned in the storm, completely without resources for several days, and without basic necessities of food and water. It was shocking for some people to see U.S. citizens in such great need—images that people more commonly associate with poor nations, not the most affluent and powerful nation in the world. But, even while many in the nation had ignored and denied the realities of poverty, the national poverty rate had in fact steadily increased for the five years prior to Katrina. And, in many U.S. cities, the infant mortality rate—thought to be a good indicator of a nation's well-being—exceeds that in far-less-developed nations.

Still, Hurricane Katrina was said by many to be a "leveling experience"— a storm that displaced hundreds of thousands of people—a mix of women and men, adults and children, people of different races, rich and poor. But did it affect all equally? The widespread devastation did displace people of many different class backgrounds. Expensive waterfront homes, often second homes for families, were destroyed along with substandard housing in the poorest areas of New Orleans and rural, coastal Mississippi. Nature does not discriminate when it comes to where a storm hits or where a flood occurs. But, on the other hand, you might ask, why was the most low-lying section of the city of New Orleans a place where mostly poor, Black people lived? Why were African Americans most of those who could not evacuate and who were forced to live—and, in some cases, die—in the horrid squalor of the Superdome and the Convention Center? Why were the poor left behind? Why was the government response so slow?

Many people asked these questions following Hurricane Katrina, and the connection between race and class was once again brought to the forefront of national consciousness—even if only temporarily. But, surveys taken after the hurricane also indicated a huge racial divide in people's opinions about whether race had affected how slowly the government responded. Two-thirds of African Americans thought the government would have responded more quickly had those most affected been White; only 17 percent of White Americans thought so (Pew Research Center 2005). At the same time, gender seemed to disappear from people's awareness, despite the fact that so many of those who appeared in the televised images of the disaster were poor women and their children. In the years that follow the hurricane, there will be many questions about who most benefits from the reconstruction of communities that were so devastated by this storm. Will it be the displaced poor? The middle-class homeowners (Black and White) who lost property in the disaster? Or will it be those already at the top of the class system—business owners who may not even reside in the region that was so devastated? Time—and some good social science research—will tell, but if sociology and history provide any early clues, then you can expect that the reconstruction of New Orleans and the Gulf will likely reproduce a social order based on race, class, and gender.

In this book, we ask students to think about race, class, and gender in ways that transform, rather than buttress, existing social arrangements. This can mean shifting one's thinking so that groups who are often silenced or ignored become heard. All social groups are located in a system of power relationships wherein your social location can shape what you know—and what others know about you. As a result, dominant forms of knowledge have been constructed largely from the experiences of the most powerful—that is, those who have the most access to systems of education and communication. Thus to acquire a more inclusive view—one that pays attention to the experiences of those in more subordinated groups—requires that you take a new frame of vision.

You can think of this as if you were taking a photograph. For years, women and people of color—and especially women of color—were totally outside people's frame of vision. But, if you move your angle of sight to in-clude those who have been overlooked, new subjects come into view. This is more than a matter of sharpening one's focus, although that is required for clarity. Instead, it means actually seeing things differently, perhaps even changing the lens you look through—thereby removing the filters (or stereo-types and misconceptions) that groups bring to what they see and know.

DEVELOPING A RACE, CLASS, AND GENDER PERSPECTIVE

In this book we ask you to think about how race, class, and gender really do matter. Thinking from a perspective that engages race, class, and gender is not just about illuminating the experiences of oppressed groups, however. It also changes how we understand the dominant culture and groups who have more power and privilege than others. For example, the development of women's studies has changed what we know and how we think about women; at the same time, it has changed what we know and how we think about men. This does not mean that women's studies is about "male-bashing." It means taking the experiences of women and men seriously and analyzing how gender, race, and class shape the experiences of both men and women—in different, but interrelated, ways. Likewise, the study of racial and ethnic groups begins by learning the diverse histories and experiences of these groups. In doing so, we transform our understanding of White experiences, too. The exclusionary thinking we have relied upon in the past simply does not reveal the intricate interconnections that exist among the different groups composing U.S. society.

It is important to know that thinking about race, class, and gender is not just a matter of studying victims. Relying too heavily on ideas about differences overemphasizes the impact of race, class, and gender on poor people, women, and people of color, rather than seeing race, class, and gender as an integral part of social structures that shape the experiences of everyone. We remind students that race, class, and gender have affected the experiences of all individuals and groups. As a result, we do not think we should talk only about women when talking about gender or only about people of color when talking about race. Because race, class, and gender affect the experiences of all, it is important to study men when analyzing gender, to study Whites when analyzing race, and to study the experiences of the affluent when analyzing class. Furthermore, we should not forget women when studying race or think only about Whites when studying gender.

So you might ask, Does reconstructing knowledge matter? To begin with, knowledge is not just some abstract thing—good to have, but not all that important. There are real consequences to having partial or distorted knowledge. First, learning about other groups helps you realize the partiality of your own perspective; furthermore, this is true for both dominant and subordinate groups. Knowing only the history of African Americans, for example, or seeing that history only in single-minded terms will not reveal the historical linkages between the oppression of African Americans and the exclusionary and exploitative treatment of other groups. This is discussed by Ronald T. Takaki in his essay included here ("A Different Mirror") on the multicultural history of American society.

Second, having misleading and incorrect knowledge leads to the formation of bad social policy—policy that then reproduces, rather than solves, social problems. Finally, knowledge is not just about content and information; it provides an orientation to the world. What you know frames how you behave and how you think about yourself and others. If what you know is wrong because it is based on exclusionary thought, you are likely to act in exclusionary ways, thereby reproducing the racism, anti-Semitism, sexism, class oppression, and homophobia of society. This may not be because you are intentionally racist, anti-Semitic, sexist, elitist, or homophobic; it may simply be because you do not know any better. Challenging oppressive race, class, and gender relations in society requires reconstructing what we know so that we have some basis from which to change these damaging and dehumanizing systems of oppression.

RACE, CLASS, AND GENDER AS A MATRIX OF DOMINATION

Race, class, and gender shape the experiences of all people in the United States. This fact has been widely documented in research and, to some extent, is commonly understood. Thus, for years, social scientists have studied the consequences of race, class, and gender inequality for different groups in society. The new framework of race, class, and gender studies presented here, however, explores how race, class, and gender operate *together* in people's lives. Fundamentally, race, class, and gender are intersecting categories of experience that affect all aspects of human life; thus, they simultaneously structure the experiences of all people in this society. At any moment, race, class, or gender may feel more salient or meaningful in a given person's life, but they are overlapping and cumulative in their effect on people's experience.

In this volume, we emphasize several core features of this intersectional framework for studying race, class, and gender. First, we emphasize *social structure* in our efforts to conceptualize intersections of race, class, and gender. We use the approach of a *matrix of domination* to analyze race, class, and gender. A matrix of domination posits multiple, interlocking levels of domination that stem from the societal configuration of race, class, and gender relations. This structural pattern affects individual consciousness, group interaction, and group access to institutional power and privileges (Collins 2000). Within this structural framework, we focus less on the similarities and differences among race, class, and gender than on the patterns of connection that join them. Because of the simultaneity of race, class, and gender in people's lives, intersections of race, class, and gender can be seen in individual stories and personal experience. In fact, much exciting work on the intersections of race, class, and gender appears in autobiographies, fiction, and personal essays. We do recognize the significance of these individual narratives and include many here, but we emphasize social structures that provide their context.

Second, studying interconnections among race, class, and gender within a context of structural power helps us understand how race, class, and gender are manifested differently, depending on their configuration with the others. Thus, one might say Black men are privileged *as men*, but this may not be true when their race and class are also taken into account. Otherwise, how can we possibly explain the particular disadvantages African American men experience as men in the criminal justice system, in education, and in the labor market? For that matter, how can we explain the experiences that Native American women undergo as Native American women—disadvantaged by the unique experiences that they have based on race, class, *and* gender—none of which is isolated from the effects of the others? Studying the connections among race, class, and gender reveals that divisions by race and by class and by gender are not as clear-cut as they may seem. White women, for example, may be disadvantaged because of gender, but privileged by race and perhaps (but not necessarily) by class. And increasing class differentiation within racial-ethnic groups reminds us that race is not a monolithic category, as can be seen in the fact that White poverty is increasing more than poverty among other groups, even while some Whites hold the most power in society.

Third, the matrix of domination approach to race, class, and gender studies is historically grounded. We have chosen to emphasize the intersections of race, class, and gender as institutional systems that have had a special impact in the United States. But race, class, and gender intersect with other categories of experience, such as sexuality, ethnicity, age, ability, religion, and nationality. But historically, they have taken varying forms from one society to the next; and within any given society, the connections among them shift. Thus, race is not inherently more important than gender, just as sexuality is not inherently more significant than class and ethnicity. Given the complex and changing relationships among these categories of analysis, we ground our analysis in the historical, institutional context of the United States. Doing so means that race, class, and gender emerge as fundamental categories of analysis in the U.S. setting, so significant that in many ways they influence all of the other categories. For example, the capitalist class relations that have characterized all phases of U.S. history have routinely privileged or penalized

groups organized by gender and by race. U.S. social institutions have reproduced economic equalities for poor people, people of color, and for women
from one generation to the next. Thus, in the United States, race, class, and
gender demonstrate visible, long-standing, material effects that in many ways
foreshadow more recently visible categories of ethnicity, religion, age, ability,
and/or sexuality. These systems of race, class, and gender have been consistently and deeply codified in U.S. laws and have had intergenerational
material effects within the capitalist class system.

DIFFERENCE, DIVERSITY, AND MULTICULTURALISM

How does the matrix of domination model differ from other ways of conceptualizing race, class, and gender relationships? We think this can be best understood by contrasting the *matrix of domination model* to what might be called
a *difference model* of race, class, and gender studies. A difference model, though
viewing some of the common processes in race, class, and gender relations,
tends to focus on unique group experiences. Books that use this framework
will likely include writings by diverse groups of people, but on closer inspec-
tion, you will see that many of these writings treat race, gender, and class
separately. While we think such studies are valuable and add to the body of
knowledge about race, class, and gender, we distinguish our work by looking
at the interrelationships among race, class, and gender, not just their additive
effects or their unique ways of being experienced.

You might think of this as the difference between thinking comparatively
versus thinking relationally. In the difference model individuals are encouraged to compare their experiences with those supposedly unlike them. When
you think comparatively, you might look at how different groups have, for
example, encountered prejudice and discrimination or you might compare
and contrast laws prohibiting interracial marriage to current debates about
same-sex marriage. These are important and interesting questions, but they
are taken a step further when you think beyond comparison to the structural
relationships between different group experiences. Thus, when you think
relationally, you see the social structures that *simultaneously* generate unique
group histories and link them together in society. You then untangle the
workings of social systems that shape the experiences of different people and
groups, and you move beyond just comparing (for example) gender oppression with race oppression or the oppression of gays and lesbians with that of
racial groups. When you recognize the systems of power that mark different

groups' experiences, you then possess the conceptual apparatus to think about changing the system, not just documenting the effects of that system on different people.

We should point out that comparative thinking can foster greater understanding and tolerance. But comparative thinking alone can also leave intact the power relations that create race, class, and gender relations. Because the concept of difference contains the unspoken question "different from what?", this framework can privilege those who are deemed to be "normal" and stigmatize people who are labeled as "different." And, because it is based on comparison, the very concept of difference fosters dichotomous, "either/or" thinking. Some difference models place people in either/or categories, as if one is either Black or White, oppressed or oppressor, powerful or powerless, normal or "different."

The language of diversity, difference, and multiculturalism encourages comparative thinking. People think comparatively when they learn about experiences other than their own and begin comparing and contrasting the experiences of different groups. This is a step beyond centering one's thinking in a single group (typically one's own), but it is nonetheless limited. For example, when students encounter studies of race, class, and gender for the first time, they often ask, "How is this group's experience like or not like my own?" This is an important question and a necessary first step, but it is not enough. For one thing, it tends to promote groups ranking the oppression of one another, as if the important thing were to determine who is most victimized. Furthermore, it frames one's understanding of different groups only within the context of other groups' experiences; thus, it can assume an artificial norm against which different groups are judged. Thinking comparatively tends to assume that race, class, and gender constitute separate and independent components of human experience that can be compared for their similarities and differences. Although thinking comparatively is an important step toward thinking more inclusively, we must go further.

Some do so by thinking in terms of an *additive model* of race, class, and gender. The additive model is reflected in terms such as *double* and *triple jeopardy*. But social inequality cannot necessarily be quantified in this fashion: Within this logic, poor African American women seemingly experience the triple oppression of race, gender, and class, whereas poor Latina lesbians encounter quadruple oppression, and so on. Adding together "differences" (thought to lie in the difference from the norm) produces a hierarchy of difference that ironically reinstalls those who are additively privileged at the top while relegating those who are additively oppressed to the bottom. We do not think of race and gender oppression in the simple additive terms implied by phrases such as *double* and *triple jeopardy*. The effects of race, class, and gender do "add up," both over time and in intensity of impact, but seeing race, class, and gender only in additive terms misses the social structural connections between them and the particular ways in which different configurations of race, class, and gender affect group experiences.

When combined with the concept of difference, additive models of thinking can foster another troubling outcome. One can begin with the concepts of race, class, and gender and continue to "add on" additional types of difference. Ethnicity, sexuality, religion, age, and ability all can be "added on" to race, class, and gender in ways that suggest that any of these forms of difference can substitute for others. This use of difference fosters a view of oppressions as equivalent and as being the same. Recognizing that difference encompasses more than race, class, and gender is a step in the right direction. But continuing to add on many distinctive forms of difference can be a never-ending process. After all, there are as many forms of difference as there are individuals. Ironically, this form of recognizing difference can erase the workings of power just as effectively as diversity initiatives.

The matrix of domination approach then also differs from just thinking about diversity. *Diversity* has become a catchword for trying to understand the complexities of race, class, and gender in the United States. What does *diversity* mean? Because the American public has become more conscious of these trends, *diversity* has become a buzzword—popularly used, but loosely defined. People use diversity to mean cultural variety, numerical representation, changing social norms, and the inequalities that characterize the status of different groups. In thinking about diversity, people have recognized that gender, age, race, sexual orientation, and ethnicity matter; thus, groups who have previously been invisible, including people of color, gays, lesbians, and bisexuals, older people, and immigrants, are now in some ways more visible. At the same time that diversity is more commonly recognized, however, these same groups continue to be defined as "other"; that is, they are perceived through dominant group values, treated in exclusionary ways, and subjected to social injustice and economic inequality. Moreover, dominant ways of thinking remain centered in the experiences of a few. As a result, groups who in total are the majority are still rendered invisible.

The movement to "understand diversity" has made people more sensitive and aware of the intersections of race, class, and gender. Thinking about diversity has also encouraged students and activists to see linkages to other categories of analysis, including sexuality, age, religion, physical disability, national identity, and ethnicity. But appreciating diversity is not the only point. The very term *diversity* implies that understanding race, class, and gender is simply a matter of recognizing the plurality of views and experiences in society—as if race, class, and gender were benign categories that foster diverse experiences instead of systems of power that produce social inequalities.

Diversity initiatives hold that the diversity created by race, class, and gender differences are pleasing and important, both to individuals and to society as a whole—so important, in fact, that diversity should be celebrated. Under diversity initiatives, ethnic foods, costumes, customs, and festivals are celebrated, and students and employees receive diversity training to heighten their multicultural awareness. Diversity initiatives also advance a notion that, despite their differences, "people are really the same." Under this view, the diversity created by race, class, and gender, although worthy of appreciation, does not and should not affect how society functions.

Certainly, opening our awareness of distinct group experiences is important, but some approaches to diversity can erase the very real differences in power that race, class, and gender create. For example, diversity initiatives have asked people to challenge the silence that has surrounded many group experiences. In this framework, people think about diversity as "listening to the voices" of a multitude of previously silenced groups. This is an important part of coming to understand race, class, and gender, but it is not enough. One problem is that people may begin hearing the voices as if they were disembodied from particular historical and social conditions—a framework that has been aggravated by postmodernist social theory. This perspective sees experience as a matter of competing discourses, personifying "voice" as if the voice or discourse itself constituted lived experience. Second, the "voices" framework suggests that any analysis is incomplete unless every voice is heard. In a sense, of course, this is true, because inclusion of silenced people is one of the goals of race/class/gender work. But in a situation where it is impossible to hear every voice, how does one decide which "voices" are more important than others? One might ask, who are the privileged listeners within these "voice" metaphors?

We think that the matrix of domination model is more analytical than either the difference, additive, or diversity frameworks *because of its focus on structural systems of power and inequality.* This means that race, class, and gender involve more than appreciating cultural diversity. The matrix of domination model requires analysis and criticism of existing systems of power and privilege; otherwise, understanding diversity becomes just one more privilege for those with the greatest access to education—something that has always been a mark of the elite class. Therefore, race, class, and gender studies mean more than just knowing the cultures of an array of human groups. Studying race, class, and gender means recognizing and analyzing the hierarchies and systems of domination that permeate society and that limit our ability to achieve true democracy and social justice.

Finally, we think it is also important to challenge the idea that race, class, and gender are important only at the level of culture—an implication of the catchword *multiculturalism*. *Culture* is traditionally defined as the "total way of life" of a group of people. It encompasses both material and symbolic components and is an important dimension of understanding human life. Analysis of culture per se, however, tends to look at the group itself, rather than at the broader conditions within which the group lives. Of course, as anthropologists know, a sound analysis of culture situates group experience within these external conditions. Nonetheless, a narrow focus on culture tends to ignore social conditions of power, privilege, and prestige. The result is that multicultural studies often seem tangled up with notions of cultural pluralism—as if knowing a culture other than one's own is the goal of a multicultural education.

Because we approach the study of race, class, and gender with an eye toward transforming thinking, we see our work as differing somewhat from the concepts implicit in the language of diversity, difference, or multiculturalism. Although we think it is important to see the diversity and plurality of different cultural forms, in our view this perspective, taken in and of itself, misses the broader point of understanding how racism, sexism, homophobia, and class relations have shaped the experience of groups. Imagine, for example, trying to study the oppression of gays and lesbians in terms of gay culture only. Obviously, doing this turns attention onto the group itself and away from the dominant society. Likewise, studying race only in terms of Latino culture or Asian American culture or African American culture, or studying women's oppression only by looking at women's culture, encourages thinking that blames the victims for their own oppression. For all of these reasons, the focus of this book is on the institutional, or structural, bases for race, class, and gender relations.

Thus, this book is not just about "understanding diversity." Developing a structural perspective on race, class, and gender is more than just understanding diversity or valuing cultural pluralism. Inclusive thinking begins with the recognition that the United States is a multicultural and diverse society. Population data and even casual observations reveal that obvious truth, but inclusive thinking is more than recognizing the plurality of experiences in this society. Understanding race, class, and gender means coming to see the systematic exclusion and exploitation of various groups. This is more than just adding in different group experiences to already established frameworks of thought. It means constructing new analyses that are focused on the centrality of race, class, and gender in the experiences of us all.

Understanding the social dynamics of race, class, and gender is central to this new vision. Studying race, class, and gender brings new facts and new perspectives to light, and it illuminates familiar things in new ways. For example, college basketball can be seen as pure entertainment, but it can also be seen as a social system in which race, class, and gender play a significant part. Also, places that appear to be all-White or all-men can be understood as products of a social system that is premised on certain race, class, and gender arrangements. Understanding the significance of race, class, and gender puts the experiences of all groups in the United States into a broader context. Furthermore, knowing how race, class, and gender operate within U.S. national borders helps you see beyond those borders, developing an awareness of how the increasingly global basis of society influences the configuration of race, class, and gender relationships in the United States.

DEVELOPING AN INCLUSIVE PERSPECTIVE

We want readers to understand that race, class, and gender are linked experiences, no one of which is more important than the others; the three are interrelated and together configure the structure of this society. You can begin to develop a more inclusive perspective by asking, How does the world look different if we put the experiences of those who have been excluded at the center of our thinking? At first, people might be tempted to simply assert the perspective and experience of their own group. Nationalist movements of different kinds have done this. They are valuable because they recognize the contributions and achievements of oppressed groups, but ultimately they are one-dimensional frameworks because they are centered in a single group experience and they encourage, rather than discourage, exclusionary thought.

Seeing inclusively is more than just seeing the world through the perspective of any one group whose views have been distorted or ignored.

Remember that group membership cuts across race, class, and gender categories. For example, one may be a working-class, Asian American woman or a Black, middle-class man or a gay, White, working-class woman. Inclusive thinking means seeing the interconnections between these experiences and not reducing a given person's or group's life to a single factor. In addition, developing inclusive thinking is more than just summing up the experiences of individual groups, as in the additive model discussed previously. Race, class, and gender are social structural categories. This means that they are embedded in the institutional structure of society. Understanding them requires a social structural analysis—by which we mean revealing the race, class, and gender patterns and processes that form the very framework of society.

We believe that thinking about the experiences of those who have been excluded from knowledge changes how we think about society, history, and culture. No longer do different groups seem just "different," "deviant," or "exotic." Rather, specific patterns of the intersections of race, class, and gender are revealed, as are the connections that exist among groups. We then learn how our different experiences are linked, both historically and now.

Once you understand that race, class, and gender are *simultaneous* and *intersecting* systems of relationship and meaning, you also can see the different ways that other categories of experience intersect in society. Age, religion, sexual orientation, nationality, physical ability, region, and ethnicity also shape systems of privilege and inequality. We have tried to integrate these different experiences throughout the book, although we could not include as much as we would have liked.

In the opening readings in this section, we begin by providing personal accounts of what exclusion means and how it feels. We have selected personal accounts that reflect the diverse experiences of race, class, gender, and/or sexual orientation. We intend for the personal nature of these accounts to build empathy between groups—an emotional stance that we think is critical to seeing linkages and connections.

Arturo Madrid, for example, shows how his experience as a young Latino student was silenced throughout his educational curriculum, leaving him to feel like an "other" in a society where he seemingly had no place, no history, no culture. For him, this involves more than just acknowledging the diverse histories, cultures, and experiences of groups who have been defined as marginal in society—what we have come to think of as "valuing diversity." But there is something more important than just valuing the diverse histories and cultures of the different groups who constitute society, and that is to recognize how groups whose experiences have been vital in the formation of society and culture have also been silenced in the construction of knowledge about this society. The result is that what we know—about the experiences of both these silenced groups and the dominant culture—is distorted and incomplete. Indeed, for that matter, ignoring such experiences also gives us a distorted view of how the nation itself has developed.

How much did you learn about the history of group oppression in your formal education? You probably touched briefly on topics such as slavery, women's suffrage, perhaps even the Holocaust, but most likely these were brief excursions from an otherwise dominant narrative that ignored people of color and women, along with others. For that matter, how much of what you study now is centered in the experiences of the most dominant groups in society? Think about the large number of social science studies that routinely make general conclusions about the population when they have been based on research done only about and by men. Or, how much of the literature you read and artistic creations that you study are the work of Asian Americans, Latinos/as, African Americans, Native Americans, gays, lesbians, or women?

By minimizing the experiences and creations of these different groups, we communicate that their work and creativity is less important and less central to the development of culture than is the history of White American men. What false or incomplete conclusions does this exclusionary thinking generate? When you learn, for example, that democracy and egalitarianism were central cultural beliefs in the early history of the United States, how do you explain the enslavement of millions of African Americans? the genocide of Native Americans? the laws against intermarriage between Asian Americans and White Americans?

This book asks you to think more inclusively. Without doing so you are prone to understand society, your own life within it, and the experiences of others through stereotypes and misleading information. If this is the basis for our knowledge about each other, then we have little ground for building more just and liberating relationships and social institutions.

In "La Güera," Cherríe Moraga writes about her developing awareness of her class, race, and sexual identity. Like the other authors here, Moraga tells us what exclusion has meant in her experience and how it feels. Her essay also reveals the intersections of race, class, and gender with the system of *compulsory heterosexuality*—that is, the institutionalized structures and beliefs that define and enforce heterosexual behavior as the only natural and permissible form of sexual expression. For Moraga, acknowledging her lesbian identity deepened her understanding of her mother's oppression as a poor Chicana. Moraga reminds us of the importance of breaking the silences that protect oppression.

Readers should keep the accounts of Madrid and Moraga in mind as they read the remainder of this book. What new experiences, understandings, theories, histories, and analyses do these readings inspire? What does it take for a member of one group (say a White male) to be willing to learn from and value the experiences of another (for example, a Chicana lesbian)? These essays show that, although we are caught in multiple systems, we can learn to see our connection to others. This is not just an intellectual exercise. As Haunani-Kay Trask shows ("From a Native Daughter"), there can also be a gap between dominant cultural narratives and people's actual experiences. As she, a native Hawaiian, tells it, the official history she learned in schools was not what she was taught in her family and community. Dominant narratives can try to justify the oppression of different groups, but the unwritten, untold subordinated truth can be a source for knowledge in pursuit of social justice.

Engaging oneself at the personal level is critical to this process of thinking differently about race, class, and gender. Changing one's mind is not just a matter of assessing facts and data, though that is important; it also requires examining one's feelings. That is why we begin with several personal narratives. Unlike more conventional forms of sociological data (such as surveys, interviews, and even direct observations), personal accounts are more likely to elicit emotional responses. Traditionally, social science has defined emotional engagement as an impediment to objectivity. Sociology, for example, has emphasized rational thought as the basis for social action and has often discouraged more personalized reflection, but the capacity to reflect on one's experience makes us distinctly human. Personal documents tap the private, reflective dimension of life, enabling us to see the inner lives of others and, in the process, revealing our own lives more completely.

The idea that objectivity is best reached only through rational thought is a specifically Western and masculine way of thinking—one that we challenge throughout this book. Including personal narratives is not meant to limit our level of understanding only to individuals. As sociologists, we study individuals in groups as a way of revealing the social structures shaping collective experiences. Through doing so, we discover our common experiences and see the impact of the social structures of race, class, and gender on our experiences. Marilyn Frye's article, "Oppression," introduces the structural perspective that lies at the heart of this book. She distinguishes oppression from suffering, pointing out that many individuals suffer in society, but that oppression is structured into the fabric of social institutions. Using the metaphor of a birdcage, Frye artfully explains the concept of social structure. Looking only at an individual wire in a cage does not reveal the network of wires that forms a cage; likewise, social structure refers to the patterns of behavior, belief, resource distribution, and social control that constitute society.

Analysis of the historical role of diverse groups is critical to understanding who we are as a society and a culture. As Ronald T. Takaki says in "A Different Mirror," this involves a debate over our national identity. Takaki makes a point of showing the common connections in the histories of African Americans, Chicanos, Irish Americans, Jews, and Native Americans. He argues that only when we understand this multidimensional history will we see ourselves in the full complexity of our humanity. Likewise, Audre Lorde writes that various forms of difference—race, sexuality, age, gender, among others—have separated and oppressed people. In a society marked by difference, she argues, we learn views of others and of ourselves that separate and divide people. For Lorde, relating across differences is critical to human survival.

Further Resources

For additional materials relating to this section, see the features on page 60 at the conclusion of this section.

References

Collins, Patricia Hill. 2000. *Black Feminist Thought: Knowledge, Consciousness, and Empowerment.* New York: Routledge.

Pew Research Center for the People and the Press. 2005. "Two-in-Three Critical of Bush's Relief Efforts." September 8. Web site: people-press.org.

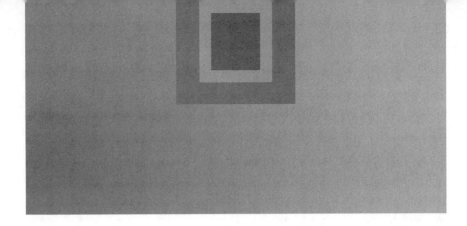

MISSING PEOPLE AND OTHERS
Joining Together to Expand the Circle

Arturo Madrid

I am a citizen of the United States, as are my parents and as were their parents, grandparents, and great-grandparents. My ancestors' presence in what is now the United States antedates Plymouth Rock, even without taking into account any American Indian heritage I might have.

I do not, however, fit those mental sets that define America and Americans. My physical appearance, my speech patterns, my name, my profession (a professor of Spanish) create a text that confuses the reader. My normal experience is to be asked, "And where are *you* from?"

My response depends on my mood. Passive-aggressive, I answer, "From here." Aggressive-passive, I ask, "Do you mean where am I originally from?" But ultimately my answer to those follow-up questions that ask about origins will be that we have always been from here.

Overcoming my resentment I will try to educate, knowing that nine times out of ten my words fall on inattentive ears. I have spent most of my adult life explaining who I am not. I am exotic, but—as Richard Rodriguez of

From *Change* 20 (May/June 1988): 55 59. Reprinted by permission.

Hunger of Memory fame so painfully found out—not exotic enough . . . not Peruvian, or Pakistani, or Persian, or whatever.

I am, however, very clearly *the other*, if only your everyday, garden-variety, domestic *other*. I've always known that I was *the other*, even before I knew the vocabulary or understood the significance of being *the other*.

I grew up in an isolated and historically marginal part of the United States, a small mountain village in the state of New Mexico, the eldest child of parents native to that region and whose ancestors had always lived there. In those vast and empty spaces, people who look like me, speak as I do, and have names like mine predominate. But the *americanos* lived among us: the descendants of those nineteenth-century immigrants who dispossessed us of our lands; missionaries who came to convert us and stayed to live among us; artists who became enchanted with our land and humanscape and went native; refugees from unhealthy climes, crowded spaces, unpleasant circumstances; and, of course, the inhabitants of Los Alamos, whose socio-cultural distance from us was moreover accentuated by the fact that they occupied a space removed from and proscribed to us. More importantly, however, they— *los americanos*—were omnipresent (and almost exclusively so) in newspapers, newsmagazines, books, on radio, in movies and, ultimately, on television.

Despite the operating myth of the day, school did not erase my otherness. It did try to deny it, and in doing so only accentuated it. To this day, schooling is more socialization than education, but when I was in elementary school—and given where I was—socialization was everything. School was where one became an American. Because there was a pervasive and systematic denial by the society that surrounded us that we were Americans. That denial was both explicit and implicit. My earliest memory of the former was that there were two kinds of churches: theirs and ours. The more usual was the implicit denial, our absence from the larger cultural, economic, political and social spaces—the one that reminded us constantly that we were *the other*. And school was where we felt it most acutely.

Quite beyond saluting the flag and pledging allegiance to it (a very intense and meaningful action, given that the U.S. was involved in a war and our brothers, cousins, uncles, and fathers were on the front lines) becoming American was learning English and its corollary—not speaking Spanish. Until very recently ours was a proscribed language—either *de jure* (by rule, by policy, by law) or *de facto* (by practice, implicitly if not explicitly; through social and political and economic pressure). I do not argue that learning English was not appropriate. On the contrary. Like it or not, and we had no basis to make any judgments on that matter, we were Americans by virtue of having been born Americans, and English was the common language of Americans. And there was a myth, a pervasive myth, that said that if we only learned to speak English well—and particularly without an accent—we would be welcomed into the American fellowship.

Senator Sam Hayakawa notwithstanding, the true text was not our speech, but rather our names and our appearance, for we would always have an accent, however perfect our pronunciation, however excellent our enunciation, however divine our diction. That accent would be heard in our pigmentation, our physiognomy, our names. We were, in short, *the other*.

Being *the other* means feeling different; is awareness of being distinct; is consciousness of being dissimilar. It means being outside the game, outside the circle, outside the set. It means being on the edges, on the margins, on the periphery. Otherness means feeling excluded, closed out, precluded, even disdained and scorned. It produces a sense of isolation, of apartness, of disconnectedness, of alienation.

Being *the other* involves a contradictory phenomenon. On the one hand being *the other* frequently means being invisible. Ralph Ellison wrote eloquently about that experience in his magisterial novel *The Invisible Man*. On the other hand, being *the other* sometimes involves sticking out like a sore thumb. What is she/he doing here?

If one is *the other*, one will inevitably be perceived unidimensionally; will be seen stereotypically; will be defined and delimited by mental sets that may not bear much relation to existing realities. There is a darker side to otherness as well. *The other* disturbs, disquiets, discomforts. It provokes distrust and suspicion. *The other* makes people feel anxious, nervous, apprehensive, even fearful. *The other* frightens, scares.

For some of us being *the other* is only annoying; for others it is debilitating; for still others it is damning. Many try to flee otherness by taking on protective colorations that provide invisibility, whether of dress or speech or manner or name. Only a fortunate few succeed. For the majority, otherness is permanently sealed by physical appearance. For the rest, otherness is betrayed by ways of being, speaking or of doing.

I spent the first half of my life downplaying the significance and consequences of otherness. The second half has seen me wrestling to understand its complex and deeply ingrained realities; striving to fathom why otherness denies us a voice or visibility or validity in American society and its institutions; struggling to make otherness familiar, reasonable, even normal to my fellow Americans.

I am also a missing person. Growing up in northern New Mexico I had only a slight sense of our being missing persons. *Hispanos*, as we called (and call) ourselves in New Mexico, were very much a part of the fabric of the society and there were Hispano professionals everywhere about me: doctors, lawyers, school teachers, and administrators. My people owned businesses, ran organizations and were both appointed and elected public officials.

To be sure, we did not own the larger businesses, nor at the time were we permitted to be part of the banking world. Other than that, however, people who looked like me, spoke like me, and had names like mine, predominated.

There was, to be sure, Los Alamos, but as I have said, it was removed from our realities.

My awareness of our absence from the larger institutional life of society became sharper when I went off to college, but even then it was attenuated by the circumstances of history and geography. The demography of Albuquerque still strongly reflected its historical and cultural origins, despite the influx of Midwesterners and Easterners. Moreover, many of my classmates at the University of New Mexico in Albuquerque were Hispanos, and even some of my professors were.

I thought that would change at UCLA, where I began graduate studies in 1960. Los Angeles already had a very large Mexican population, and that population was visible even in and around Westwood and on the campus. Many of the groundskeepers and food-service personnel at UCLA were Mexican. But Mexican-American students were few and mostly invisible, and I do not recall seeing or knowing a single Mexican-American (or, for that matter, black, Asian, or American Indian) professional on the staff or faculty of that institution during the five years I was there.

Needless to say, persons like me were not present in any capacity at Dartmouth College—the site of my first teaching appointment—and, of course, were not even part of the institutional or individual mind-set. I knew then that we—a "we" that had come to encompass American Indians, Asian Americans, black Americans, Puerto Ricans, and women—were truly missing persons in American institutional life.

Over the past three decades, the *de jure* and *de facto* segregations that have historically characterized American institutions have been under assault. As a consequence, minorities and women have become part of American institutional life, and although there are still many areas where we are not to be found, the missing persons phenomenon is not as pervasive as it once was.

However, the presence of *the other*, particularly minorities, in institutions and in institutional life, is, as we say in Spanish, *a flor de tierra;* spare plants whose roots do not go deep, a surface phenomenon, vulnerable to inclemencies of an economic, political, or social nature.

Our entrance into and our status in institutional life is not unlike a scenario set forth by my grandmother's pastor when she informed him that she and her family were leaving their mountain village to relocate in the Rio Grande Valley. When he asked her to promise that she would remain true to the faith and continue to involve herself in the life of the church, she assured him that she would and asked him why he thought she would do otherwise.

"Doña Trinidad," he told her, "in the Valley there is no Spanish church. There is only an American church." "But," she protested, "I read and speak English and would be able to worship there." Her pastor's response was: "It is possible that they will not admit you, and even if they do, they might not accept you. And that is why I want you to promise me that you are going to go to church. Because if they don't let you in through the front door, I want you to go in through the back door. And if you can't get in through the back door, go in the side door. And if you are unable to enter through the side door I want you to go in through the window. What is important is that you enter and that you stay."

Some of us entered institutional life through the front door; others through the back door; and still others through side doors. Many, if not most of us, came in through windows and continue to come in through windows. Of those who entered through the front door, some never made it past the lobby; others were ushered into corners and niches. Those who entered through back and side doors inevitably have remained in back and side rooms. And those who entered through windows found enclosures built around them. For despite the lip service given to the goal of the integration of minorities into institutional life, what has occurred instead is ghettoization, marginalization, isolation.

Not only have the entry points been limited: in addition, the dynamics have been singularly conflictive. Gaining entry and its corollary—gaining space—have frequently come as a consequence of demands made on institutions and institutional officers. Rather than entering institutions more or less passively, minorities have, of necessity, entered them actively, even aggressively. Rather than taking, they have demanded. Institutional relations have thus been adversarial, infused with specific and generalized tensions.

The nature of the entrance and the nature of the space occupied have greatly influenced the view and attitudes of the majority population within those institutions. All of us are put into the same box; that is, no matter what the individual reality, the assessment of the individual is inevitably conditioned by a perception that is held of the class. Whatever our history, whatever our record, whatever our validations, whatever our accomplishments, by and large we are perceived unidimensionally and are dealt with accordingly.

My most recent experience in this regard is atypical only in its explicitness. A few years ago I allowed myself to be persuaded to seek the presidency of a large and prestigious state university. I was invited for an interview and presented myself before the selection committee, which included members of the board of trustees. The opening question of the brief but memorable interview was directed at me by a member of that august body. "Dr. Madrid," he asked, "why does a one-dimensional person like you think he can be the president of a multi-dimensional institution like ours?"

If, as I happen to believe, the well-being of a society is directly related to the degree and extent to which all of its citizens participate in its institutions, we have a challenge before us. One of the strengths of our society—perhaps its main strength—has been a tradition of struggle against clubbishness, exclusivity, and restriction.

Today, more than ever, given the extraordinary changes that are taking place in our society, we need to take up that struggle again—irritating, grating, troublesome, unfashionable, unpleasant as it is. As educated and educator members of this society, we have a special responsibility for leading the struggle against marginalization, exclusion, and alienation.

Let us work together to assure that all American institutions, not just its precollegiate educational and penal institutions, reflect the diversity of our society. Not to do so is to risk greater alienation on the part of a growing segment of our society. It is to risk increased social tension in an already conflictive world. And ultimately it is to risk the survival of a range of institutions that, for all their defects and deficiencies, permit us the space, the opportunity, and the freedom to improve our individual and collective lot; to guide the course of our government, and to redress whatever grievances we have. Let us join together to expand, not to close the circle.

2

LA GÜERA

Cherríe Moraga

It requires something more than personal experience to gain a philosophy or point of view from any specific event. It is the quality of our response to the event and our capacity to enter into the lives of others that help us to make their lives and experiences our own.

Emma Goldman[1]

I am the very well-educated daughter of a woman who, by the standards in this country, would be considered largely illiterate. My mother was born in Santa Paula, Southern California, at a time when much of the central valley there was still farm land. Nearly thirty-five years later, in 1948, she was the only daughter of six to marry an anglo, my father.

I remember all of my mother's stories, probably much better than she realizes. She is a fine story-teller, recalling every event of her life with the vividness of the present, noting each detail right down to the cut and color of her dress. I remember stories of her being pulled out of school at the ages of five,

---

1. Alix Kates Shulman, "Was My Life Worth Living?" *Red Emma Speaks* (New York: Random House, 1972), p. 388.

seven, nine, and eleven to work in the fields, along with her brothers and sisters; stories of her father drinking away whatever small profit she was able to make for the family; of her going the long way home to avoid meeting him on the street, staggering toward the same destination. I remember stories of my mother lying about her age in order to get a job as a hat-check girl at Agua Caliente Racetrack in Tijuana. At fourteen, she was the main support of the family. I can still see her walking home alone at 3 a.m., only to turn all of her salary and tips over to her mother, who was pregnant again.

The stories continue through the war years and on: walnut-cracking factories, the Voit Rubber factory, and then the computer boom. I remember my mother doing piecework for the electronics plant in our neighborhood. In the late evening, she would sit in front of the T.V. set, wrapping copper wires into the backs of circuit boards, talking about "keeping up with the younger girls." By that time, she was already in her mid-fifties.

Meanwhile, I was college-prep in school. After classes, I would go with my mother to fill out job applications for her, or write checks for her at the supermarket. We would have the scenario all worked out ahead of time. My mother would sign the check before we'd get to the store. Then, as we'd approach the checkstand, she would say—within earshot of the cashier—"oh honey, you go 'head and make out the check," as if she couldn't be bothered with such an insignificant detail. No one asked any questions.

I was educated, and wore it with a keen sense of pride and satisfaction, my head propped up with the knowledge, from my mother, that my life would be easier than hers. I was educated; but more than this, I was "la güera": fair-skinned. Born with the features of my Chicana mother, but the skin of my anglo father, I had it made.

No one ever quite told me this (that light was right), but I knew that being light was something valued in my family (who were all Chicano, with the exception of my father). In fact, everything about my upbringing (at least what occurred on a conscious level) attempted to bleach me of what color I did have. Although my mother was fluent in it, I was never taught much Spanish at home. I picked up what I did learn from school and from overheard snatches of conversation among my relatives and mother. She often called other lower-income Mexicans "braceros," or "wet-backs," referring to herself and her family as "a different class of people." And yet, the real story was that my family, too, had been poor (some still are) and farmworkers. My mother can remember this in her blood as if it were yesterday. But this is something she would like to forget (and rightfully), for to her, on a basic economic level, being Chicana meant being "less." It was through my mother's desire to protect her children from poverty and illiteracy that we became "anglocized"; the more effectively we could pass in the white world, the better guaranteed our future.

From all of this, I experience, daily, a huge disparity between what I was born into and what I was to grow up to become. Because, (as Goldman suggests) these stories my mother told me crept under my "güera" skin. I had no choice but to enter into the life of my mother. *I had no choice.* I took her life into my heart, but managed to keep a lid on it as long as I feigned being the happy, upwardly mobile heterosexual.

When I finally lifted the lid to my lesbianism, a profound connection with my mother reawakened in me. It wasn't until I acknowledged and confronted my own lesbianism in the flesh, that my heartfelt identification with and empathy for my mother's oppression—due to being poor, uneducated, and Chicana—was realized. My lesbianism is the avenue through which I have learned the most about silence and oppression, and it continues to be the most tactile reminder to me that we are not free human beings.

You see, one follows the other. I had known for years that I was a lesbian, had felt it in my bones, had ached with the knowledge, gone crazed with the knowledge, wallowed in the silence of it. Silence *is* like starvation. Don't be fooled. It's nothing short of that, and felt most sharply when one has had a full belly most of her life. When we are not physically starving, we have the luxury to realize psychic and emotional starvation. It is from this starvation that other starvations can be recognized—if one is willing to take the risk of making the connection—if one is willing to be responsible to the result of the connection. For me, the connection is an inevitable one.

What I am saying is that the joys of looking like a white girl ain't so great since I realized I could be beaten on the street for being a dyke. If my sister's being beaten because she's Black, it's pretty much the same principle. We're both getting beaten any way you look at it. The connection is blatant; and in the case of my own family, the difference in the privileges attached to looking white instead of brown are merely a generation apart.

In this country, lesbianism is a poverty—as is being brown, as is being a woman, as is being just plain poor. The danger lies in ranking the oppressions. *The danger lies in failing to acknowledge the specificity of the oppression.* The danger lies in attempting to deal with oppression purely from a theoretical base. Without an emotional, heartfelt grappling with the source of our own oppression, without naming the enemy within ourselves and outside of us, no authentic, nonhierarchical connection among oppressed groups can take place.

When the going gets rough, will we abandon our so-called comrades in a flurry of racist/heterosexist/what-have-you panic? To whose camp, then, should the lesbian of color retreat? Her very presence violates the ranking and abstraction of oppression. Do we merely live hand to mouth? Do we merely struggle with the "ism" that's sitting on top of our own heads?

The answer is: yes, I think first we do; and we must do so thoroughly and deeply. But to fail to move out from there will only isolate us in our own oppression—will only insulate, rather than radicalize us.

To illustrate: a gay male friend of mine once confided to me that he continued to feel that, on some level, I didn't trust him because he was male; that he felt, really, if it ever came down to a "battle of the sexes," I might kill him. I admitted that I might very well. He wanted to understand the source of my distrust. I responded, "You're not a woman. Be a woman for a day. Imagine being a woman." He confessed that the thought terrified him because, to him, being a woman meant being raped by men. He *had* felt raped by men; he wanted to forget what that meant. What grew from that discussion was the realization that in order for him to create an authentic alliance with me, he must deal with the primary source of his own sense of oppression. He must, first, emotionally come to terms with what it feels like to be a victim. If he—or anyone—were to truly do this, it would be impossible to discount the oppression of others, except by again forgetting how we have been hurt.

And yet, oppressed groups are forgetting all the time. There are instances of this in the rising Black middle class, and certainly an obvious trend of such "unconsciousness" among white gay men. Because to remember may mean giving up whatever privileges we have managed to squeeze out of this society by virtue of our gender, race, class, or sexuality.

Within the women's movement, the connections among women of different backgrounds and sexual orientations have been fragile, at best. I think this phenomenon is indicative of our failure to seriously address ourselves to some very frightening questions: How have I internalized my own oppression? How have I oppressed? Instead, we have let rhetoric do the job of poetry. Even the word "oppression" has lost its power. We need a new language, better words that can more closely describe women's fear of and resistance to one another; words that will not always come out sounding like dogma.

What prompted me in the first place to work on an anthology by radical women of color was a deep sense that I had a valuable insight to contribute, by virtue of my birthright and background. And yet, I don't really understand first-hand what it feels like being shitted on for being brown. I understand much more about the joys of it—being Chicana and having family are synonymous for me. What I know about loving, singing, crying, telling stories, speaking with my heart and hands, even having a sense of my own soul comes from the love of my mother, aunts, cousins. . . .

But at the age of twenty-seven, it is frightening to acknowledge that I have internalized a racism and classism, where the object of oppression is not only someone outside of my skin, but the someone inside my skin. In fact, to a large degree, the real battle with such oppression, for all of us, begins under the skin. I have had to confront the fact that much of what I value about being Chicana, about my family, has been subverted by anglo culture and my own cooperation with it. This realization did not occur to me overnight. For example, it wasn't until long after my graduation from the private college I'd attended in Los Angeles, that I realized the major reason for my total alienation from and fear of my classmates was rooted in class and culture. CLICK.

Three years after graduation, in an apple-orchard in Sonoma, a friend of mine (who comes from an Italian Irish working-class family) says to me, "Cherríe, no wonder you felt like such a nut in school. Most of the people there were white and rich." It was true. All along I had felt the difference, but not until I had put the words "class" and "color" to the experience, did my feelings make any sense. For years, I had berated myself for not being as "free" as my classmates. I completely bought that they simply had more guts than I did—to rebel against their parents and run around the country hitchhiking, reading books and studying "art." They had enough privilege to be atheists, for chrissake. There was no one around filling in the disparity for me between their parents, who were Hollywood filmmakers, and my parents, who wouldn't know the name of a filmmaker if their lives depended on it (and precisely because their lives didn't depend on it, they couldn't be bothered). But I knew nothing about "privilege" then. White was right. Period. I could pass. If I got educated enough, there would never be any telling.

Three years after that, another CLICK. In a letter to Barbara Smith, I wrote:

> I went to a concert where Ntosake Shange was reading. There, everything exploded for me. She was speaking a language that I knew—in the deepest parts of me—existed, and that I had ignored in my own feminist studies and even in my own writing. What Ntosake caught in me is the realization that in my development as a poet, I have, in many ways, denied the voice of my brown mother—the brown in me. I have acclimated to the sound of a white language which, as my father represents it, does not speak to the emotions in my poems—emotions which stem from the love of my mother.
>
> The reading was agitating. Made me uncomfortable. Threw me into a week-long terror of how deeply I was affected. I felt that I had to start all over again. That I turned only to the perceptions of white middle-class women to speak for me and all women. I am shocked by my own ignorance.

Sitting in that auditorium chair was the first time I had realized to the core of me that for years I had disowned the language I knew best—ignored the words and rhythms that were the closest to me. The sounds of my mother and aunts gossiping—half in English, half in Spanish—while drinking cerveza in the kitchen. And the hands—I had cut off the hands in my poems. But not in conversation; still the hands could not be kept down. Still they insisted on moving.

The reading had forced me to remember that I knew things from my roots. But to remember puts me up against what I don't know. Shange's reading agitated me because she spoke with power about a world that is both alien and common to me: "the capacity to enter into the lives of others." But you can't just take the goods and run. I knew that then, sitting in the Oakland auditorium (as I know in my poetry), that the only thing worth writing about is what seems to be unknown and, therefore, fearful.

The "unknown" is often depicted in racist literature as the "darkness" within a person. Similarly, sexist writers will refer to fear in the form of the vagina, calling it "the orifice of death." In contrast, it is a pleasure to read works such as Maxine Hong Kingston's *Woman Warrior*, where fear and alienation are described as "the white ghosts." And yet, the bulk of literature in this country reinforces the myth that what is dark and female is evil. Consequently, each of us—whether dark, female, or both—has in some way *internalized* this oppressive imagery. What the oppressor often succeeds in doing is simply *externalizing* his fears, projecting them into the bodies of women, Asians, gays, disabled folks, whoever seems most "other."

> call me
> roach and presumptuous
> nightmare on your white pillow
> your itch to destroy
> the indestructible
> part of yourself
>
>   Audre Lorde[2]

But it is not really difference the oppressor fears so much as similarity. He fears he will discover in himself the same aches, the same longings as those of the people he has shitted on. He fears the immobilization threatened by his own incipient guilt. He fears he will have to change his life once he has seen himself in the bodies of the people he has called different. He fears the hatred, anger, and vengeance of those he has hurt.

This is the oppressor's nightmare, but it is not exclusive to him. We women have a similar nightmare, for each of us in some way has been both oppressed and the oppressor. We are afraid to look at how we have failed each other. We are afraid to see how we have taken the values of our oppressor into our hearts and turned them against ourselves and one another. We are afraid to admit how deeply "the man's" words have been ingrained in us.

To assess the damage is a dangerous act. I think of how, even as a feminist lesbian, I have so wanted to ignore my own homophobia, my own hatred of myself for being queer. I have not wanted to admit that my deepest personal sense of myself has not quite "caught up" with my "woman-identified" politics. I have been afraid to criticize lesbian writers who choose to "skip over" these issues in the name of feminism. In 1979, we talk of "old gay" and "butch and femme" roles as if they were ancient history. We toss them aside as merely patriarchal notions. And yet, the truth of the matter is that I have sometimes taken society's fear and hatred of lesbians to bed with me. I have sometimes hated my lover for loving me. I have sometimes felt "not woman enough" for her. I have sometimes felt "not man enough." For a lesbian trying to survive in a heterosexist society, there is no easy way around these emotions. Similarly, in a white-dominated world, there is little getting around racism and our own internalization of it. It's always there, embodied in someone we least expect to rub up against.

---

2. From "The Brown Menace or Poem to the Survival of Roaches," *The New York Head Shop and Museum* (Detroit: Broadside, 1974), p. 48.

When we do rub up against this person, *there* then is the challenge. *There* then is the opportunity to look at the nightmare within us. But we usually shrink from such a challenge.

Time and time again, I have observed that the usual response among white women's groups when the "racism issue" comes up is to deny the difference. I have heard comments like, "Well, we're open to *all* women; why don't they (women of color) come? You can only do so much. . . ." But there is seldom any analysis of how the very nature and structure of the group itself may be founded on racist or classist assumptions. More importantly, so often the women seem to feel no loss, no lack, no absence when women of color are not involved; therefore, there is little desire to change the situation. This has hurt me deeply. I have come to believe that the only reason women of a privileged class will dare to look at *how* it is that *they* oppress, is when they've come to know the meaning of their own oppression. And understand that the oppression of others hurts them personally.

The other side of the story is that women of color and working-class women often shrink from challenging white middle-class women. It is much easier to rank oppressions and set up a hierarchy, rather than take responsibility for changing our own lives. We have failed to demand that white women, particularly those who claim to be speaking for all women, be accountable for their racism.

The dialogue has simply not gone deep enough.

I have many times questioned my right to even work on an anthology which is to be written "exclusively by Third World women." I have had to look critically at my claim to color, at a time when, among white feminist ranks, it is a "politically correct" (and sometimes peripherally advantageous) assertion to make. I must acknowledge the fact that, physically, I have had a *choice* about making that claim, in contrast to women who have not had such a choice, and have been abused for their color. I must reckon with the fact that for most of my life, by virtue of the very fact that I am white-looking, I identified with and aspired toward white values, and that I rode the wave of that Southern California privilege as far as conscience would let me.

Well, now I feel both bleached and beached. I feel angry about this—the years when I refused to recognize privilege, both when it worked against me, and when I worked it, ignorantly, at the expense of others. These are not settled issues. That is why this work feels so risky to me. It continues to be discovery. It has brought me into contact with women who invariably know a hell of a lot more than I do about racism, as experienced in the flesh, as revealed in the flesh of their writing.

I think: what is my responsibility to my roots—both white and brown, Spanish-speaking and English? I am a woman with a foot in both worlds; and I refuse the split. I feel the necessity for dialogue. Sometimes I feel it urgently.

But one voice is not enough, nor two, although this is where dialogue begins. It is essential that radical feminists confront their fear of and resistance to each other, because without this, there *will* be no bread on the table. Simply, we will not survive. If we could make this connection in our heart of hearts, that if we are serious about a revolution—better—if we seriously believe there should be joy in our lives (real joy, not just "good times"), then we need one another. We women need each other. Because my/your solitary, self-asserting "go-for-the-throat-of-fear" power is not enough. The real power, as you and I well know, is collective. I can't afford to be afraid of you, nor you of me. If it takes head-on collisions, let's do it: this polite timidity is killing us.

As Lorde suggests in the passage I cited earlier, it is in looking to the nightmare that the dream is found. There, the survivor emerges to insist on a future, a vision, yes, born out of what is dark and female. The feminist movement must be a movement of such survivors, a movement with a future.

3

OPPRESSION

Marilyn Frye

It is a fundamental claim of feminism that women are oppressed. The word "oppression" is a strong word. It repels and attracts. It is dangerous and dangerously fashionable and endangered. It is much misused, and sometimes not innocently.

The statement that women are oppressed is frequently met with the claim that men are oppressed too. We hear that oppressing is oppressive to those who oppress as well as to those they oppress. Some men cite as evidence of their oppression their much-advertised inability to cry. It is tough, we are told, to be masculine. When the stresses and frustrations of being a man are cited as evidence that oppressors are oppressed by their oppressing, the word "oppression" is being stretched to meaninglessness; it is treated as though its scope includes any and all human experience of limitation or

---

From Marilyn Frye, *The Politics of Reality* (Trumansburg, NY: Crossing Press, 1983), pp. 1–16. Reprinted by permission.

suffering, no matter the cause, degree, or consequence. Once such usage has been put over on us, then if ever we deny that any person or group is oppressed, we seem to imply that we think they never suffer and have no feelings. We are accused of insensitivity; even of bigotry. For women, such accusation is particularly intimidating, since sensitivity is one of the few virtues that has been assigned to us. If we are found insensitive, we may fear we have no redeeming traits at all and perhaps are not real women. Thus are we silenced before we begin: the name of our situation drained of meaning and our guilt mechanisms tripped.

But this is nonsense. Human beings can be miserable without being oppressed, and it is perfectly consistent to deny that a person or group is oppressed without denying that they have feelings or that they suffer. . . .

The root of the word "oppression" is the element "press." *The press of the crowd; pressed into military service; to press a pair of pants; printing press; press the button.* Presses are used to mold things or flatten them or reduce them in bulk, sometimes to reduce them by squeezing out the gases or liquids in them. Something pressed is something caught between or among forces and barriers which are so related to each other that jointly they restrain, restrict or prevent the thing's motion or mobility. Mold. Immobilize. Reduce.

The mundane experience of the oppressed provides another clue. One of the most characteristic and ubiquitous features of the world as experienced by oppressed people is the double bind—situations in which options are reduced to a very few and all of them expose one to penalty, censure, or deprivation. For example, it is often a requirement upon oppressed people that we smile and be cheerful. If we comply, we signal our docility and our acquiescence in our situation. We need not, then, be taken note of. We acquiesce in being made invisible, in our occupying no space. We participate in our own erasure. On the other hand, anything but the sunniest countenance exposes us to being perceived as mean, bitter, angry, or dangerous. This means, at the least, that we may be found "difficult" or unpleasant to work with, which is enough to cost one one's livelihood; at worst, being seen as mean, bitter, angry, or dangerous has been known to result in rape, arrest, beating, and murder. One can only choose to risk one's preferred form and rate of annihilation.

Another example: It is common in the United States that women, especially younger women, are in a bind where neither sexual activity nor sexual inactivity is all right. If she is heterosexually active, a woman is open to censure and punishment for being loose, unprincipled, or a whore. The "punishment" comes in the form of criticism, snide and embarrassing remarks, being treated as an easy lay by men, scorn from her more restrained female friends. She may have to lie and hide her behavior from her parents. She must juggle the risks of unwanted pregnancy and dangerous contraceptives. On the other hand, if she refrains from heterosexual activity, she is fairly constantly harassed by men who try to persuade her into it and pressure her to "relax" and "let her hair down"; she is threatened with labels like "frigid," "uptight," "man-hater," "bitch" and "cocktease." The same parents who would be disapproving of her sexual activity may be worried by her inactivity because it suggests she is not or will not be popular, or is not sexually normal. She may be charged with lesbianism. If a woman is raped, then if she has been hetero-sexually active she is subject to the presumption that she liked it (since her activity is presumed to show that she likes sex), and if she has not been het-erosexually active, she is subject to the presumption that she liked it (since she is supposedly "repressed and frustrated"). Both heterosexual activity and het-erosexual nonactivity are likely to be taken as proof that you wanted to be raped, and hence, of course, weren't *really* raped at all. You can't win. You are caught in a bind, caught between systematically related pressures.

Women are caught like this, too, by networks of forces and barriers that expose one to penalty, loss, or contempt whether one works outside the home or not, is on welfare or not, bears children or not, raises children or not, mar-ries or not, stays married or not, is heterosexual, lesbian, both, or neither. Economic necessity; confinement to racial and/or sexual job ghettos; sexual harassment; sex discrimination; pressures of competing expectations and judgments about *women, wives,* and *mothers* (in the society at large, in racial and ethnic subcultures, and in one's own mind); dependence (full or partial) on husbands, parents, or the state; commitment to political ideas; loyalties to racial or ethnic or other "minority" groups; the demands of self-respect and responsibilities to others. Each of these factors exists in complex tension with every other, penalizing or prohibiting all of the apparently available options. And nipping at one's heels, always, is the endless pack of little things. If one dresses one way, one is subject to the assumption that one is advertising one's sexual availability; if one dresses another way, one appears to "not care about oneself" or to be "unfeminine." If one uses "strong language," one invites categorization as a whore or slut; if one does not, one invites categorization as a "lady"—one too delicately constituted to cope with robust speech or the realities to which it presumably refers.

The experience of oppressed people is that the living of one's life is con-fined and shaped by forces and barriers which are not accidental or occasional and hence avoidable, but are systematically related to each other in such a way as to catch one between and among them and restrict or penalize motion in any direction. It is the experience of being caged in: all avenues, in every direction, are blocked or booby trapped.

Cages. Consider a birdcage. If you look very closely at just one wire in the cage, you cannot see the other wires. If your conception of what is before you is determined by this myopic focus, you could look at that one wire, up and down the length of it, and be unable to see why a bird would not just fly around the wire any time it wanted to go somewhere. Furthermore, even if, one day at a time, you myopically inspected each wire, you still could not see why a bird would have trouble going past the wires to get anywhere. There is no physical property of any one wire, *nothing* that the closest scrutiny could discover, that will reveal how a bird could be inhibited or harmed by it except in the most accidental way. It is only when you step back, stop looking at the wires one by one, microscopically, and take a macroscopic view of the whole cage, that you can see why the bird does not go anywhere; and then you will see it in a moment. It will require no great subtlety of mental powers. It is perfectly *obvious* that the bird is surrounded by a network of systematically related barriers, no one of which would be the least hindrance to its flight, but which, by their relations to each other, are as confining as the solid walls of a dungeon.

It is now possible to grasp one of the reasons why oppression can be hard to see and recognize: one can study the elements of an oppressive structure with great care and some good will without seeing the structure as a whole, and hence without seeing or being able to understand that one is looking at a cage and that there are people there who are caged, whose motion and mobility are restricted, whose lives are shaped and reduced. . . .

As the cageness of the birdcage is a macroscopic phenomenon, the oppressiveness of the situations in which women live their various and different lives is a macroscopic phenomenon. Neither can be *seen* from a microscopic perspective. But when you look macroscopically you can see it—a network of forces and barriers which are systematically related and which conspire to the immobilization, reduction, and molding of women and the lives we live. . . .

4

A DIFFERENT MIRROR

Ronald T. Takaki

I had flown from San Francisco to Norfolk and was riding in a taxi to my hotel to attend a conference on multiculturalism. Hundreds of educators from across the country were meeting to discuss the need for greater cultural diversity in the curriculum. My driver and I chatted about the weather and the tourists. The sky was cloudy, and Virginia Beach was twenty minutes away. The rearview mirror reflected a white man in his forties. "How long have you

From Ronald T. Takaki, *A Different Mirror: A History of Multicultural America* (Boston: Little, Brown, 1993), pp. 1–17. Copyright © 1993 by Ronald T. Takaki. Reprinted by permission of the publisher.

been in this country?" he asked. "All my life," I replied, wincing. "I was born in the United States." With a strong southern drawl, he remarked: "I was wondering because your English is excellent!" Then, as I had many times before, I explained: "My grandfather came here from Japan in the 1880s. My family has been here, in America, for over a hundred years." He glanced at me in the mirror. Somehow I did not look "American" to him; my eyes and complexion looked foreign.

Suddenly, we both became uncomfortably conscious of a racial divide separating us. An awkward silence turned my gaze from the mirror to the passing landscape, the shore where the English and the Powhatan Indians first encountered each other. Our highway was on land that Sir Walter Raleigh had renamed "Virginia" in honor of Elizabeth I, the Virgin Queen. In the English cultural appropriation of America, the indigenous peoples themselves would become outsiders in their native land. Here, at the eastern edge of the continent, I mused, was the site of the beginning of multicultural America. Jamestown, the English settlement founded in 1607, was nearby: the first twenty Africans were brought here a year before the Pilgrims arrived at Plymouth Rock. Several hundred miles offshore was Bermuda, the "Bermoothes" where William Shakespeare's Prospero had landed and met the native Caliban in *The Tempest*. Earlier, another voyager had made an Atlantic crossing and unexpectedly bumped into some islands to the south. Thinking he had reached Asia, Christopher Columbus mistakenly identified one of the islands as "Cipango" (Japan). In the wake of the admiral, many peoples would come to America from different shores, not only from Europe but also Africa and Asia. One of them would be my grandfather. My mental wandering across terrain and time ended abruptly as we arrived at my destination. I said good-bye to my driver and went into the hotel, carrying a vivid reminder of why I was attending this conference.

Questions like the one my taxi driver asked me are always jarring, but I can understand why he could not see me as American. He had a narrow but widely shared sense of the past—a history that has viewed American as European in ancestry. "Race," Toni Morrison explained, has functioned as a "metaphor" necessary to the "construction of Americanness": in the creation of our national identity, "American" has been defined as "white."[1]

But America has been racially diverse since our very beginning on the Virginia shore, and this reality is increasingly becoming visible and ubiquitous. Currently, one-third of the American people do not trace their origins to Europe; in California, minorities are fast becoming a majority. They already predominate in major cities across the country—New York, Chicago, Atlanta, Detroit, Philadelphia, San Francisco, and Los Angeles.

This emerging demographic diversity has raised fundamental questions about America's identity and culture. In 1990, *Time* published a cover story on "America's Changing Colors." "Someday soon," the magazine announced, "white Americans will become a minority group." How soon? By 2056, most

Americans will trace their descent to "Africa, Asia, the Hispanic world, the Pacific Islands, Arabia—almost anywhere but white Europe." This dramatic change in our nation's ethnic composition is altering the way we think about ourselves. "The deeper significance of America's becoming a majority non-white society is what it means to the national psyche, to individuals' sense of themselves and their nation—their idea of what it is to be American." . . .[2]

What is fueling the debate over our national identity and the content of our curriculum is America's intensifying racial crisis. The alarming signs and symptoms seem to be everywhere—the killing of Vincent Chin in Detroit, the black boycott of a Korean grocery store in Flatbush, the hysteria in Boston over the Carol Stuart murder, the battle between white sportsmen and Indians over tribal fishing rights in Wisconsin, the Jewish-black clashes in Brooklyn's Crown Heights, the black-Hispanic competition for jobs and educational resources in Dallas, which *Newsweek* described as "a conflict of the have-nots," and the Willie Horton campaign commercials, which widened the divide between the suburbs and the inner cities.[3]

This reality of racial tension rudely woke America like a fire bell in the night on April 29, 1992. Immediately after four Los Angeles police officers were found not guilty of brutality against Rodney King, rage exploded in Los Angeles. Race relations reached a new nadir. During the nightmarish rampage, scores of people were killed, over two thousand injured, twelve thousand arrested, and almost a billion dollars' worth of property destroyed. The live televised images mesmerized America. The rioting and the murderous melee on the streets resembled the fighting in Beirut and the West Bank. The thousands of fires burning out of control and the dark smoke filling the skies brought back images of the burning oil fields of Kuwait during Desert Storm. Entire sections of Los Angeles looked like a bombed city. "Is this America?" many shocked viewers asked. "Please, can we get along here," pleaded Rodney King, calling for calm. "We all can get along. I mean, we're all stuck here for a while. Let's try to work it out."[4]

But how should "we" be defined? Who are the people "stuck here" in America? One of the lessons of the Los Angeles explosion is the recognition of the fact that we are a multiracial society and that race can no longer be defined in the binary terms of white and black. "We" will have to include Hispanics and Asians. While blacks currently constitute 13 percent of the Los Angeles population, Hispanics represent 40 percent. The 1990 census revealed that South Central Los Angeles, which was predominantly black in 1965 when the Watts rebellion occurred, is now 45 percent Hispanic. A majority of the first 5,438 people arrested were Hispanic, while 37 percent were black. Of the fifty-eight people who died in the riot, more than a third were Hispanic, and about 40 percent of the businesses destroyed were Hispanic-owned. Most of the other shops and stores were Korean-owned. The dreams of many Korean immigrants went up in smoke during the riot: two thousand Korean-owned businesses were damaged or demolished, totaling about $400 million in losses. There is evidence indicating they were targeted. "After all," explained a black gang member, "we didn't burn our community, just *their* stores."[5]

"I don't feel like I'm in America anymore," said Denisse Bustamente as she watched the police protecting the firefighters. "I feel like I am far away." Indeed, Americans have been witnessing ethnic strife erupting around the world—the rise of neo-Nazism and the murder of Turks in Germany, the ugly "ethnic cleansing" in Bosnia, the terrible and bloody clashes between Muslims and Hindus in India. Is the situation here different, we have been nervously wondering, or do ethnic conflicts elsewhere represent a prologue for America? What is the nature of malevolence? Is there a deep, perhaps primordial, need for group identity rooted in hatred for the other? Is ethnic pluralism possible for America? But answers have been limited. Television reports have been little more than thirty-second sound bites. Newspaper articles have been mostly superficial descriptions of racial antagonisms and the current urban malaise. What is lacking is historical context; consequently, we are left feeling bewildered.[6]

How did we get to this point, Americans everywhere are anxiously asking. What does our diversity mean, and where is it leading us? *How* do we work it out in the post–Rodney King era?

Certainly one crucial way is for our society's various ethnic groups to develop a greater understanding of each other. For example, how can African Americans and Korean Americans work it out unless they learn about each other's cultures, histories, and also economic situations? This need to share knowledge about our ethnic diversity has acquired new importance and has given new urgency to the pursuit for a more accurate history. . . .

While all of America's many groups cannot be covered [here], the English immigrants and their descendants require attention, for they possessed inordinate power to define American culture and make public policy. What men like John Winthrop, Thomas Jefferson, and Andrew Jackson thought as well as did mattered greatly to all of us and was consequential for everyone. A broad range of groups [is important]: African Americans, Asian Americans, Chicanos, Irish, Jews, and Indians. While together they help to explain general patterns in our society, each has contributed to the making of the United States.

African Americans have been the central minority throughout our country's history. They were initially brought here on a slave ship in 1619. Actually, these first twenty Africans might not have been slaves; rather, like most of the white laborers, they were probably indentured servants. The transformation of Africans into slaves is the story of the "hidden" origins of slavery. How and when was it decided to institute a system of bonded black labor? What happened, while freighted with racial significance, was actually conditioned by class conflicts within white society. Once established, the "peculiar institution" would have consequences for centuries to come. During the nineteenth century, the political storm over slavery almost destroyed the nation.

Since the Civil War and emancipation, race has continued to be largely defined in relation to African Americans—segregation, civil rights, the underclass, and affirmative action. Constituting the largest minority group in our society, they have been at the cutting edge of the Civil Rights Movement. Indeed, their struggle has been a constant reminder of America's moral vision as a country committed to the principle of liberty. Martin Luther King clearly understood this truth when he wrote from a jail cell: "We will reach the goal of freedom in Birmingham and all over the nation, because the goal of America is freedom. Abused and scorned though we may be, our destiny is tied up with America's destiny."[7]

Asian Americans have been here for over one hundred and fifty years, before many European immigrant groups. But as "strangers" coming from a "different shore," they have been stereotyped as "heathen," exotic, and unassimilable. Seeking "Gold Mountain," the Chinese arrived first, and what happened to them influenced the reception of the Japanese, Koreans, Filipinos, and Asian Indians as well as the Southeast Asian refugees like the Vietnamese and the Hmong. The 1882 Chinese Exclusion Act was the first law that prohibited the entry of immigrants on the basis of nationality. The Chinese condemned this restriction as racist and tyrannical. "They call us 'Chink,'" complained a Chinese immigrant, cursing the "white demons." "They think we no good! America cuts us off. No more come now, too bad!" This precedent later provided a basis for the restriction of European immigrant groups such as Italians, Russians, Poles, and Greeks. The Japanese painfully discovered that their accomplishments in America did not lead to acceptance, for during World War II, unlike Italian Americans and German Americans, they were placed in internment camps. Two-thirds of them were citizens by birth. "How could I as a 6-month-old child born in this country," asked Congressman Robert Matsui years later, "be declared by my own Government to be an enemy alien?" Today, Asian Americans represent the fastest-growing ethnic group. They have also become the focus of much mass media attention as "the Model Minority" not only for blacks and Chicanos, but also for whites on welfare and even middle-class whites experiencing economic difficulties.[8]

Chicanos represent the largest group among the Hispanic population, which is projected to outnumber African Americans. They have been in the United States for a long time, initially incorporated by the war against Mexico. The treaty had moved the border between the two countries, and the people of "occupied" Mexico suddenly found themselves "foreigners" in their "native land." As historian Albert Camarillo pointed out, the Chicano past is an integral part of America's westward expansion, also known as "manifest destiny." But while the early Chicanos were a colonized people, most of them today have immigrant roots. Many began the trek to El Norte in the early twentieth century. "As I had heard a lot about the United States," Jesus Garza recalled, "it was my dream to come here." "We came to know families from Chihuahua, Sonora, Jalisco, and Durango," stated Ernesto Galarza.

"Like ourselves, our Mexican neighbors had come this far moving step by step, working and waiting, as if they were feeling their way up a ladder." Nevertheless, the Chicano experience has been unique, for most of them have lived close to their homeland—a proximity that has helped reinforce their language, identity, and culture. This migration to El Norte has continued to the present. Los Angeles has more people of Mexican origin than any other city in the world, except Mexico City. A mostly mestizo people of Indian as well as African and Spanish ancestries, Chicanos currently represent the largest minority group in the Southwest, where they have been visibly transforming culture and society.[9]

The Irish came here in greater numbers than most immigrant groups. Their history has been tied to America's past from the very beginning. Ireland represented the earliest English frontier: the conquest of Ireland occurred before the colonization of America, and the Irish were the first group that the English called "savages." In this context, the Irish past foreshadowed the Indian future. During the nineteenth century, the Irish, like the Chinese, were victims of British colonialism. While the Chinese fled from the ravages of the Opium Wars, the Irish were pushed from their homeland by "English tyranny." Here they became construction workers and factory operatives as well as the "maids" of America. Representing a Catholic group seeking to settle in a fiercely Protestant society, the Irish immigrants were targets of American nativist hostility. They were also what historian Lawrence J. McCaffrey called "the pioneers of the American urban ghetto," "previewing" experiences that would later be shared by the Italians, Poles, and other groups from southern and eastern Europe. Furthermore, they offer contrast to the immigrants from Asia. The Irish came about the same time as the Chinese, but they had a distinct advantage: the Naturalization Law of 1790 had reserved citizenship for "whites" only. Their compatible complexion allowed them to assimilate by blending into American society. In making their journey successfully into the mainstream, however, these immigrants from Erin pursued an Irish "ethnic" strategy: they promoted "Irish" solidarity in order to gain political power and also to dominate the skilled blue-collar occupations, often at the expense of the Chinese and blacks.[10]

Fleeing pogroms and religious persecution in Russia, the Jews were driven from what John Cuddihy described as the "Middle Ages into the Anglo-American world of the *goyim* 'beyond the pale.'" To them, America represented the Promised Land. This vision led Jews to struggle not only for themselves but also for other oppressed groups, especially blacks. After the 1917 East St. Louis race riot, the Yiddish *Forward* of New York compared this antiblack violence to a 1903 pogrom in Russia: "Kishinev and St. Louis—the same soil, the same people." Jews cheered when Jackie Robinson broke into the Brooklyn Dodgers in 1947. "He was adopted as the surrogate hero by many of us growing up at the time," recalled Jack Greenberg of the NAACP Legal Defense Fund. "He was the way we saw ourselves triumphing against the forces of bigotry and ignorance." Jews stood shoulder to shoulder with blacks in the Civil Rights Movement: two-thirds of the white volunteers who went south during the 1964 Freedom Summer were Jewish. Today Jews are considered a highly successful "ethnic" group. How did they make such great socioeconomic strides? This question is often reframed by neoconservative intellectuals like Irving Kristol and Nathan Glazer to read: if Jewish immigrants were able to lift themselves from poverty into the mainstream through self-help and education without welfare and affirmative action, why can't blacks? But what this thinking overlooks is the unique history of Jewish immigrants, especially the initial advantages of many of them as literate and skilled. Moreover, it minimizes the virulence of racial prejudice rooted in American slavery.[11]

Indians represent a critical contrast, for theirs was not an immigrant experience. The Wampanoags were on the shore as the first English strangers arrived in what would be called "New England." The encounters between Indians and whites not only shaped the course of race relations, but also influenced the very culture and identity of the general society. The architect of Indian removal, President Andrew Jackson told Congress: "Our conduct toward these people is deeply interesting to the national character." Frederick Jackson Turner understood the meaning of this observation when he identified the frontier as our transforming crucible. At first, the European newcomers had to wear Indian moccasins and shout the war cry. "Little by little," as they subdued the wilderness, the pioneers became "a new product" that was "American." But Indians have had a different view of this entire process. "The white man," Luther Standing Bear of the Sioux explained, "does not understand the Indian for the reason that he does not understand America." Continuing to be "troubled with primitive fears," he has "in his consciousness the perils of this frontier continent. . . . The man from Europe is still a foreigner and an alien. And he still hates the man who questioned his path across the continent." Indians questioned what Jackson and Turner trumpeted as "progress." For them, the frontier had a different "significance": their history was how the West was lost. But their story has also been one of resistance. As Vine Deloria declared, "Custer died for your sins."[12]

By looking at these groups from a multicultural perspective, we can comparatively analyze their experiences in order to develop an understanding of their differences and similarities. Race, we will see, has been a social construction that has historically set apart racial minorities from European immigrant groups. Contrary to the notions of scholars like Nathan Glazer and Thomas Sowell, race in America has not been the same as ethnicity. A broad comparative focus also allows us to see how the varied experiences of different racial and ethnic groups occurred within shared contexts.

During the nineteenth century, for example, the Market Revolution employed Irish immigrant laborers in New England factories as it expanded cotton fields worked by enslaved blacks across Indian lands toward Mexico. Like blacks, the Irish newcomers were stereotyped as "savages," ruled by passions rather than "civilized" virtues such as self-control and hard work. The Irish saw themselves as the "slaves" of British oppressors, and during a visit to Ireland in the 1840s, Frederick Douglass found that the "wailing notes" of the Irish ballads reminded him of the "wild notes" of slave songs. The United States annexation of California, while incorporating Mexicans, led to trade with Asia and the migration of "strangers" from Pacific shores. In 1870, Chinese immigrant laborers were transported to Massachusetts as scabs to break an Irish immigrant strike; in response, the Irish recognized the need for interethnic working-class solidarity and tried to organize a Chinese lodge of the Knights of St. Crispin. After the Civil War, Mississippi planters re-cruited Chinese immigrants to discipline the newly freed blacks. During the debate over an immigration exclusion bill in 1882, a senator asked: If Indians could be located on reservations, why not the Chinese?[13]

Other instances of our connectedness abound. In 1903, Mexican and Japanese farm laborers went on strike together in California: their union officers had names like Yamaguchi and Lizarras, and strike meetings were conducted in Japanese and Spanish. The Mexican strikers declared that they were standing in solidarity with their "Japanese brothers" because the two groups had toiled together in the fields and were now fighting together for a fair wage. Speaking in impassioned Yiddish during the 1909 "uprising of twenty thousand" strikers in New York, the charismatic Clara Lemlich com-pared the abuse of Jewish female garment workers to the experience of blacks: "[The bosses] yell at the girls and 'call them down' even worse than I imagine the Negro slaves were in the South." During the 1920s, elite universities like Harvard worried about the increasing numbers of Jewish students, and new ad-missions criteria were instituted to curb their enrollment. Jewish students were scorned for their studiousness and criticized for their "clannishness." Recently, Asian-American students have been the targets of similar complaints: they have been called "nerds" and told there are "too many" of them on campus.[14]

Indians were already here, while blacks were forcibly transported to America, and Mexicans were initially enclosed by America's expanding border. The other groups came here as immigrants: for them, America repre-sented liminality—a new world where they could pursue extravagant urges and do things they had thought beyond their capabilities. Like the land itself, they found themselves "betwixt and between all fixed points of classification." No longer fastened as fiercely to their old countries, they felt a stirring to become new people in a society still being defined and formed.[15]

These immigrants made bold and dangerous crossings, pushed by polit-ical events and economic hardships in their homelands and pulled by America's demand for labor as well as by their own dreams for a better life. "By all means let me go to America," a young man in Japan begged his par-ents. He had calculated that in one year as a laborer here he could save almost a thousand yen—an amount equal to the income of a governor in Japan. "My dear Father," wrote an immigrant Irish girl living in New York, "Any man or woman without a family are fools that would not venture and come to this plentyful Country where no man or woman ever hungered." In the shtetls of Russia, the cry "To America!" roared like "wildfire." "America was in every-body's mouth," a Jewish immigrant recalled. "Businessmen talked [about] it over their accounts; the market women made up their quarrels that they might discuss it from stall to stall; people who had relatives in the famous land went around reading their letters." Similarly, for Mexican immigrants cross-ing the border in the early twentieth century, El Norte became the stuff of overblown hopes. "If only you could see how nice the United States is," they said, "that is why the Mexicans are crazy about it."[16]

The signs of America's ethnic diversity can be discerned across the con-tinent—Ellis Island, Angel Island, Chinatown, Harlem, South Boston, the Lower East Side, places with Spanish names like Los Angeles and San Antonio or Indian names like Massachusetts and Iowa. Much of what is familiar in America's cultural landscape actually has ethnic origins. The Bing cherry was developed by an early Chinese immigrant named Ah Bing. American Indians were cultivating corn, tomatoes, and tobacco long before the arrival of Columbus. The term *okay* was derived from the Choctaw word *oke*, meaning "it is so." There is evidence indicating that the name *Yankee* came from Indian terms for the English—from *eankke* in Cherokee and *Yankwis* in Delaware. Jazz and blues as well as rock and roll have African-American origins. The "Forty-Niners" of the Gold Rush learned mining techniques from the Mexicans; American cowboys acquired herding skills from Mexican *vaqueros* and adopted their range terms—such as *lariat* from *la reata*, *lasso* from *lazo*, and *stampede* from *estampida*. Songs like "God Bless America," "Easter Parade," and "White Christmas" were written by a Russian-Jewish immigrant named Israel Baline, more popularly known as Irving Berlin.[17]

Furthermore, many diverse ethnic groups have contributed to the build-ing of the American economy, forming what Walt Whitman saluted as "a vast, surging, hopeful army of workers." They worked in the South's cotton fields, New England's textile mills, Hawaii's canefields, New York's garment facto-ries, California's orchards, Washington's salmon canneries, and Arizona's copper mines. They built the railroad, the great symbol of America's indus-trial triumph. . . .

Moreover, our diversity was tied to America's most serious crisis: the Civil War was fought over a racial issue—slavery. . . .

. . . The people in our study have been actors in history, not merely victims of discrimination and exploitation. They are entitled to be viewed as subjects—as men and women with minds, wills, and voices.

> *In the telling and retelling*
> *of their stories,*
> *They create communities*
> *of memory.*

They also re-vision history. "It is very natural that the history written by the victim," said a Mexican in 1874, "does not altogether chime with the story of the victor." Sometimes they are hesitant to speak, thinking they are only "little people." "I don't know why anybody wants to hear my history," an Irish maid said apologetically in 1900. "Nothing ever happened to me worth the tellin'."[18]

But their stories are worthy. Through their stories, the people who have lived America's history can help all of us, including my taxi driver, understand that Americans originated from many shores, and that all of us are entitled to dignity. "I hope this survey do a lot of good for Chinese people," an immigrant told an interviewer from Stanford University in the 1920s. "Make American people realize that Chinese people are humans. I think very few American people really know anything about Chinese." But the remembering is also for the sake of the children. "This story is dedicated to the descendants of Lazar and Goldie Glauberman," Jewish immigrant Minnie Miller wrote in her autobiography. "My history is bound up in their history and the generations that follow should know where they came from to know better who they are." Similarly, Tomo Shoji, an elderly Nisei woman, urged Asian Americans to learn more about their roots: "We got such good, fantastic stories to tell. All our stories are different." Seeking to know how they fit into America, many young people have become listeners; they are eager to learn about the hardships and humiliations experienced by their parents and grandparents. They want to hear their stories, unwilling to remain ignorant or ashamed of their identity and past.[19]

The telling of stories liberates. By writing about the people on Mango Street, Sandra Cisneros explained, "the ghost does not ache so much." The place no longer holds her with "both arms. She sets me free." Indeed, stories may not be as innocent or simple as they seem to be. Native-American novelist Leslie Marmon Silko cautioned:

> I will tell you something about stories . . .
> They aren't just entertainment.
>   Don't be fooled.

Indeed, the accounts given by the people in this study vibrantly re-create moments, capturing the complexities of human emotions and thoughts. They also provide the authenticity of experience. After she escaped from slavery, Harriet Jacobs wrote in her autobiography: "[My purpose] is not to tell you what I have heard but what I have seen—and what I have suffered." In their sharing of memory, the people in this study offer us an opportunity to see ourselves reflected in a mirror called history.[20]

In his recent study of Spain and the New World, *The Buried Mirror*, Carlos Fuentes points out that mirrors have been found in the tombs of ancient Mexico, placed there to guide the dead through the underworld.

He also tells us about the legend of Quetzalcoatl, the Plumed Serpent: when this god was given a mirror by the Toltec deity Tezcatlipoca, he saw a man's face in the mirror and realized his own humanity. For us, the "mirror" of history can guide the living and also help us recognize who we have been and hence are. In *A Distant Mirror*, Barbara W. Tuchman finds "phenomenal parallels" between the "calamitous fourteenth century" of European society and our own era. We can, she observes, have "greater fellow-feeling for a distraught age" as we painfully recognize the "similar disarray," "collapsing assumptions," and "unusual discomfort."[21]

But what is needed in our own perplexing times is not so much a "distant" mirror, as one that is "different." While the study of the past can provide collective self-knowledge, it often reflects the scholar's particular perspective or view of the world. What happens when historians leave out many of America's peoples? What happens, to borrow the words of Adrienne Rich, "when someone with the authority of a teacher" describes our society, and "you are not in it"? Such an experience can be disorienting—"a moment of psychic disequilibrium, as if you looked into a mirror and saw nothing."[22]

Through their narratives about their lives and circumstances, the people of America's diverse groups are able to see themselves and each other in our common past. They celebrate what Ishmael Reed has described as a society "unique" in the world because "the world is here"—a place "where the cultures of the world crisscross." Much of America's past, they point out, has been riddled with racism. At the same time, these people offer hope, affirming the struggle for equality as a central theme in our country's history. At its conception, our nation was dedicated to the proposition of equality. What has given concreteness to this powerful national principle has been our coming together in the creation of a new society. "Stuck here" together, workers of different backgrounds have attempted to get along with each other.

> *People harvesting*
> *Work together unaware*
> *Of racial problems,*

wrote a Japanese immigrant describing a lesson learned by Mexican and Asian farm laborers in California.[23]

Finally, how do we see our prospects for "working out" America's racial crisis? Do we see it as through a glass darkly? Do the televised images of racial hatred and violence that riveted us in 1992 during the days of rage in Los Angeles frame a future of divisive race relations—what Arthur Schlesinger Jr. has fearfully denounced as the "disuniting of America"? Or will Americans of diverse races and ethnicities be able to connect themselves to a larger narrative? Whatever happens, we can be certain that much of our society's future will be influenced by which "mirror" we choose to see ourselves. America does not belong to one race or one group. . . . Americans have been constantly redefining their national identity from the moment of first contact on the Virginia shore. By sharing their stories, they invite us to see ourselves in a different mirror.[24]

NOTES

1. Toni Morrison, *Playing in the Dark: Whiteness in the Literary Imagination* (Cambridge, Mass., 1992), p. 47.

2. William A. Henry III, "Beyond the Melting Pot," in "America's Changing Colors," *Time*, vol. 135, no. 15 (April 9, 1990), pp. 28–31.

3. "A Conflict of the Have-Nots," *Newsweek*, December 12, 1988, pp. 28–29.

4. Rodney King's statement to the press, *New York Times*, May 2, 1992, p. 6.

5. Tim Rutten, "A New Kind of Riot," *New York Times Review of Books*, June 11, 1992, pp. 52–53; Maria Newman, "Riots Bring Attention to Growing Hispanic Presence in South-Central Area," *New York Times*, May 11, 1992, p. A10; Mike Davis, "In L.A. Burning All Illusions," *The Nation*, June 1, 1992, pp. 744–745; Jack Viets and Peter Fimrite, "S.F. Mayor Visits Riot-Torn Area to Buoy Businesses," *San Francisco Chronicle*, May 6, 1992, p. A6.

6. Rick DelVecchio, Suzanne Espinosa, and Carl Nolte, "Bradley Ready to Lift Curfew," *San Francisco Chronicle*, May 4, 1992, p. A1.

7. Abraham Lincoln, "The Gettysburg Address," in *The Annals of America*, vol. 9, *1863–1865: The Crisis of the Union* (Chicago, 1968), pp. 462–463; Martin Luther King, *Why We Can't Wait* (New York, 1964), pp. 92–93.

8. Interview with old laundryman, in "Interviews with Two Chinese," circa 1924, Box 326, folder 325, Survey of Race Relations, Stanford University, Hoover Institution Archives; Congressman Robert Matsui, speech in the House of Representatives on the 442 bill for redress and reparations, September 17, 1987, *Congressional Record* (Washington, D.C., 1987), p. 7584.

9. Albert Camarillo, *Chicanos in a Changing Society: From Mexican Pueblos to American Barrios in Santa Barbara and Southern California, 1848–1930* (Cambridge, Mass., 1979), p. 2; Juan Nepornuceno Seguín, in David J. Weber (ed.), *Foreigners in Their Native Land: Historical Roots of the Mexican Americans* (Albuquerque, N. M., 1973), p. vi; Jesus Garza, in Manuel Garnio, *The Mexican Immigrant: His Life Story* (Chicago, 1931), p. 15; Ernesto Galarza, *Barrio Boy: The Story of a Boy's Acculturation* (Notre Dame, Ind., 1986), p. 200.

10. Lawrence J. McCaffrey, *The Irish Diaspora in America* (Washington, D.C., 1984), pp. 6, 62.

11. John Murray Cuddihy, *The Ordeal of Civility: Freud, Marx, Levi Strauss, and the Jewish Struggle with Modernity* (Boston, 1987), p. 165; Jonathan Kaufman, *Broken Alliance: The Turbulent Times between Blacks and Jews in America* (New York, 1989), pp. 28, 82, 83–84, 91, 93, 106.

12. Andrew Jackson, First Annual Message to Congress, December 8, 1829, in James D. Richardson (ed.), *A Compilation of the Messages and Papers of the Presidents, 1789–1897* (Washington, D.C., 1897), vol. 2, p. 457; Frederick Jackson Turner, "The Significance of the Frontier in American History," in *The Early Writings of Frederick Jackson Turner* (Madison, Wis., 1938), pp. 185ff.; Luther Standing Bear, "What the Indian Means to America," in Wayne Moquin (ed.), *Great Documents in American*

Indian History (New York, 1973), p. 307; Vine Deloria, Jr., *Custer Died for Your Sins: An Indian Manifesto* (New York, 1969).

13. Nathan Glazer, *Affirmative Discrimination: Ethnic Inequality and Public Policy* (New York, 1978); Thomas Sowell, *Ethnic America: A History* (New York, 1981); David R. Roediger, *The Wages of Whiteness: Race and the Making of the American Working Class* (London, 1991), pp. 134–136; Dan Caldwell, "The Negroization of the Chinese Stereotype in California," *Southern California Quarterly*, vol. 33 (June 1971), pp. 123–131.

14. Thomas Almaguer, "Racial Domination and Class Conflict in Capitalist Agriculture: The Oxnard Sugar Beet Workers' Strike of 1903," *Labor History*, vol. 25, no. 3 (summer 1984), p. 347; Howard M. Sachar, *A History of the Jews in America* (New York, 1992), p. 183.

15. For the concept of liminality, see Victor Turner, *Dramas, Fields, and Metaphors: Symbolic Action in Human Society* (Ithaca, N.Y., 1974), pp. 232, 237; and Arnold Van Gennep, *The Rites of Passage* (Chicago, 1960). What I try to do is to apply liminality to the land called America.

16. Kazuo Ito, *Issei: A History of Japanese Immigrants in North America* (Seattle, 1973), p. 33; Arnold Schrier, *Ireland and the American Emigration, 1850–1900* (New York, 1970), p. 24; Abraham Cahan, *The Rise of David Levinsky* (New York, 1960; originally published in 1917), pp. 59–61; Mary Antin, quoted in Howe, *World of Our Fathers* (New York, 1983), p. 27; Lawrence A. Cardoso, *Mexican Emigration to the United States, 1897–1931* (Tucson, Ariz., 1981), p. 80.

17. Ronald Takaki, *Strangers from a Different Shore: A History of Asian Americans* (Boston, 1989), pp. 88–89; Jack Weatherford, *Native Roots: How the Indians Enriched America* (New York, 1991), pp. 210, 212; Carey McWilliams, *North from Mexico: The Spanish-Speaking People of the United States* (New York, 1968), p. 154; Stephan Themstrom (ed.), *Harvard Encyclopedia of American Ethnic Groups* (Cambridge, Mass., 1980), p. 22; Sachar, *A History of the Jews in America*, p. 367.

18. Weber (ed.), *Foreigners in Their Native Land*, p. vi; Hamilton Holt (ed.), *The Life Stories of Undistinguished Americans as Told by Themselves* (New York, 1906), p. 143.

19. "Social Document of Pany Lowe, interviewed by C. H. Burnett, Seattle, July 5, 1924," p. 6, Survey of Race Relations, Stanford University, Hoover Institution Archives; Minnie Miller, "Autobiography," private manuscript, copy from Richard Balkin; Tomo Shoji, presentation, Obana Cultural Center, Oakland, California, March 4, 1988.

20. Sandra Cisneros, *The House on Mango Street* (New York, 1991), pp. 109–110; Leslie Marmon Silko, *Ceremony* (New York, 1978), p. 2; Harriet A. Jacobs, *Incidents in the Life of a Slave Girl, written by herself* (Cambridge, Mass., 1987; originally published in 1857), p. xiii.

21. Carlos Fuentes, *The Buried Mirror: Reflections on Spain and the New World* (Boston, 1992), pp. 10, 11, 109; Barbara W. Tuchman, *A Distant Mirror: The Calamitous 14th Century* (New York, 1978), pp. xiii, xiv.

22. Adrienne Rich, *Blood, Bread, and Poetry: Selected Prose, 1979–1985* (New York, 1986), p. 199.

23. Ishmael Reed, "America: The Multinational Society," in Rick Simonson and Scott Walker (eds.), *Multi-cultural Literacy* (St. Paul, 1988), p. 160; Ito, *Issei*, p. 497.

24. Arthur M. Schlesinger, Jr., *The Disuniting of America: Reflections on a Multicultural Society* (Knoxville, Tenn., 1991); Carlos Bulosan, *America Is in the Heart: A Personal History* (Seattle, 1981), pp. 188–189.

5

FROM A NATIVE DAUGHTER

Haunani-Kay Trask

E noi'i wale mai nō ka haole, a,
'a'ole e pau nā hana a Hawai'i 'imi loa
Let the *haole* freely research us in detail
But the doings of deep delving *Hawai'i*
will not be exhausted.

—Kepelino
19th-century Hawaiian historian

When I was young the story of my people was told twice: once by my parents, then again by my school teachers. From my *'ohana* (family), I learned about the life of the old ones: how they fished and planted by the moon; shared all the fruits of their labors, especially their children; danced in great numbers for long hours; and honored the unity of their world in intricate genealogical chants. My mother said Hawaiians had sailed over thousands of miles to make their home in these sacred islands. And they had flourished, until the coming of the *haole* (whites).

At school, I learned that the "pagan Hawaiians" did not read or write, were lustful cannibals, traded in slaves, and could not sing. Captain Cook had "discovered" Hawai'i and the ungrateful Hawaiians had killed him. In revenge, the Christian god had cursed the Hawaiians with disease and death.

I learned the first of these stories from speaking with my mother and father. I learned the second from books. By the time I left for college, the books had won out over my parents, especially since I spent four long years in a missionary boarding school for Hawaiian children.

When I went away I understood the world as a place and a feeling divided in two: one *haole* (white), and the other *kānaka* (Native). When I returned ten years later with a Ph.D., the division was sharper, the lack of connection more painful. There was the world that we lived in—my ancestors, my family, and my people—and then there was the world historians described. This world, they had written, was the truth. A primitive group, Hawaiians had been ruled by bloodthirsty priests and despotic kings who owned all the land and kept our people in feudal subjugation. The chiefs were cruel, the people poor.

From Haunani Kay Trask, *From a Native Daughter* (Monroe, Maine: Common Courage Press), 1993.

But this was not the story my mother told me. No one had owned the land before the *haole* came; everyone could fish and plant, except during sacred periods. And the chiefs were good and loved their people.

Was my mother confused? What did our *kūpuna* (elders) say? They replied: Did these historians (all *haole*) know the language? Did they understand the chants? How long had they lived among our people? Whose stories had they heard?

None of the historians had ever learned our mother tongue. They had all been content to read what Europeans and Americans had written. But why did scholars, presumably well-trained and thoughtful, neglect our language? Not merely a passageway to knowledge, language is a form of knowing by itself; a people's way of thinking and feeling is revealed through its music.

I sensed the answer without needing to answer. From years of living in a divided world, I knew the historian's judgment: *There is no value in things Hawaiian; all value comes from things haole.*

Historians, I realized, were very much like missionaries. They were a part of the colonizing horde. One group colonized the spirit; the other, the mind. Frantz Fanon had been right, but not just about Africans. He had been right about the bondage of my own people: "By a kind of perverted logic, [colonialism] turns to the past of the oppressed people, and distorts, disfigures, and destroys it" (1963:210). The first step in the colonizing process, Fanon had written, was the deculturation of a people. What better way to take our culture than to remake our image? A rich historical past became small and ignorant in the hands of Westerners. And we suffered a damaged sense of people and culture because of this distortion.

Burdened by a linear, progressive conception of history and by an assumption that Euro-American culture flourishes at the upper end of that progression, Westerners have told the history of Hawai'i as an inevitable if occasionally bittersweet triumph of Western ways over "primitive" Hawaiian ways. A few authors—the most sympathetic—have recorded with deep-felt sorrow the passing of our people. But in the end, we are repeatedly told, such an eclipse was for the best.

Obviously it was best for Westerners, not for our dying multitudes. This is why the historian's mission has been to justify our passing by celebrating Western dominance. Fanon would have called this missionizing, intellectual colonization. And it is clearest in the historian's insistence that *pre-haole* Hawaiian land tenure was "feudal"—a term that is now applied, without question, in every monograph, in every schoolbook, and in every tour guide description of my people's history.

From the earliest days of Western contact my people told their guests that *no one* owned the land. The land—like the air and the sea—was for all to use and share as their birthright. Our chiefs were *stewards* of the land; they could not own or privately possess the land any more than they could sell it.

But the *haole* insisted on characterizing our chiefs as feudal landlords and our people as serfs. Thus, a European term which described a European practice founded on the European concept of private property—feudalism—was imposed upon a people halfway around the world from Europe and vastly different from her in every conceivable way. More than betraying an ignorance of Hawaiian culture and history, however, this misrepresentation was malevolent in design.

By inventing feudalism in ancient Hawai'i, Western scholars quickly transformed a spiritually based, self-sufficient economic system of land use and occupancy into an oppressive, medieval European practice of divine right ownership, with the common people tied like serfs to the land. By claiming that a Pacific people lived under a European system—that the Hawaiians lived under feudalism—Westerners could then degrade a successful system of shared land use with a pejorative and inaccurate Western term. Land tenure changes instituted by Americans and in line with current Western notions of private property were then made to appear beneficial to the Hawaiians. But in practice, such changes benefited the *haole*, who alienated the people from the land, taking it for themselves.

The prelude to this land alienation was the great dying of the people. Barely half a century after contact with the West our people had declined in number by eighty percent. Disease and death were rampant. The sandalwood forests had been stripped bare for international commerce between England and China. The missionaries had insinuated themselves everywhere. And a debt-ridden Hawaiian king (there had been no king before Western contact) succumbed to enormous pressure from the Americans and followed their schemes for dividing the land.

This is how private property land tenure entered Hawai'i. The common people, driven from their birthright, received less than one percent of the land. They starved while huge *haole*-owned sugar plantations thrived.

And what had the historians said? They had said that the Americans "liberated" the Hawaiians from an oppressive "feudal" system. By inventing a false feudal past, the historians justify—and become complicitous in—massive American theft.

Is there "evidence"—as historians call it—for traditional Hawaiian concepts of land use? The evidence is in the sayings of my people and in the words they wrote more than a century ago, much of which has been translated. However, historians have chosen to ignore any references here to shared land use. But there *is* incontrovertible evidence in the very structure of the Hawaiian language. If the historians had bothered to learn our language (as any American historian of France would learn French) they would have discovered that we show possession in two ways: through the use of an "a" possessive, which reveals acquired status, and through the use of an "o" possessive, which denotes inherent status. My body (*ko'u kino*) and my parents (*ko'u mākua*), for example, take the "o" form; most material objects, such as food (*ka'u mea'ai*) take the "a" form. But land, like one's body and one's parents, takes the "o" possessive (*ko'u 'āina*). Thus, in our way of speaking, land is inherent to the people; it is like our bodies and our parents. The people cannot exist without the land, and the land cannot exist without the people.

Every major historian of Hawai'i has been mistaken about Hawaiian land tenure. The chiefs did not own the land: they *could not* own the land. My mother was right and the *haole* historians were wrong. If they had studied our language they would have known that no one owned the land. But was their failing merely ignorance, or simple ethnocentric bias?

No, I did not believe them to be so benign. As I read on, a pattern emerged in their writing. Our ways were inferior to those of the West, to those of the historians' own culture. We were "less developed," or "immature," or "authoritarian." In some tellings we were much worse. Thus, Gavan Daws (1968), the most famed modern historian of Hawai'i, had continued a tradition established earlier by missionaries Hiram Bingham (1848; reprinted, 1981) and Sheldon Dibble (1909), by referring to the old ones as "thieves" and "savages" who regularly practiced infanticide and who, in contrast to "civilized" whites, preferred "lewd dancing" to work. Ralph Kuykendall (1938), long considered the most thorough if also the most boring of historians of Hawai'i, sustained another fiction—that my ancestors owned slaves, the outcast *kauwā*. This opinion, as well as the description of Hawaiian land tenure as feudal, had been supported by respected sociologist Andrew Lind. . . . Finally, nearly all historians had refused to accept our genealogical dating of A.D. 400 or earlier for our arrival from the South Pacific. They had, instead, claimed that our earliest appearance in Hawai'i could only be traced to A.D. 1100. Thus at least seven hundred years of our history were repudiated by "superior" Western scholarship. Only recently have archaeological data confirmed what Hawaiians had said these many centuries (Tuggle 1979).[1]

Suddenly the entire sweep of our written history was clear to me. I was reading the West's view of itself through the degradation of my own past. When historians wrote that the king owned the land and the common people were bound to it, they were saying that ownership was the only way human beings in their world could relate to the land, and in that relationship, some one person had to control both the land and the interaction between humans.

And when they said that our chiefs were despotic, they were telling of their own society, where hierarchy always results in domination. Thus any authority or elder is automatically suspected of tyranny.

And when they wrote that Hawaiians were lazy, they meant that work must be continuous and ever a burden.

And when they wrote that we were promiscuous, they meant that lovemaking in the Christian West is a sin.

And when they wrote that we were racist because we preferred our own ways to theirs, they meant that their culture needed to dominate other cultures.

And when they wrote that we were superstitious, believing in the *mana* of nature and people, they meant that the West has long since lost a deep spiritual and cultural relationship to the earth.

And when they wrote that Hawaiians were "primitive" in their grief over the passing of loved ones, they meant that the West grieves for the living who do not walk among their ancestors.

For so long, more than half my life, I had misunderstood this written record, thinking it described my own people. But my history was nowhere present. For we had not written. We had chanted and sailed and fished and built and prayed. And we had told stories through the great blood lines of memory: genealogy.

To know my history, I had to put away my books and return to the land. I had to plant *taro* in the earth before I could understand the inseparable bond between people and *'āina*. I had to feel again the spirits of nature and take gifts of plants and fish to the ancient altars. I had to begin to speak my language with our elders and leave long silences for wisdom to grow. But before anything else, I needed to learn the language like a lover so that I could rock within her and lie at night in her dreaming arms.

There was nothing in my schooling that had told me of this, or hinted that somewhere there was a longer, older story of origins, of the flowing of songs out to a great but distant sea. Only my parents' voices, over and over, spoke to me of a Hawaiian world. While the books spoke from a different world, a Western world.

And yet, Hawaiians are not of the West. We are of *Hawai'i Nei*, this world where I live, this place, this culture, this *'āina*.

What can I say, then, to Western historians of my place and people? Let me answer with a story.

A while ago I was asked to appear on a panel on the American overthrow of our government in 1893. The other panelists were all *haole*. But one was a *haole* historian from the American continent who had just published a book on what he called the American anti-imperialists. He and I met briefly in preparation for the panel. I asked him if he knew the language. He said no. I asked him if he knew the record of opposition to our annexation to America. He said there was no real evidence for it, just comments here and there. I told him that he didn't understand and that at the panel I would share the evidence. When we met in public and spoke, I said this:

There is a song much loved by our people. It was written after Hawai'i had been invaded and occupied by American marines. Addressed to our dethroned Queen, it was written in 1893, and tells of Hawaiian feelings for our land and against annexation to the United States. Listen to our lament:

Kaulana nā pua a'o Hawai'i	Famous are the children of Hawai'i
Kupa'a ma hope o ka 'āina	Who cling steadfastly to the land
Hiki mai ka 'elele o ka loko 'ino	Comes the evil-hearted with
Palapala 'ānunu me ka pākaha	A document greedy for plunder

Pane mai Hawai'i moku o Keawe	Hawai'i, island of Keawe, answers
Kokua nā hono a'o Pi'ilani	The bays of Pi'ilani [of Maui, Moloka'i, and Lana'i] help
Kako'o mai Kaua'i Mano	Kaua'i of Mano assists
Pau pu me ke one o Kakuhihewa	Firmly together with the sands of Kakuhihewa
'A'ole a'e kau i ka pūlima	Do not put the signature
Maluna o ka pepa o ka 'enemi	On the paper of the enemy
Ho'ohui 'āina kū'ai hewa	Annexation is wicked sale
I ka pono sivila a'o ke kānaka	Of the civil rights of the Hawaiian people
Mahope mākou o Lili'ūlani	We support Lili'uokalani
A loa'a 'e ka pono o ka 'āina	Who has earned the right to the land
Ha'ina 'ia mai ana ka puana	The story is told
'O ka po'e i aloha i ka 'āina	Of the people who love the land

This song, I said, continues to be sung with great dignity at Hawaiian political gatherings, for our people still share the feelings of anger and protest that it conveys.

But our guest, the *haole* historian, answered that this song, although beautiful, was not evidence of either opposition or of imperialism from the Hawaiian perspective.

Many Hawaiians in the audience were shocked at his remarks, but, in hindsight, I think they were predictable. They are the standard response of the historian who does not know the language and has no respect for its memory.

Finally, I proceeded to relate a personal story, thinking that surely such a tale could not want for authenticity since I myself was relating it. My *tūtū* (grandmother) had told my mother who had told me that at the time of the overthrow a great wailing went up throughout the islands, a wailing of weeks, a wailing of impenetrable grief, a wailing of death. But he remarked again, this too is not evidence.

And so, history goes on, written in long volumes by foreign people. Whole libraries begin to form, book upon book, shelf upon shelf. At the same time, the stories go on, generation to generation, family to family.

Which history do Western historians desire to know? Is it to be a tale of writings by their own countrymen, individuals convinced of their "unique" capacity for analysis, looking at us with Western eyes, thinking about us within Western philosophical contexts, categorizing us by Western indices, judging us by Judeo-Christian morals, exhorting us to capitalist achievements, and finally, leaving us an authoritative-because-Western record of their complete misunderstanding?

All this has been done already. Not merely a few times, but many times. And still, every year, there appear new and eager faces to take up the same telling, as if the West must continue, implacably, with the din of its own disbelief. But there is, as there has been always, another possibility. If it is truly our history Western historians desire to know, they must put down their books, and take up our practices. First, of course, the language. But later, the people, the *'āina*, the stories. Above all, in the end, the stories. Historians must listen, they must hear the generational connections, the reservoir of sounds and meanings.

They must come, as American Indians suggested long ago, to understand the land. Not in the Western way, but in the indigenous way, the way of living within and protecting the bond between people and *'āina*. This bond is cultural, and it can be understood only culturally. But because the West has lost any cultural understanding of the bond between people and land, it is not possible to know this connection through Western culture. This means that the history of indigenous people cannot be written from within Western culture. Such a story is merely the West's story of itself.

Our story remains unwritten. It rests within the culture, which is inseparable from the land. To know this is to know our history. To write this is to write of the land and the people who are born from her.

NOTES

1. See also Fornander (1878–85; reprinted, 1981). Lest one think these sources antiquated, it should be noted that there exist only a handful of modern scholarly works on the history of Hawai'i. The most respected are those by Kuykendall (1938) and Daws (1968), and a social history of the 20th century by Lawrence Fuchs (1961). Of these, only Kuykendall and Daws claim any knowledge of pre-*haole* history, while concentrating on the 19th century. However, countless popular works have relied on these two studies which, in turn, are themselves based on primary sources written in English by extremely biased, anti-Hawaiian Westerners such as explorers, traders, missionaries (e.g., Bingham [1848; reprinted, 1981] and Dibble [1909]), and sugar planters. Indeed, a favorite technique of Daws's—whose *Shoal of Time* was once the most acclaimed and recent general history—is the lengthy quotation without comment of the most racist remarks by missionaries and planters. Thus, at one point, half a page is consumed with a "white man's burden" quotation from an 1886 *Planters Monthly* article ("It is better here that the white man should rule . . . ," etc., p. 213). Daws's only comment is, "The conclusion was inescapable." To get a sense of such characteristic contempt for Hawaiians, one has but to read the first few pages, where Daws refers several times to the Hawaiians as "savages" and "thieves" and where he approvingly has Captain Cook thinking, "It was a sensible primitive who bowed before a superior civilization" (p. 2). See also—among examples too numerous to cite—his glib description of sacred *hula* as a "frivolous diversion," which, instead of work, the Hawaiians "would practice energetically in the hot sun for days on end . . . their bare brown flesh glistening with sweat" (pp. 65–66). Daws, who repeatedly displays an affection for descriptions of Hawaiian skin color, taught Hawaiian history for some years at the University of Hawai'i. He once held the Chair of Pacific History at the Australian National University's Institute of Advanced Studies.

Postscript: Since this article was written, the first scholarly history by a Native Hawaiian was published in English: *Native Land and Foreign Desires* by Lilikalā Kame'eleihiwa (Honolulu: Bishop Museum Press, 1992).

Sources:

Bingham, Hiram. 1981. *A Residence of Twenty-one Years in the Sandwich Islands.* Tokyo: Charles E. Tuttle.

Daws, Gavan. 1968. *Shoal of Time: A History of the Hawaiian Islands.* Honolulu: University of Hawai'i Press.

Dibble, Sheldon. 1909. *A History of the Sandwich Islands.* Honolulu: Thrum Publishing.

Fanon, Frantz. 1963. *The Wretched of the Earth.* New York: Grove Press.

Fornander, Abraham. 1981. *An Account of the Polynesian Race, Its Origins, and Migrations and the Ancient History of the Hawaiian People to the Times of Kamehameha I.* Routledge, Vermont: Charles E. Tuttle.

Fuchs, Lawrence H. 1961. *Hawaii Pono: A Social History.* New York: Harcourt Brace & World.

Kuykendall, Ralph. 1938. *The Hawaiian Kingdom, 1778–1854: Foundation and Transformation.* Honolulu: University of Hawai'i Press.

Tuggle, H. David. 1979. "Hawai'i," in *The Prehistory of Polynesia*, ed. Jessie D. Jennings. Cambridge: Harvard University Press.

6

AGE, RACE, CLASS, AND SEX
Women Redefining Difference

Audre Lorde

Much of Western European history conditions us to see human differences in simplistic opposition to each other: dominant/subordinate, good/bad, up/down, superior/inferior. In a society where the good is defined in terms of profit rather than in terms of human need, there must always be some group of people who, through systematized oppression, can be made to feel surplus, to occupy the place of the dehumanized inferior. Within this society, that group is made up of Black and Third World people, working-class people, older people, and women.

Paper delivered at the Copeland Colloquium, Amherst College, April 1980.

From Audre Lorde, *Sister Outsider* (Freedom, CA: Crossing Press, 1984), pp. 114–23. Reprinted by permission.

As a forty-nine-year-old Black lesbian feminist socialist mother of two, including one boy, and a member of an interracial couple, I usually find myself a part of some group defined as other, deviant, inferior, or just plain wrong. Traditionally, in american society, it is the members of oppressed, objectified groups who are expected to stretch out and bridge the gap between the actualities of our lives and the consciousness of our oppressor. For in order to survive, those of us for whom oppression is as american as apple pie have always had to be watchers, to become familiar with the language and manners of the oppressor, even sometimes adopting them for some illusion of protection. Whenever the need for some pretense of communication arises, those who profit from our oppression call upon us to share our knowledge with them. In other words, it is the responsibility of the oppressed to teach the oppressors their mistakes. I am responsible for educating teachers who dismiss my children's culture in school. Black and Third World people are expected to educate white people as to our humanity. Women are expected to educate men. Lesbians and gay men are expected to educate the heterosexual world. The oppressors maintain their position and evade responsibility for their own actions. There is a constant drain of energy which might be better used in redefining ourselves and devising realistic scenarios for altering the present and constructing the future.

Institutionalized rejection of difference is an absolute necessity in a profit economy which needs outsiders as surplus people. As members of such an economy, we have *all* been programmed to respond to the human differences between us with fear and loathing and to handle that difference in one of three ways: ignore it, and if that is not possible, copy it if we think it is dominant, or destroy it if we think it is subordinate. But we have no patterns for relating across our human differences as equals. As a result, those differences have been misnamed and misused in the service of separation and confusion.

Certainly there are very real differences between us of race, age, and sex. But it is not those differences between us that are separating us. It is rather our refusal to recognize those differences, and to examine the distortions which result from our misnaming them and their effects upon human behavior and expectation.

Racism, the belief in the inherent superiority of one race over all others and thereby the right to dominance. Sexism, the belief in the inherent superiority of one sex over the other and thereby the right to dominance. Ageism. Heterosexism. Elitism. Classism.

It is a lifetime pursuit for each one of us to extract these distortions from our living at the same time as we recognize, reclaim, and define those differences upon which they are imposed. For we have all been raised in a society where those distortions were endemic within our living. Too often, we pour the energy needed for recognizing and exploring difference into pretending those differences are insurmountable barriers, or that they do not exist at all. This results in a voluntary isolation, or false and treacherous connections. Either way, we do not develop tools for using human difference as a springboard for creative change within our lives. We speak not of human difference, but of human deviance.

Somewhere, on the edge of consciousness, there is what I call a *mythical norm*, which each one of us within our hearts knows "that is not me." In america, this norm is usually defined as white, thin, male, young, heterosexual, christian, and financially secure. It is with this mythical norm that the trappings of power reside within this society. Those of us who stand outside that power often identify one way in which we are different, and we assume that to be the primary cause of all oppression, forgetting other distortions around difference, some of which we ourselves may be practicing. By and large within the women's movement today, white women focus upon their oppression as women and ignore differences of race, sexual preference, class, and age. There is a pretense to a homogeneity of experience covered by the word *sisterhood* that does not in fact exist.

Unacknowledged class differences rob women of each others' energy and creative insight. Recently a women's magazine collective made the decision for one issue to print only prose, saying poetry was a less "rigorous" or "serious" art form. Yet even the form our creativity takes is often a class issue. Of all the art forms, poetry is the most economical. It is the one which is the most secret, which requires the least physical labor, the least material, and the one which can be done between shifts, in the hospital pantry, on the subway, and on scraps of surplus paper. Over the last few years, writing a novel on tight finances, I came to appreciate the enormous differences in the material demands between poetry and prose. As we reclaim our literature, poetry has been the major voice of poor, working class, and Colored women. A room of one's own may be a necessity for writing prose, but so are reams of paper, a typewriter, and plenty of time. The actual requirements to produce the visual arts also help determine, along class lines, whose art is whose. In this day of inflated prices for material, who are our sculptors, our painters, our photographers? When we speak of a broadly based women's culture, we need to be aware of the effect of class and economic differences on the supplies available for producing art.

As we move toward creating a society within which we can each flourish, ageism is another distortion of relationship which interferes without vision. By ignoring the past, we are encouraged to repeat its mistakes. The "generation gap" is an important social tool for any repressive society. If the younger members of a community view the older members as contemptible or suspect or excess, they will never be able to join hands and examine the living memories of the community, nor ask the all important question, "Why?" This gives rise to a historical amnesia that keeps us working to invent the wheel every time we have to go to the store for bread.

We find ourselves having to repeat and relearn the same old lessons over and over that our mothers did because we do not pass on what we have learned, or because we are unable to listen. For instance, how many times has this all been said before? For another, who would have believed that once again our daughters are allowing their bodies to be hampered and purgatoried by girdles and high heels and hobble skirts?

Ignoring the differences of race between women and the implications of those differences presents the most serious threat to the mobilization of women's joint power.

As white women ignore their built-in privilege of whiteness and define *woman* in terms of their own experience alone, then women of Color become "other," the outsider whose experience and tradition is too "alien" to comprehend. An example of this is the signal absence of the experience of women of Color as a resource for women's studies courses. The literature of women of Color is seldom included in women's literature courses and almost never in other literature courses, nor in women's studies as a whole. All too often, the excuse given is that the literatures of women of Color can only be taught by Colored women, or that they are too difficult to understand, or that classes cannot "get into" them because they come out of experiences that are "too different." I have heard this argument presented by white women of otherwise quite clear intelligence, women who seem to have no trouble at all teaching and reviewing work that comes out of the vastly different experiences of Shakespeare, Molière, Dostoyevsky, and Aristophanes. Surely there must be some other explanation.

This is a very complex question, but I believe one of the reasons white women have such difficulty reading Black women's work is because of their reluctance to see Black women as women and different from themselves. To examine Black women's literature effectively requires that we be seen as whole people in our actual complexities—as individuals, as women, as human— rather than as one of those problematic but familiar stereotypes provided in this society in place of genuine images of Black women. And I believe this holds true for the literatures of other women of Color who are not Black.

The literatures of all women of Color re-create the textures of our lives, and many white women are heavily invested in ignoring the real differences. For as long as any difference between us means one of us must be inferior, then the recognition of any difference must be fraught with guilt. To allow women of Color to step out of stereotypes is too guilt provoking, for it threatens the complacency of those women who view oppression only in terms of sex.

Refusing to recognize difference makes it impossible to see the different problems and pitfalls facing us as women.

Thus, in a patriarchal power system where whiteskin privilege is a major prop, the entrapments used to neutralize Black women and white women are not the same. For example, it is easy for Black women to be used by the power structure against Black men, not because they are men, but because they are Black. Therefore, for Black women, it is necessary at all times to separate the needs of the oppressor from our own legitimate conflicts within our communities. This same problem does not exist for white women. Black women and men have shared racist oppression and still share it, although in different ways. Out of that shared oppression we have developed joint defenses and joint vulnerabilities to each other that are not duplicated in the white community, with the exception of the relationship between Jewish women and Jewish men.

On the other hand, white women face the pitfall of being seduced into joining the oppressor under the pretense of sharing power. This possibility does not exist in the same way for women of Color. The tokenism that is sometimes extended to us is not an invitation to join power; our racial "otherness" is a visible reality that makes that quite clear. For white women there is a wider range of pretended choices and rewards for identifying with patriarchal power and its tools.

Today, with the defeat of ERA, the tightening economy, and increased conservatism, it is easier once again for white women to believe the dangerous fantasy that if you are good enough, pretty enough, sweet enough, quiet enough, teach the children to behave, hate the right people, and marry the right men, then you will be allowed to co-exist with patriarchy in relative peace, at least until a man needs your job or the neighborhood rapist happens along. And true, unless one lives and loves in the trenches it is difficult to remember that the war against dehumanization is ceaseless.

But Black women and our children know the fabric of our lives is stitched with violence and with hatred, that there is no rest. We do not deal with it only on the picket lines, or in dark midnight alleys, or in the places where we dare to verbalize our resistance. For us, increasingly, violence weaves through the daily tissues of our living—in the supermarket, in the classroom, in the elevator, in the clinic and the schoolyard, from the plumber, the baker, the saleswoman, the bus driver, the bank teller, the waitress who does not serve us.

Some problems we share as women, some we do not. You fear your children will grow up to join the patriarchy and testify against you, we fear our children will be dragged from a car and shot down in the street, and you will turn your backs upon the reasons they are dying.

The threat of difference has been no less blinding to people of Color. Those of us who are Black must see that the reality of our lives and our struggle does not make us immune to the errors of ignoring and misnaming difference. Within Black communities where racism is a living reality, differences among us often seem dangerous and suspect. The need for unity is often misnamed as a need for homogeneity, and a Black feminist vision mistaken for betrayal of our common interests as a people. Because of the continuous battle against racial erasure that Black women and Black men share, some Black women still refuse to recognize that we are also oppressed as women, and that sexual hostility against Black women is practiced not only by the white racist society, but implemented within our Black communities as well. It is a disease striking the heart of Black nationhood, and silence will not make it disappear. Exacerbated by racism and the pressures of powerlessness, violence against Black women and children often becomes a standard within our communities, one by which manliness can be measured. But these woman-hating acts are rarely discussed as crimes against Black women.

As a group, women of Color are the lowest paid wage earners in america. We are the primary targets of abortion and sterilization abuse, here and abroad. In certain parts of Africa, small girls are still being sewed shut between their legs to keep them docile and for men's pleasure. This is known as female circumcision, and it is not a cultural affair as the late Jomo Kenyatta insisted, it is a crime against Black women.

Black women's literature is full of the pain of frequent assault, not only by a racist patriarchy, but also by Black men. Yet the necessity for and history of shared battle have made us, Black women, particularly vulnerable to the false accusation that anti-sexist is anti-Black. Meanwhile, womanhating as a re-course of the powerless is sapping strength from Black communities, and our very lives. Rape is on the increase, reported and unreported, and rape is not aggressive sexuality, it is sexualized aggression. As Kalamu ya Salaam, a Black male writer points out, "As long as male domination exists, rape will exist. Only women revolting and men made conscious of their responsibility to fight sexism can collectively stop rape."[1]

Differences between ourselves as Black women are also being misnamed and used to separate us from one another. As a Black lesbian feminist comfort-able with the many different ingredients of my identity, and a woman commit-ted to racial and sexual freedom from oppression, I find I am constantly being encouraged to pluck out some one aspect of myself and present this as the meaningful whole, eclipsing or denying the other parts of self. But this is a de-structive and fragmenting way to live. My fullest concentration of energy is available to me only when I integrate all the parts of who I am, openly, allow-ing power from particular sources of my living to flow back and forth freely through all my different selves, without the restrictions of externally imposed definition. Only then can I bring myself and my energies as a whole to the service of those struggles which I embrace as part of my living.

A fear of lesbians, or of being accused of being a lesbian, has led many Black women into testifying against themselves. It has led some of us into de-structive alliances, and others into despair and isolation. In the white women's communities, heterosexism is sometimes a result of identifying with the white patriarchy, a rejection of that interdependence between women-identified women which allows the self to be, rather than to be used in the service of men. Sometimes it reflects a die-hard belief in the protective coloration of

---

1 From "Rape: A Radical Analysis, An African-American Perspective" by Kalamu ya Salaam in *Black Books Bulletin*, vol. 6, no. 4 (1980).

heterosexual relationships, sometimes a self-hate which all women have to fight against, taught us from birth.

Although elements of these attitudes exist for all women, there are particular resonances of heterosexism and homophobia among Black women. Despite the fact that woman-bonding has a long and honorable history in the African and African-american communities, and despite the knowledge and accomplishments of many strong and creative women-identified Black women in the political, social and cultural fields, heterosexual Black women often tend to ignore or discount the existence and work of Black lesbians. Part of this atitude has come from an understandable terror of Black male attack within the close confines of Black society, where the punishment for any female self-assertion is still to be accused of being a lesbian and therefore unworthy of the attention or support of the scarce Black male. But part of this need to misname and ignore Black lesbians comes from a very real fear that openly women-identified Black women who are no longer dependent upon men for their self-definition may well reorder our whole concept of social relationships.

Black women who once insisted that lesbianism was a white woman's problem now insist that Black lesbians are a threat to Black nationhood, are consorting with the enemy, are basically un-Black. These accusations, coming from the very women to whom we look for deep and real understanding, have served to keep many Black lesbians in hiding, caught between the racism of white women and the homophobia of their sisters. Often, their work has been ignored, trivialized, or misnamed, as with the work of Angelina Grimke, Alice Dunbar-Nelson, Lorraine Hansberry. Yet women-bonded women have always been some part of the power of Black communities, from our unmarried aunts to the amazons of Dahomey.

And it is certainly not Black lesbians who are assaulting women and raping children and grandmothers on the streets of our communities.

Across this country, as in Boston during the spring of 1979 following the unsolved murders of twelve Black women, Black lesbians are spearheading movements against violence against Black women.

What are the particular details within each of our lives that can be scrutinized and altered to help bring about change? How do we redefine difference for all women? It is not our differences which separate women, but our reluctance to recognize those differences and to deal effectively with the distortions which have resulted from the ignoring and misnaming of those differences.

As a tool of social control, women have been encouraged to recognize only one area of human difference as legitimate, those differences which exist between women and men. And we have learned to deal across those differences with the urgency of all oppressed subordinates. All of us have had to learn to live or work or coexist with men, from our fathers on. We have recognized and negotiated these differences, even when this recognition only continued the old dominant/subordinate mode of human relationship, where the oppressed must recognize the masters' difference in order to survive.

But our future survival is predicated upon our ability to relate within equality. As women, we must root out internalized patterns of oppression within ourselves if we are to move beyond the most superficial aspects of social change. Now we must recognize differences among women who are our equals, neither inferior nor superior, and devise ways to use each others' difference to enrich our visions and our joint struggles.

The future of our earth may depend upon the ability of all women to identify and develop new definitions of power and new patterns of relating across difference. The old definitions have not served us, nor the earth that supports us. The old patterns, no matter how cleverly rearranged to imitate progress, still condemn us to cosmetically altered repetitions of the same old exchanges, the same old guilt, hatred, recrimination, lamentation, and suspicion.

For we have, built into all of us, old blueprints of expectation and response, old structures of oppression, and these must be altered at the same time as we alter the living conditions which are a result of those structures. For the master's tools will never dismantle the master's house.

As Paulo Freire shows so well in *The Pedagogy of the Oppressed*,[2] the true focus of revolutionary change is never merely the oppressive situations which we seek to escape, but that piece of the oppressor which is planted deep within each of us, and which knows only the oppressors' tactics, the oppressors' relationships.

Change means growth, and growth can be painful. But we sharpen self-definition by exposing the self in work and struggle together with those whom we define as different from ourselves, although sharing the same goals. For Black and white, old and young, lesbian and heterosexual women alike, this can mean new paths to our survival.

> *We have chosen each other*
> *and the edge of each others battles*
> *the war is the same*
> *if we lose*
> *someday women's blood will congeal*
> *upon a dead planet*
> *if we win*
> *there is no telling*
> *we seek beyond history*
> *for a new and more possible meeting.*[3]

---

2 Seabury Press, New York, 1970.

3 From "Outlines," unpublished poem.

Suggested Readings for Part I

Collins, Patricia Hill. 2000. *Black Feminist Thought: Knowledge, Consciousness, and the Politics of Empowerment*, 2d ed. New York: Routledge.

Romero, Mary, Pierrette Hodagneu-Sotelo, and Vilma Ortiz, eds. 1997. *Challenging Fronteras: Structuring Latina and Latino Lives in the U.S.* New York: Routledge.

Takaki, Ronald. 1993. *A Different Mirror: A History of Multicultural America*. Boston: Little, Brown.

 ### InfoTrac College Edition: Search Terms

Use your access to the online library, InfoTrac College Edition, to learn more about subjects covered in this section. The following are some suggested terms for searches:

African American studies
ethnic studies
feminist studies
multicultural studies/multiculturalism

 ### InfoTrac College Edition: Bonus Reading

You can use the InfoTrac College Edition feature to find an additional reading pertinent to this section and can also search on the author's name or keywords to locate the following reading:

Guy-Sheftall, Beverly. 1997. "Whither Black Women's Studies: Interview." By Evelynn M. Hammonds. *differences: A Journal of Feminist Cultural Studies* 9 (Fall 1997): 31–45.

Beverly Guy-Sheftall is a faculty member at Spelman College—a historically Black women's college. She discusses the specific challenges of developing Black women's studies and also articulates the importance of these studies for feminism in general. How does developing such an inclusive curriculum shift the assumptions of more exclusionary thinking?

Companion Website

For additional links, quizzes, and learning tools related to this part, see the book's companion website at **http://sociology.wadsworth.com/andersen_hill_collins6e.**

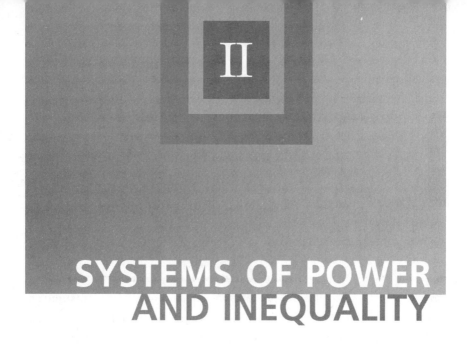

SYSTEMS OF POWER AND INEQUALITY

Margaret L. Andersen
and Patricia Hill Collins

One of the most important things to learn about race, class, and gender is that they are *systemic forms of inequality*. Although most people tend to think of them as individual characteristics (or identities), they are built into the very structure of society—and it is this social fact that drives our analysis of race, class, and gender as intersectional systems of inequality. This does not make them irrelevant as individual or group characteristics, but points you to the analysis of *social structure* to think about how race, class, and gender operate, what they mean, and how they influence people's lives.

Locating racial oppression in the structure of social institutions provides a different frame of analysis from that which would be obtained by analyzing only individuals. Using a social structural analysis of race, class, and gender turns your attention to how they work as systems of power—systems that differentially advantage and disadvantage groups depending on their social location. Moreover, this means that no one of these social facts singularly predetermines where you will be situated within this system of power and social relationships. Thus, not all men are equally powerful and not all women are equally oppressed. When you focus on the intermingling structural relationships of race, class, *and* gender, you see a more complex, ever-changing, and multidimensional social order.

To repeat, neither race nor class nor gender operate alone. They do so within a system of simultaneous, interrelated social relationships—what we have earlier called the *matrix of domination*. This means that they also engage other social facts—ethnicity, sexuality, age, disability, even the region where you live, and so forth. In this section we examine race, class, and gender from an institutional or structural perspective. And, later in the section, we examine how race, class, and gender also intersect with ethnicity, nationality, and sexuality. You will see that each of these systems of power and inequality intertwine—and they do so in different ways at different points in time. Thus, now sexuality has become more visible as a system of social subordination, but beliefs about sexuality have long served to buttress the beliefs that support racial and gender subordination. Likewise, a system of racial subordination has historically been one of the ways that class structure was created: Some accumulated property through the appropriation of other people's labor, even while groups who provided the labor that produced property for others were denied basic rights of citizenship, such as the right to vote, the right to marry, the right to own property, and the right to be considered a U.S. citizen.

Throughout Part II, you should keep the concept of *social structure* in mind. Remembering Marilyn Frye's analogy of the birdcage in Part I, be aware that race, class, and gender form a structure of social relations. This structure is supported by ideological beliefs that make things appear "normal" and "acceptable," thus clouding our awareness of how the structure operates. Thus, one of the prevailing beliefs about racism is that it is largely a thing of the past, now that formal barriers to racial discrimination have been removed. But, as Eduardo Bonilla-Silva ("Racism without Racists") points out in his formulation of *color-blind racism*, racism persists, even when it takes on new forms.

Understanding the intersections between race, class, and gender—and how they interrelate with ethnicity and sexuality—requires knowing how to conceptualize each. Although we would rather not treat them separately, we do so initially here to learn what each means and how each is manifested in different group experiences. At the same time, the readings in this section examine the connections among race, class, gender, and other important social categories—namely, ethnicity and sexuality. As we review each in turn, you will also notice several common themes.

First, *each is a socially constructed category*. That is, their significance stems not from some "natural" state, but from what they have become as the result of social and historical processes. Second, notice how *each tends to construct groups in binary (or polar opposite) terms*: man/woman, Black/White, rich/poor, gay/straight, or citizen/alien. These binary constructions create the "otherness" that we examined in the first part of this book. Third, *each is a category of individual and group identity, but note—and this is important—they are also social structures.* That is, they are not just about identity but are about group location in a system of power and inequality. Thus, when we move into Part II, you will see how they are part of the institutional fabric of society. More than being about individual and group identity, race, class, and gender—and the other systems that they intersect with—shape patterns in the labor market, families, state institutions (such as the government and the law), mass media, and so forth. This is a key difference, as we have seen, in a model that focuses solely on difference and one that focuses on the matrix of domination. That is, the matrix of domination forces you to look at social structures, while models of difference often dissolve into individual or group identities. Finally, *neither race, class, nor gender is a fixed category.* Because they are social constructions, their form—and their interrelationship—changes over time. This also means that social change is possible.

As you learn about race, class, and gender, you should keep the intersectional model in mind. One way to think about their interrelationship in a social system is to imagine a typical college basketball game. This will probably seem familiar: the players on the court, the cheerleaders moving about on the side, the band playing, fans cheering, boosters watching from the best seats, and—if the team is ranked—perhaps a television crew. Everybody seems to have a place in the game. Everybody seems to be following the rules. But what explains the patterns that we see and don't see?

Race clearly matters. The predominance of young African American men on many college basketball teams is noticeable. Why do so many young Black men play basketball? Some people argue that African Americans are simply better in areas requiring physical skills such as sports, but there is another reality: For many young Black men, sports may seem the only hope for a good job, so sports, like the military, can seem like an attractive mobility route. Perceived promises of high salaries, endorsements, and merchandise can make young people believe sports are a path to success, thus many young African American boys believe they can earn a good living playing professional sports. The odds of actually doing so are extremely slim. In truth, of the 40,000 African American boys playing high school basketball, only 35 will make it to the NBA (National Basketball Association) and only 7 of those will be starters. This makes the odds of success 0.000175 (Eitzen 1999)! But, in the face of other systematic disadvantages posed by race, some will still think this is their best chance for success.

But does a racial analysis fully explain the "rules" of college basketball? Not really. Who benefits from college basketball? Yes, players (both Black and White, and, increasingly, immigrants) get scholarships and a chance to earn college degrees. Players reap the rewards, but who really benefits? College athletics is big business, and the players make far less from it than many people believe. As amateur athletes, they are forbidden to take any payment for their skills. They are offered the hope of an NBA contract when they turn pro, or at least a college degree if they graduate. But, few actually turn pro. Indeed, few even graduate from college. Among Division I Black basketball players, 42 percent graduate from college, compared with 48 percent of White male basketball players. Among Hispanic and Native American basketball players (men), only 33 percent graduate. Interestingly, however, graduation rates among Black college athletes (including all sports) are higher than among nonathletes, most likely because of the scholarship support they receive; the reverse is true for Hispanic, Native American, and Asian students. And, among women, student-athletes also have higher graduation rates than nonathletes, as well as higher graduation rates than male student-athletes (National Collegiate Athletic Association 2005).

But winning teams also benefit educational institutions. Winning teams garner increased admissions applications, more alumni giving, higher levels of corporate support, and television revenues. Simply put, athletics is big business. Corporate sponsors want their names and products identified with winning teams and athletes; advertisers want their products promoted by winning players. Even though college athletes are forbidden to promote products, corporations create and market products in conjunction with prevailing excitement about basketball, sustained by the players' achievements. Athletic shoes, workout clothing, cars, and beer all target the consumer dollars of those who enjoy watching basketball. And how many jobs are supported by the revenues generated from the enterprise of college basketball? Of course, there are the sports reporters, team physicians, trainers, coaches, most of them defined as professionals. But there are also the service workers— preparing and selling food, cleaning the toilets and stands, maintaining the stadium. A class system defines one's place in this system of inequality, so much so that many of the service workers are invisible to the fans. So, while institutions profit the most—whether schools, product manufacturers, advertisers—there are differential benefits depending on your "rank" within the system of basketball. And the stakes get even bigger when you move beyond college into the world of professional sports.

So, do race and class fully explain the "rules" of basketball? What about gender? Only in a few schools does women's basketball draw as large an audience as men's. And certainly in the media, men's basketball is generally the public's focal point, even though women's sports are increasingly popular. In college basketball, like the pros, most of the coaches and support personnel are men, as are the camera crew and announcers. Where are the women? A few are coaches, rarely paid what the men receive—even on the most winning teams. Those closest to the action on the court may be cheerleaders—tumbling, dancing, and being thrown into the air in support of the exploits of the athletes. Others may be in the band. Some women are in the stands, cheering the team—many of them accompanied by their husbands, partners, boyfriends, parents, and children. Many work in the concession stands, fulfilling women's roles of serving others. Still others are even more invisible, left to clean the restrooms, locker rooms, and stands after the crowd goes home.

Men's behavior reveals a gendered dimension to basketball, as well. Where else are men able to put their arms around each other, slap one another's buttocks, hug each other, or cry in public without having their "masculinity" unnoticed? Sportscasters, too, bring gender into the play of sports, such as when they talk about men's heroic athletic achievements but talk about women athletes' looks or their connection to children. For that matter, look at the prominence given to men's teams in sports pages of the daily newspaper compared with sports news about women, who are typically relegated to the back pages—if their athletic accomplishments are reported at all. Sometimes what we don't see can be just as revealing as what we do see. Gender, as a feature of the game on the court, is so familiar that it may go unquestioned.

This discussion of college basketball demonstrates how race, class, and gender each provide an important, yet partial, perspective on social action. Using an intersectional model, we not only see each of them in turn but also the connections among them. In fact, race, class, and gender are so inextricably intertwined that gaining a comprehensive understanding of a basketball game requires thinking about all of them and how they work together. New questions then emerge: Why are most of those serving the food in concession stands likely to be women and men of color? How are norms of masculinity played out through sport? What class and racial ideologies are promoted through assuming that sports are a mobility route for those who try hard enough? If race, class, and gender relations are embedded in something as familiar and widespread as college basketball, to what extent are other social practices, institutions, relations, and social issues similarly structured?

Race, gender, and class divisions are deeply embedded in the structure of social institutions such as work, family, education, and the state. They shape human relationships, identities, social institutions, and the social issues that emerge from within institutions. Evelyn Nakano Glenn postulates that you can see the intersections of race, class, and gender in three realms of society: the representational realm, the realm of social interaction, and the social structural realm. The representational realm includes the symbols, language, and images that convey racial meanings in society; social interaction refers to the norms and behaviors observable in human relationships; the social structural realm involves the institutional sites where power and resources are distributed in society (Glenn 2002: 12).

This means that race, class, and gender affect all levels of our experience— our consciousness and ideas, our interaction with others, and the social institutions we live within. And, because they are interconnected, no one can be subsumed under the other. In this section of the book, although we focus on each one to provide conceptual grounding, keep in mind that race, class, and gender are connected and overlapping—in all three realms of society: the realm of ideas, interaction, and institutions.

You might begin by considering a few facts:

- The United States is in the midst of a sizable redistribution of wealth, with a greater concentration of wealth and income in the hands of a few than at most previous periods of time. At the same time, a declining share of income is going to the middle class—a class that finds its position slipping, relative to years past (Krugman 2002; DeNavas-Walt et al. 2005).
- Within class groups, racial group experiences are widely divergent. Thus, although there has been substantial growth of an African American and Latino middle class, they have a more tenuous hold on this class status than groups with more stable footing in the middle class. Furthermore, there is significant class differentiation within different racial groups (Pattillo-McCoy 1999; Massey 1993).
- Women in the top 25 percent of income groups have seen the highest wage growth of any group over the last twenty years; the lowest earning groups of women, like men, have seen wages fall, while the middle has remained flat (Mishel et al. 2005). Class differences within gender are hidden by thinking of women as a monolithic group.

- Women of color, including Latinas, African American women, Native American women, and Asian American women are concentrated in the bottom rungs of the labor market along with recent immigrant women (U.S. Department of Labor 2005).
- Poverty has been steadily increasing in the United States since 2000; it is particularly severe among women, especially among women of color and their children, but, in recent years, has risen most among White people (DeNavas-Walt et al. 2005).
- While the mass media extol the virtues of recent reforms in welfare legislation and herald a "decline in the welfare rolls," studies show that increases in family income among former welfare recipients are meager, and there has been an increase in the number of such families evicted from housing because of falling behind on rent. Families also report an increase in other material hardships—phones and utilities being cut off, for example (Lewis et al. 2002; Acker et al. 2002).
- Welfare reform is only one dimension of the shrinkage of social support systems from federal and state assistance. The shrinkage of social support is not only affecting the very poor, however. Job benefits in the form of health insurance, pensions, and so forth for all workers have declined. Following job loss, less than half of U.S. workers are currently eligible for unemployment insurance (Emsellem et al. 2002).
- At both ends of the economic spectrum there is a growth of gated communities: well-guarded, locked neighborhoods for the rich and prisons for the poor—particularly Latinos and African American men. At the same time, growth in the rate of imprisonment is highest among women (Harrison and Beck 2002; Collins and Veskel 2000).

None of these facts can be explained through an analysis that focuses only on race or class or gender. Clearly, class matters. Race matters. Gender matters. And they matter together. We turn now to defining some of the basic concepts involving the systems of power and inequality that we examine in this section.

RACE AND RACISM

Locating racial oppression in the structure of social institutions means distinguishing racism and prejudice. *Prejudice* is a hostile attitude toward a person who is presumed to have negative characteristics associated with a group to which he or she belongs. Racism is more systematic than this and is not the same thing as prejudice. Prejudice refers to people's attitudes. *Racism* is a system of power and privilege; it can be manifested in people's attitudes but is rooted in society's structure. It is reflected in the different group advantages and disadvantages, based on their location in this societal system. Racism is structured into society, not just in people's minds. As such, it is built into the very fabric of dominant institutions in the United States and has been since the founding of the nation. Joe Feagin refers to this as *systemic racism*, meaning the "complex array of anti-black practices, the unjustly gained political-economic power of whites, the continuing economic and other resource inequalities along racial lines, and the white racial ideologies and attitudes created to maintain and rationalize white privilege and power" (2000: 6).

In this definition of institutional racism, notice first that racism is part of society's structure, not just present in the minds of individual bigots. Seen in this light, people may not be individually racist but can still benefit from a system that is organized to benefit some at the expense of others, as Eduardo Bonilla-Silva points out in his essay on color-blind racism ("Racism without Racists"). *Color-blind racism* is a new form of racism in which dominant groups assume that race no longer matters—even when society is highly racially segregated and when individual and group well-being is still strongly determined by race. Many people also believe that being nonracist means being color-blind—that is, refusing to recognize or treat as significant a person's racial background and identity. But to ignore the significance of race in a society where racial groups have distinct historical and contemporary experiences is to deny the reality of their group experience. Being color-blind in a society structured on racial privilege means assuming that everybody is "White," which is why people of color might be offended by friends who say, for example, "But I never think of you as Black." This blindness to the persistent realities of race also leads to an idea that there is nothing we should be doing about it—either individually or collectively—thus racism is perpetuated. In "White Privilege and Male Privilege: Unpacking the Invisible Knapsack" Peggy McIntosh describes how the system of racial privilege becomes invisible to those who benefit from it, even though it structures the everyday life of both White people and people of color.

Racism also shapes everyday social relations. Patricia J. Williams, a noted African American legal scholar, illustrates this in her discussion of persistent discrimination in housing ("Of Race and Risk"). Despite her middle-class status, systemic racism confronts her—and other African Americans—in daily encounters. Practices of everyday racism are part of the edifice of institutional racism; yet, we often misread their meaning.

Discrimination is one of the driving forces of racism. Though it is perhaps not as overt as, for example, during Jim Crow segregation in the South, discrimination can still be seen in various patterns and practices. Indeed, segregation, though not mandated by law as it was during Jim Crow, is as stark as ever. Segregation in schools has actually increased over recent years. And, in research known as *audit studies,* researchers, one White and one Black, are matched in credentials and appearance; they pose—in person—as job or housing applicants. Audit studies find significant levels of discrimination. White job applicants in such studies are offered the job almost half of the time; Black applicants, only 11 percent of the time. White applicants are often told things such as "You are just what we are looking for." Black applicants, on the other hand, are told they do not have the right attributes for the job. Studies of employers have also found that employers hold considerable stereotypes about Black workers that prevent them from hiring them (Moss and Tilly 2001; see also the article by Philip Moss and Chris Tilly in Part III).

Another dimension of racism is that its forms change over time. Racial discrimination is no longer legal, but racism nonetheless continues to structure relations between groups and to differentiate the power that different groups have. The changing character of racism is also evident in the fact that specific racial group histories differ, but different racial groups share common experiences of racial oppression. Thus, Chinese Americans were never enslaved, but they experienced forced residential segregation and economic exploitation based on their presumed racial characteristics. Mexican Americans were never placed on federal reservations, as Native Americans have been, but in some regards both groups share the experience of colonization by White settlers. Both have experienced having their lands appropriated by White settlers; Native Americans were removed from their lands and forced into reservations, if not killed. Chicanos originally held land in what is now the American Southwest, but it was taken following the Mexican American War; in 1848 Mexico ceded huge parts of what are now California, New Mexico, Nevada, Colorado, Arizona, and Utah to the United States for $15 million. Mexicans living there were one day Mexicans, the next living in the United States, though without all the rights of citizens.

Most people assume that race is biologically fixed, an assumption that is fueled by arguments about the presumed biological basis for different forms of inequality. But the concept of race is more social than biological; scientists working on the human genome project have even found that there is no "race" gene. But you should not conclude from this that race is not "real."

It is just that its reality stems from its social significance. That is, the meaning and significance of race stems from specific social, historical, and political contexts. It is these contexts that make race meaningful, not just whatever physical differences may exist between groups.

To understand this, think about how racial categories are created, by whom, and for what purposes. Racial classification systems reflect prevailing views of race, thereby establishing groups that are presumed to be "natural." These constructed racial categories then serve as the basis for allocating resources; furthermore, once defined, the categories frame political issues and conflicts (Omi and Winant 1994). Omi and Winant define *racial formation* as "the sociohistorical process by which racial categories are created, inhabited, transformed, and destroyed" (1994: 55). In Nazi Germany, Jews were considered to be a race—a social construction that became the basis for the Holocaust. Abby L. Ferber's essay ("What White Supremacists Taught a Jewish Scholar about Identity") shows the complexities that evolve in the social construction of race. As someone who studies White supremacist groups, she sees how White racism defines her as Jewish, even while she lives in society as White. Her reflections reveal, too, the interconnections between racism and anti-Semitism (the hatred of Jewish people), reminding us of the interplay between different systems of oppression.

In understanding racial formation, we see that societies construct rules and practices that define groups in racial terms. Moreover, racial meanings constantly change as institutions evolve and as different groups contest prevailing racial definitions. Some groups are "racialized"; others, are not. Where, for example, did the term *Caucasian* come from? Although many take it to be "real" and don't think about its racist connotations, the term has racist origins. It was developed in the late eighteenth century by a German anthropologist, Johann Blumenbach. He developed a racial classification scheme that put people from the Russian Caucases at the top of the racial hierarchy because he thought Caucasians were the most beautiful and sophisticated people; darker people were put on the bottom of the list: Asians, Africans, Polynesians, and Native Americans (Hannaford 1996). It is amazing when you think about it that this term remains with us, with few questioning its racist origin and connotations.

Consider also the changing definitions of race in the U.S. census. Given the large number of multiracial groups and the increasing diversity brought about by immigration, we can no longer think of race in mutually exclusive terms. In 1860, only three "races" were presumed to exist—Whites, Blacks, and mulattoes. By 1890, however, these original three races had been joined by five others—quadroon, octoroon, Chinese, Japanese, and Indian. Ten short years later, this list shrank to five races—White, Black, Chinese, Japanese, and Indian—a situation reflecting the growth of strict segregation in the South (O'Hare 1996). Now people of mixed racial heritage present a challenge to census classifications. In the 2000 census, the U.S. government for the first time allowed people to check multiple boxes to identify themselves as more than one race. In addition, you could check "Hispanic" as a separate category. This change in the census reflects the growing number of multiracial people in the United States. The census categories are not just a matter of accurate statistics; they have significant consequences in the apportionment of societal resources. Thus, while some might argue that we should not "count" race at all, doing so is important because data on racial groups are used to enforce voting rights, to regulate equal employment opportunities, and to determine various governmental supports, among other things.

Shifting definitions of race are grounded in shifting relations of power. Recent decades have seen additional revisions to definitions of race. In particular, the experiences of Latino groups in the United States challenge longstanding racial categories of "Black" and "White." Elizabeth Martinez (in "Seeing More than Black and White") notes that White-Black relations have defined racism in the United States for centuries but that a rapidly changing population that includes diverse Latino groups is forcing Americans to reconsider the nature of racism. Color, she argues, has been the marker of race, but she challenges the dualistic thinking that has promoted this racist thinking.

The overarching structure of racial power relations means that placement in this structure leads to differences in how people see racism—or don't—and what they are willing to do about it. Thus, White Americans continue to be optimistic in their assessment of racial progress. They say that they are tired of hearing about racism and that they have done all they can to eliminate racial discrimination. People of color are less sanguine about racial progress and are more aware of the nuances of racism. Marked differences by race are still evident in employment, political representation, schooling, and other basic measures of group well-being.

CLASS

Like race, the social class system is grounded in social institutions and practices. Rather than thinking of social class as a rank held by an individual, think of social class as a series of relations that pervade the entire society and shape our social institutions and relationships with one another. Although class shapes identity and individual well-being, class is a system that differentially structures group access to economic, political, cultural, and social resources. Within the United States, the class system evolves from patterns of capitalist development, and those patterns intersect with race and gender. To begin with, the class system in the United States is marked by striking differences in income. *Income* is the amount of money brought into a household in one year. Measures of income in the United States are based on annually reported census data drawn from a sample of the population. These data show quite dramatic differences in class standing when taking gender and race into account. *Median income* is the income level above and below which half of the population lies. It is the best measure of group income standing. Thus, in 2004 median income for non-Hispanic White households was $48,977 (meaning half of such households earned more than this and half below); this is the "middle." Black households had a median income of $30,134; Hispanic households, $34,241; Asian and Pacific Islander households, $57,518 (DeNavas-Walt et al. 2005; see also Figure 1).

But this tells only part of the story. Household income is the income of a total household. What about individual earners? This is where you can see the confounding influence of gender. Among full-time, year-round workers, men earned (in 2003) $41,503 and women, $31,653. But when you also consider race, you see that income does not fall simply along lines of either race

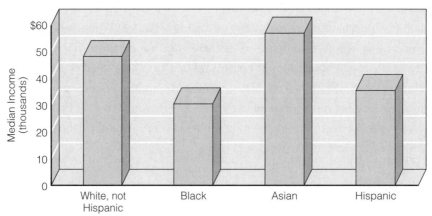

Source: DeNavas-Walt, Carmen. 2005. *Income, Poverty, and Health Insurance: Coverage in the United States: 2004,* Washington, DC: U.S. Census Bureau.

FIGURE 1 Median Household Income (2004)

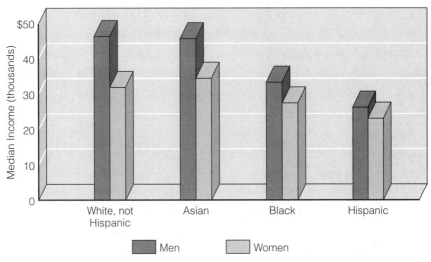

Source: U.S. Census Bureau, 2005. *Detailed Historical Tables.* www.census.gov

FIGURE 2 Median Income, Year-round, Full-time Workers

or gender (see Figure 2). White and Asian American women actually earn more than Black and, especially, Hispanic men, although there is a persistent gap within each racial-ethnic group between women and men (U.S. Census Bureau 2005). These data should lead you to be cautious about making general claims that women earn less than men—it matters *which women* and *which men* you are talking about.

Something to keep in mind is that because household income results from the income of individual workers, many households need more than one earner just to reach median levels of income. Some workers also have to hold multiple jobs to make ends meet. People who have more than one job typically do so to meet regular household expenses or to pay off debt. Although Whites (both men and women) are the group most likely to hold multiple jobs, Black and Hispanic jobholders are more likely to do so to meet basic household expenses (*Monthly Labor Review,* October 2000; www.bls.gov). In addition, workers at every class level have increased the number of hours that they work (since 1980), although it is women and those at the lower ends of the class scale who have increased their working hours the most (Mishel et al. 2005).

Differences in patterns of wealth are even more revealing than income regarding how inequality is perpetuated in society. *Wealth* is determined by adding all of one's financial assets and subtracting all debt. Income and wealth are related but are not the same thing. As important as income can be in determining one's class status, wealth is even more significant.

Consider this: Imagine two recent college graduates. They graduate in the same year, from the same college, with the same major and the identical grade point average. Both get jobs with the same salary in the same company. But, one student's parents paid all college expenses and gave her a car upon graduation. The other student worked while in school and has graduated with substantial debt from student loans. This student's family has no money to help support the new worker. Who is better off? Same salary, same credentials, but one person has a clear advantage—one that will be played out many times over as the young worker buys a home, finances her own children's education, and possibly inherits additional assets. This shows you the significance of wealth—not just income—in structuring social class.

Thus, income data indicate quite dramatic differences in class, race, and gender standing. Furthermore, wealth differences are also startling. The wealthiest 1 percent of the population control 33 percent of all wealth—the bottom 80 percent, only 16 percent (Mishel et al. 2005). For most Americans, debt, not wealth, is more common. Furthermore, 25 percent of White households, 61 percent of Black households, and 54 percent of Hispanic households have no financial assets at all (Oliver and Shapiro 1995), indicative of the vast differences in wealth holdings among different racial groups. In fact, the median net worth of White households is more than ten times that of African American and Latino households.

Wealth is especially significant because it provides a *cumulative* advantage to those who have it. Wealth helps pay for college costs for children and down payments on houses; it can cushion the impact of emergencies, such as unexpected unemployment or sudden health problems. Even small amounts of wealth can provide the cushion that averts economic disaster for families. Buying a home, investing, being free of debt, sending one's children to college, and transferring economic assets to the next generation are all instances of class advantage that add up over time and produce advantage, even beyond one's current income level. Sociologists Melvin Oliver and Thomas Shapiro (1995) have found, for example, that even Black and White Americans at the same income level, with the same educational and occupational assets, have a substantial difference in their financial assets—an average difference of $43,143 per year! This means that, even when earning the same income, the two groups are in quite different class situations—although both may be considered middle class. Furthermore, wealth produces more wealth, because inheritance allows people to transmit economic status from one generation to the next. As Thomas M. Shapiro shows ("The Hidden Cost of Being African American"), these differences in wealth contribute to the perpetuation of racial inequality across generations.

When you study class in relationship to race, you will see that overall there are wide differences in the class status of Whites and people of color, but you should be careful not to see all Whites and Asian Americans as well-off and all African Americans, Native Americans, and Latinos as poor. Consider the range of social class experiences just among Whites. Although on average White households possess higher accumulated wealth and have higher incomes than Black, Hispanic, and Native American households, large numbers of White households do not. White people also account for almost half (46 percent) of the nation's poor; and, as poverty has risen since the year 2000, it has risen most among White Americans (DeNavas-Walt et al. 2005). In addition, class experiences across racial groups can vary widely, as shown by Mary Pattillo-McCoy's research on the Black middle class in "Black Picket Fences." She shows that the Black middle class continues to experience racial segregation and, as one result, is more exposed to the risks that the Black poor experience than would be true of the White middle class.

These facts should caution us about conclusions based on *aggregate data* (that is, data that represent whole groups). Such data give you a broad picture of group differences, but they are not attentive to the more nuanced picture you see when taking into account race, class, and gender (along with other factors, such as age, level of education, occupation, and so forth). Aggregate data on Asian Americans, for example, show them as a group to be relatively well-off. But this portrayal, like the stereotypes of a model minority, obscures significant differences both when making comparisons between Asian Americans and other groups and between Asian American groups. So, for example, although Asian American median income is, in the aggregate, higher than for White Americans, this does not mean all Asian American families are better off than White families. If you look at poverty rates, you get a different picture. Ten percent of Asian Americans are poor, compared with 8.6 percent of White, non-Hispanic families (DeNavas-Walt et al. 2005). The highest rates of poverty are those for the most recent immigrant groups, including Laotians, Cambodians, Vietnamese, Chinese, and Korean immigrants (Lee 1995).

As the U.S. public witnessed following the devastation of Hurricane Katrina, poverty is more widespread than many believe it to be, even though in recent years it has been increasing. Hurricane Katrina brought renewed attention to poverty and its location in the intersection of race and class (as discussed by Jason De Parle in "Broken Levees, Unbroken Barriers"), but poverty is also a matter of gender—evidenced by the fact that women and their children are especially hard hit by poverty. Thirty-nine percent of Hispanic and Black families headed by women are poor, as are 15 percent of Asian/Pacific Islander and 24 percent of White families headed by women. Poverty rates among children are especially disturbing: in 2004, 18 percent of all children in the United States lived below the *poverty line* ($19,157 for a family of four, including two children). When adding race, the figures are even more disturbing: 34 percent of African American children, 29 percent of Hispanic children, 10 percent of Asian/Pacific Islander children, and 11 percent of White (non-Hispanic) children (those under 18 years of age) are poor—astonishing figures for one of the most affluent nations in the world (DeNavas-Walt et al. 2005; see Figures 3 and 4).

Simplistic solutions suggested by current welfare policy imply that women would not be poor if they would just get married or get a job. But the root causes of poverty lie in the distribution of wealth and capital, coupled with low wages and high unemployment among certain groups—groups whose social location is the result of race, class, and gender stratification. Keep in mind that 16 percent of workers still end up being poor; even among those working year-round and full time, 8 percent are poor. And these figures count only those whose earnings fell below the official poverty line. If you

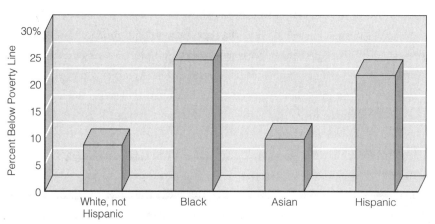

Source: DeNavas-Walt, Carmen. 2005. *Income, Poverty, and Health Insurance: Coverage in the United States: 2004.* Washington, DC: U.S. Census Bureau.

FIGURE 3 Percent Living in Poverty (2004)

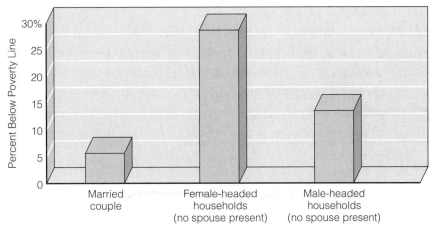

Source: DeNavas-Walt, Carmen. 2005. *Income, Poverty, and Health Insurance: Coverage in the United States: 2004.* Washington, DC: U.S. Census Bureau.

FIGURE 4 Poverty and Household Type

calculate the income received by someone working full time (40 hours a week) and year-round (52 weeks, no vacation) at the federal minimum wage ($5.50 per hour), you will see that the dollars earned ($11,440) do not even come close to the federal poverty line for a family of four ($19,157 in 2004; U.S. Census Bureau 2005).

In the United States, the social class system is also marked by differences in power. Social class is not just a matter of material difference; it is a pattern of domination in which some groups have more power than others. *Power* is the ability to influence and dominate others. This refers not just to interpersonal power but also refers to the structural power that some groups have because of their position in the class system. Groups with vast amounts of wealth, for example, can influence systems such as the media and the political process in ways that less-powerful groups cannot. Privilege in social class thus encompasses both a position of material advantage and the ability to control and influence others.

The class system is currently undergoing some profound changes, as detailed by Sklar ("Growing Gulf Between Rich and the Rest of Us"). These changes are intimately linked to patterns of economic transformation in the political economy—changes that are both global and domestic. Jobs are being exported overseas as vast multinational corporations seek to enhance their profits by promoting new markets and cutting the cost of labor. Within the United States, there is a shift from a manufacturing-based economy to a service economy, with corresponding changes in the types of jobs available and the wages attached to these jobs. Fewer skilled, decent-paying manufacturing jobs exist today than in the past. Fewer workers are covered by job benefits and unemployment insurance; only 40 percent of workers are now eligible for unemployment benefits following job loss (Emsellem et al. 2002). Wages are flat for most workers, except those at the very top. Millions of people are left with jobs that do not pay enough, in part-time or temporary work, or without any work at all.

All told, class divisions in the United States are becoming more marked. There is a growing gap between the haves and have-nots. Income growth has been greatest for those at the top end of the population—the upper 20 percent and the upper 5 percent of all income groups, regardless of race. For everyone else, income growth has remained flat. Although in every racial group, the top earners have seen the most growth in income, Black and Hispanic high-earners still earn less overall than Whites (see Figure 5). At the same time, in the nation's cities and towns, homelessness has become increasingly apparent even to casual observers. Even before Hurricane Katrina displaced hundreds of thousands of families, the number of homeless in a given year was estimated to be about two million. Families are the largest segment of the homeless population. Half of the homeless are African American; about 20 percent are children (National Coalition for the Homeless 2005).

If social class is so important in shaping life chances, why don't more people realize its significance? The answer lies in how dominant groups use ideology to explain the class system and other systems of inequality. Ideology created by dominant groups refers to a system of beliefs that simultaneously distort reality and justify the status quo. The class system in the United States has been supported through the myth that we live in a classless society. This myth serves the dominant class, making class privilege seem like something that one earns, not something that is deeply embedded in the institutions of society. The system of privilege and inequality (by race, class, and gender) is least visible to those who are most privileged and who, in turn, control the resources to define the dominant cultural belief systems. Perhaps this is why the privileged, not the poor, are more likely to believe that one gets ahead through hard work. It also helps explain why men more than women deny that patriarchy exists and why Whites more than Blacks believe racism is disappearing.

Overall, the effects of race, class, and gender manifest themselves in patterns of advantage and disadvantage. For example, in some ways—such as in rates of poverty and the racial gap in earnings in the labor market—women

Source: U.S. Census Bureau. 2002. *Historical Income Tables—Households.* Website:
www.census.gov/hhes/income/histinc/

FIGURE 5 Income Growth

of color share a class position with men of color. In other ways, women of
different races share a common class position: they all make less on average
than men of their racial group. These trends point to the need for analyzing
race, class, and gender together in thinking about inequality.

---

*In 2000 CPI-adusted dollars.
†Data not available for Hispanics in 1970;1972 data used.

GENDER

Gender, like race, is a social construction, not a biological imperative. *Gender* is rooted in social institutions and results in patterns within society that structure the relationships between women and men and that give them differing positions of advantage and disadvantage within institutions. As an identity, gender is learned; that is, through gender socialization, people construct definitions of themselves and others that are marked by gender. Like race, however, gender cannot be understood at the individual level alone. Gender is structured in social institutions, including work, families, mass media, and education.

You can see this if you think about the concept of a gendered institution. *Gendered institution* is now used to define the total patterns of gender relations that are "present in the processes, practices, images, and ideologies, and distribution of power in the various sectors of social life" (Acker 1992: 567). This term brings a much more structural analysis of gender to the forefront. Rather than seeing gender only as a matter of interpersonal relationships and learned identities, this framework focuses the analysis of gender on relations of power—just as thinking about institutional racism focuses on power relations and economic and political subordination—not just interpersonal relations. Changing gender relations is not just a matter of changing individuals. As with race and class, change requires transformation of institutional structures.

Gender, however, is not a monolithic category. Maxine Baca Zinn, Pierrette Hondagneu-Sotelo, and Michael Messner argue ("Gender through the Prism of Difference") that, although gender is grounded in specific power relations, it is important to understand that gender is constructed differently depending on the specific social locations of diverse groups. Thus race, class, nationality, sexual orientation, and other factors produce varying social and economic consequences that cannot be understood by looking at gender differences alone. These authors ask us to move beyond studying differences and instead to use multiple "prisms" to see and comprehend the complexities of multiple systems of domination—each of which shapes and is shaped by gender. Seen in this way, men appear as a less monolithic and unidimensional group as well.

Gender, race, class, and sexuality *together* construct stereotypes. Each gains meaning in relationship to the others (Glenn 2002). Thus, for Julia Alvarez ("A White Woman of Color") gender identity is intricately part of her status as Dominican, and, to complicate things further, ideals of beauty in her narrative intertwine with ideas about color. You cannot understand her experience as a woman without also locating her in the ethnic, racial, national, and migration experiences that are also part of her life. Thus, gender oppression is maintained through multiple systems—systems that are reflected in group stereotypes. These stereotypes also sexualize groups in different, but particular, ways.

Yen Le Espiritu argues in "Ideological Racism and Cultural Resistance" that *controlling images* of Asian American men and women are both racialized and sexualized. She locates the construction of these images in the institutions that produce popular culture, showing how such institutions have a stake in perpetuating race, gender, and sexual domination. Espiritu's work shows that gender stereotypes take unique forms for particular groups. Jewish American women, for example, are stereotyped as "JAPs" (Jewish American princesses), as if all were rich and privileged. This stereotype simultaneously promotes anti-Semitism and misogyny (defined as the hatred of women) at the same time that it uses an anti-Asian stereotype ("Jap") to denigrate others. For other groups, race, gender, and sexual stereotypes intertwine in different ways. Thus, African American men are stereotyped as hypermasculine and oversexed, and African American women as promiscuous, bad mothers, and nurturing "mammies" who care for everyone else, but not their own children. Latinos are stereotyped as "macho" and, like African American men, sexually passionate, but out of control. Latinas are stereotyped as either "hot" or virgin-like. Similarly, White women are sexually stereotyped in dichotomous terms as "madonnas" or "whores." Working-class women are more likely to be seen as "sluts" and upper-class women as frigid and cold. We can see that controlling images of sexuality are part of the architecture of race, class, and gender oppression (Collins 2000), revealing the interlocking systems of race, class, gender, and sexuality.

Like color-blind racism, gender ideologies may make it seem that women now have it made, even though the facts tell us otherwise. True, the gap between women's and men's income has closed, although most analysts agree that the narrowing of the gap reflects a drop in men's wages more than an increase in women's wages. And, women are more present in professional jobs—women who have become defined as the stereotypical "working woman." Despite this new image, though, most women remain concentrated in gender-segregated occupations with low wages, little opportunity for mobility, and stressful conditions. This is particularly true for women of color, who are more likely to be in occupations that are both race- and gender-segregated. And, as we have seen, among women heading their own households, poverty persists at alarmingly high rates. Income and occupational data, however, do not tell the full story for women. High rates of violence against women—whether in the home, on campus, in the workplace, or on the streets—indicate the continuing devaluation of and danger for women in this society.

Gender is also formed in the context of social institutions—family, workplaces, schools, religion, and so forth. Michael Messner shows (in "Masculinities and Athletic Careers") that sports are an important arena where gender identities and relations are formed. His study examines how boys from different racial and social class backgrounds learn about masculinity through their involvement in sports. Messner demonstrates that there is no one set of beliefs about masculinity to which all men subscribe; instead, sports shape understandings of masculinity and men's experiences in sports in race- and class-specific ways.

Taking this idea in a different direction, Thomas J. Gerschick ("Toward a Theory of Disability and Gender") analyzes how understanding disability requires an analysis of gender, as well as how gender in relationship to race and class explains dimensions of disability that might otherwise go unnoticed. Taken together, the articles in this section show the social construction of gender, its interrelationship within systems of race, class, and gender power, and the connection of gender to such factors as nationality, age, and physical ability.

ETHNICITY AND MIGRATION

Sociologists traditionally define *ethnicity* as groups who share a common culture; however, like race, ethnicity develops within the context of systems of power. Thus, the meaning and significance of ethnicity can shift over time and in different social and political contexts. For example, groups may develop a sense of heightened ethnicity in the context of specific historical events; likewise, their feeling of sharing a common group identity can result from being labeled as "outsiders" by dominant groups. Think, for example, of the heightened sense of group identity that has developed for Arab Americans in the aftermath of 9/11.

Social and historical context also shapes who becomes defined as "ethnic." Asian Americans, as an example, have developed a *panethnic* identity—that is, an identity of common experiences, even across diverse ethnic groups. But this panethnic identity has arisen from social movements that defined different Asian American groups (Chinese, Japanese, Korean, and so forth) as having common social and political experiences within the United States (Espiritu 1992). Thus, even groups given a single group identity may have diverse ethnic and cultural experiences among them, as with African Americans who may be West Indian, Dominican, U.S. born, or from other cultural origins.

Patterns in the shifting meaning of ethnicity are being influenced by the changing contours of the U.S. population. Racial-ethnic groups are a larger proportion of the U.S. population, and their numbers are expected to rise over the years ahead. One quarter of the U.S. population is now Black, Hispanic, Asian American, Pacific Islander, or Native American; by 2050, non-Hispanic Whites are predicted to make up only slightly more than half the total population. At the same time that the nation is becoming more diverse, changes are occurring regarding which groups predominate. Latinos have recently exceeded African Americans as the largest minority group in the population. Hispanic, Native American, Asian American, and African American populations are also growing more rapidly than White American populations, with the greatest growth among Hispanics and Asian Americans (Grieco and Cassidy 2001).

Immigration into the United States is only one facet of the increasing importance that ethnicity and migration play in contemporary social life. Changes in ethnicity and migration are being enacted on a world stage—a global context that increasingly links nations together in a global social order where diversity is more typical than not. You need only consult an older world atlas to get a sense of the widespread changes that characterize the current period. *World cities* have been formed that are linked through international systems of commerce; within these cities, migrants play an important role in providing the labor that is needed to keep pace with the global economy. Migrant (or "guest") workers may provide the labor for multinational corporations; or, they may provide the service work that increasingly characterizes postindustrial society. Some workers may provide agricultural labor for multinational producers of food; others do domestic labor for middle- and upper-class families whose own lives are being transformed by changes in the world economic system. Wherever you look, the world is being changed by the increasingly global basis of modern life.

Such changes indicate that globalization is not just about what is happening elsewhere in the world—as if global studies were just a matter of comparing societies. Globalization is everywhere. No nation, including the

United States, can really be understood without seeing how globalization is affecting life even at home. Patterns of life in any one society are now increasingly shaped by the connections between societies, and this is evident by looking at how ethnicity and migration are changing life in the United States. *Transnational families* are more common—that is, families whose members live and reside in different nations (often at a great distance from each other). Cultural features associated with different cultural traditions are increasingly evident, even in communities in the United States that have been thought of as "all-American" towns. Youth cultures embrace common features whether in Russia, Mexico, Japan, or the United States because of the penetration of world capitalist markets. Thus, hip-hop plays on the streets of Mexico City and salsa is heard on radio stations in the United States.

What do such changes mean for understanding ethnicity and migration in a transnational, global context? Within the formal borders of the United States, changes associated with migration are raising new questions about national identity. How will the United States define itself as a nation-state in the changing global context? How will the increased visibility of people of color in the United States, in Latin America, in Africa, in Asia, and within the borders of former European colonial powers shape the future? How are cultural representations and institutions changed in a world context marked by such an ethnic mix—both within and between countries? In this context, who gets defined as a race, and how does that map onto concepts of citizenship and the division of labor in different nations? What will it mean to be American in a nation where racial-ethnic diversity is so much a part of the national fabric?

The events of September 11, 2001, give these questions additional importance. In response to terrorism, most in the United States were catapulted into a strong sense of national identity. But, just as racial profiling was becoming increasingly criticized by the public, fears of terrorism have made it suddenly permissible to many. In the aftermath of 9/11, more restrictive immigration practices and policies have been employed; international and "ethnic" students are increasingly under surveillance; civil liberties have been restricted in the interests of national security. The events of 9/11 and the international tensions that have followed bring increasing urgency to our grappling with questions of how we can maintain a society of such great diversity within a framework of social justice.

Thus, several themes emerge in rethinking ethnicity and migration through the lens of race, class, and gender. Despite the ideology of the "melting pot," national identity in the United States has been closely linked to a history of racial privilege. As Lillian Rubin points out in "Is This a White Country, or What?" the term *American* is usually assumed to mean White. Other types of Americans, such as African Americans and Asian Americans, become distinguished from the "real" Americans by virtue of their race. More importantly, certain benefits are reserved for those deemed to be "deserving Americans."

Many Americans never "melted" into the melting pot. Many people think that race is like ethnicity and that the failure of people of color to assimilate into the mainstream as White ethnic groups purportedly have done represents an unwillingness to shed their culture. But as Mary Waters points out in "Optional Ethnicities: For Whites Only?" this view seriously misreads the meaning of both race and ethnicity in shaping American national identity. Waters suggests that White Americans of European ancestry have *symbolic ethnicity* in that their ethnic identity does not influence their lives unless they want it to. Waters contrasts this symbolic ethnic identity among many Whites with the socially enforced and imposed racial identity among African Americans. Because race operates as a physical marker in the United States, intersections of race and ethnicity operate differently for Whites and for people of color. White ethnics can thus have "ethnicity" without cost, but people of color pay the price for their ethnic identity.

We see this in Robert Smith's discussion of the increasing presence of Mexicans in the United States ("'Mexicanness' in New York"). Smith uses the concept of *racialization* to describe how groups become defined as having racial characteristics that are also the basis for their mistreatment. Although we might imagine Mexicans and Mexican Americans as an ethnic group—in that their identity comes from a commonly shared cultural background—in the context of migration, they have been redefined within the context of racial, social, and class hierarchies in the United States. As Smith argues, Mexican immigrants confront the racial segregation and discrimination that have characterized Black American experience. They are also juxtaposed against both White ethnics and other groups, such as Puerto Ricans, by social structures that place different values on groups exploited for their labor. His article shows how race and ethnicity intertwine—both between dominant and subordinate groups and among subordinate groups—those "racialized" as Black.

Despite these structural forces, however, people are not just passive victims of these social forces. Peggy Levitt ("Salsa and Ketchup: Transnational Migrants Straddle Two Worlds") shows how immigrant communities use their own institutions—whether families, community organizations, or other social networks—to provide support, as well as to sustain ties to the homelands. Nazli Kibria's research ("Migration and Vietnamese American Women") shows how Vietnamese American women and men negotiate with each other to adjust to the specific experiences they face as immigrants. By examining gender roles in Vietnamese American families, Kibria shows how women rebuild families to provide economic and social support during the transition to a new community. Her analysis reminds us that immigration and migration are not just about ethnicity and race, but are also gendered processes. Families are sites where gender is both *created* and also *contested*, as people face circumstances that require reconstruction of prior relationships. Kibria's research also emphasizes that people actively shape viable family networks and support systems that enable them to survive even in the face of cultural, economic, and social assaults. The experiences of groups migrating to the United States show both the tenacity of race, class, and gender structures *and* how people work to change these systems.

SEXUALITY

The linkage between race, class, and gender is revealed within studies of sexuality, just as sexuality is a dimension of each. For example, constructing images about Black sexuality is central to maintaining institutional racism. Similarly, beliefs about women's sexuality structure gender oppression. Thus, sexuality operates as a system of power and inequality comparable to and intersecting with the systems of race, class, and gender.

At the same time, sexuality is commodified in a capitalist society such as the United States. Jean Kilbourne shows ("You Talkin' to Me?") that the commodification of sex through advertising is especially harmful to women. The denigrating images of sex in advertising, according to Kilbourne, lead to dehumanization, as well as generating actual physical and mental harm.

Homophobia—the fear and hatred of homosexuality—supports the institutionalized power and privilege accorded to heterosexual behavior and identification. If only heterosexual forms of gender identity are labeled "normal," then gays, lesbians, and bisexuals become ostracized, oppressed, and defined as "socially deviant." Homophobia affects heterosexuals as well because it is part of the gender ideology used to distinguish "normal" men and women from those deemed deviant. Thus, young boys learn a rigid view of masculinity—one often associated with violence, bullying, and degrading others—to avoid being perceived as a "fag." The oppression of lesbians and gay men is then linked to the structure of gender in everyone's lives.

The institutionalized structures and beliefs that define and enforce heterosexual behavior as the only natural and permissible form of sexual expression are what is meant by *heterosexism*. As Jonathan Katz points out ("The Invention of Heterosexuality"), heterosexism is a specific historic construction; its meaning and presumed significance have evolved and changed at distinct historical times.

Understanding this rests on understanding sexuality, like race, gender, class, and ethnicity, as a social construction. Sexuality has a biological context, because bodies make sex pleasurable. But the real significance of sexuality lies in its social dimensions. Thus, ideas about gender in society influence how we experience sexuality and how sexuality is controlled. Homophobia is used as a mechanism to enforce the construction of "masculinity." The hatred directed toward lesbians, gays, and bisexuals is thus part of the system by which gender is created and maintained. In this regard, sexuality and gender are deeply linked.

Cornel West ("Black Sexuality: The Taboo Subject") adds another social dimension to sexuality, showing how sexuality has been used as the vehicle to support racial fears and racial subordination. Racial subordination was built on the exploitation of Black bodies—both as labor and as sexual objects. West's essay untangles multiple dimensions of racial-sexual politics. Strictures against certain interracial, sexual relationships (but not those between White men and African American women) are a way to maintain White patriarchy. And, as West points out, race mixes with both gender and sex. Without examining the ways that sexuality, race, and gender—and, we should add, class—entangle, we remain shrouded in myths and distortions about human sexuality and human relationships.

But how do race, class, gender, and sexuality interrelate? This complex question is explored in the interview by Amy Gluckman and Betsy Reed with longtime activist Barbara Smith ("Where Has Gay Liberation Gone?"). Many have argued that race, class, gender, and sexuality are similar in social relations and processes of society. Can we collapse them as similar categories of difference? Smith carefully identifies some of the ways in which race and sexuality are not similar. She notes that racial oppression is historically and structurally embedded in the founding of the United States, whereas lesbian and gay oppression was not. Differences in historical paths and varying structural arrangements should not blind us, however, to the similarities that link race, class, and gender oppression to homophobia and heterosexism. As Smith notes, similar strategies are used to oppress people by race and by sexuality. As she succinctly puts it, "Our enemies are the same. That to me is the major thing that should be pulling us together." When you use a race/class/gender framework to think about sexuality, you will see both common patterns and different realities in race, class, gender, and sexual oppression. Sexuality, for example, has not been used as an explicit category to organize the division of labor, as have race, class, and gender. Nonetheless, sexuality has been a key part of the division of labor, primarily in the form of heterosexual households where the White middle and upper classes rely on male breadwinners. But, this family form, as we have seen, has not been available to all and is currently undergoing great change. Female-headed and female-supported families have long been characteristics of families of color and are now increasingly common among White, middle-class families too. Thus, the idea of the male breadwinner—supported as it was through heterosexism—is more an ideological ideal than a reality.

Kamala Kempadoo in "Globalizing Sex Workers' Rights" raises another dimension to the discussion of sexuality—sex as work. Sex workers sell their bodies or images of their bodies for money. Kempadoo emphasizes how sex workers have organized worldwide to address issues of human rights, working conditions, and decriminalization. Her analysis links sex work to other struggles for women's rights and social justice. She also brings a global perspective to the discussion of sexuality. Sex work on a global scale is also linked to world politics about race and class, given the specific position of women of color in international sex work. Furthermore, the class politics of international relations are also apparent in the place of women in the international traffic in sex, where women's sexuality is used to promote tourism and where images of the "exotic other" are used to attract more affluent classes to various regions of the world. Kempadoo also links sexuality to processes of migration, showing how race, class, gender, and sex are part of the international traffic in women.

References

Acker, Joan, Sandra Morgen, and Lisa Gonzales. 2002. "Welfare Restructuring, Work & Poverty: Policy from Oregon." Working paper, Eugene, OR: Center for the Study of Women in Society.

Acker, Joan. 1992. "Gendered Institutions: From Sex Roles to Gendered Institutions." *Contemporary Sociology* 21 (September): 565–569.

Collins, Chuck, and Felice Veskel. 2000. *Economic Apartheid in America: A Primer on Economic Inequality and Insecurity.* New York: The New Press.

Collins, Patricia Hill. 2000. *Black Feminist Thought: Knowledge, Consciousness, and the Politics of Empowerment.* New York: Routledge.

DeNavas-Walt, Carmen, Bernadette D. Proctor, and Robert J. Mills. 2005. *Income, Poverty, and Health Insurance: Coverage in the United States: 2004.* Washington, DC: U.S. Census Bureau.

Eitzen, D. Stanley. 1999. *Fair and Foul: Beyond the Myths and Paradoxes of Sport.* Lanham, MD: Rowman and Littlefield.

Emsellem, Murray, Jessica Goldberg, Rick McHugh, Wendell Primus, Rebecca Smith, and Jeffrey Wenger. 2002. *Failing the Unemployed.* Washington, DC: Economic Policy Institute. Website: www.epinet.org.

Espiritu, Yen Le. 1992. *Asian American Panethnicity: Bridging Institutions and Identities.* Philadelphia, PA: Temple University Press.

Feagin, Joe R. 2000. *Racist America: Roots, Current Realities, and Future Reparations.* New York: Routledge.

Glenn, Evelyn Nakano. 2002. *Unequal Freedom: How Race and Gender Shaped American Citizenship and Labor.* Cambridge, MA: Harvard University Press.

Grieco, Elizabeth M., and Rachel C. Cassidy. 2001. *Overview of Race and Hispanic Origin.* Washington, DC: U.S. Census Bureau.

Hannaford, Ivan. 1996. *Race: The History of an Idea in the West.* Baltimore: Johns Hopkins University Press.

Harrison, Paige M., and Allen J. Beck. 2002. *Prisoners in 2001.* Washington, DC: U.S. Bureau of Justice Statistics. Website: www.ojp.usdoj.gov/bjs.

Krugman, Paul. 2002. "For Richer: How the Permissive Capitalism of the Boom Destroyed American Equality." *The New York Times Magazine* (October 20): 62ff.

Lee, Sharon. 1995. "Poverty and the U.S. Asian Population." *Social Science Quarterly* 75 (September): 541–559.

Lewis, Dan A., Amy Bush Stevens, and Kristen Shook Slack. 2002. *Illinois Families Study, Welfare Reform in Illinois: Is the Moderate Approach Working?* Evanston, IL: Institute for Poverty Research, Northwestern University.

Massey, Douglass S. 1993. "Latino Poverty Research: An Agenda for the 1990s." *Social Science Research Council Newsletter* 47 (March): 7–11.

Mishel, Lawrence, Jared Bernstein, and Sylvia Allegretto. 2005. *The State of Working America 2004/2005.* Washington, DC: Economic Policy Institute.

Monthly Labor Review. 2000. "At Issue: Reasons for Working Multiple Jobs." Vol. 123, No. 10. (October).

Moss, Philip I., and Chris Tilly. 2001. *Stories Employers Tell: Race, Skill, and Hiring in America (Multi City Study of Urban Inequality).* New York: Russell Sage Foundation.

National Coalition for the Homeless. 2005. *Facts about Homelessness.* Website: www.nationalhomeless.org.

National Collegiate Athletic Association. 2005. *Graduation Rates Report for NCAA-Division I Schools.* Indianapolis, IN: NCAA. Website: www.ncaa.org.

O'Hare, William P. 1996. *A New Look at Poverty in America.* Washington, DC: Population Reference Bureau.

Oliver, Melvin L., and Thomas M. Shapiro. 1995. *Black Wealth/White Wealth: A New Perspective on Racial Inequality.* New York: Routledge.

Omi, Michael, and Howard Winant. 1994. *Racial Formation in the United States: From the 1960s to the 1990s.* 2d ed. New York: Routledge.

Pattillo-McCoy, Mary. 1999. *Black Picket Fences: Privilege and Peril among the Black Middle Class.* Chicago: University of Chicago Press.

U.S. Census Bureau. 2005. *Income: Detailed Historical Table, Tables P36B–P36E.* Washington, DC: U.S. Census Bureau. Website: www.census.gov.

U.S. Department of Labor. 2005. *Employment and Earnings.* Washington, DC: U.S. Department of Labor.

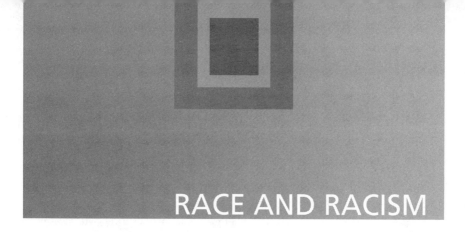

RACE AND RACISM

7

RACISM WITHOUT "RACISTS"

Eduardo Bonilla-Silva

There is a strange kind of enigma associated with the problem of racism. No one, or almost no one, wishes to see themselves as racist; still, racism persists, real and tenacious.

—Albert Memmi, *Racism*

Nowadays, except for members of white supremacist organizations, few whites in the United States claim to be "racist." Most whites assert they "don't see any color, just people"; that although the ugly face of discrimination is still with us, it is no longer the central factor determining minorities' life chances; and, finally, that like Dr. Martin Luther King Jr., they aspire to live in a society where "people are judged by the content of their character, not by the color of their skin." More poignantly, most whites insist that minorities (especially blacks) are the ones responsible for whatever "race problem" we have in this country. They publicly denounce blacks for "playing the race card," for demanding the maintenance of unnecessary and divisive race-based programs, such as affirmative action, and for crying "racism" whenever they are criticized by whites. Most whites believe that if blacks and other minorities would just stop thinking about the past, work hard, and complain less

From Eduardo Bonilla-Silva. *Racism without Racists: Color-Blind Racism and the Persistence of Racial Inequality in the United States* (Lanham, MD: Rowman and Littlefield Publishers, 2003).

(particularly about racial discrimination), then Americans of all hues could "all get along."

But regardless of whites' "sincere fictions," racial considerations shade almost everything in America. Blacks and dark-skinned racial minorities lag well behind whites in virtually every area of social life; they are about three times more likely to be poor than whites, earn about 40 percent less than whites, and have about a tenth of the net worth that whites have. They also receive an inferior education compared to whites, even when they attend integrated institutions. In terms of housing, black-owned units comparable to white-owned ones are valued at 35 percent less. Blacks and Latinos also have less access to the entire housing market because whites, through a variety of exclusionary practices by white realtors and homeowners, have been successful in effectively limiting their entrance into many neighborhoods. Blacks receive impolite treatment in stores, in restaurants, and in a host of other commercial transactions. Researchers have also documented that blacks pay more for goods such as cars and houses than do whites. Finally, blacks and dark-skinned Latinos are the targets of racial profiling by the police that, combined with the highly racialized criminal court system, guarantees their overrepresentation among those arrested, prosecuted, incarcerated, and if charged for a capital crime, executed. Racial profiling in the highways has become such a prevalent phenomenon that a term has emerged to describe it: driving while black. In short, blacks and most minorities are "at the bottom of the well."[1]

How is it possible to have this tremendous degree of racial inequality in a country where most whites claim that race is no longer relevant? More important, how do whites explain the apparent contradiction between their professed color blindness and the United States' color-coded inequality? . . . I contend that whites have developed powerful explanations—which have ultimately become justifications—for contemporary racial inequality that exculpate them from any responsibility for the status of people of color. These explanations emanate from a new racial ideology that I label *color-blind racism*. This ideology, which acquired cohesiveness and dominance in the late 1960s, explains contemporary racial inequality as the outcome of nonracial dynamics. Whereas Jim Crow racism explained blacks' social standing as the result of their biological and moral inferiority, color-blind racism avoids such facile arguments. Instead, whites rationalize minorities' contemporary status as the product of market dynamics, naturally occurring phenomena, and blacks' imputed cultural limitations. For instance, whites can attribute Latinos' high poverty rate to a relaxed work ethic ("the Hispanics are mañana, mañana, mañana—tomorrow, tomorrow, tomorrow") or residential segregation as the result of natural tendencies among groups ("Do a cat and a dog mix? I can't see it. You can't drink milk and scotch. Certain mixes don't mix.").

Color-blind racism became the dominant racial ideology as the mechanisms and practices for keeping blacks and other racial minorities "at the bottom of the well" changed. I have argued elsewhere that contemporary racial inequality is reproduced through "new racism" practices that are subtle, institutional, and apparently nonracial. In contrast to the Jim Crow era, where racial inequality was enforced through overt means (e.g., signs saying "No Niggers Welcomed Here" or shotgun diplomacy at the voting booth), today racial practices operate in "now you see it, now you don't" fashion. For example, residential segregation, which is almost as high today as it was in the past, is no longer accomplished through overtly discriminatory practices. Instead, covert behaviors such as not showing all the available units, steering minorities and whites into certain neighborhoods, quoting higher rents or prices to minority applicants, or not advertising units at all are the weapons of choice to maintain separate communities. In the economic field, "smiling face" discrimination ("We don't have jobs now, but please check later"), advertising job openings in mostly white networks and ethnic newspapers, and steering highly educated people of color into poorly remunerated jobs or jobs with limited opportunities for mobility are the new ways of keeping minorities in a secondary position. Politically, although the Civil Rights struggles have helped remove many of the obstacles for the electoral participation of people of color, "racial gerrymandering, multimember legislative districts, election runoffs, annexation of predominantly white areas, at-large district elections, and anti–single-shot devices (disallowing concentrating votes in one or two candidates in cities using at-large elections) have become standard practices to disenfranchise" people of color. Whether in banks, restaurants, school admissions, or housing transactions, the maintenance of white privilege is done in a way that defies facile racial readings. Hence, the contours of color-blind racism fit America's "new racism" quite well.

Compared to Jim Crow racism, the ideology of color blindness seems like "racism lite." Instead of relying on name calling (niggers, Spics, Chinks), color-blind racism otherizes softly ("these people are human, too"); instead of proclaiming God placed minorities in the world in a servile position, it suggests they are behind because they do not work hard enough; instead of viewing interracial marriage as wrong on a straight racial basis, it regards it as "problematic" because of concerns over the children, location, or the extra burden it places on couples. Yet this new ideology has become a formidable political tool for the maintenance of the racial order. Much as Jim Crow racism served as the glue for defending a brutal and overt system of racial oppression in the pre–Civil Rights era, color-blind racism serves today as the ideological armor for a covert and institutionalized system in the post–Civil Rights era. And the beauty of this new ideology is that it aids in the maintenance of white privilege without fanfare, without naming those who it subjects and those who it rewards. It allows a President to state things such as, "I strongly support diversity of all kinds, including racial diversity in higher education," yet, at the same time, to characterize the University of Michigan's affirmation action program as "flawed" and "discriminatory" against whites.

Thus whites enunciate positions that safeguard their racial interests without sounding "racist." Shielded by color blindness, whites can express resentment toward minorities; criticize their morality, values, and work ethic; and even claim to be the victims of "reverse racism." This is the thesis I will defend . . . to explain the curious enigma of "racism without racists."

WHITES' RACIAL ATTITUDES IN THE POST–CIVIL RIGHTS ERA

Since the late 1950s surveys on racial attitudes have consistently found that fewer whites subscribe to the views associated with Jim Crow. For example, whereas the majority of whites supported segregated neighborhoods, schools, transportation, jobs, and public accommodations in the 1940s, less than a quarter indicated they did in the 1970s. Similarly, fewer whites than ever now seem to subscribe to stereotypical views of blacks. Although the number is still high (ranging from 20 percent to 50 percent, depending on the stereotype), the proportion of whites who state in surveys that blacks are lazy, stupid, irresponsible, and violent has declined since the 1940s.

These changes in whites' racial attitudes have been explained by the survey community and commentators in four ways. First, are the *racial optimists*. This group of analysts agrees with whites' common sense on racial matters and believes the changes symbolize a profound transition in the United States. . . .

The problems with this optimistic interpretation are twofold. First, . . . relying on questions that were framed in the Jim Crow era to assess whites' racial views today produces an artificial image of progress. Since the central racial debates and the language used to debate those matters have changed, our analytical focus ought to be dedicated to the analysis of the new racial issues. Insisting on the need to rely on old questions to keep longitudinal (trend) data as the basis for analysis will, by default, produce a rosy picture of race relations that misses what is going on on the ground. Second, and more important, because of the change in the normative climate in the post–Civil Rights era, analysts must exert extreme caution when interpreting attitudinal data, particularly when it comes from single-method research designs. The research strategy that seems more appropriate for our times is mixed research designs (surveys used in combination with interviews, ethnosurveys, etc.), because it allows researchers to cross-examine their results.

A second, more numerous group of analysts exhibit what I have labeled elsewhere as the *racial pesoptimist* position. Racial pesoptimists attempt to strike a "balanced" view and suggest that whites' racial attitudes reflect progress and resistance.

. . . Despite the obvious appeal of this view in the research community (the appearance of neutrality, the pondering of "two sides," and this view's "balanced" component), racial pesoptimists are just closet optimists. Schuman, for example, has pointed out that, although "White responses to questions of principle are . . . more complex than is often portrayed . . . they nevertheless do show in almost every instance a positive movement over time."[2] Furthermore, it is his belief that the normative change in the United States is real and that the issue is that whites are having a hard time translating those norms into personal preferences.

A third group of analysts argues that the changes in whites' attitudes represent the emergence of a *symbolic racism*. This tradition is associated with the work of David Sears and his associate, Donald Kinder. They have defined symbolic racism as "a blend of anti-black affect and the kind of traditional American moral values embodied in the Protestant Ethic." According to these authors, symbolic racism has replaced biological racism as the primary way whites express their racial resentment toward minorities. In Kinder and Sanders's words:

> A new form of prejudice has come to prominence, one that is preoccupied with matters of moral character, informed by the virtues associated with the traditions of individualism. At its center are the contentions that blacks do not try hard enough to overcome the difficulties they face and that they take what they have not earned. Today, we say, prejudice is expressed in the language of American individualism.[3]

Authors in this tradition have been criticized for the slipperiness of the concept "symbolic racism," for claiming that the blend of antiblack affect and individualism is new, and for not explaining why symbolic racism came about. . . .

Despite its limitations, the symbolic racism tradition has brought attention to key elements of how whites explain racial inequality today. Whether this is "symbolic" of antiblack affect or not is beside the point and hard to assess, since as a former student of mine queried, "How does one test for the unconscious?"[4]

The fourth explanation of whites' contemporary racial attitudes is associated with those who claim that whites' racial views represent a *sense of group position*. In essence, the claim . . . is that white prejudice is an ideology to defend white privilege. Bobo and his associates have specifically suggested that because of socioeconomic changes that transpired in the 1950s and 1960s, a *laissez-faire racism* emerged that was fitting of the United States' "modern, nationwide, postindustrial free labor economy and polity."[5] Laissez-faire racism "encompasses an ideology that blames blacks themselves for their poorer relative economic standing, seeing it as the function of perceived cultural inferiority."[6]

Some of the basic arguments of authors in the symbolic and modern racism traditions and, particularly, of the laissez-faire racism view are fully compatible with my color-blind racism interpretation. Like these authors,

I argue that color-blind racism has rearticulated elements of traditional liberalism (work ethic, rewards by merit, equal opportunity, individualism, etc.) for racially illiberal goals. I also argue like them that whites today rely more on cultural rather than biological tropes to explain blacks' position in this country. Finally, I concur with most analysts of post–Civil Rights' matters in arguing that whites do not perceive discrimination to be a central factor shaping blacks' life chances.

Although most of my differences with authors in the symbolic racism and laissez-faire traditions are methodological, I have one central theoretical disagreement with them. Theoretically, most of these authors are still snarled in the prejudice problematic and thus interpret actors' racial views as *individual psychological* dispositions. . . . In contrast, my model is not anchored in actors' affective dispositions (although affective dispositions may be manifest or ideological rule is always partial). Even in periods of hegemonic rule, such as the current one, subordinate racial groups develop oppositional views. However, it would be foolish to believe that those who rule a society do not have the power to at least color (pun intended) the views of the ruled.

Racial ideology can be conceived for analytical purposes as comprising the following elements: common frames, style, and racial stories. The frames that bond together a particular racial ideology are rooted in the group-based conditions and experiences of the races and are, at the symbolic level, the representations developed by these groups to explain how the world is or ought to be. And because the group life of the various racially defined groups is based on hierarchy and domination, the ruling ideology expresses as "common sense" the interests of the dominant race, while oppositional ideologies attempt to challenge that common sense by providing alternative frames, ideas, and stories based on the experiences of subordinated races.

Individual actors employ these elements as "building blocks . . . for manufacturing versions on actions, self, and social structures" in communicative situations.[7] The looseness of the elements allows users to maneuver within various contexts (e.g., responding to a race-related survey, discussing racial issues with family, or arguing about affirmative action in a college classroom) and produce various accounts and presentations of self (e.g., appearing ambivalent, tolerant, or strong minded). This loose character enhances the legitimating role of racial ideology because it allows for accommodation of contradictions, exceptions, and new information. As Jackman points out about ideology in general: "Indeed, the strength of an ideology lies in its loose-jointed, flexible application. *An ideology is a political instrument, not an exercise in personal logic:* consistency is rigidity, the only pragmatic effect of which is to box oneself in."[8]

Before I can proceed, two important caveats should be offered. First, although whites, because of their privileged position in the racial order, form a social group (the dominant race), they are fractured along class, gender, sexual orientation, and other forms of "social cleavage." Hence, they have multiple and often contradictory interests that are not easy to disentangle and that predict *a priori* their mobilizing capacity (Do white workers have more in common with white capitalists than with black workers?). However, because all actors awarded the dominant racial position, regardless of their multiple structural locations (men or women, gay or straight, working class or bourgeois) benefit from what Mills calls the "racial contract,"[9] *most* have historically endorsed the ideas that justify the racial status quo.

Second, although not every single member of the dominant race defends the racial status quo or spouts color-blind racism, *most* do. To explain this point by analogy, although not every capitalist defends capitalism (e.g., Frederick Engels, the coauthor of *The Communist Manifesto*, was a capitalist) and not every man defends patriarchy (e.g., *Achilles Heel* is an English magazine published by feminist men), *most* do in some fashion. In the same vein, although some whites fight white supremacy and do not endorse white common sense, *most* subscribe to substantial portions of it in a casual, uncritical fashion that helps sustain the prevailing racial order.

NOTES

1. Derrick Bell, *Race, Racism and American Law* (Boston: Little, Brown, 1992).

2. Howard Schuman et al., *Racial Attitudes in America* (Cambridge, Mass.: Harvard University Press, 1997).

3. David R. Kinder and Lynn M. Sanders, *Divided by Color: Racial Politics and Democratic Ideals* (Chicago: University of Chicago Press, 1996), 106.

4. This comment was made by Susanna Dolance, a graduate student at Michigan.

5. Lawrence, Bobo and Jane A. Kluegel, and Ryan A. Smith. "Laissez-Faire Racism: the Crystallization of a Kinder, Gentler, Anti-Black Ideology," in *Racial Attitudes in the 1990s*, 15-44 (Westport, CT: Praeger, 1997).

6. Lawrence Bobo and James R. Kluegel, "Status, Ideology, and Dimensions of Whites' Racial Beliefs and Attitudes: Progress and Stagnation," in *Racial Attitudes in the 1990s*, 93–120 (Westport, CT: Praeger, 1997), 95.

7. Margaret Wetherell and Jonathan Potter, *Mapping the Language of Racism* (New York: Columbia University Press, 1992), 91.

8. My emphasis. Jackman, Mary R. 1994. *The Velvet Glove*. Berkeley: University of California Press, 69.

9. Black philosopher Charles W. Mills argues that with the advent of modern imperialism (the fifteenth and sixteenth centuries onward), whites developed a political, moral, and epistemological "racial contract" to maintain white supremacy over nonwhites. See *The Racial Contract* (Ithaca. N.Y.: Cornell University Press, 1997).

8

WHITE PRIVILEGE
Unpacking the Invisible Knapsack

Peggy McIntosh

Through work to bring materials from Women's Studies into the rest of the curriculum, I have often noticed men's unwillingness to grant that they are overprivileged, even though they may grant that women are disadvantaged. They may say they will work to improve women's status, in the society, the university, or the curriculum, but they can't or won't support the idea of lessening men's. Denials which amount to taboos surround the subject of advantages which men gain from women's disadvantages. These denials protect male privilege from being fully acknowledged, lessened, or ended.

Thinking through unacknowledged male privilege as a phenomenon, I realized that since hierarchies in our society are interlocking, there was most likely a phenomenon of white privilege which was similarly denied and protected. As a white person, I realized I had been taught about racism as something which puts others at a disadvantage, but had been taught not to see one of its corollary aspects, white privilege, which puts me at an advantage.

I think whites are carefully taught not to recognize white privilege, as males are taught not to recognize male privilege. So I have begun in an untutored way to ask what it is like to have white privilege. I have come to see white privilege as an invisible package of unearned assets which I can count on cashing in each day, but about which I was "meant" to remain oblivious. White privilege is like an invisible weightless knapsack of special provisions, maps, passports, codebooks, visas, clothes, tools, and blank checks.

Describing white privilege makes one newly accountable. As we in Women's Studies work to reveal male privilege and ask men to give up some of their power, so one who writes about having white privilege must ask, "Having described it, what will I do to lessen or end it?"

After I realized the extent to which men work from a base of unacknowledged privilege, I understood that much of their oppressiveness was unconscious. Then I remembered the frequent charges from women of color that white women whom they encounter are oppressive. I began to understand why we are justly seen as oppressive, even when we don't see ourselves that way. I began to count the ways in which I enjoy unearned skin privilege and have been conditioned into oblivion about its existence.

My schooling gave me no training in seeing myself as an oppressor, as an unfairly advantaged person, or as a participant in a damaged culture. I was taught to see myself as an individual whose moral state depended on her individual moral will. My schooling followed the pattern my colleague Elizabeth Minnich has pointed out: whites are taught to think of their lives as morally neutral, normative, and average, and also ideal, so that when we work to benefit others, this is seen as work which will allow "them" to be more like "us."

I decided to try to work on myself at least by identifying some of the daily effects of white privilege in my life. I have chosen those conditions which I think in my case *attach somewhat more to skin-color privilege* than to class, religion, ethnic status, or geographical location, though of course all these other factors are intricately intertwined. As far as I can see, my African American co-workers, friends and acquaintances with whom I come into daily or frequent contact in this particular time, place, and line of work cannot count on most of these conditions.

1. I can if I wish arrange to be in the company of people of my race most of the time.
2. If I should need to move, I can be pretty sure of renting or purchasing housing in an area which I can afford and in which I would want to live.
3. I can be pretty sure that my neighbors in such a location will be neutral or pleasant to me.
4. I can go shopping alone most of the time, pretty well assured that I will not be followed or harassed.
5. I can turn on the television or open to the front page of the paper and see people of my race widely represented.
6. When I am told about our national heritage or about "civilization," I am shown that people of my color made it what it is.
7. I can be sure that my children will be given curricular materials that testify to the existence of their race.
8. If I want to, I can be pretty sure of finding a publisher for this piece on white privilege.
9. I can go into a music shop and count on finding the music of my race represented, into a supermarket and find the staple foods which fit with my cultural traditions, into a hairdresser's shop and find someone who can cut my hair.
10. Whether I use checks, credit cards, or cash, I can count on my skin color not to work against the appearance of financial reliability.
11. I can arrange to protect my children most of the time from people who might not like them.

12. I can swear, or dress in secondhand clothes, or not answer letters, without having people attribute these choices to the bad morals, the poverty, or the illiteracy of my race.
13. I can speak in public to a powerful male group without putting my race on trial.
14. I can do well in a challenging situation without being called a credit to my race.
15. I am never asked to speak for all the people of my racial group.
16. I can remain oblivious of the language and customs of persons of color who constitute the world's majority without feeling in my culture any penalty for such oblivion.
17. I can criticize our government and talk about how much I fear its policies and behavior without being seen as a cultural outsider.
18. I can be pretty sure that if I ask to talk to "the person in charge," I will be facing a person of my race.
19. If a traffic cop pulls me over or if the IRS audits my tax return, I can be sure I haven't been singled out because of my race.
20. I can easily buy posters, postcards, picture books, greeting cards, dolls, toys, and children's magazines featuring people of my race.
21. I can go home from most meetings of organizations I belong to feeling somewhat tied in, rather than isolated, out-of-place, outnumbered, unheard, held at a distance, or feared.
22. I can take a job with an affirmative action employer without having co-workers on the job suspect that I got it because of my race.
23. I can choose public accommodation without fearing that people of my race cannot get in or will be mistreated in the places I have chosen.
24. I can be sure that if I need legal or medical help, my race will not work against me.
25. If my day, week, or year is going badly, I need not ask of each negative episode or situation whether it has racial overtones.
26. I can choose blemish cover or bandages in "flesh" color and have them more or less match my skin.

I repeatedly forgot each of the realizations on this list until I wrote it down. For me white privilege has turned out to be an elusive and fugitive subject. The pressure to avoid it is great, for in facing it I must give up the myth of meritocracy. If these things are true, this is not such a free country; one's life is not what one makes it; many doors open for certain people through no virtues of their own.

In unpacking this invisible knapsack of white privilege, I have listed conditions of daily experience which I once took for granted. Nor did I think of any of these perquisites as bad for the holder. I now think that we need a more finely differentiated taxonomy of privilege, for some of these varieties are only what one would want for everyone in a just society, and others give license to be ignorant, oblivious, arrogant and destructive.

I see a pattern running through the matrix of white privilege, a pattern of assumptions which were passed on to me as a white person. There was one main piece of cultural turf; it was my own turf, and I was among those who could control the turf. *My skin color was an asset for any move I was educated to want to make.* I could think of myself as belonging in major ways, and of making social systems work for me. I could freely disparage, fear, neglect, or be oblivious to anything outside of the dominant cultural forms. Being of the main culture, I could also criticize it fairly freely.

In proportion as my racial group was being made confident, comfortable, and oblivious, other groups were likely being made inconfident, uncomfortable, and alienated. Whiteness protected me from many kinds of hostility, distress, and violence, which I was being subtly trained to visit in turn upon people of color.

For this reason, the word "privilege" now seems to me misleading. We usually think of privilege as being a favored state, whether earned or conferred by birth or luck. Yet some of the conditions I have described here work to systematically overempower certain groups. Such privilege simply *confers dominance* because of one's race or sex.

I want, then, to distinguish between earned strength and unearned power conferred systemically. Power from unearned privilege can look like strength when it is in fact permission to escape or to dominate. But not all of the privileges on my list are inevitably damaging. Some, like the expectation that neighbors will be decent to you, or that your race will not count against you in court, should be the norm in a just society. Others, like the privilege to ignore less powerful people, distort the humanity of the holders as well as the ignored groups.

We might at least start by distinguishing between positive advantages which we can work to spread, and negative types of advantages which unless rejected will always reinforce our present hierarchies. For example, the feeling that one belongs within the human circle, as Native Americans say, should not be seen as privilege for a few. Ideally it is an *unearned entitlement.* At present, since only a few have it, it is an *unearned advantage* for them. This paper results from a process of coming to see that some of the power which I originally saw as attendant on being a human being in the U.S. consisted in *unearned advantage* and *conferred dominance.*

I have met very few men who are truly distressed about systemic, unearned male advantage and conferred dominance. And so one question for me and others like me is whether we will be like them, or whether we will get truly distressed, even outraged, about unearned race advantage and conferred dominance and if so, what we will do to lessen them. In any case, we need to do more work in identifying how they actually affect our daily lives. Many, perhaps most, of our white students in the U.S. think that racism doesn't affect them because they are not people of color; they do not see "whiteness" as a racial identity. In addition, since race and sex are not the only advantaging systems at work, we need similarly to examine the daily experience of having age advantage, or ethnic advantage, or physical ability, or advantage related to nationality, religion, or sexual orientation.

Difficulties and dangers surrounding the task of finding parallels are many. Since racism, sexism, and heterosexism are not the same, the advantaging associated with them should not be seen as the same. In addition, it is hard to disentangle aspects of unearned advantage which rest more on social class, economic class, race, religion, sex and ethnic identity than on other factors. Still, all of the oppressions are interlocking, as the Combahee River Collective Statement of 1977 continues to remind us eloquently.

One factor seems clear about all of the interlocking oppressions. They take both active forms which we can see and embedded forms which as a member of the dominant group one is taught not to see. In my class and place, I did not see myself as a racist because I was taught to recognize racism only in individual acts of meanness by members of my group, never in invisible systems conferring unsought racial dominance on my group from birth.

Disapproving of the systems won't be enough to change them. I was taught to think that racism could end if white individuals changed their attitudes. [But] a "white" skin in the United States opens many doors for whites whether or not we approve of the way dominance has been conferred on us. Individual acts can palliate, but cannot end, these problems.

To redesign social systems we need first to acknowledge their colossal unseen dimensions. The silences and denials surrounding privilege are the key political tool here. They keep the thinking about equality or equity incomplete, protecting unearned advantage and conferred dominance by making these taboo subjects. Most talk by whites about equal opportunity seems to me now to be about equal opportunity to try to get into a position of dominance while denying that *systems* of dominance exist.

It seems to me that obliviousness about white advantage, like obliviousness about male advantage, is kept strongly inculturated in the United States so as to maintain the myth of meritocracy, the myth that democratic choice is equally available to all. Keeping most people unaware that freedom of confident action is there for just a small number of people props up those in power, and serves to keep power in the hands of the same groups that have most of it already.

Though systemic change takes many decades, there are pressing questions for me and I imagine for some others like me if we raise our daily consciousness on the perquisites of being light-skinned. What will we do with such knowledge? As we know from watching men, it is an open question whether we will choose to use unearned advantage to weaken hidden systems of advantage, and whether we will use any of our arbitrarily-awarded power to try to reconstruct power systems on a broader base.

9

OF RACE AND RISK

Patricia J. Williams

Several years ago, at a moment when I was particularly tired of the unstable lifestyle that academic careers sometimes require, I surprised myself and bought a real house. Because the house was in a state other than the one where I was living at the time, I obtained my mortgage by telephone. I am a prudent little squirrel when it comes to things financial, always tucking away stores of nuts for the winter, and so I meet the criteria of a quite good credit risk. My loan was approved almost immediately.

A little while later, the contract came in the mail. Among the papers the bank forwarded were forms documenting compliance with the Fair Housing Act, which outlaws racial discrimination in the housing market. The act monitors lending practices to prevent banks from redlining—redlining being the phenomenon whereby banks circle certain neighborhoods on the map and refuse to lend in those areas. It is a practice for which the bank with which I was dealing, unbeknownst to me, had been cited previously—as well as since. In any event, the act tracks the race of all banking customers to prevent discrimination. Unfortunately, and with the creative variability of all illegality, some banks also use the racial information disclosed on the fair housing forms to engage in precisely the discrimination the law seeks to prevent.

I should repeat that to this point my entire mortgage transaction had been conducted by telephone. I should also note that I speak a Received Standard English, regionally marked as Northeastern perhaps, but not easily identifiable as black. With my credit history, my job as a law professor and, no doubt, with my accent, I am not only middle class but apparently match the cultural stereotype of a good white person. It is thus, perhaps, that the loan officer of the bank, whom I had never met, had checked off the box on the fair housing form indicating that I *was* white.

Race shouldn't matter, I suppose, but it seemed to in this case, so I took a deep breath, crossed out "white" and sent the contract back. That will teach them to presume too much, I thought. A done deal, I assumed. But suddenly the transaction came to a screeching halt. The bank wanted more money, more points, a higher rate of interest. Suddenly I found myself facing great resistance and much more debt. To make a long story short, I threatened to

---

From *The Nation*, December 29, 1997. Reprinted with permission.

sue under the act in question, the bank quickly backed down and I procured the loan on the original terms.

What was interesting about all this was that the reason the bank gave for its new-found recalcitrance was not race, heaven forbid. No, it was all about economics and increased risk: The reason they gave was that property values in that neighborhood were suddenly falling. They wanted more money to buffer themselves against the snappy winds of projected misfortune.

Initially, I was surprised, confused. The house was in a neighborhood that was extremely stable. I am an extremely careful shopper; I had uncovered absolutely nothing to indicate that prices were falling. It took my realtor to make me see the light. "Don't you get it," he sighed. "This is what always happens." And even though I suppose it was a little thick of me, I really hadn't gotten it: For of course, I was the reason the prices were in peril.

The bank's response was driven by demographic data that show that any time black people move into a neighborhood, whites are overwhelmingly likely to move out. In droves. In panic. In concert. Pulling every imaginable resource with them, from school funding to garbage collection to social workers who don't want to work in black neighborhoods. The imagery is awfully catchy, you had to admit: the neighborhood just tipping on over like a terrible accident, whoops! Like a pitcher, I suppose. All that nice fresh wholesome milk spilling out, running away . . . leaving the dark, echoing, up-ended urn of the inner city.

In retrospect, what has remained so fascinating to me about this experience was the way it so exemplified the problems of the new rhetoric of racism. For starts, the new rhetoric of race never mentions race. It wasn't race but risk with which the bank was so considered.

Second, since financial risk is all about economics, my exclusion got reclassified as just a consideration of class. There's no law against class discrimination, goes the argument, because that would represent a restraint on that basic American freedom, the ability to contract or not. If schools, trains, buses, swimming pools and neighborhoods remain segregated, it's no longer a racial problem if someone who just happens to be white keeps hiking up the price for someone who accidentally and purely by the way happens to be black. Black people end up paying higher prices for the attempt to integrate, even as the integration of oneself threatens to lower the value of one's investment.

By this measure of mortgage-worthiness, the ingredient of blackness is cast not just as a social toll but as an actual tax. A fee, an extra contribution at the door, an admission charge for the high costs of handling my dangerous propensities, my inherently unsavory properties. I was not judged based on my independent attributes or financial worth; not even was I judged by statistical profiles of what my group actually does. (For in fact, anxiety-stricken, middle-class people make grovelingly good cake-baking neighbors when not made to feel defensive by the unfortunate historical strategies of bombs, burnings or abandonment.) Rather, I was being evaluated based on what an abstraction of White Society writ large thinks we—or I—do, and that imagined "doing" was treated and thus established as a self-fulfilling prophecy. It is a dispiriting message: that some in society apparently not only devalue black people but devalue *themselves* and their homes just for having us as part of their landscape.

"I bet you'll keep your mouth shut the next time they plug you into the computer as white," laughed a friend when he heard my story. It took me aback, this postmodern pressure to "pass," even as it highlighted the intolerable logic of it all. For by these "rational" economic measures, an investment in my property suggests the selling of myself.

10

SEEING MORE THAN BLACK AND WHITE

Elizabeth Martinez

The racial and ethnic landscape has changed too much in recent years to view it with the same eyes as before. We are looking at a multi-dimensional reality in which race, ethnicity, nationality, culture and immigrant status come together with breathtakingly new results. We are also seeing global changes that have a massive impact on our domestic situation, especially the economy and labor force. For a group of Korean restaurant entrepreneurs to hire Mexican cooks to prepare Chinese dishes for mainly African-American customers, as happened in Houston, Texas, has ceased to be unusual.

The ever-changing demographic landscape compels those struggling against racism and for a transformed, non-capitalist society to resolve several strategic questions. Among them: doesn't the exclusively Black-white framework discourage the perception of common interests among people of color and thus sustain White Supremacy? Doesn't the view that only African Americans face serious institutionalized racism isolate them from potential allies? Doesn't the Black-white model encourage people of color to spend too much energy understanding our lives in relation to whiteness, obsessing about what white society will think and do?

From Elizabeth Martinez, *De Colores Means All of Us: Latina Views for a Multi-Colored Century* (Cambridge, MA: South End Press, 1998). Reprinted by permission of the South End Press.

That tendency is inevitable in some ways: the locus of power over our lives has long been white (although big shifts have recently taken place in the color of capital, as we see in Japan, Singapore and elsewhere). The oppressed have always survived by becoming experts on the oppressor's ways. But that can become a prison of sorts, a trap of compulsive vigilance. Let us liberate ourselves, then, from the tunnel vision of whiteness and behold the many colors around us! Let us summon the courage to reject outdated ideas and stretch our imaginations into the next century.

For a Latina to urge recognizing a variety of racist models is not, and should not be, yet another round in the Oppression Olympics. We don't need more competition among different social groups for the gold medal of "Most Oppressed." We don't need more comparisons of suffering between women and Blacks, the disabled and the gay, Latino teenagers and white seniors, or whatever. Pursuing some hierarchy of oppression leads us down dead-end streets where we will never find the linkage between different oppressions and how to overcome them. To criticize the exclusively Black-white framework, then, is not some resentful demand by other people of color for equal sympathy, equal funding, equal clout, equal patronage or other questionable crumbs. Above all, it is not a devious way of minimizing the centrality of the African-American experience in any analysis of racism.

The goal in re-examining the Black-white framework is to find an effective strategy for vanquishing an evil that has expanded rather than diminished. Racism has expanded partly as a result of the worldwide economic recession that followed the end of the post-war boom in the early 1970s, with the resulting capitalist restructuring and changes in the international division of labor. Those developments generated feelings of insecurity and a search for scapegoats. In the United States racism has also escalated as whites increasingly fear becoming a weakened, minority population in the next century. The stage is set for decades of ever more vicious divide-and-conquer tactics.

What has been the response from people of color to this ugly White Supremacist agenda? Instead of uniting, based on common experience and needs, we have often closed our doors in a defensive, isolationist mode, each community on its own. A fire of fear and distrust begins to crackle, threatening to consume us all. Building solidarity among people of color is more necessary than ever—but the exclusively Black-white definition of racism makes such solidarity more difficult than ever.

We urgently need twenty-first-century thinking that will move us beyond the Black-white framework without negating its historical role in the construction of U.S. racism. We need a better understanding of how racism developed both similarly and differently for various peoples, according to whether they experienced genocide, enslavement, colonization or some other structure of oppression. At stake is the building of a united anti-racist force strong enough to resist White Supremacist strategies of divide-and-conquer and move forward toward social justice for all. . . .

. . . African Americans have reason to be uneasy about where they, as a people, will find themselves politically, economically and socially with the rapid numerical growth of other folk of color. The issue is not just possible job loss, a real question that does need to be faced honestly. There is also a feeling that after centuries of fighting for simple recognition as human beings, Blacks will be shoved to the back of history again (like the back of the bus). Whether these fears are real or not, uneasiness exists and can lead to resentment when there's talk about a new model of race relations. So let me repeat: in speaking here of the need to move beyond the bipolar concept, the goal is to clear the way for stronger unity against White Supremacy. The goal is to identify our commonalities of experience and needs so we can build alliances.

The commonalities begin with history, which reveals that again and again peoples of color have had one experience in common: European colonization and/or neo-colonialism with its accompanying exploitation. This is true for all indigenous peoples, including Hawaiians. It is true for all Latino peoples, who were invaded and ruled by Spain or Portugal. It is true for people in Africa, Asia and the Pacific Islands, where European powers became the colonizers. People of color were victimized by colonialism not only externally but also through internalized racism—the "colonized mentality."

Flowing from this shared history are our contemporary commonalities. On the poverty scale, African Americans and Native Americans have always been at the bottom, with Latinos nearby. In 1995 the U.S. Census found that Latinos have the highest poverty rate, 24 percent. Segregation may have been legally abolished in the 1960s, but now the United States is rapidly moving toward resegregation as a result of whites moving to the suburbs. This leaves people of color—especially Blacks and Latinos—with inner cities that lack an adequate tax base and thus have inadequate schools. Not surprisingly, Blacks and Latinos finish college at a far lower rate than whites. In other words, the victims of U.S. social ills come in more than one color. Doesn't that indicate the need for new, inclusive models for fighting racism? Doesn't that speak to the absolutely urgent need for alliances among peoples of color?

With greater solidarity, justice for people of color could be won. And an even bigger prize would be possible: a U.S. society that advances beyond "equality," beyond granting people of color a respect equal to that given to Euro-Americans. Too often "equality" leaves whites still at the center, still embodying the Americanness by which others are judged, still defining the national character. . . .

. . . Innumerable statistics, reports and daily incidents should make it impossible to exclude Latinos and other non-Black populations of color when racism is discussed, but they don't. Police killings, hate crimes by racist individuals and murders with impunity by border officials should make it impossible, but they don't. With chilling regularity, ranch owners compel migrant workers, usually Mexican, to repay the cost of smuggling them into the United States by laboring the rest of their lives for free. The 45 Latino and Thai garment workers locked up in an El Monte, California, factory, working 18 hours a day seven days a week for $299 a month, can also be considered slaves (and one must ask why it took three years for the Immigration and Naturalization Service to act on its own reports about this horror) (*San Francisco Examiner*, August 8, 1995). Abusive treatment of migrant workers can be found all over the United States. In Jackson Hole, Wyoming, for example, police and federal agents rounded up 150 Latino workers in 1997, inked numbers on their arms and hauled them off to jail in patrol cars and a horse trailer full of manure (*Los Angeles Times*, September 6, 1997).

These experiences cannot be attributed to xenophobia, cultural prejudice or some other, less repellent term than racism. Take the case of two small Latino children in San Francisco who were found in 1997 covered from head to toe with flour. They explained they had hoped to make their skin white enough for school. There is no way to understand their action except as the result of fear in the racist climate that accompanied passage of Proposition 187, which denies schooling to the children of undocumented immigrants. Another example: Mexican and Chicana women working at a Nabisco plant in Oxnard, California, were not allowed to take bathroom breaks from the assembly line and were told to wear diapers instead. Can we really imagine white workers being treated that way? (The Nabisco women did file a suit and won, in 1997.)

No "model minority" myth protects Asians and Asian Americans from hate crimes, police brutality, immigrant-bashing, stereotyping and everyday racist prejudice. Scapegoating can even take their lives, as happened with the murder of Vincent Chin in Detroit some years ago. . . .

WHY THE BLACK-WHITE MODEL?

A bipolar model of racism has never been really accurate for the United States. Early in this nation's history. Benjamin Franklin perceived a tri-racial society based on skin color—"the lovely white" (Franklin's words), the Black, and the "tawny," as Ron Takaki tells us in *Iron Cages*. But this concept changed as capital's need for labor intensified in the new nation and came to focus on African slave labor. The "tawny" were decimated or forcibly exiled to distant areas; Mexicans were not yet available to be the main labor force. As enslaved Africans became the crucial labor force for the primitive accumulation of capital, they also served as the foundation for the very idea of whiteness—based on the concept of blackness as inferior.

Three other reasons for the Black-white framework seem obvious: numbers, geography and history. African Americans have long been the largest population of color in the United States; only recently has this begun to change. Also, African Americans have long been found in sizable numbers in most parts of the United States, including major cities, which has not been true of Latinos until recent times. Historically, the Black-white relationship has been entrenched in the nation's collective memory for some 300 years—whereas it is only 150 years since the United States seized half of Mexico and incorporated those lands and their peoples. Slavery and the struggle to end it formed a central theme in this country's only civil war—a prolonged, momentous conflict. Above all, enslaved Africans in the United States and African Americans have created an unmatched heritage of massive, persistent, dramatic and infinitely courageous resistance, with individual leaders of worldwide note.

We also find sociological and psychological explanations of the Black-white model's persistence. From the days of Jefferson onward, Native Americans, Mexicans and later the Asian/Pacific Islanders did not seem as much a threat to racial purity or as capable of arousing white sexual anxieties as did Blacks. A major reason for this must have been Anglo ambiguity about who could be called white. Most of the Mexican *ranchero* elite in California had welcomed the U.S. takeover, and Mexicans were partly European—therefore "semi-civilized"; this allowed Anglos to see them as white, unlike lower-class Mexicans. For years Mexicans were legally white, and even today we hear the ambiguous U.S. Census term "Non-Hispanic Whites."

Like Latinos, Asian Americans have also been officially counted as white in some historical periods. They have been defined as "colored" in others, with "Chinese" being yet another category. Like Mexicans, they were often seen as not really white but not quite Black either. Such ambiguity tended to put Asian Americans along with Latinos outside the prevailing framework of racism.

Blacks, on the other hand, were not defined as white, could rarely become upper-class and maintained an almost constant rebelliousness. Contemporary Black rebellion has been urban: right in the Man's face, scary. Mexicans, by contrast, have lived primarily in rural areas until a few decades ago and "have no Mau-Mau image," as one Black friend said, even when protesting injustice energetically. Only the nineteenth-century resistance heroes labeled "bandits" stirred white fear, and that was along the border, a limited area. Latino stereotypes are mostly silly: snoozing next to a cactus, eating greasy food, always being late and disorganized, rolling big Carmen Miranda eyes, shrugging with self-deprecation "me no speek good eengleesh." In other words, *not serious.* This view may be altered today by stereotypes of the gangbanger, criminal or dirty immigrant, but the prevailing image of Latinos remains that of a debased white, at best. . . .

Among other important reasons for the exclusively Black-white model, sheer ignorance leaps to mind. The oppression and exploitation of Latinos (like Asians) have historical roots unknown to most Americans. People who learn at least a little about Black slavery remain totally ignorant about how the United States seized half of Mexico or how it has colonized Puerto Rico. . . .

One other important reason for the bipolar model of racism is the stubborn self-centeredness of U.S. political culture. It has meant that the nation lacks any global vision other than relations of domination. In particular, the United States refuses to see itself as one among some 20 countries in a hemisphere whose dominant languages are Spanish and Portuguese, not English. It has only a big yawn of contempt or at best indifference for the people, languages and issues of Latin America. It arrogantly took for itself alone the name of half the western hemisphere, America, as was its "Manifest Destiny," of course.

So Mexico may be nice for a vacation and lots of Yankees like tacos, but the political image of Latin America combines incompetence with absurdity, fat corrupt dictators with endless siestas. Similar attitudes extend to Latinos within the United States. My parents, both Spanish teachers, endured decades of being told that students were better off learning French or German. The mass media complain that "people can't relate to Hispanics (or Asians)." It takes mysterious masked rebels, a beautiful young murdered singer or salsa outselling ketchup for the Anglo world to take notice of Latinos. If there weren't a mushrooming, billion-dollar "Hispanic" market to be wooed, the Anglo world might still not know we exist. No wonder that racial paradigm sees only two poles.

The exclusively Black-white framework is also sustained by the "model minority" myth, because it distances Asian Americans from other victims of racism. Portraying Asian Americans as people who work hard, study hard, obey the established order and therefore prosper, the myth in effect admonishes Blacks and Latinos: "See, anyone can make it in this society if you try hard enough. The poverty and prejudice you face are all *your* fault."

The "model" label has been a wedge separating Asian Americans from others of color by denying their commonalities. It creates a sort of racial bourgeoisie, which White Supremacy uses to keep Asian Americans from joining forces with the poor, the homeless and criminalized youth. People then see Asian Americans as a special class of yuppie: young, single, college-educated, on the white-collar track—and they like to shop for fun. Here is a dandy minority group, ready to be used against others.

The stereotype of Asian Americans as whiz kids is also enraging because it hides so many harsh truths about the impoverishment, oppression and racist treatment they experience. Some do come from middle- or upper-class families in Asia, some do attain middle-class or higher status in the U.S., and their community must deal with the reality of class privilege where it exists. But the hidden truths include the poverty of many Asian/Pacific Islander groups, especially women, who often work under intolerable conditions, as in the sweatshops. . . .

THE DEVILS OF DUALISM

Yet another cause of the persistent Black-white conception of racism is dualism, the philosophy that sees all life as consisting of two irreducible elements. Those elements are usually oppositional, like good and evil, mind and body, civilized and savage. Dualism allowed the invaders, colonizers and enslavers of today's United States to rationalize their actions by stratifying supposed opposites along race, color or gender lines. So mind is European, male and rational; body is colored, female and emotional. Dozens of other such pairs can be found, with their clear implications of superior-inferior. In the arena of race, this society's dualism has long maintained that if a person is not totally white (whatever that can mean biologically), he or she must be considered Black. . . .

Racism evolves; our models must also evolve. Today's challenge is to move beyond the Black-white dualism that has served as the foundation of White Supremacy. In taking up this challenge, we have to proceed with both boldness and infinite care. Talking race in these United States is an intellectual minefield; for every observation, one can find three contradictions and four necessary qualifications from five different racial groups. Making your way through that complexity, you have to think: keep your eyes on the prize.

11

WHAT WHITE SUPREMACISTS TAUGHT A JEWISH SCHOLAR ABOUT IDENTITY

Abby L. Ferber

A few years ago, my work on white supremacy led me to the neo-Nazi tract *The New Order*, which proclaims: "The single serious enemy facing the white man is the Jew." I must have read that statement a dozen times. Until then, I hadn't thought of myself as the enemy.

From *The Chronicle of Higher Education*, May 7, 1999, pp. B6–B7. Reprinted with permission of the author.

When I began my research for a book on race, gender, and white supremacy, I could not understand why white supremacists so feared and hated Jews. But after being immersed in newsletters and periodicals for months, I learned that white supremacists imagine Jews as the masterminds behind a great plot to mix races and, thereby, to wipe the white race out of existence.

The identity of white supremacists, and the white racial purity they espouse, requires the maintenance of secure boundaries. For that reason, the literature I read described interracial sex as "the ultimate abomination." White supremacists see Jews as threats to racial purity, the villains responsible for desegregation, integration, the civil-rights movement, the women's movement, and affirmative action—each depicted as eventually leading white women into the beds of black men. Jews are believed to be in control everywhere, staging a multipronged attack against the white race. For *WAR*, the newsletter of White Aryan Resistance, the Jew "promotes a thousand social ills . . . [f]or which you'll have to foot the bills."

Reading white-supremacist literature is a profoundly disturbing experience, and even more difficult if you are one of those targeted for elimination. Yet, as a Jewish woman, I found my research to be unsettling in unexpected ways. I had not imagined that it would involve so much self-reflection. I knew white supremacists were vehemently anti-Semitic, but I was ambivalent about my Jewish identity and did not see it as essential to who I was. Having grown up in a large Jewish community, and then having attended a college with a large Jewish enrollment, my Jewishness was invisible to me—something I mostly ignored. As I soon learned, to white supremacists, that is irrelevant.

Contemporary white supremacists define Jews as non-white: "not a religion, they are an Asiatic *race*, locked in a mortal conflict with Aryan man," according to *The New Order*. In fact, throughout white-supremacist tracts, Jews are described not merely as a separate race, but as an impure race, the product of mongrelization. Jews, who pose the ultimate threat to racial boundaries, are themselves imagined as the product of mixed-race unions.

Although self-examination was not my goal when I began, my research pushed me to explore the contradictions in my own racial identity. Intellectually, I knew that the meaning of race was not rooted in biology or genetics, but it was only through researching the white-supremacist movement that I gained a more personal understanding of the social construction of race. Reading white-supremacist literature, I moved between two worlds: one where I was white, another where I was the non-white seed of Satan; one where I was privileged, another where I was despised; one where I was safe and secure, the other where I was feared and thus marked for death.

According to white-supremacist ideology, I am so dangerous that I must be eliminated. Yet, when I put down the racist, anti-Semitic newsletters, leave my office, and walk outdoors, I am white.

Growing up white has meant growing up privileged. Sure, I learned about the historical persecutions of Jews, overheard the hushed references to distant relatives lost in the Holocaust. I knew of my grandmother's experiences with anti-Semitism as a child of the only Jewish family in a Catholic neighborhood. But those were just stories to me. Reading white supremacists finally made the history real.

While conducting my research, I was reminded of the first time I felt like an "other." Arriving in the late 1980s for the first day of graduate school in the Pacific Northwest, I was greeted by a senior graduate student with the welcome: "Oh, you're the Jewish one." It was a jarring remark, for it immediately set me apart. This must have been how my mother felt, I thought, when, a generation earlier, a college classmate had asked to see her horns. Having lived in predominantly Jewish communities, I had never experienced my Jewishness as "otherness." In fact, I did not even *feel* Jewish. Since moving out of my parents' home, I had not celebrated a Jewish holiday or set foot in a synagogue. So it felt particularly odd to be identified by this stranger as a Jew. At the time, I did not feel that the designation described who I was in any meaningful sense.

But whether or not I define myself as Jewish, I am constantly defined by others that way. Jewishness is not simply a religious designation that one may choose, as I once naïvely assumed. Whether or not I see myself as Jewish does not matter to white supremacists.

I've come to realize that my own experience with race reflects the larger historical picture for Jews. As whites, Jews today are certainly a privileged group in the United States. Yet the history of the Jewish experience demonstrates precisely what scholars mean when they say that race is a social construction.

At certain points in time, Jews have been defined as a non-white minority. Around the turn of the last century, they were considered a separate, inferior race, with a distinguishable biological identity justifying discrimination and even genocide. Today, Jews are generally considered white, and Jewishness is largely considered merely a religious or ethnic designation. Jews, along with other European ethnic groups, were welcomed into the category of "white" as beneficiaries of one of the largest affirmative-action programs in history— the 1944 GI Bill of Rights. Yet, when I read white-supremacist discourse, I am reminded that my ancestors were expelled from the dominant race, persecuted, and even killed.

Since conducting my research, having heard dozens of descriptions of the murders and mutilations of "race traitors" by white supremacists, I now carry with me the knowledge that there are many people out there who would still wish to see me dead. For a brief moment, I think that I can imagine what it must feel like to be a person of color in our society . . . but then I realize that, as a white person, I cannot begin to imagine that.

Jewishness has become both clearer and more ambiguous for me. And the questions I have encountered in thinking about Jewish identity highlight the central issues involved in studying race today. I teach a class on race and ethnicity, and usually, about midway through the course, students complain of confusion. They enter my course seeking answers to the most troubling and divisive questions of our time, and are disappointed when they discover only more questions. If race is not biological or genetic, what is it? Why, in some states, does it take just one black ancestor out of 32 to make a person legally black, yet those 31 white ancestors are not enough to make that person white? And, always, are Jews a race?

I have no simple answers. As Jewish history demonstrates, what is and is not a racial designation, and who is included within it, is unstable and changes over time—and that designation is always tied to power. We do not have to look far to find other examples: The Irish were also once considered nonwhite in the United States, and U.S. racial categories change with almost every census.

My prolonged encounter with the white-supremacist movement forced me to question not only my assumptions about Jewish identity, but also my assumptions about whiteness. Growing up "white," I felt raceless. As it is for most white people, my race was invisible to me. Reflecting the assumption of most research on race at the time, I saw race as something that shaped the lives of people of color—the victims of racism. We are not used to thinking about whiteness when we think about race. Consequently, white people like myself have failed to recognize the ways in which our own lives are shaped by race. It was not until others began identifying me as the Jew, the "other," that I began to explore race in my own life.

Ironically, that is the same phenomenon shaping the consciousness of white supremacists: They embrace their racial identity at the precise moment when they feel their privilege and power under attack. Whiteness historically has equaled power, and when that equation is threatened, their own whiteness becomes visible to many white people for the first time. Hence, white supremacists seek to make racial identity, racial hierarchies, and white power part of the natural order again. The notion that race is a social construct threatens that order. While it has become an academic commonplace to assert that race is socially constructed, the revelation is profoundly unsettling to many, especially those who benefit most from the constructs.

My research on hate groups not only opened the way for me to explore my own racial identity, but also provided insight into the question with which I began this essay: Why do white supremacists express such hatred and fear of Jews? This ambiguity in Jewish racial identity is precisely what white supremacists find so threatening. Jewish history reveals race as a social designation, rather than a God-given or genetic endowment. Jews blur the boundaries between whites and people of color, failing to fall securely on either side of the divide. And it is ambiguity that white supremacists fear most of all.

I find it especially ironic that, today, some strict Orthodox Jewish leaders also find that ambiguity threatening. Speaking out against the high rates of intermarriage among Jews and non-Jews, they issue dire warnings. Like white supremacists, they fear assaults on the integrity of the community and fight to secure its racial boundaries, defining Jewishness as biological and restricting it only to those with Jewish mothers. For both white supremacists and such Orthodox Jews, intermarriage is tantamount to genocide.

For me, the task is no longer to resolve the ambiguity, but to embrace it. My exploration of white-supremacist ideology has revealed just how subversive doing so can be: Reading white-supremacist discourse through the lens of Jewish experience has helped me toward new interpretations. White supremacy is not a movement just about hatred, but even more about fear: fear of the vulnerability and instability of white identity and privilege. For white supremacists, the central goal is to naturalize racial identity and hierarchy, to establish boundaries.

Both my own experience and Jewish history reveal that to be an impossible task. Embracing Jewish identity and history, with all their contradictions, has given me an empowering alternative to white-supremacist conceptions of race. I have found that eliminating ambivalence does not require eliminating ambiguity.

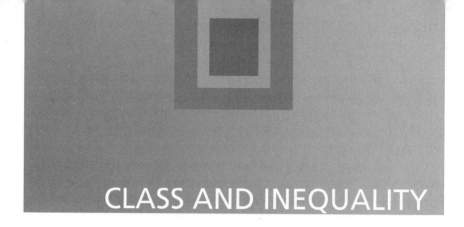

CLASS AND INEQUALITY

12

GROWING GULF BETWEEN RICH AND REST OF US

Holly Sklar

Guess which country the CIA World Factbook describes when it says, "Since 1975, practically all the gains in household income have gone to the top 20 percent of households."

If you guessed the United States, you're right.

The United States has rising levels of poverty and inequality not found in other rich democracies. It also has less mobility out of poverty.

Since 2000, America's billionaire club has gained 76 more members while the typical household has lost income and the poverty count has grown by more than 5 million people.

Poverty and inequality take a daily toll seldom seen on television. "The infant mortality rate in the United States compares with that in Malaysia—a country with a quarter the income," says the 2005 Human Development Report. "Infant death rates are higher for [black] children in Washington, D.C., than for children in Kerala, India."

Income and wealth in America are increasingly concentrated at the very top—the realm of the Forbes 400.

You could have banked $1 million a day every day for the last two years and still have far to go to make the new Forbes list of the 400 richest Americans.

It took a minimum of $900 million to get on the Forbes 400 this year. That's up $150 million from 2004.

"Surging real estate and oil prices drove up several fortunes and helped pave the way for 33 new members," Forbes notes.

Middle-class households, meanwhile, are a medical crisis or outsourced job away from bankruptcy. With 374 billionaires, the Forbes 400 will soon be billionaires only.

Bill Gates remains No. 1 on the Forbes 400 with $51 billion. Low-paid Wal-Mart workers can find Walton family heirs in five of the top 10 spots; another Wal-Mart heir ranks No. 116.

Former Bechtel president Stephen Bechtel Jr. and his son, CEO Riley Bechtel, tie for No. 109 on the Forbes 400 with $2.4 billion apiece. The politically powerful Bechtel has gotten a no-bid contract for hurricane reconstruction despite a pattern of cost overruns and shoddy work from Iraq to Boston's leaky "Big Dig" tunnel/highway project.

The Forbes 400 is a group so small they could have watched this year's Sugar Bowl from the private boxes of the Superdome.

Yet combined Forbes 400 wealth totals more than $1.1 trillion—an amount greater than the gross domestic product of Spain or Canada, the world's eighth- and ninth-largest economies.

The number of Americans in poverty is a group so large it would take the combined populations of Louisiana, Mississippi, Alabama and Texas, plus Arkansas to match it. That's according to the Census Bureau's latest count of 37 million people below the poverty line.

Millions more Americans can't afford adequate health care, housing, child care, food, transportation and other basic expenses above the official poverty thresholds, which are set too low. The poverty threshold for a single person under age 65 was just $9,827 in 2004. For a two-adult, two-child family, it was just $19,157.

By contrast, the Economic Policy Institute's Basic Family Budget Calculator says the national median basic needs budget (including taxes and tax credits) for a two-parent, two-child family was $39,984 in 2004. It was $38,136 in New Orleans and $33,636 in Biloxi, Mississippi.

America is becoming a downwardly mobile society instead of an upwardly mobile society. Median household income fell for the fifth year in a row to $44,389 in 2004—down from $46,129 in 1999, adjusting for inflation.

The Bush administration is using hurricane "recovery" to camouflage policies that will deepen inequality and poverty. They are bringing windfall profits to companies like Bechtel while suspending regulations that shore up wages for workers.

More tax cuts are in the pipeline for wealthy Americans who can afford the $17,000 watch, $160,000 coat and $10 million helicopter on the Forbes Cost of Living Extremely Well Index.

More budget cuts are in the pipeline for Medicaid, Food Stamps and other safety nets for Americans whose wages don't even cover the cost of necessities.

Without a change in course, the gulf between the rich and everyone else will continue to widen, weakening our economy and our democracy. The American Dream will be history instead of poverty.

13

TIRED OF PLAYING MONOPOLY?

Donna Langston

I. Magnin, Nordstrom, The Bon, Sears, Penneys, K mart, Goodwill, Salvation Army. If the order of this list of stores makes any sense to you, then we've begun to deal with the first question which inevitably arises in any discussion of class here in the U.S.—huh? Unlike our European allies, we in the U.S. are reluctant to recognize class differences. This denial of class divisions functions to reinforce ruling class control and domination. America is, after all, the supposed land of equal opportunity where, if you just work hard enough, you can get ahead, pull yourself up by your bootstraps. What the old bootstraps theory overlooks is that some were born with silver shoe horns. Female-headed households, communities of color, the elderly, disabled and children find themselves, disproportionately, living in poverty. If hard work were the sole determinant of your ability to support yourself and your family, surely we'd have a different outcome for many in our society. We also, however, believe in luck and, on closer examination, it certainly is quite a coincidence that the "unlucky" come from certain race, gender and class backgrounds. In order to perpetuate racist, sexist and classist outcomes, we also have to believe that the current economic distribution is unchangeable, has always existed, and probably exists in this form throughout the known universe; i.e., it's "natural." Some people explain or try to account for poverty or class position by focusing on the personal and moral merits of an individual.

From Jo Whitehorse Cochran, Donna Langston, and Carolyn Woodward, eds., *Changing Our Power: An Introduction to Women's Studies* (Dubuque, IA: Kendall-Hunt, 1988). Reprinted by permission.

If people are poor, then it's something they did or didn't do; they were lazy, unlucky, didn't try hard enough, etc. This has the familiar ring of blaming the victims. Alternative explanations focus on the ways in which poverty and class position are due to structural, systematic, institutionalized economic and political power relations. These power relations are based firmly on dynamics such as race, gender, and class.

In the myth of the classless society, ambition and intelligence alone are responsible for success. The myth conceals the existence of a class society, which serves many functions. One of the main ways it keeps the working class and poor locked into a class-based system in a position of servitude is by cruelly creating false hope. It perpetuates the false hope among the working class and poor that they can have different opportunities in life. The hope that they can escape the fate that awaits them due to the class position they were born into. Another way the rags-to-riches myth is perpetuated is by creating enough visible tokens so that oppressed persons believe they, too, can get ahead. The creation of hope through tokenism keeps a hierarchical structure in place and lays the blame for not succeeding on those who don't. This keeps us from resisting and changing the class-based system. Instead, we accept it as inevitable, something we just have to live with. If oppressed people believe in equality of opportunity, then they won't develop class consciousness and will internalize the blame for their economic position. If the working class and poor do not recognize the way false hope is used to control them, they won't get a chance to control their lives by acknowledging their class position, by claiming that identity and taking action as a group.

The myth also keeps the middle class and upper class entrenched in the privileges awarded in a class-based system. It reinforces middle- and upper-class beliefs in their own superiority. If we believe that anyone in society really can get ahead, then middle- and upper-class status and privileges must be deserved, due to personal merits, and enjoyed—and defended at all costs. According to this viewpoint, poverty is regrettable but acceptable, just the outcome of a fair game: "There have always been poor people, and there always will be."

Class is more than just the amount of money you have; it's also the presence of economic security. For the working class and poor, working and eating are matters of survival, not taste. However, while one's class status can be defined in important ways in terms of monetary income, class is also a whole lot more—specifically, class is also culture. As a result of the class you are born into and raised in, class is your understanding of the world and where you fit in; it's composed of ideas, behavior, attitudes, values, and language; class is how you think, feel, act, look, dress, talk, move, walk; class is what stores you shop at, restaurants you eat in; class is the schools you attend, the education you attain; class is the very jobs you will work at throughout your adult life. Class even determines when we marry and become mothers. Working-class women become mothers long before middle-class women receive their bachelor's degrees. We experience class at every level of our lives; class is who our friends are, where we live and work, even what kind of car we drive, if we own one, and what kind of health care we receive, if any. Have I left anything out? In other words, class is socially constructed and all-encompassing. When we experience classism, it will be because of our lack of money (i.e., choices and power in this society) and because of the way we talk, think, act, move—because of our culture.

Class affects what we perceive as and what we have available to us as choices. Upon graduation from high school, I was awarded a scholarship to attend any college, private or public, in the state of California. Yet it never occurred to me or my family that it made any difference which college you went to. I ended up just going to a small college in my town. It never would have occurred to me to move away from my family for school, because no one ever had and no one would. I was the first person in my family to go to college. I had to figure out from reading college catalogs how to apply—no one in my family could have sat down and said, "Well, you take this test and then you really should think about. . . ." Although tests and high school performance had shown I had the ability to pick up white middle-class lingo, I still had quite an adjustment to make—it was lonely and isolating in college. I lost my friends from high school—they were at the community college, vo-tech school, working, or married. I lasted a year and a half in this foreign environment before I quit college, married a factory worker, had a baby and resumed living in a community I knew. One middle-class friend in college had asked if I'd like to travel to Europe with her. Her father was a college professor and people in her family had actually travelled there. My family had seldom been able to take a vacation at all. A couple of times my parents were able—by saving all year—to take the family over to the coast on their annual two-week vacation. I'd seen the time and energy my parents invested in trying to take a family vacation to some place a few hours away; the idea of how anybody ever got to Europe was beyond me.

If class is more than simple economic status but one's cultural background as well, what happens if you're born and raised middle class, but spend some of your adult life with earnings below a middle-class income bracket—are you then working-class? Probably not. If your economic position changes, you still have the language, behavior, educational background, etc., of the middle class, which you can bank on. You will always have choices. Men who consciously try to refuse male privilege are still male; whites who want to challenge white privilege are still white. I think those who come from middle-class backgrounds need to recognize that their class privilege does not float out with the rinse water. Middle-class people can exert incredible power just by being nice and polite. The middle-class way of doing things is the standard—they're always right, just by being themselves. Beware of middle-class people who deny their privilege. Many people have times when they struggle to get shoes for the kids, when budgets are tight, etc. This isn't the same as long-term economic conditions without choices. Being working class is also generational. Examine your family's history of education, work, and standard of living. It may not be a coincidence that you share the same class status as your parents and grandparents. If your grandparents were professionals, or your parents were professionals, it's much more likely you'll be able to grow up to become a yuppie, if your heart so desires, or even if you don't think about it.

How about if you're born and raised poor or working class, yet through struggle, usually through education, you manage to achieve a different economic level: do you become middle class? Can you pass? I think some working-class people may successfully assimilate into the middle class by learning to dress, talk, and act middle class—to accept and adopt the middle-class way of doing things. It all depends on how far they're able to go. To succeed in the middle-class world means facing great pressures to abandon working-class friends and ways.

Contrary to our stereotype of the working class—white guys in overalls—the working class is not homogeneous in terms of race or gender. If you are a person of color, if you live in a female-headed household, you are much more likely to be working class or poor. The experience of Black, Latino, American Indian or Asian American working classes will differ significantly from the white working classes, which have traditionally been able to rely on white privilege to provide a more elite position within the working class. Working-class people are often grouped together and stereotyped, but distinctions can be made among the working class, working poor, and poor. Many working-class families are supported by unionized workers who pos-sess marketable skills. Most working-poor families are supported by non-unionized, unskilled men and women. Many poor families are dependent on welfare for their income.

Attacks on the welfare system and those who live on welfare are a good example of classism in action. We have a "dual welfare" system in this country whereby welfare for the rich in the form of tax-free capital gain, guaranteed loans, oil depletion allowances, etc., is not recognized as welfare. Almost everyone in America is on some type of welfare; but, if you're rich, it's in the form of tax deductions for "business" meals and entertainment, and if you're poor, it's in the form of food stamps. The difference is the stigma and humiliation connected to welfare for the poor, as compared to welfare for the rich, which is called "incentives." . . . A common focal point for complaints about "welfare" is the belief that most welfare recipients are cheaters—goodness knows there are no middle-class income tax cheaters out there. Imagine focusing the same anger and energy on the way corporations and big business cheat on their tax revenues. Now, there would be some dollars worth quibbling about. The "dual welfare" system also assigns a different degree of stigma to programs that benefit women and children . . . and programs whose recipients are primarily male, such as veterans' benefits. The implicit assumption is that mothers who raise children do not work and therefore are not deserving of their daily bread crumbs.

Anti-union attitudes are another prime example of classism in action. At best, unions have been a very progressive force for workers, women and people of color. At worst, unions have reflected the same regressive attitudes which are out there in other social structures: classism, racism, and sexism. Classism exists within the working class. The aristocracy of the working class—unionized, skilled workers—has mainly been white and male and have viewed themselves as being better than unskilled workers, the unemployed, and the poor, who are mostly women and people of color. The white working class must commit itself to a cultural and ideological transformation of racist attitudes. The history of working people, and the ways we've resisted many types of oppressions, are not something we're taught in school. Missing from our education is information about workers and their resistance.

Working-class women's critiques have focused on the following issues:

Education: White middle-class professionals have used academic jargon to rationalize and justify classism. The whole structure of education is a classist system. Schools in every town reflect class divisions: like the store list at the beginning of this article, you can list schools in your town by what classes of kids attend, and in most cities you can also list by race. The classist system is perpetuated in schools with the tracking system, whereby the "dumbs" are tracked into homemaking, shop courses and vocational school futures, while the "smarts" end up in advanced math, science, literature, and college-prep courses. If we examine these groups carefully, the coincidence of poor and working-class backgrounds with "dumbs" is rather alarming. The standard measurement of supposed intelligence is white middle-class English. If you're other than white middle class, you have to become bilingual to succeed in the educational system. If you're white middle class, you only need the language and writing skills you were raised with, since they're the standard. To do well in society presupposes middle-class background, experiences and learning for everyone. The tracking system separates those from the working class who can potentially assimilate to the middle class from all our friends, and labels us "college bound."

After high school, you go on to vocational school, community college, or college—public or private—according to your class position. Apart from the few who break into middle-class schools, the classist stereotyping of the working class as being dumb and inarticulate tracks most into vocational and low-skilled jobs. A few of us are allowed to slip through to reinforce the idea that equal opportunity exists. But for most, class position is destiny—determining our educational attainment and employment. Since we must overall abide by middle-class rules to succeed, the assumption is that we go to college in order to "better ourselves"—i.e., become more like them. I suppose it's assumed we have "yuppie envy" and desire nothing more than to be upwardly mobile individuals. It's assumed that we want to fit into their world. But many of us remain connected to our communities and families. Becoming college educated doesn't mean we have to, or want to, erase our first and natural language and value system. It's important for many of us to remain in and return to our communities to work, live, and stay sane.

Jobs: Middle-class people have the privilege of choosing careers. They can decide which jobs they want to work, according to their moral or political commitments, needs for challenge or creativity. This is a privilege denied the working class and poor, whose work is a means of survival, not choice (see Hartsock). Working-class women have seldom had the luxury of choosing between work in the home or market. We've generally done both, with little ability to purchase services to help with this double burden. Middle- and upper-class women can often hire other women to clean their houses, take care of their children, and cook their meals. Guess what class and race those "other" women are? Working a double or triple day is common for working-class women. Only middle-class women have an array of choices such as: parents put you through school, then you choose a career, then you choose when and if to have babies, then you choose a support system of working-class women to take care of your kids and house if you choose to resume your career. After the birth of my second child, I was working two part-time jobs—one loading trucks at night—and going to school during the days. While I was quite privileged because I could take my colicky infant with me to classes and the day-time job, I was in a state of continuous semi-consciousness. I had to work to support my family; the only choice I had was between school or sleep: Sleep became a privilege. A white middle-class feminist instructor at the university suggested to me, all sympathetically, that I ought to hire someone to clean my house and watch the baby. Her suggestion was totally out of my reality, both economically and socially. I'd worked for years cleaning other peoples' houses. Hiring a working-class woman to do the shit work is a middle-class woman's solution to any dilemma which her privileges, such as a career, may present her.

Mothering: The feminist critique of families and the oppressive role of mothering has focused on white middle-class nuclear families. This may not be an appropriate model for communities of class and color. Mothering and families may hold a different importance for working-class women. Within this context, the issue of coming out can be a very painful process for working-class lesbians. Due to the homophobia of working-class communities, to be a lesbian is most often to be excommunicated from your family, neighborhood, friends and the people you work with. If you're working class, you don't have such clearly demarcated concepts of yourself as an individual, but instead see yourself as part of a family and community that forms your survival structure. It is not easy to be faced with the risk of giving up ties which are so central to your identity and survival.

Individualism: Preoccupation with one's self—one's body, looks, relationships—is a luxury working-class women can't afford. Making an occupation out of taking care of yourself through therapy, aerobics, jogging, dressing for success, gourmet meals and proper nutrition, etc., may be responses that are directly rooted in privilege. The middle class has the leisure time to be preoccupied with their own problems, such as their waistlines, planning their vacations, coordinating their wardrobes, or dealing with what their mother said to them when they were five—my!

The white middle-class women's movement has been patronizing to working-class women. Its supporters think we don't understand sexism. What we don't understand is white middle-class feminism. They act as though they invented the truth, the light, and the way, which they merely need to pass along to us lower-class drudges. What they invented is a distorted form of what working-class women already know—if you're female, life sucks. Only at least we were smart enough to know that it's not just being female, but also being a person of color or class, which makes life a quicksand trap. The class system weakens all women. It censors and eliminates images of female strength. The idea of women as passive, weak creatures totally discounts the strength, self-dependence and inter-dependence necessary to survive as working-class and poor women. My mother and her friends always had a less-than-passive, less-than-enamoured attitude toward their spouses, male bosses, and men in general. I know from listening to their conversations, jokes and what they passed on to us, their daughters, as folklore. When I was five years old, my mother told me about how Aunt Betty had hit Uncle Ernie over the head with a skillet and knocked him out because he was raising his hand to hit her, and how he's never even thought about doing it since. This story was told to me with a good amount of glee and laughter. All the men in the neighborhood were told of the event as an example of what was a very acceptable response in the women's community for that type of male behavior. We kids in the neighborhood grew up with these stories of women giving husbands, bosses, the welfare system, schools, unions and men in general hell, whenever they deserved it. For me there were many role models of women taking action, control and resisting what was supposed to be their lot. Yet many white middle-class feminists continue to view feminism like math homework, where there's only supposed to be one answer. Never occurs to them that they might be talking algebra while working-class women might be talking metaphysics.

Women with backgrounds other than white middle-class experience compounded, simultaneous oppressions. We can't so easily separate our experiences by categories of gender, or race, or class, i.e., "I remember it well: on Saturday, June 3, I was experiencing class oppression, but by Tuesday, June 6, I was caught up in race oppression, then all day Friday, June 9, I was in the middle of gender oppression. What a week!" Sometimes, for example, gender and class reinforce each other. When I returned to college as a single parent after a few years of having kids and working crummy jobs—I went in for vocational testing. Even before I was tested, the white middle-class male vocational counselor looked at me, a welfare mother in my best selection from the Salvation Army racks, and suggested I quit college, go to vo-tech school and become a grocery clerk. This was probably the highest paying female working-class occupation he could think of. The vocational test results suggested I become an attorney. I did end up quitting college once again, not because of his suggestion, but because I was tired of supporting my children in ungenteel poverty. I entered vo-tech school for training as an electrician and, as one of the first women in a non-traditional field, was able to earn a living wage at a job which had traditionally been reserved for white working-class males. But this is a story for another day. Let's return to our little vocational counselor example. Was he suggesting the occupational choice of grocery clerk to me because of my gender or my class? Probably both. Let's imagine for a moment what this same vocational counselor might have advised, on sight only, to the following people:

1. A white middle-class male: doctor, lawyer, engineer, business executive.
2. A white middle-class female: close to the same suggestion as #1 if the counselor was not sexist, or, if sexist, then: librarian, teacher, nurse, social worker.
3. A middle-class man of color: close to the same suggestions as #1 if the counselor was not racist, or, if racist, then: school principal, sales, management, technician.
4. A middle-class woman of color: close to the same suggestions as #3 if counselor was not sexist; #2 if not racist; if not racist or sexist, then potentially #1.
5. A white working-class male: carpenter, electrician, plumber, welder.
6. A white working-class female—well, we already know what he told me, although he could have also suggested secretary, waitress and dental hygienist (except I'd already told him I hated these jobs).
7. A working-class man of color: garbage collector, janitor, fieldhand.
8. A working-class woman of color: maid, laundress, garment worker.

Notice anything about this list? As you move down it, a narrowing of choices, status, pay, working conditions, benefits and chances for promotions occurs. To be connected to any one factor, such as gender or class or race, can make life difficult. To be connected to multiple factors can guarantee limited economic status and poverty.

WAYS TO AVOID FACING CLASSISM

Deny Deny Deny: Deny your class position and the privileges connected to it. Deny the existence or experience of the working class and poor. You can even set yourself up (in your own mind) as judge and jury in deciding who qualifies as working class by your white middle-class standards. So if someone went to college, or seems intelligent to you, not at all like your stereotypes, they must be middle class.

Guilt Guilt Guilt: "I feel so bad, I just didn't realize!" is not helpful, but is a way to avoid changing attitudes and behaviors. Passivity—"Well, what can I do about it, anyway?"—and anger—"Well, what do they want!"—aren't too helpful either. Again, with these responses, the focus is on you and absolving the white middle class from responsibility. A more helpful remedy is to take action. Donate your time and money to local foodbanks. Don't cross picket lines. Better yet, go join a picket line.

HOW TO CHALLENGE CLASSISM

If you're middle class, you can begin to challenge classism with the following:

1. Confront classist behavior in yourself, others and society. Use and share the privileges, like time or money, which you do have.
2. Make demands on working-class and poor communities' issues—anti-racism, poverty, unions, public housing, public transportation, literacy and day care.
3. Learn from the skills and strength of working people—study working and poor people's history; take some Labor Studies, Ethnic Studies, Women Studies classes. Challenge elitism. There are many different types of intelligence: white middle-class, academic, professional intellectualism being one of them (reportedly). Finally, educate yourself, take responsibility and take action.

If you're working class, just some general suggestions (it's cheaper than therapy—free, less time-consuming and I won't ask you about what your mother said to you when you were five):

1. Face your racism! Educate yourself and others, your family, community, any organizations you belong to; take responsibility and take action. Face your classism, sexism, heterosexism, ageism, able-bodiness, adultism. . . .
2. Claim your identity. Learn all you can about your history and the history and experience of all working and poor peoples. Raise your children to be anti-racist, anti-sexist and anti-classist. Teach them the language and culture of working peoples. Learn to survive with a fair amount of anger and lots of humor, which can be tough when this stuff isn't even funny.
3. Work on issues which will benefit your community. Consider remaining in or returning to your communities. If you live and work in white middle-class environments, look for working-class allies to help you survive with your humor and wits intact. How do working-class people spot each other? We have antennae.

We need not deny or erase the differences of working-class cultures but can embrace their richness, their variety, their moral and intellectual heritage. We're not at the point yet where we can celebrate differences—not having money for a prescription for your child is nothing to celebrate. It's not time yet to party with the white middle class, because we'd be the entertainment ("Aren't they quaint? Just love their workboots and uniforms and the way they cuss!"). We need to overcome divisions among working people, not by ignoring the multiple oppressions many of us encounter, or by oppressing each other, but by becoming committed allies on all issues which affect working people: racism, sexism, classism, etc. An injury to one is an injury to all. Don't play by ruling-class rules, hoping that maybe you can live on Connecticut Avenue instead of Baltic, or that you as an individual can make it to Park Place and Boardwalk. Tired of Monopoly? Always ending up on Mediterranean Avenue? How about changing the game?

14

THE HIDDEN COST OF BEING AFRICAN AMERICAN

Thomas M. Shapiro

I met Frank and Suzanne Conway during the late-afternoon rush hour at a restaurant in Los Angeles. Recently laid off from a communications marketing firm and now taking courses to become certified to teach elementary school, Frank arrived after picking up their daughter, Logan, from day care. Suzanne arrived from her job as an operations supervisor for a money management company. The Conways loved their home in the diverse urban neighborhood of Jefferson Park, near the University of Southern California, but were gravely concerned about sending Logan to weak public schools. They talked to me at length over coffee about this community-school dilemma, their high educational hopes, and their future plans. The Conways' story and their solution to their dilemma turned out to be more common than anticipated. Because they receive generous help from their families, they are considering moving to a suburban community with highly regarded schools. Home prices there start at four times those where they live now, and Logan would grow up and go to

From Thomas M. Shapiro. 2004. *The Hidden Cost of Being African American: How Wealth Perpetuates Inequality* (New York, Oxford University Press).

school in a far more homogenous community—family wealth makes these decisions logical and desirable for some families.

Of course, as with the nearly one in three American families without financial assets, many of the family interviews did not brim over with optimistic choices and options but rather turned on how lack of family wealth severely restricts community, housing, and schooling opportunities. Like the Conways, Alice and Bob Bryant work at professional jobs and earn a middle-class income, but they do not have access to family wealth—they are asset-poor. Living in the working-class Dorchester section of Boston, they are frustrated about their inability to afford to move to a neighborhood with better schools. Doing the best they can, they are highly aware that their son, Mathew, attends only "halfway decent schools" and is not getting the "best education." The Bryants' hopes for Mathew are no different from the Conways' for Logan. What is different is their capacity to follow through on their hopes and deliver opportunities. The Conways are white and the Bryants are black. Because their incomes, professional status, and educations are nearly identical, conventional wisdom suggests that race should be at most a minor factor in opportunities available to these two families, but we will see tangible connections between family assets and race. Differing family asset capacity, which has more to do with race than with merits or accomplishments, most likely will translate into different worlds for Mathew and Logan.

Demonstrating the unique and diverse social circumstances that blacks and whites face is the best way to understand racial differences in wealth holding. The ideas I develop . . . also push the sociology of wealth in another important direction, namely, an exploration of how the uses of wealth perpetuate inequality. Together, wealth accumulation and utilization highlight the ways in which the opportunity structure contributes to massive racial wealth inequality that worsens racial inequality.

My argument is grounded in three big ideas. First, I argue that family inheritance and continuing racial discrimination in crucial areas like home-ownership are reversing gains earned in schools and on jobs and making racial inequality worse. Family inheritance is more encompassing than money passed at death, because for young adults it often includes paying for college, substantial down-payment assistance in buying a first home, and other continuing parental financial assistance. Consequently, it is virtually impossible for people of color to earn their way to equal wealth through wages. No matter how much blacks earn, they cannot preserve their occupational status for their children; they cannot outearn the wealth gap. Many believe that African Americans do not do as well as whites, other minorities, or immigrants because they spend too much money rather than save and invest in the future. They are unable to defer gratification, do not sacrifice for the future, and consume excessively. We will see how the facts speak otherwise. Second, these inheritances frequently amount to what I call transformative assets. This involves the capacity of unearned, inherited wealth to lift a family economically and socially beyond where their own achievements, jobs, and earnings would place them. These head-start assets set up different starting lines, establish different rules for success, fix different rewards for accomplishments, and ultimately perpetuate inequality. Third, the way families use head-start assets to transform their own lives—within current structures that reward them for doing so—has racial and class consequences for the homes they buy, the communities they live in, and the quality of schools their children attend. The same set of processes typically advantages whites while disadvantaging African Americans. My family interviews point to critical mechanisms of denial that insulate whites from privilege.

Homeownership is one of the bedrocks of the American Dream, and I explore homeownership as a prime way of delving into these big ideas. We are a nation of homeowners. In 2002 the homeownership rate was 68 percent, a historic high. Homeownership is by far the single most important way families accumulate wealth. Homeownership also is the way families gain access to the nicest communities, the best public services, and, most important for my argument, quality education. Homeownership is the most critical pathway for transformative assets; hence examining homeownership also keeps our eyes on contemporary discrimination in mortgage markets, the cost of home loans, residential segregation, and the way families accumulate wealth through home appreciation, all of which systematically disadvantage blacks. Homeownership appears critical to success in other areas of life as well, from how well a child does in school to better marital stability to positive civic participation to decreased domestic violence.[1] How young families acquire homes is one of the most tangible ways that the historical legacy of race plays out in the present generation and projects well into future. Understanding how young families can afford to buy homes and how this contributes greatly to the racial wealth gap brings us back full circle to the importance of family legacies.

These big ideas help us understand one of the most important issues facing America as we start the twenty-first century. African Americans were frozen out of the mainstream of American life over the first half of the last century, but since 1954 the civil rights movement has won many battles against racial injustice, and America has reached a broad national consensus in favor of a more tolerant, more inclusive society. Yet we live with a great paradox: Why is racial inequality increasing in this new era?

To fully appreciate the decisions American families like the Conways and Bryants face, we need to understand the extent, causes, and consequences of the vast increase in inequality that has taken place since the early 1970s. Inequality has increased during both Democratic and Republican administrations. Those at the top of the income distribution have increased their share the most. In fact, the slice of the income pie received by the top 1 percent of families is nearly twice as large as it was 30 years ago, and their share now is about as large as the share of the bottom 40 percent. This is not news. In *Nickel and Dimed*, liberal critic Barbara Ehrenreich tells her story of working at low-skill jobs in

America's booming service sector, jobs like waitressing, cleaning houses, and retail sales. These are the fastest-growing jobs in America, and they highlight our current work-to-welfare reform strategy. Ehrenreich's experiences illustrate how hard it is to get by in America on poverty wages. More than anything else, perhaps, Ehrenreich's personal experiences demonstrate that in today's America more than hard work is necessary for economic success. I talked to many families who live these lives for real, and we will see how rising inequality makes assets even more critical for success.

In *Wealth and Democracy*, conservative strategist Kevin Phillips argues that current laissez-faire policies are pretenses to further enrich wealthy and powerful families. Rather than philosophical principles, conservative policies of tax cuts for the wealthy, gutting the inheritance tax, and less business regulation favor wealth and property at the expense of middle-class success. The Bush administration's gradual phase-out of the estate tax privileges unearned, inherited wealth over opportunity, hard work, and accomplishment. President Bush's 2003 tax stimulus package carved 39 percent of the benefits for the wealthiest 1 percent. I will broaden the discussion of rising inequality by bringing family wealth back into the picture. Phillips concludes his book with a dire warning: "Either democracy must be renewed, with politics brought back to life, or wealth is likely to cement a new and less democratic regime— plutocracy by some other name."

An ideology that equated personal gain with benefits to society accompanied the great economic boom of the last part of the twentieth century. Even though inequality increased in the past 20 years, despite loud words and little action, policies such as affordable housing and equitable school funding that challenged that mindset simply had no chance of getting off the ground. Ironically, historically low unemployment rates went hand-in-hand with rising inequality in an America where hard work no longer means economic success. Success includes harder work, less family time, and probably more stress. The average middle-income, two-parent family now works the equivalent of 16 more weeks than it did in 1979 due to longer hours, second jobs, and working spouses.[2] The years of economic stagnation subsequent to the boom produced a dramatic increase in the number of working poor, and working homeless families are a growing concern.[3] Since late 2001, in a period marked by a declining stock market and rising unemployment, an abundance of data has provided strong evidence that lower-income households are under severe economic stress: Personal bankruptcies, automobile repossessions, mortgage foreclosures, and other indicators of bad debt all reached records in 2002.[4]

What is the role of wealth and inheritance in rising inequality? The baby boom generation, which grew up during a long period of economic prosperity right after World War II, is in the midst of benefiting from the greatest inheritance of wealth in history. One reliable source estimates that parents will bequeath $9 trillion to their adult children between 1990 and 2030.[5] Given this fact, it is no wonder that an already ineffective estate tax (due to tax planning, family trusts, and loopholes), which takes 50 percent of estates worth more than $1 million, came under such ferocious political attack during the second Clinton administration and has been effectively repealed by the Bush administration.

This wealth inheritance will exacerbate already rising inequality. Economists Robert Avery and Michael Rendall presented a benchmark statistical study in 1993 showing that most inherited wealth will be pocketed by only a few.[6] According to the study, one-third of the money will go to 1 percent of the baby boomers, who will receive about $1.6 million apiece. Another third, representing an average bequest of $336,000, will go to the next 9 percent. The final slice, divided by the remaining 90 percent of the generation, will run about $40,000 apiece. We will see how this baby boomer inheritance not only fuels inequality but also intensifies racial inequality. Few people now talk about the profound effects—economic, social, and political—of that widening gap. We can argue for the privilege of passing along more unearned inequality, or we can take a stand for fairness and equality.

THE CONTEXT OF RACIAL INEQUALITY

Writing at the beginning of the twentieth century, historian W.E.B. Du Bois emphatically declared that the problem of the century was the problem of the color line. Writing again at midcentury, Du Bois reviewed what African Americans had accomplished in education, civil rights, voting rights, occupation, income, housing, literature and arts, and science. African Americans had made progress, he noted, although it was unequal, incomplete, and accompanied by wide gaps and temporary retreats. At about the same time that Du Bois was penning his assessment in a black newspaper, the *Pittsburgh Courier*, the Nobel economist Gunnar Myrdal published the widely read *An American Dilemma*. This influential and lengthy study documented the living conditions for African Americans during the first half of the century, revealing to many for the first time the impact of systematic discrimination in the United States. These two giants helped to define racial inequality in terms of equal opportunity and discrimination and to place these issues at the heart of a nation's concern. The twisted, politically narrow, and bureaucratically unfortunate notion of "affirmative action" substituted for equal opportunity by century's end, and affirmative action continues to frame our hopes and distrust regarding race. Even though the struggle for equal opportunity is far from completed, the single-minded and narrow focus on affirmative action forces compromises with our past, obscures our present understanding of racial inequality, and restricts policy in the future.

Du Bois and Myrdal correctly identified a color line of opportunity and discrimination at the core of the twentieth-century racial equality agenda in the United States. The agenda in the twenty-first century must go further to include the challenge of closing the wealth gap, which currently is 10 cents on the dollar, if we are to make real progress toward racial equality and democracy. Understanding the racial wealth gap is the key to understanding how racial inequality is passed along from generation to generation.

The enigma of racial inequality is still a festering public and private conversation in American society. After the country's dismantling of the most oppressive racist policies and practices of its past, many have come to believe that the United States has moved beyond race and that our most pressing racial concerns should center now on race-neutrality and color-blindness. Proclaiming the success of the civil rights agenda and the dawning of a postracial age in America, books by Shelby Steele, Abigail and Stephan Thernstrom, and others influenced not only the academic debates but elite and popular opinion as well.[7] Indeed, a review of the record shows impressive gains, most particularly in the areas of law, education, jobs, and earnings. Even though progress is real, this new political sensibility about racial progress and equality incorporates illusions that mask an enduring and robust racial hierarchy and continue to hinder efforts to achieve our ideals of democracy and justice.

In fact, we can consider seriously the declining economic significance of race because the measures we have traditionally used to gauge racial inequality focus almost exclusively on salaries. The black-white earnings gap narrowed considerably throughout the 1960s and 1970s. The earnings gap has remained relatively stable since then, with inequality rising again in the 1980s and closing once more during tight labor markets in the 1990s.[8] The average black family earned 55 cents for every dollar earned by the average white family in 1989; by 2000 it reached an all-time high of 64 cents on the dollar.[9] For black men working full-time, the gains are more impressive, as their wages reached 67 percent of those of fully employed white men, up from 62 percent in 1980 and only 50 percent in 1960.[10] How much the racial wage gap has closed, why it has closed, and what it means are the subjects of academic and political debate. One study, for example, argues that the racial wage gap is really 23 percent higher than the official figures because incarceration rates hide low wages and joblessness among blacks.[11] At comparable incomes, more African American family members work to earn the same money as white families. Working longer hours and more weeks per year means that middle-income black families worked the equivalent of 12 more weeks than white families to earn the same money in 2000.[12]

The tremendous growth of the black middle class often is cited as a triumphant sign of progress toward racial equality. Indeed, the raw numbers appear to justify celebration: In 1960 a little more than three-quarters of a million black men and women were employed in middle-class occupations; by 1980 the number increased to nearly three and a third million; and nearly seven million African Americans worked in middle-class jobs in 1995.[13] This impressive growth in achieving upward mobility, however, does not tell the whole story, as some argue that stagnating economic conditions and blacks' lower-middle-class occupational profile have stalled the march into the middle class since the mid-1970s.[14]

The real story of the meaning of race in modern America, however, must include a serious consideration of how one generation passes advantage and disadvantage to the next—how individuals' starting points are determined. While ending the old ways of outright exclusion, subjugation, segregation, custom, discrimination, racist ideology, and violence, our nation continues to reproduce racial inequality, racial hierarchy, and social injustice that is very real and formidable for those who experience it.

In law, in public policy, in custom, in education, in jobs, in health, indeed, in achievements, one could argue that America is more equal today than at any time in our past. Analysts and advocates scour the annual release of official government statistics on income to detect the latest trends in racial inequality. Traditional measures of economic well-being and inequality, such as income, education, and jobs, show authentic and impressive progress toward racial equality from the mid-1960s through the early 1980s and stagnation since.[15] This is not to suggest by any stretch of the imagination that we have seen the dawning of the age of racial parity in the United States, because, indeed, wide racial gaps and discrimination persist in all of these domains. Employment discrimination, educational discrimination, environmental discrimination, and discriminatory immigration, taxation, health, welfare, and transportation policies continue.[16] Despite the passage of major civil rights reforms, most whites and blacks continue to live in highly segregated communities. To achieve perfectly integrated communities, two-thirds of either all black or all white residents would have to move across racial boundaries. The same indicators show too that progress toward racial equality has halted since the early 1980s. Vast wealth differences and hence enormous disparities in opportunities remain between equally achieving and meritorious white and black families. Progress made since the early 1960s has stalled short of equality. Familiar for Du Bois and Myrdal is the dilemma that, despite narrowed gaps in so many important areas, new generations of whites and blacks still start with vastly different sets of options and opportunities. An asset perspective examines a modern element of the American dilemma: Similar achievements by people of similar abilities do not yield comparable results.

NOTES

1. Joint Center for Housing Studies of Harvard University (2002); Ross and Yinger (2002); Boshara (2001). Data for 2002 from the third-quarter report from the Census Bureau, Department of Commerce.

2. Data from Mishel, Bernstein, and Boushey (2003). The increase in work hours primarily comes from wives working more hours and more weeks per year. The actual figure is 660 more hours worked.

3. See Otto (1999).

4. See Wedner (2002) and Andrews (2003).

5. See Avery and Rendall (1993).

6. Avery and Rendall (1993).

7. Most particularly, Steele (1990) and Thernstrom and Thernstrom (1997).

8. The narrowing of the earnings gap during the 1990s appears to have centered on black men with relatively low educations. Altonji and Blank (1999) review the economics literature on the racial earning gap.

9. Data from Mishel, Bernstein, and Boushey (2003). The specific data refer to the ratio of black-to-white median family income.

10. Data from Shkury (2001).

11. Western (2001); Western and Pettit (2002).

12. Figure from Mishel, Bernstein, and Boushey (2003).

13. Patillo-McCoy (1999) contains a good discussion of the growth and condition of the black middle class. For a statistical profile, see Smith and Horton (1997).

14. Patillo-McCoy (1999) makes this case strongly.

15. In addition to the income literature already cited, see Jargowsky (1997) for increased African American labor force participation; Grodsky and Pager (2001) for African Americans' demonstrable gains in occupational attainment; and Hout (1984) on occupational mobility. Jencks and Phillips (1998) argue that the black-white education gap has narrowed since 1970, even though large differences remain. The black-white score gap at the end of high school, for example, has narrowed substantially since 1965.

16. On employment, see Kirschenman and Neckerman (1993); Moss and Tilly (2001); Hill (1993); Feagin and Sykes (1994). On education, see Orfield, Eaton, and Jones (1997). On environment, see Bullard (1997). For residential segregation, see Massey and Denton (1993).

References

Altonji, Joseph, and Rebecca Blank. 1999. "Race and Gender in the Labor Market." In *Handbook of Labor Economics*, vol. 3, ed. Orley Ashenfelter and David Card. Amsterdam: Elsevier.

Avery, Robert, and Robert Rendall. 1993. "Estimating the Size and Distribution of the Baby Boomers' Prospective Inheritances." In *Proceedings of the Social Science Section of the American Statistical Association*. Alexandria, Va.: American Statistical Association.

Boshara, Ray. 2001. *Building Assets: A Report on the Asset-Development and IDA Field.* Washington, D.C.: Corporation for Economic Development.

Bullard, Robert, ed. 1997. *Unequal Protection: Environmental Justice and Communities of Color.* San Francisco: Sierra Club.

Feagin, Joe, and Melvin Sykes. 1994. *Living with Racism: The Black Middle-Class Experience.* Boston: Beacon.

Grodsky, Eric, and Devah Pager. 2001. "The Structure of Disadvantage: Individual and Occupational Determinants of the Black-White Wage Gap." *American Sociological Review* 66: 542–67.

Hill, Herbert. 1993. "Black Workers, Organized Labor, and Title VII of the 1964 Civil Rights Act." In *Race in America: The Struggle for Equality*, ed. Herbert Hill and James E. Hones Jr. Madison: University of Wisconsin Press.

Hout, Michael. 1984. "Occupational Mobility of Black Men, 1962 to 1973." *American Sociological Review* 49: 308–22.

Jargowsky, Paul. 1997. *Poverty and Place*. New York: Russell Sage Foundation.

Joint Center for Housing Studies of Harvard University. 2002. *The State of the Nation's Housing 2002*. Cambridge: JCHD.

Kirschenman, Joleen, and Kathryn M. Neckerman. 1991. "We'd Love to Hire Them, but . . .": The Meaning of Race for Employers." In *The Urban Underclass*, ed. Christopher Jencks and Paul E. Peterson.

Massey, Douglas, and Nancy Denton. 1993. *American Apartheid*. Cambridge: Harvard University Press.

Mishel, Lawrence, Jared Bernstein, and Heather Boushey. 2003. *The State of Working America, 2002–2003*. Ithaca: Cornell University Press.

Moss, Phillip, and Chris Tilly. 2001. *Stories Employers Tell: Race, Skill, and Hiring in America*. New York: Russell Sage Foundation.

Orfield, Gary, Susan Eaton, and Elaine Jones. 1997. *Dismantling Desegregation: The Quiet Reversal of Brown v. Board of Education*. New York: New Press.

Otto, Mary. 1999. "The Working Homeless Is a Growing Reality." *Miami Herald*. December 26.

Patillo-McCoy, Mary. 1999. *Black Picket Fences*. Chicago: University of Chicago Press.

Phillips, Kevin. 2002. *Wealth and Democracy*. New York: Broadway Books.

Ross, Stephen, and John Yinger. 2002. *The Color of Credit: Mortgage Discrimination, Research Methodology, and Fair-Lending Enforcement*. Cambridge, Mass., and London: MIT Press.

Shkury, Shimon. 2001. "Wage Differences Between White Men and Black Men in the United States of America." Master's thesis, Department of Sociology, University of Pennsylvania.

Steele, Shelby. 1990. *The Content of Our Character: A New Vision of Race in America*. New York: St. Martin's.

Thernstrom, Stephan, and Abigail Thernstrom. 1997. *America in Black and White: One Nation, Indivisible*, New York: Simon & Schuster.

Wedner, Diane. 2002. "Mortgage Delinquency Rates Reach 30-Year High." *Los Angeles Times*. September 10.

Western, Bruce. 2002. "The Impact of Incarceration on Wage Mobility and Inequality." *American Sociological Review* 67: 526–46.

Western, Bruce, and Becky Pettit. 2002. "Black-White Wage Inequality, Employment Rates, and Incarceration." Department of Sociology, Princeton University. At www.princeton.edu/~western/.

![15]

BLACK PICKET FENCES
Privilege and Peril among the Black Middle Class

Mary Pattillo-McCoy

Much of the research and media attention on African Americans is on the black poor. Welfare debates, discussions of crime and safety, urban policy initiatives, and even the cultural uproar over things like rap music are focused on the situation of poor African Americans. With more than one in four African Americans living below the official poverty line (versus approximately one in nine whites), this is a reasonable and warranted bias. But rarely do we hear the stories of the other three-fourths, or the majority of African Americans, who may be the office secretary, the company's computer technician, a project manager down the hall, or the person who teaches our children. The growth of the black middle class has been hailed as one of the major triumphs of the civil rights movement, but if we have so little information on who makes up this group and what their lives are like, how can we be so sure that triumphant progress is the full story? The optimistic assumption of the 1970s and 1980s was that upwardly mobile African Americans were quietly integrating formerly all-white occupations, businesses, neighborhoods, and social clubs. Black middle- and working-class families were moving out of all-black urban neighborhoods and into the suburbs. With these suppositions, the black middle class dropped from under the scientific lens and off the policy agenda, even though basic evidence suggests that the public celebration of black middle-class ascendance has perhaps been too hasty.

We know, for example, that a more appropriate socioeconomic label for members of the black middle class is "lower middle class." The one black doctor who lives in an exclusive white suburb and the few African American lawyers who work at a large firm are not representative of the black middle class overall (but neither are their experiences identical to those of their white colleagues). And although most white Americans are also not doctors or lawyers, the lopsided distribution of occupations for whites does favor such professional and managerial jobs, whereas the black middle class is clustered in the sales and clerical fields. Because one's occupation affects one's income, African Americans have lower earnings. Yet the inequalities run even deeper than just income. Compound and exponentiate the current differences over a history of slavery and Jim Crow, and the nearly fourteenfold wealth advantage that whites enjoy over African Americans—regardless of income, education, or occupation—needs little explanation.

We also know that the black middle class faces housing segregation to the same extent as the black poor. African Americans are more segregated from whites than any other racial or ethnic group. In fact, the black middle class likely faces the most blatant racial discrimination, in that many in its ranks can actually afford to pay for housing in predominantly white areas. Real estate agents and apartment managers can easily turn away poor African Americans by simply quoting prohibitive home costs or high rents. It takes more purposive creativity, however, to consistently steer middle-class blacks into already established African American neighborhoods by such tactics as disingenuously asserting that an apartment has just been rented when the prospective renters who show up at the property manager's door are, to his or her surprise, black. Racial segregation means that racial inequalities in employment, education, income, and wealth are inscribed in space. Predominantly white neighborhoods benefit from the historically determined and contemporarily sustained edge that whites enjoy.

Finally, we know that middle-class African Americans do not perform as well as whites on standardized tests (in school or in employment); are more likely to be incarcerated for drug offenses; are less likely to marry, and more likely to have a child without being married; and are less likely to be working. Liberals bumble when addressing these realities because, unlike housing segregation or job discrimination, of which middle-class African Americans are the clear victims, earning low grades in school or getting pregnant without a husband can easily be attributed to the bad behaviors of blacks themselves. For middle-class blacks, who ostensibly do not face the daily disadvantages of poverty, it is even more difficult to explain why they do not measure up to whites. To resolve this quandary it is essential to continuously refer back to the ways in which the black middle class *is not equal* to the white middle class. . . .

The lives of the families in Groveland* provide some answers to these questions. Groveland's approximately ninety square blocks contain a population of just under twelve thousand residents, over 95 percent of whom are African American. The 1990 median annual family income in the neighborhood is nearly $40,000, while the comparable figure for Chicago as a whole is

---

*Editors' note· Groveland is the name given to the Black middle-class neighborhood where Pattillo-McCoy conducted her research for three years.

just over $30,000. More than 70 percent of Groveland families own their own homes. By income and occupational criteria, as well as the American dream of homeownership, Groveland qualifies as a "middle-class neighborhood."

Yet this sterile description does not at all capture the neighborhood's diversity, which is critical to correctly portraying the neighborhood context of the black middle class. Groveland's unemployment rate is 12 percent, which is higher than the citywide rate, but *lower* than the percentage of unemployed residents in the neighborhoods that border Groveland. Twelve percent of Groveland's families are poor, which again makes it a bit *more* advantaged than the surrounding areas, but worse off than most of Chicago's predominantly white neighborhoods. The geography of Groveland is typical of black middle-class areas, which often sit as a kind of buffer between core black poverty areas and whites. Contrary to popular discussion, the black middle class has not out-migrated to unnamed neighborhoods outside of the black community. Instead, they are an overlooked population still rooted in the contemporary "Black Belts" of cities across the country. Some of the questions about why middle-class blacks are not at parity with middle-class whites can be answered once this fact is recognized. . . .

By the end of my research tenure in Groveland, I had seen three groups of eighth-graders graduate to high school, high school kids go on to college, and college graduates start their careers. I also heard too many stories and read too many obituaries of the teenagers who were jailed or killed along the way. The son of a police detective in jail for murder. The grandson of a teacher shot while visiting his girlfriend's house. The daughter of a park supervisor living with a drug dealer who would later be killed at a fast-food restaurant. These events were jarring, and all-too-frequent, discontinuities in the daily routine of Groveland residents. Why were some Groveland youth following a path to success, while others had concocted a recipe for certain failure? After all, these are not the stories of poor youth caught in a trap of absent opportunities, low aspirations, and harsh environments. Instead, Groveland is a neighborhood of single-family homes, old stately churches, tree-lined streets, active political and civic organizations, and concerned parents trying to maintain a middle-class way of life. These black middle-class families are a hidden population in this country's urban fabric.

The evening news hour in every major American city is filled with reports of urban crime and violence. Newspapers fill in the gaps of the more sensational tragedies about which the television could provide only a few sound bites. Rounding out the flow of urban Armageddon stories are the gossip and hearsay passed informally between neighbors, church friends, and drinking buddies. For many middle-class white Americans, the incidents they hear about in distant and troubled inner cities provide a constant symbolic threat, but an infrequent reality. For the families who live on the corner of the crime scene—overwhelmingly black or Latino, and poor—daily life is organized to avoid victimization. In the middle of these two geographically and socially distant groups lives the black middle class.

African American social workers and teachers, secretaries and nurses, entrepreneurs and government bureaucrats are in many ways the buffer between the black poor and the white middle class. When neighborhoods are changing, white middle-class families may find themselves living near low-income black families, but one group is inevitably displaced. The neighborhood becomes, once again, racially homogeneous. More than thirty years after the civil rights movement, racial segregation remains a reality in most American cities. Middle-income black families fill the residential gap between the neighborhoods that house middle-class whites and the neighborhoods where poor African Americans live. Unlike most whites, middle-class black families must contend with the crime, dilapidated housing, and social disorder in the deteriorating poor neighborhoods that continue to grow in their direction. Residents attempt to fortify their neighborhoods against this encroachment, and limit their travel and associations to other middle-class neighborhoods in the city and suburbs. Yet even with these efforts, residents of black middle-class neighborhoods share schools, grocery stores, hospitals, nightclubs, and parks with their poorer neighbors, ensuring frequent interaction within and outside the neighborhood.

The in-between position of the black middle class sets up certain crossroads for its youth. This peculiar limbo begins to explain the disparate outcomes of otherwise similar young people in Groveland. The right and wrong paths are in easy reach of neighborhood youth. Working adults are models of success. Some parents even work two jobs; while still others combine work and school to increase their chances of on-the-job promotions. All of the positive knowledge, networking, and role-model benefits that accrue to working parents are operative for many families in Groveland. But at the same time the rebellious nature of adolescence inevitably makes the wrong path a strong temptation, and there is no shortage of showy drug dealers and cocky gang members who make dabbling in deviance look fun. Youth walk a fine line between preparing for success and youthful delinquent experimentation, the consequences of which can be especially serious for black youth. . . .

. . . The black middle class is connected to the black poor through friendship and kinship ties, as well as geographically. Policies that hurt the black poor will ultimately negatively affect the black middle class. At the same time, the black middle class sits at the doorstep of middle-class privilege. Continued affirmative action, access to higher education, a plan to create real family-wage jobs, and the alleviation of residential segregation should be at the forefront of policy initiatives to support the gains already made by the black middle class. . . .

"Middle class" is a notoriously elusive category based on a combination of socioeconomic factors (mostly income, occupation, and education) and normative judgments (ranging from where people live, to what churches or clubs they belong to, to whether they plant flowers in their gardens). Among African Americans, where there has historically been less income and occupational diversity, the question of middle-class position becomes even more murky. . . .

Conversations with Groveland residents . . . underscore the fluid and complex nature of class categories among African Americans. Although most Groveland residents settle on a label somewhere between "lower middle class" and "middle class" to describe their own class position, the intermediate descriptors are plentiful. Some classification schemes focus on inequality. One resident resolved that there are the "rich," and everyone else falls into the categories of "poor, poorer, and poorest." Other words, like *ghetto, bourgie* (the shortened version of *bourgeois*), and *uppity* are normative terms that Grovelandites use to describe the intersection of standard socioeconomic measures and normative judgments of lifestyles and attitudes. Still other people talk about class in geographic terms, delineating a hierarchy of places rather than of incomes or occupations. . . .

. . . Despite continuing social and political ties, the reality of class schisms cannot be ignored. In *The Declining Significance of Race* (1978), William Julius Wilson argued that the African American community was splitting in two, with middle-class blacks improving their position relative to whites, and poor blacks becoming ever more marginalized. Civil rights legislation, especially affirmative action, worked well for African Americans poised to take advantage of educational and employment opportunities. The unsolved problem was what to do about African Americans in poverty. They were doing poorly not primarily because they were black, Wilson argued, but because they were unskilled and because the structure of the labor market had changed around them. Grounded in the conviction that social structure influences the nature of race relations, Wilson saw the growth in high-wage employment and the rise of political liberalism as fueling the diminution of race as a factor in the stratification process. The life chances of blacks were becoming more dependent on their class position. African Americans with a college education were positioned to take advantage of jobs in a service-producing economy — jobs in trade and finance, public management, and social services. And because of affirmative action legislation, firms were motivated to hire these qualified blacks.

At the same time, the situation for the black poor was stagnating, if not deteriorating. Black unemployment began to rise in the 1950s. There was not much difference in the unemployment rate for blacks and whites in 1930, but by the mid-1950s the ratio of black to white unemployment reached 2 to 1 (Farley 1985). These changes, Wilson and others argued, were the result of shifts in the mode of production. The number of well-paying manufacturing jobs in the central city had declined as a result of both technological changes and relocation. These changes permanently relegated unskilled blacks to low-wage, menial, and dead-end jobs, or pushed them out of the workforce altogether. Wilson's contribution was to direct attention to changes in the nature of production that disadvantaged unskilled blacks. His prognosis for the black middle class was relatively optimistic, a position for which he was criticized by other African American scholars. Wilson's critics rushed to prove him wrong and show that members of the new black middle class continued to face obstacles because of their race (Pinkney 1984; Willie 1979; Washington 1979, 1980; see Morris 1996 for a review).

. . . To be sure, the obstacles faced by poor blacks in a changing economy and the persistence of black poverty more generally are intolerable facts that merit considerable research and government resources. However, the research pendulum swung to the extreme, virtually ignoring the majority of African Americans who are not poor. . . .

. . . The declining interest in the status of nonpoor blacks was premature. The African American community was in a short time transformed from a population almost uniform in its poverty to one with a nascent middle class—this as recently as the 1950s. But racial disparities in occupation, income, and intergenerational mobility were not eradicated by the few years of progress. The brief period of growth spawned a kind of dismissive optimism, but the economic and social purse strings were once again pulled tight, stalling the advances made by some African Americans. The continuing inequalities between middle-class whites and African Americans attest to the persistence of racism and discrimination, albeit in quite different forms than in the Jim Crow era (Bobo, Kluegel, and Smith 1997). . . . The same stages that characterize the socioeconomic past and present of African Americans—overwhelming disadvantage, followed by progress and optimism, followed by stagnation and retrenchment—are mirrored in the spatial history (the *where*) of the black middle class. . . .

While some black families *have* integrated white neighborhoods as many commentators had predicted, the black middle class overall remains as segregated from whites as the black poor (Farley 1991). This means that the search for better neighborhoods has taken place *within* a segregated housing market. As a result, black middle-class neighborhoods are often located next to predominantly black areas with much higher poverty rates. Blacks of all socioeconomic statuses tend to be confined to a limited geographic space, which is formally designated by the discriminatory practices of banks, insurance companies, and urban planners, and symbolically identified by the formation of cultural and social institutions. . . .

. . . Historic and contemporary black residential patterns suggest the following. African Americans have long attempted to translate socioeconomic success into residential mobility, making them similar to other ethnic groups (Massey and Denton 1985). They desire to purchase better homes, safer neighborhoods, higher quality schools, and more amenities with their increased earnings. Out-migration has been a constant process. The black middle class has *always* attempted to leave poor neighborhoods, but has never been able to get very far. However, when the relative *size* of the black middle class grew, the size of its residential enclaves grew as well. *The increase in the number of black middle-class persons has led to growth in the size of black middle-class enclaves, which in turn increases the spatial distance between poor and middle-class African Americans. This greater physical separation within a segregated black community accounts for the popular belief that black middle-class out-migration is a recent and alarming trend. . . .*

The problems confronting middle-class African Americans are not solved by simply moving away from a low-income black family and next door to a middle-class white family. The fact that a neighborhood's racial makeup is frequently a proxy for the things that really count—quality of schools, security, appreciation of property values, political clout, and availability of desirable amenities—attests to the ways in which larger processes of discrimination penalize blacks at the neighborhood level. Racial inequalities perpetuate the higher poverty rate among blacks and ensure that segregated black communities will bear nearly the full burden of such inequality. The argument for residential integration is not to allow the black middle class to easily abandon black neighborhoods. Instead, more strict desegregation laws would also open the door for low-income blacks to move to predominantly white neighborhoods, where jobs and resources are unfairly clustered. Yet we need not wait for whites to accept blacks into their neighborhoods, and think of integration as the panacea for current problems. Aggressive measures must be taken to improve the socioeconomic conditions of African Americans *where they are*, by highlighting *where* the black middle class lives, it becomes apparent that concentrated urban poverty has repercussions not only for poor African Americans, but for middle-class blacks as well, while a majority of middle-class whites move farther into the hinterlands. A comprehensive antipoverty agenda would have positive benefits for African Americans as a group, and therefore for the residential environs of the black middle class— although it leaves unchallenged the desire of many blacks and even more whites to live with others of the same race.

References

Bobo, Lawrence, James R. Kluegel, and Ryan A. Smith. 1997. "Laissez-Faire Racism: The Crystallization of a Kinder, Gentler, Antiblack Ideology." In *Racial Attitudes in the 1980s*, edited by Steven A. Tuch and Jack K. Martin, 15–42. Westport, CT: Praeger.

Farley, Reynolds. 1991. "Residential Segregation of Social and Economic Groups among Blacks, 1970–1980." In *The Urban Underclass*, edited by Christopher Jencks and Paul E. Peterson, 274–298. Washington, DC: The Brookings Institution.

Farley, Reynolds. 1985. "Three Steps Forward and Two Back? Recent Changes in the Social and Economic Status of Blacks." *Ethnic and Racial Studies* 8: 4–28.

Massey, Douglas, and Nancy Denton. 1985. "Spatial Assimilation as a Socioeconomic Outcome." *American Sociological Review* 50: 94–106.

Morris, Aldon. 1996. "What's Race Got to Do With it?" *Contemporary Sociology* 25: 309–313.

Pinkney, Alfonso. 1984. *The Myth of Black Progress.* New York: Cambridge University Press.

Washington, Joseph R. 1980. *Dilemmas of the New Black Middle Class.* Philadelphia: University of Pennsylvania Afro-American Studies Program.

Washington, Joseph R., ed. 1979. *The Declining Significance of Race: A Dialogue among Black and White Social Scientists.* Philadelphia: University of Pennsylvania Afro-American Studies Program.

Willie, Charles Vert. 1979. *The Caste and Class Controversy.* Bayside, NY: General Hall.

Wilson, William Julius. 1978. *The Declining Significance of Race: Blacks and Changing American Institutions.* Chicago: University of Chicago Press.

16

BROKEN LEVEES, UNBROKEN BARRIERS

Jason De Parle

The white people got out. Most of them, anyway. If television and newspaper images can be deemed a statistical sample, it was mostly black people who were left behind. Poor black people, growing more hungry, sick and frightened by the hour as faraway officials counseled patience and warned that rescues take time.

What a shocked world saw exposed in New Orleans last week wasn't just a broken levee. It was a cleavage of race and class, at once familiar and startlingly new, laid bare in a setting where they suddenly amounted to matters of life and death. Hydrology joined sociology throughout the story line, from the settling of the flood-prone city, where well-to-do white people lived on the high ground, to its frantic abandonment.

The pictures of the suffering vied with reports of marauding, of gunshots fired at rescue vehicles and armed bands taking over the streets. The city of quaint eccentricity—of King Cakes, Mardi Gras beads and nice neighbors named Tookie—had taken a Conradian turn.

From *The New York Times*, Sept. 4, 2005, Section 4, p. 1.

In the middle of the delayed rescue, the New Orleans mayor, C.Ray Nagin, a local boy made good from a poor, black ward, burst into tears of frustration as he denounced slow moving federal officials and called for martial law.

Even people who had spent a lifetime studying race and class found themselves slack-jawed.

"This is a pretty graphic illustration of who gets left behind in this society—in a literal way," said Christopher Jencks, a sociologist glued to the televised images from his office at Harvard. Surprised to have found himself surprised, Mr. Jencks took to thinking out loud. "Maybe it's just an in-the-face version of something I already knew," he said. "All the people who don't get out, or don't have the resources, or don't believe the warning are African-American."

"It's not that it's at odds with the way I see American society," Mr. Jencks said. "But it's at odds with the way I want to see American society."

Last week it was how others saw American society, too, in images beamed across the globe. Were it not for the distinctive outlines of the Superdome, the pictures of hovering rescue helicopters might have carried a Somalian dateline. The Sri Lankan ambassador offered to help raise foreign aid.

Anyone who knew New Orleans knew that danger lurked behind the festive front. Let the good times roll, the tourists on Bourbon Street were told. Yet in every season, someone who rolled a few blocks in the wrong direction wound up in the city morgue.

Unusually poor (27.4 percent below the poverty line in 2000), disproportionately black (over two-thirds), the Big Easy is also disproportionately murderous—with a rate that was for years among the country's highest.

Once one of the most mixed societies, in recent decades, the city has become unusually segregated, and the white middle class is all but gone, moved north across Lake Pontchartrain or west to Jefferson Parish—home of David Duke, the one-time Klansman who ran for governor in 1991 and won more than half of the state's white vote.

Shortly after I arrived in town two decades ago as a fledgling reporter, I was dispatched to cover a cheerleading tryout, and I asked a grinning, half-drunk accountant where he was from, city or suburb. "White people don't live in New Orleans," he answered with a where-have-you-been disdain.

For those who loved it, its glories as well as its flaws, last week brought only heartbreak. So much of New Orleans, from its music and its food to its architecture, had shown a rainbow society at its best, even as everyone knew it was more complicated than that.

"New Orleans, first of all, is both in reality and in rhetoric an extraordinarily successful multicultural society," said Philip Carter, a developer and retired journalist whose roots in the city extend back more at least four generations. "But is also a multicultural society riven by race and class, and all this has been exposed by these stormy days. The people of our community are pitted against each other across the barricades of race and class that six months from now may be the last remaining levees in New Orleans."

No one was immune, of course. With 80 percent of the city under water, tragedy swallowed the privileged and poor, and traveled spread across racial lines.

But the divides in the city were evident in things as simple as access to a car. The 35 percent of black households that didn't have one, compared with just 15 percent among whites.

"The evacuation plan was really based on people driving out," said Craig E. Colten, a geologist at Louisiana State University and an expert on the city's vulnerable topography. "They didn't have buses. They didn't have trains."

As if to punctuate the divide, the water especially devastated the Ninth Ward, among city's poorest and lowest lying.

"Out West, there is a saying that water flows to money," Mr. Colten said. "But in New Orleans, water flows away from money. Those with resources who control where the drainage goes have always chosen to live on the high ground. So the people in the low areas were hardest hit."

Outrage grew as the week wore on, among black politicians who saw the tragedy as a reflection of a broader neglect of American cities, and in the blogosphere.

"The real reason no one is helping is because of the color of these people!" wrote "myfan88" on the Flickr blog. "This is Hotel Rwanda all over again."

"Is this what the pioneers of the civil rights movement fought to achieve, a society where many black people are as trapped and isolated by their poverty as they were by legal segregation laws?" wrote Mark Naison, director of the urban studies program at Fordham, on another blog.

One question that could not be answered last week was whether, put to a similar test, other cities would fracture along the same lines.

At one level, everything about New Orleans appears sui generis, not least its location below sea level. Many New Orleanians don't just accept the jokes about living in a Banana Republic. They spread them.

But in a quieter catastrophe, the 1995 heat wave that killed hundreds of Chicagoans, blacks in comparable age groups as whites died at higher rates—in part because they tended to live in greater social isolation, in depopulated parts of town. As in New Orleans, space intertwined with race.

And the violence? Similarly shocking scenes had erupted in Los Angeles in 1992, after the acquittal of white police officers charged with beating a black man, Rodney King. Newark, Detroit, Washington—all burned in the race riots of the 1960's. It was for residents of any major city, watching the mayhem, to feel certain their community would be immune.

With months still to go just to pump out the water that covers the city, no one can be sure how the social fault lines will rearrange. But with white flight a defining element of New Orleans in the recent past, there was already the fear in the air this week that the breached levee would leave a separated society further apart.

"Maybe we can build the levees back," said Mr. Carter. "But that sense of extreme division by class and race is going to long survive the physical reconstruction of New Orleans."

GENDER AND SEXISM

17

SEX AND GENDER THROUGH THE PRISM OF DIFFERENCE

Maxine Baca Zinn, Pierrette Hondagneu-Sotelo, and Michael Messner

"Men can't cry." "Women are victims of patriarchal oppression." "After divorces, single mothers are downwardly mobile, often moving into poverty." "Men don't do their share of housework and child care." "Professional women face barriers such as sexual harassment and a 'glass ceiling' that prevent them from competing equally with men for high-status positions and high salaries." "Heterosexual intercourse is an expression of men's power over women." Sometimes, the students in our sociology and gender studies courses balk at these kinds of generalizations. And they are right to do so. After all, some men are more emotionally expressive than some women, some women have more power and success than some men, some men do their share—or more—of housework and child care, and some women experience sex with men as both pleasurable and empowering. Indeed, contemporary gender relations are complex and changing in various directions, and as such, we need to be wary of simplistic, if handy, slogans that seem to sum up the essence of relations between women and men.

On the other hand, we think it is a tremendous mistake to conclude that "all individuals are totally unique and different," and that therefore all generalizations about social groups are impossible or inherently oppressive. In fact, we are convinced that it is this very complexity, this multifaceted nature of contemporary gender relations, that fairly begs for a sociological analysis of gender. We use the image of "the prism of difference" to illustrate our approach to developing this sociological perspective on contemporary gender relations. The *American Heritage Dictionary* defines "prism," in part, as "a homogeneous transparent solid, usually with triangular bases and rectangular sides, used to produce or analyze a continuous spectrum." Imagine a ray of light—which to the naked eye appears to be only one color— refracted through a prism onto a white wall. To the eye, the result is not an infinite, disorganized scatter of individual colors. Rather, the refracted light displays an order, a structure of relationships among the different colors—a rainbow. Similarly, we propose to use the "prism of difference" . . . to analyze a continuous spectrum of people, in order to show how gender is organized and experienced differently when refracted through the prism of sexual, racial/ethnic, social class, physical abilities, age, and national citizenship differences.

EARLY WOMEN'S STUDIES: CATEGORICAL VIEWS OF "WOMEN" AND "MEN"

. . . It is possible to make good generalizations about women and men. But these generalizations should be drawn carefully, by always asking the questions "*which* women?" and "*which* men?" Scholars of sex and gender have not always done this. In the 1960s and 1970s, women's studies focused on the differences *between* women and men rather than *among* women and men. The very concept of gender, women's studies scholars demonstrated, is based on socially defined difference between women and men. From the macro level of social institutions such as the economy, politics, and religion, to the micro level of interpersonal relations, distinctions between women and men structure social relations. Making men and women *different* from one another is the essence of gender. It is also the basis of men's power and domination. Understanding this was profoundly illuminating. Knowing that difference produced domination enabled women to name, analyze, and set about changing their victimization.

In the 1970s, riding the wave of a resurgent feminist movement, colleges and universities began to develop women's studies courses that aimed first and foremost to make women's lives visible. The texts that were developed for these courses tended to stress the things that women shared under patriarchy— having the responsibility for housework and child care, the experience or fear of men's sexual violence, a lack of formal or informal access to education, and exclusion from high-status professional and managerial jobs, political office, and religious leadership positions (Brownmiller, 1975; Kanter, 1977).

The study of women in society offered new ways of seeing the world. But the 1970s approach was limited in several ways. Thinking of gender primarily in terms of differences *between* women and men led scholars to overgeneralize about both. The concept of patriarchy led to a dualistic perspective of male privilege and female subordination. Women and men were cast as opposites. Each was treated as a homogeneous category with common characteristics and experiences. This approach *essentialized* women and men. Essentialism, simply put, is the notion that women's and men's attributes and indeed women and men themselves are categorically different. From this perspective, male control and coercion of women produced conflict between the sexes. The feminist insight originally introduced by Simone De Beauvoir in 1953— that women, as a group, had been socially defined as the "other" and that men had constructed themselves as the subjects of history, while constructing women as their objects—fueled an energizing sense of togetherness among many women. As college students read books such as *Sisterhood Is Powerful* (Morgan, 1970), many of them joined organizations that fought—with some success—for equality and justice for women.

THE VOICES OF "OTHER" WOMEN

Although this view of women as an oppressed "other" was empowering for certain groups of women, some women began to claim that the feminist view of universal sisterhood ignored and marginalized their major concerns. It soon became apparent that treating women as a group united in its victimization by patriarchy was biased by too narrow a focus on the experiences and perspectives of women from more privileged social groups. "Gender" was treated as a generic category, uncritically applied to women. Ironically, this analysis, which was meant to unify women, instead produced divisions between and among them. The concerns projected as "universal" were removed from the realities of many women's lives. For example, it became a matter of faith in second-wave feminism that women's liberation would be accomplished by breaking down the "gendered public-domestic split." Indeed, the feminist call for women to move out of the kitchen and into the workplace resonated in the experiences of many of the college-educated white women who were inspired by Betty Friedan's 1963 book, *The Feminine Mystique*. But the idea that women's movement into workplaces was itself empowering or liberating seemed absurd or irrelevant to many working-class women and women of color. They were already working for wages, as had many of their mothers and grandmothers, and did not consider access to jobs and public life "liberating." For many of these women, liberation had more to do with organizing in communities and workplaces—often alongside men—for better schools, better pay, decent benefits, and other policies to benefit their neighborhoods, jobs, and families. The feminism of the 1970s did not seem to address these issues.

As more and more women analyzed their own experiences, they began to address the power relations that created differences among women and the part that privileged women played in the oppression of others. For many women of color, working-class women, lesbians, and women in contexts outside the United States (especially women in non-Western societies), the focus on male domination was a distraction from other oppressions. Their lived experiences could support neither a unitary theory of gender nor an ideology of universal sisterhood. As a result, finding common ground in a universal female victimization was never a priority for many groups of women.

Challenges to gender stereotypes soon emerged. Women of varied races, classes, national origins, and sexualities insisted that the concept of gender be broadened to take their differences into account (Baca Zinn et. al., 1986; Hartmann, 1976; Rich, 1980; Smith, 1977). Many women began to argue that their lives were affected by their location in a number of different hierarchies: as African Americans, Latinas, Native Americans, or Asian Americans in the race hierarchy; as young or old in the age hierarchy; as heterosexual, lesbian, or bisexual in the sexual orientation hierarchy; and as women outside the Western industrialized nations, in subordinated geopolitical contexts. These arguments made it clear that women were not victimized by gender alone but by the historical and systematic denial of rights and privileges based on other differences as well.

MEN AS GENDERED BEINGS

As the voices of "other" women in the mid- to late 1970s began to challenge and expand the parameters of women's studies, a new area of scholarly inquiry was beginning to stir—a critical examination of men and masculinity. To be sure, in those early years of gender studies, the major task was to conduct studies and develop courses about the lives of women in order to begin to correct centuries of scholarship that rendered invisible women's lives, problems, and accomplishments. But the core idea of feminism—that "femininity" and women's subordination is a social construction—logically led to an examination of the social construction of "masculinity" and men's power. Many of the first scholars to take on this task were psychologists who were concerned with looking at the social construction of "the male sex role" (e.g., Pleck, 1981). By the late 1980s, there was a growing interdisciplinary collection of studies of men and masculinity, much of it by social scientists (Brod, 1987; Kaufman, 1987; Kimmel, 1987; Kimmel & Messner, 1989).

Reflecting developments in women's studies, the scholarship on men's lives tended to develop three themes: First, what we think of as "masculinity" is not a fixed, biological essence of men, but rather is a social construction that shifts and changes over time as well as between and among various national and cultural contexts. Second, power is central to understanding gender as a relational construct, and the dominant definition of masculinity is largely about expressing difference from—and superiority over—anything considered "feminine." And third, there is no singular "male sex role." Rather, at any given time there are various masculinities. R. W. Connell (1987; 1995; 2002) has been among the most articulate advocates of this perspective. Connell argues that hegemonic masculinity (the dominant form of masculinity at any given moment) is constructed in relation to femininities *as well as* in relation to various subordinated or marginalized masculinities. For example, in the United States, various racialized masculinities (e.g., as represented by African American men, Latino immigrant men, etc.) have been central to the construction of hegemonic (white middle-class) masculinity. This "othering" of racialized masculinities helps to shore up the privileges that have been historically connected to hegemonic masculinity. When viewed this way, we can better understand hegemonic masculinity as part of a system that includes gender as well as racial, class, sexual, and other relations of power.

The new literature on men and masculinities also begins to move us beyond the simplistic, falsely categorical, and pessimistic view of men simply as a privileged sex class. When race, social class, sexual orientation, physical abilities, immigrant, or national status are taken into account, we can see that in some circumstances, "male privilege" is partly—sometimes substantially— muted (Kimmel & Messner, 2004). Although it is unlikely that we will soon see a "men's movement" that aims to undermine the power and privileges that are connected with hegemonic masculinity, when we begin to look at "masculinities" through the prism of difference, we can begin to see similarities and possible points of coalition between and among certain groups of women and men (Messner, 1998). Certain kinds of changes in gender relations—for instance, a national family leave policy for working parents—might serve as a means of uniting particular groups of women and men.

GENDER IN INTERNATIONAL CONTEXTS

It is an increasingly accepted truism that late twentieth-century increases in transnational trade, international migration, and global systems of production and communication have diminished both the power of nation-states and the significance of national borders. A much more ignored issue is the extent to which gender relations—in the United States and elsewhere in the world—are increasingly linked to patterns of global economic restructuring. Decisions made in corporate headquarters located in Los Angeles, Tokyo, or London may have immediate repercussions on how women and men thousands of miles away organize their work, community, and family lives

(Sassen, 1991). It is no longer possible to study gender relations without giving attention to global processes and inequalities. . . .

Around the world, women's paid and unpaid labor is key to global development strategies. Yet it would be a mistake to conclude that gender is molded from the "top down." What happens on a daily basis in families and workplaces simultaneously constitutes and is constrained by structural transnational institutions. For instance, in the second half of the twentieth century young, single women, many of them from poor rural areas, were (and continue to be) recruited for work in export assembly plants along the U.S.-Mexico border, in East and Southeast Asia, in Silicon Valley, in the Caribbean, and in Central America. While the profitability of these multinational factories depends, in part, on management's ability to manipulate the young women's ideologies of gender, the women . . . do no not respond passively or uniformly, but actively resist, challenge, and accommodate. At the same time, the global dispersion of the assembly line has concentrated corporate facilities in many U.S. cities, making available myriad managerial, administrative, and clerical jobs for college educated women. Women's paid labor is used at various points along this international system of production. Not only employment but also consumption embodies global interdependencies. There is a high probability that the clothing you are wearing and the computer you use originated in multinational corporate headquarters and in assembly plants scattered around third world nations. And if these items were actually manufactured in the United States, they were probably assembled by Latin American and Asian-born women.

Worldwide, international labor migration and refugee movements are creating new types of multiracial societies. While these developments are often discussed and analyzed with respect to racial differences, gender typically remains absent. As several commentators have noted, the white feminist movement in the United States has not addressed issues of immigration and nationality. Gender, however, has been fundamental in shaping immigration policies (Chang, 1994; Hondagneu-Sotelo, 1994). Direct labor recruitment programs generally solicit either male or female labor (e.g., Filipina nurses and Mexican male farm workers), national disenfranchisement has particular repercussions for women and men, and current immigrant laws are based on very gendered notions of what constitutes "family unification." As Chandra Mohanty suggests, "analytically these issues are the contemporary metropolitan counterpart of women's struggles against colonial occupation in the geographical third world" (1991:23). Moreover, immigrant and refugee women's daily lives often challenge familiar feminist paradigms. The occupations in which immigrant and refugee women concentrate—paid domestic work, informal sector street vending, assembly or industrial piece work performed in the home—often blur the ideological distinction between work and family and between public and private spheres (Hondagneu-Sotelo, 2001; Parrenas, 2001).

FROM PATCHWORK QUILT TO PRISM

All of these developments—the voices of "other" women, the study of men and masculinities, and the examination of gender in transnational contexts—have helped redefine the study of gender. By working to develop knowledge that is inclusive of the experiences of all groups, new insights about gender have begun to emerge. Examining gender in the context of other differences makes it clear that nobody experiences themselves as solely gendered. Instead, gender is configured through cross-cutting forms of difference that carry deep social and economic consequences.

By the mid-1980s, thinking about gender had entered a new stage, which was more carefully grounded in the experiences of diverse groups of women and men. This perspective is a general way of looking at women and men and understanding their relationships to the structure of society. Gender is no longer viewed simply as a matter of two opposite categories of people, males and females, but a range of social relations among differently situated people. Because centering on difference is a radical challenge to the conventional gender framework, it raises several concerns. If we think of all the systems that converge to simultaneously influence the lives of women and men, we can imagine an infinite number of effects these interconnected systems have on different women and men. Does the recognition that gender can be understood only contextually (meaning that there is no singular "gender" per se) make women's studies and men's studies newly vulnerable to critics in the academy? Does the immersion in difference throw us into a whirlwind of "spiraling diversity" (Hewitt, 1992:316) whereby multiple identities and locations shatter the categories "women" and "men"?

. . . We take a position directly opposed to an empty pluralism. Although the categories "woman" and "man" have multiple meanings, this does not reduce gender to a "postmodern kaleidoscope of lifestyles. Rather, it points to the *relational* character of gender" (Connell, 1992:736). Not only are masculinity and femininity relational, but different *masculinities* and *femininities* are interconnected through other social structures such as race, class, and nation. The concept of relationality suggests that "the lives of different groups are interconnected even without face-to-face relations (Glenn, 2002:14). The meaning of "woman" is defined by the existence of women of different races and classes. Being a white woman in the United States is meaningful only insofar as it is set apart from and in contradistinction to women of color.

Just as masculinity and femininity each depend on the definition of the other to produce domination, differences *among* women and *among* men are also created in the context of structured relationships. Some women derive benefits from their race and class position and from their location in the global economy, while they are simultaneously restricted by gender. In other words, such women are subordinated by patriarchy, yet their relatively privileged positions within hierarchies of race, class, and the global political economy intersect to create for them an expanded range of opportunities, choices, and ways of living. They may even use their race and class advantage to minimize some of the consequences of patriarchy and/or to oppose other women. Similarly, one can become a man in opposition to other men. For example, "the relation between heterosexual and homosexual men is central, carrying heavy symbolic freight. To many people, homosexuality is the *negation* of masculinity. . . . Given that assumption, antagonism toward homosexual men may be used to define masculinity" (Connell, 1992:736).

In the past decade, viewing gender through the prism of difference has profoundly reoriented the field (Acker, 1999; Glenn, 1999, 2002; Messner, 1996; West & Fenstermaker, 1995). Yet analyzing the multiple constructions of gender does not just mean studying groups of women and groups of men as different. It is clearly time to go beyond what we call the "patchwork quilt" phase in the study of women and men—that is, the phase in which we have acknowledged the importance of examining differences within constructions of gender, but do so largely by collecting together a study here on African American women, a study there on gay men, a study on working-class Chicanas, and so on. This patchwork quilt approach too often amounts to no more than "adding difference and stirring." The result may be a lovely mosaic, but like a patchwork quilt, it still tends to overemphasize boundaries rather than to highlight bridges of interdependency. In addition, this approach too often does not explore the ways that social constructions of femininities and masculinities are based on and reproduce relations of power. In short, we think that the substantial quantity of research that has now been done on various groups and subgroups needs to be analyzed within a framework that emphasizes differences and inequalities not as discrete areas of separation, but as interrelated bands of color that together make up a spectrum. . . .

References

Acker, Joan. 1999. "Rewriting Class, Race and Gender: Problems in Feminist Rethinking" Pp. 44–69 in Myra Marx Ferree, Judith Lorber, and Beth B. Hess (eds.), *Revisioning Gender*. Thousand Oaks, CA: Sage Publications.

Baca Zinn, M., L., Weber Cannon, E., Higgenbotham, & B., Thornton Dill. 1986. "The Costs of Exclusionary Practices in Women's Studies," *Signs: Journal of Women in Culture and Society 11:* 290–303.

Brod, Harry (ed.). 1987. *The Making of Masculinities: The New Men's Studies*. Boston: Allen & Unwin.

Brownmiller, Susan. 1975. *Against Our Will: Men, Women, and Rape*. New York: Simon & Schuster.

Chang, Grace. 1994. "Undocumented Latinas: The New 'Employable Mothers.'" Pp. 259–285 in Evelyn Nakano Glenn, Grace Chang, and Linda Rennie Forcey (eds.), *Mothering, Ideology, Experience, and Agency*. New York and London: Routledge.

Connell, R. W. 1987. *Gender and Power*. Stanford, CA: Stanford University Press.

Connell, R. W. 1992. "A Very Straight Gay: Masculinity, Homosexual Experience, and the Dynamics of Gender," *American Sociological Review* 57: 735–751.

Connell, R. W. 1995. *Masculinities*. Berkeley: University of California Press.

Connell, R. W. 2002. *Gender*. Cambridge: Polity.

De Beauvoir, Simone. 1953. *The Second Sex*. New York: Knopf.

Glenn, Evelyn Nakano. 1999. "The Social Construction and Institutionalization of Gender and Race: An Integrative Framework," Pp. 3–43 in Myra Marx Ferree, Judith Lorber, and Beth B. Hess (eds.), *Revisioning Gender*. Thousand Oaks. CA: Sage Publications.

Glenn, Evelyn Nakano. 2002. *Unequal Sisterhood: How Race and Gender Shaped American Citizenship and Labor*. Cambridge, MA: Harvard University Press. 2002.

Hartmann, Heidi. 1976. "Capitalism, Patriarchy, and Job Segregation by Sex," *Signs: Journal of Women in Culture and Society 1*(3), part 2, spring: 137–167.

Hewitt, Nancy A. 1992. "Compounding Differences," *Feminist Studies 18:* 313–326.

Hondagneu-Sotelo, Pierrette. 1994. *Gendered Transitions: Mexican Experiences of Immigration*. Berkeley: University of California Press.

Hondagneu-Sotelo, Pierrette. 2001. *Doméstica: Immigrant Workers Cleaning and Caring in the Shadows of Affluence*. Berkeley: University of California Press.

Kanter, Rosabeth Moss. 1977. *Men and Women of the Corporation*. New York: Basic Books.

Kaufman, Michael. 1987. *Beyond Patriarchy: Essays by Men on Pleasure, Power, and Change*. Toronto and New York: Oxford University Press.

Kimmel, Michael S. (ed.). 1987. *Changing Men: New Directions in Research on Men and Masculinity*. Newbury Park, CA: Sage.

Kimmel, Michael S. 1996. *Manhood in America: A Cultural History*. New York: Free Press.

Kimmel, Michael S. & Michael A. Messner (eds.). 1989. *Men's Lives*. New York: Macmillan.

Kimmel, Michael S. & Michael A. Messner (eds.). 2004. *Men's Lives*, 6th ed. Boston: Pearson A and B.

Messner, Michael A. 1996. "Studying Up on Sex," *Sociology of Sport Journal 13:* 221–237.

Messner, Michael A. 1998. *Politics of Masculinities: Men in Movements*. Thousand Oaks, CA: Sage Publications.

Mohanty, Chandra Talpade. 1991. "Cartographies of Struggle: Third World Women and the Politics of Feminism." Pp. 51–80 in Chandra Talpade Mohanty, Ann Russo, and Lourdes Torres, (eds.), *Third World Women and the Politics of Feminism*. Bloomington: Indiana University Press.

Morgan, Robin. 1970. *Sisterhood Is Powerful: An Anthology of Writing from the Women's Liberation Movement*. New York: Vintage Books.

Parrenas, Rhacel Salazar. 2001. *Servants of Globalization: Women, Migration and Domestic Work*. Stanford: Stanford University Press.

Pleck, J. H. 1976. "The Male Sex Role: Definitions, Problems, and Sources of Change," *Journal of Social Issues 32:* 155–164.

Rich, Adrienne. 1980. "Compulsory Heterosexuality and the Lesbian Experience," *Signs: Journal of Women in Culture and Society 5:* 631–660.

Sassen, Saskia. 1991. *The Global City: New York, London, Tokyo.* Princeton: Princeton University Press.

Smith, Barbara. 1977. *Toward a Black Feminist Criticism.* Freedom, CA: Crossing Press.

West, Candace & Sarah Fenstermaker. 1995. "Doing Difference," *Gender & Society 9:* 8-37.

18

IDEOLOGICAL RACISM AND CULTURAL RESISTANCE
Constructing Our Own Images

Yen Le Espiritu

... A central aspect of racial exploitation centers on defining people of color as "the other" (Said 1979). The social construction of Asian American "otherness"—through such controlling images as the Yellow Peril, the model minority, the Dragon Lady, and the China Doll—is "the precondition for their cultural marginalization, political impotence, and psychic alienation from mainstream American society" (Hamamoto 1994, p. 5). As indicated by these stereotypes, representations of gender and sexuality figure strongly in the articulation of racism. These racist stereotypes collapse gender and sexuality: Asian men have been constructed as hypermasculine, in the image of the "Yellow Peril," but also as effeminate, in the image of the "model minority," and Asian women have been depicted as superfeminine, in the image of the "China Doll," but also as castrating, in the image of the "Dragon Lady" (Mullings 1994, pp. 279–280; Okihiro 1995). As Mary Ann Doane (1991) suggested, sexuality is "indissociable from the effects of polarization and differentiation, often linking them to structures of power and domination" (p. 217). In the Asian American case, the gendering of ethnicity—the process whereby white ideology assigns selected gender characteristics to

From Yen Le Espiritu, *Asian American Women and Men* (Thousand Oaks, CA: Alta Maria Press, 1997). Reprinted by permission of Rowman & Littlefield Publishers, Inc.

various ethnic "others"—cast Asian American men and women as simultaneously masculine and feminine but also as neither masculine nor feminine. On
the one hand, as part of the Yellow Peril, Asian American men and women
have been depicted as a *masculine* threat that needs to be contained. On the
other hand, both sexes have been skewed toward the female side: an indication of the group's marginalization in U.S. society and its role as the compli-
ant "model minority" in contemporary U.S. cultural ideology. Although an
apparent disjunction, both the feminization and masculinization of Asian
men and women exist to define and confirm the white man's superiority
(Kim 1990).

THE YELLOW PERIL

In the United States, Asia and America—East and West—are viewed as mutually exclusive binaries (Kim 1993, p. viii). Within this exclusive binary system,
Asian Americans, even as citizens, are designated Asians, not Americans.
Characterizing Asian Americans as "permanent houseguests in the house of
America," Sau-Ling Cynthia Wong (1993) stated that "Asian Americans are
put in the niche of the 'unassimilable alien': . . . they are alleged to be self-
disqualified from full American membership by materialistic motives, questionable political allegiance, and, above all, outlandish, overripe, 'Oriental'
cultures" (p. 6). Sonia Shah (1994) defined this form of "cultural discrimination" as a "peculiar blend of cultural and sexist oppression based on our accents, our clothes, our foods, our values and our commitments" (p. 182). This
cultural discrimination brands Asians as perpetual foreigners and thus perpetuates the notion of their alleged racial unassimilability. For example, although
Japanese Americans have lived in the United States since the turn of the century, many television programs, such as *Happy Days* (1974–1984) and *Gung
Ho* (1986–1987), have continued to portray them as newly arrived foreigners
(Hamamoto 1994, p. 13).

As the unassimilable alien, Asian Americans embody for many other
Americans the "Yellow Peril"—the threat that Asians will one day unite and
conquer the world. This threat includes military invasion and foreign trade
from Asia, competition to white labor from Asian labor, the alleged moral
degeneracy of Asian people, and potential miscegenation between whites
and Asians (Wu 1982, p. 1). Between 1850 and 1940, U.S. popular media
consistently portrayed Asian men as a military threat to the security and welfare of the United States *and* as a sexual danger to innocent white women
(Wu 1982). In numerous dime novels, movies, and comic strips, Asians
appeared as feral, rat-faced men lusting after virginal white women. Arguing
for racial purity, these popular media depicted Asian-white sexual union as
"at best, a form of beastly sodomy, and, at worst, a Satanic marriage"
(Hoppenstand 1983, p. 174). In these popular depictions, the white man was

the desirable sexual partner and the hero who rescued the white woman from "a fate worse than death" (Hoppenstand 1983, pp. 174–175). By the mid-1880s, hundreds of garishly illustrated and garishly written dime novels were being disseminated among a wide audience, sporting such sensational titles as *The Bradys and the Yellow Crooks*, *The Chase for the Chinese Diamonds*, *The Opium Den Detective*, and *The Stranglers of New York*. As portrayed in these dime novels, the Yellow Peril was the Chinatown district of a big city "in which decent, honest white folk never ventured" (Hoppenstand 1983, p. 177).

In 20th-century U.S. popular media, the Japanese joined the Chinese as a perceived threat to Europe and the United States (Wu 1982, p. 2). In 1916, William Randolph Hearst produced and distributed *Petria*, a movie about a group of fanatical Japanese who invade the United States and attempt to rape a white woman (Quinsaat 1976, p. 265). After the Japanese bombing of Pearl Harbor on December 7, 1941, the entire Yellow Peril stereotype be-came incorporated in the nation's war propaganda, quickly whipping white Americans into a war fever. Along with the print media, Hollywood cranked up its anti-Japanese propaganda and produced dozens of war films that cen-tered on the Japanese menace. The fiction of the Yellow Peril stereotype be-came intertwined with the fact of the United States' war with Japan, and the two became one in the mind-set of the American public (Hoppenstand 1983, pp. 182–183). It was fear of the Yellow Peril—fear of the rise of nonwhite people and their contestation of white supremacy—that led to the declaration of martial law in Hawaii on December 7, 1941, and to the internment of over 110,000 Japanese on the mainland in concentration camps (Okihiro 1994, p. 137). In subsequent decades, reflecting changing geopolitical concerns, U.S. popular media featured a host of new Yellow Peril stereotypes. During the 1950s Cold War years, in television programs as well as in movies, the Communist Chinese evildoers replaced the Japanese monster; during the Vietnam war of the 1970s, the Vietnamese Communists emerged as the new Oriental villains.

Today, Yellow Perilism takes the forms of the greedy, calculating, and clever Japanese businessman aggressively buying up U.S. real estate and cul-tural institutions *and* the superachieving but nonassimilating Asian Americans (Hagedorn 1993, p. xxii). In a time of rising economic powers in Asia, de-clining economic opportunities in the United States, and growing diversity among America's people, this new Yellow Perilism—the depiction of Asian and Asian Americans as economic and cultural threats to mainstream United States—supplies white Americans with a united identity and provides ideo-logical justification for U.S. isolationist policy toward Asia, increasing restric-tions against Asian (and Latino) immigration, and the invisible institutional racism and visible violence against Asians in the United States (Okihiro 1994, pp. 138–139).

THE RACIAL CONSTRUCTION
OF ASIAN AMERICAN MANHOOD

Like other men of color, Asian American men have been excluded from white-based cultural notions of the masculine. Whereas white men are depicted both as virile and as protectors of women, Asian men have been characterized both as asexual *and* as threats to white women. It is important to note the historical contexts of these seemingly divergent representations of Asian American manhood. The racist depictions of Asian men as "lascivious and predatory" were especially pronounced during the nativist movement against Asians at the turn of the [20th] century (Frankenberg 1993, pp. 75–76). The exclusion of Asian women from the United States and the subsequent establishment of bachelor societies eventually reversed the construction of Asian masculinity from "hypersexual" to "asexual" and even "homosexual." The contemporary model-minority stereotype further emasculates Asian American men as passive and malleable. Disseminated and perpetuated through the popular media, these stereotypes of the emasculated Asian male construct a reality in which social and economic discrimination against these men appears defensible. As an example, the desexualization of Asian men naturalized their inability to establish conjugal families in pre-World War II United States. Gliding over race-based exclusion laws that banned the immigration of most Asian women and antimiscegenation laws that prohibited men of color from marrying white women, these dual images of the eunuch and the rapist attributed the "womanless households" characteristics of pre-war Asian America to Asian men's lack of sexual prowess and desirability.

A popular controlling image applied to Asian American men is that of the sinister Oriental—a brilliant, powerful villain who plots the destruction of Western civilization. Personified by the movie character of Dr. Fu Manchu, this Oriental mastermind combines Western science with Eastern magic and commands an army of devoted assassins (Hoppenstand 1983, p. 178). Though ruthless, Fu Manchu lacks masculine heterosexual prowess (Wang 1988, p. 19), thus privileging heterosexuality. Frank Chin and Jeffrey Chan (1972), in a critique of the desexualization of Asian men in Western culture, described how the Fu Manchu character undermines Chinese American virility:

> Dr. Fu, a man wearing a long dress, batting his eyelashes, surround by muscular black servants in loin cloths, and with his habit of caressingly touching white men on the leg, wrist, and face with his long fingernails is not so much a threat as he is a frivolous offense to white manhood. (p. 60)

In another critique that glorifies male aggression, Frank Chin (1972) contrasted the neuterlike characteristics assigned to Asian men to the sexually aggressive images associated with other men of color. "Unlike the white stereotype of the evil black stud, Indian rapist, Mexican macho, the evil of the evil Dr. Fu Manchu was not sexual, but homosexual" (p. 66). However, Chin failed to note that as a homosexual, Dr. Fu (and by extension, Asian men) threatens and offends white masculinity—and therefore needs to be contained ideologically and destroyed physically.

Whereas the evil Oriental stereotype marks Asian American men as the white man's enemy, the stereotype of the sexless Asian sidekick—Charlie Chan, the Chinese laundryman, the Filipino houseboy—depicts Asian men as devoted and impotent, eager to please. William Wu (1982) reported that the Chinese servant "is the most important single image of the Chinese immigrants" in American fiction about Chinese Americans between 1850 and 1940 (p. 60). More recently, such diverse television programs as *Bachelor Father* (1957–1962), *Bonanza* (1959–1973), *Star Trek* (1966–1969), and *Falcon Crest* (1981–1990) all featured the stock Chinese bachelor domestic who dispenses sage advice to his superiors in addition to performing traditional female functions within the household (Hamamoto 1994, p. 7). By trapping Chinese men (and by extension, Asian men) in the stereotypical "feminine" tasks of serving white men, American society erases the figure of the Asian "masculine" plantation worker in Hawaii or railroad construction worker in the western United States, thus perpetuating the myth of the androgynous and effeminate Asian man (Goellnicht 1992, p. 198). This feminization, in turn, confines Asian immigrant men to the segment of the labor force that performs women's work.

The motion picture industry has been key in the construction of Asian men as sexual deviants. In a study of Asians in the U.S. motion pictures, Eugene Franklin Wong (1978) maintained that the movie industry filmically castrates Asian males to magnify the superior sexual status of white males (p. 27). As on-screen sexual rivals of whites, Asian males are neutralized, unable to sexually engage Asian women and prohibited from sexually engaging white women. By saving the white women from sexual contact with the racial "other," the motion picture industry protects the Anglo-American, bourgeois male establishment from any challenges to its hegemony (Marchetti 1993, p. 218). At the other extreme, the industry has exploited on the most potent aspects of the Yellow Peril discourses—the sexual danger of contact between the races—by concocting a sexually threatening portrayal of the licentious and aggressive Yellow Man lusting after the White Woman (Marchetti 1993, p. 3). Heedful of the larger society's taboos against Asian male–white female sexual union, white male actors donning "yellowface"—instead of Asian male actors—are used in these "love scenes." Nevertheless, the message of the perverse and animalistic Asian male attacking helpless white women is clear (Wong 1978). Though depicting sexual aggression, this image of the rapist, like that of the eunuch, casts Asian men as sexually undesirable. As Wong

(1978) succinctly stated, in Asian male–white female relations, "There can be rape, but there cannot be romance" (p. 25). Thus, Asian males yield to the sexual superiority of the white males who are permitted filmically to maintain their sexual dominance over both white women and women of color. A young Vietnamese American man describes the damaging effect of these stereotypes on his self-image:

> Every day I was forced to look into a mirror created by white society and its media. As a young Asian man, I shrank before white eyes. I wasn't tall, I wasn't fair, I wasn't muscular, and so on. Combine that with the enormous insecurities any pubescent teenager feels, and I have no difficulty in knowing now why I felt naked before a mass of white people. (Nguyen 1990, p. 23)

White cultural and institutional racism against Asian males is also reflected in the motion picture industry's preoccupation with the death of Asians—a filmic solution to the threats of the Yellow Peril. In a perceptive analysis of Hollywood's view of Asians in films made from the 1930s to the 1960s, Tom Engelhardt (1976) described how Asians, like Native Americans, are seen by the movie industry as inhuman invaders, ripe for extermination. He argued that the theme of the nonhumanness of Asians prepares the audience to accept, without flinching, "the levelling and near-obliteration of three Asian areas in the course of three decades" (Engelhardt 1976, p. 273). The industry's death theme, though applying to all Asians, is mainly focused on Asian males, with Asian females reserved for sexual purposes (Wong 1978, p. 35). Especially in war films, Asian males, however advantageous their initial position, inevitably perish at the hands of the superior white males (Wong 1978, p. 34).

THE RACIAL CONSTRUCTION
OF ASIAN AMERICAN WOMANHOOD

Like Asian men, Asian women have been reduced to one-dimensional caricatures in Western representation. The condensation of Asian women's multiple differences into gross character types—mysterious, feminine, and nonwhite—obscures the social injustice of racial, class, and gender oppression (Marchetti 1993, p. 71). Both Western film and literature promote dichotomous stereotypes of the Asian woman: Either she is the cunning Dragon Lady or the servile Lotus Blossom Baby (Tong 1994, p. 197). Though connoting two extremes, these stereotypes are interrelated: Both eroticize Asian women as exotic "others"—sensuous, promiscuous, but untrustworthy. Whereas American popular culture denies "manhood" to Asian men, it endows Asian women with an excess of "womanhood," sexualizing them but also impugning their sexuality. In this process, both sexism and racism have been blended together to produce the sexualization of white racism (Wong 1978, p. 260). Linking the controlling images of Asian men and women, Elaine Kim (1990) suggested that Asian women are portrayed as sexual for the same reasons that men are asexual: "Both exist to define the white man's virility and the white man's superiority" (p. 70).

As the racialized exotic "others," Asian American women do not fit the white-constructed notions of the feminine. Whereas white women have been depicted as chaste and dependable, Asian women have been represented as promiscuous and untrustworthy. In a mirror image of the evil Fu Manchu, the Asian woman was portrayed as the castrating Dragon Lady who, while puffing on her foot-long cigarette holder, could poison a man as easily as she could seduce him. "With her talon-like six-inch fingernails, her skin-tight satin dress slit to the thigh," the Dragon Lady is desirable, deceitful, and dangerous (Ling 1990, p. 11). In the 1924 film *The Thief of Baghdad*, Anna May Wong, a pioneer Chinese American actress, played a handmaid who employed treachery to help an evil Mongol prince attempt to win the hand of the Princess of Baghdad (Tajima 1989, p. 309). In so doing, Wong unwittingly popularized a common Dragon Lady social type: treacherous women who are partners in crime with men of their own kind. The publication of *Daughter of Fu Manchu* (1931) firmly entrenched the Dragon Lady image in white consciousness. Carrying on her father's work as the champion of Asian hegemony over the white race, Fah Lo Sue exhibited, in the words of American studies scholar, William F. Wu, "exotic sensuality, sexual availability to a white man, and a treacherous nature" (cited in Tong 1994, p. 197). A few years later, in 1934, Milton Caniff inserted into his adventure comic strip *Terry and the Pirates* another version of the Dragon Lady who "combines all the best features of past moustache twirlers with the lure of the handsome wench" (Hoppenstand 1983, p. 178). As such, Caniff's Dragon Lady fuses the image of the evil male Oriental mastermind with that of the Oriental prostitute first introduced some 50 years earlier in the dime novels.

At the opposite end of the spectrum is the Lotus Blossom stereotype, reincarnated throughout the years as the China Doll, the Geisha Girl, the War Bride, or the Vietnamese prostitute—many of whom are the spoils of the last three wars fought in Asia (Tajima 1989, p. 309). Demure, diminutive, and deferential, the Lotus Blossom Baby is "modest, tittering behind her delicate ivory hand, eyes downcast, always walking ten steps behind her man, and, best of all, devot[ing] body and soul to serving him" (Ling 1990, p. 11). Interchangeable in appearance and name, these women have no voice; their "nonlanguage" includes uninterpretable chattering, pidgin English, giggling, or silence (Tajima 1989). These stereotypes of Asian women as submissive and dainty sex objects not only have impeded women's economic mobility but also have fostered an enormous demand for X-rated films and pornographic materials featuring Asian women in bondage, for "Oriental" bathhouse workers in U.S. cities, and for Asian mail-order brides (Kim 1984, p. 64).

SEXISM, RACISM, AND LOVE

The racialization of Asian manhood and womanhood upholds white masculine hegemony. Cast as sexually available, Asian women become yet another possession of the white man. In motion pictures and network programs, interracial sexuality, though rare, occurs principally between a white male and an Asian female. A combination of sexism and racism makes this form of miscegenation more acceptable: Race mixing between an Asian male and a white female would upset not only racial taboos but those that attend patriarchal authority as well (Hamamoto 1994, p. 39). Whereas Asian men are depicted as either the threatening rapist or the impotent eunuch, white men are endowed with the masculine attributes with which to sexually attract the Asian woman. Such popular television shows as *Gunsmoke* (1955–1975) and *How the West Was Won* (1978–1979) clearly articulate the theme of Asian female sexual possession by the white male. In these shows, only white males have the prerogative to cross racial boundaries and to choose freely from among women of color as sex partners. Within a system of racial and gender oppression, the sexual possession of women and men of color by white men becomes yet another means of enforcing unequal power relations (Hamamoto 1994, p. 46).

The preference for white male–Asian female is also prevalent in contemporary television news broadcasting, most recently in the 1993–1995 pairing of Dan Rather and Connie Chung as coanchors of the *CBS Evening News*. Today, virtually every major metropolitan market across the United States today has at least one Asian American female newscaster (Hamamoto 1994, p. 245). While female Asian American anchorpersons—Connie Chung, Tritia Toyota, Wendy Tokuda, and Emerald Yeh—are popular television news figures, there is a nearly total absence of Asian American men. Critics argue that this is so because the white male hiring establishment, and presumably the larger American public, feels more comfortable (i.e., less threatened) seeing a white male sitting next to a minority female at the anchor desk than the reverse. Stephen Tschida of WDBJ-TV (Roanoke, Virginia), one of only a handful of male Asian American television news anchors, was informed early in his career that he did not have the proper "look" to qualify for the anchorperson position. Other male broadcast news veterans have reported being passed over for younger, more beauteous, female Asian Americans (Hamamoto 1994, p. 245). This gender imbalance sustains the construction of Asian American women as more successful, assimilated, attractive, and desirable than their male counterparts. . . .

CONCLUSION

Ideological representations of gender and sexuality are central in the exercise and maintenance of racial, patriarchal, and class domination. In the Asian American case, this ideological racism has taken seemingly contrasting forms: Asian men have been cast as both hypersexual and asexual, and Asian women have been rendered both superfeminine and masculine. Although in apparent disjunction, both forms exist to define, maintain, and justify white male supremacy. The racialization of Asian American manhood and womanhood underscores the interconnections of race, gender, and class. As categories of difference, race and gender relations do not parallel but intersect and confirm each other, and it is the complicity among these categories of difference that enables U.S. elites to justify and maintain their cultural, social, and economic power. Responding to the ideological assaults on their gender identities, Asian American cultural workers have engaged in a wide range of oppositional projects to defend Asian American manhood and womanhood. In the process, some have embraced a masculinist cultural nationalism, a stance that marginalizes Asian American women and their needs. Though sensitive to the emasculation of Asian American men, Asian American feminists have pointed out that Asian American nationalism insists on a fixed masculinist identity, thus obscuring gender differences. Though divergent, both the nationalist and feminist positions advance the dichotomous stance of man or woman, gender or race or class, without recognizing the complex relationality of these categories of oppression. It is only when Asian Americans recognize the intersections of race, gender, and class that we can transform the existing hierarchical structure.

References

Chin, F. (1972). Confessions of the Chinatown cowboy. *Bulletin of Concerned Asian Scholars, 4*(3), 66.

Chin. F., & Chan, J. P. (1972). Racist love. In R. Kostelanetz (Ed.), *Seeing through shuck* (pp. 65–79). New York: Ballantine.

Doane, M. A. (1991). *Femme fatales: Feminism, film theory, psychoanalysis.* New York: Routledge.

Engelhardt, T. (1976). Ambush at Kamikaze Pass. In E. Gee (Ed.), *Counterpoint: Perspectives on Asian America* (pp. 270–279). Los Angeles: University of California at Los Angeles, Asian American Studies Center.

Frankenberg, R. (1993). *White women, race matters: The social construction of whiteness.* Minneapolis: University of Minnesota Press.

Goellnicht, D. C. (1992). Tang Ao in America: Male subject positions in *China Men.* In S. G. Linn & A. Ling (Eds.), *Reading the literatures of Asian America* (pp. 191–212). Philadelphia: Temple University Press.

Hagedorn, J. (1993). Introduction: "Role of dead man require very little acting." In J. Hagedorn (Ed.), *Charlie Chan is dead: An anthology of contemporary Asian American fiction* (pp. xxi–xxx). New York: Penguin.

Hamamoto, D. Y. (1994). *Monitored peril: Asian Americans and the politics of representation.* Minneapolis: University of Minnesota Press.

Hoppenstand, G. (1983). Yellow devil doctors and opium dens: A survey of the yellow peril stereotypes in mass media entertainment. In C. D. Geist & J. Nachbar (Eds.), *The popular culture reader* (3rd ed., pp. 171–185). Bowling Green, OH: Bowling Green University Press.

Kim, E. (1984). Asian American writers: A bibliographical review. *American Studies International, 22*, 2.

Kim, E. (1990). "Such opposite creatures": Men and women in Asian American literature. *Michigan Quarterly Review, 29*, 68–93.

Kim, E. (1993). Preface. In J. Hagedorn (Ed.), *Charlie Chan is dead: An anthology of Contemporary Asian American fiction* (pp. vii–xiv). New York: Penguin.

Ling, A. (1990). *Between worlds: Women writers of Chinese ancestry.* New York: Pergamon.

Marchetti, G. (1993). *Romance and the "Yellow Peril": Race, sex, and discursive strategies in Hollywood fiction.* Berkeley: University of California Press.

Mullings, L. (1994). Images, ideology, and women of color. In M. Baca Zinn & B. T. Dill (Eds.), *Women of color in U.S. society* (pp. 265–289). Philadelphia: Temple University Press.

Nguyen, V. (1990, December 7). Growing up in white America. *Asian Week*, p. 23.

Okihiro, G. Y. (1994). *Margins and mainstreams: Asians in American history and culture.* Seattle: University of Washington Press.

Okihiro, G. Y. (1995, November). *Reading Asian bodies, reading anxieties.* Paper presented at the University of California, San Diego Ethnic Studies Colloquium, La Jolla.

Quinsaat, J. (1976). Asians in the media. The shadows in the spotlight. In E. Gee (Ed.), *Counterpoint: Perspectives on Asian America* (pp. 264–269). Los Angeles: University of California at Los Angeles, Asian American Studies Center.

Said, E. (1979). *Orientalism.* New York: Random House.

Shah, S. (1994). Presenting the Blue Goddess: Toward a national, Pan-Asian Feminist agenda. In K. Aguilar-San Juan (Ed.), *The state of Asian America: Activism and resistance in the 1990s* (pp. 147–158). Boston: South End.

Tajima, R. (1989). Lotus blossoms don't bleed: Images of Asian women. In Asian Women United of California (Ed.), *Making waves: An anthology of writings by and about Asian American women* (pp. 308–317). Boston: Beacon.

Tong, B. (1994). *Unsubmissive women: Chinese prostitutes in nineteenth-century San Francisco.* Norman: University of Oklahoma Press.

Wang, A. (1988). Maxine Hong Kingston's reclaiming of America: The birthright of the Chinese American male. *South Dakota Review, 26*, 18–29.

Wong, E. F. (1978). *On visual media racism: Asians in the American motion pictures.* New York: Arno.

Wong, S.-L. C. (1993). *Reading Asian American literature: From necessity to extravagance.* Princeton, NJ: Princeton University Press.

Wu, W. F. (1982). *The Yellow Peril: Chinese Americans in American fiction 1850–1940.* Hamden, CT: Archon.

19

A WHITE WOMAN OF COLOR

Julia Álvarez

Growing up in the Dominican Republic, I experienced racism within my own family—though I didn't think of it as racism. But there was definitely a hierarchy of beauty, which was the main currency in our daughters-only family. It was not until years later, from the vantage point of this country and this education, that I realized that this hierarchy of beauty was dictated by our coloring. We were a progression of whitening, as if my mother were slowly bleaching the color out of her children.

The oldest sister had the darkest coloring, with very curly hair and "coarse" features. She looked the most like Papi's side of the family and was considered the least pretty. I came next, with "good hair," and skin that back then was a deep olive, for I was a tomboy—another dark mark against me—who would not stay out of the sun. The sister right after me had my skin color, but she was a good girl who stayed indoors, so she was much paler, her hair a golden brown. But the pride and joy of the family was the baby. She was the one who made heads turn and strangers approach asking to feel her silken hair. She was white white, an adjective that was repeated in describing her color as if to deepen the shade of white. Her eyes were brown, but her hair was an unaccountable towheaded blond. Because of her coloring, my father was teased that there must have been a German milkman in our neighborhood. How could *she* be *his* daughter? It was clear that this youngest child resembled Mami's side of the family.

It was Mami's family who were *really* white. They were white in terms of race and white also in terms of class. From them came the fine features, the pale skin, the lank hair. Her brothers and uncles went to schools abroad and had important businesses in the country. They also emulated the manners and habits of North Americans. Growing up, I remember arguments at the supper table on whether or not it was proper to tie one's napkin around one's neck, on how much of one's arm one could properly lay on the table, on whether spaghetti could be eaten with the help of a spoon. My mother, of course, insisted on all the protocol of knives and forks and on eating a little portion of everything served; my father, on the other hand, defended our eating whatever we wanted, with our hands if need be, so we could "have fun" with our food. My mother would snap back that we looked like *jibaritas* who should be living out in the country. Of course, that was precisely where my father's family came from.

Not that Papi's family weren't smart and enterprising, all twenty-five brothers and sisters. (The size of the family in and of itself was considered very country by some members of Mami's family.) Many of Papi's brothers had gone to the university and become professionals. But their education was totally island—no fancy degrees from Andover and Cornell and Yale, no summer camps or school songs in another language. Papi's family still lived in the interior versus the capital, in old-fashioned houses without air conditioning, decorated in ways my mother's family would have considered, well, tasteless. I remember antimacassars on the backs of rocking chairs (which were the living-room set), garish paintings of flamboyant trees, ceramic planters with plastic flowers in bloom. They were *criollos*—creoles—rather than cosmopolitans, expansive, proud, colorful. (Some members had a sixth finger on their right—or was it their left hand?) Their features were less aquiline than Mother's family's, the skin darker, the hair coarse and curly. Their money still had the smell of the earth on it and was kept in a wad in their back pockets, whereas my mother's family had money in the Chase Manhattan Bank, most of it with George Washington's picture on it, not Juan Pablo Duarte's.

It was clear to us growing up then that lighter was better, but there was no question of discriminating against someone because he or she was dark-skinned. Everyone's family, even an elite one like Mami's, had darker-skinned members. All Dominicans, as the saying goes, have a little black behind the ears. So, to separate oneself from those who were darker would have been to divide *una familia*, a sacrosanct entity in our culture. Neither was white blood necessarily a sign of moral or intellectual or political superiority. All one has to do is page through a Dominican history book and look at the number of dark-skinned presidents, dictators, generals, and entrepreneurs to see that power has not resided exclusively or even primarily among the whites on the island. The leadership of our country has been historically "colored."

But being black was something else. A black Dominican was referred to as a "dark Indian" (*indio oscuro*)—unless you wanted to come to blows with him, that is. The real blacks were the Haitians who lived next door and who occupied the Dominican Republic for twenty years, from 1822 to 1844, a fact that can still so inflame the Dominican populace you'd think it had happened last year. The denial of the Afro-Dominican part of our culture reached its climax during the dictatorship of Trujillo, whose own maternal grandmother was Haitian. In 1937, to protect Dominican race purity, Trujillo ordered the overnight genocide of thousands (figures range from 4,000 to 20,000) of Haitians by his military, who committed this atrocity using only machetes and knives in order to make this planned extermination look like a "spontaneous" border skirmish. He also had the Dominican Republic declared a white nation despite of the evidence of the mulatto senators who were forced to pass this ridiculous measure.

So, black was not so good, kinky hair was not so good, thick lips not so good. But even if you were *indio oscuro conpelo malo y una bemba de aquí a Bani*, you could still sit in the front of the bus and order at the lunch counter—or the equivalent thereof. There was no segregation of races in the halls of power. But in the aesthetic arena—the one to which we girls were relegated as females—lighter was better. Lank hair and pale skin and small, fine features were better. All I had to do was stay out of the sun and behave myself and I could pass as a pretty white girl.

Another aspect of my growing up also greatly influenced my thinking on race. Although I was raised in the heart of a large family, my day-to-day caretakers were the maids. Most of these women were dark-skinned, some of Haitian background. One of them, Misiá, had been spared the machetes of the 1937 massacre when she was taken in and hidden from the prowling *guardias* by the family. We children spent most of the day with these women. They tended to us, nursed us when we were sick, cradled us when we fell down and scraped an elbow or knee (as a tomboy, there was a lot of this scraping for me), and most important, they told us stories of *los santos* and *el baroón del cementerio*, of *el cuco* and *las ciguapas*, beautiful dark-skinned creatures who escaped capture because their feet were turned backwards so they left behind a false set of footprints. These women spread the wings of our imaginations and connected us deeply to the land we came from. They were the ones with the stories that had power over us.

We arrived in Nueva York in 1960, before the large waves of Caribbean immigrants created little Habanas, little Santo Domingos, and little San Juans in the boroughs of the city. Here we encountered a whole new kettle of wax—as my malapropping Mami might have said. People of color were treated as if they were inferior, prone to violence, uneducated, untrustworthy, lazy—all the "bad" adjectives we were learning in our new language. Our dark-skinned aunt, Tía Ana, who had lived in New York for several decades and so was the authority in these matters, recounted stories of discrimination on buses and subways. These American were so blind! One drop of black and you were black. Everyone back home would have known that Tía Ana was not black: she had "good hair" and her skin color was a light *indio*. All week, she worked in a *factoria* in the Bronx, and when she came to visit us on Saturdays to sew our school clothes, she had to take three trains to our nice neighborhood where the darkest face on the street was usually her own.

We were lucky we were white Dominicans or we would have had a much harder time of it in this country. We would have encountered a lot more prejudice than we already did, for white as we were, we found that our Latinoness, our accents, our habits and smells, added "color" to our complexion. Had we been darker, we certainly could not have bought our mock Tudor house in Jamaica Estates. In fact, the African American family who moved in across the street several years later needed police protection because of threats. Even so, at the local school, we endured the bullying of classmates. "Go back to where you came from!" they yelled at my sisters and me in the playground. When some of them started throwing stones, my mother made up her mind that we were not safe and began applying to boarding schools where privilege transformed prejudice into patronage.

"So where are you from?" my classmates would ask.

"Jamaica Estates," I'd say, an edge of belligerence to my voice. It was obvious from my accent, if not my looks, that I was not *from* there in the way they meant being from somewhere.

"I mean *originally*."

And then it would come out, the color, the accent, the cousins with six fingers, the smell of garlic.

By the time I went off to college, a great explosion of American culture was taking place on campuses across the country. The civil rights movement, the Vietnam War and subsequent peace movement, the women's movement, were transforming traditional definitions of American identity. Ethnicity was in: my classmates wore long braids like Native Americans and peasant blouses from Mexico and long, diaphanous skirts and dangly earrings from India. Suddenly, my foreignness was being celebrated. This reversal felt affirming but also disturbing. As huipils, serapes, and embroidered dresses proliferated about me, I had the feeling that my ethnicity had become a commodity. I resented it.

When I began looking for a job after college, I discovered that being a white Latina made me a nonthreatening minority in the eyes of these employers. My color was a question *only* of culture, and if I kept my cultural color to myself, I was "no problem." Each time I was hired for one of my countless "visiting appointments"—they were never permanent "invitations," mind you—the inevitable questionnaire would accompany my contract in which I was to check off my RACE: CAUCASIAN, BLACK, NATIVE AMERICAN, ASIAN, HISPANIC, OTHER. How could a Dominican divide herself in this way? Or was I really a Dominican anymore? And what was a Hispanic? A census creation—there is no such culture—how could it define who I was at all? Given this set of options, the truest answer might have been to check off OTHER.

For that was the way I had begun to think of myself. Adrift from any Latino community in this country, my culture had become an internal homeland, periodically replenished by trips "back home." But as a professional woman on my own, I felt less and less at home on the island. My values, the loss of my Catholic faith, my lifestyle, my wardrobe, my hippy ways, and my feminist ideas separated me from my native culture. I did not subscribe to many of the mores and constraints that seemed to be an intrinsic part of that culture. And since my culture had always been my "color," by rejecting these mores I had become not only Americanized but whiter.

If I could have been a part of a Latino community in the United States, the struggle might have been, if not easier, less private and therefore less isolating. These issues of acculturation and ethnicity would have been struggles to share with others like me. But all my North American life I had lived in shifting academic communities—going to boarding schools, then college, and later teaching wherever I could get those yearly appointments—and these communities reflected the dearth of Latinos in the profession. Except for friends in Spanish departments, who tended to have come from their countries of origin to teach rather than being raised in this country as I was, I had very little daily contact with Latinos.

Where I looked for company was where I had always looked for company since coming to this country: in books. At first the texts that I read and taught were the ones prescribed to me, the canonical works which formed the content of the bread-and-butter courses that as a "visiting instructor" I was hired to teach. These texts were mostly written by white male writers from Britain and the United States, with a few women thrown in and no Latinos. Thank goodness for the occasional creative writing workshop where I could bring in the multicultural authors I wanted. But since I had been formed in this very academy, I was clueless where to start. I began to educate myself by reading, and that is when I discovered that there were others out there like me, hybrids who came in a variety of colors and whose ethnicity and race were an evolving process, not a rigid paradigm or a list of boxes, one of which you checked off.

This discovery of my ethnicity on paper was like a rebirth. I had been going through a pretty bad writer's block: the white page seemed impossible to fill with whatever it was I had in me to say. But listening to authors like Maxine Hong Kingston, Toni Morrison, Gwendolyn Brooks, Langston Hughes, Maya Angelou, June Jordan, and to Lorna Dee Cervantes, Piri Thomas, Rudolfo Anaya, Edward Rivera, Ernesto Galarza (that first wave of Latino writers), I began to hear the language "in color." I began to see that literature could reflect the otherness I was feeling, that the choices in fiction and poetry did not have to be bleached out of their color or simplified into either/or. A story could allow for the competing claims of different parts of ourselves and where we came from.

Ironically, it was through my own stories and poems that I finally made contact with Latino communities in this country. As I published more, I was invited to read at community centers and bilingual programs. Latino students, who began attending colleges in larger numbers in the late seventies and eighties, sought me out as a writer and teacher "of color." After the publication of *How the García Girls Lost Their Accents*, I found that I had become a sort of spokesperson for Dominicans in this country, a role I had neither sought nor accepted. Of course, some Dominicans refused to grant me any status as a "real" Dominican because I was "white." With the color word there was also a suggestion of class. My family had not been among the waves of economic immigrants that left the island in the seventies, a generally darker-skinned, working-class group, who might have been the maids and workers in my mother's family house. We had come in 1960, political refugees, with no money but with "prospects": Papi had a friend who was the doctor at the Waldorf Astoria and who helped him get a job; Mami's family had money in the Chase Manhattan Bank they could lend us. We had changed class in America—from Mami's elite family to middle-class spics—but our background and education and most especially our pale skin had made mobility easier for us here. We had not undergone the same kind of race struggles as other Dominicans; therefore, we could not be "real" Dominicans.

What I came to understand and accept and ultimately fight for with my writing is the reality that ethnicity and race are not fixed constructs or measurable quantities. What constitutes our ethnicity and our race—once there is literally no common ground beneath us to define it—evolves as we seek to define and redefine ourselves in new contexts. My Latino-ness is not something someone can take away from me or leave me out of with a definition. It is in my blood: it comes from that mixture of biology, culture, native language, and experience that makes me a different American from one whose family comes from Ireland or Poland or Italy. My Latino-ness is also a political choice. I am choosing to hold on to my ethnicity and native language even if I can "pass." I am choosing to color my Americanness with my Dominicanness even if it came in a light shade of skin color.

I hope that as Latinos, coming from so many different countries and continents, we can achieve solidarity in this country as the mix that we are. I hope we won't shoot ourselves in the foot in order to maintain some sort of false "purity" as the glue that holds us together. Such an enterprise is bound to fail. We need each other. We can't afford to reject the darker or lighter varieties, and to do so is to have absorbed a definition of ourselves as exclusively one thing or the other. And haven't we learned to fear that word "exclusive"? This reductiveness is absurd when we are talking about a group whose very definition is that of a mestizo race, a mixture of European, indigenous, African, and much more. Within this vast circle, shades will lighten and darken into overlapping categories. If we cut them off, we diminish our richness and we plant a seed of ethnic cleansing that is the root of the bloodshed we have seen in Bosnia and the West Bank and Rwanda and even our own Los Angeles and Dominican Republic.

As we Latinos redefine ourselves in America, making ourselves up and making ourselves over, we have to be careful, in taking up the promises of America, not to adopt its limiting racial paradigms. Many of us have shed customs and prejudices that oppressed our gender, race, or class on our native islands and in our native countries. We should not replace these with modes of thinking that are divisive and oppressive of our rich diversity. Maybe as a group that embraces many races and differences, we Latinos can provide a positive multicultural, multiracial model to a divided America.

![20]

MASCULINITIES AND ATHLETIC CAREERS

Michael Messner

. . . It is now widely accepted in sport sociology that social institutions such as the media, education, the economy, and (a more recent and controversial addition to the list) the black family itself all serve to systematically channel disproportionately large numbers of young black men into football, basketball, boxing, and baseball, where they are subsequently "stacked" into low-prestige and high-risk positions, exploited for their skills, and finally, when their bodies are used up, excreted from organized athletics at a young age with no transferable skills with which to compete in the labor market (Edwards 1984; Eitzen and Purdy 1986; Eitzen and Yetman 1977).

While there are racial differences in involvement in sports, class, age, and educational differences seem more significant. Rudman's (1986) initial analysis revealed profound differences between whites' and blacks' orientations to sports. Blacks were found to be more likely than whites to view sports favorably, to incorporate sports into their daily lives, and to be affected by the outcome of sporting events. However, when age, education, and social class were factored into the analysis, Rudman found that race did not explain whites' and blacks' different orientations. Blacks' affinity to sports is best explained by their tendency to be clustered disproportionately in lower-income groups.

The 1980s has ushered in what Wellman (1986, p. 43) calls a "new political linguistics of race," which emphasizes cultural rather than structural causes (and solutions) to the problems faced by black communities. The advocates of the cultural perspective believe that the high value placed on sports by black communities has led to the development of unrealistic hopes in millions of black youths. They appeal to family and community to bolster other choices based upon a more rational assessment of "reality." Visible black role models in many other professions now exist, they say, and there is ample evidence which proves that sports careers are, at best, a bad gamble.

Author's note: Parts of this article were presented as papers at the American Sociological Association Annual Meeting, Chicago, in August 1987, and at the North American Society for the Sociology of Sport Annual Meeting in Edmonton, Alberta, in November 1987. I thank Maxime Baca Zinn, Bob Blauner, Bob Dunn, Pierrette Hondagneu-Sotelo, Carol Jacklin, Michael Kimmel, Judith Lorber, Don Sabo, Barrie Thorne, and Carol Warren for constructive comments on earlier versions of this article.

From *Gender & Society* 3 (March 1989): 71–88. Reprinted by permission of Sage Publications, Inc.

Critics of the cultural perspective have condemned it as conservative and victim blaming. But it can also be seen as a response to the view of black athletes as little more than unreflexive dupes of an all-powerful system, which ignores the importance of agency. Gruneau (1983) has argued that sports must be examined within a theory that views human beings as active subjects who are operating within historically constituted structural constraints. Gruneau's reflexive theory rejects the simplistic views of sports as either a realm of absolute oppression or an arena of absolute freedom and spontaneity. Instead, he argues, it is necessary to construct an understanding of how and why participants themselves actively make choices and construct and define meaning and a sense of identity within the institutions [in which] they find themselves.

None of these perspectives considers the ways that gender shapes men's definitions of meaning and choices. Within the sociology of sport, gender as a process that interacts with race and class is usually ignored or taken for granted—except when it is *women* athletes who are being studied. Sociologists who are attempting to come to grips with the experiences of black men in general, and in organized sports in particular, have almost exclusively focused their analytic attention on the variable "black," while uncritically taking "men" as a given. Hare and Hare (1984), for example, view masculinity as a biologically determined tendency to act as a provider and protector that is thwarted for black men by socioeconomic and racist obstacles. Staples (1982) does view masculinity largely as a socially produced script, but he accepts this script as a given, preferring to focus on black men's blocked access to male role fulfillment. These perspectives on masculinity fail to show how the male role itself, as it interacts with a constricted structure of opportunity, can contribute to locking black men into destructive relationships and lifestyles (Franklin 1984; Majors 1986).

This article will examine the relationships among male identity, race, and social class by listening to the voices of former athletes. I will first briefly describe my research. Then I will discuss the similarities and differences in the choices and experiences of men from different racial and social class backgrounds. Together, these choices and experiences help to construct what Connell (1987) calls "the gender order." Organized sports, it will be suggested, is a practice through which men's separation from and power over women is embodied and naturalized at the same time that hegemonic (white, heterosexual, professional-class) masculinity is clearly differentiated from marginalized and subordinated masculinities.

DESCRIPTION OF RESEARCH

Between 1983 and 1985, I conducted 30 open-ended, in-depth interviews with male former athletes. My purpose was to add a critical understanding of male gender identity to Levinson's (1978) conception of the "individual lifecourse"—specifically, to discover how masculinity develops and changes as a man interacts with the socially constructed world of organized sports. Most of the men I interviewed had played the U.S. "major sports"—football, basketball, baseball, track. At the time of the interview, each had been retired from playing organized sports for at least 5 years. Their ages ranged from 21 to 48, with the median, 33. Fourteen were black, 14 were white, and 2 were Hispanic. Fifteen of the 16 black and Hispanic men had come from poor or working-class families, while the majority (9 of 14) of the white men had come from middle-class or professional families. Twelve had played organized sports through high school, 11 through college, and 7 had been professional athletes. All had at some time in their lives based their identities largely on their roles as athletes and could therefore be said to have had athletic careers.

MALE IDENTITY AND ORGANIZED SPORTS

... For the men in my study, the rule-bound structure of organized sports became a context in which they struggled to construct a masculine positional identity.

All of the men in this study described the emotional salience of their earliest experiences in sports in terms of relationships with other males. It was not winning and victories that seemed important at first; it was something "fun" to do with fathers, older brothers or uncles, and eventually with same-aged peers. As a man from a white, middle-class family said, "The most important thing was just being out there with the rest of the guys—being friends." A 32-year-old man from a poor Chicano family, whose mother had died when he was 9 years old, put it more succinctly:

> What I think sports did for me is it brought me into kind of an instant family. By being on a Little League team, or even just playing with kids in the neighborhood, it brought what I really wanted, which was some kind of closeness.

Though sports participation may have initially promised "some kind of closeness," by the ages of 9 or 10, the less skilled boys were already becoming alienated from—or weeded out of—the highly competitive and hierarchical system of organized sports. Those who did experience some early successes received recognition from adult males (especially fathers and older brothers) and held higher status among peers. As a result, they began to pour more and more of their energies into athletic participation. It was only after they learned that they would get recognition from other people for being a good athlete—indeed, that this attention was contingent upon *being a winner*—that performance and winning (the dominant values of organized sports) became extremely important. For some, this created pressures that served to lessen or eliminate the fun of athletic participation (Messner 1987a, 1987b).

While feminist psychoanalytic and developmental theories of masculinity are helpful in explaining boys' early attraction and motivations in organized sports, the imperatives of core gender identity do not fully determine the contours and directions of the life course. As Rubin (1985) and Levinson (1978) have pointed out, an understanding of the lives of men must take into account the processual nature of male identity as it unfolds through interaction between the internal (psychological ambivalences) and the external (social, historical, and institutional) contexts.

To examine the impact of the social contexts, I divided my sample into two comparison groups. In the first group were 10 men from higher-status backgrounds, primarily white, middle-class, and professional families. In the second group were 20 men from lower-status backgrounds, primarily minority, poor, and working-class families. While my data offered evidence for the similarity of experiences and motivations of men from poor backgrounds, independent of race, I also found anecdotal evidence of a racial dynamic that operates independently of social class. However, my sample was not large enough to separate race and class, and so I have combined them to make two status groups.

In discussing these two groups, I will focus mainly on the high school years. During this crucial period, the athletic role may become a master status for a young man, and he is beginning to make assessments and choices about his future. It is here that many young men make a major commitment to—or begin to back away from—athletic careers.

Men from Higher-Status Backgrounds

The boyhood dream of one day becoming a professional athlete—a dream shared by nearly all the men interviewed in this study—is rarely realized. The sports world is extremely hierarchical. The pyramid of sports careers narrows very rapidly as one climbs from high school, to college, to professional levels of competition (Edwards 1984; Harris and Eitzen 1978; Hill and Lowe 1978). In fact, the chances of attaining professional status in sports are approximately 4/100,000 for a white man, 2/100,000 for a black man, and 3/100,000 for a Hispanic man in the United States (Leonard and Reyman 1988). For many young athletes, their dream ends early when coaches inform them that they are not big enough, strong enough, fast enough, or skilled enough to compete at the higher levels. But six of the higher-status men I interviewed did not wait for coaches to weed them out. They made conscious decisions in high school or in college to shift their attentions elsewhere—usually toward educational and career goals. Their decision not to pursue an athletic career appeared to them in retrospect to be a rational decision based on the growing knowledge of how very slim their chances were to be successful in the sports world. For instance, a 28-year-old white graduate student said:

> By junior high I started to realize that I was a good player—maybe even one of the best in my community—but I realized that there were all these people all over the country and how few will get to play pro sports. By high school, I still dreamed of being a pro—I was a serious athlete, I played hard—but I knew it wasn't heading anywhere. I wasn't going to play pro ball.

A 32-year-old white athletic director at a small private college had been a successful college baseball player. Despite considerable attention from professional scouts, he had decided to forgo a shot at a baseball career and to enter graduate school to pursue a teaching credential. As he explained this decision:

> At the time I think I saw baseball as pissing in the wind, really. I was married, I was 22 years old with a kid. I didn't want to spend 4 or 5 years in the minors with a family. And I could see I wasn't a superstar; so it wasn't really worth it. So I went to grad school. I thought that would be better for me.

Perhaps most striking was the story of a high school student body president and top-notch student who was also "Mr. Everything" in sports. He was named captain of his basketball, baseball, and football teams and achieved All-League honors in each sport. This young white man from a middle-class family received attention from the press and praise from his community and peers for his athletic accomplishments, as well as several offers of athletic scholarships from universities. But by the time he completed high school, he had already decided to quit playing organized sports. As he said:

> I think in my own mind I kind of downgraded the stardom thing. I thought that was small potatoes. And sure, that's nice in high school and all that, but on a broad scale, I didn't think it amounted to all that much. So I decided that my goal's to be a dentist, as soon as I can.

In his sophomore year of college, the basketball coach nearly persuaded him to go out for the team, but eventually he decided against it:

> I thought, so what if I can spend two years playing basketball? I'm not going to be a basketball player forever and I might jeopardize my chances of getting into dental school if I play.

He finished college in three years, completed dental school, and now, in his mid-30s, is again the epitome of the successful American man: a professional with a family, a home, and a membership in the local country club.

How and why do so many successful male athletes from higher-status backgrounds come to view sports careers as "pissing in the wind," or as "small potatoes"? How and why do they make this early assessment and choice to shift from sports and toward educational and professional goals? The white, middle-class institutional context, with its emphasis on education and income, makes it clear to them that choices exist and that the pursuit of an athletic career is not a particularly good choice to make. Where the young male once found sports to be a convenient institution within which to construct masculine status, the postadolescent and young adult man from a higher-status background simply *transfers* these same strivings to other institutional contexts: education and careers.

For the higher-status men who had chosen to shift from athletic careers, sports remained important on two levels. First, having been a successful high school or college athlete enhances one's adult status among other men in the community—but only as a badge of masculinity that is *added* to his professional status. In fact, several men in professions chose to be interviewed in their offices, where they publicly displayed the trophies and plaques that attested to their earlier athletic accomplishments. Their high school and college athletic careers may have appeared to them as "small potatoes," but many successful men speak of their earlier status as athletes as having "opened doors" for them in their present professions and in community affairs. Similarly, Farr's (1988) research on "Good Old Boys Sociability Groups" shows how sports, as part of the glue of masculine culture, continues to facilitate "dominance bonding" among privileged men long after active sports careers end. The college-educated, career-successful men in Farr's study rarely express overtly sexist, racist, or classist attitudes; in fact, in their relationships with women, they "often engage in expressive intimacies" and "make fun of exaggerated 'machismo'" (p. 276). But though they outwardly conform more to what Pleck (1982) calls "the modern male role," their informal relationships within their sociability groups, in effect, affirm their own gender and class status by constructing and clarifying the boundaries between themselves and women and lower-status men. This dominance bonding is based largely upon ritual forms of sociability (camaraderie, competition), "the superiority of which was first affirmed in the exclusionary play activities of young boys in groups" (Farr 1988, p. 265).

In addition to contributing to dominance bonding among higher-status adult men, sports remains salient in terms of the ideology of gender relations. Most men continued to watch, talk about, and identify with sports long after their own disengagement from athletic careers. Sports as a mediated spectacle provides an important context in which traditional conceptions of masculine superiority—conceptions recently contested by women—are shored up. As a 32-year-old white professional-class man said of one of the most feared professional football players today:

> A woman can do the same job as I can do—maybe even be my boss. But I'll be damned if she can go out on the football field and take a hit from Ronnie Lott.

Violent sports as spectacle provide linkages among men in the project of the domination of women, while at the same time helping to construct and clarify differences among various masculinities. The statement above is a clear identification with Ronnie Lott *as a man*, and the basis of the identification is the violent male body. As Connell (1987, p. 85) argues, sports is an important organizing institution for the embodiment of masculinity. Here, men's power over women becomes naturalized and linked to the social distribution of violence. Sports, as a practice, suppresses natural (sex) similarities, constructs differences, and then, largely through the media, weaves a structure of symbol and interpretation around these differences that naturalizes them (Hargreaves 1986, p. 112). It is also significant that the man who made the above statement about Ronnie Lott was quite aware that he (and perhaps 99 percent of the rest of the U.S. male population) was probably as incapable as most women of taking a "hit" from someone like Lott and living to tell of it. For middle-class men, the "tough guys" of the culture industry—the Rambos, the Ronnie Lotts who are fearsome "hitters," who "play hurt"—are the heroes who "prove" that "we men" are superior to women. At the same time, they play the role of the "primitive other," against whom higher-status men define themselves as "modern" and "civilized."

Sports, then, is important from boyhood through adulthood for men from higher-status backgrounds. But it is significant that by adolescence and early adulthood, most of these young men have concluded that sports *careers* are not for them. Their middle-class cultural environment encourages them to decide to shift their masculine strivings in more "rational" directions: education and nonsports careers. Yet their previous sports participation continues to be very important to them in terms of constructing and validating their status within privileged male peer groups and within their chosen professional careers. And organized sports, as a public spectacle, is a crucial locus around which ideologies of male superiority over women, as well as higher-status men's superiority over lower-status men, are constructed and naturalized.

Men from Lower-Status Backgrounds

For the lower-status young men in this study, success in sports was not an added proof of masculinity; it was often their only hope of achieving public masculine status. A 34-year-old black bus driver who had been a star athlete in three sports in high school had neither the grades nor the money to attend college, so he accepted an offer from the U.S. Marine Corps to play on their baseball team. He ended up in Vietnam, where a grenade blew four fingers off his pitching hand. In retrospect, he believed that his youthful focus on sports stardom and his concomitant lack of effort in academics made sense:

> You can go anywhere with athletics—you don't have to have brains. I mean, I didn't feel like I was gonna go out there and be a computer expert, or

something that was gonna make a lot of money. The only thing I could do and live comfortably would be to play sports—just to get a contract—doesn't matter if you play second or third team in the pros, you're gonna make big bucks. That's all I wanted, a confirmed livelihood at the end of my ventures, and the only way I could do it would be through sports. So I tried. It failed, but that's what I tried.

Similar, and even more tragic, is the story of a 34-year-old black man who is now serving a life term in prison. After a career-ending knee injury at the age of 20 abruptly ended what had appeared to be a certain road to professional football fame and fortune, he decided that he "could still be rich and famous" by robbing a bank. During his high school and college years, he said, he was nearly illiterate:

I'd hardly ever go to classes and they'd give me *C*s. My coaches taught some of the classes. And I felt, "So what? They *owe* me that! I'm an *athlete!* I thought that was what I was born to do—to play sports—and everybody understood that.

Are lower-status boys and young men simply duped into putting all their eggs into one basket? My research suggested that there was more than "hope for the future" operating here. There were also immediate psychological reasons that they chose to pursue athletic careers. By the high school years, class and ethnic inequalities had become glaringly obvious, especially for those who attended socioeconomically heterogeneous schools. Cars, nice clothes, and other signs of status were often unavailable to these young men, and this contributed to a situation in which sports took on an expanded importance for them in terms of constructing masculine identities and status. A white, 36-year-old man from a poor, single-parent family who later played professional baseball had been acutely aware of his low-class status in his high school:

I had one pair of jeans, and I wore them every day. I was always afraid of what people thought of me—that this guy doesn't have anything, that he's wearing the same Levi's all the time, he's having to work in the cafeteria for his lunch. What's going on? I think that's what made me so shy. . . . But boy, when I got into sports, I let it all hang out—[laughs]—and maybe that's why I became so good, because I was frustrated, and when I got into that element, they gave me my uniform in football, basketball, and baseball, and I didn't have to worry about how I looked, because then it was *me* who was coming out, and not my clothes or whatever. And I think that was the drive.

Similarly, a 41-year-old black man who had a 10-year professional football career described his insecurities as one of the few poor blacks in a mostly white, middle-class school and his belief that sports was the one arena in which he could be judged solely on his merit:

I came from a poor family, and I was very sensitive about that in those days. When people would say things like "Look at him—he has dirty pants on,"

> I'd think about it for a week. [But] I'd put my pants on and I'd go out on the football field with the intention that I'm gonna do a job. And if that calls on me to hurt you, I'm gonna do it. It's as simple as that. I demand respect just like everybody else.

"Respect" was what I heard over and over when talking with the men from lower-status backgrounds, especially black men. I interpret this type of respect to be a crystallization of the masculine quest for recognition through public achievement, unfolding within a system of structured constraints due to class and race inequities. The institutional context of education (sometimes with the collusion of teachers and coaches) and the constricted structure of opportunity in the economy made the pursuit of athletic careers appear to be the most rational choice to these young men.

The same is not true of young lower-status women. Dunkle (1985) points out that from junior high school through adulthood, young black men are far more likely to place high value on sports than are young black women, who are more likely to value academic achievement. There appears to be a gender dynamic operating in adolescent male peer groups that contributes toward their valuing sports more highly than education. Franklin (1986, p. 161) has argued that many of the normative values of the black male peer group (little respect for nonaggressive solutions to disputes, contempt for nonmaterial culture) contribute to the constriction of black men's views of desirable social positions, especially through education. In my study, a 42-year-old black man who did succeed in beating the odds by using his athletic scholarship to get a college degree and eventually becoming a successful professional said:

> By junior high, you either got identified as an athlete, a thug, or a bookworm. It's very important to be seen as somebody who's capable in some area. And you *don't* want to be identified as a bookworm. I was very good with books, but I was kind of covert about it. I was a closet bookworm. But with sports, I was *somebody;* so I worked very hard at it.

For most young men from lower-status backgrounds, the poor quality of their schools, the attitudes of teachers and coaches, as well as the antieducation environment within their own male peer groups, made it extremely unlikely that they would be able to succeed as students. Sports, therefore, became *the* arena in which they attempted to "show their stuff." For these lower-status men, as Baca Zinn (1982) and Majors (1986) argued in their respective studies of Chicano men and black men, when institutional resources that signify masculine status and control are absent, physical presence, personal style, and expressiveness take on increased importance. What Majors (1986, p. 6) calls "cool pose" is black men's expressive, often aggressive, assertion of masculinity. This self-assertion often takes place within a social context in which the young man is quite aware of existing social inequities. As the black bus driver, referred to above, said of his high school years:

> See, the rich people use their money to do what they want to do. I use my ability. If you wanted to be around me, if you wanted to learn something about sports, I'd teach you. But you're gonna take me to lunch. You're gonna let me use your car. See what I'm saying? In high school I'd go where I wanted to go. I didn't have to be educated. I was well-respected. I'd go somewhere, and they'd say, "Hey, that's Mitch Harris,[1] yeah, that's a bad son of a bitch!"

Majors (1986) argues that although "cool pose" represents a creative survival technique within a hostile environment, the most likely long-term effect of this masculine posturing is educational and occupational dead ends. As a result, we can conclude, lower-status men's personal and peer-group responses to a constricted structure of opportunity—responses that are rooted, in part, in the developmental insecurities and ambivalences of masculinity—serve to lock many of these young men into limiting activities such as sports.

SUMMARY AND CONCLUSIONS

This research has suggested that within a social context that is stratified by social class and by race, the choice to pursue—or not to pursue—an athletic career is explicable as an individual's rational assessment of the available means to achieve a respected masculine identity. For nearly all of the men from lower-status backgrounds, the status and respect that they received through sports was temporary—it did not translate into upward mobility. Nonetheless, a strategy of discouraging young black boys and men from involvement in sports is probably doomed to fail, since it ignores the continued existence of structural constraints. Despite the increased number of black role models in nonsports professions, employment opportunities for young black males have actually deteriorated. . . .

But it would be a mistake to conclude that we simply need to breed socioeconomic conditions that make it possible for poor and minority men to mimic the "rational choices" of white, middle-class men. If we are to build an appropriate understanding of the lives of all men, we must critically analyze white middle-class masculinity, rather than uncritically taking it as a normative standard. To fail to do this would be to ignore the ways in which organized sports serve to construct and legitimate gender differences and inequalities among men and women.

Feminist scholars have demonstrated that organized sports give men from all backgrounds a means of status enhancement that is not available to young women. Sports thus serve the interests of all men in helping to construct and legitimize their control of public life and their domination of women (Bryson 1987; Hall 1987; Theberge 1987). Yet concrete studies are suggesting that men's experiences within sports are not all of a piece. Brian Pronger's (1990) research suggests that gay men approach sports differently than straight men do, with a sense of "irony." And my research suggests that although sports are important for men from both higher- and lower-status backgrounds, there are crucial differences. In fact, it appears that the meaning that most men give to their athletic strivings has more to do with competing for status among men than it has to do with proving superiority over women. How can we explain this seeming contradiction between the feminist claim that sports links all men in the domination of women and the research findings that different groups of men relate to sports in very different ways?

. . . Connell's (1987) concept of the "gender order" is useful. The gender order is a dynamic process that is constantly in a state of play. Moving beyond static gender-role theory and reductionist concepts of patriarchy that view men as an undifferentiated group which oppresses women, Connell argues that at any given historical moment, there are competing masculinities— some hegemonic, some marginalized, some stigmatized. Hegemonic masculinity (that definition of masculinity which is culturally ascendant) is constructed in relation to various subordinated masculinities as well as in relation to femininities. The project of male domination of women may tie all men together, but men share very unequally in the fruits of this domination.

These are key insights in examining the contemporary meaning of sports. Utilizing the concept of the gender order, we can begin to conceptualize how hierarchies of race, class, age, and sexual preference among men help to construct and legitimize men's overall power and privilege over women. And how, for some black, working-class, or gay men, the false promise of sharing in the fruits of hegemonic masculinity often ties them into their marginalized and subordinate statuses within hierarchies of intermale dominance. For instance, black men's development of what Majors (1986) calls "cool pose" within sports can be interpreted as an example of creative resistance to one form of social domination (racism); yet it also demonstrates the limits of an agency that adopts other forms of social domination (masculinity) as its vehicle. As Majors (1990) points out:

> Cool Pose demonstrates black males' potential to transcend
> oppressive conditions in order to express themselves *as men.* [Yet] it ultimately
> does not put black males in a position to live and work in more egalitarian
> ways with women, nor does it directly challenge male hierarchies.

Indeed, as Connell's (1990) analysis of an Australian "Iron Man" shows, the commercially successful, publicly acclaimed athlete may embody all that is valued in present cultural conceptions of hegemonic masculinity—physical strength, commercial success, supposed heterosexual virility. Yet higher-status men, while they admire the public image of the successful athlete, may also look down on him as a narrow, even atavistic, example of masculinity. For these higher-status men, their earlier sports successes are often status enhancing and serve to link them with other men in ways that continue to exclude women. Their decisions not to pursue athletic careers are equally important signs of their status vis-à-vis other men. Future examinations of the contemporary meaning and importance of sports to men might take as a fruitful point of departure that athletic participation, and sports as public spectacle, serve to provide linkages among men in the project of the domination of women, while at the same time helping to construct and clarify differences and hierarchies among various masculinities.

NOTE

1. "Mitch Harris" is a pseudonym.

References

Baca Zinn, M. 1982. "Chicano Men and Masuclinity." *Journal of Ethnic Studies* 10:29–44.

Bryson, L. 1987. "Sport and the Maintenance of Masculine Hegemony." *Women's Studies International Forum* 10:349–60.

Connell, R. W. 1987. *Gender and Power*. Stanford, CA: Stanford University Press.

——. 1990. "An Iron Man: The Body and Some Contradictions of Hegemonic Masculinity." In *Sport, Men, and the Gender Order: Critical Feminist Perspectives*, edited by M. A. Messner and D. S. Sabo. Champaign, IL: Human Kinetics.

Dunkle, M. 1985. "Minority and Low-Income Girls and Young Women in Athletics." *Equal Play* 5 (Spring-Summer): 12–13.

Edwards, H. 1984. "The Collegiate Athletic Arms Race: Origins and Implications of the 'Rule 48' Controversy." *Journal of Sport and Social Issues* 8:4–22.

Eitzen, D. S. and D. A. Purdy. 1986. "The Academic Preparation and Achievement of Black and White College Athletes." *Journal of Sport and Social Issues* 10:15–29.

Eitzen, D. S. and N. B. Yetman. 1977. "Immune From Racism?" *Civil Rights Digest* 9:3–13.

Farr, K. A. 1988. "Dominance Bonding Through the Good Old Boys Sociability Group." *Sex Roles* 18:259–77.

Franklin, C. W. II. 1984. *The Changing Definition of Masculinity*. New York: Plenum.

——. 1986. "Surviving the Institutional Decimation of Black Males: Causes, Consequences, and Intervention." In *The Making of Masculinities: The New Men's Studies*, edited by H. Brod, pp. 155–70. Winchester, MA: Allen & Unwin.

Gruncau, R. 1983. *Class, Sports, and Social Development*. Amherst: University of Massachusetts Press.

Hall, M. A. (ed.). 1987. "The Gendering of Sport, Leisure, and Physical Education." *Women's Studies International Forum* 10:361–474.

Hare, N. and J. Hare. 1984. *The Endangered Black Family: Coping with the Unisexualization and Coming Extinction of the Black Race.* San Francisco, CA: Black Think Tank.

Hargreaves, J. A. 1986. "Where's the Virtue? Where's the Grace? A Discussion of the Social Production of Gender Through Sport." *Theory, Culture and Society* 3:109–21.

Harris, D. S. and D. S. Eitzen. 1978. "The Consequences of Failure in Sport." *Urban Life* 7:177–88.

Hill, P. and B. Lowe. 1978. "The Inevitable Metathesis of the Retiring Athlete." *International Review of Sport Sociology* 9:5–29.

Leonard, W. M. II and J. M. Reyman. 1988. "The Odds of Attaining Professional Athlete Status: Refining the Computations." *Sociology of Sport Journal* 5:162–69.

Levinson, D. J. 1978. *The Seasons of a Man's Life.* New York: Ballantine.

Majors, R. 1986. "Cool Pose: The Proud Signature of Black Survival." *Changing Men: Issues in Gender, Sex, and Politics* 17:5–6.

——. 1990. "Cool Pose: Black Masculinity in Sports." In *Sport, Men, and the Gender Order: Critical Feminist Perspectives,* edited by M. A. Messner and D. S. Sabo. Champaign, IL: Human Kinetics.

Messner, M. 1987a. "The Meaning of Success: The Athletic Experience and the Development of Male Identity." In *The Making of Masculinities: The New Men's Studies,* edited by H. Brod, pp. 193–209. Winchester, MA: Allen & Unwin.

——. 1987b. "The Life of a Man's Seasons: Male Identity in the Lifecourse of the Athlete." In *Changing Men: New Directions in Research on Men and Masculinity,* edited by M. S. Kimmel, pp. 53–67. Newbury Park, CA: Sage.

Pleck, J. H. 1982. *The Myth of Masculinity.* Cambridge: MIT Press.

Pronger, B. 1990. "Gay Jocks: A Phenomenology of Gay Men in Athletics." In *Sport, Men, and the Gender Order: Critical Feminist Perspectives,* edited by M. A. Messner and D. S. Sabo. Champaign, IL: Human Kinetics.

Rubin, L. B. 1985. *Just Friends: The Role of Friendship in Our Lives.* New York: Harper & Row.

Rudman, W. J. 1986. "The Sport Mystique in Black Culture." *Sociology of Sport Journal* 3:305–19.

Staples, Robert. 1982. *Black Masculinity.* New York: Black Scholar Press.

Theberge, N. 1987. "Sport and Women's Empowerment." *Women's Studies International Forum* 10:387–93.

Wellman, D. 1986. "The New Political Linguistics of Race." *Socialist Review* 87/88: 43–62.

21

TOWARD A THEORY OF DISABILITY AND GENDER

Thomas J. Gerschick

As feminist theory has developed, scholars increasingly have attended to how gender intersects with other social characteristics, including sexual orientation, class, and race and ethnicity, to shape the perceptions, experiences, and life chances of women and men. More recently, activists and scholars have applied feminist insights, theory, and methods to the intersection of disability and gender.[1] However, comprehensive theories about the relationship between disability and gender remain elusive. This essay contributes to the development of such theory by addressing the following questions: How does disability affect the gendering process? How does it affect the experience of gender? How does having a disability affect women's and men's abilities to enact gender? In what ways are the experiences of women and men with disabilities similar and different?[2]

Developing a theory of disability and gender provides insight into the lives of a large number of people. The U.S. Census Bureau estimates that in 1994 more than 20.6 percent of the U.S. population, or about fifty-four million people, had some level of physical or mental disability; for 9.9 percent of the population, or twenty-six million people, this disability was severe (McNeil 1997, 1).[3] After women, then, people with disabilities represent the largest minority population in the United States. Given that the likelihood of developing a disability increases with age, and given that the baby-boom generation is aging, the proportion of the U.S. population with disabilities will likely continue to increase. Moreover, accounting for the experiences of women and men with disabilities makes feminist theories of gender more inclusive, complex, and nuanced. Finally, a theory of the relation between gender and disability provides another tool that people with disabilities can use to understand and challenge their oppression.

In order to contextualize the experiences of women and men with physical disabilities, we need to attend to three sets of social dynamics: the stigma assigned to disability, gender as an interactional process, and the importance of the body to enacting gender.

From: *Signs: Journal of Women in Culture and Society* 2000, vol. 25, no. 4.

To have a disability is not only a physical or mental condition; it is also a social and stigmatized one (Goffman 1963). As anthropologist Robert Murphy observes, "Stigmatization is less a by-product of disability than its substance. The greatest impediment to a person's taking full part in this society are not his physical flaws, but rather the tissue of myths, fears, and misunderstandings that society attaches to them" (1990, 113). Thus, stigmatization is embedded in the daily interactions between people with disabilities and the temporarily able-bodied.[4] In order to enact gender, people with disabilities must be recognized by others as "appropriately" masculine or feminine (West and Zimmerman 1987). Much is at stake in this process, as one's sense of self rests precariously on other's validation or rejection of one's gender performance. Successful enactment bestows status and acceptance; failure invites embarrassment and humiliation (West and Zimmerman 1987). Thus, people with disabilities are engaged in an asymmetrical power relationship with their temporarily able-bodied counterparts.

Bodies are central to achieving recognition as appropriately gendered beings. Bodies operate socially as canvases on which gender is displayed and kinesthetically as the mechanisms by which it is physically enacted. Thus, the bodies of people with diabilities make them vulnerable to being denied recognition as women and men. The type of disability, its visibility, its severity, and whether it is physical or mental in origin mediate the degree to which the body of a person with a disability is socially compromised. For instance, a severe case of the Epstein-Barr virus can lead to disability; however, typically the condition is not readily apparent and, as a consequence, does not trigger stigmatization and devaluation. Conversely, having quadriplegia and using a wheelchair for mobility is highly visual, is perceived to be severe, and frequently elicits invalidation.[5] Moreover, the degree to which a person with a disability is legitimized or delegitimized is context-specific and has both material and nonmaterial consequences.

Disability affects the gendering process in many ways. My current research suggests that the age of onset combines with the type, severity, and visibility of a person's disability to influence the degree to which she or he is taught and subjected to gendered expectations. As C. West and D.H. Zimmerman (1987) note, no one escapes being gendered, including people with disabilities. However, all people do not experience the same degree and type of gender socialization and expectations. For instance, if an infant has a congenital disability and if that disability is severe, as in the case of spina bifida, parents and others in the infant's social world will assign her or him to sex and gender categories but will likely hold fewer gender expectations than for an infant who has a milder disability, such as a visual impairment. Conversely, when the onset of a disability occurs later in a child's life, she or he already will have experienced a significant amount of gender socialization and internalized many gendered expectations. Thus, her or his struggles for social validation as a woman or man will begin with a different level of awareness and commitment to gender. For people with disabilities, then, gendering is conditional.

Furthermore, theories of gender presume that everyone has the same ability to learn, understand, respond to, and be held accountable for gendered expectations. However, for people with a mental disability, these abilities are compromised to different degrees. For example, a person with profound mental retardation may not be able to comprehend many aspects of gender and consequently would largely be beyond the reach of sanctions, while the same does not hold true for a person with a learning disability. Additionally, mental illness can vary individuals' gender enactment. Kay Redfield Jamison (1995), for instance, eloquently describes how her gender performance varied depending on whether she was manic or depressed.

Although women and men with disabilities share similar experiences of devaluation, isolation, marginalization, and discrimination, their fortunes diverge in important ways. Two stigmatized statuses converge in the lives of women with disabilities, further diminishing their already devalued gender status. As M. Fine and A. Asch note, they experience "sexism without the pedestal" (1988, 1). Conversely, for men with physical disabilities, masculine gender privilege collides with the stigmatized status of having a disability, thereby causing status inconsistency, as having a disability erodes much, but not all, masculine privilege.

Although there is much that we do not know regarding the extent of violence that people with disbilities experience, research suggests that children with disabilities are 70 percent more likely to be physically or sexually abused than their able-bodied counterparts (Crosse, Kaye, and Ratnofsky 1993). This abuse is likely to be chronic rather than episodic and to be perpetuated by someone the victim knows, such as a family member or personal attendant (Sobsey and Doe 1991). Furthermore, this abuse is gendered; females with disabilities are more likely to be sexually assaulted, whereas males with disabilities are more likely to experience other forms of physical abuse (Sobsey, Randall, and Parrila 1997). Thus, having a disability exacerbates one of the worst, most direct elements of oppression.

In the contemporary United States, to be perceived as physically attractive is to be socially and sexually desirable. As a result of their invalidated condition, women and men with disabilities are constrained in their opportunities to nurture and to be nurtured, to be loved and to love, and to become parents if they so desire (Fine and Asch 1988, 13). Writer Susan Hannaford explains, "I discovered on becoming officially defined as 'disabled' that I lost my previous identity as a sexually attractive being" (1985, 17). This dynamic, in addition to being mediated by degree, type, and severity of disability, may also be gendered. For example, Hannaford maintains that women are four times as likely as men to divorce after developing a disability (18) and only one-third to one-fourth as likely to marry (76). Fine and Asch (1988, 12–23) provide a range of supporting evidence. Ironically, this may also mean that women with disabilities are less likely than their able-bodied counterparts to be limited by many of the gendered expectations and roles that feminists have challenged.

Women and men with physical disabilities are also economically more vulnerable than nondisabled people. Among people of working age, women with disabilities are less likely to participate in the labor force than both nondisabled women and men with disabilities. This gap varies by gender and the severity of the disability. For instance, according to the U.S. Census Bureau, nondisabled women's labor force participation rate in 1994 was 74.5 percent. For women with a mild disability, the percentage dropped to 68.4 percent, and it plunged to 24.7 percent for women with severe disabilities. For men, the respective numbers were 89.9 percent, 85.1 percent, and 27.8 percent (McNeil 1997). Women with disabilities are also more susceptible to being tracked into low-wage service-sector jobs.

Similarly, gender and the severity of one's disability affect median monthly earnings. Among women 21–64 years of age in 1994, median monthly earnings were $1,470 among those with no disability, $1,200 among those with a nonsevere disability, and $1,000 among those with a severe disability. Comparable figures for men were $2,190, $1,857, and $1,262 (McNeil 1997). As a consequence, women and men with disabilities are poorer than their able-bodied counterparts, and women with disabilities fare worst of all (LaPlante et al. 1999).

In brief summary, disability has a profound effect on the material and nonmaterial experience of gender. Yet, there is still much we do not know about this dynamic: How and under what conditions do social characteristics such as race, class, age, and sexual orientation further mediate the relationship between gender and disability? How does gender affect the experience of disability? How do the dynamics identified in this essay vary by culture in a global context? How might the stigmatization and marginalization that women and men with disabilities face contribute to the creation of alternative gender identities? As we enter a new millennium, I encourage the readers . . . to take up these questions and to add further inquiries of their own so that we can soon develop more comprehensive theories about the relationship between disability and gender.

NOTES

1. See Fine and Asch 1988; Hillyer 1993; Morris 1993a, 1993b; Gerschick and Miller 1995; Wendell 1996, 1997; Gerschick 1998.

2. Space limitations necessitate that I focus on disabilities primarily in the United States in this essay. See Lynn and Wilkinson 1993 for a number of international perspectives on women and disability.

3. McNeil 1997 provides Census Bureau definitions and measures of disability.

4. I intentionally use the term *temporarily able-bodied* to highlight the facts that aging is often disabling and that many of us will develop a disability during our lifetime. In 1994,

e.g., the disability rate among the U.S. population ages 65–79 years was 47.3 percent; for those ages 80 years and older, it rose to 71.5 percent (McNeil 1997).

5. Of course, the degree to which one's body is compromised is also affected by other social characteristics, including race and ethnicity, social class, age and sexual orientation. Unfortunately, exploring these other characteristics is beyond the scope of this essay.

References

Crosse, S. B., E. Kaye, and A. C. Ratnofsky. 1993. *Report on the Maltreatment of Children with Disabilities.* Washington, D.C.: National Center on Child Abuse and Neglect.

Fine, M., and A. Asch. 1988. "Introduction: Beyond Pedestals." In *Women with Disabilities: Essays in Psychology, Culture, and Politics,* ed. M. Fine and A. Asch, 1–37. Philadelphia: Temple University Press.

Gerschick, T. J. 1998. "Sisyphus in a Wheelchair: Men with Physical Disabilities Confront Gender Domination." In *Everyday Inequalities: Critical Inquiries,* ed. J. O'Brien and J. A. Howard, 189–211. Oxford: Blackwell.

Gerschick, T. J., and A. S. Miller. 1995. "Coming to Terms: Masculinity and Physical Disability." In *Men's Health and Illness: Gender, Power, and the Body,* 183–204. Thousand Oaks, Calif.: Sage.

Goffman, E. 1963. *Stigma: Notes on the Management of Spoiled Identity.* New York: Touchstone.

Hannaford, S. 1985. *Living Outside Inside: A Disabled Woman's Experience.* Berkeley, Calif.: Canterbury.

Hillyer, B. 1993. *Feminism and Disability.* Norman: University of Oklahoma Press.

Jamison, K. R. 1995. *An Unquiet Mind.* New York: Knopf.

LaPlante, M. P., J. Kennedy, H. S. Kaye, and B. L. Wenger. 1999. *Disability and Employment.* Available on-line at http://dsc.ucsf.edu/default.html.

Lynn, M., and S. Wilkinson, eds. 1993. "Women and Disability," special issue of *Canadian Woman Studies,* vol. 13, no. 4.

McNeil, J. M. 1997. *Americans with Disabilities, 1994–95.* Current Population Report No. P70-61. Washington, D.C.: Bureau of the Census.

Morris, J. 1993a. "Feminism and Disability." *Feminist Review,* no. 43 (Spring): 57–70.

———. 1993b. "Gender and Disability." In *Disabling Barriers—Enabling Environments,* ed. J. Swain, v: Finkelstein, S. French, and M. Oliver, 85–92. Thousand Oaks, Calif.: Sage.

Murphy, R. F. 1990. *The Body Silent.* New York: Norton.

Sobsey, D., and T. Doe. 1991. "Patterns of Sexual Abuse and Assault." *Sexuality and Disability* 9(3): 243–59.

Sobsey, D., W. Randall, and R. K. Parrila. 1997. "Gender Differences in Abused Children with and without Disabilities." *Child Abuse and Neglect* 21(8):707–20.

Wendell, S. 1996. *The Rejected Body: Feminist Philosophical Reflections on Disability.* New York: Routledge.

———. 1997. "Toward a Feminist Theory of Disability." In *The Disability Studies Reader,* ed. L. Davis, 260–78. New York: Routledge.

West, C., and D. H. Zimmerman. 1987. "Doing Gender." *Gender & Society* 1(2):125–51.

ETHNICITY AND NATIONALITY

22

"IS THIS A WHITE COUNTRY, OR WHAT?"

Lillian B. Rubin

"They're letting all these coloreds come in and soon there won't be any place left for white people," broods Tim Walsh, a thirty-three-year-old white construction worker. "It makes you wonder: Is this a white country, or what?"

It's a question that nags at white America, one perhaps that's articulated most often and most clearly by the men and women of the working class. For it's they who feel most vulnerable, who have suffered the economic contractions of recent decades most keenly, who see the new immigrants most clearly as direct competitors for their jobs.

It's not whites alone who stew about immigrants. Native-born blacks, too, fear the newcomers nearly as much as whites—and for the same economic reasons. But for whites the issue is compounded by race, by the fact that the newcomers are primarily people of color. For them, therefore, their economic anxieties have combined with the changing face of America to create a profound uneasiness about immigration—a theme that was sounded by nearly 90 percent of the whites I met, even by those who are themselves first-generation, albeit well-assimilated, immigrants.

Sometimes they spoke about this in response to my questions; equally often the subject of immigration arose spontaneously as people gave voice to their concerns. But because the new immigrants are dominantly people of color, the discourse was almost always cast in terms of race as well as immigration, with the talk slipping from immigration to race and back again as if these are not two separate phenomena. "If we keep letting all them foreigners in, pretty soon there'll be more of them than us and then what will this country be like?" Tim's wife, Mary Anne, frets. "I mean, this is *our* country, but the way things are going, white people will be the minority in our own country. Now does that make any sense?"

Such fears are not new. Americans have always worried about the strangers who came to our shores, fearing that they would corrupt our society, dilute our culture, debase our values. So I remind Mary Anne, "When your ancestors came here, people also thought we were allowing too many foreigners into the country. Yet those earlier immigrants were successfully integrated into the American society. What's different now?"

"Oh, it's different, all right," she replies without hesitation. "When my people came, the immigrants were all white. That makes a big difference." . . .

Listening to Mary Anne's words I was reminded again how little we Americans look to history for its lessons, how impoverished is our historical memory. For, in fact, being white didn't make "a big difference" for many of those earlier immigrants. The dark-skinned Italians and the eastern European Jews who came in the late nineteenth and early twentieth centuries didn't look very white to the fair-skinned Americans who were here then. Indeed, the same people we now call white—Italians, Jews, Irish—were seen as another race at that time. Not black or Asian, it's true, but an alien other, a race apart, although one that didn't have a clearly defined name. Moreover, the racist fears and fantasies of native-born Americans were far less contained then than they are now, largely because there were few social constraints on their expression.

When, during the nineteenth century, for example, some Italians were taken for blacks and lynched in the South, the incidents passed virtually unnoticed. And if Mary Anne and Tim Walsh, both of Irish ancestry, had come to this country during the great Irish immigration of that period, they would have found themselves defined as an inferior race and described with the same language that was used to characterize blacks: "low-browed and savage, grovelling and bestial, lazy and wild, simian and sensual."[1] Not only during that period but for a long time afterward as well, the U.S. Census Bureau counted the Irish as a distinct and separate group, much as it does today with the category it labels "Hispanic."

But there are two important differences between then and now, differences that can be summed up in a few words: the economy and race. Then, a growing industrial economy meant that there were plenty of jobs for both immigrant and native workers, something that can't be said for the contracting economy in which we live today. True, the arrival of the immigrants, who were more readily exploitable than native workers, put Americans at a disadvantage and created discord between the two groups. Nevertheless, work was available for both.

Then, too, the immigrants—no matter how they were labeled, no matter how reviled they may have been—were ultimately assimilable, if for no other reason than that they were white. As they began to lose their alien ways, it became possible for native Americans to see in the white ethnics of yesteryear a reflection of themselves. Once this shift in perception occurred, it was possible for the nation to incorporate them, to take them in, chew them up, digest them, and spit them out as Americans—with subcultural variations not always to the liking of those who hoped to control the manners and mores of the day, to be sure, but still recognizably white Americans.

Today's immigrants, however, are the racial other in a deep and profound way. . . . And integrating masses of people of color into a society where race conciousness lies at the very heart of our central nervous system raises a whole new set of anxieties and tensions. . . .

The increased visibility of other racial groups has focused whites more self-consciously than ever on their own racial identification. Until the new immigration shifted the complexion of the land so perceptibly, whites didn't think of themselves as white in the same way that Chinese know they're Chinese and African-Americans know they're black. Being white was simply a fact of life, one that didn't require any public statement, since it was the definitive social value against which all others were measured. "It's like everything's changed and I don't know what happened," complains Marianne Bardolino. "All of a sudden you have to be thinking all the time about these race things. I don't remember growing up thinking about being white like I think about it now. I'm not saying I didn't know there was coloreds and whites; it's just that I didn't go along thinking, *Gee, I'm a white person.* I never thought about it at all. But now with all the different colored people around, you have to think about it because they're thinking about it all the time."

"You say you feel pushed now to think about being white, but I'm not sure I understand why. What's changed?" I ask.

"I told you," she replies quickly, a small smile covering her impatience with my question. "It's because they think about what they are, and they want things their way, so now I have to think about what I am and what's good for me and my kids." She pauses briefly to let her thoughts catch up with her tongue, then continues. "I mean, if somebody's always yelling at you about being black or Asian or something, then it makes you think about being white. Like, they want the kids in school to learn about their culture, so then I think about being white and being Italian and say: What about my culture? If they're going to teach about theirs, what about mine?"

To which America's racial minorities respond with bewilderment. "I don't understand what white people want," says Gwen Tomalson. "They say if black kids are going to learn about black culture in school, then white people want their kids to learn about white culture. I don't get it. What do they think kids have been learning about all these years? It's all about white people and how they live and what they accomplished. When I was in school you wouldn't have thought black people existed for all our books ever said about us."

As for the charge that they're "thinking about race all the time," as Marianne Bardolino complains, people of color insist that they're forced into it by a white world that never lets them forget. "If you're Chinese, you can't forget it, even if you want to, because there's always something that reminds you," Carol Kwan's husband, Andrew, remarks tartly. "I mean, if Chinese kids get good grades and get into the university, everybody's worried and you read about it in the papers."

While there's little doubt that racial anxieties are at the center of white concerns, our historic nativism also plays a part in escalating white alarm. The new immigrants bring with them a language and an ethnic culture that's vividly expressed wherever they congregate. And it's this also, the constant reminder of an alien presence from which whites are excluded, that's so troublesome to them.

The nativist impulse isn't, of course, given to the white working class alone. But for those in the upper reaches of the class and status hierarchy—those whose children go to private schools, whose closest contact with public transportation is the taxi cab—the immigrant population supplies a source of cheap labor, whether as nannies for their children, maids in their households, or workers in their businesses. They may grouse and complain that "nobody speaks English anymore," just as working-class people do. But for the people who use immigrant labor, legal or illegal, there's a payoff for the inconvenience—a payoff that doesn't exist for the families in this study but that sometimes costs them dearly. For while it may be true that American workers aren't eager for many of the jobs immigrants are willing to take, it's also true that the presence of a large immigrant population—especially those who come from developing countries where living standards are far below our own—helps to make these jobs undesirable by keeping wages depressed well below what most American workers are willing to accept. . . .

It's not surprising, therefore, that working-class women and men speak so angrily about the recent influx of immigrants. They not only see their jobs and their way of life threatened, they feel bruised and assaulted by an environment that seems suddenly to have turned color and in which they feel like strangers in their own land. So they chafe and complain: "They come here to take advantage of us, but they don't really want to learn our ways," Beverly Sowell, a thirty-three-year old white electronics assembler, grumbles irritably. "They live different than us; it's like another world how they live. And they're so clannish. They keep to themselves, and they don't even *try* to learn English. You go on the bus these days and you might as well be in a foreign country; everybody's talking some other language, you know, Chinese or Spanish or something. Lots of them have been here a long time, too, but they don't care; they just want to take what they can get."

But their complaints reveal an interesting paradox, an illuminating glimpse into the contradictions that beset native-born Americans in their relations with those who seek refuge here. On the one hand, they scorn the immigrants; on the other, they protest because they "keep to themselves." It's the same contradiction that dominates black-white relations. Whites refuse to integrate blacks but are outraged when they stop knocking at the door, when they move to sustain the separation on their own terms—in black theme houses on campuses, for example, or in the newly developing black middle-class suburbs.

I wondered, as I listened to Beverly Sowell and others like her, why the same people who find the lifeways and languages of our foreign-born population offensive also care whether they "keep to themselves."

"Because like I said, they just shouldn't, that's all," Beverly says stubbornly. "If they're going to come here, they should be willing to learn our ways—you know what I mean, be real Americans. That's what my grandparents did, and that's what they should do."

"But your grandparents probably lived in an immigrant neighborhood when they first came here, too," I remind her.

"It was different," she insists. "I don't know why; it was. They wanted to be Americans; these here people now, I don't think they do. They just want to take advantage of this country. . . .

"Everything's changed, and it doesn't make sense. Maybe you get it, but I don't. We can't take care of our own people and we keep bringing more and more foreigners in. Look at all the homeless. Why do we need more people here when our own people haven't got a place to sleep?"

"Why do we need more people here?"—a question Americans have asked for two centuries now. Historically, efforts to curb immigration have come during economic downturns, which suggests that when times are good, when American workers feel confident about their future, they're likely to be more generous in sharing their good fortune with foreigners. But when the economy falters, as it did in the 1990s, and workers worry about having to compete for jobs with people whose standard of living is well below their own, resistance to immigration rises. "Don't get me wrong; I've got nothing against these people," Tim Walsh demurs. "But they don't talk English, and they're used to a lot less, so they can work for less money than guys like me can. I see it all the time; they get hired and some white guy gets left out."

It's this confluence of forces—the racial and cultural diversity of our new immigrant population; the claims on the resources of the nation now being made by those minorities who, for generations, have called America their home; the failure of some of our basic institutions to serve the needs of our people; the contracting economy, which threatens the mobility aspirations of working-class families—all these have come together to leave white workers feeling as if everyone else is getting a piece of the action while they get nothing. "I feel like white people are left out in the cold," protests Diane Johnson, a twenty-eight-year-old white single mother who believes she lost a job as a bus driver to a black woman. "First it's the blacks; now it's all those other colored people, and it's like everything always goes their way. It seems like a white person doesn't have a chance anymore. It's like the squeaky wheel gets the grease, and they've been squeaking and we haven't," she concludes angrily.

Until recently, whites didn't need to think about having to "squeak"—at least not specifically as whites. They have, of course, organized and squeaked at various times in the past—sometimes as ethnic groups, sometimes as workers. But not as whites. As whites they have been the dominant group, the favored ones, the ones who could count on getting the job when people of color could not. Now suddenly there are others—not just individual others but identifiable groups, people who share a history, a language, a culture, even a color—who lay claim to some of the rights and privileges that formerly had been labeled "for whites only." And whites react as if they've been betrayed, as if a sacred promise has been broken. They're white, aren't they? They're *real* Americans, aren't they? This is their country, isn't it?

The answers to these questions used to be relatively unambiguous. But not anymore. Being white no longer automatically assures dominance in the politics of a multiracial society. Ethnic group politics, however, has a long and fruitful history. As whites sought a social and political base on which to stand, therefore, it was natural and logical to reach back to their ethnic past. Then they, too, could be "something"; they also would belong to a group; they would have a name, a history, a culture, and a voice. "Why is it only the blacks or Mexicans or Jews that are 'something'?" asks Tim Walsh. "I'm Irish, isn't that something, too? Why doesn't that count?"

In reclaiming their ethnic roots, whites can recount with pride the tribulations and transcendence of their ancestors and insist that others take their place in the line from which they have only recently come. "My people had a rough time, too. But nobody gave us anything, so why do we owe them something? Let them pull their share like the rest of us had to do," says Al Riccardi, a twenty-nine-year-old white taxi driver.

From there it's only a short step to the conviction that those who don't progress up that line are hampered by nothing more than their own inadequacies or, worse yet, by their unwillingness to take advantage of the opportunities offered them. "Those people, they're hollering all the time about discrimination," Al continues, without defining who "those people" are. "Maybe once a long time ago that was true, but not now. The problem is that a lot of those people are lazy. There's plenty of opportunities, but you've got to be willing to work hard."

He stops a moment, as if listening to his own words, then continues, "Yeah, yeah, I know there's a recession on and lots of people don't have jobs. But it's different with some of those people. They don't really want to work, because if they did, there wouldn't be so many of them selling drugs and getting in all kinds of trouble."

"You keep talking about 'those people' without saying who you mean," I remark.

"Aw c'mon, you know who I'm talking about," he says, his body shifting uneasily in his chair. "It's mostly the black people, but the Spanish ones, too."

In reality, however, it's a no-win situation for America's people of color, whether immigrant or native born. For the industriousness of the Asians comes in for nearly as much criticism as the alleged laziness of other groups. When blacks don't make it, it's because, whites like Al Riccardi insist, their culture doesn't teach respect for family; because they're hedonistic, lazy, stupid, and/or criminally inclined. But when Asians demonstrate their ability to overcome the obstacles of an alien language and culture, when the Asian family seems to be the repository of our most highly regarded traditional values, white hostility doesn't disappear. It just changes its form. Then the accomplishments of Asians, the speed with which they move up the economic ladder, aren't credited to their superior culture, diligence, or intelligence—even when these are granted—but to the fact that they're "single minded," "untrustworthy," "clannish drones," "narrow people" who raise children who are insufficiently "well rounded."[2] . . .

Not surprisingly, as competition increases, the various minority groups often are at war among themselves as they press their own particular claims, fight over turf, and compete for an ever-shrinking piece of the pie. In several African-American communities, where Korean shopkeepers have taken the place once held by Jews, the confrontations have been both wrenching and tragic. A Korean grocer in Los Angeles shoots and kills a fifteen-year-old black girl for allegedly trying to steal some trivial item from the store.[3] From New York City to Berkeley, California, African-Americans boycott Korean shop owners who, they charge, invade their neighborhoods, take their money, and treat them disrespectfully.[4] But painful as these incidents are for those involved, they are only symptoms of a deeper malaise in both communities— the contempt and distrust in which the Koreans hold their African-American neighbors, and the rage of blacks as they watch these new immigrants surpass them.

Latino-black conflict also makes headlines when, in the aftermath of the riots in South Central Los Angeles, the two groups fight over who will get the lion's share of the jobs to rebuild the neighborhood. Blacks, insisting that they're being discriminated against, shut down building projects that don't include them in satisfactory numbers. And indeed, many of the jobs that formerly went to African-Americans are now being taken by Latino workers. In an article entitled "Black vs. Brown," Jack Miles, an editorial writer for the *Los Angeles Times*, reports that "janitorial firms serving downtown Los Angeles have almost entirely replaced their unionized black work force with non-unionized immigrants."[5] . . .

But the disagreements among America's racial minorities are of little interest or concern to most white working-class families. Instead of conflicting groups, they see one large mass of people of color, all of them making claims that endanger their own precarious place in the world. It's this perception that has led some white ethnics to believe that reclaiming their ethnicity alone is not enough, that so long as they remain in their separate and distinct groups, their power will be limited. United, however, they can become a formidable countervailing force, one that can stand fast against the threat posed by minority demands. But to come together solely as whites would diminish their impact and leave them open to the charge that their real purpose is simply to retain the privileges of whiteness. A dilemma that has been resolved, at least for some, by the birth of a new entity in the history of American ethnic groups—the "European-Americans."[6] . . .

At the University of California at Berkeley, for example, white students and their faculty supporters insisted that the recently adopted multicultural curriculum include a unit of study of European-Americans. At Queens College in New York City, where white ethnic groups retain a more distinct presence, Italian-American students launched a successful suit to win recognition as a disadvantaged minority and gain the entitlements accompanying that status, including special units of Italian-American studies.

White high school students, too, talk of feeling isolated and, being less sophisticated and wary than their older sisters and brothers, complain quite openly that there's no acceptable and legitimate way for them to acknowledge a white identity. "There's all these things for all the different ethnicities, you know, like clubs for black kids and Hispanic kids, but there's nothing for me and my friends to join," Lisa Marshall, a sixteen-year-old white high school student, explains with exasperation. "They won't let us have a white club because that's supposed to be racist. So we figured we'd just have to call it something else, you know, some ethnic thing, like Euro-Americans. Why not? They have African-American clubs."

Ethnicity, then, often becomes a cover for " white," not necessarily because these students are racist but because racial identity is now such a prominent feature of the discourse in our social world. In a society where racial consciousness is so high, how else can whites define themselves in ways that connect them to a community and, at the same time, allow them to deny their racial antagonisms?

Ethnicity and race—separate phenomena that are now inextricably entwined. Incorporating newcomers has never been easy, as our history of controversy and violence over immigration tells us.[7] But for the first time, the new immigrants are also people of color, which means that they tap both the nativist and racist impulses that are so deeply a part of American life. As in the past, however, the fear of foreigners, the revulsion against their strange customs and seemingly unruly ways, is only part of the reason for the anti-immigrant attitudes that are increasingly being expressed today. For whatever xenophobic suspicions may arise in modern America, economic issues play a critical role in stirring them up.

NOTES

1. David R. Roediger, *The Wages of Whiteness* (New York: Verso, 1991), p. 133.

2. These were, and often still are, the commonly held stereotypes about Jews. Indeed, the Asian immigrants are often referred to as "the new Jews."

3. Soon Ja Du, the Korean grocer who killed fifteen-year-old Latasha Harlins, was found guilty of voluntary manslaughter and sentenced to four hundred hours of community service, a $500 fine, reimbursement of funeral costs to the Harlins family, and five years' probation.

4. The incident in Berkeley didn't happen in the black ghetto, as most of the others did. There, the Korean grocery store is near the University of California campus, and the woman involved in the incident is an African-American university student who was Maced by the grocer after an argument over a penny.

5. Jack Miles, "Blacks vs. Browns," *Atlantic Monthly* (October 1992), pp. 41–68.

6. For an interesting analysis of what he calls "the transformation of ethnicity," see Richard D. Alba, *Ethnic Identity* (New Haven, CT: Yale University Press, 1990).

7. In the past, many of those who agitated for a halt to immigration were immigrants or native-born children of immigrants. The same often is true today. As anti-immigrant sentiment grows, at least some of those joining the fray are relatively recent arrivals. One man in this study, for example—a fifty-two-year-old immigrant from Hungary— is one of the leaders of an anti-immigration group in the city where he lives.

References

Alba, Richard D. *Ethnic Identity.* New Haven: Yale University Press, 1990.

Roediger, David R. *The Wages of Whiteness.* New York: Verso, 1991.

23

OPTIONAL ETHNICITIES
For Whites Only?

Mary C. Waters

What does it mean to talk about ethnicity as an option for an individual? To argue that an individual has some degree of choice in their ethnic identity flies in the face of the commonsense notion of ethnicity many of us believe

From Silvia Pedraza and Rubén G. Rumbaut, eds., *Origins and Destinies: Immigration, Race and Ethnicity in America* (Belmont, CA: Wadsworth, 1996), pp. 444–54. Reprinted by permission.

in—that one's ethnic identity is a fixed characteristic, reflective of blood ties and given at birth. However, social scientists who study ethnicity have long concluded that while ethnicity is based on a *belief* in a common ancestry, ethnicity is primarily a *social* phenomenon, not a biological one (Alba 1985, 1990; Barth 1969; Weber [1921] 1968, p. 389). The belief that members of an ethnic group have that they share a common ancestry may not be a fact. There is a great deal of change in ethnic identities across generations through intermarriage, changing allegiances, and changing social categories. There is also a much larger amount of change in the identities of individuals over their lives than is commonly believed. While most people are aware of the phenomenon known as "passing"—people raised as one race who change at some point and claim a different race as their identity—there are similar life course changes in ethnicity that happen all the time and are not given the same degree of attention as "racial passing."

White Americans of European ancestry can be described as having a great deal of choice in terms of their ethnic identities. The two major types of options White Americans can exercise are (1) the option of whether to claim any specific ancestry, or to just be "White" or American, [Lieberson (1985) called these people "unhyphenated Whites"] and (2) the choice of which of their European ancestries to choose to include in their description of their own identities. In both cases, the option of choosing how to present yourself on surveys and in everyday social interactions exists for Whites because of social changes and societal conditions that have created a great deal of social mobility, immigrant assimilation, and political and economic power for Whites in the United States. Specifically, the option of being able to not claim any ethnic identity exists for Whites of European background in the United States because they are the majority group—in terms of holding political and social power, as well as being a numerical majority. The option of choosing among different ethnicities in their family backgrounds exists because the degree of discrimination and social distance attached to specific European backgrounds has diminished over time. . . .

SYMBOLIC ETHNICITIES FOR WHITE AMERICANS

What do these ethnic identities mean to people and why do they cling to them rather than just abandoning the tie and calling themselves American? My own field research with suburban Whites in California and Pennsylvania found that later-generation descendants of European origin maintain what are called "symbolic ethnicities." Symbolic ethnicity is a term coined by Herbert Gans (1979) to refer to ethnicity that is individualistic in nature and without real social cost for the individual. These symbolic identifications are essentially leisure-time activities, rooted in nuclear family traditions and reinforced by the voluntary enjoyable aspects of being ethnic (Waters 1990).

Richard Alba (1990) also found later-generation Whites in Albany, New York, who chose to keep a tie with an ethnic identity because of the enjoyable and voluntary aspects to those identities, along with the feelings of specialness they entailed. An example of symbolic ethnicity is individuals who identify as Irish, for example, on occasions such as Saint Patrick's Day, on family holidays, or for vacations. They do not usually belong to Irish American organizations, live in Irish neighborhoods, work in Irish jobs, or marry other Irish people. The symbolic meaning of being Irish American can be constructed by individuals from mass media images, family traditions, or other intermittent social activities. In other words, for later-generation White ethnics, ethnicity is not something that influences their lives unless they want it to. In the world of work and school and neighborhood, individuals do not have to admit to being ethnic unless they choose to. And for an increasing number of European-origin individuals whose parents and grandparents have intermarried, the ethnicity they claim is largely a matter of personal choice as they sort through all of the possible combinations of groups in their genealogies. . . .

RACE RELATIONS AND SYMBOLIC ETHNICITY

However much symbolic ethnicity is without cost for the individual, there is a cost associated with symbolic ethnicity for the society. That is because symbolic ethnicities of the type described here are confined to White Americans of European origin. Black Americans, Hispanic Americans, Asian Americans, and American Indians do not have the option of a symbolic ethnicity at present in the United States. For all of the ways in which ethnicity does not matter for White Americans, it does matter for non-Whites. Who your ancestors are does affect your choice of spouse, where you live, what job you have, who your friends are, and what your chances are for success in American society, if those ancestors happen not to be from Europe. The reality is that White ethnics have a lot more choice and room for maneuver than they themselves think they do. The situation is very different for members of racial minorities, whose lives are strongly influenced by their race or national origin regardless of how much they may choose not to identify themselves in terms of their ancestries.

When White Americans learn the stories of how their grandparents and great-grandparents triumphed in the United States over adversity, they are usually told in terms of their individual efforts and triumphs. The important role of labor unions and other organized political and economic actors in their social and economic successes are left out of the story in favor of a generational story of individual Americans rising up against communitarian, Old World intolerance, and New World resistance. As a result, the "individualized" voluntary, cultural view of ethnicity for Whites is what is remembered.

One important implication of these identities is that they tend to be very individualistic. There is a tendency to view valuing diversity in a pluralist environment as equating all groups. The symbolic ethnic tends to think that all groups are equal; everyone has a background that is their right to celebrate and pass on to their children. This leads to the conclusion that all identities are equal and all identities in some sense are interchangeable—"I'm Italian American, you're Polish American. I'm Irish American, you're African American." The important thing is to treat people as individuals and all equally. However, this assumption ignores the very big difference between an individualistic symbolic ethnic identity and a socially enforced and imposed racial identity.

My favorite example of how this type of thinking can lead to some severe misunderstandings between people of different backgrounds is from the *Dear Abby* advice column. A few years back a person wrote in who had asked an acquaintance of Asian background where his family was from. His acquaintance answered that this was a rude question and he would not reply. The bewildered White asked Abby why it was rude, since he thought it was a sign of respect to wonder where people were from, and he certainly would not mind anyone asking HIM about where his family was from. Abby asked her readers to write in to say whether it was rude to ask about a person's ethnic background. She reported that she got a large response, that most non-Whites thought it was a sign of disrespect, and Whites thought it was flattering:

> Dear Abby,
> I am 100 percent American and because I am of Asian ancestry I am often asked "What are you?" It's not the personal nature of this question that bothers me, it's the question itself. This query seems to question my very humanity. "What am I? Why I am a person like everyone else!"
>
> Signed, A REAL AMERICAN
>
> Dear Abby,
> Why do people resent being asked what they are? The Irish are so proud of being Irish, they tell you before you even ask. Tip O'Neill has never tried to hide his Irish ancestry.
>
> Signed, JIMMY.
> (Reprinted by permission of Universal Press Syndicate)

In this exchange Jimmy cannot understand why Asians are not as happy to be asked about their ethnicity as he is, because he understands his ethnicity and theirs to be separate but equal. Everyone has to come from somewhere—his family from Ireland, another's family from Asia—each has a history and each should be proud of it. But the reason he cannot understand the perspective of the Asian American is that all ethnicities are not equal; all are not symbolic, costless, and voluntary. When White Americans equate their own symbolic ethnicities with the socially enforced identities of non-White Americans, they obscure the fact that the experiences of Whites and non-Whites have been qualitatively different in the United States and that the current identities of individuals partly reflect that unequal history.

In the next section I describe how relations between Black and White students on college campuses reflect some of these asymmetries in the understanding of what a racial or ethnic identity means. While I focus on Black and White students in the following discussion, you should be aware that the myriad other groups in the United States—Mexican Americans, American Indians, Japanese Americans—all have some degree of social and individual influences on their identities, which reflect the group's social and economic history and present circumstance.

RELATIONS ON COLLEGE CAMPUSES

Both Black and White students face the task of developing their race and ethnic identities. Sociologists and psychologists note that at the time people leave home and begin to live independently from their parents, often ages eighteen to twenty-two, they report a heightened sense of racial and ethnic identity as they sort through how much of their beliefs and behaviors are idiosyncratic to their families and how much are shared with other people. It is not until one comes in close contact with many people who are different from oneself that individuals realize the ways in which their backgrounds may influence their individual personality. This involves coming into contact with people who are different in terms of their ethnicity, class, religion, region, and race. For White students, the ethnicity they claim is more often than not a symbolic one—with all of the voluntary, enjoyable, and intermittent characteristics I have described above.

Black students at the university are also developing identities through interactions with others who are different from them. Their identity development is more complicated than that of Whites because of the added element of racial discrimination and racism, along with the "ethnic" developments of finding others who share their background. Thus Black students have the positive attraction of being around other Black students who share some cultural elements, as well as the need to band together with other students in a reactive and oppositional way in the face of racist incidents on campus.

Colleges and universities across the country have been increasing diversity among their student bodies in the last few decades. This has led in many cases to strained relations among students from different racial and ethnic backgrounds. The 1980s and 1990s produced a great number of racial incidents and high racial tensions on campuses. While there were a number of racial incidents that were due to bigotry, unlawful behavior, and violent or vicious attacks, much of what happens among students on campuses involves a low level of tension and awkwardness in social interactions.

Many Black students experience racism personally for the first time on campus. The upper-middle-class students from White suburbs were often isolated enough that their presence was not threatening to racists in their high schools. Also, their class background was known by their residence and this may have prevented attacks being directed at them. Often Black students at the university who begin talking with other students and recognizing racial slights will remember incidents that happened to them earlier that they might not have thought were related to race.

Black college students across the country experience a sizeable number of incidents that are clearly the result of racism. Many of the most blatant ones that occur between students are the result of drinking. Sometimes late at night, drunken groups of White students coming home from parties will yell slurs at single Black students on the street. The other types of incidents that happen include being singled out for special treatment by employees, such as being followed when shopping at the campus bookstore, or going to the art museum with your class and the guard stops you and asks for your I.D. Others involve impersonal encounters on the street—being called a nigger by a truck driver while crossing the street, or seeing old ladies clutch their pocketbooks and shake in terror as you pass them on the street. For the most part these incidents are not specific to the university environment, they are the types of incidents middle-class Blacks face every day throughout American society, and they have been documented by sociologists (Feagin 1991).

In such a climate, however, with students experiencing these types of incidents and talking with each other about them, Black students do experience a tension and a feeling of being singled out. It is unfair that this is part of their college experience and not that of White students. Dealing with incidents like this, or the ever-present threat of such incidents, is an ongoing developmental task for Black students that takes energy, attention, and strength of character. It should be clearly understood that this is an asymmetry in the "college experience" for Black and White students. It is one of the unfair aspects of life that results from living in a society with ongoing racial prejudice and discrimination. It is also very understandable that it makes some students angry at the unfairness of it all, even if there is no one to blame specifically. It is also very troubling because, while most Whites do not create these incidents, some do, and it is never clear until you know someone well whether they are the type of person who could do something like this. So one of the reactions of Black students to these incidents is to band together.

In some sense then, as Blauner (1992) has argued, you can see Black students coming together on campus as both an "ethnic" pull of wanting to be together to share common experiences and community, and a "racial" push of banding together defensively because of perceived rejection and tension from Whites. In this way the ethnic identities of Black students are in some sense similar to, say, Korean students wanting to be together to share experiences.

And it is an ethnicity that is generally much stronger than, say, Italian Americans. But for Koreans who come together there is generally a definition of themselves as "different from" Whites. For Blacks reacting to exclusion, there is a tendency for the coming together to involve both being "different from" but also "opposed to" Whites.

The anthropologist John Ogbu (1990) has documented the tendency of minorities in a variety of societies around the world, who have experienced severe blocked mobility for long periods of time, to develop such oppositional identities. An important component of having such an identity is to describe others of your group who do not join in the group solidarity as devaluing and denying their very core identity. This is why it is not common for successful Asians to be accused by others of "acting White" in the United States, but it is quite common for such a term to be used by Blacks and Latinos. The oppositional component of a Black identity also explains how Black people can question whether others are acting "Black enough." On campus, it explains some of the intense pressures felt by Black students who do not make their racial identity central and who choose to hang out primarily with non-Blacks. This pressure from the group, which is partly defining itself by not being White, is exacerbated by the fact that race is a physical marker in American society. No one immediately notices the Jewish students sitting together in the dining hall, or the one Jewish student sitting surrounded by non-Jews, or the Texan sitting with the Californians, but everyone notices the Black student who is or is not at the "Black table" in the cafeteria.

An example of the kinds of misunderstandings that can arise because of different understandings of the meanings and implications of symbolic versus oppositional identities concerns questions students ask one another in the dorms about personal appearances and customs. A very common type of interaction in the dorm concerns questions Whites ask Blacks about their hair. Because Whites tend to know little about Blacks, and Blacks know a lot about Whites, there is a general asymmetry in the level of curiosity people have about one another. Whites, as the numerical majority, have had little contact with Black culture; Blacks, especially those who are in college, have had to develop bicultural skills—knowledge about the social worlds of both Whites and Blacks. Miscommunication and hurt feelings about White students' questions about Black students' hair illustrate this point. One of the things that happens freshman year is that White students are around Black students as they fix their hair. White students are generally quite curious about Black students' hair— they have basic questions such as how often Blacks wash their hair, how they get it straightened or curled, what products they use on their hair, how they comb it, etc. Whites often wonder to themselves whether they should ask these questions. One thought experiment Whites perform is to ask themselves whether a particular question would upset them. Adopting the "do unto others" rule, they ask themselves, "If a Black person was curious about my hair would I get upset?" The answer usually is "No, I would be happy to tell them."

Another example is an Italian American student wondering to herself, "Would I be upset if someone asked me about calamari?" The answer is no, so she asks her Black roommate about collard greens, and the roommate explodes with an angry response such as, "Do you think all Black people eat watermelon too?" Note that if this Italian American knew her friend was Trinidadian American and asked about peas and rice the situation would be more similar and would not necessarily ignite underlying tensions.

Like the debate in *Dear Abby*, these innocent questions are likely to lead to resentment. The issue of stereotypes about Black Americans and the assumption that all Blacks are alike and have the same stereotypical cultural traits has more power to hurt or offend a Black person than vice versa. The innocent questions about Black hair also bring up a number of asymmetries between the Black and White experience. Because Blacks tend to have more knowledge about Whites than vice versa, there is not an even exchange going on, the Black freshman is likely to have fewer basic questions about his White roommate than his White roommate has about him. Because of the differences historically in the group experiences of Blacks and Whites there are some connotations to Black hair that don't exist about White hair. (For instance, is straightening your hair a form of assimilation, do some people distinguish between women having "good hair" and "bad hair" in terms of beauty and how is that related to looking "White"?) Finally, even a Black freshman who cheerfully disregards or is unaware that there are these asymmetries will soon slam into another asymmetry if she willingly answers every innocent question asked of her. In a situation where Blacks make up only 10 percent of the student body, if every non-Black needs to be educated about hair, she will have to explain it to nine other students. As one Black student explained to me, after you've been asked a couple of times about something so personal you begin to feel like you are an attraction in a zoo, that you are at the university for the education of the White students.

INSTITUTIONAL RESPONSES

Our society asks a lot of young people. We ask young people to do something that no one else does as successfully on such a wide scale—that is to live together with people from very different backgrounds, to respect one another, to appreciate one another, and to enjoy and learn from one another. The successes that occur every day in this endeavor are many, and they are too often overlooked. However, the problems and tensions are also real, and they will not vanish on their own. We tend to see pluralism working in the United States in much the same way some people expect capitalism to work. If you put together people with various interests and abilities and resources, the "invisible hand" of capitalism is supposed to make all the parts work together in an economy for the common good.

There is much to be said for such a model—the invisible hand of the market can solve complicated problems of production and distribution better than any "visible hand" of a state plan. However, we have learned that unequal power relations among the actors in the capitalist marketplace, as well as "externalities" that the market cannot account for, such as long-term pollution, or collusion between corporations, or the exploitation of child labor, means that state regulation is often needed. Pluralism and the relations between groups are very similar. There is a lot to be said for the idea that bringing people who belong to different ethnic or racial groups together in institutions with no interference will have good consequences. Students from different backgrounds will make friends if they share a dorm room or corridor, and there is no need for the institution to do any more than provide the locale. But like capitalism, the invisible hand of pluralism does not do well when power relations and externalities are ignored. When you bring together individuals from groups that are differentially valued in the wider society and provide no guidance, there will be problems. In these cases the "invisible hand" of pluralist relations does not work, and tensions and disagreements can arise without any particular individual or group of individuals being "to blame." On college campuses in the 1990s some of the tensions between students are of this sort. They arise from honest misunderstandings, lack of a common background, and very different experiences of what race and ethnicity mean to the individual.

The implications of symbolic ethnicities for thinking about race relations are subtle but consequential. If your understanding of your own ethnicity and its relationship to society and politics is one of individual choice, it becomes harder to understand the need for programs like affirmative action, which recognize the ongoing need for group struggle and group recognition, in order to bring about social change. It also is hard for a White college student to understand the need that minority students feel to band together against discrimination. It also is easy, on the individual level, to expect everyone else to be able to turn their ethnicity on and off at will, the way you are able to, without understanding that ongoing discrimination and societal attention to minority status makes that impossible for individuals from minority groups to do. The paradox of symbolic ethnicity is that it depends upon the ultimate goal of a pluralist society, and at the same time makes it more difficult to achieve that ultimate goal. It is dependent upon the concept that all ethnicities mean the same thing, that enjoying the traditions of one's heritage is an option available to a group or an individual, but that such a heritage should not have any social costs associated with it.

As the Asian Americans who wrote to *Dear Abby* make clear, there are many societal issues and involuntary ascriptions associated with non-White identities. The developments necessary for this to change are not individual but societal in nature. Social mobility and declining racial and ethnic sensitivity are closely associated. The legacy and the present reality of discrimination on the basis of race or ethnicity must be overcome before the ideal of a pluralist society, where all heritages are treated equally and are equally available for individuals to choose or discard at will, is realized.

References

Alba, Richard D. 1985. *Italian Americans: Into the Twilight of Ethnicity.* Englewood Cliffs, NJ: Prentice-Hall.

——. 1990. *Ethnic Identity: The Transformation of White America.* New Haven: Yale University Press.

Barth, Frederick. 1969. *Ethnic Groups and Boundaries.* Boston: Little, Brown.

Blauner, Robert. 1992. "Talking Past Each Other: Black and White Languages of Race." *American Prospect* (Summer): 55–64.

Feagin, Joe R. 1991. "The Continuing Significance of Race: Anti-Black Discrimination in Public Places." *American Sociological Review* 56: 101–17.

Gans, Herbert. 1979. "Symbolic Ethnicity: The Future of Ethnic Groups and Cultures in America." *Ethnic and Racial Studies* 2: 1–20.

Lieberson, Stanley. 1985. *Making It Count: The Improvement of Social Research and Theory.* Berkeley: University of California Press.

Ogbu, John. 1990. "Minority Status and Literacy in Comparative Perspective." *Daedalus* 119: 141–69.

Waters, Mary C. 1990. *Ethnic Options: Choosing Identities in America.* Berkeley: University of California Press.

Weber, Max. [1921]/1968. *Economy and Society: An Outline of Interpretive Sociology.* Eds. Guenther Roth and Claus Wittich, trans. Ephraim Fischoff. New York: Bedminister Press.

24

SALSA AND KETCHUP
Transnational Migrants Straddle Two Worlds

Peggy Levitt

The suburb, with its expensive homes with neatly-trimmed lawns and sport-utility-vehicles, seems like any other well-to-do American community. But the mailboxes reveal a difference: almost all are labeled "Patel" or "Bhagat."

From *Contexts*, Vol. 3, Issue 2, pp. 20–26. American Sociological Association, ISSN 1536 6052 © 2004. All rights reserved.

Over the past two decades, these families moved from the small towns and villages of Gujarat State on the west coast of India, first to rental apartments in northeastern Massachusetts and then to their own homes in subdivisions outside Boston. Casual observers watching these suburban dwellers work, attend school, and build religious congregations might conclude that yet another wave of immigrants is successfully pursuing the American dream. A closer look, however, reveals that they are pursuing Gujarati dreams as well. They send money back to India to open businesses or improve family homes and farms. They work closely with religious leaders to establish Hindu communities in the United States and also to strengthen religious life in their homeland. Indian politicians at the state and national level court these emigrants' contributions to India's political and economic development.

The Gujarati experience illustrates a growing trend among immigrants to the United States and Europe. In the 21st century, many people will belong to two societies at the same time. Researchers call those who maintain strong, regular ties to their homelands and who organize aspects of their lives across national borders "transnational migrants." They assimilate into the country that receives them, while sustaining strong ties to their homeland. Assimilation and transnational relations are not mutually exclusive; they happen simultaneously and influence each other. More and more, people earn their living, raise their family, participate in religious communities, and express their political views across national borders.

Social scientists have long been interested in how newcomers become American. Most used to argue that to move up the ladder, immigrants would have to abandon their unique customs, language and values. Even when it became acceptable to retain some ethnic customs, most researchers still assumed that connections to homelands would eventually wither. To be Italian American or Irish American would ultimately have much more to do with the immigrant experience in America than with what was happening back in Italy or Ireland. Social scientists increasingly recognize that the host-country experiences of some migrants remain strongly influenced by continuing ties to their country of origin and its fate.

These transnational lives raise fundamental issues about 21st century society. What are the rights and responsibilities of people who belong to two nations? Both home- and host-country governments must decide whether and how they will represent and protect migrants and what they can demand from them in return. They may have to revise their understandings of "class" or "race" because these terms mean such different things in each country. For example, expectations about how women should balance work and family vary considerably in Latin America and in the United States. Both home- and host-country social programs may have to be reformulated, taking into account new challenges and new opportunities that arise when migrants keep one foot in each of two worlds.

TWO CASES: DOMINICANS AND GUJARATIS IN BOSTON

My research among the Dominican Republic and Gujarati immigrants who have moved to Massachusetts over the past three decades illustrates the changes that result in their origin and host communities. Migration to Boston from the Dominican village of Miraflores began in the late 1960s. By the early 1990s, nearly two-thirds of the 550 households in Miraflores had relatives in the Boston area, most around the neighborhood of Jamaica Plain, a few minutes from downtown. Migration has transformed Miraflores into a transnational village. Community members, wherever they are, maintain such strong ties to each other that the life of this community occurs almost simultaneously in two places. When someone is ill, cheating on their spouse, or finally granted a visa, the news spreads as fast on the streets of Jamaica Plain, Boston as it does in Miraflores, Dominican Republic.

Residents of Miraflores began to migrate because it became too hard to make a living at farming. As more and more people left the fields of the Dominican Republic for the factories of Boston, Miraflores suffered economically. But as more and more families began to receive money from relatives in the United States (often called "remittances"), their standard of living improved. Most households can now afford the food, clothing, and medicine for which previous generations struggled. Their homes are filled with the TVs, VCRs, and other appliances their migrant relatives bring them. Many have been able to renovate their houses, install indoor plumbing, even afford air conditioning. With money donated in Boston and labor donated in Miraflores, the community built an aqueduct and baseball stadium, and renovated the local school and health clinic. In short, most families live better since migration began, but they depend on money earned in the United States to do so.

Many of the Mirafloreños in Boston live near and work with one another, often at factories and office-cleaning companies where Spanish is the predominant language. They live in a small neighborhood, nestled within the broader Dominican and Latino communities. They participate in the PTA and in the neighborhood organizations of Boston, but feel a greater commitment toward community development in Miraflores. They are starting to pay attention to elections in the United States, but it is still Dominican politics that inspires their greatest passion. When they take stock of their life's accomplishments, it is the Dominican yardstick that matters most.

The transnational character of Mirafloreños' lives is reinforced by connections between the Dominican Republic and the United States. The Catholic Church in Boston and the Church on the island cooperate because each feels responsible for migrant care. All three principal Dominican political parties campaign in the United States because migrants make large contributions and also influence how relatives back home vote. No one can run for president in the Dominican Republic, most Mirafloreños agree, if he or she does not campaign in New York. Conversely, mayoral and gubernatorial candidates in the northeastern United States now make obligatory pilgrimages to Santo Domingo. Since remittances are one of the most important sources of foreign currency, the Dominican government instituted policies to encourage migrants' long-term participation without residence. For example, under the administration of President Leonel Fernández (1996–2000), the government set aside a certain number of apartments for Dominican emigrants in every new construction project it supported. When they come back to visit, those of Dominican origin, regardless of their passport, go through the customs line for Dominican nationals at the airport and are not required to pay a tourist entry fee.

RELIGIOUS TIES

The people from Miraflores illustrate one way migrants balance transnational ties and assimilation, with most of their effort focused on their homeland. The Udah Bhagats, a subcaste from Gujarat State, make a different set of choices. They are more fully integrated into certain parts of American life, and their homeland ties tend to be religious and cultural rather than political. Like Gujaratis in general, the Udah Bhagats have a long history of transnational migration. Some left their homes over a century ago to work as traders throughout East Africa. Many of those who were forced out of Africa in the 1960s by local nationalist movements moved on to the United Kingdom and the United States instead of moving back to India. Nearly 600 families now live in the greater Boston region.

The Udah Bhagats are more socially and economically diverse than the Mirafloreños. Some migrants came from small villages where it is still possible to make a good living by farming. Other families, who had moved to Gujarati towns a generation ago, owned or were employed by small businesses there. Still others, from the city of Baroda, worked in engineering and finance before migrating. About half of the Udah Bhagats now in Massachusetts work in factories or warehouses, while the other half work as engineers, computer programmers or at the small grocery stores they have purchased. Udah Bhagats in Boston also send remittances home, but for special occasions or when a particular need arises, and the recipients do not depend on them. Some still own a share in the family farm or have invested in Gujarati businesses, like one man who is a partner in a computer school. Electronics, clothing, and appliances from the United States line the shelves of homes in India, but the risidents have not adopted western lifestyles as much as the Mirafloreños. The Gujarati state government has launched several initiatives to stimulate investment by "Non-Resident Gujaratis," but these are not central to state economic development policy.

In the United States, both professional and blue-collar Gujaratis work alongside native-born Americans; it is their family and religious life that is still tied to India. Some Bhagat families have purchased houses next door to each other. In an American version of the Gujarati extended family household, women still spend long hours preparing food and sending it across the street to friends and relatives. Families gather in one home to do *puja*, or prayers, in the evenings. Other families live in mixed neighborhoods, but they too spend much of their free time with other Gujaratis. Almost everyone still speaks Gujarati at home. While they are deeply grateful for the economic opportunities that America offers, they firmly reject certain American values and want to hold fast to Indian culture.

As a result, Udah Bhagats spend evenings and weekends at weddings and holiday celebrations, prayer meetings, study sessions, doing charitable work, or trying to recruit new members. Bhagat families conduct these activities within religious organizations that now operate across borders. Rituals, as well as charitable obligations, have been redefined so they can be fulfilled in the United States but directly supervised by leaders back in India. For example, the Devotional Associates of Yogeshwar or the Swadhyaya movement requires followers back in Gujarat to dedicate time each month to collective farming and fishing activities; their earnings are then donated to the poor. An example of such charitable work in Boston is families meeting on weekends to assemble circuit boards on sub-contract for a computer company. For the Udah Bhagats, religious life not only reaffirms their homeland ties but also erects clear barriers against aspects of American life they want to avoid. Not all Indians are pleased that Hindu migrants are so religious in America. While some view the faithful as important guardians of the religious flame, others claim that emigrants abroad are the principal underwriters of the recent wave of Hindu nationalism plaguing India, including the Hindu-Muslim riots that took place in Ahmedabad in 2002.

THE RISE OF TRANSNATIONAL MIGRATION

Not all migrants are transnational migrants, and not all who take part in transnational practices do so all the time. Studies by Alejandro Portes and his colleagues reveal that fewer than 10 percent of the Dominican, Salvadoran, and Colombian migrants they surveyed regularly participated in transnational economic and political activities. But most migrants do have occasional transnational contacts. At some stages in their lives, they are more focused on their country of origin, and at other times more committed to their host nation. Similarly, they climb two different social ladders. Their social status may improve in one country and decline in the other.

Transnational migration is not new. In the early 1900s, some European immigrants also returned to live in their home countries or stayed in America while being active in economic and political affairs at home. But improvements in telecommunications and travel make it cheaper and easier to remain in touch than ever before. Some migrants stay connected to their homelands daily through e-mail or phone calls. They keep their fingers on the pulse of everyday life and weigh in on family affairs in a much more direct way than their earlier counterparts. Instead of threatening the disobedient grandchild with the age-old refrain, "wait until your father comes home," the grandmother says, "wait until we call your mother in Boston."

The U.S. economy welcomes highly-educated, professional workers from abroad, but in contrast to the early 20th century, is less hospitable to low-skilled industrial workers or those not proficient in English. Because of poverty in their country of origin and insecurity in the United States, living across borders has become a financial necessity for many less skilled migrant workers. At the same time, many highly skilled, professional migrants choose to live transnational lives; they have the money and know-how to take advantage of economic and political opportunities in both settings. These days, America tolerates and even celebrates ethnic diversity—indeed, for some people, remaining "ethnic" is part of being a true American—which also makes long-term participation in the homeland and putting down roots in the United States easier.

Nations of origin are also increasingly supportive of long distance citizenship, especially countries that depend on the remittances and political clout of migrants. Immigrants are no longer forced to choose between their old and new countries as they had to in the past. Economic self-sufficiency remains elusive for small, non-industrialized countries and renders them dependent on foreign currency, much of it generated by migrants. Some national governments actually factor emigrant remittances into their macro-economic policies and use them to prove credit-worthiness. Others, such as the Philippines, actively promote their citizens as good workers to countries around the world. Transnational migrants become a key export and their country of origin's main connection to the world economy. By footing the bill for school and road construction back home, transnational migrants meet goals that weak home governments cannot. The increasingly interdependent global economy requires developing nations to tie themselves more closely to trade partners. Emigrant communities are also potential ambassadors who can foster closer political and economic relations.

THE AMERICAN DREAM GOES TRANSNATIONAL

Although few immigrants are regularly active in two nations, their efforts, combined with those of immigrants who participate occasionally, add up. They can transform the economy, culture and everyday life of whole regions in their countries of origin. They transform notions about gender relations, democracy, and what governments should and should not do. For instance, many young women in Miraflores, Dominican Republican, no longer want to marry men who have not migrated because they want husbands who will share the housework and take care of the children as the men who have been to the United States do. Other community members argue that Dominican politicians should be held accountable just like Bill Clinton was when he was censured for his questionable real estate dealings and extramarital affairs.

Transnational migration is therefore not just about the people who move. Those who stay behind are also changed. The American-born children of migrants are also shaped by ideas, people, goods, and practices from outside— in their case, from the country of origin—that they may identify with during particular periods in their lives. Although the second generation will not be involved with their ancestral homes in the same ways and with the same intensity as their parents, even those who express little interest in their roots know how to activate these connections if and when they decide to do so. Some children of Gujaratis go back to India to find marriage partners and many second-generation Pakistanis begin to study Islam when they have children. Children of Mirafloreños born in the United States participate actively in fund-raising efforts for Miraflores. Even Dominican political parties have established chapters of second-generation supporters in the United States.

Transnational migrants like the Mirafloreños and the Udah Bhagats in Boston challenge both the host and the origin nations' understanding of citizenship, democracy, and economic development. When individuals belong to two countries, even informally, are they protected by two sets of rights and subject to two sets of responsibilities? Which states are ultimately responsible for which aspects of their lives? The Paraguayan government recently tried to intercede on behalf of a dual national sentenced to death in the United States, arguing that capital punishment is illegal in Paraguay. The Mexican government recently issued a special consular ID card to all Mexican emigrants, including those living without formal authorization in the United States. More than 100 cities, 900 police departments, 100 financial institutions, and 13 states accept the cards as proof of identity for obtaining a drivers' license or opening a bank account. These examples illustrate the ways in which countries of origin assume partial responsibility for emigrants and act on their behalf.

Transnational migration also raises questions about how the United States and other host nations should address immigrant poverty. For example, should transnationals qualify for housing assistance in the United States at the same time that they are building houses back home? What about those who cannot fully support themselves here because they continue to support families in their homelands? Transnational migration also challenges policies of the nations of origin. For example, should social welfare and community development programs discriminate between those who are supported by remittances from the United States and those who have no such outside support? Ideally, social programs in the two nations should address issues of common concern in coordination with one another.

There are also larger concerns about the tension between transnational ties and local loyalties. Some outside observers worry when they see both home country and U.S. flags at a political rally. They fear that immigrants' involvement in homeland politics means that they are less loyal to the United States. Assimilation and transnational connections, however, do not have to conflict. The challenge is to find ways to use the resources and skills that migrants acquire in one context to address issues in the other. For example, Portes and his colleagues find that transnational entrepreneurs are more likely to be U.S. citizens, suggesting that becoming full members of their new land helped them run successful businesses in their countries of origin. Similarly, some Latino activists use the same organizations to promote participation in American politics that they use to mobilize people around homeland issues. Some of the associations created to promote Dominican businesses in New York also played a major role in securing the approval of dual citizenship on the island.

These are difficult issues and some of our old solutions no longer work. Community development efforts directed only at Boston will be inadequate if they do not take into account that Miraflores encompasses Boston and the island and that significant energy and resources are still directed toward Miraflores. Education and health outcomes will suffer if policymakers do not consider the many users who circulate in and out of two medical and school systems. As belonging to two places becomes increasingly common, we need approaches to social issues that not only recognize, but also take advantage of, these transnational connections.

25

"MEXICANNESS" IN NEW YORK
Migrants Seek New Place in Old Racial Order

Robert Smith

Over the past decade, one of the more dramatic population developments in the United States has been the burgeoning of the Mexican community all along the eastern seaboard. Population experts predict that within ten years

From *North American Congress on Latin America (NACLA) Report on the Americas*, 35, (September/October) 14–17. Reprinted by permission of the publisher.

Mexicans will be the largest minority on the east coast—from Florida to New England. In many places, especially those with relatively small minority populations, such as some towns in New York's Hudson Valley or on the Delmarva Peninsula just east of Washington, DC, they already are. This growth has been especially striking in New York City. From a population that barely existed in the early 1980s, Mexican New Yorkers now number in the hundreds of thousands. The U.S. Census Bureau enumerated over 260,000 Mexicans in New York State in 2000, of whom more than 180,000 were estimated to be in New York City. Allowing for the undercount—many Mexican New Yorkers are undocumented—this means there are probably 450,000–500,000 Mexicans in the state and 300,000 in the city alone.

The new migrants to New York are predominantly from the Mixteca region of southern Mexico, a region that includes large parts of the states of Puebla, Oaxaca and Guerrero. It is a poor, hot agricultural region, called *"tierra caliente,"* that has sent migrant workers to the United States in small numbers since the 1940s, and from which migration to the United States has been accelerating since Mexico's rural economy went into long-term crisis in the late 1980s.

The new immigrants, willing to put in long, hard days of work, have been welcomed by the city's low-wage employers, though their children have received a more ambiguous welcome in the city's schools and neighborhoods. And as the third-largest Latino group in the city, with an enormous potential for growth, Mexicans are beginning to draw the attention of New York's political and community leaders. How their "Mexicanness" will be defined in New York's complex web of ethnicities remains to be seen. Answers will emerge as they begin to negotiate their way through the city's system of social and racial hierarchies.[1]

Mexicans do not fit "naturally" into any one spot in New York's social and racial hierarchies. They enter New York both as immigrants and as Latinos. As immigrants they face—and many have internalized—expectations that they conform to an "immigrant analogy" according to which they will work hard and sacrifice their personal well-being so that their children and grandchildren can prosper. As Latinos, they confront social networks that are heavily "racialized"—networks in which ethnic groups are represented on a continuum that runs from black to white. They face the standard U.S. representations of race, based on the "original sin" of slavery, with "whiteness" signalling that a group is fit for full membership in society. Their immigrant bargain is, in fact, implicitly juxtaposed to the situation of native-born blacks: the native-born do not sacrifice, and they therefore will not prosper.

But the racial categories in New York City are complicated by two things. On the one hand, there are nuanced degrees of white ethnicity and racialization due in part to the presence of first-generation white immigrants such as Greeks, Russians and Italians. On the other hand, African-Americans share the most stigmatized position at the bottom of the hierarchy with a Latino group, Puerto Ricans. Many Puerto Ricans possess phenotypes that most Americans would consider "black," and experience consonant levels of racial segregation and discrimination; but they also speak Spanish and are immigrants. Hence, many Mexican parents and their New York-born children wonder whether their futures will look more like the hard lives they associate with Puerto Ricans and blacks or more like the upwardly mobile lives they associate with white ethnic immigrants. They wonder—worriedly—whether they will become a marginalized, racialized minority or an incorporated ethnic group?[2]

Writing in the 1930s, W.E.B. Du Bois mused that poor southern whites got a "public, psychological wage" by being white that enabled them to feel superior to blacks despite the many commonalities in their material living conditions. Historian David Roediger has used Du Bois' insight to analyze how the "Irish became white." When Irish immigrants started coming to the United States in significant numbers in the 1830s, they had much in common with African-Americans. Both groups did America's dirty work, both were victimized by systematic racism, and they often lived side by side in the poorest parts of northern cities. Roediger answers the question of how the Irish came to not only distance themselves from blacks but to embrace an anti-black racism by analyzing their racialized mobilization by the Catholic Church and the Democratic Party. What the Irish had learned, in essence, was that to be full members of U.S. society, one had not simply to be "not black" but also in many instances "anti-black."[3] This dynamic of incorporation has lived on through generations in a situation in which immigration to the United States is seen simultaneously as a struggle-and-prosper story—the "immigrant analogy"—and one in which generations of immigrants have succeeded by differentiating themselves from blacks, who are understood to form an underclass.

My research with Mexicans in New York over the last fifteen years has yielded a complex picture of responses to the need to define oneself within racialized hierarchies.[4] The immigrant first generation usually has responded by embracing the immigrant analogy, though in different ways in different contexts. In the labor market, for example, Mexican workers frequently confront complex and contradictory forms of ethnic solidarity.[5] While many Korean, Greek, Italian and native-born employers explicitly or implicitly compare Mexican immigrants to native-born blacks and Puerto Ricans, hence treating them as part of the out-group, they also see them as immigrants like themselves, or like their immigrant predecessors, hence part of their in-group. This leads to an emphasis by employers on their own similarities with their Mexican immigrant employees, and the difference of both from native minorities. I have heard many an employer identify with his Mexican employees. A Greek restaurant owner, for example, extolled to me the virtues of Mexican employees while in the same breath he disparaged African-Americans. With tears in his eyes, he told me about working 12-hour days like his Mexican workers, saying, "When I came to this country I was a good Mexican." The willingness of Mexican immigrants to work hard makes them different from native-born workers, he said, and he detailed how they moved up step by step from being busboys, to dishwashers, to cooks.[6] In addition to African-Americans and Puerto Ricans, native-born whites are occasionally included in these unfavorable comparisons.

Within this social context, racialization—the logic of moral and civic worth based on one's ethnic or racial affiliation—takes place within the Mexican community itself. For example, while some parents express no preferences regarding who their children date, many parents do not want their children to date African-Americans or in some cases Puerto Ricans, even though they themselves may have black and Puerto Rican friends, or even relatives through marriage. Many parents talk of how Puerto Ricans helped them when they came to New York many years earlier, when there were fewer Spanish speakers, but lament what they see as the Puerto Rican population's miserable social conditions. In particular, many Mexican immigrants and their U.S.-born children point to what they see as the tendency of Puerto Rican young men to engage in crime, especially against Mexicans, the propensity of Puerto Rican young women to get pregnant, and the tendency of many Puerto Ricans to depend on government assistance. This is frequently expressed as evidence of the "Americanization" that robs Puerto Ricans of their culture and leaves them vulnerable to the urban vices that Mexicans can resist. . . .

. . . Americanization among Puerto Ricans is seen as a cause of their having failed, while Mexicans are seen to be insulated by their culture from such erosions of values. To be sure, many in the first or second generation do not buy into the immigrant analogy. A second generation woman notes the tendency of Mexicans to assert that they are different from blacks and Puerto Ricans, but is critical of it: "They don't want to be like them," she says of her young compatriots, "but I believe they are, because I believe they do the same things. Why do they have to have a gang? Supposedly that's only blacks and Puerto Ricans. You know, and why do they have to go around drinking 'forties' . . . the big bottles of beer? Mexicans?"[7]

This woman has identified a potential problem in the collective self-image of much of the Mexican community in New York. If that self-image is premised on a juxtaposition with African-Americans and Puerto Ricans, it is being challenged by rising indicators of social distress resulting from the settlement and incorporation of Mexicans in New York. Despite increasing numbers of upwardly mobile second-generation youth, these indicators show increasing numbers of young people, born in Mexico and in the United States, who leave school or join gangs, or become pregnant at an early age. The formation of youth gangs grows out of the migration process itself and the often hostile reception that Mexican youth get here. Concretely, many second generation youth see that their lives are very similar to the blacks and

Puerto Ricans with whom they share neighborhoods, parks and schools. Many see limited employment options, little payback from schooling, and feel that the larger society and its institutions think they will fail.

. . . According to the Census, Mexicans as a group went from having one of the highest per capita incomes of all Latinos in New York in 1980 (when the community was smaller) to having one of the lowest in 1990. By 1990, Mexicans also had the largest percentage of 16–19 year olds not in school and not graduated: 47% versus 22% for Dominicans and Puerto Ricans, 18% for blacks and 8% for whites. Part of the reason for these indicators of social distress is the huge surge in Mexican youth migration during the 1990s; younger people earn less, and teen migrants often do not enter school.

The figures are disquieting for members of the Mexican community. Social psychologists have observed that a positive ethnic identity is usually associated with greater life success, but for many of these young people, self image is formed around an identity that includes being vulnerable on the street, seeing relatively few people who have succeeded through school, and facing the prospect of years of poorly paid hard work.

. . . Among adolescent Mexicans, there has been no single way of adapting to New York life. In addition to the young Mexicans who are dropping out of school at alarming rates, some upwardly mobile youth have used their Mexican ethnicity to differentiate themselves from other minorities in their schools and neighborhoods, whom they see as not serious about school. "Being Mexican helps us do better" describes how many of these adolescents understand themselves. There are other, "cosmopolitan," adolescents who see Mexicanness as only one identity among many, and there is a small group that dissociates itself from Mexicans in public places and identifies instead, in most cases, with upwardly mobile blacks. They see these successful black students as role models whose success they wish to emulate. They fear that if they hang around with other Mexicans they will be pressured to cut school a lot or eventually drop out.

And the results of adolescent engagements with racialized social relations have sometimes been ironic. For example, many Mexican youth, especially boys, now fear being "stepped up to"—stopped by others to verify if they are in a rival gang or not—by members of Mexican gangs more than they fear confrontation with blacks or Puerto Ricans. Most Mexican gang confrontations actually involve conflicts with other Mexicans, not Puerto Ricans or African-Americans. Other Mexican youth I have interviewed report that they are not stepped up to because they "look Dominican" or "look Ecuadorian," and hence are let pass uninspected.

All this suggests recent immigrants and their allies should step up their fight for an immigrant policy that includes more bilingual education, programs for parents to learn English, summer and after school programs for youth and tighter links between U.S. institutions and the communities from which immigrants come. Such a policy, of course, would have to be linked to the rebirth of anti-poverty efforts on behalf of the entire population.

For now, as Mexicans enter the political, social and economic worlds of New York, they do so within the pervasive and dangerous context of racialization. Immigration is not a straight "struggle and prosper" story. We should take note of how the Irish and other "formerly non-white" immigrants became white, and what this means for how immigrants, past and present, have learned and internalized what it means to be "American."

NOTES

1. See Robert Smith, "Mexicans: Social, Educational, Economic and Political Problems and Prospects in New York," in Nancy Foner, ed., *New Immigrants in New York* (New York: Columbia University Press, 2001).

2. For Mexicans in California, the answer will be different than for those in New York. In California, there has already been a racialization and stigmatization of Chicanos, despite the fact that there has been significant upward mobility in the population there as well, especially among women. See Dowell Myers and Cynthia Cranford, "Temporal Differentiation in the Occupational Mobility of Immigrant and Native-Born Latina Workers," *American Sociological Review*, Vol. 63, No. 1, February, 1998, pp. 68–93. It is also interesting that the comments I have heard usually compare Mexicans to Puerto Ricans and blacks or other minorities, and not with whites. Part of the reason for this is that the lifeworlds of most Mexicans and Mexican Americans, especially youth, do not include too many whites. Many of the people we have interviewed for our projects report not knowing many whites, except for teachers or employers, and that most of their classmates, workmates, or people they see in the parks or in their neighborhoods, are black or Latino.

3. David Roediger, *The Wages of Whiteness* (New York: Verso, 1991), especially chapters 1 and 7. See also Joel Ignatiev, *How the Irish Became White* (New York: Routledge, 1995) and Matthew Jacobson, *Whiteness of a Different Color: European Immigrants and the Alchemy of Race* (Cambridge: Harvard University Press, 1998).

4. This work can be consulted in a variety of venues: Robert Smith, "'Los Ausentes Siempre Presentes': The Imagining, Making and Politics of Community Between Ticuani, Puebla, Mexico and New York City," Doctoral Dissertation, Department of Political Science, Columbia University, 1995; "Mexicans in New York City: Membership and Incorporation of New Immigrant Group," in Sherrie L. Baver and Gabriel Haslip-Viera, eds. *Latinos in New York* (South Bend: University of Notre Dame Press, 1996); "Gender, Race and Schools in Educational and Work Outcomes of Second Generation Mexican Americans in New York," in Marcelo Suarez-Orozco and Mariela Paez, eds., *Latinos in the 21st Century* (Berkeley: University of California Press, 2001); "Mexicans," in Foner, ed. See also Robert Smith, Hector Cordero-Guzman and Ramon Grosfoguel, "Introduction: New Analytical Perspectives on Migration, Race and Transnationalization" in Cordero-Guzman, Smith and Grosfoguel, eds., Migration, Race and Transnationalization in a Changing New York (Philadelphia: Temple University Press, 2001); and Robert Smith, *Migration, Settlement and Transnational Life*, 2002. Research assistance during 1998–2000 by Sara Guerrero Rippberger, Sandra Lara, Agustin Vecino, Carolina Pérez, Griscelda Pérez, Linda Rodriguez and Lisa Peterson is gratefully acknowledged.

5. I call this "doubly bounded solidarity." It is my adaptation of the concept of bounded solidarity as developed by Alejandro Portes and his colleagues. See Portes' chapters in Portes, *The Economic Sociology of Immigration* (New York: Russell Sage Foundation, 1995). Also see Min Zhou, "Segmented Assimilation: Issues, Controversies, and Recent Research on the New Second Generation," in Charles Hirschman, Philip Kasinitz, and Josh DeWind, eds., *Handbook of International Migration: The American Experience* (New York: Russell Sage Foundation, 1999), pp. 196–212.

6. Author's interview, 1993, New York City.

7. Author's interview, 1997, New York City.

26

MIGRATION AND VIETNAMESE AMERICAN WOMEN
Remaking Ethnicity

Nazli Kibria

VIETNAMESE AMERICANS AND THE RISE IN WOMEN'S POWER

My research on the adaptive strategies of a community of Vietnamese refugees in Philadelphia revealed some of the ways in which women and men struggled and clashed with each other in efforts to shape the social organization of family and community life. From 1983 to 1985, I gathered information on family life and gender relations through participant observation in household and community settings, as well as in-depth interviews with women and men in the ethnic community.

The Vietnamese of the study were recent immigrants who had arrived in the United States during the late 1970s and early 1980s. Most were from urban, middle-class backgrounds in southern Vietnam. At the time of the study, over 30 percent of the adult men in the households of study were unemployed. Of the men who were employed, over half worked in low-paying, unskilled jobs in the urban service sector or in factories located in the outlying areas of the city. Women tended to work periodically, occupying jobs in the informal economic sector as well as in the urban service economy. Eight of the twelve households had members who collected public assistance. Both the family economy and informal community exchange networks were important means by which the households dealt with economic scarcities. Family and community were of tremendous economic salience to the group, as they were important resources for survival in the face of a rather inhospitable economic and social environment.

As suggested by the high rate of the men's unemployment, settlement in the United States had generated some shifts in power in favor of the women in the group. Traditional Vietnamese family and gender relations were modeled on Confucian principles, which placed women in subordination to men in every aspect of life. A key aspect of the social and economic oppression of women in traditional Vietnamese life was the patrilineal extended household. Its organization dictated that women married at a young age, following which they entered the household of their husband's father. This structure ensured the concentration of economic resources in the hands of men and men's control of women through the isolation of women from their families of origin.[1]

It is important to note the deep-seated changes in traditional family and gender structures in Vietnam during this century. War and urbanization eroded the structure of the patrilineal extended household. While unemployment was high in the cities, men from middle-class backgrounds were able to take advantage of the expansion of middle-level positions in the government bureaucracy and army. Such occupational opportunities were more limited for women: the women study participants indicated that they engaged in seasonal and informal income-generating activities or worked in low-level jobs in the growing war-generated service sector in the cities. The transition from rural to urban life had generated a shift in the basis of men's control over economic and social resources. However, families relied on men's income to maintain a middle-class standard of living. Thus women remained in a position of economic subordination to men, a situation that served to sustain the ideals of the traditional family system and men's authority in the family. Restrictions on women's sexuality were important for middle-class families who sought to distinguish themselves from the lower social strata. My data suggest that families were especially conscious of the need to distance themselves from poorer "fallen" women who had become associated with the prostitution generated by the American military presence.

Within the Vietnamese American community of study, I found several conditions that were working to undermine the bases on which male authority had rested in Vietnam. Most important, for the Vietnamese men, the move to the United States had involved a profound loss of social economic status. Whereas in pre-1975 Vietnam the men held middle-class occupations, in the United States they had access to largely unskilled, low-status, and low-paying jobs. Also, because of their difficulties with English and their racial-ethnic status, the men found themselves disadvantaged within social arenas of the dominant society. Compounding these problems was the dearth of strong formal ethnic organizations in the community that could have served as a vehicle for the men's political assertion into the dominant society.

As a result of these losses, the comparative access of men and women to the resources of the dominant society had to some extent become equalized. In contrast to the experiences of the men, migration had not significantly altered the position of the women in the economy. As in Vietnam, the women tended to work sporadically, sometimes in family businesses or, more commonly, in temporary jobs in the informal and service sector economies of the city. However, the economic contributions of women to the family budget had risen in proportion to those of the men. I have suggested that in modern, urban South Vietnam the force and legitimacy of male authority had rested heavily on the ability of men to ensure a middle-class status and standard of living for their families. In the United States, the ability of men to fulfull this expectation had been eroded. Among the men, there was widespread concern about the consequences of this situation for their status in the family, as is revealed by the words of a former lieutenant of the South Vietnamese army: "In Vietnam, the man earns and everyone depends on him. In most families, one or two men could provide for the whole family. Here the man finds he can never make enough money to take care of the family. His wife has to work, his children have to work, and so they look at him in a different way. The man isn't strong anymore, like he was in Vietnam."

Such changes had opened up the possibilities for a renegotiation of gender relations, and were the cause of considerable conflict between men and women in the family and community. The shifts in power had also enhanced the ability of women to construct and channel familial and ethnic resources in ways that they chose. Previously I suggested that the changes in the balance of power between men and women generated by migration are crucial to understanding the manner and degree to which immigrant family and community reveal themselves to be gender contested. How, then, did the fairly drastic shift in the gender balance of power among the Vietnamese Americans reflect itself in the ability of the men and women in this group to influence family and community life? In the following section, I describe some of the ways in which gender interests and conflict shaped family and community life for the Vietnamese Americans.

FAMILY AND ETHNICITY AS GENDER CONTESTED

One of the most intriguing and important strategies of Vietnamese American adaptation that I observed was the rebuilding of kinship networks. Family ties had undergone tremendous disruption in the process of escape from Vietnam and resettlement in the United States. Despite this, the households of the group tended to be large and extended. The process by which this occurred was one in which the study participants actively worked to reconstruct family networks by building kin relationships. In order for this to take place, the criteria for inclusion in the family had become extremely flexible. Thus close friends were often incorporated into family groups as fictive kin. Also, relationships with relatives who were distant or vaguely known in Vietnam were elevated in importance. Perhaps most important for women, the somewhat greater significance traditionally accorded the husband's kin had receded in importance.[2] Given the scarcity of relatives in the United States, such distinctions were considered a luxury, and the demands of life made the rebuilding of family a valuable, if not a necessary, step in the process of adaptation to the dominant society.

While important for the group as a whole, the reconstruction of kinship as it took place had some special advantages for women. One consequence of the more varied and inclusive nature of the kinship network was that women were rarely surrounded exclusively by the husband's relatives and/or friends. As a result, they were often able to turn to close fictive kin and perhaps members of their families of origin for support during conflicts with men in the family. Another condition that enhanced the power of married women in the family was that few had to deal with the competing authority of their mother-in-law in the household, because elderly women have not been among those likely to leave Vietnam.

The reconstruction of kinship thus had important advantages for women, particularly as it moved the Vietnamese perhaps even further from the ideal model of the patrilineal extended household that it had been in the past. But women were not simply passive beneficiaries of the family rebuilding process. Rather, they played an active part in family reconstruction, attempting to shape family boundaries in ways that were to their advantage. I found women playing a vital part in creating fictive kin by forging close ties. And women were often important, if not central, "gatekeepers" to the family group and household. Thus the women helped to decide such matters as whether the marriage of a particular family member was a positive event and could be taken as an opportunity to expand kinship networks. At other times the women passed judgment on current or potential family members, as to whether they had demonstrated enough commitment to such important familial obligations as the sharing of economic and social resources with kin.

Although women undoubtedly played an important part in family reconstruction, their control over decisions about family membership was by no means exclusive or absolute. In fact, the question of who was legitimately included in the family group was often a source of tension within families, particularly between men and women. The frequency of disputes over this issue stemmed in part from the fluidity and subsequent uncertainty about family boundaries, as well as the great pressures often placed on individuals to subordinate their needs to those of the family collective. Beyond this, I also suggest that disputes over boundaries arose from the fundamental underlying gender divisions in the family. That is, the different interests of women and men in the family spurred efforts to shape the family in ways that were of particular advantage to them. For the reasons I have previously discussed, the Vietnamese American women had greater influence and opportunity in the shaping of family in the United States than they had in the past. The women tended to use this influence to construct family groups that extended their power in the family.

In one case that I observed, considerable tension developed between a couple named Nguyet and Phong concerning the sponsorship[3] of Nguyet's nephew and his family from a refugee camp in Southeast Asia. Nguyet and Phong had been together with their three children (two from Nguyet's previous marriage) for about seven years, since they had met in a refugee camp in Thailand. Phong remained married to a woman who was still living in Vietnam with his children, a fact that was the source of some stress for Nguyet and Phong. The issue of the nephew's sponsorship seemed to exacerbate tensions in the relationship. Phong did not want to undertake the sponsorship because of the potentially heavy financial obligations it entailed. He also confessed that he was worried that Nguyet would leave him after the nephew's arrival, a threat often made by Nguyet during their quarrels. Finally, he talked of how Nguyet's relationship with the nephew was too distant to justify the sponsorship. Nguyet had never even met the nephew, who was the son of a first cousin rather than of a sibling.

Confirming some of Phong's fears, Nguyet saw the presence of the nephew and his family as a potentially important source of support for herself. She spoke of how she had none of "my family" in the country, in comparison with Phong, whose sister lived in the city. She agreed that she did not know much about her nephew, but nonetheless felt that his presence would ease her sense of isolation and also would provide a source of aid if her relationship with Phong deteriorated. Eventually she proceeded with the sponsorship, but only after a lengthy dispute with Phong.

While the issue of sponsorship posed questions about kinship in an especially sharp manner, there were other circumstances under which women and men clashed over family boundaries. When kin connections could not be questioned (for example, in the case of a sibling), what came under dispute was the commitment of the particular person involved to familial norms and obligations. One of my woman respondents fought bitterly with her older brother about whether their male cousin should live with them. Her brother objected to the cousin's presence in the household on the grounds that he had not responded to their request for a loan of money two years ago. The woman respondent wanted to overlook this breach of conduct because of her extremely close relationship with the cousin, who had been her "best friend" in Vietnam.

Regardless of the particular circumstances, gender conflict seemed an important part of the family reconstruction process. Women and men shared an interest in creating and maintaining a family group that was large and cohesive enough to provide economic and social support. However, their responses to the family reconstruction process were framed by their differing interests, as men and women, within the family. Men and women attempted to channel family membership in ways that were to their advantage, such that their control over the resources of the family group was enhanced.

Gender divisions and conflicts also entered into the community life of the group. The social networks of the Vietnamese American women were central to the dynamics and organization of the ethnic community. They served to organize and regulate exchange between households. While "hanging out" at informal social gatherings, I observed women exchanging information, money, goods, food, and tasks such as child care and cooking. Given the precarious economic situation of the group, these exchanges played an important role in ensuring the economic survival and stability of the households. The women's centrality to these social networks gave them the power not only to regulate household exchange but also to act as agents of social control in the community in a more general sense. I found that women, through the censure of gossip and the threat of ostracism, played an important part in defining community norms. In short, the relative rise in power that had accrued to the Vietnamese American women as a result of migration expressed itself in their considerable influence over the organization and dynamics of the ethnic community. Like kinship, community life was a negotiated arena, one over which women and men struggled to gain control.

The gender-contested quality of ethnic forms was also apparent in the efforts of women to reinterpret traditional Vietnamese familial ideologies on their own terms. In general, the Vietnamese American women continued to espouse and support traditional ideologies of gender relations as important ideals. For example, when asked during interviews to describe the "best" or ideal roles of men and women in the family, most of my respondents talked of a clear division of roles in which women assumed primary responsibility for maintaining the home and taking care of the children, and men for the economic support of the family. Most felt that household decisions should be made jointly, although the opinion of the man was seen to carry more weight. About half of those interviewed felt that a wife should almost always obey her husband. Even more widespread were beliefs in the importance of restrictions on female (but not male) sexuality before marriage.

While women often professed such beliefs, their relationship to traditional ideologies was active rather than passive and inflexible. In other words, the women tended to emphasize certain aspects of the traditional familial ideology over others. In particular, they emphasized parental authority and the obligation of men to sacrifice individual needs and concerns in order to fulfill the needs of the family, traditional precepts they valued and hoped to preserve in the United States. The women's selective approach to Vietnamese "tradition" emerged most clearly in situations of conflict between men and women in the family. In such disputes, women selectively used the traditional ideologies to protect themselves and to legitimate their actions and demands (Kibria 1990). Thus, husbands who were beating their wives were attacked by other women in the community on the grounds that they (the husbands) were inadequate breadwinners. The women focused not on the husband's treatment of his wife but on his failure to fulfill his family caretaker role. Through this selective emphasis, the women managed to condemn the delinquent husband without appearing to depart from "tradition." In short, for the Vietnamese American women, migration had resulted in a greater ability to shape family and community life.

CONCLUSION

For immigrant women, ethnic ties and institutions may be both a source of resistance and support, and of patriarchal oppression. Through an acknowledgment of this duality we can arrive at a fuller understanding of immigrant women's lives: one that captures the multifaceted constraints as well as the resistances that are offered by immigrant women to the oppressive forces in their lives. In patterns similar to those noted by studies of other racial-ethnic groups (Stack 1974; Baca Zinn 1975), the Vietnamese Americans presented in this [article] relied on family and community for survival and resistance. Their marginal status made the preservation of these institutions an important priority.

Like other racial-ethnic women, the ability of the Vietnamese American women to shape ethnicity was constrained by their social-structural location in the dominant society. These women saw the traditional family system as key to their cultural autonomy and economic security in American society. Migration may have equalized the economic resources of the men and women, but it had not expanded the economic opportunities of the women enough to make independence from men an attractive economic reality. The Vietnamese American women, as is true for other women of color, were especially constrained in their efforts to "negotiate" family and community in that they faced triple disadvantages (the combination of social class, racial-ethnic, and gender statuses) in their dealings with the dominant society.

Recognition of the role of ethnic institutions in facilitating immigrant adaptation and resistance is essential. However, it is equally important to not lose sight of gender divisions and conflicts, and the ways in which these influence the construction of ethnic institutions. Feminist scholars have begun to explore the diverse ways in which immigrant women manipulate family and community to enhance their own power, albeit in ways that are deeply constrained by the web of multiple oppressions that surround them (Andezian 1986; Bhachu 1986; Kibria 1990). Such work begins to suggest the complexity of immigrant women's relationship to ethnic structures, which is informed by both strength and oppression.

NOTES

1. Some scholars stress the fact that the reality of women's lives was far different from that suggested by these Confucian ideals. Women in traditional Vietnam also had a relatively favorable economic position in comparison with Chinese women due to Vietnamese women's rights of inheritance as well as their involvement in commercial activities (see Hickey 1964; Keyes 1977). Despite these qualifications, there is little to suggest that the economic and social subordination of women was not a fundamental reality in Vietnam.

2. Hy Van Luong (1984) has noted the importance of two models of kinship in Vietnamese life, one that is patrilineal-oriented and another in which bilateral kin are of significance. Thus the flexible, encompassing conceptions of family that I found among the group were not entirely new, but had their roots in Vietnamese life; however, they had acquired greater significance in the context of the United States.

3. Refugee resettlement in the United States involves a system of sponsorship by family members or other interested parties who agree to assume part of the responsibility for taking care of those sponsored for a period of time after their arrival.

References

Andezian, Sossie. 1986. "Women's Roles in Organizing Symbolic Life: Algerian Female Immigrants in France." Pp. 254–266 in *International Migration: The Female Experience*, edited by R. J. Simon and C. B. Brettell. Totowa, N.J.: Rowman and Allenheld.

Baca Zinn, Maxine. 1975. "Political Familism: Toward Sex Role Equality in Chicano Families." *Aztlan* 6, no. 1: 13–26.

Bhachu, Parminder K. 1986. "Work, Dowry and Marriage Among East African Sikh Women in the U.K." Pp. 241–254 in *International Migration: The Female Experience*, edited by R. J. Simon and C. B. Brettell. Totowa, N.J.: Rowman and Allenheld.

Hickey, Gerald C. 1964. *Village in Vietnam*. New Haven: Yale University Press.

Keyes, Charles F. 1977. *The Golden Peninsula*. New York: Macmillan.

Kibria, Nazli. 1990. "Power, Patriarchy and Gender Conflict in the Vietnamese Immigrant Community." *Gender & Society* 4, no. 1 (March): 9–24.

Luong, Hy Van. 1984. "'Brother' and 'Uncle': An Analysis of Rules, Structural Contradictions and Meaning in Vietnamese Kinship." *American Anthropologist* 86, no. 2: 290–313.

Stack, Carol. 1974. *All Our Kin*. New York: Harper & Row.

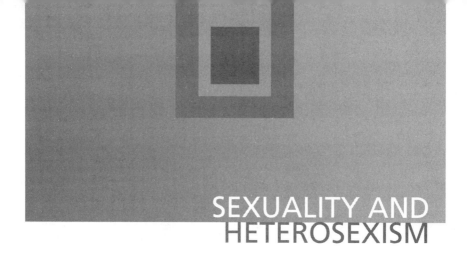

SEXUALITY AND HETEROSEXISM

27

"YOU TALKIN' TO ME?"

Jean Kilbourne

. . . We live in a culture in which it is difficult not to feel trapped in a false self, not to feel that one's body is simply an "object among other objects in the world." This is especially true for women, since our bodies are routinely used as objects to sell every imaginable kind of product, from chainsaws to chewing gum. This affects all of us—but how could it not retraumatize people who were treated as objects in childhood? . . .

Many ads feature just a part of a woman's body—a derriere, a headless torso. An ad for an Internet terminal features a woman bending over. The copy says, "Your butt. It's practically a fixation. You look at it in the mirror. You exercise it. You dress it, so it looks good. You pinch it, for firmness, like a melon. How can we help improve it? Sit on it, and find out." Imagine—a part of one's body is being referred to as a separate object, "like a melon." How difficult it is to feel "embodied" in such a world? No wonder research studies keep finding that many women are depressed by exposure to advertisements and women's magazines.

We may not be conscious of this, but we are affected. I've been studying these issues for decades and I still feel awful almost every time I read a fashion

From Jean Kilbourne. 1999. *Can't Buy My Love: How Advertising Changes How We Think and Feel.* New York: reprinted and edited with the permission of The Free Press, a division of Simon & Shuster Adult Publishing Group. All rights reserved.

magazine. My belly to too round (ever since I gave birth to my daughter), my skin marred by sunspots and wrinkles, my teeth not white enough, my nails not perfect. It's easy to write this off as trivial vanity, but the impact can be deep and serious. It makes it difficult for a woman to feel safe, at home in her body and, therefore, in the world. . . .

It is almost impossible to imagine what our popular culture would look like if women's bodies weren't objectified and dismembered. We are so used to this that it is hard to believe that it has not always been so. In fact, the eroticized imagery of women has been part of the general cultural landscape, not relegated to the world of pornography and sex clubs, for only the past fifty years or so. It is true that there have been erotic images of women in art for centuries, but mass technology has made it possible for these images to constantly surround us. Unlike art, advertising always yokes these images to products. The point is not to arouse desire for the woman, but to arouse desire for the product. Robert Schultz describes these images as "scattered like parks or resorts, little retreats for the male imagination, strokes to the ego and hooks for commerce."

I've been talking about the exploitation of women in advertising since the late 1960s and it was the subject of my 1979 film *Killing Us Softly: Advertising's Image of Women*. It is certainly no longer news. However, it is more extreme and pervasive than ever before. Women's bodies are not only used to attract attention to the product in increasingly absurd ways, as when a nude woman is used to sell a watch or breasts are used to sell fishing line, but increasingly the woman's body morphs into the product, as in the ad for "the Sak." And this objectification is related to addiction and substance abuse in ways that are complex and that have not been explored.

It is becoming clearer that this objectification has consequences, one of which is the effect that it has on sexuality and desire. Sex in advertising and the media is often criticized from a puritanical perspective—there's too much of it, it's too blatant, it will encourage kids to be promiscuous, and so forth. But sex in advertising has far more to do with trivializing sex than promoting it, with narcissism than with promiscuity, with consuming than with connecting. The problem is not that it is sinful, but that it is synthetic and cynical.

Sexual images in advertising and throughout the media define what is sexy and, more important, who is sexy. To begin with, sex in advertising in the mass media is almost entirely heterosexist—lesbian, gay, or bisexual sex is rarely even implied in the mainstream media (aside from the occasional male fantasy of lesbianism as two beautiful women waiting for Dick to arrive). We are surrounded by images of young, beautiful heterosexual couples with perfect hard bodies having sex. Women are portrayed as sexually desirable only if they are young, thin, carefully polished and groomed, made up, depilated, sprayed, and scented—rendered quite unerotic, in fact—and men are conditioned to seek such partners and to feel disappointed if they fail.

We never see eroticized images of older people, imperfect people, people with disabilities. The gods have sex, the rest of us watch—and judge our own imperfect sex lives against the fantasy of constant desire and sexual fulfillment portrayed in the media. To a great extent, the images define desirability—our own as well as others'. We can never measure up. Inevitably, this affects our self-images and radically distorts reality. "You have the right to remain sexy," says an ad featuring a beautiful young woman, her legs spread wide, but the subtext is "only if you look like this." And she is an object—available, exposed, essentially passive. She has the right to remain sexy, but not the right to be actively sexual.

Just as women and girls are offered a kind of ersatz defiance through drinking and smoking that interferes with true rebellion, so are we offered a pseudo-sexuality, a sexual mystique, that makes it far more difficult to discover our own unique and authentic sexuality. How sexy can a woman be who hates her body? She can act sexy, but can she feel sexy? How fully can she surrender to passion if she is worried that her thighs are too heavy or her stomach too round, if she can't bear to be seen in the light, or if she doesn't like the fragrance of her own genitals?

In the world of advertising, only young people have sex. Not only are young women valued only for their sexuality, but the rest of us end up in a culture arrested in adolescence, surrounded by teenage fantasies of sex and romance, a culture that idealizes the very things that make real intimacy impossible—impulsive gratification, narcissism, distance and disconnection, romanticism, and eternal youth. Sex in advertising is about a constant state of desire and arousal—never about intimacy or fidelity or commitment. This not only makes intimacy impossible—it erodes real desire. The endless pursuit of passion is fueled by a sense of inner deadness, emptiness—and it is doomed to failure, like any addiction. Passion inevitably wanes and one is alone again, empty.

When we think about it, the people in ads aren't sexy because of anything unique to them. They have no personal histories. They mostly look alike and are interchangeable. They very rarely look at each other. "The only downside to female guests that stay over for breakfast is they leave with your nicest shirts," says an ad featuring a man getting dressed. His back is to the young woman in his bed, who is covering herself up as if embarrassed. People in ads like this aren't lovers—they are the users and the used. They are sexy because of the products they use. The jeans, the perfume, the car are sexy in and of themselves. The answer to the question posed by one ad, "What attracts?" is the perfume being advertised, which means these particular partners are irrelevant. They could easily be with anyone else who happened to be wearing Jovan musk. Advertising even tells us that "Shi Cashmere is sexier than skin!" Often the people in the ads are grim—there is no humor, no quirkiness, none of the individuality that defines the truly erotic.

Although the sexual sell, overt and subliminal, is at a fever pitch in most advertising, depictions of sex as an important and profound human activity are notably absent. It is a cold and oddly passionless sex that surrounds us. A sense of joy is also absent; the models generally look either hostile or bored. Passionate sex is one way that we can experience the oceanic, the transcendence of our own boundaries. But this can only occur between subjects, not objects. Sex certainly cannot and does not always have to be sacred and transcendent, but it is tragic for a culture when that possibility is diminished or lost. As psychologist Linda Pollock says, sexual pleasure is significantly more important and, at the same time, significantly less important than our culture holds it to be.

This notion that sexiness and sex appeal come from without rather than within is one of advertising's most damaging messages. Real sexiness has to do with a passion for life, individuality, uniqueness, vitality. It has nothing to do with products or with all the bored, perfect-looking models embracing that we see all around us. If Jeremy Iggers's definition of the erotic as "a heightened sense of aliveness" is true, then surely, in a world in which beautiful people so often look more dead than alive, it is the car ads that most promise an erotic experience. We live in a culture that is sex-crazed and sex-saturated, but strangely *unerotic.*

Advertising constantly confuses real sexuality with narcissism. Identical models parade alone through the commercials, caressing their own soft skin, stroking and hugging their bodies, shaking their long silky manes, sensually bathing and applying powders and lotions, and then admiring themselves at length in the mirror. We're subjected to a steady barrage of messages telling us that all that matters is the immediate fulfillment of our needs and desires. "We are hedonists and we want what feels good," declares a Nike ad. We are the heroes of every ad. "You deserve a break today." "Go for it." As an ad for a bath product says, "Entering Willow Lake. Population: One. You."

"A celebration of laughter . . . love . . . and intense happiness," says the ad for Amarige perfume. But all we see is a woman who seems to be in the throes of orgasm caressing her own throat. We don't need partners any more. This is perfect disconnection.

This has been taken even further in some recent ads where the models are literally kissing themselves. Supermodel Linda Evangelista appears in one such ad as a woman and a man. Transvestite RuPaul is featured in another, in which RuPaul the guy nuzzles RuPaul the babe. She is no doubt wearing "Narcisse" perfume and he "Egoiste."

This adolescent attitude toward sex is further reflected and reinforced by all the ads (and situation comedies and films) that turn sex into a dirty joke. Countless ads use sophomoric double entendres, such as "We keep it up longer" (for a radio station), "Your ability to score has just improved" (for a video game), and "You never forget your first time" (for alcohol and for a discount store). An ad for shoes in a British magazine aimed at young people features a photo of a blonde in the throes of passion (or dead—it's hard to tell) and the copy, "Half way up Mount Caroline. Realised I'd forgotten my safety gear. Made a speedy descent." An American ad for cruises asks the question, "What's your idea of fun?" A beautiful woman slyly replies, "Licking the salt off my husband's margarita." When sexual jokes are used to sell everything from rice to roach-killer, from cars to carpets, it's hard to remember that sex can unite two souls, can inspire awe. Individually these ads are harmless enough, sometimes even funny, but the cumulative effect is to degrade and devalue sex.

I do not mean to imply for a minute that sex has to be romantic, soft, nice, domesticated. We inevitably objectify ourselves and each other sexually, which is fine as long as there is reciprocity, as long as we all can be subjects as well, and never merely objects. As Ann Snitow says, "The danger of objectification and fragmentation depend on context. . . . The antipornography campaign introduces misleading goals into our struggle when it intimates that in a feminist world we will never objectify anyone, never take the part for the whole, never abandon ourselves to the mindlessness or the intensities of feeling that link sex with childhood, death, the terrors and pleasures of the oceanic." Far from abandoning the erotic, we need to take it back from the commercial culture that monopolizes it.

Perhaps most important, advertising and the popular culture define human connection almost entirely in terms of sex, thus overemphazing the relative importance of sex in our lives (and marriages) and underemphasizing other important things (friendship, loyalty, fun, the love of children, community). According to poet Robert Hass, the art of the pornographer "consists in the absence of scale." There is no sense of scale in advertising, no sense of what is of greater or lesser importance. Life is rich and varied, with so many aspects that are important and meaningful—political, occupational, educational, creative, artistic, religious, and spiritual aspects. Sex is certainly one of these important aspects but, as Sut Jhally says, "Never in history has the *iconography* of a culture been so obsessed or possessed by questions of sexuality and gender." Men's magazines are filled with erotic images of perfect women (which also litter our highways and fill our TV screens). And women's magazines are filled with desperate articles about how to keep our men sexually happy—explicit instructions for fellatio, recommendations to try new things like anal sex.

The magazines for single women, like *Cosmopolitan*, are breathless, risque ("Drive Him Wild in Bed: The Surprising Places He Wants You to Touch," "Be the Best Sex of His Life," and "Rated X: Sex Lessons of a Paris Madam" are typical cover stories). The ones for wives and mothers are more instructive (how to have romantic quickies, revive your sex life with a weekend in the Caribbean). When I read these magazines, I can almost feel the fatigue between the lines—oh, my God, in addition to working full-time and spending "quality time" with the children and remembering everyone's birthday and being responsible for all the planning of our lives and all the emotional work of the marriage, I also have to schedule passionate interludes and put on a garter belt and stockings and learn the latest sexual positions. No wonder I need a drink or a cigarette or a pint of ice cream. . . .

In a world filled with fast-food chains and junk-food advertising, many people are deliberately starving themselves or gorging themselves into oblivion. Consuming food for which we have no real appetite, we are never satisfied and lose our ability to gauge our own hunger. In a similar way, the barrage of constant sexual images and perfect bodies being offered up to us like delectable pastries (or perhaps popsicles) leave us sexually numb and out of touch with our own desire. We can get almost any kind of ethnic food in our own hometowns these days, and we also have more sexual choices than ever before in terms of partners and techniques. But when eating is divorced from hunger and appetite and sex is divorced from desire and relationships, both experiences become onanistic, solitary, unfulfilling.

Of course, all these sexual images aren't intended to sell us on sex—they are intended to sell us on shopping. The desire they want to inculcate is not for orgasm but for more gismos. This is the intent of the advertisers—but an unintended consequence is the effect these images have on real sexual desire and real lives. When sex is a commodity, there is always a better deal. The wreckage that ensues when people try to emulate the kind of sexuality glorified in the ads and the popular culture is everywhere, from my house to the White House. And many who choose not to act on these impulsive sexual mandates nonetheless end up worrying that something is wrong with them, with their flawed and ordinary and all-too-human relationships.

So, all these blatant sexual images that surround us actually are more likely to lead to disconnection rather than to connection. And substance abuse and addiction, especially for women, is often a response to disconnection. Advertising doesn't cause this disconnection, of course, just as it doesn't cause addiction. But it does objectify women's bodies, making it more difficult for women to feel safely "embodied" and thus furthering a sense of dissociation. And it creates a climate in which disconnection and dissociation are normalized, even glorified and eroticized. And finally it deliberately offers addictive products—alcohol, cigarettes, food—as a way to cope with the pain this causes.

Far from improving, the situation continues to get worse. We are so used to blatant sexual images these days that advertisers have to constantly push the envelope in order to attract our attention, to break through the clutter. Increasingly, in order to shock us into paying attention, they borrow images from the world of pornography—which is a world of violence, a world of utter disconnection.

28

WHERE HAS GAY LIBERATION GONE?
An Interview with Barbara Smith

Amy Gluckman and Betsy Reed

The links between homophobia and sexism have been analyzed a lot, but the linkages between homophobia and other forms of oppression, especially class and race oppression, haven't been thought about or analyzed as much. What connections do you see between, first of all, gay oppression and our economic system, and issues of class?

I think that's really a very complicated issue. I often say that, unlike racial oppression, lesbian and gay oppression is not economically linked, and is not structurally and historically linked, to the founding of this country and of capitalism in the United States. This country was not founded on homophobia; it was founded on slavery and racism and, before that, prior to the importation of slaves, it was founded on the genocide of the indigenous people who lived here, which also had profound racial consequences and rationales. I think that sometimes, certain lesbians and gay men get very upset when I and others—I'm not the only person who would say it—put that kind of analysis out because they think it means that I'm saying that lesbian and gay oppression is not serious. That's not what I'm saying at all.

Do you think that extends into the future? In other words, would you say that capitalism could go along its merry way and assimilate gay people and provide gay rights, but otherwise remain the same?

. . . As with all groups, I think that our economic system has the most implications for lesbians and gay men when their class position makes them vulnerable to that economic system. So in other words, it's not that in general being lesbian or gay puts you into a critical relationship to capitalism, it's that a large proportion of lesbians and gay men are poor or working class, but of course they're completely invisible the way the movement's politics are defined now.

So much of this society is about consumerism. As long as lesbians and gay men are characterized as people who have huge amounts of disposable income and who are kind of fun and trendy—nice entertainment type people, k. d. langs and Martinas, just a little on the edge but not really that

From Amy Gluckman and Betsy Reed, eds. *Homo Economics: Capitalism, Community, and Lesbian and Gay Life* (New York: Routledge, 1997), pp. 195–207. Reprinted by permission.

threatening—as long as they're characterized in that way, probably capitalism can incorporate them. If they begin to think about how extending lesbian and gay rights fully might shake up the patriarchal nuclear family and the economic arrangements that are tied to that, then that might be the point at which capitalists would say, "Well no, I don't think we can include that." As long as it's about k. d. lang and Cindy Crawford on the cover of *Vanity Fair*, capitalism doesn't have any problem with that because that's nothing but an image. . . .

. . . Right-wing organizations have used inflated income information about gays and lesbians to try to drum up homophobia, which is almost a direct appeal to people's economic frustration. As an organizer, have you encountered that? To what extent do you think that the backlash against lesbian and gay rights has to do with the degree to which people in this country under capitalism are economically exploited and might seek a hateful outlet for that?

What they say is that these people do not qualify as a disenfranchised group because look at their income levels, as if the only way you could be disenfranchised is by income or lack of access to it. When they tell the untruth that all of us are economically privileged, of course that fans it. I can't say that I have personally seen that myth being picked up. When I come into contact with straight people, it's usually Black people. And it's usually around Black issues.

I don't know that the economic thing is such an issue for heterosexual Black communities; I think it's the moral thing. It's not so much that those white gays are rich, it's that those white gays are sinners, they're going against God. And they're also white, so they must be racist. And if you are a Black lesbian or gay man, then you must be a racial traitor. Those are the kinds of things that I hear, not so much that they're so rich. But I think there's an assumption on the part of most people of color that *most* white people are better off than we are anyway. It's an assumption that in some cases is accurate and in some cases is a myth that is perpetuated to keep people apart who should be in solidarity with each other because of class. It's a myth that keeps people away from each other, because there are some real commonalities between white and poor and being of color and poor. . . .

Can you say more about the links that you see between racism and gay oppression?

All of the different kinds of oppression are tied to each other, particularly when it comes to the kinds of repression and oppression that are practiced against different groups of people. When you look at a profile of how people who are oppressed experience their oppression, you see such similar components: demonization, scapegoating, police brutality, housing segregation, lack of access to certain jobs and employment, even the taking away of children—custody. They have done that to poor women of color and to poor women from time out of mind. This is not a new phenomenon that women who had children couldn't keep them because the state intervened. It's just that this group of people—lesbians and some gay men—are now experiencing the same thing. There are many similarities in what we experience. And also the same people who are hounding the usual scapegoat target groups, they're hounding the lesbian and gay community too. Our enemies are the same. That to me is the major thing that should be pulling us together.

The militant right wing in this country has targeted the lesbian and gay community, but they have targeted other groups, too. And they're really being quite successful during this time period. Does the Oklahoma City bombing have anything to do with the fate of the lesbian and gay community? Absolutely it does! The Oklahoma bombing epitomizes what dire straits the country is in as a whole, and if we had a responsible lesbian/gay/bisexual/transgendered people movement, it would be asking questions like, "Okay, what is our movement supposed to be doing now, post–Oklahoma City?" That really should have been a wake-up call.

We need to look at why those people are so antigovernment. The press never explains; all it gave us after the bombing was, "They're antigovernment and they're very upset over Waco." The reason those people are so antigovernment is that they think this government is a Zionist conspiracy that privileges Black savages. That's what they think. It's never explained that the reason they're so antigovernment is because they're white supremacists, they're anti-Semitic, they're homophobic, and they're definitely opposed to women's freedom too.

You asked about race and lesbian and gay oppression. One of the things that I wanted to say early on is that the clearest responses that I have to that are out of my own experience as a person who has those identities linked. I think that the clearest answers come from those of us who simultaneously experience these oppressions; however, identity politics has been so maligned during this period that I almost hesitate to bring it up, because I don't want people to think I'm saying that the only reason it makes a difference is because it's bothering *me*. Of course, I am concerned about these issues because in my own life and experience I know what struggle is about, I know what oppression is about, and I have seen and experienced suffering myself.

That's not the only reason I am an activist, though. I care about everyone who is under siege. Some people think that because I'm so positively pro-Black and because I speak out against racism at every turn, that I don't really care if white people are suffering. Quite to the contrary. I care about all people who are not getting a fair shake, who are not getting an equal chance to fulfill their maximum potential and to live without fear and to have the basic things that every human needs: shelter, clothing, quality health care, meaningful and fairly compensated work, love and caring and freedom to express and to create, all those things that make life worth living. How limited would my politics be if I was only concerned about people like me! Given who I am as a Black woman and a lesbian and a person from a working-class home who is a socialist opposed to the exploitation of capitalism, well maybe that isn't so narrow. But what if I only cared about other Black lesbians? I would be sitting on the head of a pin.

The best heroes and the best heroines that we have throughout history have been those people who have gone beyond the narrow expectations that their demographic profile would lead you to expect. . . .

Those privileged, white gay men you mentioned that you view as setting the agenda currently—suppose homophobia could be eased in some ways. What stake do they have in other forms of oppression being ended?

The systems of oppression really do tie together. The plans and the strategies for oppressing and repressing our various groups are startlingly similar, and a society that is unjust, it's like cancer or a bleeding ulcer or something. You can't contain it. I guess it was Martin Luther King who said that when you have injustice anywhere, you really have it everywhere. It poisons the body politic of the society as a whole, and therefore you can't have singular solutions. Those white gay men who have disposable income and who think that all they need to do is get rid of the most blatant homophobia in corporate, government, and military settings, in the legal system and on TV, and everything else will fall into place, that they'll have a nice life in their little enclaves—they're dreaming. Let's say they got rid of homophobia in those places that I mentioned—which is not really getting rid of homophobia, it's getting rid of it in places that make their lives difficult—but suppose they were able to do that. If they were living in or near a city that has imploded, like Los Angeles, because of racial and economic exploitation and oppression, then how free are they going to be? I don't know why people can't understand how interconnected our fates are as creatures on the planet. . . .

One of the arguments people make for single-issue activism is that the gay community is too diverse to agree on an entire multi-issue agenda. They say, "We'll never get anywhere if we have to agree on everything else, so we're just going to work on one thing that we do agree about."

. . . If gay rights were put in place tomorrow, my behind would still be on fire. I would still be in ultimate danger here, because racism is still in the saddle. And so is class oppression, and so is sexual oppression. So getting a middle-of-the-road, mainstream gay rights agenda passed, how's that going to stop me from being raped? How's that going to help me not get breast cancer? How is it going to help the environment not get poisoned? How is it going to help the children of my community to have a chance for a decent life?

29

GLOBALIZING SEX WORKERS' RIGHTS

Kamala Kempadoo

When I first heard about prostitutes organizing for their rights in Suriname in 1993, I was both excited and puzzled by the news. Was it a singular incident spurred by an outsider, or did it reflect a local movement? I wanted to know. Also, in this part of the world, were women serious about staying in the sex industry or anxious to have prostitution abolished? What were the aims of such an organization, and who were the activists? Was this an isolated group, and what was the response to this initiative from the rest of the women's movement in this corner of South America? Questions outweighed any answer I could find in libraries or books—I decided to travel to Suriname to find out more. . . .

SEX WORKER, PROSTITUTE OR WHORE?

Identity, rights, working conditions, decriminalization, and legitimacy have been central issues collectively addressed by prostitutes for many years. Through these struggles the notion of the sex worker has emerged as a counterpoint to traditionally derogatory names, under the broad banner of a prostitutes' rights movement, with some parts recovering and valorizing the name and identity of "whore." In this [work] we have chosen the term "sex worker" to reflect the current use throughout the world, although . . . "sex worker" and "prostitute" are used interchangeably. It is a term that suggests we view prostitution not as an identity—a social or a psychological characteristic of women, often indicated by "whore"—but as an income-generating activity or form of labor for women and men. The definition stresses the social location of those engaged in sex industries as working people.

The idea of the sex worker is inextricably related to struggles for the recognition of women's work, for basic human rights and for decent working conditions. The definition emphasizes flexibility and variability of sexual labor as well as its similarities with other dimensions of working people's lives. Sex work is experienced as an integral part of many women's and men's

---

From Kamala Kempadoo and J. Doezema, *Global Sex Workers: Rights, Resistence, and Redefinition* (New York: Routledge, 1998), pp. 1–28. Reproduced by permission of Routledge, Inc., part of the Taylor & Francis Group.

lives around the world, and not necessarily as the sole defining activity around which their sense of self or identity is shaped. Moreover, commercial sex work . . . is not always a steady activity, but may occur simultaneously with other forms of income-generating work such as domestic service, informal commercial trading, market-vending, shoeshining or office work. Sex work can also be quite short-lived or be a part of an annual cycle of work—in few cases are women and men engaged full-time or as professionals. Consequently, in one person's lifetime, sex work is commonly just one of the multiple activities employed for generating income, and very few stay in prostitution for their entire adulthood. In most cases, sex work is not for individual wealth but for family well-being or survival; for working class women to clothe, feed and educate their children; and for young women and men to sustain themselves when the family income is inadequate. For many, sex work means migration away from their hometown or country. For others, it is associated with drug use, indentureship or debt-bondage. For the majority, participation in sex work entails a life in the margins.

The concept of sex work emerged in the 1970s through the prostitutes' rights movement in the United States and Western Europe. . . . Defining human activity or work as the way in which basic needs are met and human life produced and reproduced, Than-Dam Truong argues that activities involving purely sexual elements of the body and sexual energy should also be considered vital to the fulfillment of basic human needs: for both procreation and bodily pleasure.[1] Truong thus introduces the concept of sexual labor to capture the notion of the utilization of sexual elements of the body and as a way of understanding a productive life force that is employed by women and men. In this respect she proposes that sexual labor be considered similar to other forms of labor that humankind performs to sustain itself—such as mental and manual labor, all of which involve specific parts of the body and particular types of energy and skills. Furthermore, she points out, the social organization of sexual labor has taken a variety of forms in different historical contexts and political economies, whereby there is no universal form or appearance of either prostitution or sex work. Instead, she proposes, analyses of prostitution need to address and take into account the specific ways in which sexual subjectivity, sexual needs and desires are constructed in specific contexts. Wet-nursing, temple prostitution, "breeding" under slavery, surrogate child-bearing, donor sex, commercial sex and biological reproduction can thus be seen as illustrations of historical and contemporary ways in which sexual labor has been organized for the re-creation and replenishment of human and social life.

Perhaps one of the most confounding dimensions in the conceptualization of prostitution as labor concerns the relation that exists in many people's minds between sexual acts and "love," and with prevailing ideas that without love, sexual acts are harmful and abusive. After all, isn't sex supposed to be about consensual sharing of our "most personal, private, erotic, sensitive parts of our physical and psychic being," as some would argue?[2] And aren't women in particular harmed or violated by sexual acts that are not intimate? In such perspectives, the sale of one's sexual energies is confused with a particular morality about sexual relations and essentialist cultural interpretations are imposed upon the subject. This conflation of sex with the highest form of intimacy presupposes a universal meaning of sex, and ignores changing perceptions and values as well as the variety of meanings that women and men hold about their sexual lives. . . .

. . . There is a persistent pattern through much of history that positions the social gendered category "women" as the sellers or providers of sexual labor and "men" as the group deriving profits and power from the interactions. The subordination of the female and the feminine is the overriding factor for this arrangement in a variety of cultural, national and economic contexts, producing stigmas and social condemnation of persons who defy the socially defined boundaries of womanhood. Categories of "good" and "bad" women (virgin/whore, madonna/prostitute, chaste/licentious women) exist in most patriarchal societies, where the "bad" girl becomes the trope for female sexuality that threatens male control and domination. Female sexual acts that serve women's sexual or economic interests are, within the context of masculin-ist hegemony, dangerous, immoral, perverted, irresponsible and indecent. Construed in this fashion, the image of the whore disciplines and divides women, forcing some to conform to virginity, domesticity and monogamy and demonizing those who transgress these boundaries. Sex work positions women in dominant discourse as social deviants and outcasts. Today the majority of the world's sex workers are women, working within male-dominated businesses and industries, yet while the social definition of the provider of sexual labor is often closely associated with specific cultural constructions of femininity, and "the prostitute" rendered virtually synonymous with "woman," these gendered relations are clearly also being contested and redefined in different ways throughout the world. Various trends acutely challenge the tendency to essentialize the sex worker with biological notions of gender. In the Caribbean for example, so-called romance tourism is based on the sale by men of "love" to North American and European women, and "rent-a-dreads" and beach boys dominate the sex trade in the tourism industry in some islands.[3] . . . Thai sex workers in Japan report to sometimes buy sex for their own pleasure from male strippers, Brazilian "miches"—young male hustlers—get by through selling sex to other men, and in Europe and Malaysia male-to-female transgender sex workers also service men. Across the globe, "genetic" men and boys engage in sex work, selling sex to both men and women in homosexual and heterosexual relations, as feminine and masculine subjects. Nevertheless, even with the increasing visibility of genetic men and boys in sex work, gender inequality and discrimination remain evident. . . .

Children, both boys and girls, are also increasingly evident in prostitution, particularly in Third World settings, making the picture of gendered relations even more complex. However, child participation in sex industries invariably raises other questions and problems than those to do with gender, and it is within the international debates on "child prostitution" that a discourse of sexual labor and sex work is also apparent. While some attribute the rise of adolescents and pre-pubescent children in prostitution to the insatiable sexual appetites of depraved western men, or to cultural preferences in Third World countries for sex with virgins, a highly compelling explanation involves an analysis of the global political economy and processes of development and underdevelopment. Studies by the International Labor Organization (ILO) show that the proliferation of earning activity by children is associated with the development process "with its intrinsic features of population and social mobility, urbanization, and progressive monetization of all forms of human activity," and the growth of the modern tourist industry based on the accumulation of wealth and disposable incomes in the industrialized world.[4] The disruption that such development brings to the organization of production in developing countries, draws children into marginal and servile occupations sometimes requiring parents to deploy the income-generating capacity of their children in order to ensure that the household survives. The research suggests we include child prostitution in the context of the global exploitation of child labor in order to effectively address the problem. Such understandings of child labor undergird various child worker movements around the world. . . .

Sex work, as we understand it here, is not a universal or ahistorical category, but is subject to change and redefinition. It is clearly not limited to prostitution or to women, but certainly encompasses what is generally understood to fall into these two categories. However, even though human sexual and emotional resources have been organized and managed in different ways and acquired different meanings, capital accumulation, liberal free market politics and the commodification of waged labor has transformed various social arrangements in a consistent fashion. . . .

If sexual labor is seen to be subject to exploitation, as with any other labor, it can also be considered as a basis for mobilization in struggles for working conditions, rights and benefits and for broader resistances against the oppression of working peoples, paralleling situations in other informal and unregulated sectors. And by recognizing sexual labor in this fashion, it is possible to identify broader strategies for change. . . . The conceptualization of prostitutes, whores, strippers, lap dancers, escorts, exotic dancers, etc., as "sex workers" insists that working women's common interests can be articulated within the context of broader (feminist) struggles against the devaluation of "women's" work and gender exploitation within capitalism. . . .

SEX WORK AND RACISM

Besides the location of women in the sex trade as workers, migrants and agents we address the specificity of racism in positioning Third World sex workers in international relations. . . .

. . . Images of "the exotic" are entwined with ideologies of racial and ethnic difference: the "prostitute" is defined as "other" in comparison to the racial or ethnic origin of the client. Such boundaries, between which women are defined as "good" and "bad," or woman and whore, reinforce sexual relations intended for marriage and family and sets limits on national and ethnic membership. The brown or black woman is regarded as a desirable, tantalizing, erotic subject, suitable for temporary or non-marital sexual intercourse—the ideal "outside" woman—and rarely seen as a candidate for a long-term commitment, an equal partner, or as a future mother. She thus represents the unknown or forbidden yet is positioned in dominant discourse as the subordinated "other." . . . It is not simply grinding poverty that underpins a woman's involvement in prostitution. Race and ethnicity are equally important factors for any understanding of contemporary sex industries. . . . Prostitution is a realm of contradictions. Thus, even with the heightened exoticization of the sexuality of Third World women and men, they are positioned within the global sex industry second to white women. White sex workers invariably work in safer, higher paid and more comfortable environments; brown women—Mulatas, Asians, Latinas—form a middle class; and Black women are still conspicuously overrepresented in the poorest and most dangerous sectors of the trade, particularly street work. Whiteness continues to represent the hegemonic ideal of physical and sexual attractiveness and desirability, and white sexual labor is most valued within the global sex industry. . . .

. . . Some prostitutes' rights advocates assume that western development, capitalist modernization and industrialization will enable women in developing countries to exercise choice and attain "freedom." Seen to be trapped in underdeveloped states, Third World prostitutes continue to be positioned in this discourse as incapable of making decisions about their own lives, forced by overwhelming external powers completely beyond their control into submission and slavery. Western women's experience is thus made synonymous with assumptions about the inherent superiority of industrialized capitalist development and Third World women placed in categories of pre-technological "backwardness," inferiority, dependency and ignorance. . . .

Third World and anti-racist feminisms have over the past two decades intensely critiqued the universalism and totalizing effect of unnuanced western (feminist) theorizing—modernist and postmodernist—arguing that many of the concepts and theories produced about women's oppression are, and have been for many years, grounded in struggles of middle-class white women and may be quite antithetical to other women's experiences, if not representative of imperialist feminist thought. Nevertheless the need for feminist theory to engage with racialized sexual subjectivities in tandem with the historical weight of imperialism, colonialism and racist constructions of power has only been raised recently in the context of this feminist theorizing on prostitution. In view of histories of the oversexualization of non-western women in western cultures and the colonial legacies of the rape and sexual abuse of indigenous, and other Third World women, a hesitancy to explore topics of Third World women's sexual agency and subjectivity in prostitution is quite understandable. Yet in an era when women can no longer be defined exclusively as victims, where Third World women speak for themselves in various forums, where increasingly analyses have shifted focus from simple hierarchies and dichotomies to the problematization of multiple spaces, seemingly contradictory social locations and plural sites of power, it would seem that experiences, identities and struggles of women in the global sex industry cannot be neglected. . . .

TRANSNATIONAL SEX WORK AND THE GLOBAL ECONOMY

. . . Since the 1970s a global restructuring of capitalist production and investment has taken place and this can be seen to have wide-scale gendered implications and, by association, an impact on sex industries and sex work internationally. New corporate strategies to increase profit have developed, involving the movement of capital from industrial centers to countries with cheap labor, the circumvention of unionized labor, and so-called flexible employment policies. Unemployment and temporary work plagues the industrialized centers as well as "developing" countries. . . .

The emerging global economic order has already wreaked havoc on women's lives. Recent studies document an increasing need of women to contribute to the household economy through waged labor, yet having to deal with declining real wages, lower wage structures than men and longer working hours. Seasonal or flexible employment is the norm for women all over the world. Skilled and unskilled female workers constitute the main labor force in the new export-oriented industries—for shoe, toy, textile and garment production, in agribusinesses and electronic factories—where they are faced with poor working conditions, are continually threatened with unemployment due to automation and experience mass dismissals due to relocations of whole sectors of the industry. In many instances, minimum wage, health and safety laws are overridden by the transnational corporations in these new production zones, leaving women workers in particularly hazardous situations. Furthermore, with disruptions to traditional household and family structures, women are increasingly becoming heads of households, providing and nurturing the family. With dwindling family resources and the western emphasis on the independent nuclear family, women must also increasingly rely on the state for provisions such as maternity leave and child-care, yet fewer funds are allocated by governments for social welfare and programs. Informal sector work and "moonlighting" is growing and engagement in the booming sex industries fills a gap created by globalization.

Migration is a road many take to seek other opportunities and to break away from oppressive local conditions caused by globalization. A 1996 ILO report describes the "feminization" of international labor migration as "one of the most striking economic and social phenomena of recent times." This "phenomenon" according to the authors of the report, is most pronounced in Asian countries where women are migrating as "autonomous, economic agents" in their own right, "trying to seize economic opportunities overseas."[5] The Philippines has put more women onto the overseas labor market than any other country in the world.[6] Within all this dislocation and movement, some migrant women become involved in sex work.

However, laws prohibiting or regulating prostitution and migration, particularly from the South, combine to create highly complex and oppressive situations for women if they become involved in sex work once abroad. The illegal movement of persons for work elsewhere, commonly known as "trafficking" also becomes a very real issue for those who are being squeezed on all sides and have few options other than work in underground and informal sectors. Traffickers take advantage of the illegality of commercial sex work and migration, and are able to exert an undue amount of power and control over those seeking political or economic refuge or security. In such cases, it is the laws that prevent legal commercial sex work and immigration that form the major obstacles.

A related dimension to globalization with the expansion of sex industries, a heightened necessity for transnational migration for work, and increasing immiseration of women worldwide, is the spread of AIDS. Paul Farmer links the pandemic in sub-Saharan Africa to the social realities of the migrant labor system, rapid urbanization, high levels of war with military mobilization, landlessness and poverty that have been exacerbated by an economic crises caused by "poor terms of trade, the contradictions of post-colonial economies which generate class disparities and burdensome debt service" since the mid 1970s.[7] These factors, he contends, are intricately intertwined with pervasive gender inequality and specific socially constructed meanings of gender and sex, creating a very complex situation regarding the epidemiology and, consequently, the prevention of AIDS. . . .

. . . Sex workers are continually blamed for the spread of the disease, with Eurocentric racist notions of cultural difference compounding the effect for Third World populations. Consequently, inappropriate methods of intervention have been introduced and sex workers burdened with having to take responsibility for the prevention and control of the disease. . . .

THE GLOBAL MOVEMENT

. . . Sex workers in Third World and other non-western countries have been busy, taking action, demonstrating against injustices they face, and demanding human, civil, political and social rights. Thus not only was an Ecuadorian association formed in 1982, but they held a sex workers' strike in 1988. In Brazil, a national prostitutes conference took place in 1987, giving rise to the establishment of the National Network of Prostitutes, Da Vida. In Montevideo, Uruguay, AMEPU inaugurated its childcare center and new headquarters after making its first public appearance in the annual May Day march in 1988. The Network of Sex Work Projects, founded in 1991, began to make links with sex workers' rights and health care projects in the Asian and Pacific region, slowly creating a truly international network that today includes at least forty different projects and groups in as many different countries around the world. 1992 witnessed the founding of the Venezuelan Association of Women for Welfare and Mutual Support (AMBAR), with the Chilean group Association for the Rights of Women, "Angela Lina" (APRODEM) and the Mexican Unión Única following suit in 1993. Two national congresses were held by the Ecuadorian sex workers' rights association in 1993 and 1994. The Maxi Linder Association in Suriname, the Indian Mahila Samanwaya Committee, and the Colombian Association of Women (Cormujer), were also all established by 1994. In the same year, around 400 prostitutes staged a protest against the closing of a brothel in Lima, Peru, with the slogan "We Want to Work, We Want to Work" and in Paramaribo, Suriname, sex workers made a first mass public appearance on AIDS Day, marching through the city with the banner "No Condom, No Pussy," drawing attention to their demands for safe sex. Also, 1994 witnessed the founding of The Sex Worker Education and Advocacy Taskforce (SWEAT) in South Africa. In 1996, groups in Japan and the Dominican Republic—Sex Workers! Encourage, Empower, Trust and Love Yourselves! (SWEETLY) and Movement of United Women (MODEMU)—were formed, and in the same year the Indian organization held its first congress in Calcutta, as well as organizing several protests and demonstrations against harassment and brutality. In 1997, with the help of AMBAR in Venezuela, the Association for Women in Solidarity (AMAS) became the first Nicaraguan group, comprised mainly of street workers. Other sex worker organizations have been reported to exist in Indonesia, Tasmania, Taiwan, and Turkey. . . .

While this list of organizations is not exhaustive, and keeps growing, we must keep in mind that each group has a history that pre-dates its formal founding date. Sex workers as individuals and in informal groups have battled against stigmas and discriminatory laws, denounced social and political injustices, and fought for their basic human rights in non-western settings for many years and there are often several years of organized activity before a formal organization appears on the map. . . .

. . . While clearly there is a need for autonomous organizing and consolidation of each group's position, within its own political, economic and cultural context, it is evident that sex workers do not view the struggle as isolated from that of other members of society. As prostitutes, migrant workers, transgenders, family breadwinners, single parents, HIV-positives, or teenagers, many recognize the multiple arenas in which their lives play, and consequently the multiple facets of social life that must be addressed. Gay, lesbian, bisexual, and transgender organizations, legal and human rights activists, health care workers, labor unions, and other sex industry workers are potential allies in the struggle to transform sexual labor into work that is associated with dignity, respect and decent working conditions. The coalitions that are taking shape through everyday resistances of sex workers also brings new meanings to the women's movement and feminism.

NOTES

1. Than-Dam Truong, *Sex, Money and Morality: Prostitution and Tourism in South East Asia* (London: Zed Books, 1990).

2. A position argued by Kathleen Barry, *The Prostitution of Sexuality: The Global Exploitation of Women* (New York: New York University Press, 1995).

3. Clayton M. Press, Jr. "Reputation and Respectability Considered: Hustling in a Tourist Setting." *Caribbean Issues* 4 (1978): 109–19; and Deborah Pruitt and Suzanne LaFont, "For Love and Money: Romance Tourism in Jamaica," *Annals of Tourism Research* 22, no. 2 (1995), 422–40.

4. Maggie Black, *In the Twilight Zone: Child Workers in the Hotel, Tourism and Catering Industry* (Geneva: International Labour Office, 1995).

5. International Labor Organization. Web site: www.ilo.org.

6. Ninotchka Rosca, "The Philippines' Shameful Export," *The Nation* (April 17, 1995).

7. Paul Farmer, "Women, Poverty, and AIDS," in *Women, Poverty and AIDS: Sex, Drugs and Structural Violence*, ed. Paul Farmer, Margaret Connors, and Janie Simmons (Monroe, Me: Common Courage Press, 1996), p. 71.

30

BLACK SEXUALITY
The Taboo Subject

Cornel West

Americans are obsessed with sex and fearful of black sexuality. The obsession has to do with a search for stimulation and meaning in a fast-paced, market-driven culture; the fear is rooted in visceral feelings about black bodies fueled by sexual myths of black women and men. The dominant myths draw black women and men either as threatening creatures who have the potential for sexual power over whites, or as harmless, desexed underlings of a white culture. There is Jezebel (the seductive temptress), Sapphire (the evil, manipulative bitch), or Aunt Jemima (the sexless, long-suffering nurturer). There is Bigger Thomas (the mad and mean predatory craver of white women), Jack Johnson, the super performer—be it in athletics, entertainment, or sex—who excels others naturally and prefers women of a lighter hue), or Uncle Tom (the spineless, sexless—or is it impotent?—sidekick of whites). The myths offer distorted, dehumanized creatures whose bodies—color of skin, shape of nose and lips, type of hair, size of hips—are already distinguished from the white norm of beauty and whose feared sexual activities are deemed disgusting, dirty, or funky and considered less acceptable.

Yet the paradox of the sexual politics of race in America is that, behind closed doors, the dirty, disgusting, and funky sex associated with black people is often perceived to be more intriguing and interesting, while in public spaces talk about black sexuality is virtually taboo. Everyone knows it is virtually impossible to talk candidly about race without talking about sex. Yet most social scientists who examine race relations do so with little or no reference to how sexual perceptions influence racial matters. My thesis is that black sexuality is a taboo subject in white and black America and that a candid dialogue about black sexuality between and within these communities is requisite for healthy race relations in America.

The major cultural impact of the 1960s was not to demystify black sexuality but rather to make black bodies more accessible to white bodies *on an equal basis*. The history of such access up to that time was primarily one of brutal white rape and ugly white abuse. The Afro-Americanization of white youth—given the disproportionate black role in popular music and athletics—has put white kids in closer contact with their own bodies and facilitated more humane interaction with black people. Listening to Motown records in the sixties or dancing to hip hop music in the nineties may not lead one to question the sexual myths of black women and men, but when white and black kids buy the same Billboard hits and laud the same athletic heroes the result is often a shared cultural space where some humane interaction takes place.

This subterranean cultural current of interracial interaction increased during the 1970s and 1980s even as racial polarization deepened on the political front. We miss much of what goes on in the complex development of race relations in America if we focus solely on the racial card played by the Republican Party and overlook the profound multicultural mix of popular culture that has occurred in the past two decades. In fact, one of the reasons Nixon, Reagan, and Bush had to play a racial card, that is, had to code their language about race, rather than simply call a spade a spade, is due to the changed *cultural* climate of race and sex in America. The classic scene of Senator Strom Thurmond—staunch segregationist and longtime opponent of interracial sex and marriage—strongly defending Judge Clarence Thomas—married to a white woman and an alleged avid consumer of white pornography—shows how this change in climate affects even reactionary politicians in America.

Needless to say, many white Americans still view black sexuality with disgust. And some continue to view their own sexuality with disgust. Victorian morality and racist perceptions die hard. But more and more white Americans are willing to interact sexually with black Americans *on an equal basis*—even if the myths still persist. I view this as neither cause for celebration nor reason for lament. Anytime two human beings find genuine pleasure, joy, and love, the stars smile and the universe is enriched. Yet as long as that pleasure, joy, and love is still predicated on myths of black sexuality, the more fundamental challenge of humane interaction remains unmet. Instead, what we have is white access to black bodies on an equal basis—but not yet the demythologizing of black sexuality.

This demythologizing of black sexuality is crucial for black America because much of black self-hatred and self-contempt has to do with the refusal of many black Americans to love their own black bodies—especially their black noses, hips, lips, and hair. Just as many white Americans view black sexuality with disgust, so do many black Americans—but for very different reasons and with very different results. White supremacist ideology is based first and foremost on the degradation of black bodies in order to control them. One of the best ways to instill fear in people is to terrorize them. Yet this fear is best sustained by convincing them that their bodies are ugly, their intellect is inherently underdeveloped, their culture is less civilized, and their future warrants less concern than that of other peoples. Two hundred and forty-four years of slavery and nearly a century of institutionalized terrorism in the form of segregation, lynchings, and second-class citizenship in America were aimed at precisely this devaluation of black people. This white supremacist venture was, in the end, a relative failure—thanks to the courage and creativity of millions of black people and hundreds of exceptional white folk like John Brown, Elijah Lovejoy, Myles Horton, Russell Banks, Anne Braden, and others. Yet this white dehumanizing endeavor has left its toll in the psychic scars and personal wounds now inscribed in the souls of black folk. These scars and wounds are clearly etched on the canvass of black sexuality.

How does one come to accept and affirm a body so despised by one's fellow citizens? What are the ways in which one can rejoice in the intimate moments of black sexuality in a culture that questions the aesthetic beauty of one's body? Can genuine human relationships flourish for black people in a society that assaults black intelligence, black moral character, and black possibility?

These crucial questions were addressed in those black social spaces that affirmed black humanity and warded off white contempt—especially in black families, churches, mosques, schools, fraternities, and sororities. These precious black institutions forged a mighty struggle against the white supremacist bombardment of black people. They empowered black children to learn against the odds and supported damaged black egos so they could keep fighting; they preserved black sanity in an absurd society in which racism ruled unabated; and they provided opportunities for black love to stay alive. But these grand yet flawed black institutions refused to engage one fundamental issue: *black sexuality*. Instead, they ran from it like the plague. And they obsessively condemned those places where black sexuality was flaunted: the streets, the clubs, and the dance-halls.

Why was this so? Primarily because these black institutions put a premium on black survival in America. And black survival required accommodation with and acceptance from white America. Accommodation avoids any sustained association with the subversive and transgressive—be it communism or miscegenation. Did not the courageous yet tragic lives of Paul Robeson and Jack Johnson bear witness to this truth? And acceptance meant that only "good" negroes would thrive—especially those who left black sexuality at the door when they "entered" and "arrived." In short, struggling black institutions made a Faustian pact with white America: avoid any substantive engagement with black sexuality and your survival on the margins of American society is, at least, possible.

White fear of black sexuality is a basic ingredient of white racism. And for whites to admit this deep fear even as they try to instill and sustain fear in blacks is to acknowledge a weakness—a weakness that goes down to the bone. Social scientists have long acknowledged that interracial sex and marriage is the most *perceived* source of white fear of black people—just as the repeated castrations of lynched black men cries out for serious psycho-cultural explanation.

Black sexuality is a taboo subject in America principally because it is a form of black power over which whites have little control—yet its visible manifestations evoke the most visceral of white responses, be it one of seductive obsession or downright disgust. On the one hand, black sexuality among blacks simply does not include whites, nor does it make them a central point of reference. It proceeds as if whites do not exist, as if whites are invisible and simply don't matter. This form of black sexuality puts black agency center stage with no white presence at all. This can be uncomfortable for white people accustomed to being the custodians of power.

On the other hand, black sexuality between blacks and whites proceeds based on underground desires that Americans deny or ignore in public and over which laws have no effective control. In fact, the dominant sexual myths of black women and men portray whites as being "out of control"—seduced, tempted, overcome, overpowered by black bodies. This form of black sexuality makes white passivity the norm—hardly an acceptable self-image for a white-run society.

Of course, neither scenario fully accounts for the complex elements that determine how any particular relationship involving black sexuality *actually* takes place. Yet they do accent the crucial link between black sexuality and black power in America. In this way, to make black sexuality a taboo subject is to silence talk about a particular kind of power black people are perceived to have over whites. On the surface, this "golden" side is one in which black people simply have an upper hand sexually over whites given the dominant myths in our society.

. . . Black male sexuality differs from black female sexuality because black men have different self-images and strategies of acquiring power in the patriarchal structures of white America and black communities. Similarly, black male heterosexuality differs from black male homosexuality owing to the self-perceptions and means of gaining power in the homophobic institutions of white America and black communities. The dominant myth of black male sexual prowess makes black men desirable sexual partners in a culture obsessed with sex. In addition, the Afro-Americanization of white youth has been more a male than a female affair given the prominence of male athletes and the cultural weight of male pop artists. This process results in white youth—male and female—imitating and emulating black male styles of walking, talking, dressing, and gesticulating in relation to others. One irony of our present moment is that just as young black men are murdered, maimed, and imprisoned in record numbers, their styles have become disproportionately influential in shaping popular culture. For most young black men, power is acquired by stylizing their bodies over space and time in such a way that their bodies reflect their uniqueness and provoke fear in others. To be "bad" is good not simply because it subverts the language of the dominant white culture but also because it imposes a unique kind of order for young black men on their own distinctive chaos and solicits an attention that makes others pull back with some trepidation. This young black male style is a form of self-identification and resistance in a hostile culture; it also is an instance of machismo identity ready for violent encounters. Yet in a patriarchal society, machismo identity is expected and even exalted—as with Rambo and Reagan. Yet a black machismo style solicits primarily sexual encounters with women and violent encounters with other black men or aggressive police. In this way, the black male search for power often reinforces the myth of black male sexual prowess—a myth that tends to subordinate black and white women as objects of sexual pleasure. This search for power also usually results in a direct confrontation with the order-imposing authorities of the status quo, that is, the police or criminal justice system. The prevailing cultural crisis of many black men is the limited stylistic options of self-image and resistance in a culture obsessed with sex yet fearful of black sexuality.

This situation is even bleaker for most black gay men who reject the major stylistic option of black machismo identity, yet who are marginalized in white America and penalized in black America for doing so. In their efforts to be themselves, they are told they are not really "black men," not machismo-identified. Black gay men are often the brunt of talented black comics like Arsenio Hall and Damon Wayans. Yet behind the laughs lurks a black tragedy of major proportions: the refusal of white and black America to entertain seriously new stylistic options for black men caught in the deadly endeavor of rejecting black machismo identities.

The case of black women is quite different, partly because the dynamics of white and black patriarchy affect them differently and partly because the degradation of black female heterosexuality in America makes black female lesbian sexuality a less frightful jump to make. This does not mean that black lesbians suffer less than black gays—in fact, they suffer more, principally owing to their lower economic status. But this does mean that the subculture of black lesbians is fluid and the boundaries are less policed precisely because black female sexuality in general is more devalued, hence more marginal in white and black America.

The dominant myth of black female sexual prowess constitutes black women as desirable sexual partners—yet the central role of the ideology of white female beauty attenuates the expected conclusion. Instead of black women being the most sought after "objects of sexual pleasure"—as in the case of black men—white women tend to occupy this "upgraded," that is, degraded, position primarily because white beauty plays a weightier role in sexual desirability for women in racist patriarchal America. The ideal of female beauty in this country puts a premium on lightness and softness mythically associated with white women and downplays the rich stylistic manners associated with black women. This operation is not simply more racist to black women than that at work in relation to black men; it also is more devaluing of women in general than that at work in relation to men in general. This means that black women are subject to more multilayered bombardments of racist assaults than black men in addition to the sexist assaults they receive from black men. Needless to say, most black men—especially professional ones—simply recycle this vulgar operation along the axis of lighter hues that results in darker black women bearing more of the brunt than their already devalued lighter sisters. The psychic bouts with self-confidence, the existential agony over genuine desirability, and the social burden of bearing and usually nurturing black children under these circumstances breeds a spiritual strength of black women unbeknownst to most black men and nearly all other Americans.

As long as black sexuality remains a taboo subject, we cannot acknowledge, examine, or engage these tragic psychocultural facts of American life. Furthermore, our refusal to do so limits our ability to confront the overwhelming realities of the AIDS epidemic in America in general and in black America in particular. Although the dynamics of black male sexuality differ from those of black female sexuality, new stylistic options of self-image and resistance can be forged only when black women and men do so together. This is so not because all black people should be heterosexual or with black partners, but rather because all black people—including black children of so-called "mixed" couples—are affected deeply by the prevailing myths of black sexuality. These myths are part of a wider network of white supremacist lies whose authority and legitimacy must be undermined. In the long run, there is simply no way out for all of us other than living out the truths we proclaim about genuine humane interaction in our psychic and sexual lives. Only by living against the grain can we keep alive the possibility that the visceral feelings about black bodies fed by racist myths and promoted by market-driven quests for stimulation do not forever render us obsessed with sexuality and fearful of each other's humanity.

31

THE INVENTION OF HETEROSEXUALITY

Jonathan Ned Katz

Heterosexuality is old as procreation, ancient as the lust of Eve and Adam. That first lady and gentleman, we assume, perceived themselves, behaved, and felt just like today's heterosexuals. We suppose that heterosexuality is unchanging, universal, essential: ahistorical.

Contrary to that common sense conjecture, the concept of heterosexuality is only one particular historical way of perceiving, categorizing, and imagining the social relations of the sexes. Not ancient at all, the idea of heterosexuality is a modern invention, dating to the late nineteenth century. The heterosexual belief, with its metaphysical claim to eternity, has a particular, pivotal place in the social universe of the late nineteenth and twentieth centuries that it did not inhabit earlier. This essay traces the historical process by which the heterosexual idea was created as ahistorical and taken-for-granted. . . .

By not studying the heterosexual idea in history, analysts of sex, gay and straight, have continued to privilege the "normal" and "natural" at the expense of the "abnormal" and "unnatural." Such privileging of the norm accedes to its domination, protecting it from questions. By making the normal the object of a thoroughgoing historical study we simultaneously pursue a pure truth and a sex-radical and subversive goal: we upset basic preconceptions. We discover that the heterosexual, the normal, and the natural have a history of changing definitions. Studying the history of the term challenges its power.

Contrary to our usual assumption, past Americans and other peoples named, perceived, and socially organized the bodies, lusts, and intercourse of the sexes in ways radically different from the way we do. If we care to understand this vast past sexual diversity, we need to stop promiscuously projecting our own hetero and homo arrangement. Though lip service is often paid to the distorting, ethnocentric effect of such conceptual imperialism, the category heterosexuality continues to be applied uncritically as a universal analytical tool. Recognizing the time-bound and culturally specific character of the heterosexual category can help us begin to work toward a thoroughly historical view of sex. . . .

Before Heterosexuality: Early Victorian True Love, 1820–1860

In the early nineteenth-century United States, from about 1820 to 1860, the heterosexual did not exist. Middle-class white Americans idealized a True Womanhood, True Manhood, and True Love, all characterized by "purity"— the freedom from sensuality.[1] Presented mainly in literary and religious texts, this True Love was a fine romance with no lascivious kisses. This ideal contrasts strikingly with late nineteenth- and twentieth-century American incitements to a hetero sex.[2]

Early Victorian True Love was only realized within the mode of proper procreation, marriage, the legal organization for producing a new set of correctly gendered women and men. Proper womanhood, manhood, and progeny—not a normal male-female eros—was the main product of this mode of engendering and of human reproduction.

The actors in this sexual economy were identified as manly men and womanly women and as procreators, not specifically as erotic beings or heterosexuals. Eros did not constitute the core of a heterosexual identity that inhered, democratically, in both men and women. True Women were defined by their distance from lust. True Men, though thought to live closer to carnality, and in less control of it, aspired to the same freedom from concupiscence.

Legitimate natural desire was for procreation and a proper manhood or womanhood; no heteroerotic desire was thought to be directed exclusively and naturally toward the other sex; lust in men was roving. The human body was thought of as a means towards procreation and production; penis and vagina were instruments of reproduction, not of pleasure. Human energy, thought of as a closed and severely limited system, was to be used in producing children and in work, not wasted in libidinous pleasures.

The location of all this engendering and procreative labor was the sacred sanctum of early Victorian True Love, the home of the True Woman and True Man—a temple of purity threatened from within by the monster masturbator, an archetypal early Victorian cult figure of illicit lust. The home of True Love was a castle far removed from the erotic exotic ghetto inhabited most notoriously then by the prostitute, another archetypal Victorian erotic monster. . . .

Late Victorian Sex-Love: 1860–1892

"Heterosexuality" and "homosexuality" did not appear out of the blue in the 1890s. These two eroticisms were in the making from the 1860s on. In late Victorian America and in Germany, from about 1860 to 1892, our modern idea of an eroticized universe began to develop, and the experience of a heterolust began to be widely documented and named. . . .

In the late nineteenth-century United States, several social factors converged to cause the eroticizing of consciousness, behavior, emotion, and identity that became typical of the twentieth-century Western middle class. The transformation of the family from producer to consumer unit resulted in a change in family members' relation to their own bodies; from being an instrument primarily of work, the human body was integrated into a new economy, and began more commonly to be perceived as a means of consumption and pleasure. Historical work has recently begun on how the biological human body is differently integrated into changing modes of production, procreation, engendering, and pleasure so as to alter radically the identity, activity, and experience of that body.[3]

The growth of a consumer economy also fostered a new pleasure ethic. This imperative challenged the early Victorian work ethic, finally helping to usher in a major transformation of values. While the early Victorian work ethic had touted the value of economic production, that era's procreation ethic had extolled the virtues of human reproduction. In contrast, the late Victorian economic ethic hawked the pleasures of consuming, while its sex ethic praised an erotic pleasure principle for men and even for women.

In the late nineteenth century, the erotic became the raw material for a new consumer culture. Newspapers, books, plays, and films touching on sex, "normal" and "abnormal," became available for a price. Restaurants, bars, and baths opened, catering to sexual consumers with cash. Late Victorian entrepreneurs of desire incited the proliferation of a new eroticism, a commoditized culture of pleasure.

In these same years, the rise in power and prestige of medical doctors allowed these upwardly mobile professionals to prescribe a healthy new sexuality. Medical men, in the name of science, defined a new ideal of male-female relationships that included, in women as well as men, an essential, necessary, normal eroticism. Doctors, who had earlier named and judged the sex-enjoying woman a "nymphomaniac," now began to label women's *lack* of sexual pleasure a mental disturbance, speaking critically, for example, of female "frigidity" and "anesthesia."[4]

By the 1880s, the rise of doctors as a professional group fostered the rise of a new medical model of Normal Love, replete with sexuality. The new Normal Woman and Man were endowed with a healthy libido. The new theory of Normal Love was the modern medical alternative to the old Cult of True Love. The doctors prescribed a new sexual ethic as if it were a morally neutral, medical description of health. The creation of the new Normal Sexual had its counterpart in the invention of the late Victorian Sexual Pervert. The attention paid the sexual abnormal created a need to name the sexual normal, the better to distinguish the average him and her from the deviant it.

Heterosexuality: The First Years, 1892–1900

In the periodization of heterosexual American history suggested here, the years 1892 to 1900 represent "The First Years" of the heterosexual epoch, eight key years in which the idea of the heterosexual and homosexual were initially and tentatively formulated by U.S. doctors. The earliest-known American use of the word "heterosexual" occurs in a medical journal article by Dr. James G. Kiernan of Chicago, read before the city's medical society on March 7, 1892, and published that May—portentous dates in sexual history.[5] But Dr. Kiernan's heterosexuals were definitely not exemplars of normality. Heterosexuals, said Kiernan, were defined by a mental condition, "psychical hermaphroditism." Its symptoms were "inclinations to both sexes." These heterodox sexuals also betrayed inclinations "to abnormal methods of gratification," that is, techniques to insure pleasure without procreation. Dr. Kiernan's heterogeneous sexuals did demonstrate "traces of the normal sexual appetite" (a touch of procreative desire). Kiernan's normal sexuals were implicitly defined by a monolithic other-sex inclination and procreative aim. Significantly, they still lacked a name.

Dr. Kiernan's article of 1892 also included one of the earliest-known uses of the word "homosexual" in American English. Kiernan defined "Pure homosexuals" as persons whose "general mental state is that of the opposite sex." Kiernan thus defined homosexuals by their deviance from a gender norm. His heterosexuals displayed a double deviance from both gender and procreative norms.

Though Kiernan used the new words heterosexual and homosexual, an old procreative standard and a new gender norm coexisted uneasily in his thought. His word heterosexual defined a mixed person and compound urge, abnormal because they wantonly included procreative and non-procreative objectives, as well as same-sex and different-sex attractions.

That same year, 1892, Dr. Krafft-Ebing's influential *Psychopathia Sexualis* was first translated and published in the United States.[6] But Kiernan and Krafft-Ebing by no means agreed on the definition of the heterosexual. In Krafft-Ebing's book, "hetero-sexual" was used unambiguously in the modern sense to refer to an erotic feeling for a different sex. "Homosexual" referred unambiguously to an erotic feeling for a "same sex." In Krafft-Ebing's volume, unlike Kiernan's article, heterosexual and homosexual were clearly distinguished from a third category, a "psycho-sexual hermaphroditism," defined by impulses toward both sexes.

Krafft-Ebing hypothesized an inborn "sexual instinct" for relations with the "opposite sex," the inherent "purpose" of which was to foster procreation. Krafft-Ebing's erotic drive was still a reproductive instinct. But the doctor's clear focus on a different-sex versus same-sex sexuality constituted a historic, epochal move from an absolute procreative standard of normality toward a new norm. His definition of heterosexuality as other-sex attraction provided the basis for a revolutionary, modern break with a centuries-old procreative standard.

It is difficult to overstress the importance of that new way of categorizing. The German's mode of labeling was radical in referring to the biological sex, masculinity or femininity, and the pleasure of actors (along with the procreant purpose of acts). Krafft-Ebing's heterosexual offered the modern world a new norm that came to dominate our idea of the sexual universe, helping to change it from a mode of human reproduction and engendering to a mode of pleasure. The heterosexual category provided the basis for a move from a production-oriented, procreative imperative to a consumerist pleasure principle—an institutionalized pursuit of happiness. . . .

Only gradually did doctors agree that heterosexual referred to a normal, "other-sex" eros. This new standard-model heterosex provided the pivotal term for the modern regularization of eros that paralleled similar attempts to standardize masculinity and femininity, intelligence, and manufacturing.[7] The idea of heterosexuality as the master sex from which all others deviated was (like the idea of the master race) deeply authoritarian. The doctors' normalization of a sex that was hetero proclaimed a new heterosexual separatism—an erotic apartheid that forcefully segregated the sex normals from the sex perverts. The new, strict boundaries made the emerging erotic world less polymorphous—safer for sex normals. However, the idea of such creatures as heterosexuals and homosexuals emerged from the narrow world of medicine to become a commonly accepted notion only in the early twentieth century. In 1901, in the comprehensive *Oxford English Dictionary*, "heterosexual" and "homosexual" had not yet made it.

The Distribution of the Heterosexual Mystique: 1900–1930

In the early years of this heterosexual century the tentative hetero hypothesis was stabilized, fixed, and widely distributed as the ruling sexual orthodoxy: The Heterosexual Mystique. Starting among pleasure-affirming urban working-class youths, southern blacks, and Greenwich Village bohemians as defensive subculture, heterosex soon triumphed as dominant culture.[8]

In its earliest version, the twentieth-century heterosexual imperative usually continued to associate heterosexuality with a supposed human "need," "drive," or "instinct" for propagation, a procreant urge linked inexorably with carnal lust as it had not been earlier. In the early twentieth century, the falling birth rate, rising divorce rate, and "war of the sexes" of the middle class were matters of increasing public concern. Giving vent to heteroerotic emotions was thus praised as enhancing baby-making capacity, marital intimacy, and family stability. (Only many years later, in the mid-1960s, would heteroeroticism be distinguished completely, in practice and theory, from procreativity and male-female pleasure sex justified in its own name.)

The first part of the new sex norm—hetero—referred to a basic gender divergence. The "oppositeness" of the sexes was alleged to be the basis for a universal, normal, erotic attraction between males and females. The stress on the sexes' "oppositeness," which harked back to the early nineteenth century, by no means simply registered biological differences of females and males. The early twentieth-century focus on physiological and gender dimorphism reflected the deep anxieties of men about the shifting work, social roles, and power of men over women, and about the ideals of womanhood and manhood. That gender anxiety is documented, for example, in 1897, in *The New York Times*' publication of the Reverend Charles Parkhurst's diatribe against female "andromaniacs," the preacher's derogatory, scientific-sounding name for women who tried to "minimize distinctions by which manhood and womanhood are differentiated."[9] The stress on gender difference was a conservative response to the changing social-sexual division of activity and feeling which gave rise to the independent "New Woman" of the 1880s and eroticized "Flapper" of the 1920s.

The second part of the new hetero norm referred positively to sexuality. That novel upbeat focus on the hedonistic possibilities of male-female conjunctions also reflected a social transformation—a revaluing of pleasure and procreation, consumption and work in commercial, capitalist society. The democratic attribution of a normal lust to human females (as well as males) served to authorize women's enjoyment of their own bodies and began to undermine the early Victorian idea of the pure True Woman—a sex-affirmative action still part of women's struggle. The twentieth-century Erotic Woman also undercut the nineteenth-century feminist assertion of women's moral superiority, cast suspicions of lust on women's passionate romantic friendships with women, and asserted the presence of a menacing female monster, "the lesbian."[10] . . .

In the perspective of heterosexual history, this early twentieth-century struggle for the more explicit depiction of an "opposite-sex" eros appears in a curious new light. Ironically, we find sex-conservatives, the social purity advocates of censorship and repression, fighting against the depiction not just of sexual perversity but also of the new normal hetero-sexuality. That a more open depiction of normal sex had to be defended against forces of propriety confirms the claim that heterosexuality's predecessor, Victorian True Love, had included no legitimate eros. . . .

The Heterosexual Steps Out: 1930–1945

In 1930, in *The New York Times*, heterosexuality first became a love that dared to speak its name. On April 20th of that year, the word "heterosexual" is first known to have appeared in *The New York Times Book Review*. There, a critic described the subject of André Gide's *The Immoralist* proceeding "from a heterosexual liaison to a homosexual one." The ability to slip between sexual categories was referred to casually as a rather unremarkable aspect of human possibility. This is also the first known reference by *The Times* to the new hetero/homo duo.[11]

In September the second reference to the hetero/homo dyad appeared in *The New York Times Book Review*, in a comment on Floyd Dell's *Love in the Machine Age*. This work revealed a prominent antipuritan of the 1930s using the dire threat of homosexuality as his rationale for greater heterosexual freedom. *The Times* quoted Dell's warning that current abnormal social conditions kept the young dependent on their parents, causing "infantilism, prostitution and homosexuality." Also quoted was Dell's attack on the "inculcation of purity" that "breeds distrust of the opposite sex." Young people, Dell said, should be "permitted to develop normally to heterosexual adulthood." "But," *The Times* reviewer emphasized, "such a state already exists, here and now." And so it did. Heterosexuality, a new gender-sex category, had been distributed from the narrow, rarified realm of a few doctors to become a nationally, even internationally, cited aspect of middle-class life.[12] . . .

Heterosexual Hegemony: 1945–1965

The "cult of domesticity" following World War II—the reassociation of women with the home, motherhood, and child-care; men with fatherhood and wage work outside the home—was a period in which the predominance of the hetero norm went almost unchallenged, an era of heterosexual hegemony. This was an age in which conservative mental-health professionals reasserted the old link between heterosexuality and procreation. In contrast, sex-liberals of the day strove, ultimately with success, to expand the heterosexual ideal to include within the boundaries of normality a wider-than-ever range of nonprocreative, premarital, and extramarital behaviors. But sex-liberal reform actually helped to extend and secure the dominance of the heterosexual idea, as we shall see when we get to Kinsey.

The postwar sex-conservative tendency was illustrated in 1947, in Ferdinand Lundberg and Dr. Marynia Farnham's books, *Modern Woman: The Lost Sex*. Improper masculinity and femininity was exemplified, the authors decreed, by "engagement in heterosexual relations . . . with the complete intent to see to it that they do not eventuate in reproduction."[13] Their procreatively defined heterosex was one expression of a postwar ideology of fecundity that, internalized and enacted dutifully by a large part of the population, gave rise to the postwar baby boom.

The idea of the feminine female and masculine male as prolific breeders was also reflected in the stress, specific to the late 1940s, on the homosexual as sad symbol of "sterility"—that particular loaded term appears incessantly in comments on homosex dating to the fecund forties.

In 1948, in *The New York Times Book Review*, sex liberalism was in ascendancy. Dr. Howard A. Rusk declared that Alfred Kinsey's just published report on *Sexual Behavior in the Human Male* had found "wide variations in sex concepts and behavior." This raised the question: "What is 'normal' and 'abnormal'?" In particular, the report had found that "homosexual experience is much more common than previously thought," and "there is often a mixture of both homo and hetero experience."[14]

Kinsey's counting of orgasms indeed stressed the wide range of behaviors and feelings that fell within the boundaries of a quantitative, statistically accounted heterosexuality. Kinsey's liberal reform of the hetero/homo dualism widened the narrow, old hetero category to accord better with the varieties of social experience. He thereby contradicted the older idea of a monolithic, qualitatively defined, natural procreative act, experience, and person.[15]

Though Kinsey explicitly questioned "whether the terms 'normal' and 'abnormal' belong in a scientific vocabulary," his counting of climaxes was generally understood to define normal sex as majority sex. This quantified norm constituted a final, society-wide break with the old qualitatively defined reproductive standard. Though conceived of as purely scientific, the statistical definition of the normal as the-sex-most-people-are-having substituted a new, quantitative moral standard for the old, qualitative sex ethic—another triumph for the spirit of capitalism.

Kinsey also explicitly contested the idea of an absolute, either/or antithesis between hetero and homo persons. He denied that human beings "represent two discrete populations, heterosexual and homosexual." The world, he ordered, "is not to be divided into sheep and goats." The hetero/homo division was not nature's doing: "Only the human mind invents categories and tries to force facts into separated pigeon-holes. The living world is a continuum."[16]

With a wave of the taxonomist's hand, Kinsey dismissed the social and historical division of people into heteros and homos. His denial of heterosexual and homosexual personhood rejected the social reality and profound subjective force of a historically constructed tradition which, since 1892 in the United States, had cut the sexual populaton in two and helped to establish the social reality of a heterosexual and homosexual identity.

On the one hand, the social construction of homosexual persons has led to the development of a powerful gay liberation identity politics based on an ethnic group model. This has freed generations of women and men from a deep, painful, socially induced sense of shame, and helped to bring about a society-wide liberalization of attitudes and responses to homosexuals.[17] On the other hand, contesting the notion of homosexual and heterosexual persons was one early, partial resistance to the limits of the hetero/homo construction. Gore Vidal, rebel son of Kinsey, has for years been joyfully proclaiming:

> there is no such thing as a homosexual or a heterosexual person. There are only homo- or heterosexual acts. Most people are a mixture of impulses if not practices, and what anyone does with a willing partner is of no social or cosmic significance.
>
> So why all the fuss? In order for a ruling class to rule, there must be arbitrary prohibitions. Of all prohibitions, sexual taboo is the most useful because sex involves everyone. . . . we have allowed our governors to divide the population into two teams. One team is good, godly, straight; the other is evil, sick, vicious.[18]

Heterosexuality Questioned: 1965–1982

By the late 1960s, anti-establishment counterculturalists, fledgling feminists, and homosexual-rights activists had begun to produce an unprecedented critique of sexual repression in general, of women's sexual repression in particular, of marriage and the family—and of some forms of heterosexuality. . . .

HETEROSEXUAL HISTORY: OUT OF THE SHADOWS

Our brief survey of the heterosexual idea suggests a new hypothesis. Rather than naming a conjunction old as Eve and Adam, heterosexual designates a word and concept, a norm and role, an individual and group identity, a behavior and feeling, and a peculiar sexual-political institution particular to the late nineteenth and twentieth centuries.

Because much stress has been placed here on heterosexuality as word and concept, it seems important to affirm that heterosexuality (and homosexuality) came into existence before it was named and thought about. The formulation of the heterosexual idea did not create a heterosexual experience or behavior; to suggest otherwise would be to ascribe determining power to labels and concepts. But the titling and envisioning of heterosexuality did play an important role in consolidating the construction of the heterosexual's social existence. Before the wide use of the word "heterosexual," I suggest, women and men did not mutually lust with the same profound, sure sense of normalcy that followed the distribution of "heterosexual" as universal sanctifier.

According to this proposal, women and men make their own sexual histories. But they do not produce their sex lives just as they please. They make their sexualities within a particular mode of organization given by the past and altered by their changing desire, their present power and activity, and their vision of a better world. That hypothesis suggests a number of good reasons for the immediate inauguration of research on a historically specific heterosexuality.

The study of the history of the heterosexual experience will forward a great intellectual struggle still in its early stages. This is the fight to pull heterosexuality, homosexuality, and all the sexualities out of the realm of nature and biology [and] into the realm of the social and historical. Feminists have explained to us that anatomy does not determine our gender destinies (our masculinities and femininities). But we've only recently begun to consider that *biology does not settle our erotic fates.* The common notion that biology determines the object of sexual desire, or that physiology and society together cause sexual orientation, are determinisms that deny the break existing between our bodies and situations and our desiring. Just as the biology of our hearing organs will never tell us why we take pleasure in Bach or delight in Dixieland, our female or male anatomies, hormones, and genes will never tell us why we yearn for women, men, both, other, or none. That is because desiring is a self-generated project of individuals within particular historical cultures. Heterosexual history can help us see the place of values and judgments in the construction of our own and others' pleasures, and to see how our erotic tastes—our aesthetics of the flesh—are socially institutionalized through the struggle of individuals and classes.

The study of heterosexuality in time will also help us to recognize the *vast historical diversity of sexual emotions and behaviors*—a variety that challenges the monolithic heterosexual hypothesis. John D'Emilio and Estelle Freedman's *Intimate Matters: A History of Sexuality in America* refers in passing to numerous substantial changes in sexual activity and feeling: for example, the widespread use of contraceptives in the nineteenth century, the twentieth-century incitement of the female orgasm, and the recent sexual conduct changes by gay men in response to the AIDS epidemic. It's now a commonplace of family history that people in particular classes feel and behave in substantially different ways under different, historical conditions. Only when we stop assuming an invariable essence of heterosexuality will we begin the research to reveal the full variety of sexual emotions and behaviors.

The historical study of the heterosexual experience can help us *understand the erotic relationships of women and men in terms of their changing modes of social organization.* Such modal analysis actually characterizes a sex history well underway. This suggests that the eros-gender-procreation system (the social ordering of lust, femininity and masculinity, and baby-making) has been linked closely to a society's particular organization of power and production. To understand the subtle history of heterosexuality we need to look carefully at correlations between (1) society's organization of eros and pleasure; (2) its mode of engendering persons as feminine or masculine (its making of women and men); (3) its ordering of human reproduction; and (4) its dominant political economy. This General Theory of Sexual Relativity proposes that substantial historical changes in the social organization of eros, gender, and procreation have basically altered the activity and experience of human beings within those modes.

A historical view locates heterosexuality and homosexuality in time, helping us distance ourselves from them. This distancing can help us formulate new questions that clarify our long-range sexual-political goals: What has been and is the social function of sexual categorizing? Whose interests have been served by the division of the world into heterosexual and homosexual? Do we dare not draw a line between those two erotic species? Is some sexual naming socially necessary? Would human freedom be enhanced if the sex-biology of our partners in lust was of no particular concern, and had no name? In what kind of society could we all more freely explore our desire and our flesh?

As we move [into the year 2000], a new sense of the historical making of the heterosexual and homosexual suggests that these are ways of feeling, acting, and being with each other that we can together unmake and radically remake according to our present desire, power, and our vision of a future political-economy of pleasure.

NOTES

1. Barbara Welter, "The Cult of True Womanhood: 1820–1860," *American Quarterly*, vol. 18 (Summer 1966); Welter's analysis is extended here to include True Men and True Love.

2. Some historians have recently told us to revise our idea of sexless Victorians: their experience and even their ideology, it is said, were more erotic than we previously thought. Despite the revisionists, I argue that "purity" was indeed the dominant, early Victorian, white middle-class standard. For the debate on Victorian sexuality see John

D'Emilio and Estelle Freedman, *Intimate Matters: A History of Sexuality in America* (New York: Harper & Row, 1988), p. xii.

3. See, for example, Catherine Gallagher and Thomas Laqueur, eds., "The Making of the Modern Body: Sexuality and Society in the Nineteenth Century," *Representations*, no. 14 (Spring 1986) (republished, Berkeley: University of California Press, 1987).

4. This reference to females reminds us that the invention of heterosexuality had vastly different impacts on the histories of women and men. It also differed in its impact on lesbians and heterosexual women, homosexual and heterosexual men, the middle class and working class, and on different religious, racial, national, and geographic groups.

5. Dr. James G. Kieman, "Responsibility in Sexual Perversion," *Chicago Medical Recorder*, vol. 3 (May 1892), pp. 185–210.

6. R. von Krafft-Ebing, *Psychopathia Sexualis, with Especial Reference to Contrary Sexual Instinct: A Medico-Legal Study*, trans. Charles Gilbert Chaddock (Philadelphia: F. A. Davis, 1892), from the 7th and revised German ed. Preface, November 1892.

7. For the standardization of gender see Lewis Terman and C. C. Miles, *Sex and Personality, Studies in Femininity and Masculinity* (New York: McGraw Hill, 1936). For the standardization of intelligence see Lewis Terman, *Stanford-Binet Intelligence Scale* (Boston: Houghton Mifflin, 1916). For the standardization of work, see "scientific management" and "Taylorism" in Harry Braverman, *Labor and Monopoly Capital: The Degradation of Work in the Twentieth Century* (New York: Monthly Review Press, 1974).

8. See D'Emilio and Freedman, *Intimate Matters*, pp. 194–201, 231, 241, 295–96; Ellen Kay Trimberger, "Feminism, Men, and Modern Love: Greenwich Village, 1900–1925," in *Powers of Desire: The Politics of Sexuality*, ed. Ann Snitow, Christine Stansell, Sharon Thompson (New York: Monthly Review Press, 1983), pp. 131–52; Kathy Peiss, "'Charity Girls' and City Pleasures: Historical Notes on Working Class Sexuality, 1880–1920," in *Powers of Desire*, pp. 74–87; and Mary P. Ryan, "The Sexy Saleslady: Psychology, Heterosexuality, and Consumption in the Twentieth Century," in her *Womanhood in America*, 2nd ed. (New York: Franklin Watts, 1979), pp. 151–82.

9. [Rev. Charles Parkhurst], "Woman. Calls Them Andromaniacs. Dr. Parkhurst So Characterizes Certain Women Who Passionately Ape Everything That Is Mannish. Woman Divinely Preferred. Her Supremacy Lies in Her Womanliness, and She Should Make the Most of It—Her Sphere of Best Usefulness the Home," *The New York Times*, May 23, 1897, p. 16:1.

10. See Lisa Duggan, "The Social Enforcement of Heterosexuality and Lesbian Resistance in the 1920s," in *Class, Race, and Sex: The Dynamics of Control*, ed. Amy Swerdlow and Hanah Lessinger (Boston: G. K. Hall, 1983), pp. 75–92; Rayna Rapp and Ellen Ross, "The Twenties Backlash: Compulsory Heterosexuality, the Consumer Family, and the Waning of Feminism," in *Class, Race, and Sex*; Christina Simmons, "Companionate Marriage and the Lesbian Threat," *Frontiers*, vol. 4, no. 3 (Fall 1979), pp. 54–59; and Lillian Faderman, *Surpassing the Love of Men* (New York: William Morrow, 1981).

11. Louis Kronenberger, review of André Gide, *The Immoralist*, *New York Times Book Review*, April 20, 1930, p. 9.

12. Henry James Forman, review of Floyd Dell, *Love in the Machine Age* (New York: Farrar & Rinehart), *New York Times Book Review*, September 14, 1930, p. 9.

13. Ferdinand Lundberg and Dr. Marynia F. Farnham, *Modern Woman: The Lost Sex* (New York: Harper, 1947).

14. Dr. Howard A. Rusk, *New York Times Book Review*, January 4, 1948, p. 3.

15. Alfred Kinsey, Wardell B. Pomeroy, Clyde E. Martin, *Sexual Behavior in the Human Male* (Philadelphia: W. B. Saunders, 1948), pp. 199–200.

16. Kinsey, *Sexual Behavior*, pp. 637, 639.

17. See Steven Epstein, "Gay Politics, Ethnic Identity: The Limits of Social Constructionism," *Socialist Review* 93/93 (1987), pp. 9–54.

18. Gore Vidal, "Someone to Laugh at the Squares With" [Tennessee Williams], *New York Review of Books*, June 13, 1985; reprinted in his *At Home: Essays, 1982–1988* (New York: Random House, 1988), p. 48.

Suggested Readings for Part II

Andersen, Margaret L. 2006. *Thinking about Women: Sociological Perspectives on Sex and Gender*, 7th ed. Boston, MA: Allyn & Bacon.

Collins, Chuck, and Felice Veskel. 2000. *Economic Apartheid in America: A Primer on Economic Inequality and Insecurity*. New York: The New Press.

Ehrenreich, Barbara. 2001. *Nickel and Dimed: On (Not) Getting By in America*. New York: Metropolitan Books.

Espiritu, Yen Le. 1997. *Asian American Women and Men*. Thousand Oaks: Sage.

Feagin, Joe. 2000. *Racist America: Roots, Current Realities, and Future Reparations*. New York: Routledge.

Oliver, Melvin, and Thomas Shapiro. 1995. *Black Wealth/White Wealth: A New Perspective on Racial Inequality*. New York: Routledge.

 ### InfoTrac College Edition: Search Terms

Use your access to the online library, InfoTrac College Edition, to learn more about subjects covered in this section. The following are some suggested terms for searches:

gender segregation wealth
homophobia White privilege
institutional racism working poor
model minority

  ### InfoTrac College Edition: Bonus Reading

You can use the InfoTrac College Edition feature to find an additional reading pertinent to this section and can also search on the author's name or keywords to locate the following reading:

Byng, Michelle D. 1998. "Mediating Discrimination: Resisting Oppression among African-American Muslim Women." *Social Problems* 45 (November): 473–487.

Through detailed interviews with Muslim women in the United States, Michelle Byng uses a race/class/gender framework to show how Muslim women construct their identities even in the face of discrimination. Her research shows not only how discrimination operates, but, just as importantly, how women resist the oppressive consequences of discrimination. What does her research suggest about how people construct their identities and visions of the world even in the context of race, class, and gender oppression?

What unique challenges do Muslim women face, and what lessons do other women learn from them?

Companion Website

For additional links, quizzes, and learning tools related to this part, see the book's companion website, at **http://sociology.wadsworth.com /andersen _hill_collins6e.**

THE STRUCTURE OF
SOCIAL INSTITUTIONS

*Margaret L. Andersen
and Patricia Hill Collins*

In the United States and globally, social institutions exert a powerful influence on everyday life. Social institutions are also important channels for societal penalties and privileges. The type of work you do, the structure of your family, whether your religion will be recognized or suppressed, the kind of education you receive, the images you see of yourself in the media, and how you are treated by the state are all shaped by the social institutions of the society where you live. People rely on institutions to meet their needs, although social institutions do so better for some groups than others. When a specific institution (such as the economy) fails them, people often appeal to another institution (such as the state) for redress. In this sense, institutions are both sources of support and sources of repression.

The concept of an institution is abstract, because there is no thing or object that one can point to as an institution. *Social institutions* are the established societal patterns of behavior organized around particular purposes. The economy is an institution, as are the family, the media, education, and the state —important societal institutions examined here. Each is organized around a specific purpose; in the case of the economy, for example, its purpose is the production, distribution, and consumption of goods and services. Within a given institution, there may be various patterns, such as different family structures, but as a whole, institutions are general patterns of behavior that emerge because of the specific societal conditions in which groups live. Institutions do change over time, both as societal conditions evolve and as groups challenge specific institutional structures, but they are also enduring and persistent, even in the face of active efforts to change them. Institutions confront people from birth and live on after people die.

Across all societies, institutions are patterned by intersections of race, class, gender, sexuality, age, ethnicity, and disability (among others), and, as a result, their effects on social institutions differ from one society to the next. Each society has a distinctive history and institutional configuration of social inequalities. Within the United States, race, class, and gender constitute fundamental categories that shape American social institutions that serve as basic conduits for social inequalities. Moreover, social institutions are interconnected. We think the interrelationships among institutions are especially apparent when studied in the context of race, class, and gender. Race, class, and gender oppression rests on a network of interconnected social institutions. Understanding the interconnections between institutions helps us see that we are all part of one historically created system that finds structural form in interrelated social institutions.

Despite their significance, dominant American ideology portrays institutions as neutral in their treatment of different groups; indeed, the liberal framework of the law allegedly makes access to public institutions (such as education and work) gender and race blind. Still, institutions differentiate on the basis of race, class, and gender. As the readings included here show, institutions are actually structured on the basis of race, class, and gender relations.

As an example, think of the economy. Economic institutions in American society are founded on capitalism—an economic system based on the pursuit of profit and the principle of private ownership. Such a system creates class inequality since, in simple terms, the profits of some stem from the exploitation of the labor of others. Race and gender further divide the U.S. capitalist economy, resulting in labor and consumer markets that routinely advantage some and disadvantage others. In particular, corporate and government

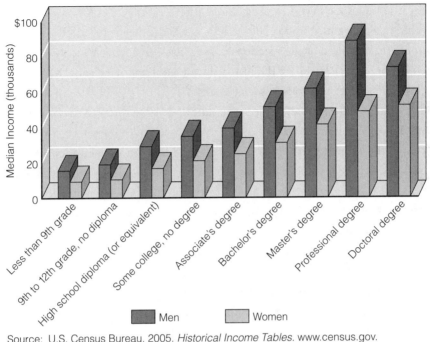

Source: U.S. Census Bureau. 2005. *Historical Income Tables*. www.census.gov.

FIGURE 1 Median Income by Educational Attainment (2003)

structures create jobs for some while leaving others underemployed or without work.

Those with jobs encounter a dual labor market that includes: (1) a primary labor market characterized by relatively high wages, opportunities for advancement, employee benefits, and rules of due process that protect workers' rights; and, (2) a secondary labor market (where most women and minorities are located) characterized by low wages, little opportunity for advancement, few benefits, and little protection for workers. One result of the dual labor market is the persistent wage gap between men and women (see Figure 1) and between Whites and people of color—even when they have the same level of education. Women tend to be clustered in jobs that employ mostly women workers; such jobs have been economically devalued as a result. Gender segregation and race segregation intersect in the dual labor market, so women of color are most likely to be working in occupations where most of the other workers are also women of color. At the same time, men of color are segregated into particular segments of the market, too. Indeed, there is a direct connection between gender and race segregation and wages, because wages are lowest in occupations where women of color predominate (U.S. Department of Labor 2005). This is what it means to say that institutions are structured by intersections of race, class, and gender: Institutions are built from and then reflect the historical and contemporary patterns of race, class, and gender relations in society.

As a second example, think of the state. The state refers to the organized system of power and authority in society. This includes the government, the police, the military, and the law (as reflected in both social policy and the civil and criminal justice system). The state is supposed to protect all citizens, regardless of their race, class, and gender (as well as other characteristics, such as disability and age); yet, like other gendered institutions, state policies routinely privilege men. This means not only that the majority of powerful people in the state are men (such as elected officials, judges, police, and the military) but, just as important, that the state works to protect men's interests. Policies about reproductive rights provide a good example. They are largely enacted by men, but have an important effect on women. Similarly, welfare policies designed to encourage people to work are based on the model of men's experiences, because they presume that staying home to care for one's children is not working. In this sense, the state is a gendered institution.

Most people do not examine the institutional structure of society when thinking about intersections of race, class, and gender. The individualist framework of dominant American culture sees race, class, gender, ethnicity, sexuality, and age as attributes of individuals, instead of seeing them as systems of power and inequality that are embedded in institutional structures. People do, of course, have identities of race, class, and gender, and these identities have an enormous impact on individual experience. However, seeing race, class, and gender from an individual viewpoint overlooks how profoundly embedded these identities are in the structure of American institutions. Moving historically marginalized groups to the center of analysis clarifies the importance of social institutions as links between individual experience and larger structures of race, class, and gender.

In this section of the book we examine how social institutions structure systems of power and inequality of race, class, gender, ethnicity, and sexuality that, in turn, structure those very same social institutions. We look at five important social institutions: work and the economic system; families; cultural institutions that reproduce ideas, such as the media; education and social welfare policies; and state institutions and violence. Each institution can be shown to have a unique impact on different groups (such as the discriminatory treatment of African American men by the criminal justice system). At the same time, each institution and its interrelationship with other institutions can be seen as specifically structured through the dynamics of race, class, and gender relations.

WORK AND ECONOMIC TRANSFORMATION

Structural transformations in the global economy have dramatically changed the conditions under which all people work. Three basic transformations currently affect the character of work. First, employers have turned to new technologies and job export to cut the costs of labor and to increase profitability. In some cases, new technologies have made some jobs obsolete. In other cases, where technology could not replace workers, jobs have been exported to countries where workers work for lower wages. Race, class, and gender frame how individual workers encounter these dual processes of "de-skilling" and job export.

Second, the new global economy has spurred the growth of the service sector. Here the dual economy operates by creating high-paying service work for skilled, college-educated workers (accountants, marketing representatives, etc.) and low-paying service work for everyone else (food service workers, nursing home aides, child care workers, and domestic workers, for example). With this growing service sector comes a shift in the kinds of skills required of workers. Here, too, race, gender, and class intersect in privileging and penalizing groups of workers. In "'Soft' Skills and Race," Philip Moss and Chris Tilly show how the "soft skills" of having the ability to interact with a range of people and demonstrating motivation to employers are increasingly important skills in the service economy. African American men, in particular, are perceived as lacking these skills and as a result are less likely to be hired for certain types of jobs.

Finally, global economic interdependence means that national borders no longer match up with corporations and the products that they make. Instead, products may be manufactured and assembled in a variety of places. This has fostered major population migrations; workers migrate in search of jobs and economic opportunities. The influx of new immigrant workers is nothing new in the United States. Domestic service captures these trends of "de-skilling," the growth of the service sector, and migration in search of economic opportunity. Pierrette Hondagneu-Sotelo's article "Doméstica" details how immigrant women from a few non-European nations are the newest generation of domestic workers. Service work has long served as an entry point to the labor market for poor women and women of color (Hondagneu-Sotelo 2001).

These changes have brought new opportunities for some groups—those positioned to benefit from the changes—while, for others, they have meant massive economic dislocation. The 30 million people who make up the working poor are the one group most affected by these economic trends. Katherine Newman points out in "The Invisible Poor" that powerful media images erroneously equate poverty with Black, undeserving welfare mothers. Instead, people on welfare are not the largest group of poor people in the United States. Rather, the working poor whose earnings do not allow them to afford decent housing, health care, child care, and nutrition constitute the largest group. Many are young workers, are mothers with children, and/or are African American or Latino or immigrants. Moreover, economic dislocation is not confined to workers in bad jobs. Kenneth W. Brown's experiences with "The Indignities of Unemployment" show that even workers in good jobs can be negatively affected by these economic trends.

FAMILIES

Families are another primary social institution profoundly influenced by intersecting systems of race, class, and gender. Historically, the family has been presumed to be the world of women: the ideology of the family (i.e., dominant belief systems about the family) purports that families are places for nurturing, love, and support—characteristics that have been associated with women. This ideal identifies women with the private world of the family and men with the public sphere of work. Family ideology, of course, only projects an ideal, because the large number of working mothers shows that few families actually fit the presumed ideal. Nonetheless, the ideology of the family provides a standard against which all families are judged. Moreover, the ideology of the family is class and race specific; that is, it ignores and distorts the family experiences of African Americans, Latinos, and most Whites.

Bonnie Thornton Dill's essay, "Our Mothers' Grief," shows that for African American, Chinese American, and Mexican American women, family structure is deeply affected by the relationships of families to the structures of race, class, and gender. Dill's historical analysis of racial-ethnic women and their families in "Our Mothers' Grief" examines diverse patterns of family organization directly influenced by a group's placement in the larger political economy. Just as the political economy of the nineteenth century affected women's experience in families, the political economy of the late twentieth century shapes family relations for women and men of all races.

The articles in this section illustrate several points that have emerged from feminist studies of families (e.g., see Thorne 1992). First, the family is not monolithic. The now widely acknowledged diversity among families refutes the idea that there is a normative family: White, middle-class, with children, organized around a heterosexual married couple (preferably with the wife not employed), and needing little support from relatives or neighbors. As the experiences of African Americans, Latinos, lesbians, gays, Asian Americans, and others reveal, this so-called normal family actually represents a minority perspective. Traditional myths about the American family mask the diversity of families in the United States. For example, one important myth about all families is that they are racially homogeneous. As Erica Chito Childs points out in "Navigating Interracial Borders," many individuals challenge the myth by marrying across racial boundaries. At the same time, Childs notes that navigating the Black/White border can encounter far more resistance than expected (Childs 2005).

Second, in this context of the idealized family, the best way to analyze families is to look at their underlying structures. For example, many presume that families are formed around a heterosexual norm. But as Kath Weston points out in "Straight Is to Gay as Family Is to No Family," gays and lesbians also participate in their families of origin and create families of their own. Claiming sexual identities as gay, lesbian, or bisexual does not mean relinquishing family or, worse yet, being defined as anti-family or as being a threat to family. Gay and lesbian partners often form permanent relationships, often including children. Although such partnerships are not uniformly legally recognized, they are part of the diversity among families. Raising children in diverse family environments so that they appreciate not only their own families, but also diverse ways of forming families, is a challenge in a society that devalues gays and lesbians and people of color.

Third, the dominant ideology that has glorified the family routinely distorts the actual behavior of women, people of color, children, and the elderly. Annette Lareau's study ("Unequal Childhoods") of how class and race foster unequal childhoods among America's children examines one such distortion. Lareau shows how children from different social classes and racial groups encounter very different opportunity structures. The very concept of American childhood varies tremendously by race, class, and gender.

A fourth theme that has emerged from new studies of families concerns family boundaries. The boundaries separating family, work, and other institutions are more fluid than was previously believed. No institution is isolated from another. Changes in the economy, for example, affect family structures; moreover, this effect is reciprocal, because changes in the family generate changes in the economy. The situation of working mothers challenges this assumption of the separation of work and family. The behavior of employed women of color, that the presumed dichotomy between the public and private spheres is false, is especially evident in light of the experience of people of color. Racial-ethnic families have rarely been provided the protection and privacy that the alleged split between public and private assumes. From welfare policy to reproductive rights, this dichotomy is based on the myth that families are insulated from the society around them.

A final theme concerns how immigration and the family experiences of new ethnic groups shape ideas about family. The experiences of groups migrating to the United States shows both the tenacity of race, class, and gender structures *and* how people work to change these systems. In "Chappals and Gym Shorts" Almas Sayeed depicts living as an Indian Muslim woman in Kansas—a place historically seen as quintessentially "American." She describes the complexity of negotiating the multiple and different cultural spheres that, as she says, "interlink" in her experience. Her narrative shows how her ethnic status, her gender, her religion, and her community all shape her identity as a feminist Islamic woman.

Recentering one's thinking about the family by understanding the interconnections of race, class, and gender reveals new understandings about families and the myths that have pervaded assumptions about family experience. In particular, ideology that presents families as peaceful, loving, nurturing spaces masks the underlying conflicts that are embedded in family systems. Although we do not examine family violence directly here, we know that violence stems from the gender, race, and class conflicts that are encouraged in a sexist, racist, and class-based society. In addition, we think of family violence not only as that which occurs between family members, but also as that which happens to families as they confront the institutional structures of race, class, and gender oppression.

MEDIA AND CULTURE

Work, family, and other social institutions are patterned by race, class, and gender, yet many people do not see these patterns and even may claim that they do not exist. The effects of economic restructuring on people of color and women and the differences manifested as Americans try to meet the American family ideal can be difficult to understand. How can race, class, and gender exert such a powerful influence on our everyday lives, yet remain so invisible?

The products of cultural institutions, such as movies, books, television, advertisements in the mass media, the statistics and documents produced by government, and the textbooks, curriculum materials, and teaching methods of schools, explain in part why race, class, and gender relations are obscured. These and other cultural institutions reproduce ideas by identifying which ideas are valuable, which are not, and which should not be heard at all. In this way, the ideas of groups that are privileged within race, class, and gender relations are routinely heard, whereas the ideas of groups who are disadvantaged are silenced.

In part, invisibility and silencing result from deeply entrenched ideas about race, class, and gender in the social fabric of the United States. Because beliefs about race, class, and gender are so ordinary, they often go unnoticed. Robert Moore points this out in his essay on "Racist Stereotyping in the English Language." Moore's analysis of the negative connotations associated with uses of the term "black" and the almost uniformly positive connotations that accompany the term "white" reveal a pattern that, for most people, is hidden in plain sight. In everyday social interaction, people invoke these negative and positive meanings associated with "black" and "white" without stopping to think about them at all. This everyday use obscures the historical origins of these meanings and makes the meanings of "black" and "white" appear to be natural and timeless rather than socially constructed.

Mass media and similar cultural institutions have the ability to do harm to those stigmatized by them. The articles in this section remind us that the ideas produced by these cultural institutions are far from benign because they uphold social policies and affect individuals. Placing his analysis in a global human rights context, Ward Churchill discusses how American national identity has been constructed against the interests of Native Americans. He suggests that, while Native American symbolism and imagery is ubiquitous in the United States, the derogatory use of Native American mascots and the like for sports teams stereotypes and stigmatizes contemporary Native

Americans. Ironically, while Native Americans continue to experience what Churchill discusses as genocidal policies, distorted ideas about Native American culture continue to be celebrated at college and professional sporting events. Churchill feels so strongly about the damage done to Native Americans by pervasive negative symbolism that he views this practice as criminal. On a more personal note, Judith Ortiz Cofer points out how burdensome it can be to continually encounter the "Myth of the Latin Woman" wherever she goes.

Certain cultural institutions have gained greater importance in the context of global economic restructuring. With the emergence of a global, mass media that circulates via television, music videos, cable, radio, and the Internet to all parts of the globe, racist and sexist ideas can travel quickly. Thus, those who control mass media are in a position to shape the basic ideas of society that come to be seen as truth. Gregory Mantsios's essay "Media Magic: Making Class Invisible" explores how mass media have been central in shaping ideas about social class. His work identifies the growing significance of mass media in framing how people think about class, race, and gender.

Sports and leisure constitute another cultural institution that is growing in importance. As a cultural institution, sports have a central place in the social lives of millions. Boys and girls from different racial and social class backgrounds learn about masculinity and femininity through their involvement in figure skating versus hockey, gymnastics versus wrestling, or golf versus double Dutch. Julianne Malveaux's article on basketball captures the contradictions of sports as a major vehicle for American ideas of gender and race. Despite her understanding of the ways in which basketball limits the horizons of its largely African American players and broadens those of predominantly White coaches, corporate sponsors, and television audiences, Malveaux still loves basketball. These are the contradictions of contemporary patterns of race, class, and gender—exploitation can be profitable and entertaining.

Mass media, sports, and others cultural institutions can help reproduce and mask social inequalities of race, class, and gender, but these same cultural institutions can be sites for challenging longstanding oppressions. In this sense, cultural institutions are rarely all good or all bad—more often, they are a little bit of both. The music industry generally and hip hop culture in particular illustrate these tendencies. Through their lyrics and their endorsement of liquor, gym shoes, and lavish lifestyles, many hip hop artists uphold prevailing ideas about race, class, and gender hierarchies. At the same time, hip hop has sparked a renewed activism in many African American and Latino youth. Mass media images are often the site of struggles between those who hold traditional views of race, class, and gender oppression as natural and inevitable and people of color, women, poor people, and other historically excluded groups who challenge these inequalities (Dyson 2001).

STATE INSTITUTIONS AND SOCIAL WELFARE

Race, class, and gender are fundamental in the construction of the American nation-state and its policies, just as the state is fundamental in shaping and defining these categories. Because the state is the system of legitimated power and authority in society, government policies determine people's rights. As the history of Jim Crow legislation shows, the U.S. government has often upheld exclusionary practices. At the same time, as the Civil Rights Movement and subsequent civil rights legislation of the 1960s demonstrates, the state can be an important albeit reluctant ally in challenging unjust social policies.

Social policies can be developed on behalf of disadvantaged groups, and historically the state has had a significant role in developing such policies. The state can negotiate groups' rights and organize people's access to state and societal resources. Government can solve problems that individuals cannot solve on their own, although many people are now cynical about the state's ability to do so. Public confidence in government has eroded, with many observers believing that the government is incapable of solving social problems that they see as being caused by individual failure. Indeed, in recent years, the state has been more involved in dismantling social supports than in providing assistance for those in need.

In this context, because ideally education prepares people to compete within the job market, the importance of education as a responsibility of the state has increased. Yet American education has recently and frequently been described as an institution in crisis. People worry that children are not learning in school. High school dropout rates, especially among students from poor and working-class families, reveal deep problems in the system of education. The sheer cost of post-secondary education makes it inaccessible to many. All of these factors contribute to the continuing disparity in the educational attainment of different groups (Kozol 1991).

In "Can Education Eliminate Race, Class, and Gender Inequality?" Roslyn Arlin Mickelson and Stephen Samuel Smith show how schools promote inequalities of race, class, and gender. Their analysis reveals the interplay between school policies that perpetuate existing hierarchies (such as credential inflation) and belief systems about race, class, and gender that are embedded in the so-called hidden curriculum. Students encounter these structures and belief systems while young, when their identities assume major importance. Schools thus become key sites where the inequalities of race, class, and gender are fostered and resisted.

Social welfare policy constitutes an important area of struggle where intersections of race, class, and gender within the American nation-state are highly visible. On the one hand, as Chuck Collins points out in "Aid to Dependent Corporations," welfare for the rich is rarely identified as such. Because affluent White men run American corporations and the social welfare state itself, social welfare policies that benefit this group disappear from public scrutiny. In contrast, social welfare policies reserved for the least powerful members of American society—people of color, women, children, and immigrant groups—become highly visible, publicly debated, and often stigmatized. In "Welfare Reform, Family Hardship, and Women of Color," Linda Burnham details the negative effects of contemporary welfare policy on women. Burnham suggests that the family hardship experienced by women of color in the United States be placed in a human rights context.

The social welfare state may be responsible for generating policies that attack problems of poverty, racism, and sexism, yet actual policies may be ineffective if they draw too heavily on commonsense ideas of race, class, and gender (Neubeck and Cazenave 2001). Through a discussion of eugenics, the authors of "Race, Poverty and Disability: Three Strikes and You're Out! Or Are You?" examine how common ways of thinking about disability intersect with similar thinking about race and poverty. Proponents of eugenics believed in "higher" and "lower" races and supported state-sponsored programs to control the population of lower race. The article details how eugenics thinking may have disappeared from official public policy, yet its spirit persists in influencing contemporary public policy toward people of color living with disabilities in poverty. In "Just Choices: Women of Color, Reproductive Health, and Human Rights," the women of the Sistersong collective take a closer look at how social policies that value some groups of citizens over others affect the reproductive choices of women of color (Roberts 1997).

STATE INSTITUTIONS AND VIOLENCE

The violence permeating the United States is a pressing social issue. School shootings, snipers, and street criminals dominate the news and project the idea that violence is rampant. Usually violence is depicted as the action of crazed individuals who are socially maladjusted, angry, or desperate. Although this may be the case for some, deeper questions about violence are raised when we think about violence in the context of race, class, and gender relations. Who is perceived as violent shifts, as does who we see as victims of violence. The consequences of violence in society are numerous, not the least of which is the fear that images of violence create and the action of the state toward those perceived as violent. How can we apply our knowledge of race, class, and gender to understanding violence?

It is important to see violence not as acts of individual social deviance but as one outcome of how the state sanctions a politics of race, class, and gender that permeates a range of social institutions. C. Matthew Snipp's essay "The First Americans" details the historical role of the state in forcing Native Americans from their homes and subordinating them to a new system of state control. Genocide, forced relocation, and regulation by state law have shaped Native American experience; state processes, whether in the form of war, legislation, or social policy, have contributed to the current place of Native Americans in U.S. society. At the same time, as Snipp notes, groups are resilient as they face adversity and often turn to the state for assistance. The history of civil rights legislation shows that the state can be an invaluable resource for addressing the wrongs of race, class, and gender injustice. In this sense, the state is both a source of oppression and an avenue for seeking justice.

Violent acts, the threat of violence, and more generalized policies based on the use of force find organizational homes in state institutions of social control—primarily the police, the military, and the criminal justice system. Intersections of race, class, and gender shape all of these institutions. In "Policing the National Body: Sex, Race, and Criminalization," Jael Silliman demonstrates how intersections of race, class, and gender shape state power. Silliman links policies such as aggressive policing and the increasing incarceration of African American, Latino, and poor White men; the assault on reproductive rights of women of color; and the search of immigrants of color by the Immigration and Naturalization Service under the pretext of national security as part of an overarching system of policing the body politic.

Violence simultaneously permeates a range of other social institutions. Some social institutions are known for their use of force, while others are less peaceful than they appear. Men's violence against women and children (whether physical, emotional, or sexual) in families of all social classes and racial/ethnic compositions contradicts the dominant belief that the home is a place of tranquility and love. Sexual harassment on the job as a dimension of social control belies the belief that men and women encounter a similar work environment. In the media, depicting rape as pleasurable to women and portraying violence against Native Americans, Asian Americans, and African Americans in numerous movies as justified contributes to a generalized belief system condoning violence. Thus, violence is both hated and condoned in a society where the meaning, commission, and consequences of violence are deeply tied to race, class, and gender inequality.

When it comes to violence, it is important to remember that the police, the military, and the criminal justice system play an important part in punishing certain forms of violence while ignoring others. Through the policies themselves and differential enforcement of policies, state institutions shape what counts as violence. In this way, state policies link individual acts of violence to the more routine, systemic violence that reflects social inequalities of race, class, and gender. To illustrate this historically, lynchings of African American men can be seen as the random acts of unruly mobs; yet, the failure to arrest, prosecute, and convict those who did the lynching is powerful testament to public endorsement of these seemingly individual acts of violence. Likewise, rape appears to be a private act, but it occurs as part of a generalized climate that condones violence against women. Yet race, class, and gender have shaped the very definition of rape and the treatment afforded rape survivors and their rapists. In "Rape, Racism, and the Law," Jennifer Wriggins examines how the legal system's treatment of rape has disproportionately targeted Black men for punishment and made Black women especially vulnerable by denying their sexual subordination. Although violence may be experienced individually, it occurs in specific organizational and institutional contexts shaped by race, class, and gender.

Because the state is the major social institution that is authorized to use violence, actions of the police, the criminal justice system, and the military constitute important parts of how race, class, and gender operate. The military is especially important in that it constitutes the legitimate use of force, typically in defense of American foreign policy. In "Military Mirrors a

Working-Class America," David M. Halbfinger and Steven A. Holmes show how race, class, and gender affect the composition of who joins the military and who goes to fight America's wars. Working-class kids from small towns and inner cities alike join the military, primarily in search of opportunities that elude them in their home communities. Yet if ideas about American citizenship are refracted through the lens of race, class, gender, ethnicity, and sexuality, one might ask who they defend and toward what ends? Working-class kids fight America's wars, yet who decides what those wars shall be? These are tough questions that get at the heart of the connections between the state and its legitimate use of force. Yet they are questions that are unlikely to be answered without attending to the complexities of race, class, and gender arguments.

One must ask, how can the United States build a national community that adheres to principles of fairness and justice with such a diverse population? Thinking about violence brings a new dimension to this complex question. After the events of 9/11, most in the United States felt fearful about violence—particularly terrorism and international war. For many in the United States who had been less touched in the past by threats of violence, these were new fears. But, as Desiree Taylor points out ("How Safe Is America?"), feeling unsafe is not new for many—those who, because of their class, their race, their sexual orientation, and/or their gender, have never been safe within the United States. For Taylor, cries to defend freedom and democracy in the face of terrorist threats must be accompanied with the realization that justice and freedom have long been denied to many living within the United States. The point is not to dismiss people's fears about new threats, but to create a new nation where race, class, and gender justice within the United States are as important to us as our position in the world.

References

Childs, Erica Chito. 2005. *Navigating Interracial Borders: Black-White Couples and Their Social Worlds.* New Brunswick, N.J.: Rutgers University Press.

Dyson, Michael Eric. 2001. *Holler If You Hear Me: Searching for Tupac Shakur.* New York: Basic Civitas Books.

Hondagneu-Sotelo, Pierrette. 2001. *Doméstica: Immigrant Workers Cleaning and Caring in the Shadows of Affluence.* Berkeley: University of California Press.

Neubeck, Kenneth J. and Noel A. Cazenave. 2001. *Welfare Racism: Playing the Race Card against America's Poor.* New York: Routledge.

Kozol, Jonathan. 1991. *Savage Inequalities: Children in America's Schools.* New York: Harper Collins.

Roberts, Dorothy. 1997. *Killing the Black Body: Race, Reproduction, and the Meaning of Liberty.* New York: Vintage.

Thorne, Barrie, with Marilyn Yalom. 1992. *Rethinking the Family: Some Feminist Questions,* rev. ed. Boston: Northeastern University Press.

U.S. Department of Labor. January 2005. *Employment and Earnings.* Washington, D.C.: U.S. Government Printing Office.

WORK AND ECONOMIC TRANSFORMATION

32

RACE, CLASS, GENDER, AND WOMEN'S WORKS

Teresa Amott and Julie Matthaei

What social and economic factors determine and differentiate women's work lives? Why is it, for instance, that the work experiences of African American women are so different from those of European American women? Why have some women worked outside the home for pay, while others have provided for their families through unpaid work in the home? Why are most of the wealthy women in the United States of European descent, and why are so many women of color poor? . . .

Throughout U.S. history, economic differences among women (and men) have been constructed and organized along a number of social categories. In our analysis, we focus on the three categories which we see as most central—gender, race-ethnicity, and class—with less discussion of others, such as age, sexual preference, and religion. We see these three social categories as interconnected, historical processes of domination and subordination. Thinking about gender, race-ethnicity, and class, then, necessitates thinking historically about power and economic exploitation. . . .

From Teresa Amott and Julie Matthaei, *Race, Gender, and Work: A Multicultural Economic History of Women in the United States*, 2d ed. (Boston: South End Press, 1996). Reprinted with permission of South End Press.

GENDER, RACE-ETHNICITY, AND CLASS PROCESSES: HISTORICAL AND INTERCONNECTED

The concepts of gender, race-ethnicity, and class are neither trans-historical nor independent. Hence, it is artificial to discuss them outside of historical time and place, and separately from one another. At the same time, without such a set of concepts, it is impossible to make sense of women's disparate economic experiences.

Gender, race-ethnicity, and class are not natural or biological categories which are unchanging over time and across cultures. Rather, these categories are socially constructed: they arise and are transformed in history, and themselves transform history. Although societies rationalize them as natural or god-given, ideas of appropriate feminine and masculine behavior vary widely across history and culture. Concepts and practices of race-ethnicity, usually justified by religion or biology, also vary over time, reflecting the politics, economics, and ideology of a particular time and, in turn, reinforcing or transforming politics, economics, and ideology. For example, nineteenth-century European biologists Louis Agassiz and Count Arthur de Gobineau developed a taxonomy of race which divided humanity into separate and unequal racial species; this taxonomy was used to rationalize European colonization of Africa and Asia, and slavery in the United States. Class is perhaps the most historically specific category of all, clearly dependent upon the particular economic and social constellation of a society at a point in time. Still, notions of class as inherited or genetic continue to haunt us, harkening back to earlier eras in which lowly birth was thought to cause low intelligence and a predisposition to criminal activity.

Central to the historical transformation of gender, race-ethnicity, and class processes have been the struggles of subordinated groups to redefine or transcend them. For example, throughout the development of capitalism, workers' consciousness of themselves as workers and their struggles against class oppression have transformed capitalist-worker relationships, expanding workers' rights and powers. In the nineteenth century, educated white women escaped from the prevailing, domestic view of womanhood by arguing that homemaking included caring for the sick and the needy through volunteer work, social homemaking careers, and political organizing. In the 1960s, the transformation of racial-ethnic identity into a source of solidarity and pride was essential to movements of people of color, such as the Black Power and American Indian movements.

Race-ethnicity, gender, and class are interconnected, interdetermining historical processes, rather than separate systems. This is true in two senses, which we will explore in more detail below. First, it is often difficult to determine whether an economic practice constitutes class, race, or gender oppression: for example, slavery in the U.S. South was at the same time a system of class oppression (of slaves by owners) and of racial-ethnic oppression (of Africans by Europeans). Second, a person does not experience these different processes of domination and subordination independently of one another; in philosopher Elizabeth Spelman's metaphor, gender, race-ethnicity, and class are not separate "pop-beads" on a necklace of identity. Hence, there is no generic gender oppression which is experienced by all women regardless of their race-ethnicity or class. As Spelman puts it:

> . . . in the case of much feminist thought we may get the impression that a woman's identity consists of a sum of parts neatly divisible from one another, parts defined in terms of her race, gender, class, and so on. . . . On this view of personal identity (which might also be called pop-bead metaphysics), my being a woman means the same whether I am white or Black, rich or poor, French or Jamaican, Jewish or Muslim.[1]

The problems of "pop-bead metaphysics" also apply to historical analysis. In our reading of history, there is no common experience of gender across race-ethnicity and class, of race-ethnicity across class and gender lines, or of class across race-ethnicity and gender.

With these caveats in mind, let us examine the processes of gender, class, and race-ethnicity, their importance in the histories of women's works, and some of the ways in which these processes have been intertwined.

Gender

. . . Gender differences in the social lives of men and women are based on, but are not the same thing as, biological differences between the sexes. Gender is rooted in societies' beliefs that the sexes are naturally distinct and opposed social beings. These beliefs are turned into self-fulfilling prophecies through sex-role socialization: the biological sexes are assigned distinct and often unequal work and political positions, and turned into socially distinct genders.

Economists view the sexual division of labor as central to the gender differentiation of the sexes. By assigning the sexes to different and complementary tasks, the sexual division of labor turns them into different and complementary genders. . . . The work of males is at least partially, if not wholly, different from that of females, making "men" and "women" different economic and social beings. Sexual divisions of labor, not sexual difference alone, create difference and complementarity between "opposite" sexes. These differences, in turn, have been the basis for marriage in most societies. . . .

The concept of gender certainly helps us understand women's economic histories. . . . Each racial-ethnic group has had a sexual division of labor which has barred individuals from the activities of the opposite sex. Gender processes do differentiate women's lives in many ways from those of the men in their own racial-ethnic and class group. Further, gender relations in all groups tend to assign women to the intra-familial work of childrearing, as well as to place women in a subordinate position to the men of their class and racial-ethnic group.

But as soon as we have written these generalizations, exceptions pop into mind. Gender roles do not always correspond to sex. Some American Indian tribes allowed individuals to choose among gender roles: a female, for example, could choose a man's role, do men's work, and marry another female who lived out a woman's role. In the nineteenth century, some white females "passed" as men in order to escape the rigid mandates of gender roles. In many of these cases, women lived with and loved other women.

Even though childrearing is women's work in most societies, many women do not have children, and others do not perform their own child care or domestic work. Here, class is an especially important differentiating process. Upper-class women have been able to use their economic power to reassign some of the work of infant care—sometimes even breastfeeding—to lower-class women of their own or different racial-ethnic groups. These women, in turn, may have been forced to leave their infants alone or with relatives or friends. Finally, gender complementarity has not always led to social and economic inequality; for example, many American Indian women had real control over the home and benefited from a more egalitarian sharing of power between men and women.

Since the processes of sex-role socialization are historically distinct in different times and different cultures, they result in different conceptions of appropriate gender behavior. Both African American and Chicana girls, for instance, learn how to be women—but both must learn the specific gender roles which have developed within their racial-ethnic and class group and historical period. For example, for white middle-class homemakers in the 1950s, adherence to the concept of womanhood discouraged paid employment, while for poor Black women it meant employment as domestic servants for white middle-class women. Since racial-ethnic and class domination have differentiated the experiences of women, one cannot assume, as do many feminist theorists and activists, that all women have the same experience of gender oppression—or even that they will be on the same side of a struggle, not even when some women define that struggle as "feminist."

Not only is gender differentiation and oppression not a universal experience which creates a common "women's oppression," the sexual divisions of labor and family systems of people of color have been systematically disrupted by racial-ethnic and class processes. In the process of invasion and conquest, Europeans imposed their notions of male superiority on cultures with more egalitarian forms of gender relations, including many American Indian and African tribes. At the same time, European Americans were quick to abandon their notion of appropriate femininity when it conflicted with profits; for example, slave owners often assigned slave women to backbreaking labor in the fields.

Racial-ethnic and class oppression have also disrupted family life among people of color and the white working class. Europeans interfered with family relations within subordinated racial-ethnic communities through rape and forced cohabitation. Sometimes whites encouraged or forced reproduction, as when slaveowners forced slave women into sexual relations. On the other hand, whites have often used their power to curtail reproduction among peoples of color, and aggressive sterilization programs were practiced against Puerto Ricans and American Indians as late as the 1970s. Beginning in the late nineteenth century, white administrators took American Indian children from their parents to "civilize" them in boarding schools where they were forbidden to speak their own languages or wear their native dress. Slaveowners commonly split up slave families through sale to different and distant new owners. Nevertheless, African Americans were able to maintain strong family ties, and even augmented these with "fictive" or chosen kin. From the mid-nineteenth through the mid-twentieth centuries, many Asians were separated from their spouses or children by hiring policies and restrictions on immigration. Still, they maintained family life within these split households, and eventually succeeded in reuniting, sometimes after generations. Hence, for peoples of color, having children and maintaining families have been an essential part of the struggle against racist oppression. Not surprisingly, many women of color have rejected the white women's movement view of the family as the center of "women's oppression."

These examples reveal the limitations of gender as a single lens through which to view women's economic lives. Indeed, any attempt to understand women's experiences using gender alone cannot only cause misunderstanding, but can also interfere with the construction of broad-based movements against the oppressions experienced by women.

Race-Ethnicity

Like gender, race-ethnicity is based on a perceived physical difference, and rationalized as "natural" or "god-given." But whereas gender creates difference and inequality according to biological sex, race-ethnicity differentiates individuals according to skin color or other physical features.

In all of human history, individuals have lived in societies with distinct languages, cultures, and economic institutions; these ethnic differences have been perpetuated by intermarriage within, but rarely between, societies. However, ethnic differences can exist independently of a conception of race, and without a practice of racial-ethnic domination such as the Europeans practiced over the last three centuries. . . .

Does the concept of race-ethnicity help us understand the economic history of women in the United States? Certainly, for white racial-ethnic domination has been a central force in U.S. history. European colonization of North America entailed the displacement and murder of the continent's indigenous peoples, rationalized by the racist view that American Indians were savage heathens. The economy of the South was based on a racial-ethnic system, in which imported Africans were forced to work for white landowning families as slaves. U.S. military expansion in the nineteenth century brought more lands under U.S. control—the territories of northern Mexico (now the Southwest), the Philippines, and Puerto Rico—incorporating their peoples into the racial-ethnic hierarchy. And from the mid-nineteenth century onward, Asians were brought into Hawaii's plantation system to work for whites as semi-free laborers. In the twentieth century, racial-ethnic difference and inequality have been perpetuated by the segregation of people of color into different and inferior jobs, living conditions, schools, and political positions, and by the prohibition of intermarriage with whites in some states up until 1967.

Race-ethnicity is a key concept in understanding women's economic histories. But it is not without limitations. First, racial-ethnic processes have never operated independently of class and gender. In the previous section on gender, we saw how racial domination distorted gender and family relations among people of color. Racial domination has also been intricately linked to economic or class domination. As social scientists Michael Omi (Asian American) and Howard Winant (European American) explain, the early European arguments that people of color were without souls had direct economic meaning:

> At stake were not only the prospects for conversion, but the types of treatment to be accorded them. The expropriation of property, the denial of political rights, the introduction of slavery and other forms of coercive labor, as well as outright extermination, all presupposed a worldview which distinguished Europeans—children of God, human beings, etc.—from "others." Such a worldview was needed to explain why some should be "free" and others enslaved, why some had rights to land and property while others did not.[2]

Indeed, many have argued that racial theories only developed after the economic process of colonization had started, as a justification for white domination of peoples of color.

The essentially economic nature of early racial-ethnic oppression in the United States makes it difficult to isolate whether peoples of color were subordinated in the emerging U.S. economy because of their race-ethnicity or their economic class. Whites displaced American Indians and Mexicans to obtain their land. Whites imported Africans to work as slaves and Asians to work as contract laborers. Puerto Ricans and Filipinas/os were victims of further U.S. expansionism. Race-ethnicity and class intertwined in the patterns of displacement for land, genocide, forced labor, and recruitment from the seventeenth through the twentieth centuries. While it is impossible, in our minds, to determine which came first in these instances—race-ethnicity or class—it is clear that they were intertwined and inseparable.

Privileging racial-ethnic analysis also leads one to deny the existence of class differences, both among whites and among people of color, which complicate and blur the racial-ethnic hierarchy. A racial-ethnic analysis implies that all whites are placed above all peoples of color. . . .

. . . A minority of the dominated race is allowed some upward mobility and ranks economically above whites. At the same time, however, all whites have some people of color below them. For example, there are upper-class Black, Chicana, and Puerto Rican women who are more economically privileged than poor white women; however, there are always people of color who are less economically privileged than the poorest white woman. Finally, class oppression operates among women of the same racial-ethnic group.

A third problem with the analysis of racial domination is that such domination has not been a homogeneous process. Each subordinated racial-ethnic group has been oppressed and exploited differently by whites: for example, American Indians were killed and displaced, Africans were enslaved, and Filipinas/os and Puerto Ricans were colonized. Whites have also dominated whites; some European immigrant groups, particularly Southern and Eastern Europeans, were subjected to segregation and violence. In some cases, people of color have oppressed and exploited those in another group: Some American Indian tribes had African slaves; some Mexicans and Puerto Ricans displaced and murdered Indians and had African slaves. Because of these differences, racial oppression does not automatically bring unity of peoples of color across their own racial-ethnic differences, and feminists of color are not necessarily in solidarity with one another.

To sum up, we see that, as with gender, the concept of race-ethnicity is essential to our analysis of women's works. However, divorcing this concept from gender and class, again, leads to problems in both theory and practice.

Class

. . . We believe that the concepts of class and exploitation are crucial to understanding the work lives of women in early U.S. history, as well as in the modern, capitalist economy. Up through the nineteenth century, different class relations organized production in different regions of the United States. The South was dominated by slave agriculture; the Northeast by emerging industrial capitalism; the Southwest (then part of Mexico) by the *hacienda* system which carried over many elements of the feudal manor into large-scale production for the market; the rural Midwest by independent family farms that produced on a small scale for the market; and the American Indian West by a variety of tribal forms centered in hunting and gathering or agriculture, many characterized by cooperative, egalitarian economic relations. Living within these different labor systems, and in different class positions within them, women led very different economic lives.

By the late nineteenth century, however, capitalism had become the dominant form of production, displacing artisans and other small producers along with slave plantations and tribal economies. Today, wage labor accounts for over 90 percent of employment; self employment, including family businesses, accounts for the remaining share. With the rise of capitalism, women were brought into the same labor system, and polarized according to the capitalist-wage laborer hierarchy.

At the same time as the wage labor form specific to capitalism became more prevalent, capitalist class relations became more complex and less transparent. Owners of wealth (stocks and bonds) now rarely direct the production process; instead, salaried managers, who may or may not own stock in the company, take on this function. While the capitalist class may be less identifiable, it still remains a small and dominant elite. . . .

Class can be a powerful concept in understanding women's economic lives, but there are limits to class analysis if it is kept separate from race-ethnicity and gender. First, as we saw in the race section above, the class relations which characterized the early U.S. economy were also racial-ethnic and gender formations. Slave owners were white and mostly male, slaves were Black. The displaced tribal economies were the societies of indigenous peoples. Independent family farmers were whites who farmed American Indian lands; they organized production in a patriarchal manner, with women and children's work defined by and subordinated to the male household head and property owner. After establishing their dominance in the pre-capitalist period, white men were able to perpetuate and institutionalize this dominance in the emerging capitalist system, particularly through the monopolization of managerial and other high-level jobs.

Second, the sexual division of labor within the family makes the determination of a woman's class complicated—determined not simply by her relationship to the production process, but also by that of her husband or father. For instance, if a woman is not in the labor force but her husband is a capitalist, then we might wish to categorize her as a member of the capitalist class. But what if that same woman worked as a personnel manager for a large corporation, or as a salesperson in an elegant boutique? Clearly, she derives upper-class status and access to income from her husband, but she is also, in her own right, a worker. Conversely, when women lose their husbands through divorce, widowhood, or desertion, they often change their class position in a downward direction. A second gender-related economic process overlooked by class analysis is the unpaid household labor performed by women for their fathers, husbands, and children—or by other women, for pay.

Third, while all workers are exploited by capitalists, they are not equally exploited, and gender and race-ethnicity play important roles in this differentiation. Men and women of the same racial-ethnic group have rarely performed the same jobs—this sex-typing and segregation is the labor market form of the sexual division of labor we studied above. Further, women of different racial-ethnic groups have rarely been employed at the same job, at least not within the same workplace or region. This racial-ethnic typing and segregation has both reflected and reinforced the racist economic practices upon which the U.S. economy was built.

Thus, jobs in the labor force hierarchy tend to be simultaneously race-typed and gender-typed. Picture in your mind a registered nurse. Most likely, you thought of a white woman. Picture a doctor. Again, you imagined a person of a particular gender (probably a man), and a race (probably a white person). If you think of a railroad porter, it is likely that a Black man comes to mind. Almost all jobs tend to be typed in such a way that stereotypes make it difficult for persons of the "wrong" race and/or gender to train for or obtain the job. Of course, there are regional and historical variations in the typing of jobs. On the West Coast, for example, Asian men performed much of the paid domestic work during the nineteenth century because women were in such short supply. In states where the African American population is very small, such as South Dakota or Vermont, domestic servants and hotel chambermaids are typically white. Nonetheless, the presence of variations in race-gender typing does not contradict the idea that jobs tend to take on racial-ethnic and gender characteristics with profound effects on the labor market opportunities of job-seekers. . . .

. . . The racial-ethnic and gender processes operating in the labor market have transposed white and male domination from pre-capitalist structures into the labor market's class hierarchy. This hierarchy can be described by grouping jobs into different labor market sectors or segments: "primary," "secondary," and "underground." . . . The primary labor market—which has been monopolized by white men—offers high salaries, steady employment, and upward mobility. Its upper tier consists of white-collar salaried or self-employed workers with high status, autonomy, and, often, supervisory capacity. Wealth increases access to this sector, since it purchases elite education and provides helpful job connections. . . .

The lower tier of the primary sector, which still yields high earnings but involves less autonomy, contains many unionized blue-collar jobs. White working-class men have used union practices, mob violence, and intimidation to monopolize these jobs. By World War II, however, new ideologies of worker solidarity, embodied in the mass industrial unions, began to overcome the resistance of white male workers to the employment of people of color and white women in these jobs.

In contrast to both these primary tiers, the secondary sector offers low wages, few or no benefits, little opportunity for advancement, and unstable employment. People of color and most white women have been concentrated in these secondary sector jobs, where work is often part-time, temporary, or seasonal, and pay does not rise with increasing education or experience. Jobs in both tiers of the primary labor market have generally yielded family wages, earnings high enough to support a wife and children who are not in the labor force for pay. Men of color in the secondary sector have not been able to earn enough to support their families, and women of color have therefore participated in wage labor to a much higher degree than white women whose husbands held primary sector jobs.

Outside of the formal labor market is the underground sector, where the most marginalized labor force groups, including many people of color, earn their livings from illegal or quasi-legal work. This sector contains a great variety of jobs, including drug trafficking, crime, prostitution, work done by undocumented workers, and sweatshop work which violates labor standards such as minimum wages and job safety regulations.

NOTES

1. Elizabeth V. Spelman, *Inessential Woman: Problems of Exclusion in Feminist Thought* (Boston: Beacon Press, 1988).

2. Michael Omi and Howard Winant, *Racial Formation in the United States* (New York: Routledge & Kegan Paul, 1986), p. 58.

33

THE INDIGNITIES OF UNEMPLOYMENT

Kenneth W. Brown

I am a number, a statistic, a peak on a national bar graph. I am not physically or mentally disabled. But I am financially disabled; I am unemployed.

I am unemployed after nearly 14 years of being a loyal, hardworking employee. I bought into the company philosophy, followed the company credo and worked hard to help accomplish the corporate goal. As I was coddled, supported, and groomed, I grew to believe that I was an important member of the corporate family, only to be unceremoniously dumped after I had served my purpose and was no longer needed or welcomed, like a bastard son at a family reunion.

I am making every effort to find work. I have made countless phone inquiries, answered many classified ads and contacted people I have not spoken

---

From *Essence* 26 (September 1995): 56. Reprinted by permission.

to in years, looking for job leads. I have attended job fairs in search of another chance to rejoin corporate America, struggling to maintain my sense of dignity as I walked about the crowded rooms—looking along with so many others for the next opportunity to reenter the economic mainstream.

As unemployment refuses to loosen its grasp, I find it increasingly difficult to remain hopeful, positive, and confident. Prolonged unemployment can do a number on your psyche, your soul, and your spirit. Unemployment can make you question your skills and abilities. And it can damage your self-esteem. I don't care how much confidence you have; unemployment can shake that confidence.

As I search for my next position, I do so with growing reluctance and trepidation. When I prepare for the next job interview, I practice my responses to the questions about myself, my strengths, my weaknesses, and my future goals.

I make sure I speak the King's English with perfect enunciation, ever mindful not to let street slang or my ethnicity slip into my conversation.

I often wonder whether my white counterparts are as conscious of their diction as I am of mine. I also wonder whether I am selling out or compromising myself too much. Do white men wonder if they are being too forceful, too eager to please, too assertive? Do they agonize as much as I do over how to appear skilled and capable without intimidating the people who have the power to hire? The thought of always keeping these ideas in mind is exhausting and sad. Is this the cross that African-American men and women must bear in order to be accepted into corporate America?

Unemployment can make you question your faith and spiritual foundation. I pray for my unemployment to end. I pray for direction and guidance. I also pray for the day when I do not have to wonder whether my blackness is a barrier to reentry into the labor force. I am still waiting for a response. Unemployment makes me wonder if anyone is listening.

Being unemployed also makes me question my manhood. I was raised to be a responsible household member who would carry my share of the weight. But now that I am no longer holding up my end of the financial bargain, my wife and I exist on a single income: hers. While I am fortunate that she has been supportive throughout my long period of unemployment, I must fight hard against seeing myself as a failure or loser. I have never before considered myself a loser, and I refuse to be one. Every day I must remind myself that being without a job does not make me less of a man.

Some good things have resulted from my unemployment. I have gained a renewed awareness of life's blessings: the value of true friends and the love, support, encouragement and prayers of family. In many ways I have become a stronger person. I have resolved to survive unemployment. I resolve to become a statistic for working Americans, and not just another African-American male without a job.

34

"SOFT" SKILLS AND RACE

Philip Moss and Chris Tilly

The growth of "soft" or social skills is a factor that has been neglected in research on the racial gap in labor market outcomes, despite the fact that employer surveys have repeatedly identified such skills as the most important hiring criterion for entry-level jobs (Capelli 1995). In this study, therefore, we examined the relationship between employer racial attitudes and their hiring practices, with special attention given to their use of soft skills. We defined soft skills as skills, abilities, and traits that pertain to personality, attitude, and behavior rather than to formal or technical knowledge. Based on 56 face-to-face interviews with employers, we sought to learn how employment gatekeepers conceived of soft skills in relation to hiring Black men for entry-level jobs.

According to our findings, employers reported an increasing need for soft skills—driven, they said, by heightened competitive pressure—and they rated Black men poorly in terms of such skills. Thus, the heightened competition that propels current business restructuring appears to contribute to increased labor market inequality by race. . . .

THE GROWING IMPORTANCE OF SOFT SKILLS

Again, we defined soft skills as skills, abilities, and traits that pertain to personality, attitude, and behavior rather than to formal or technical knowledge. Two clusters of soft skills were important to the employers surveyed. The first, *interaction*, involves ability to interact with customers, coworkers, and supervisors. This cluster includes friendliness, teamwork, ability to fit in, and appropriate affect, grooming, and attire. The interaction category is related to concepts of *emotional labor* (Hochschild 1983; Wharton 1993) and *nurturant social skills* (England 1992; Kilbourne, England, & Beron 1994). A second cluster, *motivation*, takes in characteristics such as enthusiasm, positive work attitude, commitment, dependability, and willingness to learn. We distinguish both from hard skills, including skills in math, reading, and writing;

From *Work and Occupations* 23 (August 1996): 252–76 © 1996 Sage Publications, Inc. Reprinted by permission of Sage Publications, Inc.

knowledge of particular job procedures; "brightness;" ability to learn; educational attainment; and physical strength.

Interaction and motivation skills differ from one another, and in much of our analysis, we distinguish between the two. However, we grouped them together under the rubric of soft skills because employers often subsumed both in terms like *attitude* and because many employers viewed both as more immutable than hard skills. Of course, soft skills are in part culturally defined, and therefore employer assessments of soft skills will be confounded by differences in culture and by racial stereotyping. Indeed, the word *skills* is to some extent a misnomer, although employers most definitely conceptualize these attributes as contributing to individual productivity differences.

We asked almost all interviewees to identify the most important qualities they looked for when hiring entry-level workers. As Table 1 shows, interaction skills were by far the most important qualification in retail. Motivation and hard skills received roughly equal emphasis in auto parts and insurance. Only in the public sector were hard skills mentioned most often. Overall, 86% of respondents included soft skills in their list of the most important hiring criteria, and almost half mentioned soft skills first in that list. . . .

Respondents in all four industries stated that competitive pressures have led to growing soft-skill needs (Moss & Tilly 1996). For instance, auto makers are pushing their suppliers to cut costs and increase quality. In response, many of the parts manufacturers are escalating basic and technical skill requirements. Some, however, are demanding more soft skills as well. For instance, a human resource manager at an alloy casting plant told us:

> Hiring used to be based on 90% experience, 10% attitude or work ethic.
> I find that changing . . . due to the [emphasis on] team work and total quality.
> Attitudes and people getting along with one another . . . —this is a big part
> now. I would almost say it's 50% to 60% being experience and the other
> 40% being attitude, work ethic, teamwork.

In retail clothing, heightened emphasis on customer service—again, spurred by intensified competition—has led companies to screen more carefully for soft skills when hiring sales clerks. One discount clothing chain has

Table 1 Most Important Qualities Looked for in Entry-Level Employees

Industry	Frequency With Which Each Category Was Mentioned (Percent)		
	Hard Skills	Interaction	Motivation
Auto parts manufacturing	58	32	63
Retail clothing	22	78	39
Insurance	67	67	78
Public sector	100	60	60

NOTE: Informants typically mentioned more than one desired quality.

adopted the slogan "fast, fun, and friendly." According to a regional personnel representative for the chain, this means that now

> I tell my . . . personnel managers, "If they don't smile, don't hire them."
> I don't care how well-educated they are, how well-versed they are in retail,
> if they can't smile, they're not going to make a customer feel welcome.
> And we don't want them in our store.

On the other hand, respondents reported declining hard skill needs among sales clerks, due to optical scanning equipment and computerized cash registers.

Insurance companies increasingly demand computer literacy among their clerical workers. In addition, financial deregulation has heightened competition, leading insurers to adopt several strategies: downsizing, reorganization of work, and greater stress on customer service. As one human resource manager put it, "on a scale of 1 to 10 it [customer relations] is a 9.999. . . . There is much more emphasis now being placed on it."

Finally, in the public sector, budget cuts have combined with political demands for greater productivity and quality of service. In our public sector interviews, two thirds of respondents reported that they were looking for more skilled people. Although some of these respondents noted a greater need for some basic or technical skill, all mentioned a need for greater customer skills—in jobs ranging from clerk-typist to hospital housekeeper.

SOFT SKILLS AND RACE IN THE EYES OF EMPLOYERS

The emphasis employers place on soft skills disadvantages Black male job applicants. This is because many employers see Black men as lacking in precisely the skills they consider increasingly important. Indeed, in our sample, the employers placing the greatest emphasis on soft skills were those most likely to have negative views of Black men as workers. The views employers hold of Black men in this regard were partly stereotype, partly cultural gap, and partly an accurate perception of the skills that many less educated Black men bring to the labor market. . . .

Interaction Skills

Employers voiced two main sets of concerns about the ability of Black men to interact effectively with customers and coworkers. First, a substantial minority of respondents—32%—described Black men as defensive, hostile, or having a difficult "attitude." The content of these comments ranged widely. A Latino store manager in a Black area of Los Angeles, who hires mostly Latinos, flatly stated, "You know, a lot of people are afraid, they [Black men] project a certain image that makes you back off. . . . They're really scary." When asked, "How much of that do you think is perception, how much do you think is actually reality?" he responded, "I think 80% is reality. 80% of it's factual."

Other respondents stated that managers see Black men as difficult to control. For example, the Black female personnel manager of a Detroit retail store commented,

> Employers are sometimes intimidated by an uneducated Black male to come in. Their appearance really isn't up to par, their language, how they go about an interview. Whereas females Black or White, most people do feel, "I could control this person." . . . A lot of times people are physically intimidated by Black men. . . . The majority of our employers are not Black. And if you think that person may be a problem, [that] young Black men normally are bad, or [that] the ones in this area [are], you say, "I'm not going to hire that person, because I don't want trouble."

A White female personnel official from a Los Angeles public sector department offered a related perspective, laying part of the blame with White supervisors:

> . . . And I also think that part of the problem is that the supervisors and managers of these people have their own sets of expectations and their own sets of goals that don't address the diversity of these people, and it's kind of like, well, hell, if they're going to come work for me, they're going to damn well do it my way. . . . And my own personal feeling is that a lot of these young Black men who are being tough scare some of their supervisors. And so rather than address their behavior problems and deal with the issues, they will back away until they can find a way to get rid of them. We have a tendency to fear what we're not real familiar with.

Although a few respondents provided this level of detail, most of the negative responses were far briefer: "a lot of Black males have a chip on their shoulder," or "I get a strong sense of, with Black males at times of a hostility, of 'I deserve so and so, this belongs to me.'"

Our questions probed primarily for generalizations, but some respondents noted variation within race and gender categories. Even the store manager who described Black men as "really scary" added, "You know, there's a lot of Black males that are nice; they usually project a different image. They don't want to project the same image as gangsters."

In addition to negative views of the demeanor of Black men, we found that many retail employers saw the racial composition of employment itself as an issue for customers. The Black male personnel manager of a large retail store located in a Detroit-area suburban mall stated that because the labor market area is 90% Black, "we are forced to have an Affirmative Action program for nonminorities in this particular store." In fact, the store has shifted away from walk-in applications to in-store or mail recruiting from the store's customer base. Given that the mall sits in an integrated suburb of Detroit, his statement implies a fear that an all-Black workforce would erode the White suburban customer base.

In subsequent interviews, we asked retail informants explicitly about attempts to keep the racial mix of store employees similar to that of customers. Seven of the 10 retail informants whom we asked, responded that this was indeed a management concern. Not all of them approved of the customer attitudes to which they were responding. For example, a White female personnel manager at a Los Angeles store said,

> At [a store she was posted at previously] we had a lot of customer complaints because it's primarily White, and we were always getting complaints that there were all Black employees and it's because they were Black. That would be the first thing the customer would bring up was "Black." It was because they were Black that they didn't do their job right.

Nonetheless, this informant and others—Black, White, and Latino alike—viewed the goal of race-matching staff with customers as a legitimate management objective.

Motivation

Forty percent of respondents voiced perceptions of Black men as unmotivated employees. Once again, comments varied widely in substance. A Latino female personnel officer of a Los Angeles retail distribution warehouse, whose workforce is 72% Latino and only 6% Black, stated, "Black men are lazy. . . . Who is going to turn over? The uneducated Black." The White male owner of a small Detroit area plastic parts plant (46% Black, 54% White) said that in his experience, Black men "just don't care—like everybody owes them." "Black kids don't want to work," was the opinion of a White male owner of a small auto parts rebuilding shop in Los Angeles, whose workforce was entirely Hispanic female. "Black men are not responsible," added a Latino female personnel supervisor for a Los Angeles auto parts manufacturer located next to a major Black area but with a workforce that was 85% Latino and less than 1% Black.

This is still a minority viewpoint. The majority of respondents stated that they saw no differences in work ethic by race, although surely, in some cases, they were simply proffering the socially approved response. As in the case of interaction, some respondents discussed variation within race/gender categories. A number of employers invoked such variation to dismiss racial differences:

> We have problem employees, who choose not to come to work as often as others, but that cuts across all racial lines, you know, so no, I wouldn't say that's the case as a blanket statement. We have problem people, but they're

> just problem people. Some of them happen to be Black and some of them happen to be White, but I wouldn't say it's any better or worse in any one group or the other.

Other managers attributed apparent racial differences to class or neighborhood effects. Yet others noted distinctions within racial groups but still rated Black employees lower on average. For example, in a Los Angeles area discount store where the main workforce was Latino, the manager opined:

> I think the Hispanic people have a very serious work ethic. I have a lot of respect for them. They take pride in what they do. Some of the Black folks that I've worked with do, but I'd say a majority of them are just there putting in the time and kind of playing around.

In fact, although only a minority of respondents questioned the work ethic of Blacks, a substantial majority agreed with the idea that immigrants have a stronger work ethic than native-born workers—81% of Detroit respondents who ventured an opinion on this agreed, and 88% of Los Angeles respondents. This bodes ill for less-skilled Black workers, particularly in Los Angeles, because they increasingly compete with immigrant workers for jobs. . . .

How and Why Employers Form These Perceptions

Employers indicated that they based their perceptions of Black men on experiences with past and present employees, on impressions of applicants, and on more general impressions from the media and from experiences outside work. About half of respondents referred to their own employees, sometimes arguing that the immediacy of these observations rendered them objective. Stated a store manager,

> I think [Black men] feel things should be given to them and not earned. And because of that, they don't earn the right to keep jobs. Now that may be, you know, someone would say I may have an attitude problem, but that, I just look at pure facts. I mean with the people that I've had work for me. . . .

. . . In a number of cases, informants pleaded ignorance due to a lack of Black applicants: "It's hard for us to say [why Black men do poorly in the labor market], because we don't have a large enough community, so we don't interview very many Blacks, and we don't reject many Blacks."

Other employers, especially those in White or Hispanic areas, referred to contact with Blacks outside the workplace. A White male insurance manager outside Detroit reported:

> I am involved and attend an urban church, and we attend there working with the homeless and the retarded and people of that nature, [and] unless something is done to help these Black males, it is just a sorry situation.

Although no respondent specifically cited the media as a source for their impressions of Black men, the impact of the media was evident, as in these two comments by White Detroit area manufacturing managers:

> Manager 1: We have a lot guys out there with cocaine in their pocket and Uzis in the trunk.

> Manager 2: I think a lot of [the difficulty Black men face in the labor market] is based on their inability to complete schooling early on, for whatever reason. I don't know a lot of the statistics of the Black race but I do see that. I think that is a good fact. . . . It's going to take unfortunately a heck of a long time to fully eliminate discrimination. We hear about it in the news still, and it's a shame.

. . . Even more important than how employers form their perceptions of Black men is why they hold these views. We argue that the negative views are a complicated combination of stereotypes, realities, and conflicting cultures. The evidence that stereotypes are involved is straightforward. On the one hand, some respondents voiced clearly stereotypical attitudes: "Black men are lazy. . . . They've got no respect for anyone"; and "I'm no doctor . . . but I'm convinced, having dealt with grievance and unrest . . . that Black men, and to some extent Black women, do not deal with stress physically as well as some other races."

On the other hand, certain managers charged that other managers harbored stereotypical views:

> People have a tendency, . . . even if they don't voice it, they deal with their stereotypes. It's easy to identify someone as a female or identify someone as Black male or a White male. And so whatever it is that they have of their expectations of those people, they will project that.

In particular, some managers claimed that their peers engaged in statistical discrimination or generalized from a visible but unrepresentative subset of Black men:

> I think that many employers may feel that because of the large numbers of Black males who are in prison and have problems, that there is a tendency for those who are out and in the workforce to do mischievous things. That's unfortunate.

And one informant, a Black female manager at a Detroit area utility, contended that employers hold Blacks to a different standard than Whites:

> When Blacks and Hispanics and whomever come into the work group, and they are not part of the majority, then one thing they need to know is that they cannot always do what they see others doing, and that is key. That is a lesson that needs to be taught. I think the rules aren't always the same, and it may

> not always be intentional. A lot is institutional and lot of it is people just not understanding others.

We believe that the perceptions stated by employers contain an element of reality as well. We have no independent way of verifying the statements employers made. However, some comments offered substantial detail and specificity, and some referred to "objective" measures such as absenteeism. . . .

Wilson (1987) argued that soft-skill problems are the product of poor neighborhoods; a number of our informants argued instead that such skills—and particularly motivation—are endogenous to the workplace and labor market. As a Black human resource official of a Detroit-area insurer expressed it,

> I think business drives the work ethic. . . . If business is lax . . . then people have casual attitudes about their jobs. . . . You are one thing up to the point of entering the business world, but then you are something else. I'm not the same person I was 15 years ago. I had to take on certain thoughts and attitudes whether I liked it or not.

Several others agreed that motivation is more a function of management than of the workforce. When asked about racial differences in the work ethic, a White male manager of contracted public-sector workers mused,

> I think it's how you motivate each group. Two or three years ago, I would have probably said, well, the Black race isn't as motivated as the Oriental or the Hispanic. But I've seen that if you motivate, that you have to motivate each group differently.

A White male public-sector human resource official added that work ethic may vary by job:

> If I take security, or I take the basic labor jobs, I'm not so sure that when they were Caucasian-dominated 20 years ago, that people weren't leaning on a shovel and goldbricking. Many times, the classifications we normally associate with being more lazy or finding ways to avoid work, are the entry-level, lower skilled ones. And now those happen to be dominated by Blacks and to a lesser extent Hispanics right now.

A small number of informants also argued that workers can be trained to relate well to customers. Even a store manager who commented that "it does take a certain kind of person" to be "fast, fun, and friendly," added, "but if you work with a person, I think that you could pretty much [get them to] be fast, fun, and friendly." . . .

In addition to stereotype and reality, interviewees spoke of cultural gaps between young Black men and their supervisors, coworkers, and customers—especially as an explanation of difficulties in interaction. A Black human resource manager at an insurance company described the problems of cultural translation:

> I think that, as I attend executive meetings, and in many cases, I'm the only Black man there, the cultural diversity and the strangeness that different people bring to one another—oftentimes people aren't prepared to receive what another person may be prepared to offer. And I think that through that lack of communication, a lot of times things are misunderstood. When problems occur, if I work for you and you had a problem with me, you may not know how to approach me and vice versa, I may not know how to approach you.

White respondents also referred to "a difference in understanding," but were more likely to pose it as a failure of the Black men themselves: "[Young Black men] don't present themselves well to the employer, just because they don't know, they don't realize how they're communicating, or not communicating." This conforms with the view, expressed in focus groups by young, inner-city Black and Latino men, that code switching—being able to present oneself and communicate in ways acceptable to majority White culture—is the most important skill needed to find and keep a job (Jobs for the Future 1995). . . .

CONCLUSIONS

We find that due to competitive pressure, employers are demanding more soft skills, even in low-skill jobs. Soft skills include interaction and motivation, and employers are valuing both more highly. However, many managers perceive Black men as possessing fewer soft skills, along both dimensions. Thus, the same increases in competitive pressure that drive corporate downsizing and restructuring are contributing to widening racial inequality in labor market outcomes.

Employers base their perceptions of Black men on assessments of current or past employees and applicants, as well as interaction outside the workplace, and media images of Blacks. Three factors underlie negative evaluations of Black men as workers: racial stereotypes, cultural differences between employers and young Black men, and actual skill differences. The actual skill differences themselves are in part endogenous to the work situation. Moreover, in a work world characterized by increasing levels of interaction, racially biased attitudes held by customers or coworkers of other racial groups can themselves lead to lower measured productivity—that is, productivity differences can be the direct result of discrimination.

References

Capelli, P. (1995). Is the "skills gap" really about attitudes? *California Management Review, 37*(4), 108–124.

England, P. (1992). *Comparable worth: Theories and evidence.* New York: Aldine de Gruyter.

Hochschild, A. R. (1983). *The managed heart: Commercialization of human feeling.* Berkeley: University of California Press.

Jobs for the Future. (1995). Information from focus groups of young, inner city men of color, for work in progress. Unpublished manuscripts. Boston, MA: Author, for the Annie E. Casey Foundation.

Kilbourne, B. S., England, P., & Beron, K. (1994). Effects of changing individual, occupational, and industrial characteristics on changes in earnings: Intersections of race and gender. *Social Forces, 72,* 1149–1176.

Moss, P., & Tilly, C. (1996). *Growing demand for "soft" skills in four industries: Evidence from in-depth employer interviews* (Working Paper No. 93). New York: Russell Sage Foundation.

Wharton, A. (1993). The affective consequences of service work: Managing emotions on the job. *Work and Occupations, 20*(2), 205–232.

Wilson, W. J. (1987). *The truly disadvantaged.* Chicago: University of Chicago Press.

35

THE INVISIBLE POOR

Katherine S. Newman

Forty years ago, when it first began to dawn on this prosperous nation that the end of the Great Depression had not cured widespread poverty, popular representations of the poor focused on Kentucky hollows where Appalachian children sat on wooden stoops, their bellies swollen and faces blank. Miners whose livelihoods had disappeared with the end of the coal boom were left behind like refugees from another era, their families consigned to a threadbare existence. We understood that these were working folk who had fallen on hard times. The whole country reeled at the thought that such desperate

---

conditions existed in the heartland—among good (white) people—and the war on poverty was born in order to lift up the downtrodden.

In the intervening years, however, as many writers have noted, poverty has been racialized. Even though the majority of the poor are still white and working—as they were in the 1930s and thereafter—the public impression is quite clearly the reverse: poverty wears a black face and is presumed to follow from an unwillingness to enter the labor force. As Herbert Gans explains in his compelling book *The War Against the Poor*, the tendency to racialize the undeserving, the objects of society's contempt, is of long standing. The English poor laws of the mid-nineteenth century distinguished sharply between the shiftless and the working poor, associating the former with the Irish, who were regarded as an undesirable racial caste. In the United States, successive waves of immigrants have taken their place in the unholy category of the undeserving poor, including the Italians, the Slavs, and the Eastern European Jews who filled the boweries of the eastern seaboard in the early twentieth century.

But the Great Migration of African-Americans out of the rural South to the industrialized cities of the North in the twentieth century altered forever the racial dynamics of urban poverty. And urban poverty has long been far more visible, to the media and hence to the public at large, than its rural counterpart, however devastating the latter may be. Initially pulled by war-related job opportunities and pushed by agricultural mechanization that put a damper on southern demands for labor, blacks flooded into cities like Chicago, Milwaukee, Akron, New York, Pittsburgh, and elsewhere, only to be met by intense white hostility and overt policies of containment. They were confined in segregated communities that rapidly became overcrowded. . . .

As the jobs that initially sustained the northern migrants began to dry up, the consequences of extreme segregation became all too evident: places like the Cabrini-Green housing project were devastated and volatile. The underground economy and the welfare system were all that remained as forms of subsistence in some projects, and the association of African-Americans who were not gainfully employed with the damning label of "undeserving poor" took root. It was an easy linkage to make in a country obsessed by race.

It is also misleading because in fact the largest group of poor people in the United States are not those on welfare. They are the working poor whose earnings are so meager that despite their best efforts, they cannot afford decent housing, diets, health care, or child care. The debilitating conditions that impinge upon the working poor—substandard housing, crumbling schools, inaccessible health care—are hardly different from those that surround their nonworking counterparts. For many, indeed, these difficulties are measurably worse because too many of the working poor lack access to government supports that cushion those out of the labor force: subsidized housing, medical care, and food stamps.

DEFINING WORKING POVERTY

Debates over how to define poverty have raged for many years now, and not just because scholars love to argue: federal dollars ebb and flow depending on the definition. The technicalities of these debates need not concern us, but some of the principles that underlie them are relevant because they determine whose lives we are talking about when we use the term "working poor." . . .

We might want to think of the working poor as those employees who receive the minimum wage. This is hardly a perfect measure, for many of these minimum-wage earners are young people who live with their middle-class families. While their earnings are low, they do not live in poor households. Still, this is not universally true: only 36 percent of minimum-wage workers are teenagers; 42 percent are adults twenty-five years old and older. Some scholars dismiss the problems of minimum-wage workers because so many of them are women who work part-time (and are therefore presumed to be bringing in "pin money" rather than the necessities of life). While 65 percent of the nation's low-wage workers are women, the gender picture changes dramatically when we examine only *full-time*, year-round minimum wage workers: about 60 percent of them are men. . . .

When readers picture this low-wage workforce, they are likely to imagine hamburger flippers. Service workers of this kind are indeed among the working poor. Yet a surprisingly varied group of American employees take home wages low enough to pull their households below the poverty line. Household service workers (housekeepers, child care workers, and cooks) had a poverty rate of 21.8 percent during 1996. The rate for dental assistants, bartenders, hairdressers, and waitresses was 13.2 percent, and that for operators, fabricators, and laborers was 8 percent.

AGE, FAMILY STATUS, EDUCATION, AND RACE

With these definitions of the working poor in mind, we might ask who they are in a sociological sense: what kinds of people find themselves in this category? The short answer is that the nation's young, its single parents, the poorly educated, and minorities are more likely than other workers to be poor.

As America's youth enter an increasingly inhospitable labor market, they have found themselves at a disadvantage over those who preceded them in better years. Poverty rates for young workers have nearly doubled in the last twenty years. Family status has a powerful impact on the working poor as well. Not surprisingly, families in which both husband and wife work are the least likely to be poor. Working single mothers, on the other hand, are the most likely to be poor—the poverty rate of families supported by single mothers is almost four times that of married-couple families with at least one worker. Single-parent families with mothers at the helm are almost twice as likely to be poor as families maintained solely by men, a reflection of the weak position of women in the labor market. But the predicament for single men should not be understated: 10 percent of America's working men who maintain families without a wife suffer poverty as well. Clearly, lacking a second earner—male or female—a low-wage worker is at great risk for falling below the poverty line.

We know that our changing economy favors the well-educated. Their incomes have risen while high school dropouts have seen a precipitous loss in their wages and their employment rates and a concomitant increase in their poverty. . .

Race complicates this picture. In an all-too-familiar story of America's racial divide, we discover that the white population has a significantly lower proportion of working poor (5.4 percent using the BLS* definition) than either African-Americans (13.3 percent) or Hispanics (14.6 percent). This is not just a matter of educational disadvantage concentrated among minorities: African-Americans in the labor force are more likely to be poor than their white counterparts at all levels of the educational continuum. . . .

. . . The clamor over welfare reform that crested in 1996 further tightened the linkage in the public mind between the indigent poor and the whole concept of poverty. The . . . data presented here suggest that this is a relatively minor part of the problem. More important by far are the trends that have increased the size of the *working* population that canr ot make ends meet and the millions of children growing up in their households.

THE WORKING POOR IN HARLEM

Central Harlem is one of the poorest parts of New York City. Nearly 30 percent of its households were on public assistance in 1990. Poverty stands at 40 percent. Harlem's walls are laden with graffiti, windows are frequently shattered, and housing projects—magnets for troublemakers—rise above the skyline and dominate the once-elegant brownstones that are now boarded up, their stoops crumbling in decay. Running through the middle of this enclave is a bustling commercial strip, 125th Street (Martin Luther King, Jr. Boulevard), that has a long and glorious history as the crucible of the Harlem Renaissance. The Apollo Theatre, still the grand center of Harlem culture, is on 125th Street, as is a large state office building, named after one of the most famous of the community's native sons, Adam Clayton Powell, Jr.

Harlem residents do much of their shopping along 125th Street, for it is there that the most accessible drugstores, clothing shops, furniture marts, and fast food restaurants are to be found. To buy anything at a fancier store requires a subway trip or bus ride to another neighborhood. Shopping is

---

*Editors' note: Bureau of Labor Statistics.

therefore a community ritual, a constant public parade through the heart of America's best-known African-American enclave.

The main thoroughfare is also the place many Harlem residents turn to when they try to find work. Hence it is also the place where I began to look for the working-poor families. . . . I found them by way of four fast food restaurants that cater to the African-American and Latino clientele in the center of Harlem and on its periphery, where immigrant families from the Dominican Republic and Puerto Rico cluster. Beginning with fast food eateries was not an accident, for the stereotype of hamburger-flipping as the emblematic low-wage job turns out to be quite accurate. *More than one in every fifteen Americans has worked in the fast food industry.* Minority youth are a big part of this labor force: some one in eight of them has worked in the business. Hence the public image of the "McJob" accords fairly well with reality, for the fast food industry is a critical gateway into the labor market for thousands of people who live in inner-city neighborhoods. It is from this starting point that they hope to launch careers that will take them out of the minimum-wage bracket into a job that pays enough to sustain a family.

As is true in any study of a particular occupational group, fast food workers do not necessarily represent the entire universe of low-wage workers. One could just as usefully study people who scan in groceries in supermarkets or clerks in low-priced clothing shops. The question naturally arises, then, how far we can generalize from the experience of Harlem's fast food workers to the working poor elsewhere in the country. . . .

Race/Ethnicity

Nearly all of the residents of central Harlem are African-American. But the workforce we encountered in Harlem's fast food establishments was far more diverse: only slightly over half of its workers are black. A large group, nearly one-quarter, are immigrants who were either born in the Dominican Republic and immigrated to New York as children or first-generation Americans of Dominican parentage. They are members of one of the fastest growing groups of newcomers to New York. . . .

Sons and daughters of Dominican immigrants tend to live in enclaves dominated by friends, family members, and other co-ethnics, communities where most children begin life as monolingual speakers of Spanish. Eventually, of course, they learn the English language and American ways as they move through New York's school system and rub shoulders with outsiders who do not share their culture. Nonetheless, the identification they feel with their fellow immigrants—an identity reinforced by frequent visits and long stays in their "homeland"—is so strong that they think of themselves as Dominican even though many were born in New York.

Sixteen percent of the people whom we encountered in the restaurant workforce were Latinos from elsewhere in the Caribbean, principally Puerto

Rico, which has for decades sent workers to the U.S. mainland for jobs, and pulled them back with family ties that run deep. Return migration, or, rather, circular patterns of migration, are so common in this community that a hybrid culture has developed: the Nuyoricans. Puerto Ricans are the largest Hispanic group in New York; one-half of all the Latinos in the city are of Puerto Rican origin. In fact, they are among the largest ethnic groups of any kind, numbering nearly a million and increasing at a rapid rate. . . .

Puerto Ricans and Dominicans represent the two largest groups of Latino immigrants in New York City. They are also among the poorest of the city's residents: Hispanics have median household incomes that are two-thirds of the median for whites or less, and their poverty rates are at least one and a half times greater than those for whites. Nuyoricans and Dominicans, who are important entrants to Harlem's low-wage economy, are also among the poorest of the city's Hispanics, falling well behind the smaller and more prosperous groups of Argentines, Panamanians, and Peruvians. . . .

. . . Although the two groups of Latinos are comparable in many respects (age, fertility, family structure), Puerto Ricans tend to have higher earnings. Dominicans in New York—and in my study—tend to make up for this disadvantage by increasing the number of people per household who are in the labor market. Both groups, however, are at great risk for joining the ranks of the working poor. In this they resemble the native-born African-Americans in Harlem, whose options are similarly limited by the pressures of racial discrimination, an imploding labor market, and a weak educational system that does little to position New York's poverty population for the good jobs that remain.

Age

We usually think of a fast food job as a youngster's first stepping-stone into the labor market, a part-time foray for pocket money and a forestate of an adult lifetime of full-time employment. In most of the nation's suburbs, and in some of its more affluent cities, that is exactly who occupies this employment niche. Not so in central Harlem. . . . While a significant number of high-school-age kids are working in these restaurants, most of the employees are considerably older. Seventy percent of the workers we interviewed are over nineteen. Thirty-five percent are well into adulthood, twenty-three years old and older. This stands in marked contrast to national figures on the fast food workforce. Nationwide, nearly three-quarters of the workers in this industry are twenty years old or younger, with more than one-quarter in the high-school-age group. No doubt the differences reflect the relative paucity of opportunities in a depressed economy like that of central Harlem. Older people have fewer better-paying prospects and are therefore "pushing down" into jobs that would qualify as entry-level way stations elsewhere.

When we look at the local age figures for African-Americans, the contrast with the national average-aged worker grows sharper. . . . One-half of the African-Americans in this workforce are twenty-three years old and older, reflecting once again the more restricted nature of the labor market opportunities open to them. Dominicans, by contrast, look more like the stereotypical young worker in a hamburger flipping job: half of them are in the youngest age group and only 16 percent are as old as the majority of black fast food workers.

Education

Fast food jobs are often thought to act as magnets, pulling young people away from school, distracting their attention from the kind of "human capital" investment that will pay off in the long run. . . . Contrary to prevailing stereotypes of fast food workers as high school dropouts—these inner-city workers are both quite strongly attached to the educational enterprise and better educated as a group than we might have expected. About 70 percent of the youngest workers (fifteen-to-eighteen-year-olds) are in a regular high school program, and another 10 percent are enrolled in an alternative high school. Eight percent are going to college. Less than 10 percent, most of whom are immigrant workers who completed their schooling in Latin America, are completely detached from the world of education. . . .

For many people in these age groups, education is an ongoing process that will continue for many years into adulthood. It is instructive, then, to consider what they hope to accomplish over the long run—what the *aspirations* of these low-wage workers look like. Perhaps in part because of their encounter with the raw world of low-wage employment and their desire to find something better over the long run, Burger Barn employees have very high expectations for their educational futures. Over half of the youngest workers expect to go on to college. African-Americans have higher educational goals than do their Latino counterparts, and part-time workers (many of whom are taking courses while working) expect to do better than those who work full-time.

Whether these aspirations will be realized or not is hard to forecast, but the data on the actual enrollment patterns of these fast food workers are not particularly encouraging. The older the workers, the less likely they are to be enrolled in courses of any kind, and most of those who are in school are taking vocational, technical, or para-professional courses, rather than liberal arts courses of the kind that is typical for the four-year institutions they aspire to attend. Older workers with adult responsibilities may find higher education out of reach.

Still, we see an extraordinary commitment to higher education in aspiration if not in practice, even among those fast food employees who are already quite a bit older than the normal middle-class college student. The numbers reflect what we found in the course of many months of conversation with Harlem's low-wage workers: an enduring belief in education as an essential credential for mobility in the labor market. This portrait could not possibly be farther from the stereotypical picture of the inner-city minority (usually described as a high school dropout with no appreciation of the value of education).

Gender

We have known for some time that low-wage work is often women's work. Nationally, women are concentrated in the jobs that cluster at the bottom of the income distribution. Fast food jobs, prototypical examples of low-wage work, are overwhelmingly held by females in the United States: in 1984, two-thirds of this labor force was female. Not so in Harlem. Nearly half of the workers in these ghetto restaurants were men. This suggests that men face a steeper uphill battle in finding better jobs in communities like Harlem, ultimately "slipping down" into sectors that, elsewhere, would be largely women's employment preserves.

Family/Household Structure

There are many ways to describe . . . Harlem's fast food labor force, and we have already encountered some—race, gender, and age being among the most common demographic descriptors. One other needs to be added, however, if we are to understand who these people are: family structure. In suburban America, we would expect to find that the fast food labor force was composed mainly of young people who are living at home with their parents and passing through this work experience as a way station to a more remunerative future. We already know that Harlem's restaurant workers are older. But what kinds of families do these low-wage workers come from, or more particularly, what do the households they live in look like?

Almost one-third of these Harlem workers live with a single parent (overwhelmingly a mother). Only 13 percent of these workers are children living in a nuclear household (with both parents). Over half of the workers we studied are over the age of eighteen, but still live with their parents or other relatives. These are young adults who cannot earn enough money to launch independent lives and are therefore forced to remain at home, where resources can be pooled and poverty managed collaboratively in the family.

More than one-third of these Harlem workers were parents trying to support families on the strength of these minimum-wage positions. Very few had children under the age of six, most likely because it is so hard to pay for child care out of wages this low. Those who did have young children were older (twenty-five to thirty-four) and worked full-time; one-third were trying to make ends meet alone, as single parents.

The literature on the urban underclass posits a physical separation of welfare recipients and working people, a separation that supposedly underwrites divergent cultures. Aid to Families with Dependent Children, we are told, spawned negative socialization patterns, most especially an unfamiliarity with (or lack of appreciation for) the world of work. When we look at real families, though, we find that what look like separate worlds to the Bureau of Labor Statistics are whole family units that combine work and welfare, and always have.

Twenty-nine percent of central Harlem's households received support from the welfare system in 1995. However, many of the same families also contained members who were in the labor force. Indeed, among restaurant workers, about one-quarter were living in households where someone was receiving AFDC income, though wages remain the overwhelming source of family support for virtually all of these households. Two in five of the Burger Barn workers are the only formally employed person in their household. This is more than designer sneakers and gold chains: the income these young workers receive is a critical source of support in poor households in Harlem.

Rather than paint welfare and work as different worlds, it makes far more sense to describe them as two halves of a single coin, as an integrated economic system at the very bottom of our social structure. Kyesha's family is a clear example of this fusion. Her mother needs the income her working child brings into the house; Kyesha needs the subsidies (housing, medical care, etc.) that state aid provides to her mother. Only because the two domains are linked can this family manage to make ends meet, and then just barely. Of course, many of these restaurant workers are in families that have no contact with the state welfare system at all. Instead, they are wage workers whose family members are also working for a living. Our understanding of their parents' occupational situations is complicated by the fractured family structure that so many are embedded in: 27 percent of their fathers are deceased, and 14 percent of their mothers as well. Since very few of the people we studied were over the age of forty, this suggests a pattern of early mortality among their parents, with all the difficulties this brings about in the lives of young people. Divorce and the incidence of never-married mothers produce enough distance between children and their fathers that many know only that their fathers are alive, and are not aware of what they do for a living.

Still, we do know something about the employment patterns of the parents of our restaurant workers. Over half of their mothers are working, with medical services—hospitals, home care agencies, and nursing homes—providing by far the largest source of employment. The health care industry was one of the few sectors that continued to grow in New York City throughout the relentless recession of the early 1990s; it absorbed many of the inner city's working poor.

What we know about the fathers of these fast food workers is probably less reliable than the information about mothers, simply because the ties between children and their fathers are more tenuous. Nonetheless, 46 percent of the fathers are reported by their sons and daughters to be employed. For many of them, we have no information about their occupation at all because their children do not know where they work. Those for whom we have information are employed as skilled craftsmen and transportation workers. The rest are scattered in janitorial services, factory labor, and retail trades. A number of them are retired and 10 percent are presently unemployed but once worked. . . .

Ongoing changes in the American economy have pulled the rug out from under the low-wage labor market. The continued fiscal instability of cities like New York is spurring cuts in public employment and critical services. Federal government retrenchment has reduced funding for everything from housing subsidies to Medicaid. These trends conspire to make the problems of the working poor more severe than they used to be. That's the bad news. The good news is that despite all of these difficulties, the nation's working poor continue to seek their salvation in the labor market. That such a commitment persists when the economic rewards are so minimal is testimony to the durability of the work ethic, to the powerful reach of mainstream American culture, which has always placed work at the center of our collective moral existence.

Reference

Gans, Herbert. 1995. *The War Against the Poor.* New York: Basic Books.

36

DOMÉSTICA

Pierrette Hondagneu-Sotelo

Particular regional formations have historically characterized the racialization of paid domestic work in the United States. Relationships between domestic employees and employers have always been imbued with racial meanings: white "masters and mistresses" have been cast as pure and superior, and "maids

From Pierrette Hondagneu-Sotelo, *Doméstica: Immigrant Workers Caring and Cleaning in America* (Berkeley: University of California Press, 2001) pp. 13–22. Reprinted by permission of the University of California Press.

and servants," drawn from specific racial-ethnic groups (varying by region), have been cast as dirty and socially inferior. The occupational racialization we see now in Los Angeles or New York City continues this American legacy, but it also draws to a much greater extent on globalization and immigration.

In the United States today, immigrant women from a few non-European nations are established as paid domestic workers. These women—who hail primarily from Mexico, Central America, and the Caribbean and who are perceived as "nonwhite" in Anglo-American contexts—hold various legal statuses. Some are legal permanent residents or naturalized U.S. citizens, many as beneficiaries of the 1986 Immigration Reform and Control Act's amnesty-legalization program. Central American women, most of whom entered the United States after the 1982 cutoff date for amnesty, did not qualify for legalization, so in the 1990s they generally either remained undocumented or held a series of temporary work permits, granted to delay their return to war-ravaged countries. Domestic workers who are working without papers clearly face extra burdens and risks: criminalization of employment, denial of social entitlements, and status as outlaws anywhere in the nation. If they complain about their jobs, they may be threatened with deportation. Undocumented immigrant workers, however, are not the only vulnerable ones. In the 1990s, even legal permanent residents and naturalized citizens saw their rights and privileges diminish, as campaigns against illegal immigration metastasized into more generalized xenophobic attacks on all immigrants, including those here with legal authorization. Immigration status has clearly become an important axis of inequality, one interwoven with relations of race, class, and gender, and it facilitates the exploitation of immigrant domestic workers.

Yet race and immigration are interacting in an important new way, which Latina immigrant domestic workers exemplify: their position as "foreigners" and "immigrants" allows employers, and the society at large, to perceive them as outsiders and thereby overlook the contemporary racialization of the occupation. Immigration does not trump race but, combined with the dominant ideology of a "color-blind" society, manages to shroud it.

With few exceptions, domestic work has always been reserved for poor women, for immigrant women, and for women of color; but over the last century, paid domestic workers have become more homogenous, reflecting the subordinations of both race and nationality/immigration status. In the late nineteenth century, this occupation was the most likely source of employment for U.S.-born women. In 1870, according to the historian David M. Katzman, two-thirds of all nonagricultural female wage earners worked as domestics in private homes. The proportion steadily declined to a little over one-third by 1900, and to one-fifth by 1930. Alternative employment opportunities for women expanded in the mid- and late twentieth century, so by 1990, fewer than 1 percent of employed American women were engaged in domestic work. Census figures, of course, are notoriously unreliable in documenting this increasingly undocumentable, "under-the-table" occupation, but the trend is clear: paid domestic work has gone from being *either* an immigrant woman's job *or* a minority woman's job to one that is now filled by women who, as Latina and Caribbean immigrants, embody subordinate status both racially and as immigrants.

Regional racializations of the occupation were already deeply marked in the late nineteenth and early twentieth centuries, as the occupation recruited women from subordinate racial-ethnic groups. In northeastern and midwestern cities of the late nineteenth century, single young Irish, German, and Scandinavian immigrants and women who had migrated from the country to the city typically worked as live-in "domestic help," often leaving the occupation when they married. During this period, the Irish were the main target of xenophobic vilification. With the onset of World War I, European immigration declined and job opportunities in manufacturing opened up for whites, and black migration from the South enabled white employers to recruit black women for domestic jobs in the Northeast. Black women had always predominated as a servant caste in the South, whether in slavery or after, and by 1920 they constituted the single largest group in paid domestic work in both the South and the Northeast. Unlike European immigrant women, black women experienced neither individual nor intergenerational mobility out of the occupation, but they succeeded in transforming the occupation from one characterized by live-in arrangements, with no separation between work and social life, to live-out "day work"—a transformation aided by urbanization, new interurban transportation systems, and smaller urban residences.

In the Southwest and the West of the late nineteenth and early twentieth centuries, the occupation was filled with Mexican American and Mexican immigrant women, as well as Asian, African American, and Native American women and, briefly, Asian men. Asian immigrant men were among the first recruits for domestic work in the West. California exceptionalism—its Anglo-American conquest from Mexico in 1848, its ensuing rapid development and overnight influx of Anglo settlers and miners, and its scarcity of women—initially created many domestic jobs in the northern part of the territory for Chinese "houseboys," laundrymen, and cooks, and later for Japanese men, followed by Japanese immigrant women and their U.S.-born daughters, the nisei, who remained in domestic work until World War II. Asian American women's experiences . . . provide an intermediate case of intergenerational mobility out of domestic work between that of black and Chicana women who found themselves, generation after generation, stuck in the occupational ghetto of domestic work and that of European immigrant women of the early twentieth century who quickly moved up the mobility ladder.

For Mexican American women and their daughters, domestic work became a dead-end job. From the 1880s until World War II, it provided the largest source of nonagricultural employment for Mexican and Chicana women throughout the Southwest. During this period, domestic vocational training

schools, teaching manuals, and Americanization efforts deliberately chan-
neled them into domestic jobs. Continuing well into the 1970s throughout
the Southwest, and up to the present in particular regions, U.S.-born Mexican
American women have worked as domestics. Over that time, the job has
changed. Much as black women helped transform the domestic occupation
from live-in to live-out work in the early twentieth century, Chicanas in the
Southwest increasingly preferred contractual housecleaning work . . . to
live-in or daily live-out domestic work.

While black women dominated the occupation throughout the nation
during the 1950s and 1960s, there is strong evidence that many left it during
the late 1960s. The 1970 census marked the first time that domestic work did
not account for the largest segment of employed black women; and the proportion of black women in domestic work continued to drop dramatically in
the 1970s and 1980s, falling from 16.4 percent in 1972 to 7.4 percent in 1980,
then to 3.5 percent by the end of the 1980s. By opening up public-sector jobs
to black women, the Civil Rights Act of 1964 made it possible for them to
leave private domestic service. Consequently, both African American and
Mexican American women moved into jobs from which they had been previously barred, as secretaries, sales clerks, and public-sector employees, and
into the expanding number of relatively low-paid service jobs in convalescent
homes, hospitals, cafeterias, and hotels.

These occupational adjustments and opportunities did not go unnoticed.
In a 1973 *Los Angeles Times* article, a manager with thirty years of experience in
domestic employment agencies reported, "Our Mexican girls are nice, but the
blacks are hostile." Speaking very candidly about her contrasting perceptions
of Latina immigrant and African American women domestic workers, she said
of black women, "you can feel their anger. They would rather work at Grant's
for $1.65 an hour than do housework. To them it denotes a lowering of self."
By the 1970s black women in the occupation were growing older, and their
daughters were refusing to take jobs imbued with servitude and racial subordination. Domestic work, with its historical legacy in slavery, was roundly
rejected. Not only expanding job opportunities but also the black power movement, with its emphasis on self-determination and pride, dissuaded younger
generations of African American women from entering domestic work.

It was at this moment that newspaper reports, census data, and anecdotal
accounts first register the occupation's demographic shift toward Latina
immigrants, a change especially pronounced in areas with high levels of
Latino immigration. In Los Angeles, for example, the percentage of African
American women working as domestics in private households fell from 35 percent to 4 percent from 1970 to 1990, while foreign-born Latinas increased
their representation from 9 percent to 68 percent. Again, since census counts
routinely underestimate the poor and those who speak limited or no English,
the women in this group may represent an even larger proportion of private
domestic workers.

Ethnographic case studies conducted not only in Los Angeles but also in Washington, D.C., San Francisco, San Diego, Houston, El Paso, suburban areas of Long Island, and New York City provide many details about the experiences of Mexican, Caribbean, and Central American women who now predominate in these metropolitan centers as nanny/housekeepers and housecleaners. Like the black women who migrated from the rural South to northern cities in the early twentieth century, Latina immigrant women newly arrived in U.S. cities and suburbs in the 1970s, 1980s, and 1990s often started as live-ins, sometimes first performing unpaid household work for kin before taking on very low paying live-in jobs for other families. Live-in jobs, shunned by better-established immigrant women, appeal to new arrivals who want to minimize their living costs and begin sending their earnings home. Vibrant social networks channel Latina immigrants into these jobs, where the long hours and the social isolation can be overwhelming. As time passes, many of the women seek live-out domestic jobs. Despite the decline in live-in employment arrangements at the century's midpoint, the twentieth century ended in the United States much as it began, with a resurgence of live-in jobs filled by women of color—now Latina immigrants.

Two factors of the late twentieth century were especially important in creating this scenario. First, . . . globalization has promoted higher rates of immigration. The expansion of U.S. private investment and trade; the opening of U.S. multinational assembly plants (employing mostly women) along the U.S.-Mexico border and in Caribbean and Central American nations, facilitated by government legislative efforts such as the Border Industrialization Program, the North American Free Trade Agreement, and the Caribbean Basin Initiative; the spreading influence of U.S. mass media; and U.S. military aid in Central America have all helped rearrange local economies and stimulate U.S.-bound migration from the Caribbean, Mexico, and Central America. Women from these countries have entered the United States at a propitious time for families looking to employ housecleaners and nannies.

Second, increased immigration led to the racialized xenophobia of the 1990s. The rhetoric of these campaigns shifted focus, from attacking immigrants for lowering wages and competing for jobs to seeking to bar immigrants' access to social entitlements and welfare. In the 1990s, legislation codified this racialized nativism, in large part taking aim at women and children. In 1994 California's Proposition 187, targeting Latina immigrants and their children, won at the polls; and although its denial of all public education and of publicly funded health care was ruled unconstitutional by the courts, the vote helped usher in new federal legislation. In 1996 federal welfare reform, particularly the Immigration Reform Act and Individual Responsibility Act (IRAIRA), codified the legal and social disenfranchisement of legal permanent residents and undocumented immigrants. At the same time, language—and in particular the Spanish language—was becoming racialized; virulent "English Only" and anti-bilingual education campaigns and ballot initiatives spread.

Because Latina immigrants are disenfranchised as immigrants and foreigners, Americans can overlook the current racialization of the job. On the one hand, racial hostilities and fears may be lessened as increasing numbers of Latina and Caribbean nannies care for tow-headed children. As Sau-ling C. Wong suggests in an analysis of recent films, "in a society undergoing radical demographic and economic changes, the figure of the person of color patiently mothering white folks serves to allay racial anxieties."[1] Stereotypical images of Latinas as innately warm, loving, and caring certainly round out this picture. Yet on the other hand, the status of these Latinas as immigrants today serves to legitimize their social, economic, and political subordination and their disproportionate concentration in paid domestic work.

Such legitimation makes it possible to ignore American racism and discrimination. Thus the abuses that Latina domestic workers suffer in domestic jobs can be explained away because the women themselves are foreign and unassimilable. If they fail to realize the American Dream, according to this distorted narrative, it is because they are lazy and unmotivated or simply because they are "illegal" and do not merit equal opportunities with U.S.-born American citizens. Contemporary paid domestic work in the United States remains a job performed by women of color, by black and brown women from the Caribbean, Central America, and Mexico. This racialization of domestic work is masked by the ideology of "a color-blind society" and by the focus on immigrant "foreignness."

GLOBAL TRENDS IN PAID DOMESTIC WORK

Just as paid domestic work has expanded in the United States, so too it appears to have grown in many other postindustrial societies—in Canada and in parts of Europe—in the "newly industrialized countries" (NICs) of Asia, and in the oil-rich nations of the Middle East. Around the globe Caribbean, Mexican, Central American, Peruvian, Sri Lankan, Indonesian, Eastern European, and Filipina women—the latter in disproportionately great numbers—predominate in these jobs. Worldwide, paid domestic work continues its long legacy as a racialized and gendered occupation, but today divisions of nation and citizenship are increasingly salient. Rhacel Parreñas, who has studied Filipina domestic workers, refers to this development as the "international division of reproductive labor," and Anthony Richmond has called it part of a broad, new "global apartheid."[2]

. . . We must remember that the inequality of nations is a key factor in the globalization of contemporary paid domestic work. This inequality has had three results. First, around the globe, paid domestic work is increasingly performed by women who leave their own nations, their communities, and often their families of origin to do it. Second, the occupation draws not only women from the poor socioeconomic classes but also women of relatively high status in their own countries—countries that colonialism made much poorer than those countries where they go to do domestic work. Thus it is not unusual to find middle-class, college-educated women working in other nations as private domestic workers. Third, the development of service-based economies in postindustrial nations favors the international migration of women laborers. Unlike in earlier industrial eras, today the demand for gendered labor favors migrant women's services.

Nations use vastly different methods to "import" domestic workers from other countries. Some countries have developed highly regulated, government-operated, contract labor programs that have institutionalized both the recruitment and working conditions of migrant domestic workers. Canada and Hong Kong exemplify this approach. Since 1981 the Canadian federal government has formally recruited thousands of women to work as live-in nanny/housekeepers for Canadian families. Most come from third world countries, the majority in the 1980s from the Caribbean and in the 1990s from the Philippines; and once in Canada, they must remain in live-in domestic service for two years, until they obtain their landed immigrant status, the equivalent of the U.S. "green card." During this period, they must work in conditions reminiscent of formal indentured servitude and they may not quit their jobs or collectively organize to improve job conditions.

Similarly, since 1973 Hong Kong has relied on the formal recruitment of domestic workers, mostly Filipinas, to work on a full-time, live-in basis for Chinese families. Of the 150,000 foreign domestic workers in Hong Kong in 1995, 130,000 hailed from the Philippines, with smaller numbers drawn from Thailand, Indonesia, India, Sri Lanka, and Nepal. Just as it is now rare to find African American women employed in private domestic work in Los Angeles, so too have Chinese women vanished from the occupation in Hong Kong. . . .

In the larger global context, the United States remains distinctive, as it follows a more laissez-faire approach to incorporating immigrant women into paid domestic work. Unlike in Hong Kong and Canada, here there is no formal government system or policy to legally contract with foreign domestic workers. In the past, private employers in the United States were able to "sponsor" individual immigrant women working as domestics for their green cards, sometimes personally recruiting them while they were vacationing or working in foreign countries, but this route is unusual in Los Angeles today. For such labor certification, the sponsor must document that there is a shortage of labor able to perform a particular, specialized job—and in Los Angeles and many other parts of the country, demonstrating a shortage of domestic workers has become increasingly difficult. And it is apparently unnecessary, as the significant demand for domestic workers in the United States is largely filled not through formal channels but through informal recruitment from the growing number of Caribbean and Latina immigrant women who are already living (legally or illegally) in the United States. The Immigration and Naturalization Service, the federal agency charged with stopping illegal migration, has historically served the interest of domestic employers and winked at the hiring of undocumented immigrant women in private homes.

As we compare the hyperregulated employment systems in Hong Kong and Canada with the U.S. approach to domestic work, we must distinguish between the regulation of labor and the regulation of foreign domestic workers. . . . Here, the United States is again an exception. U.S. labor regulations *do* cover private domestic work—but no one knows about them. . . . Domestic workers' wages and hours are governed by state and federal law, and special regulations cover such details as limits on permissible deductions for breakage and for boarding costs of live-in workers. These regulations did not fall from the sky: they are the result of several important, historic campaigns organized by and for paid domestic workers. Most U.S. employers now know . . . about their obligations for employment taxes—though these obligations are still widely ignored—but few employers and perhaps fewer employees know about the labor laws pertaining to private domestic work. It's almost as though these regulations did not exist. At the same time, the United States does not maintain separate immigration policies for domestic workers, of the sort that mandate live-in employment or decree instant deportation if workers quit their jobs.

This duality has two consequences. On the one hand, both the absence of hyperregulation of domestic workers and the ignorance about existing labor laws further reinforce the belief that paid domestic work is not a real job. Domestic work remains an arrangement that is thought of as private: it remains informal, "in the shadows," and outside the purview of the state and other regulating agencies. On the other hand, the absence of state monitoring of domestic job contracts and of domestic workers' personal movement, privacy, and bodily adornment suggests an opening to upgrade domestic jobs in the United States. Unlike in Hong Kong and Canada, for example, where state regulations prevent Filipina domestic workers from quitting jobs that they find unsatisfactory or abusive, in Los Angeles, Latina immigrant domestic workers can . . . quit their jobs. Certainly they face limited options when they seek jobs outside of private homes, but it is important to note that they are not yoked by law to the same boss and the same job.

The absence of a neocolonialist, state-operated, contractual system for domestic work thus represents an opportunity to seek better job conditions. The chance of success might be improved if existing labor regulations were strengthened, if domestic workers were to work at collective organizing, and if informational and educational outreach to the domestic workers were undertaken. But to be effective, these efforts must occur in tandem with a new recognition that the relationships in paid domestic work are relations of employment.

NOTES

1. Sau-ling C. Wong. 1994. "Diverted Mothering: Representations of Caregivers of Color in the Age of Multiculturalism." pp. 67–91 in *Mothering: Ideology, Experience, and Agency*, edited by Evelyn Nakano Glenn, Grace Chang, and Linda Pennie Forcey. New York: Routledge, p. 69.

2. Rhacel Salazar Parreñas. 2000. "Migrant Filipina Domestic Workers and the International Division of Reproductive Labor." *Gender & Society* 14:560–580; Anthony Richmond. 1994. *Global Apartheid: Refugees, Racism, and the New World Order*. Toronto: Oxford University Press.

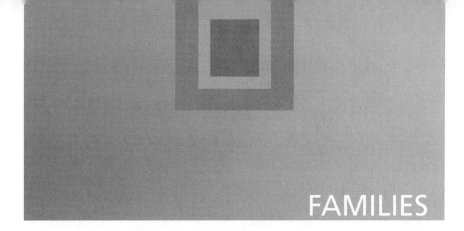

FAMILIES

37

OUR MOTHERS' GRIEF
*Racial-Ethnic Women and
the Maintenance of Families*

Bonnie Thornton Dill

REPRODUCTIVE LABOR[1] FOR WHITE WOMEN IN EARLY AMERICA

In eighteenth- and nineteenth-century America, the lives of white[2] women in the United States were circumscribed within a legal and social system based on patriarchal authority. This authority took two forms: public and private. The social, legal, and economic position of women in this society was controlled through the private aspects of patriarchy and defined in terms of their relationship to families headed by men. The society was structured to confine white wives to reproductive labor within the domestic sphere. At the same time, the formation, preservation, and protection of families among white settlers was seen as crucial to the growth and development of American society. Building, maintaining, and supporting families was a concern of the State and of those organizations that prefigured the State. Thus, while white women had few legal rights as women, they were protected through public forms of patriarchy that acknowledged and supported their

From *Journal of Family History* 13 (1988): 415–31. Reprinted by permission.

family roles of wives, mothers, and daughters because they were vital instruments for building American society. . . .

In colonial America, white women were seen as vital contributors to the stabilization and growth of society. They were therefore accorded some legal and economic recognition through a patriarchal family structure. . . .

Throughout the colonial period, women's reproductive labor in the family was an integral part of the daily operation of small-scale family farms or artisan's shops. According to Kessler-Harris (1981), a gender-based division of labor was common, but not rigid. The participation of women in work that was essential to family survival reinforced the importance of their contributions to both the protection of the family and the growth of society.

Between the end of the eighteenth and mid-nineteenth century, what is labeled the "modern American family" developed. The growth of industrialization and an urban middle class, along with the accumulation of agrarian wealth among Southern planters, had two results that are particularly pertinent to this discussion. First, class differentiation increased and sharpened, and with it, distinctions in the content and nature of women's family lives. Second, the organization of industrial labor resulted in the separation of home and family and the assignment to women of a separate sphere of activity focused on childcare and home maintenance. Whereas men's activities became increasingly focused upon the industrial competitive sphere of work, "women's activities were increasingly confined to the care of children, the nurturing of the husband, and the physical maintenance of the home" (Degler 1980, p. 26).

This separate sphere of domesticity and piety became both an ideal for all white women as well as a source of important distinctions between them. As Matthaei (1982) points out, tied to the notion of wife as homemaker is a definition of masculinity in which the husband's successful role performance was measured by his ability to keep his wife in the homemaker role. The entry of white women into the labor force came to be linked with the husband's assumed inability to fulfill his provider role.

For wealthy and middle-class women, the growth of the domestic sphere offered a potential for creative development as homemakers and mothers. Given ample financial support from their husband's earnings, some of these women were able to concentrate their energies on the development and elaboration of the more intangible elements of this separate sphere. They were also able to hire other women to perform the daily tasks such as cleaning, laundry, cooking, and ironing. Kessler-Harris cautions, however, that the separation of productive labor from the home did not seriously diminish the amount of physical drudgery associated with housework, even for middle-class women. . . . In effect, household labor was transformed from economic productivity done by members of the family group to home maintenance; childcare and moral uplift done by an isolated woman who perhaps supervised some servants.

Working-class white women experienced this same transformation but their families' acceptance of the domestic code meant that their labor in the home intensified. Given the meager earnings of working-class men, working-class families had to develop alternative strategies to both survive and keep the wives at home. The result was that working-class women's reproductive labor increased to fill the gap between family need and family income. Women increased their own production of household goods through things such as canning and sewing; and by developing other sources of income, including boarders and homework. A final and very important source of other income was wages earned by the participation of sons and daughters in the labor force. In fact, Matthaei argues that "the domestic homemaking of married women was supported by the labors of their daughters" (1982, p. 130). . . .

Another way in which white women's family roles were socially acknowledged and protected was through the existence of a separate sphere for women. The code of domesticity, attainable for affluent women, became an ideal toward which nonaffluent women aspired. Notwithstanding the personal constraints placed on women's development, the notion of separate spheres promoted the growth and stability of family life among the white middle class and became the basis for working-class men's efforts to achieve a family wage, so that they could keep their wives at home. Also, women gained a distinct sphere of authority and expertise that yielded them special recognition.

During the eighteenth and nineteenth centuries, American society accorded considerable importance to the development and sustenance of European immigrant families. As primary laborers in the reproduction and maintenance of family life, women were acknowledged and accorded the privileges and protections deemed socially appropriate to their family roles. This argument acknowledges the fact that the family structure denied these women many rights and privileges and seriously constrained their individual growth and development. Because women gained social recognition primarily through their membership in families, their personal rights were few and privileges were subject to the will of the male head of the household. Nevertheless, the recognition of women's reproductive labor as an essential building block of the family, combined with a view of the family as the cornerstone of the nation, distinguished the experiences of the white, dominant culture from those of racial ethnics.

Thus, in its founding, American society initiated legal, economic, and social practices designed to promote the growth of family life among European colonists. The reception colonial families found in the United States contrasts sharply with the lack of attention given to the families of racial-ethnics. Although the presence of racial-ethnics was equally as important for the growth of the nation, their political, economic, legal, and social status was quite different.

REPRODUCTIVE LABOR AMONG
RACIAL-ETHNICS IN EARLY AMERICA

Unlike white women, racial-ethnic women experienced the oppressions of a patriarchal society but were denied the protections and buffering of a patriarchal family. Their families suffered as a direct result of the organization of the labor systems in which they participated.

Racial-ethnics were brought to this country to meet the need for a cheap and exploitable labor force. Little attention was given to their family and community life except as it related to their economic productivity. Labor, and not the existence or maintenance of families, was the critical aspect of their role in building the nation. Thus they were denied the social structural supports necessary to make *their* families a vital element in the social order. Family membership was not a key means of access to participation in the wider society. The lack of social, legal, and economic support for racial-ethnic families intensified and extended women's reproductive labor, created tensions and strains in family relationships, and set the stage for a variety of creative and adaptive forms of resistance.

AFRICAN-AMERICAN SLAVES

Among students of slavery, there has been considerable debate over the relative "harshness" of American slavery, and the degree to which slaves were permitted or encouraged to form families. It is generally acknowledged that many slaveowners found it economically advantageous to encourage family formation as a way of reproducing and perpetuating the slave labor force. This became increasingly true after 1807 when the importation of African slaves was explicitly prohibited. The existence of these families and many aspects of their functioning, however, were directly controlled by the master. In other words, slaves married and formed families but these groupings were completely subject to the master's decision to let them remain intact. One study has estimated that about 32 percent of all recorded slave marriages were disrupted by sale, about 45 percent by death of a spouse, about 10 percent by choice, with the remaining 13 percent not disrupted at all (Blassingame 1972, pp. 90–92). African slaves thus quickly learned that they had a limited degree of control over the formation and maintenance of their marriages and could not be assured of keeping their children with them. The threat of disruption was perhaps the most direct and pervasive cultural assault[3] on families that slaves encountered. Yet there were a number of other aspects of the slave system which reinforced the precariousness of slave family life.

In contrast to some African traditions and the Euro-American patterns of the period, slave men were not the main provider or authority figure in the family. The mother-child tie was basic and of greatest interest to the slave-owner because it was critical in the reproduction of the labor force.

In addition to the lack of authority and economic autonomy experienced by the husband-father in the slave family, use of the rape of women slaves as a weapon of terror and control further undermined the integrity of the slave family. . . . The slave family, therefore, was at the heart of a peculiar tension in the master-slave relationship. On the one hand, slaveowners sought to encourage familial ties among slaves because, as Matthaei (1982) states: ". . . these provided the basis of the development of the slave into a self-conscious socialized human being" (p. 81). They also hoped and believed that this socialization process would help children learn to accept their place in society as slaves. Yet the master's need to control and intervene in the familial life of the slaves is indicative of the other side of this tension. Family ties had the potential for becoming a competing and more potent source of allegiance than the slavemaster himself. Also, kin were as likely to socialize children in forms of resistance as in acts of compliance.

It was within this context of surveillance, assault, and ambivalence that slave women's reproductive labor took place. She and her menfolk had the task of preserving the human and family ties that could ultimately give them a reason for living. They had to socialize their children to believe in the possibility of a life in which they were not enslaved. The slave woman's labor on behalf of the family was, as Davis (1971) has pointed out, the only labor the slave engaged in that could not be directly appropriated by the slave-owner for his own profit. Yet, its indirect appropriation, as labor crucial to the reproduction of the slaveowner's labor force, was the source of strong ambivalence for many slave women. Whereas some mothers murdered their babies to keep them from being slaves, many sought within the family sphere a degree of autonomy and creativity denied them in other realms of the society. The maintenance of a distinct African-American culture is testimony to the ways in which slaves maintained a degree of cultural autonomy and resisted the creation of a slave family that only served the needs of the master.

Gutman (1976) provides evidence of the ways in which slaves expressed a unique Afro-American culture through their family practices. He provides data on naming patterns and kinship ties among slaves that flies in the face of the dominant ideology of the period. That ideology argued that slaves were immoral and had little concern for or appreciation of family life.

Yet Gutman demonstrated that within a system which denied the father authority over his family, slave boys were frequently named after their fathers, and many children were named after blood relatives as a way of maintaining family ties. Gutman also suggested that after emancipation a number of slaves took the names of former owners in order to reestablish family ties that had been disrupted earlier. On plantation after plantation, Gutman found considerable evidence of the building and maintenance of extensive kinship ties among slaves. In instances where slave families had been disrupted, slaves in new communities reconstituted the kinds of family and kin ties that came to characterize Black family life throughout the South. These patterns included, but were not limited to, a belief in the importance of marriage as a long-term commitment, rules of exogamy that included marriage between first cousins, and acceptance of women who had children outside of marriage. Kinship networks were an important source of resistance to the organization of labor that treated the individual slave, and not the family, as the unit of labor (Caulfield 1974).

Another interesting indicator of the slaves' maintenance of some degree of cultural autonomy has been pointed out by Wright (1981) in her discussion of slave housing. Until the early 1800s, slaves were often permitted to build their housing according to their own design and taste. During that period, housing built in an African style was quite common in the slave quarters. By 1830, however, slaveowners had begun to control the design and arrangement of slave housing and had introduced a degree of conformity and regularity to it that left little room for the slave's personalization of the home. Nevertheless, slaves did use some of their own techniques in construction and often hid it from their masters. . . .

Housing is important in discussions of family because its design reflects sociocultural attitudes about family life. The housing that slaveowners provided for their slaves reflected a view of Black family life consistent with the stereotypes of the period. While the existence of slave families was acknowledged, it certainly was not nurtured. Thus, cabins were crowded, often containing more than one family, and there were no provisions for privacy. Slaves had to create their own. . . .

Perhaps most critical in developing an understanding of slave women's reproductive labor is the gender-based division of labor in the domestic sphere. The organization of slave labor enforced considerable equality among men and women. The ways in which equality in the labor force was translated into the family sphere is somewhat speculative. . . .

. . . We know, for example, that slave women experienced what has recently been called the "double day" before most other women in this society. Slave narratives (Jones 1985; White 1985; Blassingame 1977) reveal that women had primary responsibility for their family's domestic chores. They cooked (although on some plantations meals were prepared for all of the slaves), sewed, cared for their children, and cleaned house, all after completing a full day of labor for the master. Blassingame (1972) and others have pointed out that slave men engaged in hunting, trapping, perhaps some gardening, and furniture making as ways of contributing to the maintenance of their families. Clearly, a gender-based division of labor did exist within the family and it appears that women bore the larger share of the burden for housekeeping and child care. . . .

Black men were denied the male resources of a patriarchal society and therefore were unable to turn gender distinctions into female subordination, even if that had been their desire. Black women, on the other hand, were denied support and protection for their roles as mothers and wives and thus had to modify and structure those roles around the demands of their labor. Thus, reproductive labor for slave women was intensified in several ways: by the demands of slave labor that forced them into the double-day of work; by the desire and need to maintain family ties in the face of a system that gave them only limited recognition; by the stresses of building a family with men who were denied the standard social privileges of manhood; and by the struggle to raise children who could survive in a hostile environment.

This intensification of reproductive labor made networks of kin and quasi-kin important instruments in carrying out the reproductive tasks of the slave community. Given an African cultural heritage where kinship ties formed the basis of social relations, it is not at all surprising that African American slaves developed an extensive system of kinship ties and obligations (Gutman 1976; Sudarkasa 1981). Research on Black families in slavery provides considerable documentation of participation of extended kin in childrearing, childbirth, and other domestic, social, and economic activities (Gutman 1976; Blassingame 1972; Genovese and Miller 1974). . . .

With individual households, the gender-based division of labor experienced some important shifts during emancipation. In their first real opportunity to establish family life beyond the controls and constraints imposed by a slavemaster, family life among Black sharecroppers changed radically. Most women, at least those who were wives and daughters of able-bodied men, withdrew from field labor and concentrated on their domestic duties in the home. Husbands took primary responsibility for the fieldwork and for relations with the owners, such as signing contracts on behalf of the family. Black women were severely criticized by whites for removing themselves from field labor because they were seen to be aspiring to a model of womanhood that was considered inappropriate for them. This reorganization of female labor, however, represented an attempt on the part of Blacks to protect women from some of the abuses of the slave system and to thus secure their family life. It was more likely a response to the particular set of circumstances that the newly freed slaves faced than a reaction to the lives of their former masters. Jones (1985) argues that these patterns were "particularly significant" because at a time when industrial development was introducing a labor system that divided male and female labor, the freed Black family was establishing a pattern of joint work and complementary tasks between males and females that was reminiscent of the preindustrial American families. Unfortunately, these former slaves had to do this without the institutional supports that white farm families had in the midst of a sharecropping system that deprived them of economic independence.

CHINESE SOJOURNERS

An increase in the African slave population was a desired goal. Therefore, Africans were permitted and even encouraged at times to form families subject to the authority and whim of the master. By sharp contrast, Chinese people were explicitly denied the right to form families in the United States through both law and social practice. Although male laborers began coming to the United States in sizable numbers in the middle of the nineteenth century, it was more than a century before an appreciable number of children of Chinese parents were born in America. Tom, a respondent in Nee and Nee's (1973) book, *Longtime Californ'*, says: "One thing about Chinese men in America was you had to be either a merchant or a big gambler, have lot of side money to have a family here. A working man, an ordinary man, just can't!" (p. 80).

Working in the United States was a means of gaining support for one's family with an end of obtaining sufficient capital to return to China and purchase land. The practice of sojourning was reinforced by laws preventing Chinese laborers from becoming citizens, and by restrictions on their entry into this country. Chinese laborers who arrived before 1882 could not bring their wives and were prevented by law from marrying whites. Thus, it is likely that the number of Chinese-American families might have been negligible had it not been for two things: the San Francisco earthquake and fire in 1906, which destroyed all municipal records; and the ingenuity and persistence of the Chinese people who used the opportunity created by the earthquake to increase their numbers in the United States. Since relatives of citizens were permitted entry, American-born Chinese (real and claimed) would visit China, report the birth of a son, and thus create an entry slot. Years later the slot could be used by a relative or purchased. The purchasers were called "paper sons." Paper sons became a major mechanism for increasing the Chinese population, but it was a slow process and the sojourner community remained predominantly male for decades.

The high concentration of males in the Chinese community before 1920 resulted in a split-household form of family. . . .

The women who were in the United States during this period consisted of a small number who were wives and daughters of merchants and a larger percentage who were prostitutes. Hirata (1979) has suggested that Chinese prostitution was an important element in helping to maintain the split-household family. In conjunction with laws prohibiting intermarriage, Chinese prostitution helped men avoid long-term relationships with women in the United States and ensured that the bulk of their meager earnings would continue to support the family at home.

The reproductive labor of Chinese women, therefore, took on two dimensions primarily because of the split-household family form. Wives who remained in China were forced to raise children and care for in-laws on the meager remittances of their sojourning husband. Although we know few details about their lives, it is clear that the everyday work of bearing and maintaining children and a household fell entirely on their shoulders. Those women who immigrated and worked as prostitutes performed the more nurturant aspects of reproductive labor, that is, providing emotional and sexual companionship for men who were far from home. Yet their role as prostitute was more likely a means of supporting their families at home in China than a chosen vocation.

The Chinese family system during the nineteenth century was a patriarchal one wherein girls had little value. In fact, they were considered only temporary members of their father's family because when they married, they became members of their husband's families. They also had little social value: girls were sold by some poor parents to work as prostitutes, concubines, or servants. This saved the family the expense of raising them, and their earnings also became a source of family income. For most girls, however, marriages were arranged and families sought useful connections through this process.

With the development of a sojourning pattern in the United States, some Chinese women in those regions of China where this pattern was more prevalent would be sold to become prostitutes in the United States. Most, however, were married off to men whom they saw only once or twice in the 20- or 30-year period during which he was sojourning in the United States. Her status as wife ensured that a portion of the meager wages he earned would be returned to his family in China. This arrangement required considerable sacrifice and adjustment on the part of wives who remained in China and those who joined their husbands after a long separation. . . .

Despite these handicaps, Chinese people collaborated to establish the opportunity to form families and settle in the United States. In some cases it took as long as three generations for a child to be born on United States soil. . . .

CHICANOS

Africans were uprooted from their native lands and encouraged to have families in order to increase the slave labor force. Chinese people were immigrant laborers whose "permanent" presence in the country was denied. By contrast, Mexican-Americans were colonized and their traditional family life was disrupted by war and the imposition of a new set of laws and conditions of labor. The hardships faced by Chicano families, therefore, were the result of the United States colonization of the indigenous Mexican population, accompanied by the beginnings of industrial development in the region. The treaty of Guadalupe Hidalgo, signed in 1848, granted American citizenship to Mexicans living in what is now called the Southwest. The American takeover, however, resulted in the gradual displacement of Mexicans from the land and their incorporation into a colonial labor force (Barrera 1979). In addition, Mexicans who immigrated into the United States after 1848 were also absorbed into the labor force.

Whether natives of Northern Mexico (which became the United States after 1848) or immigrants from Southern Mexico, Chicanos were a largely peasant population whose lives were defined by a feudal economy and a daily struggle on the land for economic survival. Patriarchal families were important instruments of community life and nuclear family units were linked together through an elaborate system of kinship and godparenting. Traditional life was characterized by hard work and a fairly distinct pattern of sex-role segregation. . . .

As the primary caretakers of hearth and home in a rural environment, *Las Chicanas* labor made a vital and important contribution to family survival. . . .

Although some scholars have argued that family rituals and community life showed little change before World War I (Saragoza 1983), the American conquest of Mexican lands, the introduction of a new system of labor, the loss of Mexican-owned land through the inability to document ownership, plus the transient nature of most of the jobs in which Chicanos were employed, resulted in the gradual erosion of this pastoral way of life. Families were uprooted as the economic basis for family life changed. Some immigrated from Mexico in search of a better standard of living and worked in the mines and railroads. Others who were native to the Southwest faced a job market that no longer required their skills and moved into mining, railroad, and agricultural labor in search of a means of earning a living. According to Camarillo (1979), the influx of Anglo[4] capital into the pastoral economy of Santa Barbara rendered obsolete the skills of many Chicano males who had worked as ranchhands and farmers prior to the urbanization of that economy. While some women and children accompanied their husbands to the railroad and mine camps, they often did so despite prohibitions against it. Initially many of these camps discouraged or prohibited family settlement.

The American period (post-1848) was characterized by considerable transiency for the Chicano population. Its impact on families is seen in the growth of female-headed households, which was reflected in the data as early as 1860. Griswold del Castillo (1979) found a sharp increase in female-headed households in Los Angeles, from a low of 13 percent in 1844 to 31 percent in 1880. Camarillo (1979, p. 120) documents a similar increase in Santa Barbara from 15 percent in 1844 to 30 percent by 1880. These increases appear to be due not so much to divorce, which was infrequent in this Catholic population, but to widowhood and temporary abandonment in search of work. Given the hazardous nature of work in the mines and railroad camps, the death of a husband, father or son who was laboring in these sites was not uncommon. Griswold del Castillo (1979) reports a higher death rate among men than women in Los Angeles. The rise in female-headed households, therefore, reflects the instabilities and insecurities introduced into women's lives as a result of the changing social organization of work.

One outcome, the increasing participation of women and children in the labor force was primarily a response to economic factors that required the modification of traditional values. . . .

Slowly, entire families were encouraged to go to railroad workcamps and were eventually incorporated into the agricultural labor market. This was a response both to the extremely low wages paid to Chicano laborers and to the preferences of employers who saw family labor as a way of stabilizing the workforce. For Chicanos, engaging all family members in agricultural work was a means of increasing their earnings to a level close to subsistence for the entire group and of keeping the family unit together. . . .

While the extended family has remained an important element of Chicano life, it was eroded in the American period in several ways. Griswold del Castillo (1979), for example, points out that in 1845 about 71 percent of Angelenos lived in extended families and that by 1880, fewer than half did. This decrease in extended families appears to be a response to the changed economic conditions and to the instabilities generated by the new sociopolitical structure. Additionally, the imposition of American law and custom ignored and ultimately undermined some aspects of the extended family. The extended family in traditional Mexican life consisted of an important set of familial, religious, and community obligations. Women, while valued primarily for their domesticity, had certain legal and property rights that acknowledged the importance of their work, their families of origin and their children. . . .

In the face of the legal, social, and economic changes that occurred during the American period, Chicanas were forced to cope with a series of dislocations in traditional life. They were caught between conflicting pressures to maintain traditional women's roles and family customs and the need to participate in the economic support of their families by working outside the home. During this period the preservation of some traditional customs became an important force for resisting complete disarray. . . .

Of vital importance to the integrity of traditional culture was the perpetuation of the Spanish language. Factors that aided in the maintenance of other aspects of Mexican culture also helped in sustaining the language. However, entry into English-language public schools introduced the children and their families to systematic efforts to erase their native tongue. . . .

Another key factor in conserving Chicano culture was the extended family network, particularly the system of *compadrazgo* or godparenting. Although the full extent of the impact of the American period on the Chicano extended family is not known, it is generally acknowledged that this family system, though lacking many legal and social sanctions, played an important role in the preservation of the Mexican community (Camarillo 1979, p. 13). In Mexican society, godparents were an important way of linking family and community through respected friends or authorities. Named at the important rites of passage in a child's life, such as birth, confirmation, first communion, and marriage, *compadrazgo* created a moral obligation for godparents to act as guardians, to provide financial assistance in times of need, and to substitute in case of the death of a parent. Camarillo (1979) points out that in traditional society these bonds cut across class and racial lines. . . .

The extended family network—which included godparents—expanded the support groups for women who were widowed or temporarily abandoned and for those who were in seasonal, part-, or full-time work. It suggests, therefore, the potential for an exchange of services among poor people whose income did not provide the basis for family subsistence. . . . This family form is important to the continued cultural autonomy of the Chicano community.

CONCLUSION: OUR MOTHERS' GRIEF

Reproductive labor for Afro-American, Chinese-American, and Mexican-American women in the nineteenth century centered on the struggle to maintain family units in the face of a variety of cultural assaults. Treated primarily as individual units of labor rather than as members of family groups, these women labored to maintain, sustain, stabilize, and reproduce their families while working in both the public (productive) and private (reproductive) spheres. Thus, the concept of reproductive labor, when applied to women of color, must be modified to account for the fact that labor in the productive sphere was required to achieve even minimal levels of family subsistence. Long after industrialization had begun to reshape family roles among middle-class white families, driving white women into a cult of domesticity, women of color were coping with an extended day. This day included subsistence labor outside the family and domestic labor within the family. For slaves, domestics, migrant farm laborers, seasonal factory-workers, and prostitutes, the distinctions between labor that reproduced family life and which economically sustained it were minimized. The expanded workday was one of the primary ways in which reproductive labor increased.

Racial-ethnic families were sustained and maintained in the face of various forms of disruption. Yet racial-ethnic women and their families paid a high price in the process. High rates of infant mortality, a shortened life span, the early onset of crippling and debilitating disease provided some insight into the costs of survival.

The poor quality of housing and the neglect of communities further increased reproductive labor. Not only did racial-ethnic women work hard outside the home for a mere subsistence, they worked very hard inside the home to achieve even minimal standards of privacy and cleanliness. They were continually faced with disease and illness that directly resulted from the absence of basic sanitation. The fact that some African women murdered their children to prevent them from becoming slaves is an indication of the emotional strain associated with bearing and raising children while participating in the colonial labor system.

We have uncovered little information about the use of birth control, the prevalence of infanticide, or the motivations that may have generated these or other behaviors. We can surmise, however, that no matter how much children were accepted, loved, or valued among any of these groups of people, their futures in a colonial labor system were a source of grief for their mothers. For those children who were born, the task of keeping them alive, of helping them to understand and participate in a system that exploited them, and the challenge of maintaining a measure—no matter how small—of cultural integrity, intensified reproductive labor.

Being a racial-ethnic woman in nineteenth-century American society meant having extra work both inside and outside the home. It meant having a contradictory relationship to the norms and values about women that were being generated in the dominant white culture. As pointed out earlier, the notion of separate spheres of male and female labor had contradictory outcomes for the nineteenth-century whites. It was the basis for the confinement of women to the household and for much of the protective legislation that subsequently developed. At the same time, it sustained white families by providing social acknowledgment and support to women in the performance of their family roles. For racial-ethnic women, however, the notion of separate spheres served to reinforce their subordinate status and became, in effect, another assault. As they increased their work outside the home, they were forced into a productive labor sphere that was organized for men and "desperate" women who were so unfortunate or immoral that they could not confine their work to the domestic sphere. In the productive sphere, racial-ethnic women faced exploitative jobs and depressed wages. In the reproductive sphere, however, they were denied the opportunity to embrace the dominant ideological definition of "good" wife or mother. In essence, they were faced with a double-bind situation, one that required their participation in the labor force to sustain family life but damned them as women, wives, and mothers because they did not confine their labor to the home. Thus, the conflict between ideology and reality in the lives of racial-ethnic women during the nineteenth century sets the stage for stereotypes, issues of self-esteem, and conflicts around gender-role prescriptions that surface more fully in the twentieth century. Further, the tensions and conflicts that characterized their lives during this period provided the impulse for community activism to jointly address the inequities, which they and their children and families faced.

NOTES

1. The term *reproductive labor* is used to refer to all of the work of women in the home. This includes but is not limited to: the buying and preparation of food and clothing, provision of emotional support and nurturance for all family members, bearing children, and planning, organizing, and carrying out a wide variety of tasks associated

with their socialization. All of these activities are necessary for the growth of patriarchal capitalism because they maintain, sustain, stabilize, and *reproduce* (both biologically and socially) the labor force.

2. The term *white* is a global construct used to characterize peoples of European descent who migrated to and helped colonize America. In the seventeenth century, most of these immigrants were from the British Isles. However, during the time period covered by this article, European immigrants became increasingly diverse. It is a limitation of this article that time and space does not permit a fuller discussion of the variations in the white European immigrant experience. For the purposes of the argument made herein and of the contrast it seeks to draw between the experiences of mainstream (European) cultural groups and that of racial/ethnic minorities, the differences among European settlers are joined and the broad similarities emphasized.

3. Cultural assaults, according to Caulfield (1974), are benign and systematic attacks on the institutions and forms of social organization that are fundamental to the maintenance and flourishing of a group's culture.

4. This term is used to refer to white Americans of European ancestry.

References

Barrera, Mario. 1979. *Race and Class in the Southwest*. South Bend, IN: Notre Dame University Press.

Blassingame, John. 1972. *The Slave Community: Plantation Life in the Antebellum South*. New York: Oxford University Press.

———. 1977. *Slave Testimony: Two Centuries of Letters, Speeches, Interviews, and Autobiographies*. Baton Rouge, LA: Louisiana State University Press.

Camarillo, Albert. 1979. *Chicanos in a Changing Society*. Cambridge, MA: Harvard University Press.

Caulfield, Mina Davis. 1974. "Imperialism, the Family, and Cultures of Resistance." *Socialist Review* 4(2)(October): 67–85.

Davis, Angela. 1971. "The Black Woman's Role in the Community of Slaves." *Black Scholar* 3(4)(December): 2–15.

Degler, Carl. 1980. *At Odds*. New York: Oxford University Press.

Genovese, Eugene D., and Elinor Miller, eds. 1974. *Plantation, Town, and County: Essays on the Local History of American Slave Society*. Urbana: University of Illinois Press.

Griswold del Castillo, Richard. 1979. *The Los Angeles Barrio: 1850–1890*. Los Angeles: The University of California Press.

Gutman, Herbert. 1976. *The Black Family in Slavery and Freedom: 1750–1925*. New York: Pantheon.

Hirata, Lucie Cheng. 1979. "Free, Indentured, Enslaved: Chinese Prostitutes in Nineteenth-Century America." *Signs* 5 (Autumn): 3–29.

Jones, Jacqueline. 1985. *Labor of Love, Labor of Sorrow*. New York: Basic Books.

Kessler-Harris, Alice. 1981. *Women Have Always Worked*. Old Westbury: The Feminist Press.

Matthaei, Julie. 1982. *An Economic History of Women in America*. New York: Schocken Books.

Nee, Victor G., and Brett de Bary Nee. 1973. *Longtime Californ'*. New York: Pantheon Books.

Saragoza, Alex M. 1983. "The Conceptualization of the History of the Chicano Family: Work, Family, and Migration in Chicanos." Research Proceedings of the Symposium on Chicano Research and Public Policy. Stanford, CA: Stanford University, Center for Chicano Research.

Wright, Deborah Gray. 1985. *Ar'n't I a Woman?: Female Slaves in the Plantation South.* New York: W. W. Norton.

Wright, Gwendolyn. 1981. *Building the Dream: A Social History of Housing in America.* New York: Pantheon Books.

38

NAVIGATING INTERRACIAL BORDERS: BLACK-WHITE COUPLES AND THEIR SOCIAL WORLDS

Erica Chito Childs

The 1967 Academy Award–winning movie *Guess Who's Coming to Dinner* concluded with a warning from a white father to his daughter and her "Negro" fiancé. That same year, the Supreme Court overturned any laws against interracial marriage as unconstitutional. Yet how does the contemporary U.S. racial landscape compare? In this ever-changing world of race and color, where do black-white couples fit, and has this unimaginable opposition disappeared?

While significant changes have occurred in the realm of race relations largely from the civil rights struggle of the 1960s, U.S. society still has racial borders. Most citizens live, work, and socialize with others of the same race— as if living within borders, so to speak—even though there are no longer legal barriers such as separate facilities or laws against intermarriage. Yet if these largely separate racial worlds exist, what social world(s) do black-white couples live in and how do they navigate these racial borders? Even more important, how do white communities and black communities view and respond to black-white couples? In other words, do they navigate the racial borders by enforcing, ignoring, or actively trying to dismantle them? My goal is to explore these issues to better understand the contemporary beliefs and practices surrounding black-white couples. . . . My data comes from varied sources, including

From Erica Chito Childs, *Navigating Interracial Borders: Black-White Couples and Their Social World* (New Brunswick:NJ Rutgers University Press, © 2005.)

Web sites, black-white couples, Hollywood films, white communities, and black communities. . . .

. . . My own story also brought me to this research. The social world of black-white couples is the world I navigate. From my own experiences, I have seen the ways most whites respond to an interracial relationship. Growing up white, second-generation Portuguese in a predominantly white Rhode Island suburb, race never was an issue, or at least not one I heard about. After moving to Los Angeles during high school and beginning college, I entered into a relationship with an African American man (who I eventually married), never imagining what it would bring. My family did not disown me or hurl racial slurs. Still, in many ways I learned what it meant to be an "interracial couple" and how this was not what my family, community, or countless unknown individuals had scripted for me. Not many whites ever said outright that they were opposed to the relationship, yet their words and actions signaled otherwise.

One of the most telling examples occurred a few years into our relationship. An issue arose when my oldest sister's daughter wanted to attend her prom with an African American schoolmate she was dating. My sister and her husband refused to let him in the house the night of the prom or any other time because, they said, he was "not right" for her. It was clear to everyone, however, that skin color was the problem. To this day, my niece will tell you that her parents would never have accepted her with a black man. Yet my sister and her family never expressed any opposition to my relationship and even seemed supportive, in terms of inviting us over to their house, giving wedding and holiday gifts, and so forth. Although my sister never openly objected to my relationship, she drew the line with her daughter—quite literally enforcing a racial boundary to protect her daughter and family from blackness. For me, this personal story and the countless stories of other interracial couples point to the necessity of examining societal attitudes, beliefs, images, and practices regarding race and, more specifically, black-white relations. Interracial couples—because of their location on the line between white and black—often witness or bring forth racialized responses from both whites and blacks. As with my sister, opposition may exist yet is not visible until a close family member or friend becomes involved or wants to become involved interracially. . . .

INTERRACIAL RELATIONSHIPS AS A MINER'S CANARY

It is these community and societal responses, as well as the images and beliefs produced and reproduced about these unions that provide the framework within which to understand the issue of interracial couplings. Underlying these responses and images is a racial ideology, or, in other words, a dominant discourse, that posits interracial couples and relationships as deviant. Still, the significance of these discourses and what exactly they reveal about race in society can be hard to see. For some of us the effects of race are all too clear, while for others race—and the accompanying advantages and disadvantages—remain invisible. As a white woman, it was only through my relationship, and raising my two children, that I came to see how race permeates everything in society. Being white yet now part of a multiracial family, I experienced, heard, and even thought things much differently than before, primarily because whites and blacks responded to me differently than before. I think of the metaphor of the "miner's canary"—the canaries miners use to alert them to a poisonous atmosphere. In *The Miner's Canary: Enlisting Race, Resisting Power, Transforming Power*, Lani Guinier and Gerald Torres argue that the experiences of racial minorities, like the miner's canary, can expose the underlying problems in society that ultimately affect everyone, not just minorities. In many ways, the experiences of black-white couples are a miner's canary, revealing problems of race that otherwise can remain hidden, especially to whites. The issues surrounding interracial couples—racialized/sexualized stereotypes, perceptions of difference, familial opposition, lack of community acceptance—should not be looked at as individual problems, but rather as a reflection of the larger racial issues that divide the races. Since interracial couples exist on the color-line in society—a "borderland" between white and black—their experiences and the ways communities respond to these relationships can be used as a lens through which we can understand contemporary race relations. . . .

LIFE ON THE BORDER: NARRATIVES OF BLACK-WHITE COUPLES

From 1999 to 2001, I interviewed fifteen black-white heterosexual couples who were referred to me through personal and professional contacts, and some of whom I encountered randomly in public. They ranged in age from twenty to sixty-nine and all were in committed relationships of two to twenty-five years. Nine were married. The couples' education levels varied. All respondents had finished high school or its equivalent; twenty-one respondents had attended some college and/or had received a bachelor's degree; and four respondents had advanced degrees. The socioeconomic status of the couples ranged from working class to upper middle class. The respondents included a college student, waitress, manager, factory worker, university professor, social worker, salesperson, and postal worker. All couples lived in the northeastern United States, from Maine to Pennsylvania, yet many of the couples had traveled extensively and had lived in other parts of the country, including California, Florida, and the South.

I interviewed the couples together, since I was interested in their experiences, accounts, narratives, and the ways they construct their lives and create their "selves" and their identities as "interracial couples." The interviews lasted for two to three hours, and I ended up with more than forty hours of interview data. . . . These accounts are seen not only as "descriptions, opinions, images, or attitudes about race relations but also as 'systems of knowledge' and 'systems of values' in their own right, used for the discovery and organization of reality."

THE SEPARATE WORLDS OF WHITES AND BLACKS

To explore the larger cultural and sociopolitical meanings that black-white couplings have for both the white and black communities in which they occur, a significant portion of this work is based on original qualitative research in white communities and black communities about their ideas, beliefs, and views on interracial sexuality and marriage. Community research was conducted to further explore the responses to interracial couples that are found in social groups and communities—family, friends, neighbors, religious groups, schools, etc. The ways that these couples provide the occasion for groups to express and play out their ideas and prejudices about race and sex are integral to understanding the social construction of interracial couples. . . .

A black person and a white person coming together has been given many names—miscegenation, amalgamation, race mixing, and jungle fever—conjuring up multiple images of sex, race, and taboo. Black-white relationships and marriages have long been viewed as a sign of improving race relations and assimilation, yet these unions have also been met with opposition from both white and black communities. Overall, there is an inherent assumption that interracial couples are somehow different from same-race couples. Within the United States, the responses to black-white couplings have ranged from disgust to curiosity to endorsement, with the couples being portrayed as many things—among them, deviant, unnatural, pathological, exotic, but always sexual. Even the way that couples are labeled or defined as "interracial" tells us something about societal expectations. We name what is different. For example, a male couple is more likely to be called a "gay couple" than a gender-mixed couple is to be called a "heterosexual couple."

Encompassed by the history of race relations and existing interracial images, how do black-white couples view themselves, their relationships, and the responses of their families and communities? And how do they interpret these familial and community responses? Black-white couples, like all of us, make meaning out of their experiences in the available interpretive frameworks and often inescapable rules of race relations in this country. . . .

Black-white couples come together across the boundaries of race and perceived racial difference seemingly against the opposition of their communities. This is not to say, however, that the couples are free from racialized thinking, whether it be in their use of color-blind discourse or their own racial preferences, such as to date only interracially or to live in all-white neighborhoods. Nonetheless, these couples create multiracial families, not only creating multiracial families of their own but also changing the racial dynamic of the families from which they come. What significance does this have for the institution of family, and how does this play out for the white and black families to whom it occurs?

It might be expected that the family is the source of the greatest hostility toward interracial relationships. It is in families that the meanings and attachments to racial categories are constructed and learned; one's family is often "the most critical site for the generation and reproduction of racial formations." This includes who is and is not an acceptable marriage partner. In white and black families, certain discourses are used when discussing black-white relationships that reproduce the image of these unions as different, deviant, even dangerous. Interracial relationships and marriage often bring forth certain racialized attitudes and beliefs about family and identity that otherwise may have remained hidden. The ways that white and black families understand and respond to black-white interracial couples and the racialized discourses they use are inextricably tied to ideas of family, community, and identity. White and black families' (and communities') interpretations and responses to interracial couples are part of these available discourses on race and race relations in our society. Many times, black-white couples provide the occasion for families to express and play out their ideas and prejudices about race and sex, which is integral to understanding the social construction of "interracial couples" within America today.

ALL IN THE FAMILY: WHITE FAMILIES

Among whites, the issue of interracial marriage is often a controversial topic, and even more so when they are asked to discuss their own views of their family's views. The white community respondents in this study were hesitant to discuss their personal views on family members becoming involved interracially. One strategy used by the respondents was to discuss other families they knew rather than their own views. For example, during the white focus group interviews, the first responses came from two individuals who had some experience or knowledge of interracial couples or families. Sara discussed a friend who adopted two "very dark" black children and how white people would stare at her and the children in public. Anne mentioned her niece who married a black man and said "the family is definitely against it," which causes them problems.

In group interviews with white college students, a number of the students also used stories about other interracial families they knew to explain why their family would prefer they marry someone of the same race. One college student said her family would have a problem with her marrying interracially, explaining that their opinion is based on their experiences with an interracial family in their neighborhood. She had babysat for this family and, according to her, they had "social issues because the dad was *real dark* and the mom was white, and the kids just had major issues." Her choice of words reveals the importance of color and the use of a discursive strategy such as referring to the children as a problem and not the relationship itself. . . .

White "Concern" and Preference

For the white college students interviewed, the role of family is key and certainly influences their decisions not to date interracially. The majority of white students expressed verbally or by raising their hand that their parents, white parents in general, would have a difficult time with an interracial partner for a number of reasons. Yet their parents' opposition was described in nonracial terms, much like their own views. For example, one white male student said, "All parents find something wrong [with the person their child chooses] if they're not exactly as they imagined. My parents would be *surprised* because [an interracial relationship] is not what they are expecting, so it would be difficult in that sense." Many students simply stated something to the effect of "my parents aren't prejudiced; they just wouldn't want me to marry a black guy."

Other students described their families' views against interracial dating as based on the meanings of family and marriage in general. For example, one male student stated that his parents would have a problem with an interracial relationship, because "they brought me up to date within [my] race. They're not like racist, but [they say] just keep with your own culture, be proud of who you are and carry that on to your kids." Some students cited the difference between dating and marriage. As one female college student said, "It becomes more of an issue when you get to be juniors or seniors, because you start thinking long-term, about what your parents will say, and dating a black person just isn't an option." Another student described dating interracially in similar terms: "Dating's not an issue, they always encouraged [me] to interact with all people. For the future and who you're gonna spend the rest of your life with, there's a difference between being with someone of the same race and someone of a different race, [interracial marriage] is not like it's wrong but . . . just that it would be too difficult."

In one of the discussions of family with the white college students, an interesting incident occurred. One of the male students, who was vocal throughout the focus group, sat listening to the other students and looking around the room. Finally he interrupted the discussion: "Are you kidding me? . . . parents would shit, they'd have a freaking heart attack. [*He dramatically grabs the front of his shirt and imitates a growling father's voice*]. "Uhh, son, how could you do this to us, the family?" Everyone laughed at his performance, but this student's use of humor to depict his father (or a white father in general) having "a heart attack" is an interesting discursive strategy. Although he presented it in a comical way, his statement does not seem unrealistic to the group. Often, jocular speech is used to convey a serious message in order to avoid being labeled racist or prejudiced.

When asked why their families would respond in these ways to an interracial relationship, the group largely cited the "opposition of the larger society" as the reason why they and/or their family personally would prefer that their family not become involved interracially. Among the white college students, parents were described as "concerned about how difficult it would be." . . .

IT'S A FAMILY AFFAIR: BLACK FAMILIES

Black families, like white families, can operate as a deterrent to interracial relationships. A family member becoming involved with a white individual is seen as problematic on a number of levels, yet the black families often raised different issues than the white families, such as the importance of "marrying black" and the negative meanings attached to becoming involved interracially. These issues figured prominently among the black partners, the black community respondents, and even black popular culture.

Among the black college students and community respondents, a main issue was the emphasis on marrying within their race, explicitly identifying race as the issue, unlike the white communities. Most students discussed how their parents would have a problem. One black female student stated, "My family would outright disown me" (which received a number of affirmations from the group). Another college student commented on the beliefs her family instilled in her: "My family raised me to be very proud of who I am, a black woman, and they instilled in me the belief that I would never want to be with anyone but a strong black man." Other students described incidents or comments they had heard that let them know they were expected to marry black. Similarly, Leslie, a black community respondent, stated she was raised by her parents to date anyone, but they were "adamant about me marrying black." She added that they told her not to "even think about marrying interracially." Allen also stated that his parents told him that "high school dating is fine but not marriage, ohhh nooo!" Couples like Gwen and Bill, Chris and Victoria, and others also recounted how the black partner's family had more difficulty accepting the relationship when they realized that the couple was getting married as opposed to just dating.

A significant piece of black familial opposition involves the perceived racism of whites in the larger society. Black families were described as having a hard time accepting a family member getting involved with a white person because of lingering racism and a distrust in whites in general. For example, one black college student stated that her family would have a problem if she brought home a white man, "because they would always be wondering what his family was saying, you know, do they talk about me behind my back?" Other students' responses echoed these views, such as one student who remarked, "My mom would have a problem with it. She just doesn't trust white people."

Also, black community members such as Alice and Jean argued that their opposition to a family member getting involved with a white person was based on the belief that the white individual (or their white family/neighborhood) would mistreat their family member. All but two of the black community members expressed the concern that since white society is racist there is no reason to become involved with a white person. . . .

The black families related to this study objected to having a white person in their family and intimate social circles because they viewed whites as the "enemy" and their presence as a sign that the black partner is not committed to his or her community or family. Not surprisingly, black individuals opposed interracial marriage much more than interracial dating, primarily because marriage represents a legitimation of the union and formally brings the white partner into the family.

Despite such opposition, the black college students argued that black families are still more accepting than white families. . . .

While white families discourage their family members from engaging in interracial relationships to maintain white privilege, black families discourage these unions to maintain the strength and solidarity of black communities. Black families view interracial relationships as a loss in many ways—the loss of individuals to white society, the weakening of families and communities, and the devaluing of blackness. . . .

FAMILY MATTERS

. . . The familial responses discussed throughout the research clearly demonstrate how images of oneself and one's family is linked to the concept of race and otherness, especially within the construction of families, both white and black. White families often objected to the idea of a member dating interracially, not because they met the black individual and were confronted with overwhelming "racial" differences, but because they were merely responding based on their ideas and beliefs about interracial relationships and blacks in general. . . .

Being in an interracial relationship often brings forth problems within families, since white and black families overwhelmingly want to remain monoracial. . . .

This . . . highlights how difficult it is to negotiate issues of race and family. Discussing race and, more important, views on interracial relationships in nonracial terms often makes it even more difficult for individuals to challenge and confront their family's views. By using phrases such as "It's not my personal preference" or "I just worry about the problems you will face in society," families and individuals are able to oppose interracial relationships without appearing prejudiced or racist. A family member's opposition, however, is also tied to the issue of identity—the identity of the family and the individuals involved. Families express concern over the identities of the biracial children who will be produced, and in many ways there is a tendency for white families to worry that the children will be "too black," and the black families worry about the children being "more white." The white individuals who enter into a relationship with a black person are seen as "less white" and as tainting the white family, while the black individuals who get involved are seen as "not black enough" and as leaving their blackness behind. All of these fears and beliefs demonstrate the centrality of race to the constructions of families and identities and, more important, the socially constructed nature of race, if one's relationship can change one's "race" in this society still divided by racial boundaries. Ultimately, black-white couples and biracial children are forced to exist somewhere in between, with or without their families.

39

STRAIGHT IS TO GAY AS FAMILY IS TO NO FAMILY

Kath Weston

IS "STRAIGHT" TO "GAY" AS "FAMILY" IS TO "NO FAMILY"?

For years, and in an amazing variety of contexts, claiming a lesbian or gay identity has been portrayed as a rejection of "the family" and a departure from kinship. In media portrayals of AIDS, Simon Watney . . . observes that "we are invited to imagine some absolute divide between the two domains of 'gay life' and 'the family,' as if gay men grew up, were educated, worked and lived our lives in total isolation from the rest of society." Two presuppositions lend a dubious credence to such imagery: the belief that gay men and lesbians do not have children or establish lasting relationships, and the belief that they invariably alienate adoptive and blood kin once their sexual identities become

From Kath Weston, *Families We Choose: Lesbians, Gays, Kinship* (New York: Columbia University Press, 1991), pp. 22–29. Reprinted by permission of Columbia University Press.

known. By presenting "the family" as a unitary object, these depictions also imply that everyone participates in identical sorts of kinship relations and subscribes to one universally agreed-upon definition of family.

Representations that exclude lesbians and gay men from "the family" invoke what Blanche Wiesen Cook . . . has called "the assumption that gay people do not love and do not work," the reduction of lesbians and gay men to sexual identity, and sexual identity to sex alone. In the United States, sex apart from heterosexual marriage tends to introduce a wild card into social relations, signifying unbridled lust and the limits of individualism. If heterosexual intercourse can bring people into enduring association via the creation of kinship ties, lesbian and gay sexuality in these depictions isolates individuals from one another rather than weaving them into a social fabric. To assert that straight people "naturally" have access to family, while gay people are destined to move toward a future of solitude and loneliness, is not only to tie kinship closely to procreation, but also to treat gay men and lesbians as members of a nonprocreative species set apart from the rest of humanity. . . .

It is but a short step from positioning lesbians and gay men somewhere beyond "the family"—unencumbered by relations of kinship, responsibility, or affection—to portraying them as a menace to family and society. A person or group must first be outside and other in order to invade, endanger, and threaten. My own impression from fieldwork corroborates Frances Fitzgerald's . . . observation that many heterosexuals believe not only that gay people have gained considerable political power, but also that the absolute number of lesbians and gay men (rather than their visibility) has increased in recent years. Inflammatory rhetoric that plays on fears about the "spread" of gay identity and of AIDS finds a disturbing parallel in the imagery used by fascists to describe syphilis at mid-century, when "the healthy" confronted "the degenerate" while the fate of civilization hung in the balance. . . .

A long sociological tradition in the United States of studying "the family" under siege or in various states of dissolution lent credibility to charges that this institution required protection from "the homosexual threat." . . .

. . . By shifting without signal between reproduction's meaning of physical procreation and its sense as the perpetuation of society as a whole, the characterization of lesbians and gay men as nonreproductive beings links their supposed attacks on "the family" to attacks on society in the broadest sense. Speaking of parents who had refused to accept her lesbian identity, a Jewish woman explained, "They feel like I'm finishing off Hitler's job." The plausibility of the contention that gay people pose a threat to "the family" (and, through the family, to ethnicity) depends upon a view of family grounded in heterosexual relations, combined with the conviction that gay men and lesbians are incapable of procreation, parenting, and establishing kinship ties.

Some lesbians and gay men . . . had embraced the popular equation of their sexual identities with the renunciation of access to kinship, particularly when first coming out. "My image of gay life was very lonely, very weird, no

family," Rafael Ortiz recollected. "I assumed that my family was gone now—
that's it." After Bob Korkowski began to call himself gay, he wrote a series of
poems in which an orphan was the central character. Bob said the poetry
expressed his fear of "having to give up my family because I was queer." When
I spoke with Rona Bren after she had been home with the flu, she told me that
whenever she was sick, she relived old fears. That day she had remembered
her mother's grim prediction: "You'll be a lesbian and you'll be alone the rest
of your life. Even a dog shouldn't be alone."

Looking backward and forward across the life cycle, people who equated
their adoption of a lesbian or gay identity with a renunciation of family did so
in the double-sided sense of fearing rejection by the families in which they
had grown up, and not expecting to marry or have children as adults. Although
few in numbers, there were still those who had considered "going straight" or
getting married specifically in order to "have a family." Vic Kochifos thought
he understood why:

> It's a whole lot easier being straight in the world than it is being gay. . . .
> You have built-in loved ones: wife, husband, kids, extended family. It just works
> easier. And when you want to do something that requires children, and you
> want to have a feeling of knowing that there's gonna be someone around
> who cares about you when you're 85 years old, there are thoughts that go
> through your head, sure. There must be. There's a way of doing it gay, but
> it's a whole lot harder, and it's less secure.

Bernie Margolis had been sexually involved with men since he was in his
teens, but for years had been married to a woman with whom he had several
children. At age 67 he regretted having grown to adulthood before the current
discussion of gay families, with its focus on redefining kinship and constructing new sorts of parenting arrangements.

> I didn't want to give up the possibility of becoming a family person. Of having
> kids of my own to carry on whatever I built up. . . . My mother was always
> talking about she's looking forward to the day when she would bring her
> children under the canopy to get married. It never occurred to her that I
> wouldn't be married. It probably never occurred to me either.

The very categories "good family person" and "good family man" had seemed
to Bernie intrinsically opposed to a gay identity. In his fifties at the time
I interviewed him, Stephen Richter attributed never having become a father
to "not having the relationship with the woman." Because he had envisioned
parenting and procreation only in the context of a heterosexual relationship,
regarding the two as completely bound up with one another, Stephen had
never considered children an option.

Older gay men and lesbians were not the only ones whose adult lives had
been shaped by ideologies that banish gay people from the domain of kinship.
Explaining why he felt uncomfortable participating in "family occasions," a

young man who had no particular interest in raising a child commented, "When families get together, what do they talk about? Who's getting married, who's having children. And who's not, okay? Well, look who's not." Very few of the lesbians and gay men I met believed that claiming a gay identity automatically requires leaving kinship behind. In some cases people described this equation as an outmoded view that contrasted sharply with revised notions of what constitutes a family.

Well-meaning defenders of lesbian and gay identity sometimes assert that gays are not inherently "anti-family," in ways that perpetuate the association of heterosexual identity with exclusive access to kinship. Charles Silverstein . . . , for instance, contends that lesbians and gay men may place more importance on maintaining family ties than heterosexuals do because gay people do not marry and raise children. Here the affirmation that gays and lesbians are capable of fostering enduring kinship ties ends up reinforcing the implication that they cannot establish "families of their own," presumably because the author regards kinship as unshakably rooted in heterosexual alliance and procreation. In contrast, discourse on gay families cuts across the politically loaded couplet of "pro-family" and "anti-family" that places gay men and lesbians in an inherently antagonistic relation to kinship solely on the basis of their nonprocreative sexualities. "Homosexuality is not what is breaking up the Black family," declared Barbara Smith . . . , a black lesbian writer, activist, and speaker at the 1987 Gay and Lesbian March on Washington. "Homophobia is. My Black gay brothers and my Black lesbian sisters are members of Black families, both the ones we were born into and the ones we create."

At the height of gay liberation, activists had attempted to develop alternatives to "the family," whereas by the 1980s many lesbians and gay men were struggling to legitimate gay families as a form of kinship. . . . Gay or chosen families might incorporate friends, lovers, or children, in any combination. Organized through ideologies of love, choice, and creation, gay families have been defined through a contrast with what many gay men and lesbians . . . called "straight," "biological," or "blood" family. If families we choose were the families lesbians and gay men created for themselves, straight family represented the families in which most had grown to adulthood.

What does it mean to say that these two categories of family have been defined through contrast? One thing it emphatically does *not* mean is that heterosexuals share a single coherent form of family (although some of the lesbians and gay men doing the defining believed this to be the case). I am not arguing here for the existence of some central, unified kinship system vis-à-vis which gay people have distinguished their own practice and understanding of family. In the United States, race, class, gender, ethnicity, regional origin, and context all inform differences in household organization, as well as differences in notions of family and what it means to call someone kin.

In any relational definition, the juxtaposition of two terms gives meaning to both. Just as light would not be meaningful without some notion of darkness, so gay or chosen families cannot be understood apart from the families lesbians and gay men call "biological," "blood," or "straight." Like others in their society, most gay people . . . considered biology a matter of "natural fact." When they applied the terms "blood" and "biology" to kinship, however, they tended to depict families more consistently organized by procreation, more rigidly grounded in genealogy, and more uniform in their conceptualization than anthropologists know most families to be. For many lesbians and gay men, blood family represented not some naturally given unit that provided a base for all forms of kinship, but rather a procreative principle that organized only one possible *type* of kinship. In their descriptions they situated gay families at the opposite end of a spectrum of determination, subject to no constraints beyond a logic of "free" choice that ordered membership. To the extent that gay men and lesbians mapped "biology" and "choice" onto identities already opposed to one another (straight and gay, respectively), they polarized these two types of family along an axis of sexual identity.

The following chart recapitulates the ideological transformation generated as lesbians and gay men began to inscribe themselves within the domain of kinship.

What this chart presents is not some static substitution set, but a historically motivated succession. To move across or down the chart is to move through time. Following along from left to right, time appears as process, periodized with reference to the experience of coming out. In the first opposition, coming out defines the transition from a straight to a gay identity. For the person who maintains an exclusively biogenetic notion of kinship, coming out can mark the renunciation of kinship, the shift from "family" to "no family" portrayed in the second opposition. In the third line, individuals who accepted the possibility of gay families after coming out could experience themselves making a transition from the biological or blood families in which they had grown up to the establishment of their own chosen families.

Moving from top to bottom, the chart depicts the historical time that inaugurated contemporary discourse on gay kinship. "Straight" changes from a category with an exclusive claim on kinship to an identity allied with a specific kind of family symbolized by biology or blood. Lesbians and gay men, originally relegated to the status of people without family, later lay claim to a distinctive type of family characterized as families we choose or create. While dominant cultural representations have asserted that straight is to gay as family is to no family (lines 1 and 2), at a certain point in history gay people began to contend that straight is to gay as blood family is to chosen families (lines 1 and 3).

What provided the impetus for this ideological shift? Transformations in the relation of lesbians and gay men to kinship are inseparable from sociohistorical developments: changes in the context for disclosing a lesbian or gay identity to others, attempts to build urban gay "community," cultural inferences about relationships between "same-gender" partners, and the lesbian baby boom associated with alternative (artificial) insemination. . . . If . . . kinship is something people use to act as well as to think, then its transformations should have unfolded not only on the "big screen" of history, but also on the more modest stage of day-to-day life, where individuals have actively engaged novel ideological distinctions and contested representations that would exclude them from kinship.

40

UNEQUAL CHILDHOODS

Annette Lareau

Laughing and yelling, a white fourth-grader named Garrett Tallinger splashes around in the swimming pool in the backyard of his four-bedroom home in the suburbs on a late spring afternoon. As on most evenings, after a quick dinner his father drives him to soccer practice. This is only one of Garrett's many activities. His brother has a baseball game at a different location. There are evenings when the boys' parents relax, sipping a glass of wine. Tonight is not one of them. As they rush to change out of their work clothes and get the children ready for practice, Mr. and Mrs. Tallinger are harried.

Only ten minutes away, a Black fourth-grader, Alexander Williams, is riding home from a school open house. His mother is driving their beige, leather-upholstered Lexus. It is 9:00 P.M. on a Wednesday evening. Ms. Williams is

---

From Annette Lareau, *Unequal Childhoods: Class, Race, and Family Life* (Los Angeles: University of California Press, © 2003.) Reprinted by permission.

tired from work and has a long Thursday ahead of her. She will get up at 4:45 A.M. to go out of town on business and will not return before 9:00 P.M. On Saturday morning, she will chauffeur Alexander to a private piano lesson at 8:15 A.M., which will be followed by a choir rehearsal and then a soccer game. As they ride in the dark, Alexander's mother, in a quiet voice, talks with her son, asking him questions and eliciting his opinions.

Discussions between parents and children are a hallmark of middle-class child rearing. Like many middle-class parents, Ms. Williams and her husband see themselves as "developing" Alexander to cultivate his talents in a concerted fashion. Organized activities, established and controlled by mothers and fathers, dominate the lives of middle-class children such as Garrett and Alexander. By making certain their children have these and other experiences, middle-class parents engage in a process of *concerted cultivation*. From this, a robust sense of entitlement takes root in the children. This sense of entitlement plays an especially important role in institutional settings, where middle-class children learn to question adults and address them as relative equals.

Only twenty minutes away, in blue-collar neighborhoods, and slightly farther away, in public housing projects, childhood looks different. Mr. Yanelli, a white working-class father, picks up his son Little Billy, a fourth-grader, from an after-school program. They come home and Mr. Yanelli drinks a beer while Little Billy first watches television, then rides his bike and plays in the street. Other nights, he and his Dad sit on the sidewalk outside their house and play cards. At about 5:30 P.M. Billy's mother gets home from her job as a house cleaner. She fixes dinner and the entire family sits down to eat together. Extended family are a prominent part of their lives. Ms. Yanelli touches base with her "entire family every day" by phone. Many nights Little Billy's uncle stops by, sometimes bringing Little Billy's youngest cousin. In the spring, Little Billy plays baseball on a local team. Unlike for Garrett and Alexander, who have at least four activities a week, for Little Billy, baseball is his only organized activity outside of school during the entire year. Down the road, a white working-class girl, Wendy Driver, also spends the evening with her girl cousins, as they watch a video and eat popcorn, crowded together on the living room floor.

Farther away, a Black fourth-grade boy, Harold McAllister, plays outside on a summer evening in the public housing project in which he lives. His two male cousins are there that night, as they often are. After an afternoon spent unsuccessfully searching for a ball so they could play basketball, the boys had resorted to watching sports on television. Now they head outdoors for a twilight water balloon fight. Harold tries to get his neighbor, Miss Latifa, wet. People sit in white plastic lawn chairs outside the row of apartments. Music and television sounds waft through the open windows and doors.

The adults in the lives of Billy, Wendy, and Harold want the best for them. Formidable economic constraints make it a major life task for these parents to put food on the table, arrange for housing, negotiate unsafe neighborhoods, take children to the doctor (often waiting for city buses that do not come), clean children's clothes, and get children to bed and have them ready for school the next morning. But unlike middle-class parents, these adults do not consider the concerted development of children, particularly through organized leisure activities, an essential aspect of good parenting. Unlike the Tallingers and Williamses, these mothers and fathers do not focus on concerted cultivation. For them, the crucial responsibilities of parenthood do not lie in eliciting their children's feelings, opinions, and thoughts. Rather, they see a clear boundary between adults and children. Parents tend to use directives: they tell their children what to do rather than persuading them with reasoning. Unlike their middle-class counterparts, who have a steady diet of adult organized activities, the working-class and poor children have more control over the character of their leisure activities. Most children are free to go out and play with friends and relatives who typically live close by. Their parents and guardians facilitate the *accomplishment of natural growth*. Yet these children and their parents interact with central institutions in the society, such as schools, which firmly and decisively promote strategies of concerted cultivation in child rearing. For working-class and poor families, the cultural logic of child rearing at home is out of synch with the standards of institutions. As a result, while children whose parents adopt strategies of concerted cultivation appear to gain a sense of entitlement, children such as Billy Yanelli, Wendy Driver, and Harold McAllister appear to gain an emerging sense of distance, distrust, and constraint in their institutional experiences.

America may be the land of opportunity, but it is also a land of inequality. This research identifies the largely invisible but powerful ways that parents' social class impacts chilren's life experiences. It shows, using indepth observations and interviews with middle-class (including members of the upper-middle-class), working-class, and poor families, that inequality permeates the fabric of the culture. . . . I report the results of intensive observational research for a total of twelve families when their children were nine and ten years old. I argue that key elements of family life cohere to form a cultural logic of child rearing. In other words, the differences among families seem to cluster together in meaningful patterns. In this historical moment, middle-class parents tend to adopt a cultural logic of child rearing that stresses the concerted cultivation of children. Working-class and poor parents, by contrast, tend to undertake the accomplishment of natural growth. In the accomplishment of natural growth, children experience long stretches of leisure time, child-initiated play, clear boundaries between adults and children, and daily interactions with kin. Working-class and poor children, despite tremendous economic strain, often have more "childlike" lives, with autonomy from adults and control over their extended leisure time. Although middle-class children miss out on kin relationships and leisure time, they appear to (at least potentially) gain important institutional advantages. From the experience of concerted cultivation, they acquire skills that could be valuable in the future when they enter the world of work. Middle-class white and Black children in my study did exhibit some key differences; yet the biggest gaps were not within social classes but, as I show, across them. It is these class differences and how they are enacted in family life and child rearing that shape the ways children view themselves in relation to the rest of the world.

CULTURAL REPERTOIRES

Professionals who work with children, such as teachers, doctors, and counselors, generally agree about how children should be raised. Of course, from time to time they may disagree on the ways standards should be enacted for an individual child or family. For example, teachers may disagree about whether or not parents should stop and correct a child who mispronounces a word while reading. Counselors may disagree over whether a mother is being too protective of her child. Still, there is little dispute among professionals on the broad principles for promoting educational development in children through proper parenting. These standards include the importance of talking with children, developing their educational interests, and playing an active role in their schooling. Similarly, parenting guidelines typically stress the importance of reasoning with children and teaching them to solve problems through negotiation rather than with physical force. Because these guidelines are so generally accepted, and because they focus on a set of practices concerning how parents should raise children, they form a *dominant set of cultural repertoires* about how children should be raised. This widespread agreement among professionals about the broad principles for child rearing permeates our society. A small number of experts thus potentially shape the behavior of a large number of parents.

Professionals' advice regarding the best way to raise children has changed regularly over the last two centuries. From strong opinions about the merits of bottle feeding, being stern with children, and utilizing physical punishment (with dire warnings of problematic outcomes should parents indulge children), there have been shifts to equally strongly worded recommendations about the benefits of breast feeding, displaying emotional warmth toward children, and using reasoning and negotiation as mechanisms of parental control. Middle-class parents appear to shift their behaviors in a variety of spheres more rapidly and more thoroughly than do working-class or poor parents. As professionals have shifted their recommendations from bottle feeding to breast feeding, from stern approaches to warmth and empathy, and from spanking to time-outs, it is middle-class parents who have responded most promptly. Moreover, in recent decades, middle-class children in the United States have had to face the prospect of "declining fortunes." Worried about how their children will get ahead, middle-class parents are increasingly determined to make sure that their children are not excluded from any opportunity that might eventually contribute to their advancement.

Middle-class parents who comply with current professional standards and engage in a pattern of concerted cultivation deliberately try to stimulate their children's development and foster their cognitive and social skills. The commitment among working-class and poor families to provide comfort, food, shelter, and other basic support requires ongoing effort, given economic challenges and the formidable demands of child rearing. But it stops short of the deliberate cultivation of children and their leisure activities that occurs in middle-class families. For working-class and poor families, sustaining children's natural growth is viewed as an accomplishment.

What is the outcome of these different philosophies and approaches to child rearing? Quite simply, they appear to lead to the *transmission of differential advantages* to children. In this study, there was quite a bit more talking in middle-class homes than in working-class and poor homes, leading to the development of greater verbal agility, larger vocabularies, more comfort with authority figures, and more familiarity with abstract concepts. Importantly, children also developed skill differences in interacting with authority figures in institutions and at home. Middle-class children such as Garrett Tallinger and Alexander Williams learn, as young boys, to shake the hands of adults and look them in the eye. In studies of job interviews, investigators have found that potential employees have less than one minute to make a good impression. Researchers stress the importance of eye contact, firm handshakes, and displaying comfort with bosses during the interview. In poor families like Harold McAllister's, however, family members usually do not look each other in the eye when conversing. In addition, as Elijah Anderson points out, they live in neighborhoods where it can be dangerous to look people in the eye too long. The types of social competence transmitted in the McAllister family are valuable, but they are potentially less valuable (in employment interviews, for example) than those learned by Garrett Tallinger and Alexander Williams.

The white and Black middle-class children in this study also exhibited an emergent version of the *sense of entitlement* characteristic of the middle-class. They acted as though they had a right to pursue their own individual preferences and to actively manage interactions in institutional settings. They appeared comfortable in these settings; they were open to sharing information and asking for attention. Although some children were more outgoing than others, it was common practice among middle-class children to shift interactions to suit *their* preferences. Alexander Williams knew how to get the doctor to listen to his concerns (about the bumps under his arm from his new deodorant). His mother explicitly trained and encouraged him to speak up with the doctor. Similarly, a Black middle-class girl, Stacey Marshall, was taught by her mother to expect the gymnastics teacher to accommodate her individual learning style. Thus, middle-class children were trained in "the rules of the game" that govern interactions with institutional representatives.

They were not conversant in other important social skills, however, such as organizing their time for hours on end during weekends and summers, spending long periods of time away from adults, or hanging out with adults in a nonobtrusive, subordinate fashion. Middle-class children also learned (by imitation and by direct training) how to make the rules work in their favor. Here, the enormous stress on reasoning and negotiation in the home also has a potential advantage for future institutional negotiations. Additionally, those in authority responded positively to such interactions. Even in fourth grade, middle-class children appeared to be acting on their own behalf to gain advantages. They made special requests of teachers and doctors to adjust procedures to accommodate their desires.

The working-class and poor children, by contrast, showed an emerging *sense of constraint* in their interactions in institutional settings. They were less likely to try to customize interactions to suit their own preferences. Like their parents, the children accepted the actions of persons in authority (although at times they also covertly resisted them). Working-class and poor parents sometimes were not as aware of their children's school situation (as when their children were not doing homework). Other times, they dismissed the school rules as unreasonable. For example, Wendy Driver's mother told her to "punch" a boy who was pestering her in class; Billy Yanelli's parents were proud of him when he "beat up" another boy on the playground, even though Billy was then suspended from school. Parents also had trouble getting "the school" to respond to their concerns. When Ms. Yanelli complained that she "hates" the school, she gave her son a lesson in powerlessness and frustration in the face of an important institution. Middle-class children such as Stacey Marshall learned to make demands on professionals, and when they succeeded in making the rules work in their favor they augmented their "cultural capital" (i.e., skills individuals inherit that can then be translated into different forms of value as they move through various institutions) for the future. When working-class and poor children confronted institutions, however, they generally were unable to make the rules work in their favor nor did they obtain capital for adulthood. Because of these patterns of legitimization, children raised according to the logic of concerted cultivation can gain advantages, in the form of an emerging sense of entitlement, while children raised according to the logic of natural growth tend to develop an emerging sense of constraint.

SOCIAL STRATIFICATION AND INDIVIDUALISM

Public discourse in America typically presents the life accomplishments of a person as the result of her or his individual qualities. Songs like "I Did It My Way," memoirs, television shows, and magazine articles, celebrate the individual. Typically, individual outcomes are connected to individual effort and talent, such as being a "type A" personality, being a hard worker, or showing leadership. These cultural beliefs provide a framework for Americans' views of inequality.

Indeed, Americans are much more comfortable recognizing the power of individual initiative than recognizing the power of social class. Studies show that Americans generally believe that responsibility for their accomplishments rests on their individual efforts. Less than one-fifth see "race, gender, religion, or class as very important for 'getting ahead in life.'" Compared to Europeans, individuals in the United States are much more likely to believe they can improve their standard of living. Put differently, Americans believe in the American dream: "The American dream that we were all raised on is a simple but powerful one—if you work hard and play by the rules, you should be given a chance to go as far as your God-given ability will take you." This American ideology that each individual is responsible for his or her life outcomes is the expressed belief of the vast majority of Americans, rich and poor.

Yet there is no question that society is stratified. . . . Highly valued resources such as the possession of wealth; having an interesting, well-paying, and complex job; having a good education; and owning a home, are not evenly distributed throughout the society. Moreover, these resources are transferred across generations: One of the best predictors of whether a child will one day graduate from college is whether his or her parents are college graduates. Of course, relations of this sort are not absolute: Perhaps two-thirds of the members of society ultimately reproduce their parents' level of educational attainment, while about one-third take a different path. Still, there is no question that we live in a society characterized by considerable gaps in resources or, put differently, by substantial *inequality*. . . . I demonstrate the existence of a cultural logic of child rearing that tends to differ according to families' social class positions. I see these interweaving practices as coming together in a messy but still recognizable way. In contrast to many, I suggest that social class does have a powerful impact in shaping the daily rhythms of family life. . . .

THE POWER OF SOCIAL CLASS

In the United States, people disagree about the importance of social class in daily life. Many Americans believe that this country is fundamentally *open*. They assume the society is best understood as a collection of individuals. They believe that people who demonstrate hard work, effort, and talent are likely to achieve upward mobility. Put differently, many Americans believe in the American Dream. In this view, children should have roughly equal life chances. The extent to which life chances vary can be traced to differences in aspirations, talent, and hard work on the part of individuals. This perspective rejects the notion that parents' social location systematically shapes children's life experiences and outcomes. Instead, outcomes are seen as resting more in the hands of individuals. . . .

THE LIMITS OF SOCIAL CLASS

Among the families we observed, some aspects of daily life did not vary systematically by social class. There were episodes of laughter, emotional connection, and happiness as well as quiet comfort in every family. Harold McAllister and his mother laughed together as he almost dropped his hot dog but then, in an awkward grab, caught it. After a baseball game, Mr. Williams rubbed Alexander's head affectionately and called him "handsome." Ms. Handlon gave her daughter a big squeeze around her shoulders after the Christmas Eve pageant, and Melanie beamed. One summer afternoon, Mr. Yanelli and Billy played cards together, sitting cross-legged on the sidewalk. These moments of connection seemed deeply meaningful to both children and parents in all social classes, even as they take different shape by social class, in terms of language, activity, and character.

All the families we observed also had rituals: favorite meals they often ate, television programs they watched, toys or games that were very important, family outings they looked forward to, and other common experiences. The content of their rituals varied (especially by social class); what did not vary was that the children enjoyed these experiences and they provided a sense of membership in a family. Also, in all social classes, a substantial part of the children's days was spent in repetitive rituals: getting up, making the bed, taking a shower, getting dressed, brushing hair and teeth, eating breakfast, finding school books and papers, and waiting for adults to get ready. These moments were interspersed with hours, days, and weeks of household work, tedious demands, mundane tasks, and tension. This was true for all families, regardless of social class. Nor were any families immune to life tragedies: across all social classes there were premature deaths due to car accidents or suicides. Across all social classes children and parents had different temperaments: some were shy and quiet; some were outgoing and talkative. Some had a sense of humor and some did not. The degree of organization and orderliness in daily life also did not vary systematically by social class. Some houses were clean and some were a disaster. Some of the messiest ones were middle-class homes in which the entryway was a paragon of order but the living spaces, particularly the upstairs, were in a tumble. Despite the formidable differences among the families detailed in each home, after a few visits, the research assistants and I found that the surroundings felt normal, comfortable, and safe. Put differently, they all felt like home.

CONCERTED CULTIVATION AND THE
ACCOMPLISHMENT OF NATURAL GROWTH

Despite these important areas of shared practices, social class made a significant difference in the routines of children's daily lives. The white and Black middle-class parents engaged in practices of *concerted cultivation*. In these families, parents actively fostered and assessed their children's talents, opinions, and skills. They scheduled their children for activities. They reasoned with them. They hovered over them and outside the home they did not hesitate to intervene on the children's behalf. They made a deliberate and sustained effort to stimulate children's development and to cultivate their cognitive and social skills. The working-class and poor parents viewed children's development as unfolding spontaneously, as long as they were provided with comfort, food, shelter, and other basic support. I have called this cultural logic of child rearing the *accomplishment of natural growth*. As with concerted cultivation, this commitment, too, required ongoing effort; sustaining children's natural growth despite formidable life challenges is properly viewed as accomplishment. Parents who relied on natural growth generally organized their children's lives so they spent time in and around home, in informal play with peers, siblings, and cousins. As a result, the children had more autonomy regarding leisure time and more opportunities for child-initiated play. They also were more responsible for their lives outside the home. Unlike in middle-class families, adult-organized activities were uncommon. Instead of the relentless focus on reasoning and negotiation that took place in middle-class families, there was less speech (including less whining and badgering) in working-class and poor homes. Boundaries between adults and children were clearly marked; parents generally used language not as an aim in itself but more as a conduit for social life. Directives were common. In their institutional encounters, working-class and poor parents turned over responsibility to professionals; when parents did try to intervene, they felt that they were less capable and less efficacious than they would have liked. While working-class and poor children differed in important ways, particularly in the stability of their lives, surprisingly there was not a major difference between them in their cultural logic of child rearing. Instead, in this study the cultural divide appeared to be between the middle class and everyone else. . . .

HOW DOES IT MATTER?

Both concerted cultivation and the accomplishment of natural growth offer intrinsic benefits (and burdens) for parents and their children. Nevertheless, these practices are accorded different social values by important social institutions. There are signs that some family cultural practices, notably those associated with concerted cultivation, give children advantages that other cultural practices do not.

In terms of the rhythms of daily life, both concerted cultivation and the accomplishment of natural growth have advantages and disadvantages. Middle-class children learn to develop and value an individualized sense of self. Middle-class children are allowed to participate in a variety of coveted activities: gymnastics, soccer, summer camps, and so on. These activities improve their skills and teach them, as Mr. Tallinger noted, to be better athletes than their parents were at comparable ages. They learn to handle moments of humiliation on the field as well as moments of glory. Middle-class children learn, as Mr. Williams noted, the difference between baroque and classical music. They learn to perform. They learn to present themselves. But this cultivation has a cost. Family schedules are disrupted. Dinner hours are very hard to arrange. Siblings such as Spencer and Sam Tallinger spend dreary hours waiting at athletic fields and riding in the car going from one event to another. Family life, despite quiet interludes, is frequently frenetic. Parents, especially mothers, must reconcile conflicting priorities, juggling events whose deadlines are much tighter than the deadlines connected to serving meals or getting children ready for bed. The domination of children's activities can take a toll on families. At times, everyone in the middle-class families— including ten-year-old children—seemed exhausted. Thus, there are formidable costs, as well as benefits to this child-rearing approach.

Working-class and poor children also had advantages, as well as costs, from the cultural logic of child rearing they experienced. Working-class and poor children learned to entertain themselves. They played outside, creating their own games, as Tyrec Taylor did with his friends. They did not complain of being bored. Working-class and poor children also appeared to have boundless energy. They did not have the exhaustion that we saw in middle-class children the same age. Some working-class and poor children longed to be in organized activities—Katie Brindle wanted to take ballet and Harold McAllister wanted to play football. When finances, a lack of transportation, and limited availability of programs conspired to prevent or limit their participation, they were disappointed. Many were also deeply aware of the economic constraints and the limited consumption permitted by their family's budget. Living spaces were small, and often there was not much privacy. The television was almost always on and, like many middle-class children growing up in the 1950s, working-class and poor children watched unrestricted amounts of television. As a result, family members spent more time together in shared space than occurred in middle-class homes. Indeed, family ties were very strong, particularly among siblings. Working-class and poor children also developed very close ties with their cousins and other extended family members.

Within the home, these two approaches to child rearing each have identifiable strengths and weaknesses. When we turn to examining institutional dynamics outside the home, however, the unequal benefits of middle-class children's lives compared to working-class and poor children's lives become clearer. In crucial ways, middle-class family members appeared reasonably comfortable and entitled, while working-class and poor family members appeared uncomfortable and constrained. . . .

This pattern occurred in school interactions, as well. Some working-class and poor parents had warm and friendly relations with educators. Overall, however, working-class and poor parents in this study had much more distance or separation from the school than did middle-class mothers.

Other working-class and poor parents also appeared baffled, intimidated, and subdued in parent-teacher conferences. Ms. Driver, frantically worried because Wendy, a fourth-grader, was not yet able to read, resisted intervening, saying, "I don't want to jump into anything and find it is the wrong thing." When working-class and poor parents did try to intervene in their children's educational experiences, they often felt ineffectual. . . .

Overall, the routine rituals of family life are not equally legitimized in the broader society. Parents' efforts to reason with children (even two-year-olds) are seen as more educationally valuable than parents' use of directives. Spending time playing soccer or baseball is deemed by professionals as more valuable than time spent watching television. Moreover, differences in the cultural logic of child rearing are attached to unequal currency in the broader society. The middle-class strategy of concerted cultivation appears to have greater promise of being capitalized into social profits than does the strategy of the accomplishment of natural growth found in working-class and poor homes.

41

CHAPPALS AND GYM SHORTS
An Indian Muslim Woman in the Land of Oz

Almas Sayeed

It was finals week during the spring semester of my sophomore year at the University of Kansas, and I was buried under mounds of papers and exams. The stress was exacerbated by long nights, too much coffee and a chronic, building pain in my permanently splintered shins (left over from an old sports injury). Between attempting to understand the nuances of Kant's *Critique of Pure Reason* and applying the latest game-theory models to the 1979 Iranian revolution, I was regretting my decision to pursue majors in philosophy, women's studies *and* international studies.

My schedule was not exactly permitting much down time. With a full-time school schedule, a part-time job at Lawrence's domestic violence shelter and preparations to leave the country in three weeks, I was grasping to hold onto what little sanity I had left. Wasn't living in Kansas supposed to be more laid-back than this? After all, Kansas was the portal to the magical land of Oz, where wicked people melt when doused with mop water and bright red, sparkly shoes could substitute for the services of American Airlines, providing a quick getaway. Storybook tales aside, the physical reality of this period was that my deadlines were inescapable. Moreover, the most pressing of these deadlines was completely non-school related: my dad, on his way home to Wichita, was coming for a brief visit. This would be his first stay by himself, without Mom to accompany him or act as a buffer.

Dad visited me the night before my most difficult exam. Having just returned from spending time with his family—a group of people with whom he historically had an antagonistic relationship—Dad seemed particularly relaxed in his stocky six-foot-four frame. Wearing one of the more subtle of his nineteen cowboy hats, he arrived at my door, hungry, greeting me in Urdu, our mother tongue, and laden with gifts from Estée Lauder for his only daughter. Never mind that I rarely wore makeup and would have preferred to see the money spent on my electric bill or a stack of feminist theory books from my favorite used bookstore. If Dad's visit was going to include a conversation about how little I use beauty products, I was not going to be particularly receptive.

"Almas," began my father from across the dinner table, speaking in his British-Indian accent infused with his love of Midwestern colloquialisms, "You know that you won't be a spring chicken forever. While I was in Philadelphia, I realized how important it is for you to begin thinking about our culture, religion and your future marriage plans. I think it is time we began a two-year marriage plan so you can find a husband and start a family. I think twenty-two will be a good age for you. You should be married by twenty-two."

I needed to begin thinking about the "importance of tradition" and be married by twenty-two? This, from the only Indian man I knew who had Alabama's first album on vinyl and loved to spend long weekends in his rickety, old camper near Cheney Lake, bass fishing and listening to traditional Islamic Quavali music? My father, in fact, was in his youth crowned "Mr. Madras," weightlifting champion of 1965, and had left India to practice medicine and be an American cowboy in his spare time. But he wanted *me* to aspire to be a "spring chicken," maintaining some unseen hearth and home to reflect my commitment to tradition and culture.

Dad continued, "I have met a boy that I like for you very much. Masoud's son, Mahmood. He is a good Muslim boy, tells great jokes in Urdu and is a promising engineer. We should be able to arrange something. I think you will be very happy with him!" Dad concluded with a satisfied grin.

Masoud, Dad's cousin? This would make me and Mahmood distant relatives of some sort. And Dad wants to "arrange something"? I had brief visions of being paraded around a room, serving tea to strangers in a sari or a shalwar kameez (a traditional South Asian outfit for women) wearing a long braid and chappals (flat Indian slippers), while Dad boasted of my domestic capabilities to increase my attractiveness to potential suitors. I quickly flipped through my mental Rolodex of rhetorical devices, acquired during years of women's studies classes and found the card blank. No doubt, even feminist scholar Catherine MacKinnon would have been rendered speechless sitting across the table in a Chinese restaurant speaking to my overzealous father.

It is not that I hadn't already dealt with the issue. In fact, we had been here before, ever since the marriage proposals began (the first one came when I was fourteen). Of course, when they first began, it was a family joke, as my parents understood that I was to continue my education. The jokes, however, were always at my expense: "You received a proposal from a nice boy living in our mosque. He is studying medicine," my father would come and tell me with a huge, playful grin. "I told him that you weren't interested because you are too busy with school. And anyway you can't cook or clean." My father found these jokes particularly funny, given my dislike of household chores. In this way, the eventuality of figuring out how to deal with these difficult issues was postponed with humor.

Dad's marriage propositions also resembled conversations that we had already had about my relationship to Islamic practices specific to women, some negotiated in my favor and others simply shelved for the time being. Just a year ago, Dad had come to me while I was home for the winter holidays, asking me to begin wearing *hijab*, the traditional headscarf worn by Muslim women. I categorically refused, maintaining respect for those women who chose to do so. I understood that for numerous women, as well as for Dad, hijab symbolized something much more than covering a woman's body or hair; it symbolized a way to adhere to religious and cultural traditions in order to prevent complete Western immersion. But even my sympathy for this concern didn't change my feeling that hijab constructed me as a woman first and a human being second. Veiling seemed to reinforce the fact that inequality between the sexes was a natural, inexplicable phenomenon that is impossible to overcome, and that women should cover themselves, accommodating an unequal hierarchy, for the purposes of modesty and self-protection. I couldn't reconcile these issues and refused my father's request to don the veil. Although there was tension—Dad claimed I had yet to have my religious awakening— he chose to respect my decision.

Negotiating certain issues had always been part of the dynamic between my parents and me. It wasn't that I disagreed with them about everything. In fact, I had internalized much of the Islamic perspective of the female body while simultaneously admitting to its problematic nature (To this day, I would rather wear a wool sweater than a bathing suit in public, no matter how sweltering the weather). Moreover, Islam became an important part of differentiating myself from other American kids who did not have to find a balance between two opposing cultures. Perhaps Mom and Dad recognized the need to concede certain aspects of traditional Islamic norms, because for all intents and purposes, I had been raised in the breadbasket of America.

By the time I hit adolescence, I had already established myself outside of the social norm of the women in my community. I was an athletic teenager, a competitive tennis player and a budding weightlifter. After a lot of reasoning with my parents, I was permitted to wear shorts to compete in tennis tournaments, but I was not allowed to show my legs or arms (no tank tops) outside of sports. It was a big deal for my parents to have agreed to allow me to wear shorts in the first place. The small community of South Asian Muslim girls my age, growing up in Wichita, became symbols of the future of our community in the United States. Our bodies became the sites to play out cultural and religious debates. Much in the same way that Lady Liberty had come to symbolize idealized stability in the *terra patria* of America, young South Asian girls in my community were expected to embody the values of a preexisting social structure. We were scrutinized for what we said, what we wore, being seen with boys in public and for lacking grace and piety. Needless to say, because of disproportionate muscle mass, crooked teeth, huge Lucy glasses, and a disposition to walk pigeon-toed, I was not among the favored.

To add insult to injury, Mom nicknamed me "Amazon Woman," lamenting the fact that she—a beautiful, petite lady—had produced such a graceless, unfeminine creature. She was horrified by how freely I got into physical fights with my younger brother and armwrestled boys at school. She was particularly frustrated by the fact that I could not wear her beautiful Indian jewelry, especially her bangles and bracelets, because my wrists were too big. Special occasions, when I had to slather my wrists with tons of lotion in order to squeeze my hands into her tiny bangles, often bending the soft gold out of shape, caused us both infinite amounts of grief. I was the snot-nosed, younger sibling of the Bollywood (India's Hollywood) princess that my mother had in mind as a more appropriate representation of an Indian daughter. Rather, I loved sports, sports figures and books. I hated painful makeup rituals and tight jewelry.

It wasn't that I had a feminist awakening at an early age. I was just an obnoxious kid who did not understand the politics raging around my body. I did not possess the tools to analyze or understand my reaction to this process of social conditioning and normalization until many years later, well after I had left my parents' house and the Muslim community in Wichita. By positioning me as a subject of both humiliation and negotiation, Mom and Dad had inadvertently laid the foundations for me to understand and scrutinize the process of conditioning women to fulfill particular social obligations.

What was different about my dinner conversation with Dad that night was a sense of immediacy and detail. Somehow discussion about a "two-year marriage plan" seemed to encroach on my personal space much more than had previous jokes about my inability to complete my household chores or pressure to begin wearing hijab. I was meant to understand that that when it came to marriage, I was up against an invisible clock (read: social norms) that would dictate how much time I had left: how much time I had left to remain desirable, attractive and marriageable. Dad was convinced that it was his duty to ensure my long-term security in a manner that reaffirmed traditional Muslim culture in the face of an often hostile foreign community. I recognized that the threat was not as extreme as being shipped off to India in order to marry someone I had never met. The challenge was far more subtle than this. I was being asked to choose my community; capitulation through arranged marriage would show my commitment to being Indian, to being a good Muslim woman and to my parents by providing that they had raised me with a sense of duty and the willingness to sacrifice for my culture, religion and family.

There was no way to tell Dad about my complicated reality. Certain characteristics of my current life already indicated failure by such standards. I was involved in a long-term relationship with a white man, whose father was a prison guard on death row, an occupation that would have mortified my upper-middle-class, status-conscious parents. I was also struggling with an insurmountable crush on an *actress* in the Theater and Film Department. I was debating my sexuality in terms of cultural compatibility as well as gender. Moreover, there was no way to tell Dad that my social circle was supportive of these nontraditional romantic explorations. My friends in college had radically altered my perceptions of marriage and family. Many of my closest friends, including my roommates, were coming to terms with their own life-choices, having recently come out of the closet but unable to tell their families about their decisions. I felt inextricably linked to this group of women, who, like me, often had to lead double lives. The immediacy of fighting for issues such as queer rights, given the strength and beauty of my friends' romantic relationships, held far more appeal for me than the topics of marriage and security that my father broached over our Chinese dinner. There was no way to explain to my loving, charismatic, steadfastly religious father, who was inclined to the occasional violent outburst, that a traditional arranged marriage not only conflicted with the feminist ideology I had come to embrace, but it seemed almost petty in the face of larger, more pressing issues.

Although I had no tools to answer my father that night at dinner, feminist theory had provided me with the tools to understand *why* my father and I were engaged in the conversation in the first place. I understood that in his mind, Dad was fulfilling his social obligation as father and protector. He worried about my economic stability and, in a roundabout way, my happiness. Feminism and community activism had enabled me to understand these things as part of a proscribed role for women. At the same time, growing up in Kansas and coming to feminism here meant that I had to reconcile a number of different issues. I am a Muslim, first-generation Indian, feminist woman studying in a largely homogeneous white, Christian community in Midwestern America. What sacrifices are necessary for me to retain my familial relationships as well as a sense of personal autonomy informed by Western feminism?

The feminist agenda in my community is centered on ending violence against women, fighting for queer rights and maintaining women's reproductive choices. As such, the way that I initially became involved with this community was through community projects such as "Womyn Take Back the Night," attending pride rallies and working at the local domestic violence shelter. I am often the only woman of color in feminist organizations and at feminist events. Despite having grown up in the Bible belt, it is difficult for me to relate to stories told by my closest friends of being raised on cattle ranches and farms, growing up Christian by default and experiencing the strict social norms of small, religious communities in rural Kansas. Given the context of this community—a predominantly white, middle-class, college town—I have difficulty explaining that my feminism has to address issues like, "I should be able to wear *both* hijab *and* shorts if I chose to." The enormity of our agenda leaves little room to debate issues equally important but applicable only to me, such as the meaning of veiling, arranged marriages versus dating and how the north-south divide uniquely disadvantages women in the developing world.

It isn't that the women in my community ever turned to me and said, "Hey you, brown girl, stop diluting our priorities." To the contrary, the majority of active feminists in my community are eager to listen and understand my sometimes divergent perspective. We have all learned to share our experiences as women, students, mothers, partners and feminists. We easily relate to issues of male privilege, violence against women and figuring out how to better appreciate the sacrifices made by our mothers. From these commonalities we have learned to work together, creating informal social networks to complete community projects.

The difficulty arises when trying to put this theory and discussion into practice. Like last year, when our organization, the Womyn's Empowerment Action Coalition, began plans for the Womyn Take Back the Night march and rally, a number of organizers were eager to include the contribution of a petite, white belly dancer in the pre-march festivities. When I voiced my concern that historically belly dancing had been used as a way to objectify women's bodies in the Middle East, one of my fellow organizers (and a very good friend) laughed and called me a prude: "We're in Kansas, Almas," she said. "It doesn't mean the same thing in our culture. It is different here than over *there*." I understood what she meant, but having just returned from seven months in the West Bank, Palestine two months before, for me over there *was* over here. In the end, the dance was included while I wondered about our responsibility to women outside of the United States and our obligation to address the larger social, cultural issues of the dance itself.

To reconcile the differences between my own priorities and those of the women I work with, I am learning to bridge the gap between the Western white women (with the occasional African-American or Chicana) feminist canon and my own experience as a first-generation Indian Muslim woman living in the Midwest. I struggle with issues like cultural differences, colonialism, Islam and feminism and how they relate to one another. The most difficult part has been to get past my myopic vision of simply laying feminist theory written by Indian, Muslim or postcolonial theorists on top of American-Western feminism. With the help of feminist theory and other feminists, I am learning to dissect Western models of feminism, trying to figure out what aspects of these models can be applied to certain contexts. To this end, I have had the privilege of participating in projects abroad, in pursuit of understanding feminism in other contexts.

For example, while living with my extended family in India, I worked for a micro-credit affiliate that advised women on how to get loans and start their own businesses. During this time I learned about the potential of micro-enterprise as a weapon against the feminization of poverty. Last year, I spent a semester in the West Bank, Palestine studying the link between women and economics in transitional states and beginning to understand the importance of women's efforts during revolution. These experiences have been invaluable to me as a student of feminism and women's mobilization efforts. They have also shaped my personal development, helping me understand where the theoretical falls short of solving for the practical. In Lawrence, I maintain my participation in local feminist projects. Working in three different contexts has highlighted the amazing and unique ways in which feminism develops in various cultural settings yet still maintains certain commonalities.

There are few guidebooks for women like me who are trying to negotiate the paradigm of feminism in two different worlds. There is a delicate dance here that I must master—a dance of negotiating identity within interlinking cultural spheres. When faced with the movement's expectations of my commitment to local issues, it becomes important for me to emphasize that differences in culture and religion are also "local issues." This has forced me to change my frame of reference, developing from a rebellious tomboy who resisted parental imposition to a budding social critic, learning how to be a committed feminist and still keep my cultural, religious and community ties. As for family, we still negotiate despite the fact that Dad's two-year marriage plan has yet to come to fruition in this, my twenty-second year.

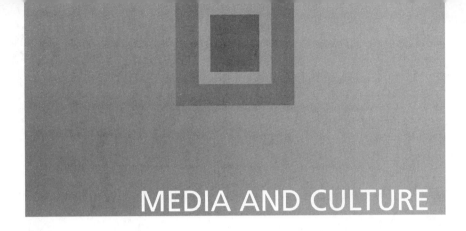

MEDIA AND CULTURE

42

RACIST STEREOTYPING IN THE ENGLISH LANGUAGE

Robert B. Moore

LANGUAGE AND CULTURE

An integral part of any culture is its language. Language not only develops in conjunction with a society's historical, economic and political evolution; it also reflects that society's attitudes and thinking. Language not only *expresses* ideas and concepts but actually *shapes* thought.[1] If one accepts that our dominant white culture is racist, then one would expect our language—an indispensable transmitter of culture—to be racist as well. Whites, as the dominant group, are not subjected to the same abusive characterization by our language that people of color receive. Aspects of racism in the English language that will be discussed in this essay include terminology, symbolism, politics, ethnocentrism, and context.

Before beginning our analysis of racism in language we would like to quote part of a TV film review which shows the connection between language and culture.[2]

From Paula S. Rothenberg, ed., *Racism and Sexism: An Integrated Study* (New York: St. Martin's Press, 1988), pp. 269–79. Reprinted by permission of the Council on Interracial Books for Children c/o Lawrence Jordan Literary Agency, 345 West 121st Street, NY, NY 10027.

Depending on one's culture, one interacts with time in a very distinct fashion. One example which gives some cross-cultural insights into the concept of time is language. In Spanish, a watch is said to "walk." In English, the watch "runs." In German, the watch "functions." And in French, the watch "marches." In the Indian culture of the Southwest, people do not refer to time in this way. The value of the watch is displaced with the value of "what time it's getting to be." Viewing these five cultural perspectives of time, one can see some definite emphasis and values that each culture places on time. For example, a cultural perspective may provide a clue to why the negative stereotype of the slow and lazy Mexican who lives in the "Land of Manana" exists in the Anglo value system, where time "flies," the watch "runs" and "time is money."

A SHORT PLAY ON "BLACK" AND "WHITE" WORDS

Some may blackly (angrily) accuse me of trying to blacken (defame) the English language, to give it a black eye (a mark of shame) by writing such black words (hostile). They may denigrate (to cast aspersions; to darken) me by accusing me of being blackhearted (malevolent), of having a black outlook (pessimistic, dismal) on life, of being a blackguard (scoundrel)—which would certainly be a black mark (detrimental fact) against me. Some may black-brow (scowl at) me and hope that a black cat crosses in front of me because of this black deed. I may become a black sheep (one who causes shame or embarrassment because of deviation from the accepted standards), who will be blackballed (ostracized) by being placed on a blacklist (list of undesirables) in an attempt to blackmail (to force or coerce into a particular action) me to retract my words. But attempts to blackjack (to compel by threat) me will have a Chinaman's chance of success, for I am not a yellow-bellied Indian-giver of words, who will whitewash (cover up or gloss over vices or crimes) a black lie (harmful, inexcusable). I challenge the purity and innocence (white) of the English language. I don't see things in black and white (entirely bad or entirely good) terms, for I am a white man (marked by upright firmness) if there ever was one. However, it would be a black day when I would not "call a spade a spade," even though some will suggest a white man calling the English language racist is like the pot calling the kettle black. While many may be niggardly (grudging, scanty) in their support, others will be honest and decent—and to them I say, that's very white of you (honest, decent).

The preceding is of course a white lie (not intended to cause harm), meant only to illustrate some examples of racist terminology in the English language.

OBVIOUS BIGOTRY

Perhaps the most obvious aspect of racism in language would be terms like "nigger," "spook," "chink," "spic," etc. While these may be facing increasing social disdain, they certainly are not dead. Large numbers of white Americans continue to utilize these terms. "Chink," "gook," and "slant-eyes" were in common usage among U.S. troops in Vietnam. An NBC nightly news broadcast, in February 1972, reported that the basketball team in Pekin, Illinois, was called the "Pekin Chinks" and noted that even though this had been protested by Chinese Americans, the term continued to be used because it was easy, and meant no harm. Spiro Agnew's widely reported "fat Jap" remark and the "little Jap" comment of lawyer John Wilson, during the Watergate hearings, are surface indicators of a deep-rooted Archie Bunkerism.

Many white people continue to refer to Black people as "colored," as for instance in a July 30, 1975, *Boston Globe* article on a racist attack by whites on a group of Black people using a public beach in Boston. One white person was quoted as follows:

> We've always welcomed good colored people in South Boston but we will not tolerate radical blacks or Communists. . . . Good colored people are welcome in South Boston, black militants are not.

Many white people may still be unaware of the disdain many African Americans have for the term "colored," but it often appears that whether used intentionally or unintentionally, "colored" people are "good" and "know their place," while "Black" people are perceived as "uppity" and "threatening" to many whites. Similarly, the term "boy" to refer to African American men is now acknowledged to be a demeaning term, though still in common use. Other terms such as "the pot calling the kettle black" and "calling a spade a spade" have negative racial connotations but are still frequently used, as for example when President Ford was quoted in February 1976 saying that even though Daniel Moynihan had left the U.N., the U.S. would continue "calling a spade a spade."

COLOR SYMBOLISM

The symbolism of white as positive and black as negative is pervasive in our culture, with the black/white words used in the beginning of this essay only one of many aspects. "Good guys" wear white hats and ride white horses, "bad guys" wear black hats and ride black horses. Angels are white, and devils are black. The definition of *black* includes "without any moral light or goodness, evil, wicked, indicating disgrace, sinful," while that of *white* includes "morally pure, spotless, innocent, free from evil intent."

A children's TV cartoon program, *Captain Scarlet*, is about an organization called Spectrum, whose purpose is to save the world from an evil extraterrestrial force called the Mysterons. Everyone in Spectrum has a color name—Captain Scarlet, Captain Blue, etc. The one Spectrum agent who has been mysteriously taken over by the Mysterons and works to advance their evil aims is Captain Black. The person who heads Spectrum, the good organization out to defend the world, is Colonel White.

Three of the dictionary definitions of white are "fairness of complexion, purity, innocence." These definitions affect the standards of beauty in our culture, in which whiteness represents the norm. "Blondes have more fun" and "Wouldn't you really rather be a blonde" are sexist in their attitudes toward women generally, but are racist white standards when applied to third world women. A 1971 *Mademoiselle* advertisement pictured a curly-headed, ivory-skinned woman over the caption, "When you go blonde go all the way," and asked: "Isn't this how, in the back of your mind, you always wanted to look? All wide-eyed and silky blonde down to there, and innocent?" Whatever the advertising people meant by this particular woman's innocence, one must remember that "innocent" is one of the definitions of the word white. This standard of beauty when preached to all women is racist. The statement "Isn't this how, in the back of your mind, you always wanted to look?" either ignores third world women or assumes they long to be white.

Time magazine in its coverage of the Wimbledon tennis competition between the black Australian Evonne Goolagong and the white American Chris Evert described Ms. Goolagong as "the dusky daughter of an Australian sheepshearer," while Ms. Evert was "a fair young girl from the middle-class groves of Florida." *Dusky* is a synonym of "black" and is defined as "having dark skin; of a dark color; gloomy; dark; swarthy." Its antonyms are "fair" and "blonde." *Fair* is defined in part as "free from blemish, imperfection, or anything that impairs the appearance, quality, or character: pleasing in appearance, attractive; clean; pretty; comely." By defining Evonne Goolagong as "dusky," *Time* technically defined her as the opposite of "pleasing in appearance; attractive; clean; pretty; comely."

The studies of Kenneth B. Clark, Mary Ellen Goodman, Judith Porter and others indicate that this persuasive "rightness of whiteness" in U.S. culture affects children before the age of four, providing white youngsters with a false sense of superiority and encouraging self-hatred among third world youngsters.

ETHNOCENTRISM OR FROM A WHITE PERSPECTIVE

Some words and phrases that are commonly used represent particular perspectives and frames of reference, and these often distort the understanding of the reader or listener. David R. Burgest[3] has written about the effect of using the terms "slave" or "master." He argues that the psychological impact of the statement referring to "the master raped his slave" is different from the impact of the same statement substituting the words: "the white captor raped an African woman held in captivity."

> Implicit in the English usage of the "master-slave" concept is ownership of the "slave" by the "master," therefore, the "master" is merely abusing his property (slave). In reality, the captives (slave) were African individuals with human worth, right and dignity and the term "slave" denounces that human quality thereby making the mass rape of African women by white captors more acceptable in the minds of people and setting a mental frame of reference for legitimizing the atrocities perpetuated against African people.

The term slave connotes a less than human quality and turns the captive person into a thing. For example, two McGraw-Hill Far Eastern Publishers textbooks (1970) stated, "At first it was the slaves who worked the cane and they got only food for it. Now men work cane and get money." Next time you write about slavery or read about it, try transposing all "slaves" into "African people held in captivity," "Black people forced to work for no pay" or "African people stolen from their families and societies." While it is more cumbersome, such phrasing conveys a different meaning.

PASSIVE TENSE

Another means by which language shapes our perspective has been noted by Thomas Greenfield,[4] who writes that the achievements of Black people—and Black people themselves—have been hidden in

> the linguistic ghetto of the passive voice, the subordinate clause, and the "understood" subject. The seemingly innocuous distinction (between active/passive voice) holds enormous implications for writers and speakers. When it is effectively applied, the rhetorical impact of the passive voice—the art of making the creator or instigator of action totally disappear from a reader's perception—can be devastating.

For instance, some history texts will discuss how European immigrants came to the United States seeking a better life and expanded opportunities, but will note that "slaves *were brought* to America." Not only does this omit the destruction of African societies and families, but it ignores the role of northern merchants and southern slaveholders in the profitable trade in human beings. Other books will state that "the continental railroad *was built*," conveniently omitting information about the Chinese laborers who built much of it or the oppression they suffered.

Another example. While touring Monticello, Greenfield noted that the tour guide

> made all the black people of Monticello disappear through her use of the passive voice. While speaking of the architectural achievements of Jefferson in the active voice, she unfailingly shifted to passive when speaking of the work performed by Negro slaves and skilled servants.

Noting a type of door that after 166 years continued to operate without need for repair, Greenfield remarks that the design aspect of the door was much simpler than the actual skill and work involved in building and installing it. Yet his guide stated: "Mr. Jefferson designed these doors . . ." while "the doors were installed in 1809." The workers who installed those doors were African people whom Jefferson held in bondage. The guide's use of the passive tense enabled her to dismiss the reality of Jefferson's slaveholding. It also meant that she did not have to make any mention of the skills of those people held in bondage.

POLITICS AND TERMINOLOGY

"Culturally deprived," "economically disadvantaged" and "underdeveloped" are other terms which mislead and distort our awareness of reality. The application of the term "culturally deprived" to third world children in this society reflects a value judgment. It assumes that the dominant whites are cultured and all others without culture. In fact, third world children generally are bicultural, and many are bilingual, having grown up in their own culture as well as absorbing the dominant culture. In many ways, they are equipped with skills and experiences which white youth have been deprived of, since most white youth develop in a monocultural, monolingual environment. Burgest[5] suggests that the term "culturally deprived" be replaced by "culturally dispossessed," and that the term "economically disadvantaged" be replaced by "economically exploited." Both these terms present a perspective and implication that provide an entirely different frame of reference as to the reality of the third world experience in U.S. society.

Similarly, many nations of the third world are described as "underdeveloped." These less wealthy nations are generally those that suffered under colonialism and neo-colonialism. The "developed" nations are those that exploited their resources and wealth. Therefore, rather than referring to these countries as "underdeveloped," a more appropriate and meaningful designation might be "over exploited." Again, transpose this term next time you read about "underdeveloped nations" and note the different meaning that results.

Terms such as "culturally deprived," "economically disadvantaged" and "underdeveloped" place the responsibility for their own conditions on those being so described. This is known as "Blaming the Victim."[6] It places responsibility for poverty on the victims of poverty. It removes the blame from those in power who benefit from, and continue to permit, poverty.

Still another example involves the use of "non-white," "minority" or "third world." While people of color are a minority in the U.S., they are part of the vast majority of the world's population, in which white people are a distinct minority. Thus, by utilizing the term minority to describe people of color in the U.S., we can lose sight of the global majority/minority reality—a fact of some importance in the increasing and interconnected struggles of people of color inside and outside the U.S.

To describe people of color as "non-white" is to use whiteness as the standard and norm against which to measure all others. Use of the term "third world" to describe all people of color overcomes the inherent bias of "minority" and "non-white." Moreover, it connects the struggles of third world people in the U.S. with the freedom struggles around the globe.

The term third world gained increasing usage after the 1955 Bandung Conference of "non-aligned" nations, which represented a third force outside of the two world superpowers. The "first world" represents the United States, Western Europe and their sphere of influence. The "second world" represents the Soviet Union and its sphere. The "third world" represents, for the most part, nations that were, or are, controlled by the "first world" or West. For the most part, these are nations of Africa, Asia and Latin America.

"LOADED" WORDS AND NATIVE AMERICANS

Many words lead to a demeaning characterization of groups of people. For instance, Columbus, it is said, "discovered" America. The word *discover* is defined as "to gain sight or knowledge of something previously unseen or unknown; to discover may be to find some existent thing that was previously unknown." Thus, a continent inhabited by millions of human beings cannot be "discovered." For history books to continue this usage represents a Eurocentric (white European) perspective on world history and ignores the existence of, and the perspective of, Native Americans. "Discovery," as used in the Euro-American context, implies the right to take what one finds, ignoring the rights of those who already inhabit or own the "discovered" thing.

Eurocentrism is also apparent in the usage of "victory" and "massacre" to describe the battles between Native Americans and whites. *Victory* is defined in the dictionary as "a success or triumph over an enemy in battle or war; the decisive defeat of an opponent." *Conquest* denotes the "taking over of control by the victor, and the obedience of the conquered." *Massacre* is defined as "the unnecessary, indiscriminate killing of a number of human beings, as in barbarous warfare or persecution, or for revenge or plunder." *Defend* is described as "to ward off attack from; guard against assault or injury; to strive to keep safe by resisting attack."

Eurocentrism turns these definitions around to serve the purpose of distorting history and justifying Euro-American conquest of the Native American homelands. Euro-Americans are not described in history books as invading Native American lands, but rather as defending *their* homes against "Indian" attacks. Since European communities were constantly encroaching on land already occupied, then a more honest interpretation would state that it was the Native Americans who were "warding off," "guarding" and "defending" their homelands.

Native American victories are invariably defined as "massacres," while the indiscriminate killing, extermination and plunder of Native American nations by Euro-Americans is defined as "victory." Distortion of history by the choice of "loaded" words used to describe historical events is a common racist practice. Rather than portraying Native Americans as human beings in highly defined and complex societies, cultures and civilizations, history books use such adjectives as "savages," "beasts," "primitive," and "backward." Native people are referred to as "squaw," "brave," or "papoose" instead of "woman," "man," or "baby."

Another term that has questionable connotations is *tribe*. The *Oxford English Dictionary* defines this noun as "a race of people; now applied especially to a primary aggregate of people in a primitive or barbarous condition, under a headman or chief." Morton Fried,[7] discussing "The Myth of Tribe," states that the word "did not become a general term of reference to American Indian society until the nineteenth century. Previously, the words commonly used for Indian populations were 'nation' and 'people.'" Since "tribe" has assumed a connotation of primitiveness or backwardness, it is suggested that the use of "nation" or "people" replace the term whenever possible in referring to Native American peoples.

The term *tribe* invokes even more negative implications when used in reference to American peoples. As Evelyn Jones Rich[8] has noted, the term is "almost always used to refer to third world people and it implies a stage of development which is, in short, a put-down."

"LOADED" WORDS AND AFRICANS

Conflicts among diverse peoples within African nations are often referred to as "tribal warfare," while conflicts among the diverse peoples within European countries are never described in such terms. If the rivalries between the Ibo and the Hausa and Yoruba in Nigeria are described as "tribal," why not the rivalries between Serbs and Slavs in Yugoslavia, or Scots and English in Great Britain, Protestants and Catholics in Ireland, or the Basques and the Southern Spaniards in Spain? Conflicts among African peoples in a particular nation have religious, cultural, economic and/or political roots. If we can analyze the roots of conflicts among European peoples in terms other than "tribal warfare," certainly we can do the same with African peoples, including correct reference to the ethnic groups or nations involved. For example, the terms "Kaffirs," "Hottentot" or "Bushmen" are names imposed by white Europeans. The correct names are always those by which a people refer to themselves. (In these instances Xhosa, Khoi-Khoin and San are correct.[9])

The generalized application of "tribal" in reference to Africans—as well as the failure to acknowledge the religious, cultural and social diversity of African peoples—is a decidedly racist dynamic. It is part of the process whereby Euro-Americans justify, or avoid confronting, their oppression of third world peoples. Africa has been particularly insulted by this dynamic, as witness the pervasive "darkest Africa" image. This image, widespread in Western culture, evokes an Africa covered by jungles and inhabited by "un-civilized," "cannibalistic," "pagan," "savage" peoples. This "darkest Africa" image avoids the geographical reality. Less than 20 percent of the African continent is wooded savanna, for example. The image also ignores the history of African cultures and civilizations. Ample evidence suggests this distortion of reality was developed as a convenient rationale for the European and American slave trade. The Western powers, rather than exploiting, were civ-ilizing and Christianizing "uncivilized" and "pagan savages" (so the rational-ization went). This dynamic also served to justify Western colonialism. From Tarzan movies to racist children's books like *Doctor Dolittle* and *Charlie and the Chocolate Factory*, the image of "savage" Africa and the myth of "the white man's burden" has been perpetuated in Western culture.

A 1972 *Time* magazine editorial lamenting the demise of *Life* magazine, stated that the "lavishness" of *Life*'s enterprises included "organizing safaris into darkest Africa." The same year, the *New York Times*' C. L. Sulzberger wrote that Africa has "a history as dark as the skins of many of its people." Terms such as "darkest Africa," "primitive," "tribe" ("tribal") or "jungle," in reference to Africa, perpetuate myths and are especially inexcusable in such large circulation publications.

Ethnocentrism is similarly reflected in the term "pagan" to describe tra-ditional religions. A February 1973 *Time* magazine article on Uganda stated, "Moslems account for only 500,000 of Uganda's 10 million people. Of the remainder, 5,000,000 are Christians and the rest pagan." *Pagan* is defined as "Heathen, a follower of a polytheistic religion; one that has little or no reli-gion and that is marked by a frank delight in and uninhibited seeking after sensual pleasures and material goods." *Heathen* is defined as "Unenlightened; an unconverted member of a people or nation that does not acknowledge the God of the Bible. A person whose culture or enlightenment is of an inferior grade, especially an irreligious person." Now, the people of Uganda, like almost all Africans, have serious religious beliefs and practices. As used by Westerners, "pagan" connotes something wild, primitive and inferior—another term to watch out for.

The variety of traditional structures that African people live in are their "houses," not "huts." A *hut* is "an often small and temporary dwelling of simple construction." And to describe Africans as "natives" (noun) is derogatory terminology—as in, "the natives are restless." The dictionary definition of *native* includes: "one of a people inhabiting a territorial area at the time of its discovery or becoming familiar to a foreigner; one belonging to a people having a less complex civilization." Therefore, use of "native," like use of "pagan" often implies a value judgment of white superiority.

QUALIFYING ADJECTIVES

Words that would normally have positive connotations can have entirely different meanings when used in a racial context. For example, C. L. Sulzberger, the columnist of the *New York Times*, wrote in January 1975, about conversations he had with two people in Namibia. One was the white South African administrator of the country and the other a member of SWAPO, the Namibian liberation movement. The first is described as "Dirk Mudge, who as senior elected member of the administration is a kind of acting Prime Minister. . . ." But the second person is introduced as "Daniel Tijongarero, an intelligent Herero tribesman who is a member of SWAPO. . . ." What need was there for Sulzberger to state that Daniel Tijongarero is "intelligent"? Why not also state that Dirk Mudge was "intelligent"—or do we assume he wasn't?

A similar example from a 1968 *New York Times* article reporting on an address by Lyndon Johnson stated, "The President spoke to the well-dressed Negro officials and their wives." In what similar circumstances can one imagine a reporter finding it necessary to note that an audience of white government officials was "well-dressed"?

Still another word often used in a racist context is "qualified." In the 1960s white Americans often questioned whether Black people were "qualified" to hold public office, a question that was never raised (until too late) about white officials like Wallace, Maddox, Nixon, Agnew, Mitchell, et al. The question of qualifications has been raised even more frequently in recent years as white people question whether Black people are "qualified" to be hired for positions in industry and educational institutions. "We're looking for a qualified Black" has been heard again and again as institutions are confronted with affirmative action goals. Why stipulate that Blacks must be "qualified," when for others it is taken for granted that applicants must be "qualified"?

SPEAKING ENGLISH

Finally, the depiction in movies and children's books of third world people speaking English is often itself racist. Children's books about Puerto Ricans or Chicanos often connect poverty with a failure to speak English or to speak it well, thus blaming the victim and ignoring the racism which affects third world people regardless of their proficiency in English. Asian characters speak a stilted English ("Honorable so and so" or "Confucius say") or have a speech impediment ("roots or ruck," "very solly," "flied lice"). Native American characters speak another variation of stilted English ("Boy not hide. Indian take boy."), repeat certain Hollywood-Indian phrases ("Heap big" and "Many moons") or simply grunt out "Ugh" or "How." The repeated use of these language characterizations functions to make third world people seem less intelligent and less capable than the English-speaking white characters.

WRAP-UP

A *Saturday Review* editorial[10] on "The Environment of Language" stated that language

> . . . has as much to do with the philosophical and political conditioning of a society as geography or climate. . . . people in Western cultures do not realize the extent to which their racial attitudes have been conditioned since early childhood by the power of words to ennoble or condemn, augment or detract, glorify or demean. Negative language infects the subconscious of most Western people from the time they first learn to speak. Prejudice is not merely imparted or superimposed. It is metabolized in the bloodstream of society. What is needed is not so much a change in language as an awareness of the power of words to condition attitudes. If we can at least recognize the underpinnings of prejudice, we may be in a position to deal with the effects.

To recognize the racism in language is an important first step. Consciousness of the influence of language on our perceptions can help to negate much of that influence. But it is not enough to simply become aware of the effects of racism in conditioning attitudes. While we may not be able to change the language, we can definitely change our usage of the language. We can avoid using words that degrade people. We can make a conscious effort to use terminology that reflects a progressive perspective, as opposed to a distorting perspective. It is important for educators to provide students with opportunities to explore racism in language and to increase their awareness of it, as well as learning terminology that is positive and does not perpetuate negative human values.

NOTES

1. Simon Podair, "How Bigotry Builds Through Language," *Negro Digest*, March 1967.

2. Jose Armas, "Antonia and the Mayor: A Cultural Review of the Film," *The Journal of Ethnic Studies*, Fall 1975.

3. David R. Burgest, "The Racist Use of the English Language," *Black Scholar*, Sept. 1973.

4. Thomas Greenfield, "Race and Passive Voice at Monticello," *Crisis*, April 1975.

5. David R. Burgest, "Racism in Everyday Speech and Social Work Jargon," *Social Work*, July 1973.

6. William Ryan, *Blaming the Victim*, Pantheon Books, 1971.

7. Morton Fried, "The Myth of Tribe," *National History*, April 1975.

8. Evelyn Jones Rich, "Mind Your Language," *Africa Report*, Sept./Oct. 1974.

9. Steve Wolf, "Catalogers in Revolt Against LC's Racist, Sexist Headings," *Bulletin of Interracial Books for Children*, Vol. 6, Nos. 3&4, 1975.

10. "The Environment of Language," *Saturday Review*, April 8, 1967.

Also see:

Roger Bastide, "Color, Racism and Christianity," *Daedalus*, Spring 1967.

Kenneth J. Gergen, "The Significance of Skin Color in Human Relations," *Daedalus*, Spring 1967.

Lloyd Yabura, "Towards a Language of Humanism," *Rhythm*, Summer 1971.

UNESCO, "Recommendations Concerning Terminology in Education on Race Questions," June 1968.

43

CRIMES AGAINST HUMANITY

Ward Churchill

If nifty little "pep" gestures like the "Indian Chant" and the "Tomahawk Chop" are just good clean fun, then let's spread the fun around, shall we?

During the past couple of seasons, there has been an increasing wave of controversy regarding the names of professional sports teams like the Atlanta "Braves," Cleveland "Indians," Washington "Redskins," and Kansas City "Chiefs." The issue extends to the names of college teams like Florida State University "Seminoles," University of Illinois "Fighting Illini," and so on, right on down to high school outfits like the Lamar (Colorado) "Savages." Also involved have been team adoption of "mascots," replete with feathers, buckskins, beads, spears, and "warpaint" (some fans have opted to adorn

From Ward Churchill, "Crimes Against Humanity," *Z Magazine* 6 (March 1993): 43–47. Reprinted by permission of the author.

themselves in the same fashion), and nifty little "pep" gestures like the "Indian Chant" and "Tomahawk Chop."

A substantial number of American Indians have protested that use of native names, images, and symbols as sports team mascots and the like is, by definition, a virulently racist practice. Given the historical relationship between Indians and non-Indians during what has been called the "Conquest of America," American Indian Movement leader (and American Indian Anti-Defamation Council founder) Russell Means has compared the practice to contemporary Germans naming their soccer teams the "Jews," "Hebrews," and "Yids," while adorning their uniforms with grotesque caricatures of Jewish faces taken from the Nazis' anti-Semitic propaganda of the 1930s. Numerous demonstrations have occurred in conjunction with games—most notably during the November 15, 1992 match-up between the Chiefs and Redskins in Kansas City—by angry Indians and their supporters.

In response, a number of players—especially African Americans and other minority athletes—have been trotted out by professional team owners like Ted Turner, as well as university and public school officials, to announce that they mean not to insult but to honor native people. They have been joined by the television networks and most major newspapers, all of which have editorialized that Indian discomfort with the situation is "no big deal," insisting that the whole thing is just "good, clean fun." The country needs more such fun, they've argued, and "a few disgruntled Native Americans" have no right to undermine the nation's enjoyment of its leisure time by complaining. This is especially the case, some have argued, "in hard times like these." It has even been contended that Indian outrage at being systematically degraded—rather than the degradation itself—creates "a serious barrier to the sort of intergroup communication so necessary in a multicultural society such as ours."

Okay, let's communicate. We are frankly dubious that those advancing such positions really believe their own rhetoric, but, just for the sake of argument, let's accept the premise that they are sincere. If what they say is true, then isn't it time we spread such "inoffensiveness" and "good cheer" around among *all* groups so that *everybody* can participate *equally* in fostering the round of national laughs they call for? Sure it is—the country can't have too much fun or "intergroup involvement"—so the more, the merrier. Simple consistency demands that anyone who thinks the Tomahawk Chop is a swell pastime must be just as hearty in their endorsement of the following ideas—by the logic used to defend the defamation of American Indians—should help us all really start yukking it up.

First, as a counterpart to the Redskins, we need an NFL team called "Niggers" to honor Afro-Americans. Half-time festivities for fans might include a simulated stewing of the opposing coach in a large pot while players and cheerleaders dance around it, garbed in leopard skins and wearing fake bones in their noses. This concept obviously goes along with the kind of gaiety attending the Chop, but also with the actions of the Kansas City Chiefs, whose team members—prominently including black team members—lately appeared on a poster looking "fierce" and "savage" by way of wearing Indian regalia. Just a bit of harmless "morale boosting," says the Chiefs' front office. You bet.

So that the newly formed Niggers sports club won't end up too out of sync while expressing the "spirit" and "identity" of Afro-Americans in the above fashion, a baseball franchise—let's call this one the "Sambos"—should be formed. How about a basketball team called the "Spearchuckers"? A hockey team called the "Jungle Bunnies"? Maybe the "essence" of these teams could be depicted by images of tiny black faces adorned with huge pairs of lips. The players could appear on TV every week or so gnawing on chicken legs and spitting watermelon seeds at one another. Catchy, eh? Well, there's "nothing to be upset about," according to those who love wearing "war bonnets" to the Super Bowl or having "Chief Illiniwik" dance around the sports arenas of Urbana, Illinois.

And why stop there? There are plenty of other groups to include. Hispanics? They can be "represented" by the Galveston "Greasers" and San Diego "Spics," at least until the Wisconsin "Wetbacks" and Baltimore "Beaners" get off the ground. Asian Americans? How about the "Slopes," "Dinks," "Gooks," and "Zipperheads?" Owners of the latter teams might get their logo ideas from editorial page cartoons printed in the nation's newspapers during World War II: slant-eyes, buck teeth, big glasses, but nothing racially insulting or derogatory, according to the editors and artists involved at the time. Indeed, this Second World War–vintage stuff can be seen as just another barrel of laughs, at least by what current editors say are their "local standards" concerning American Indians.

Let's see. Who's been left out? Teams like the Kansas City "Kikes," Hanover "Honkies," San Leandro "Shylocks," Daytona "Dagos," and Pittsburgh "Polacks" will fill a certain social void among white folk. Have a religious belief? Let's all go for the gusto and gear up the Milwaukee "Mackerel Snappers" and Hollywood "Holy Rollers." The Fighting Irish of Notre Dame can be rechristened the "Drunken Irish" or "Papist Pigs." Issues of gender and sexual preferences can be addressed through creation of teams like the St. Louis "Sluts," Boston "Bimbos," Detroit "Dykes," and the Fresno "Fags." How about the Gainesville "Gimps" and Richmond "Retards," so the physically and mentally impaired won't be excluded from our fun and games?

Now, don't go getting "overly sensitive" out there. None of this is demeaning or insulting, at least not when it's being done to Indians. Just ask the folks who are doing it, or their apologists like Andy Rooney in the national media. They'll tell you—as in fact they *have* been telling you—that there's been no harm done, regardless of what their victims think, feel, or say. The situation is exactly the same as when those with precisely the same mentality used to insist that Step 'n' Fetchit was okay, or Rochester on the *Jack Benny Show*, or Amos and Andy, Charlie Chan, the Frito Bandito, or any of the other cutesy symbols making up the lexicon of American racism. Have we communicated yet?

Let's get just a little bit real here. The notion of "fun" embodied in rituals like the Tomahawk Chop must be understood for what it is. There's not a single non-Indian example used above which can be considered socially acceptable in even the most marginal sense. The reasons are obvious enough. So why is it different where American Indians are concerned? One can only conclude that, in contrast to the other groups at issue, Indians are (falsely) perceived as being too few, and therefore too weak, to defend themselves effectively against racist and otherwise offensive behavior.

Fortunately, there are some glimmers of hope. A few teams and their fans have gotten the message and have responded appropriately. Stanford University, which opted to drop the name "Indians" from Stanford, has experienced no resulting drop-off in attendance. Meanwhile, the local newspaper in Portland, Oregon, recently decided its long-standing editorial policy prohibiting use of racial epithets should include derogatory team names. The Redskins, for instance, are now referred to as "the Washington team," and will continue to be described in this way until the franchise adopts an inoffensive moniker (newspaper sales in Portland have suffered no decline as a result).

Such examples are to be applauded and encouraged. They stand as figurative beacons in the night, proving beyond all doubt that it is quite possible to indulge in the pleasure of athletics without accepting blatant racism into the bargain.

NUREMBERG PRECEDENTS

On October 16, 1946, a man named Julius Streicher mounted the steps of a gallows. Moments later he was dead, the sentence of an international tribunal composed of representatives of the United States, France, Great Britain, and the Soviet Union having been imposed. Streicher's body was then cremated, and—so horrendous were his crimes thought to have been—his ashes dumped into an unspecified German river so that "no one should ever know a particular place to go for reasons of mourning his memory."

Julius Streicher had been convicted at Nuremberg, Germany, of what were termed "Crimes Against Humanity." The lead prosecutor in his case— Justice Robert Jackson of the United States Supreme Court—had not argued that the defendant had killed anyone, nor that he had personally committed any especially violent act. Nor was it contended that Streicher had held any particularly important position in the German government during the period in which the so-called Third Reich had exterminated some 6,000,000 Jews, as well as several million Gypsies, Poles, Slavs, homosexuals, and other unter-menschen (subhumans).

The sole offense for which the accused was ordered put to death was in having served as publisher/editor of a Bavarian tabloid entitled *Der Sturmer* during the early-to-mid 1930s, years before the Nazi genocide actually began. In this capacity, he had penned a long series of virulently anti-Semitic editorials and "news" stories, usually accompanied by cartoons and other images graphically depicting Jews in extraordinarily derogatory fashion. This, the prosecution asserted, had done much to "dehumanize" the targets of his distortion in the mind of the German public. In turn, such dehumanization had made it possible—or at least easier—for average Germans to later indulge in the outright liquidation of Jewish "vermin." The tribunal agreed, holding that Streicher was therefore complicit in genocide and deserving of death by hanging.

During his remarks to the Nuremberg tribunal, Justice Jackson observed that, in implementing its sentences, the participating powers were morally and legally binding themselves to adhere forever after to the same standards of conduct that were being applied to Streicher and the other Nazi leaders. In the alternative, he said, the victorious allies would have committed "pure murder" at Nuremberg—no different in substance from that carried out by those they presumed to judge—rather than establishing the "permanent benchmark for justice" which was intended.

Yet in the United States of Robert Jackson, the indigenous American Indian population had already been reduced, in a process which is ongoing to this day, from perhaps 12.5 million in the year 1500 to fewer than 250,000 by the beginning of the 20th century. This was accomplished, according to official sources, "largely through the cruelty of [Euro-American] settlers," and an informal but clear governmental policy which had made it an articulated goal to "exterminate these red vermin," or at least whole segments of them.

Bounties had been placed on the scalps of Indians—any Indians—in places as diverse as Georgia, Kentucky, Texas, the Dakotas, Oregon, and California, and had been maintained until resident Indian populations were decimated or disappeared altogether. Entire peoples such as the Cherokee had been reduced to half their size through a policy of forced removal from their homelands east of the Mississippi River to what were then considered less preferable areas in the West.

Others, such as the Navajo, suffered the same fate while under military guard for years on end. The United States Army had also perpetrated a long series of wholesale massacres of Indians at places like Horseshoe Bend, Bear River, Sand Creek, the Washita River, the Marias River, Camp Robinson, and Wounded Knee.

Through it all, hundreds of popular novels—each competing with the next to make Indians appear more grotesque, menacing, and inhuman—were sold in the tens of millions of copies in the U.S. Plainly, the Euro-American public was being conditioned to see Indians in such a way as to allow their eradication to continue. And continue it did until the Manifest Destiny of the U.S.—a direct precursor to what Hitler would subsequently call Lebens-raumpolitik (the politics of living space)—was consummated.

By 1900, the national project of "clearing" Native Americans from their land and replacing them with "superior" Anglo-American settlers was complete: the indigenous population had been reduced by as much as 98 percent while approximately 97.5 percent of their original territory had "passed" to the invaders. The survivors had been concentrated, out of sight and mind of the public, on scattered "reservations," all of them under the self-assigned "plenary" (full) power of the federal government. There was, of course, no Nuremberg-style tribunal passing judgment on those who had fostered such circumstances in North America. No U.S. official or private citizen was ever imprisoned—never mind hanged—for implementing or propagandizing what had been done. Nor had the process of genocide afflicting Indians been completed. Instead, it merely changed form.

Between the 1880s and the 1980s, nearly half of all Native American children were coercively transferred from their own families, communities, and cultures to those of the conquering society. This was done through compulsory attendance at remote boarding schools, often hundreds of miles from their homes, where native children were kept for years on end while being systematically "deculturated" (indoctrinated to think and act in the manner of Euro-Americans rather than Indians). It was also accomplished through a pervasive foster home and adoption program—including "blind" adoptions, where children would be permanently denied information as to who they were/are and where they'd come from—placing native youths in non-Indian homes.

The express purpose of all this was to facilitate a U.S. governmental policy to bring about the "assimilation" (dissolution) of indigenous societies. In other words, Indian cultures as such were to be caused to disappear. Such policy objectives are directly contrary to the United Nations 1948 Convention on Punishment and Prevention of the Crime of Genocide, an element of international law arising from the Nuremberg proceedings. The forced "transfer of the children" of a targeted "racial, ethnical, or religious group" is explicitly prohibited as a genocidal activity under the Convention's second article.

Article II of the Genocide Convention also expressly prohibits involuntary sterilization as a means of "preventing births among" a targeted population. Yet, in 1975, it was conceded by the U.S. government that its Indian Health Service (IHS), then a subpart of the Bureau of Indian Affairs (BIA), was even then conducting a secret program of involuntary sterilization that had affected approximately 40 percent of all Indian women. The program was allegedly discontinued, and the IHS was transferred to the Public Health Service, but no one was punished. In 1990, it came out that the IHS was inoculating Inuit children in Alaska with Hepatitis-B vaccine. The vaccine had already been banned by the World Health Organization as having a demonstrated correlation with the HIV-Syndrome which is itself correlated to AIDS. As this is written, a "field test" of Hepatitis-A vaccine, also HIV-correlated, is being conducted on Indian reservations in the northern plains region.

The Genocide Convention makes it a "crime against humanity" to create conditions leading to the destruction of an identifiable human group, as such. Yet the BIA has utilized the government's plenary prerogatives to negotiate mineral leases "on behalf of" Indian peoples paying a fraction of standard royalty rates. The result has been "super profits" for a number of preferred U.S. corporations. Meanwhile, Indians, whose reservations ironically turned out to be in some of the most mineral-rich areas of North America, which makes us, the nominally wealthiest segment of the continent's population, live in dire poverty.

By the government's own data in the mid-1980s, Indians received the lowest annual and lifetime per capita incomes of any aggregate population group in the United States. Concomitantly, we suffer the highest rate of infant mortality, death by exposure and malnutrition, disease, and the like. Under such circumstances, alcoholism and other escapist forms of substance abuse are endemic in the Indian community, a situation which leads both to a general physical debilitation of the population and a catastrophic accident rate. Teen suicide among Indians is several times the national average.

The average life expectancy of a reservation-based Native American man is barely 45 years; women can expect to live less than three years longer.

Such itemizations could be continued at great length, including matters like the radioactive contamination of large portions of contemporary Indian Country, the forced relocation of traditional Navajos, and so on. But the point should be made: genocide, as defined in international law, is a continuing fact of day-to-day life (and death) for North America's native peoples. Yet there has been—and is—only the barest flicker of public concern about, or even consciousness of, this reality. Absent any serious expression of public outrage, no one is punished and the process continues.

A salient reason for public acquiescence before the ongoing holocaust in Native North America has been a continuation of the popular legacy, often through more effective media. Since 1925, Hollywood has released more than 2,000 films, many of them rerun frequently on television, portraying Indians as strange, perverted, ridiculous, and often dangerous things of the past. Moreover, we are habitually presented to mass audiences one-dimensionally, devoid of recognizable human motivations and emotions; Indians thus serve as props, little more. We have thus been thoroughly and systematically dehumanized.

Nor is this the extent of it. Everywhere, we are used as logos, as mascots, as jokes: "Big-Chief" writing tablets, "Red Man" chewing tobacco, "Winnebago" campers, "Navajo" and "Cherokee" and "Pontiac" and "Cadillac" pickups and automobiles. There are the Cleveland "Indians," the Kansas City "Chiefs," the Atlanta "Braves" and the Washington "Redskins" professional sports teams—not to mention those in thousands of colleges, high schools, and elementary schools across the country—each with their own degrading caricatures and parodies of Indians and/or things Indian. Pop fiction continues in the same vein, including an unending stream of New Age manuals purporting to expose the inner works of indigenous spirituality in everything from pseudo-philosophical to do-it-yourself styles. Blond yuppies from Beverly Hills amble about the country claiming to be reincarnated 17th century Cheyenne Ushamans ready to perform previously secret ceremonies.

In effect, a concerted, sustained, and in some ways accelerating effort has gone into making Indians unreal. It is thus of obvious importance that the American public begin to think about the implications of such things the next time they witness a gaggle of face-painted and war-bonneted buffoons doing the "Tomahawk Chop" at a baseball or football game. It is necessary that they think about the implications of the grade-school teacher adorning their child in turkey feathers to commemorate Thanksgiving. Think about the significance of John Wayne or Charlton Heston killing a dozen "savages" with a single bullet the next time a western comes on TV. Think about why Land-o-Lakes finds it appropriate to market its butter with the stereotyped image of an "Indian princess" on the wrapper. Think about what it means when non-Indian academics profess—as they often do—to "know more about Indians than Indians do themselves." Think about the significance of charlatans like Carlos Castaneda and Jamake Highwater and Mary Summer Rain and Lynn Andrews churning out "Indian" bestsellers, one after the other, while Indians typically can't get into print.

Think about the real situation of American Indians. Think about Julius Streicher. Remember Justice Jackson's admonition. Understand that the treatment of Indians in American popular culture is not "cute" or "amusing" or just "good, clean fun."

Know that it causes real pain and real suffering to real people. Know that it threatens our very survival. And know that this is just as much a crime against humanity as anything the Nazis ever did. It is likely that the indigenous people of the United States will never demand that those guilty of such criminal activity be punished for their deeds. But the least we have the right to expect—indeed, to demand—is that such practices finally be brought to a halt.

44

MEDIA MAGIC
Making Class Invisible

Gregory Mantsios

Of the various social and cultural forces in our society, the mass media is arguably the most influential in molding public consciousness. Americans spend an average twenty-eight hours per week watching television. They also spend an undetermined number of hours reading periodicals, listening to the radio, and going to the movies. Unlike other cultural and socializing institutions, ownership and control of the mass media is highly concentrated. Twenty-three corporations own more than one-half of all the daily newspapers, magazines, movie studios, and radio and television outlets in the United States.[1] The number of media companies is shrinking and their control of the industry is expanding. And a relatively small number of media outlets is producing and packaging the majority of news and entertainment programs. For the most part, our media is national in nature and single-minded (profit-oriented) in purpose. This media plays a key role in defining our cultural tastes, helping us locate ourselves in history, establishing our national identity, and ascertaining the range of national and social possibilities. In this essay, we will examine the way the mass media shapes how people think about each other and about the nature of our society.

The United States is the most highly stratified society in the industrialized world. Class distinctions operate in virtually every aspect of our lives, determining the nature of our work, the quality of our schooling, and the health and safety of our loved ones. Yet remarkably, we, as a nation, retain illusions about living in an egalitarian society. We maintain these illusions, in large part, because the media hides gross inequities from public view. In those instances when inequities are revealed, we are provided with messages that obscure the nature of class realities and blame the victims of class-dominated society for their own plight. Let's briefly examine what the news media, in particular, tells us about class.

From Paula Rothenberg, ed., *Race, Class, and Gender in the United States: An Integrated Study*, 4th ed. (New York: St. Martin's Press, 1998). Reprinted with permission of the author.

ABOUT THE POOR

The news media provides meager coverage of poor people and poverty. The coverage it does provide is often distorted and misleading.

The Poor Do Not Exist

For the most part, the news media ignores the poor. Unnoticed are forty million poor people in the nation—a number that equals the entire population of Maine, Vermont, New Hampshire, Connecticut, Rhode Island, New Jersey, and New York combined. Perhaps even more alarming is that the rate of poverty is increasing twice as fast as the population growth in the United States. Ordinarily, even a calamity of much smaller proportion (e.g., flooding in the Midwest) would garner a great deal of coverage and hype from a media usually eager to declare a crisis, yet less than one in five hundred articles in the *New York Times* and one in one thousand articles listed in the *Readers Guide to Periodic Literature* are on poverty. With remarkably little attention to them, the poor and their problems are hidden from most Americans.

When the media does turn its attention to the poor, it offers a series of contradictory messages and portrayals.

The Poor Are Faceless

Each year the Census Bureau releases a new report on poverty in our society and its results are duly reported in the media. At best, however, this coverage emphasizes annual fluctuations (showing how the numbers differ from previous years) and ongoing debates over the validity of the numbers (some argue the number should be lower, most that the number should be higher). Coverage like this desensitizes us to the poor by reducing poverty to a number. It ignores the human tragedy of poverty—the suffering, indignities, and misery endured by millions of children and adults. Instead, the poor become statistics rather than people.

The Poor Are Undeserving

When the media does put a face on the poor, it is not likely to be a pretty one. The media will provide us with sensational stories about welfare cheats, drug addicts, and greedy panhandlers (almost always urban and Black). Compare these images and the emotions evoked by them with the media's treatment of middle-class (usually white) "tax evaders," celebrities who have a "chemical dependency," or wealthy businesspeople who use unscrupulous means to "make a profit." While the behavior of the more affluent offenders is considered an "impropriety" and a deviation from the norm, the behavior of the poor is considered repugnant, indicative of the poor in general, and worthy of our indignation and resentment.

The Poor Are an Eyesore

When the media does cover the poor, they are often presented through the eyes of the middle class. For example, sometimes the media includes a story about community resistance to a homeless shelter or storekeeper annoyance with panhandlers. Rather than focusing on the plight of the poor, these stories are about middle-class opposition to the poor. Such stories tell us that the poor are an inconvenience and an irritation.

The Poor Have Only Themselves to Blame

In another example of media coverage, we are told that the poor live in a personal and cultural cycle of poverty that hopelessly imprisons them. They routinely center on the Black urban population and focus on perceived personality or cultural traits that doom the poor. While the women in these stories typically exhibit an "attitude" that leads to trouble or a promiscuity that leads to single motherhood, the men possess a need for immediate gratification that leads to drug abuse or an unquenchable greed that leads to the pursuit of fast money. The images that are seared into our mind are sexist, racist, and classist. Census figures reveal that most of the poor are white not Black or Hispanic, that they live in rural or suburban areas not urban centers, and hold jobs at least part of the year.[2] Yet, in a fashion that is often framed in an understanding and sympathetic tone, we are told that the poor have inflicted poverty on themselves.

The Poor Are Down on Their Luck

During the Christmas season, the news media sometimes provides us with accounts of poor individuals or families (usually white) who are down on their luck. These stories are often linked to stories about soup kitchens or other charitable activities and sometimes call for charitable contributions. These "Yule time" stories are as much about the affluent as they are about the poor: they tell us that the affluent in our society are a kind, understanding, giving people—which we are not.* The series of unfortunate circumstances that

---

*American households with incomes of less than $10,000 give an average of 5.5 percent of their earning to charity or to a religious organization, while those making more than $100,000 a year give only 2.9 percent. After changes in the 1986 tax code reduced the benefits of charitable giving, taxpayers earning $500,000 or more slashed their average donation by nearly one-third. Furthermore, many of these acts of benevolence do not help the needy. Rather than provide funding to social service agencies that aid the poor, the voluntary contributions of the wealthy go to places and institutions that entertain, inspire, cure, or educate wealthy Americans—art museums, opera houses, theaters, orchestras, ballet companies, private hospitals, and elite universities. (Robert Reich, "Secession of the Successful," *New York Times Magazine*, February 17, 1991, p. 43.)

have led to impoverishment are presumed to be a temporary condition that will improve with time and a change in luck.

Despite appearances, the messages provided by the media are not entirely disparate. With each variation, the media informs us what poverty is not (i.e., systemic and indicative of American society) by informing us what it is. The media tells us that poverty is either an aberration of the American way of life (it doesn't exist, it's just another number, it's unfortunate but temporary) or an end product of the poor themselves (they are a nuisance, do not deserve better, and have brought their predicament upon themselves).

By suggesting that the poor have brought poverty upon themselves, the media is engaging in what William Ryan has called "blaming the victim."[3] The media identifies in what ways the poor are different as a consequence of deprivation, then defines those differences as the cause of poverty itself. Whether blatantly hostile or cloaked in sympathy, the message is that there is something fundamentally wrong with the victims—their hormones, psychological makeup, family environment, community, race, or some combination of these—that accounts for their plight and their failure to lift themselves out of poverty.

But poverty in the United States is systemic. It is a direct result of economic and political policies that deprive people of jobs, adequate wages, or legitimate support. It is neither natural nor inevitable: there is enough wealth in our nation to eliminate poverty if we chose to redistribute existing wealth or income. The plight of the poor is reason enough to make the elimination of poverty the nation's first priority. But poverty also impacts dramatically on the non-poor. It has a dampening effect on wages in general (by maintaining a reserve army of unemployed and underemployed anxious for any job at any wage) and breeds crime and violence (by maintaining conditions that invite private gain by illegal means and rebellion-like behavior, not entirely unlike the urban riots of the 1960s). Given the extent of poverty in the nation and the impact it has on us all, the media must spin considerable magic to keep the poor and the issue of poverty and its root causes out of the public consciousness.

ABOUT EVERYONE ELSE

Both the broadcast and the print news media strive to develop a strong sense of "we-ness" in their audience. They seek to speak to and for an audience that is both affluent and like-minded. The media's solidarity with affluence, that is, with the middle and upper class, varies little from one medium to another. Benjamin DeMott points out, for example, that the *New York Times* understands affluence to be intelligence, taste, public spirit, responsibility, and a readiness to rule and "conceives itself as spokesperson for a readership awash in these qualities."[4] Of course, the flip side to creating a sense of "we," or "us," is establishing a perception of the "other." The other relates back to the faceless, amoral, undeserving, and inferior "underclass." Thus, the world according to the news media is divided between the "underclass" and everyone else. Again the messages are often contradictory.

The Wealthy Are Us

Much of the information provided to us by the news media focuses attention on the concerns of a very wealthy and privileged class of people. Although the concerns of a small fraction of the populace, they are presented as though they were the concerns of everyone. For example, while relatively few people actually own stock, the news media devotes an inordinate amount of broadcast time and print space to business news and stock market quotations. Not only do business reports cater to a particular narrow clientele, so do the fashion pages (with $2,000 dresses), wedding announcements, and the obituaries. Even weather and sports news often have a class bias. An all news radio station in New York City, for example, provides regular national ski reports. International news, trade agreements, and domestic policies issues are also reported in terms of their impact on business climate and the business community. Besides being of practical value to the wealthy, such coverage has considerable ideological value. Its message: the concerns of the wealthy are the concerns of us all.

The Wealthy (as a Class) Do Not Exist

While preoccupied with the concerns of the wealthy, the media fails to notice the way in which the rich as a class of people create and shape domestic and foreign policy. Presented as an aggregate of individuals, the wealthy appear without special interests, interconnections, or unity in purpose. Out of public view are the class interests of the wealthy, the interlocking business links, the concerted actions to preserve their class privileges and business interests (by running for public office, supporting political candidates, lobbying, etc.). Corporate lobbying is ignored, taken for granted, or assumed to be in the public interest. (Compare this with the media's portrayal of the "strong arm of labor" in attempting to defeat trade legislation that is harmful to the interests of working people.) It is estimated that two-thirds of the U.S. Senate is composed of millionaires.[5] Having such a preponderance of millionaires in the Senate, however, is perceived to be neither unusual nor antidemocratic; these millionaire senators are assumed to be serving "our" collective interests in governing.

The Wealthy Are Fascinating and Benevolent

The broadcast and print media regularly provide hype for individuals who have achieved "super" success. These stories are usually about celebrities and superstars from the sports and entertainment world. Society pages and gossip columns serve to keep the social elite informed of each others' doings, allow the rest of us to gawk at their excesses, and help to keep the American dream alive. The print media is also fond of feature stories on corporate empire builders. These stories provide an occasional "insider's" view of the private and corporate life of industrialists by suggesting a rags to riches account of corporate success. These stories tell us that corporate success is a series of smart moves, shrewd acquisitions, timely mergers, and well thought out executive suite shuffles. By painting the upper class in a positive light, innocent of any wrongdoing (labor leaders and union organizations usually get the opposite treatment), the media assures us that wealth and power are benevolent. One person's capital accumulation is presumed to be good for all. The elite, then, are portrayed as investment wizards, people of special talent and skill, who even their victims (workers and consumers) can admire.

The Wealthy Include a Few Bad Apples

On rare occasions, the media will mock selected individuals for their personality flaws. Real estate investor Donald Trump and New York Yankees owner George Steinbrenner, for example, are admonished by the media for deliberately seeking publicity (a very un-upper class thing to do); hotel owner Leona Helmsley was caricatured for her personal cruelties; and junk bond broker Michael Milkin was condemned because he had the audacity to rob the rich. Michael Parenti points out that by treating business wrongdoings as isolated deviations from the socially beneficial system of "responsible capitalism," the media overlooks the features of the system that produce such abuses and the regularity with which they occur. Rather than portraying them as predictable and frequent outcomes of corporate power and the business system, the media treats abuses as if they were isolated and atypical. Presented as an occasional aberration, these incidents serve not to challenge, but to legitimate, the system.[6]

The Middle Class Is Us

By ignoring the poor and blurring the lines between the working people and the upper class, the news media creates a universal middle class. From this perspective, the size of one's income becomes largely irrelevant: what matters is that most of "us" share an intellectual and moral superiority over the disadvantaged. As *Time* magazine once concluded, "Middle America is a state of mind."[7] "We are all middle class," we are told, "and we all share the same concerns": job security, inflation, tax burdens, world peace, the cost of food and housing, health care, clean air and water, and the safety of our streets. While the concerns of the wealthy are quite distinct from those of the middle class (e.g., the wealthy worry about investments, not jobs), the media convinces us that "we [the affluent] are all in this together."

The Middle Class Is a Victim

For the media, "we" the affluent not only stand apart from the "other"—the poor, the working class, the minorities, and their problems—"we" are also victimized by the poor (who drive up the costs of maintaining the welfare roles), minorities (who commit crimes against us), and by workers (who are greedy and drive companies out and prices up). Ignored are the subsidies to the rich, the crimes of corporate America, and the policies that wreak havoc on the economic well-being of middle America. Media magic convinces us to fear, more than anything else, being victimized by those less affluent than ourselves.

The Middle Class Is Not a Working Class

The news media clearly distinguishes the middle class (employees) from the working class (i.e., blue collar workers) who are portrayed, at best, as irrelevant, outmoded, and a dying breed. Furthermore, the media will tell us that the hardships faced by blue collar workers are inevitable (due to progress), a result of bad luck (chance circumstances in a particular industry), or a product of their own doing (they priced themselves out of a job). Given the media's presentation of reality, it is hard to believe that manual, supervised, unskilled, and semiskilled workers actually represent more than 50 percent of the adult working population.[8] The working class, instead, is relegated by the media to "the other."

In short, the news media either lionizes the wealthy or treats their interests and those of the middle class as one in the same. But the upper class and the middle class do not share the same interests or worries. Members of the upper class worry about stock dividends (not employment), they profit from inflation and global militarism, their children attend exclusive private schools, they eat and live in a royal fashion, they call on (or are called upon by) personal physicians, they have few consumer problems, they can escape whenever they want from environmental pollution, and they live on streets and travel to other areas under the protection of private police forces.*[9]

---

*The number of private security guards in the United States now exceeds the number of public police officers. (Robert Reich, "Secession of the Successful," *New York Times Magazine*, February 17, 1991, p. 42.)

The wealthy are not only a class with distinct life-styles and interests, they are a ruling class. They receive a disproportionate share of the country's yearly income, own a disproportionate amount of the country's wealth, and contribute a disproportionate number of their members to governmental bodies and decision-making groups—all traits that William Domhoff, in his classic work *Who Rules America*, defined as characteristic of a governing class.[10]

This governing class maintains and manages our political and economic structures in such a way that these structures continue to yield an amazing proportion of our wealth to a minuscule upper class. While the media is not above referring to ruling classes in other countries (we hear, for example, references to Japan's ruling elite),[11] its treatment of the news proceeds as though there were no such ruling class in the United States.

Furthermore, the news media inverts reality so that those who are working class and middle class learn to fear, resent, and blame those below, rather than those above them in the class structure. We learn to resent welfare, which accounts for only two cents out of every dollar in the federal budget (approximately $10 billion) and provides financial relief for the needy,* but learn little about the $11 billion the federal government spends on individuals with incomes in excess of $100,000 (not needy),[12] or the $17 billion in farm subsidies, or the $214 billion (twenty times the cost of welfare) in interest payments to financial institutions.

Middle-class whites learn to fear African Americans and Latinos, but most violent crime occurs within poor and minority communities and is neither interracial† nor interclass. As horrid as such crime is, it should not mask the destruction and violence perpetrated by corporate America. In spite of the fact that 14,000 innocent people are killed on the job each year, 100,000 die prematurely, 400,000 become seriously ill, and 6 million are injured from work-related accidents and diseases, most Americans fear government regulation more than they do unsafe working conditions.

Through the media, middle-class—and even working-class—Americans learn to blame blue collar workers and their unions for declining purchasing power and economic security. But while workers who managed to keep their jobs and their unions struggled to keep up with inflation, the top 1 percent of American families saw their average incomes soar 80 percent in the last decade.[13] Much of the wealth at the top was accumulated as stockholders and

---

*A total of $20 billion is spent on welfare when you include all state funding. But the average state funding also comes to only two cents per state dollar.

† In 92 percent of the murders nationwide the assailant and the victim are of the same race (46 percent are white/white, 46 percent are black/black), 5.6 percent are black on white, and 2.4 percent are white on black. (FBI and Bureau of Justice Statistics, 1985–1986, quoted in Raymond S. Franklin, *Shadows of Race and Class*, University of Minnesota Press, Minneapolis, 1991, p. 108.)

corporate executives moved their companies abroad to employ cheaper labor (56 cents per hour in El Salvador) and avoid paying taxes in the United States. Corporate America is a world made up of ruthless bosses, massive layoffs, favoritism and nepotism, health and safety violations, pension plan losses, union busting, tax evasions, unfair competition, and price gouging, as well as fast buck deals, financial speculation, and corporate wheeling and dealing that serve the interests of the corporate elite, but are generally wasteful and destructive to workers and the economy in general.

It is no wonder Americans cannot think straight about class. The mass media is neither objective, balanced, independent, nor neutral. Those who own and direct the mass media are themselves part of the upper class, and neither they nor the ruling class in general have to conspire to manipulate public opinion. Their interest is in preserving the status quo, and their view of society as fair and equitable comes naturally to them. But their ideology dominates our society and justifies what is in reality a perverse social order—one that perpetuates unprecedented elite privilege and power on the one hand and widespread deprivation on the other. A mass media that did not have its own class interests in preserving the status quo would acknowledge that inordinate wealth and power undermines democracy and that a "free market" economy can ravage a people and their communities.

NOTES

1. Martin Lee and Norman Solomon, *Unreliable Sources*, Lyle Stuart (New York, 1990), p. 71. See also Ben Bagdikian, *The Media Monopoly*, Beacon Press (Boston, 1990).

2. Department of Commerce, Bureau of the Census, "Poverty in the United States: 92," *Current Population Reports, Consumer Income*, Series P60-185, pp. xi, xv, 1.

3. William Ryan, *Blaming the Victim*, Vintage (New York, 1971).

4. Benjamin Demott, *The Imperial Middle*, William Morrow (New York, 1990), p. 123.

5. Fred Barnes, "The Zillionaires Club," *The New Republic*, January 29, 1990, p. 24.

6. Michael Parenti, *Inventing Reality*, St. Martin's Press (New York, 1986), p. 109.

7. *Time*, January 5, 1979, p. 10.

8. Vincent Navarro, "The Middle Class—A Useful Myth," *The Nation*, March 23, 1992, p. 1.

9. Charles Anderson, *The Political Economy of Social Class*, Prentice Hall (Englewood Cliffs, N.J., 1974), p. 137.

10. William Domhoff, *Who Rules America*, Prentice Hall (Englewood Cliffs, N.J., 1967), p. 5.

11. Lee and Solomon, *Unreliable Sources*, p. 179.

12. *Newsweek*, August 10, 1992, p. 57.

13. *Business Week*, June 8, 1992, p. 86.

45

THE MYTH OF THE LATIN WOMAN
I Just Met a Girl Named María

Judith Ortiz Cofer

On a bus trip to London from Oxford University, where I was earning some graduate credits one summer, a young man, obviously fresh from a pub, spotted me and as if struck by inspiration went down on his knees in the aisle. With both hands over his heart he broke into an Irish tenor's rendition of "María" from *West Side Story*. My politely amused fellow passengers gave his lovely voice the round of gentle applause it deserved. Though I was not quite as amused, I managed my version of an English smile: no show of teeth, no extreme contortions of the facial muscles—I was at this time of my life practicing reserve and cool. Oh, that British control, how I coveted it. But María had followed me to London, reminding me of a prime fact of my life: you can leave the Island, master the English language, and travel as far as you can, but if you are a Latina, especially one like me who so obviously belongs to Rita Moreno's gene pool, the Island travels with you.

This is sometimes a very good thing—it may win you that extra minute of someone's attention. But with some people, the same things can make *you* an island—not so much a tropical paradise as an Alcatraz, a place nobody wants to visit. As a Puerto Rican girl growing up in the United States and wanting like most children to "belong," I resented the stereotype that my Hispanic appearance called forth from many people I met.

Our family lived in a large urban center in New Jersey during the sixties, where life was designed as a microcosm of my parents' casas on the island. We spoke in Spanish, we ate Puerto Rican food bought at the bodega, and we practiced strict Catholicism complete with Saturday confession and Sunday mass at a church where our parents were accommodated into a one-hour Spanish mass slot, performed by a Chinese priest trained as a missionary for Latin America.

As a girl I was kept under strict surveillance, since virtue and modesty were, by cultural equation, the same as family honor. As a teenager I was instructed on how to behave as a proper señorita. But it was a conflicting message girls got, since the Puerto Rican mothers also encouraged their

From Judith Ortiz Cofer, *The Latin Deli: Prose & Poetry* (Athens: University of Georgia Press, 1993). Copyright © 1993 by Judith Ortiz Cofer. Reprinted by permission of the publisher.

daughters to look and act like women and to dress in clothes our Anglo friends and their mothers found too "mature" for our age. It was, and is, cultural, yet I often felt humiliated when I appeared at an American friend's party wearing a dress more suitable to a semiformal than to a playroom birthday celebration. At Puerto Rican festivities, neither the music nor the colors we wore could be too loud. I still experience a vague sense of letdown when I'm invited to a "party" and it turns out to be a marathon conversation in hushed tones rather than a fiesta with salsa, laughter, and dancing—the kind of celebration I remember from my childhood.

I remember Career Day in our high school, when teachers told us to come dressed as if for a job interview. It quickly became obvious that to the barrio girls, "dressing up" sometimes meant wearing ornate jewelry and clothing that would be more appropriate (by mainstream standards) for the company Christmas party than as daily office attire. That morning I had agonized in front of my closet, trying to figure out what a "career girl" would wear because, essentially, except for Marlo Thomas on TV, I had no models on which to base my decision. I knew how to dress for school: at the Catholic school I attended we all wore uniforms; I knew how to dress for Sunday mass, and I knew what dresses to wear for parties at my relatives' homes. Though I do not recall the precise details of my Career Day outfit, it must have been a composite of the above choices. But I remember a comment my friend (an Italian-American) made in later years that coalesced my impressions of that day. She said that at the business school she was attending the Puerto Rican girls always stood out for wearing "everything at once." She meant, of course, too much jewelry, too many accessories. On that day at school, we were simply made the negative models by the nuns who were themselves not credible fashion experts to any of us. But it was painfully obvious to me that to the others, in their tailored skirts and silk blouses, we must have seemed "hopeless" and "vulgar." Though I now know that most adolescents feel out of step much of the time, I also know that for the Puerto Rican girls of my generation that sense was intensified. The way our teachers and classmates looked at us that day in school was just a taste of the culture clash that awaited us in the real world, where prospective employers and men on the street would often misinterpret our tight skirts and jingling bracelets as a come-on.

Mixed cultural signals have perpetuated certain stereotypes—for example, that of the Hispanic woman as the "Hot Tamale" or sexual firebrand. It is a one-dimensional view that the media have found easy to promote. In their special vocabulary, advertisers have designated "sizzling" and "smoldering" as the adjectives of choice for describing not only the foods but also the women of Latin America. From conversations in my house I recall hearing about the harassment that Puerto Rican women endured in factories where the "boss men" talked to them as if sexual innuendo was all they understood and, worse, often gave them the choice of submitting to advances or being fired.

It is custom, however, not chromosomes, that leads us to choose scarlet over pale pink. As young girls, we were influenced in our decisions about clothes and colors by the women—older sisters and mothers who had grown up on a tropical island where the natural environment was a riot of primary colors, where showing your skin was one way to keep cool as well as to look sexy. Most important of all, on the island, women perhaps felt freer to dress and move more provocatively, since, in most cases, they were protected by the traditions, mores, and laws of a Spanish/Catholic system of morality and machismo whose main rule was: *You may look at my sister, but if you touch her I will kill you.* The extended family and church structure could provide a young woman with a circle of safety in her small pueblo on the Island; if a man "wronged" a girl, everyone would close in to save her family honor.

This is what I have gleaned from my discussions as an adult with older Puerto Rican women. They have told me about dressing in their best party clothes on Saturday nights and going to the town's plaza to promenade with their girlfriends in front of the boys they liked. The males were thus given an opportunity to admire the women and to express their admiration in the form of *piropos:* erotically charged street poems they composed on the spot. I have been subjected to a few piropos while visiting the Island, and they can be outrageous, although custom dictates that they must never cross into obscenity. This ritual, as I understand it, also entails a show of studied indifference on the woman's part; if she is "decent," she must not acknowledge the man's impassioned words. So I do understand how things can be lost in translation. When a Puerto Rican girl dressed in her idea of what is attractive meets a man from the mainstream culture who has been trained to react to certain types of clothing as a sexual signal, a clash is likely to take place. The line I first heard based on this aspect of the myth happened when the boy who took me to my first formal dance leaned over to plant a sloppy overeager kiss painfully on my mouth, and when I didn't respond with sufficient passion said in a resentful tone: "I thought you Latin girls were supposed to mature early"—my first instance of being thought of as a fruit or vegetable—I was supposed to *ripen,* not just grow into womanhood like other girls.

It is surprising to some of my professional friends that some people, including those who should know better, still put others "in their place." Though rarer, these incidents are still commonplace in my life. It happened to me most recently during a stay at a very classy metropolitan hotel favored by young professional couples for their weddings. Late one evening after the theater, as I walked toward my room with my new colleague (a woman with whom I was coordinating an arts program), a middle-aged man in a tuxedo, a young girl in satin and lace on his arm, stepped directly into our path. With his champagne glass extended toward me, he exclaimed, "Evita!"

Our way blocked, my companion and I listened as the man half-recited, half-bellowed "Don't Cry for Me, Argentina." When he finished, the young girl said: "How about a round of applause for my daddy?" We complied, hoping this would bring the silly spectacle to a close. I was becoming aware that our little group was attracting the attention of the other guests. "Daddy" must have perceived this too, and he once more barred the way as we tried to walk past him. He began to shout-sing a ditty to the tune of "La Bamba"—except the lyrics were about a girl named María whose exploits all rhymed with her name and gonorrhea. The girl kept saying "Oh, Daddy" and looking at me with pleading eyes. She wanted me to laugh along with the others. My companion and I stood silently waiting for the man to end his offensive song. When he finished, I looked not at him but at his daughter. I advised her calmly never to ask her father what he had done in the army. Then I walked between them and to my room. My friend complimented me on my cool handling of the situation. I confessed to her that I really had wanted to push the jerk into the swimming pool. I knew that this same man—probably a corporate executive, well educated, even worldly by most standards—would not have been likely to regale a white woman with a dirty song in public. He would perhaps have checked his impulse by assuming that she could be somebody's wife or mother, or at least *somebody* who might take offense. But to him, I was just an Evita or a María: merely a character in his cartoon-populated universe.

Because of my education and my proficiency with the English language, I have acquired many mechanisms for dealing with the anger I experience. This was not true for my parents, nor is it true for the many Latin women working at menial jobs who must put up with stereotypes about our ethnic group such as: "They make good domestics." This is another facet of the myth of the Latin women in the United States. Its origin is simple to deduce. Work as domestics, waitressing, and factory jobs are all that's available to women with little English and few skills. The myth of the Hispanic menial has been sustained by the same media phenomenon that made "Mammy" from *Gone with the Wind* America's idea of the black woman for generations; María, the housemaid or counter girl, is now indelibly etched into the national psyche. The big and the little screens have presented us with the picture of the funny Hispanic maid, mispronouncing words and cooking up a spicy storm in a shiny California kitchen.

This media-engendered image of the Latina in the United States has been documented by feminist Hispanic scholars, who claim that such portrayals are partially responsible for the denial of opportunities for upward mobility among Latinas in the professions. I have a Chicana friend working on a Ph.D. in philosophy at a major university. She says her doctor still shakes his head in puzzled amazement at all the "big words" she uses. Since I do not wear my diplomas around my neck for all to see, I too have on occasion been sent to that "kitchen," where some think I obviously belong.

One such incident that has stayed with me, though I recognize it as a minor offense, happened on the day of my first public poetry reading. It took place in Miami in a boat-restaurant where we were having lunch before the event. I was nervous and excited as I walked in with my notebook in hand. An older woman motioned me to her table. Thinking (foolish me) that she wanted me to autograph a copy of my brand new slender volume of verse, I went over. She ordered a cup of coffee from me, assuming that I was the wait-ress. Easy enough to mistake my poems for menus, I suppose. I know that it wasn't an intentional act of cruelty, yet with all the good things that happened that day, I remember that scene most clearly, because it reminded me of what I had to overcome before anyone would take me seriously. In retrospect I un-derstand that my anger gave my reading fire, that I have almost always taken doubts in my abilities as a challenge—and that the result is, most times, a feeling of satisfaction at having won a convert when I see the cold, appraising eyes warm to my words, the body language change, the smile that indicates that I have opened some avenue for communication. That day I read to that woman and her lowered eyes told me that she was embarrassed at her little faux pas, and when I willed her to look up to me, it was my victory, and she graciously allowed me to punish her with my full attention. We shook hands at the end of the reading, and I never saw her again. She has probably forgot-ten the whole thing but maybe not.

Yet I am one of the lucky ones. My parents made it possible for me to ac-quire a stronger footing in the mainstream culture by giving me the chance at an education. And books and art have saved me from the harsher forms of ethnic and racial prejudice that many of my Hispanic *compañeras* have had to endure. I travel a lot around the United States, reading from my books of poetry and my novel, and the reception I most often receive is one of positive interest by people who want to know more about my culture. There are, how-ever, thousands of Latinas without the privilege of an education or the entrée into society that I have. For them life is a struggle against the misconceptions perpetuated by the myth of the Latina as whore, domestic, or criminal. We cannot change this by legislating the way people look at us. The transforma-tion, as I see it, has to occur at a much more individual level. My personal goal in my public life is to try to replace the old pervasive stereotypes and myths about Latinas with a much more interesting set of realities. Every time I give a reading, I hope the stories I tell, the dreams and fears I examine in my work, can achieve some universal truth which will get my audience past the particu-lars of my skin color, my accent, or my clothes.

I once wrote a poem in which I called us Latinas "God's brown daugh-ters." This poem is really a prayer of sorts, offered upward, but also, through the human-to-human channel of art, outward. It is a prayer for communica-tion, and for respect. In it, Latin women pray "in Spanish to an Anglo God / with a Jewish heritage," and they are "fervently hoping / that if not omnipo-tent, / at least He be bilingual."

46

GLADIATORS, GAZELLES, AND GROUPIES
Basketball Love and Loathing

Julianne Malveaux

The woman in me loves the sheer physical impact of a basketball game. I don't dwell on the fine points, the three-point shot or the overtime, and can't even tell you which teams make me sweat (though I could have told you twenty years ago). I can tell you, though, how much I enjoy watching mostly black men engage in an elegantly (and sometimes inelegantly) skilled game, and how engrossing the pace and physicality can be. In my younger days, I spent hours absorbed by street basketball games, taking the subway to watch the Rucker Pros in upper Manhattan, hanging on a bench near the basketball courts on West Fourth Street in the Village. I didn't consider myself a basketball groupie—I was a nerd who liked the game. Still, there is something about muscled, scantily clad men (the shorts have gotten longer in the 1990s) that spoke to me. Once I even joked that watching basketball games was like safe sex in the age of AIDS. Yes, the woman in me, even in my maturity, loves the physical impact of a basketball game, a game where muscles strain, sweat flies, and intensity demands attention.

The feminist in me abhors professional basketball and the way it reinforces gender stereotypes. Men play, women watch. Men at the center, women at the periphery, and eagerly so. Men making millions, women scheming to get to some of the millions through their sex and sexuality. The existence of the Women's National Basketball Association hardly ameliorates my loathing for the patriarchal underbelly of the basketball sport, since women players are paid a scant fraction of men's pay and attract a fraction of the live and television audience. To be sure, women's basketball will grow and develop and perhaps even provide men with role models of what sportsmanship should be. I am also emphatically clear that basketball isn't the only patriarchy in town. Despite women's participation in politics it, too, is a patriarchy, with too many women plying sex and sexuality as their stock in trade, as the impeachment imbroglio of 1998–99 reminds us.

From Todd Boyd and Kenneth L. Shropshire, eds., *Basketball Jones: America Above the Rim* (New York: New York University Press, 2000), pp. 51–58. Reprinted by permission of New York University Press.

The race person in me has mixed feelings about basketball. On one hand, I enjoy seeing black men out there making big bank, the kind of bank they can't make in business, science, or more traditional forms of work. On the other hand, I'm aware of the minuscule odds that any high school hoopster will become a Michael Jordan. If some young brothers spent less time on the hoops and more in the labs, perhaps the investment of time in chemistry would yield the same mega-millions that professional basketball does. This is hardly the sole fault of the youngsters with NBA aspirations. It is also the responsibility of coaches to introduce a reality check to those young people whose future focus is exclusively on basketball. And it is society's responsibility to make sure there are opportunities for young men, especially young African American men, outside basketball. The athletic scholarship should not be the sole passport to college for low-income young men. Broader access to quality education must be a societal mandate; encouraging young African American men to focus on higher education is critical to our nation's fullest development.

Professional basketball bears an unfortunate similarity to an antebellum plantation, with some coaches accustomed to barking orders and uttering racial expletives to get maximum performance from their players. While few condone the fact that Latrell Sprewell, then of the Golden State Warriors, choked his coach P. J. Carlesimo in 1997, many understand that rude, perhaps racist, but certainly dismissive treatment motivated his violent action. The race of coaches, writers, and commentators, in contrast to that of the players, often has broader racial implications. White players whose grammar needs a boost often get it from sportswriters, who make them sound far more erudite than they are. The same writers quote black players with exaggerated, cringe-producing broken English—"dis," "dat," "dese," and "dose"—almost a parody of language. White commentators frequently remark on the "natural talent" of black players, compared to the skill of white ones. Retired white players are more likely to get invitations to coach and manage than are their black counterparts.

Despite this plantation tension, there are those who tout the integration in basketball as something lofty and desirable and the sport itself as one that teaches discipline, teamwork, and structure. In *Values of the Game*, former New Jersey senator and 2000 presidential candidate Bill Bradley describes the game as one of passion, discipline, selflessness, respect, perspective, courage, and other virtues. Though Bradley took a singular position as a senator in lifting up the issue of police brutality around the Rodney King beating, his record on race matters is otherwise relatively unremarkable. But Bradley gets credit for being far more racially progressive than he actually is because he, a white man, played for the New York Knicks for a decade, living at close quarters with African American men.

As onerous as I find the basketball plantation, the race person in me wonders why I am so concerned about the gladiators. Few if any of them exhibit anything that vaguely resembles social consciousness. Michael Jordan, for example, passed on the opportunity to make a real difference in the 1990 North Carolina Senate race between the former Charlotte mayor and Democratic candidate, the African American architect Harvey Gantt, and the ultra-conservative and racially manipulative Republican senator Jesse Helms, preferring to save his endorsements for Nike. Charles Barkley once arrogantly crowed that he was not a role model, ignoring the biblical adage that much is expected of those to whom much is given. Few of the players, despite their millions, invest in the black community and in black economic development. Magic Johnson is a notable exception, with part ownership in a Los Angeles–based black bank and development of a theater chain that has the potential for revitalizing otherwise abandoned inner-city communities. Johnson's example notwithstanding, basketball players are more likely to make headlines for their shenanigans than for giving back to the community.

With my mixed feelings, love and loathing, why pay attention to basketball at all? Why not tune it out as forcefully as I tune out anything else I'm disinterested in? The fact is that it is nearly impossible to tune out, turn off, or ignore basketball. It is a cultural delimiter, a national export, a medium through which messages about race, gender, and power are transmitted not only nationally but also internationally. As Walter LaFeber observes in his book, *Michael Jordan and the New Global Capitalism*, Mr. Jordan's imagery has been used not only to sell the basketball game and Nike shoes but to make hundreds of millions of dollars for both Mr. Jordan and the companies he represents. Jordan is not to be faulted for brokering his skill into millions of dollars. Still, the mode and methods of his enrichment make the game of basketball a matter of intellectual curiosity as one explores the way in which capitalism and popular culture intersect. Jordan's millions, interesting as they may be, are less interesting than the way in which media have created his iconic status in both domestic and world markets and offered him up as a role model of the reasonable, affable African American man, the antithesis of "bad boy" trash talkers who so frequently garner headlines.

From a gender perspective, too, there is another set of questions. What would a woman have to do to achieve the same influence, iconic status, and bankability as Jordan? Is it even conceivable, in a patriarchal world, that a woman could earn, gain, or be invented in as iconic a status as a Michael Jordan? A woman might sing—but songbirds come and go and aren't often connected with international marketing of consumer products. She might dance—but that, too, would not turn into international marketability. She might possess the dynamic athleticism of the tennis-playing Williams sisters, Venus and Serena, or she might have the ethereal beauty of a Halle Berry. In either case, her product identification would solely be connected with "women's" products—hair, beauty, and women's sports items. The commercial heavy lifting has been left to the big boys, or to one big boy in particular, Michael Jordan.

To be sure, the public acceptance of women's sports has changed. Thanks to Title IX, women's sports get better funding and more attention at the college level than they did only decades ago. After several fits and starts, the professional women's basketball league seems to be doing well, although not as well as the NBA. In time this may change, but my informal survey of male basketball fans suggests that some find women's basketball simply less entertaining than the NBA. "When women start dunking and trash talking, more people will start watching," said a man active in establishing Midnight Basketball teams in urban centers. If this is the case, then it raises questions both about women's basketball and about the tension between male players and officials about on-court buffoonery. Do officials kill the goose that laid the golden egg when they ask a Dennis Rodman to "behave himself"?

My ire is not about gender envy; it is about imagery and the replication of gender-oppressive patterns by using basketball, especially, to connect an image of sportsmanship, masculinity, with product identification. In a commercial context that promotes this connection, there is both a subtle and a not-so-subtle message about the status of women.

There is also a set of subtle messages about race and race relations that emerges when African American men are used in the same way that African American women were used in the "trade cards" of the early twentieth century. In the patriarchal context, hoopsters become hucksters while the invisible (white) male role as power broker is reinforced. In too many ways the rules and profit of the game reinforce the rules, profit, and history of American life, with iconic gladiators serving as symbols and servants of multinational interests. Black men who entertain serve as stalkers for white men who measure profits. Neutered black men can join their white colleagues in chachinging cash registers but can never unlock the golden handcuffs and the platinum muzzles that limit their ability to generate independent opinions. Women? Always seen, never heard. Ornamental or invisible assets. Pawns in an unspoken game.

A subtext of the basketball culture relegates women, especially African American women, to a peripheral, dependent, and soap-operatic role. These women are sometimes seen as sources of trouble (as in the imbroglio with the Washington then Bullets, now Wizards, where apparently false rape charges spotlighted the lives of two players and perhaps changed the long-term composition of the team). Or they are depicted (for example, in a 1998 *Sports Illustrated* feature) as predatory sperm collectors, whose pregnancies are part of a "plot" to collect child support from high-earning hoopsters.

There are aspects to some women's behavior in relationship with basketball stars that are hardly laudable. (Some of this is detailed in the fictional *Homecourt Advantage*, written by two basketball significant others.) At the same time, it is clear that this behavior is more a symptom than a cause of predatory patriarchy. After all, no one forces a player into bed or into a relationship with an unscrupulous woman. But conditions often make a player irresistible to women whose search for legitimacy comes through attachment to a man.

The disproportionate attention and influence that the basketball lifestyle gives some men makes them thoroughly irresistible to some women. This begs the question: In a patriarchy, just what can women do to attain the same influence and irresistibility? In a patriarchy, male games are far more intriguing than female games. Women, spectators, can watch and attach themselves to high-achieving gladiators. There is little that they can do, in the realm of sport, capitalism, and imagery, to gain the same access that men have. Again, this is not restricted to basketball but is a reflection of gender roles in our society. One might describe this as the "Hillary Rodham Clinton dilemma." Does a woman gain more power and influence by developing her own career or by attaching herself to a powerful man?

This dilemma may be a short-term one, given changes in the status of women in our society. Still, a range of scholars have noted that while women have come a long way, with higher incomes, higher levels of labor-force participation, and increased representation in executive ranks, at the current pace, income equality (which may not be the equivalent of the breakdown of patriarchy) will occur in the middle of the twenty-first century.

Those who depict the basketball culture have been myopic in their focus on the men who shoot hoops, because their coverage has ignored the humanity of the women who hover around hoopsters like moths drawn to a flame. Those writers who are eager to write about the "paternity ward" or about "Darwin's athletes" might also ask how the gender relations in basketball replicate or differ from gender relations in our society. Unfortunately, gender relations in basketball are too often the norm in society. Men play, women watch. To the extent that the basketball culture is elevated, women's roles are denigrated. Why are we willing to endow male hoopsters with a status that no woman can attain in our society? Sedentary men sing the praises of male hoopsters, sit enthralled and engrossed by their games, thus elevating a certain form of achievement in our society. This behavior is seen as normal, even laudable. Yet it takes women, often the daughters or sisters of these enthralled men, out of the iconic, high-achievement mix and pushes them to the periphery of a culture that reveres the athletic achievement derived from the combination of basketball prowess and patriarchy.

The combination of prowess and patriarchy denigrates the groupie who is attracted by the bright lights, but it also dehumanizes the swift gazelle, the gladiator, and the hoopster, whose humanity is negated by his basketball identity. Media coverage depicts young men out of control, trash-talking, wild-walking, attention-grabbing icons. Men play, women watch. Were there other center stages, this would be of limited interest. But the fact is that this stage is one from which other stages reverberate. Men play, women watch, in politics, economics, technology, and sports. And it is "blown up" into international cultural supremacy in basketball.

This woman watches, with love and loathing, the way basketball norms reinforce those that exist in our society. It is a triumph of patriarchy, this exuberance of masculine physicality. It is a reminder to women that feminism notwithstanding, we have yet to gain economic and cultural equivalency with Michael Jordan's capitalist dominance. While we should not, perhaps, ask men to walk away from arenas in which they can dominate, we must ask ourselves why there is no equivalent space for us; why the basketball tenet that men play, women watch, reverberates in so many other sectors of our society.

References

Bradley, Bill. *Values of the Game*. New York: Artisan Press, 1998.

Ewing, Rita, and Crystal McCrary. *Homecourt Advantage*. New York: Avon Books, 1998.

Frey, Darcy. *The Last Shot: City Street, Basketball Dreams*. Boston: Houghton Mifflin, 1994.

Hoberman, John. *Darwin's Athletes: How Sport Has Damaged Black America and Preserved the Myth of Race*. New York: Mariner Books, 1997.

LaFeber, Walter. *Michael Jordan and the New Global Capitalism*. New York: W. W. Norton & Co., 1999.

Wahl, Grant, and L. Jon Wertheim. "Paternity Ward." *Sports Illustrated*, May 4, 1998, at 62.

47

CAN EDUCATION ELIMINATE RACE, CLASS, AND GENDER INEQUALITY?

Roslyn Arlin Mickelson and Stephen Samuel Smith

INTRODUCTION

Parents, politicians, and educational policy makers share the belief that a "good education" is *the* meal ticket. It will unlock the door to economic opportunity and thus enable disadvantaged groups or individuals to improve their lot dramatically.[1] This belief is one of the assumptions that has long been part of the American Dream. According to the putative dominant ideology, the United States is basically a meritocracy in which hard work and individual effort are rewarded, especially in financial terms.[2] Related to this central belief are a series of culturally enshrined misconceptions about poverty and wealth. The central one is that poverty and wealth are the result of individual inadequacies or strengths rather than the results of the distributive mechanisms of the capitalist economy. A second misconception is the belief that everyone is the master of her or his own fate. The dominant ideology assumes that American society is open and competitive, a place where an individual's status depends on talent and motivation, not inherited position, connections, or privileges linked to ascriptive characteristics like gender or race. To compete fairly, everyone must have access to education free of the fetters of family background, gender, and race. Since the middle of this century, the reform policies of the federal government have been designed, at least officially, to enhance individuals' opportunities to acquire education. The question we will explore in this essay is whether expanding educational opportunity is enough to reduce the inequalities of race, social class, and gender which continue to characterize U.S. society.

We begin by discussing some of the major educational policies and programs of the past forty-five years that sought to reduce social inequality through expanding equality of educational opportunity. This discussion highlights the success and failures of programs such as school desegregation, compensatory education, Title IX, and job training. We then focus on the barriers these programs face in actually reducing social inequality. Our point is that inequality is so deeply rooted in the structure and operation of the U.S. political economy, that, at best, educational reforms can play only a limited role in ameliorating such inequality. In fact, there is considerable evidence that indicates that, for poor and many minority children, education helps legitimate, if not actually reproduce, significant aspects of social inequality in their lives. Finally, we speculate about education's potential role in individual and social transformation.

First, it is necessary to distinguish among equality, equality of opportunity, and equality of educational opportunity. The term *equality* has been the subject of extensive scholarly and political debate, much of which is beyond the scope of this essay. Most Americans reject equality of life conditions as a goal, because it would require a fundamental transformation of our basic economic and political institutions, a scenario most are unwilling to accept. As Ralph Waldo Emerson put it, "The genius of our country has worked out our true policy—opportunity."

The distinction between equality of opportunity and equality of outcome is important. Through this country's history, equality has most typically been understood in the former way. Rather than a call for the equal distribution of money, property, or many other social goods, the concern over equality has been with equal opportunity in pursuit of these goods. In the words of Jennifer Hochschild, "So long as we live in a democratic capitalist society—that is, so long as we maintain the formal promise of political and social equality while encouraging the practice of economic inequality—we need the idea of equal opportunity to bridge that otherwise unacceptable contradiction."[3] To use a current metaphor: If life is a game, the playing field must be level; if life is a race, the starting line must be in the same place for everyone. For the playing field to be level, many believe education is crucial because it gives individuals the wherewithal to compete in the allegedly meritocratic system. In America, then, *equality* is really understood to mean *equality of opportunity*, which itself hinges on *equality of educational opportunity*.

THE SPOTTY RECORD OF FEDERAL EDUCATIONAL REFORMS

In the past [fifty] years, a series of educational reforms initiated at the national level has been introduced into local school systems. All of the reforms aimed to move education closer to the ideal of equality of educational opportunity. Here we discuss several of these reforms, and how the concept of equality of educational opportunity has evolved. Given the importance of race and racism in U.S. history, many of the federal education policies during this period attempted to redress the most egregious forms of inequality based on race.

School Desegregation

Although American society has long claimed to be based on equality of opportunity, the history of race relations suggests the opposite. Perhaps the most influential early discussion of this disparity was Gunnar Myrdal's *An American Dilemma*, published in 1944. The book vividly exposed the contradictions between the ethos of freedom, justice, equality of opportunity and the actual experiences of African Americans in the United States.[4]

The links among desegregation, expanded educational opportunity, and the larger issue of equality of opportunity are very clear from the history of the desegregation movement. This movement, whose first phase culminated in the 1954 *Brown* decision outlawing *de jure* segregation in school, was the first orchestrated attempt in U.S. history to directly address inequality of educational opportunity. The NAACP strategically chose school segregation to be the camel's nose under the tent of the Jim Crow (segregated) society. That one of the nation's foremost civil rights organizations saw the attack on segregated schools as the opening salvo in the battle against society-wide inequality is a powerful example of the American belief that education has a pivotal role in promoting equality of opportunity.

Has desegregation succeeded? This is really three questions: First, to what extent are the nation's schools desegregated? Second, have desegregation efforts enhanced students' academic outcomes? Third, what are the long-term outcomes of desegregated educational experiences?

Since 1954, progress toward the desegregation of the nation's public schools has been uneven and limited. Blacks experienced little progress in desegregation until the mid-1960s when, in response to the civil rights movement, a series of federal laws, executive actions, and judicial decisions resulted in significant gains, especially in the South. Progress continued until 1988, when the effects of a series of federal court decisions and various local and national political developments precipitated marked trends toward the resegregation of Black students. Nationally, in 1994–1995, 33 percent of Black students attended majority White schools compared with the approximately 37 percent who attended majority White schools for much of the 1980s.[5]

Historically, Latinos were relatively less segregated than African Americans. However, from the mid-1960s to the mid-1990s there was a steady increase in the percentage of the Latino students who attended segregated schools. As a result, education for Latinos is now more segregated than it is for Blacks.

Given the long history of legalized segregation in the south, it is ironic that the South's school systems are now generally the country's most *de*segregated, while those in the northeast are the most intensely segregated. However, even desegregated schools are often resegregated at the classroom level by tracking or ability grouping. There is a strong relationship between race and social class, and racial isolation is often an outgrowth of residential segregation and socioeconomic background.

Has desegregation helped to equalize educational outcomes? A better question might be which desegregation programs under what circumstances accomplish which goals? Evidence from recent desegregation research suggests that, overall, children benefit academically and socially from well-run programs. Black students enjoy modest academic gains, while the academic achievement of White children is not hurt, and in some cases is helped, by desegregation. In school systems which have undergone desegregation efforts, the racial gap in educational outcomes has generally been reduced, but not eliminated.

More important than short-term academic gains are the long-term consequence of desegregation for Black students. Compared to those who attended racially isolated schools, Black adults who experienced desegregated education as children are more likely to attend multiracial colleges and graduate from them, work in higher-status jobs, live in integrated neighborhoods, assess their abilities more realistically when choosing an occupation, and to report interracial friendships.[6]

Despite these modest, but positive, outcomes, in the last decade of the twentieth century, most American children attend schools segregated by race, ethnicity, and social class. Consequently, [fifty] years of official federal interventions aimed at achieving equality of educational opportunity through school desegregation have only made small steps toward achieving that goal; children from different race and class backgrounds continue to receive segregated and, in many respects, unequal educations. . . .

Title IX

Title IX of the 1972 Higher Education Act is the primary federal law prohibiting sex discrimination in education. It states, "No person in the United States shall, on the basis of sex, be excluded from participation in, be denied benefit of, or be subjected to discrimination under any program or activity receiving Federal financial assistance." Until Title IX's passage, gender inequality in educational opportunity received minimal legislative attention. The act mandates gender equality of treatment in admission, courses, financial aid, counseling services, employment, and athletics.

The effect of Title IX upon college athletics has been especially controversial. While women constitute 53 percent of undergraduates, they are only 37 percent of college athletes. This is undoubtedly due to the complex interaction between institutional practices and gender-role socialization over the life course. Certainly, the fact that the vast majority of colleges spend much more money on recruiting and scholarships for male athletes contributes to the disparities.

In spring 1997, the U.S. Supreme Court refused to review a lower court's ruling in *Brown v. Cohen* that states in essence that Title IX requires universities to provide equal athletic opportunities for male and female students regardless of cost. Courts have generally upheld the following three-pronged test for compliance: (1) the percentage of athletes who are females should reflect the percentage of students who are female; (2) there must be a continuous record of expanding athletic opportunities for females athletes; and (3) schools must accommodate the athletic interests and abilities of female students. As of the ruling, very few universities were in compliance with the law.

Gender discrimination exists in other areas of education where it takes a variety of forms. For example, in K–12 education official curricular materials frequently feature a preponderance of male characters. Male and female characters typically exhibit traditional gender roles. Vocational education at the high school and college level remains gender-segregated to some degree. School administrators at all levels are overwhelmingly male although most teachers in elementary and secondary schools are female. In higher education, the situation is more complex. Faculty women in academia are found disproportionately in the lower ranks, are less likely to be promoted, and continue to earn less than their male colleagues.

Like the laws and policies aimed at eliminating race differences in school processes and outcomes, those designed to eliminate gender differences in educational opportunities have, at best, only narrowed them. Access to educational opportunity in the United States remains unequal for people of different gender, race, ethnic, and socioeconomic backgrounds.

EQUALITY OF EDUCATIONAL OPPORTUNITY AND EQUALITY OF INCOME

Despite the failures of . . . many programs to eliminate the inequality of educational opportunity over the past 45 years, there is one indicator of substantial progress: measured in median years, the gap in educational attainment between Blacks and Whites, and between males and females, has all but disappeared. In 1997, the median educational attainment of most groups was slightly more than twelve years. In the 1940s, by contrast, White males and females had a median educational attainment of just under nine years, African American males about five years, and African American women about six.

However, the main goal of educational reform is not merely to give all groups the opportunity to receive the same quality and quantity of education. According to the dominant ideology, the ultimate goal of these reforms is to provide equal educational opportunity in order to facilitate equal access to jobs, housing, and various other aspects of the American dream. It thus becomes crucial to examine whether the virtual elimination of the gap in educational attainment has been accompanied by a comparable decrease in other measures of inequality.

Of the various ways inequality can be measured, income is one of the most useful. Much of a person's social standing and access to the good things in life depends on his or her income.[7] Unfortunately, the dramatic progress in narrowing the gap in educational attainment has not been matched by a comparable narrowing of the gap in income inequality. Median individual earnings by race and gender indicate that White men still earn significantly more than any other group. Black men trail White men, and all women earn significantly less than all men. Even when occupation, experience, and level of education are controlled, women earn less than men, and Black men earn less than White men. It is only Black and White women with comparable educational credentials in similar jobs who earn about the same.

The discrepancy between the near elimination of the gap in median educational attainment and the ongoing gaps in median income is further evidence that addressing the inequality of educational opportunity is woefully insufficient for addressing broader sources of inequality throughout society.

This discrepancy can be explained by the nature of the U.S. political economy. The main cause of income inequality is the structure and operation of U.S. capitalism, a set of institutions which scarcely have been affected by the educational reforms discussed earlier. Greater equality of educational opportunity has not led to a corresponding decrease in income inequality because educational reforms do not create more good-paying jobs, affect gender-segregated and racially segmented occupational structures, or limit the mobility of capital either between regions of the country or between the United States and other countries. For example, no matter how good an education White working-class or minority youth may receive, it does nothing to alter the fact that thousands of relatively good paying manufacturing jobs have left northern inner cities for northern suburbs, the sunbelt, or foreign countries.

Many argue that numerous service jobs remain or that new manufacturing positions have been created in the wake of this capital flight. But these pay less than the departed manufacturing jobs, are often part-time or temporary, and frequently do not provide benefits. Even middle-class youth are beginning to fear the nature of the jobs which await them once they complete their formal education. Without changes in the structure and operation of the capitalist economy, educational reforms alone cannot markedly improve the social and economic position of disadvantaged groups. This is the primary reason that educational reforms do little to affect the gross social inequalities that inspired them in the first place.

BEYOND ATTAINMENT: THE PERSISTENCE OF EDUCATIONAL INEQUALITY

Educational reforms have not led to greater overall equality for several additional reasons. While race and gender gaps in educational attainment have narrowed considerably, educational achievement remains highly differentiated by social class, gender, and race. Many aspects of school processes and curricular content are deeply connected to race, social class, and gender inequality. But gross measures of educational outputs, such as median years of schooling completed, mask these indicators of inequality.

Not all educational experiences are alike. Four years of public high school in Beverly Hills are quite different from four years in an inner-city school. Family background, race, and gender have a great deal to do with whether a person goes to college and which institution of higher education she or he attends. The more privileged the background, the more likely a person is to attend an elite private university.

For example, according to Jacobs, women trail men slightly in representation in high status institutions of higher education because women are less likely to attend engineering programs and are more likely to be part-time students (who are themselves more likely to attend lower status institutions such as community colleges). Gender segregation in fields of study remains marked, with women less likely than men to study in scientific and mathematical fields. Furthermore, there is substantial race and ethnic segregation between institutions of higher education. Asian-Americans and Latinos are more segregated from Whites than are African-Americans. Whites and Asian-Americans are more likely to attend higher status universities than are African-Americans and Latinos.[8]

These patterns of race and gender segregation in higher education have direct implications for gender and race gaps in occupational and income attainment. Math and science degree recipients are more likely to obtain more lucrative jobs. A degree from a state college is not as competitive as one from an elite private university. Part of the advantage of attending more prestigious schools comes from the social networks to which a person has access and can join.

Another example of persistent inequality of educational opportunity is credential inflation. Even though women, minorities, and members of the working class now obtain higher levels of education than they did before, members of more privileged social groups gain even higher levels of education. At the same time, the educational requirements for the best jobs (those with the highest salaries, benefits, agreeable working conditions, autonomy, responsibility) are growing. Those with the most education from the best schools tend to be the top candidates for the best jobs. Because people from more privileged backgrounds are almost always in a better position to gain these desirable educational credentials, members of the working class, women, and minorities are still at a competitive disadvantage. Due to the dynamics of credential inflation, educational requirements previously necessary for the better jobs and now within the reach of many dispossessed groups are inadequate and insufficient in today's labor market. The credential inflation process keeps the already privileged one step (educational credential) ahead of the rest of the job seekers.[9]

One additional aspect of the persistent inequalities in educational opportunities concerns what sociologists of education call the hidden curriculum. This concept refers to two separate but related processes. The first is that the content and process of education differ for children according to their race, gender, and class. The second is that these differences reflect and thus help reproduce the inequalities based on race, gender, and class that characterize U.S. society as a whole.

One aspect of the hidden curriculum is the formal curriculum's ideological content. Anyon's work on U.S. history texts demonstrates that children from more privileged backgrounds are more likely to be exposed to rich, sophisticated, and complex materials than are their working-class counterparts.[10] Another aspect of the hidden curriculum concerns the social organization of the school and the classroom. Some hidden curriculum theorists suggest that tracking, ability grouping, and conventional teacher-centered classroom interactions contribute to the reproduction of the social relations of production at the workplace. Lower-track classrooms are disproportionately filled with working-class and minority students. Students in lower tracks are more likely than those in higher tracks to be assigned repetitive exercises with low levels of cognitive challenge. Lower-track students are likely to work individually and to lack classroom experience with problem solving or other independent, creative activities. Such activities are more conducive to preparing students for working-class jobs than for professional and managerial positions. Correspondence principle theorists argue that educational experiences from preschool to high school are designed to differentially prepare students for their ultimate positions in the work force, and that a student's placement in various school programs is strongly related to her or his race and class origin. Critics charge that the correspondence principle has been applied in too deterministic and mechanical a fashion. Evidence abounds of student resistance to class, gender, and race differentiated education.[11] This is undoubtedly why so many students drop out or graduate from high school with minimal levels of literacy and formal skills. Nonetheless, hidden curriculum theory offers a compelling contribution to explanations of how and why school processes and outcomes are so markedly different according to the race, gender, and social class of students.

CONCLUSION

In this [essay] we have argued that educational reforms alone cannot reduce inequality. Nevertheless, education remains important to any struggle to reduce inequality. Moreover, education is more than a meal ticket; it is intrinsically worthwhile and crucially important for the survival of democratic society. Many of the programs discussed in this essay contribute to the enhancement of individuals' cognitive growth and thus promote important nonsexist, nonracist attitudes and practices. Many of these programs also make schools somewhat more humane places for adults and children. Furthermore, education, even reformist liberal education, contains the seeds of individual and social transformation. Those of us committed to the struggle against inequality cannot be paralyzed by the structural barriers that make it impossible for education to eliminate inequality. We must look upon the schools as arenas of struggle against race, gender, and social class inequality.

NOTES

1. This essay draws on an article by Roslyn Arlin Mickelson that appeared as "Education and the Struggle Against Race, Class and Gender Inequality," *Humanity and Society* 11(4) (1987): 440–64.

2. Ascertaining whether a set of beliefs constitutes the dominant ideology in a particular society involves a host of difficult theoretical and empirical questions. For this reason we use the term *putative dominant ideology*. For discussion of these questions, see Nicholas Abercrombie et al., *The Dominant Ideology Thesis* (London: George Allen & Unwin, 1980); James C. Scott, *Weapons of the Weak* (New Haven: Yale University Press, 1985); Stephen Samuel Smith, "Political Acquiescence and Beliefs About State Coercion" (unpublished Ph.D. dissertation, Stanford University, 1990).

3. Jennifer Hochschild, "The Double-Edged Sword of Equal Educational Opportunity." Paper presented at the meeting of the American Education Research Association, Washington, D.C., April 22, 1987.

4. Gunnar Myrdal, *An American Dilemma: The Negro Problem and Modern Democracy* (New York: Harper & Row, 1944).

5. Gary Orfield, Mark D. Bachmeier, David R. James, and Tamela Eitle, "Deepening Segregation in American Public Schools" (Cambridge, MA: Harvard Project on School Desegregation, 1997).

6. Amy Stuart Wells and Robert L. Crain, "Perpetuation Theory and the Long-Term Effects of School Desegregation," *Review of Educational Research* 64(4) (1994): 531–55.

7. To be sure, income does not measure class-based inequality, but there is a positive correlation between income and class. Income has the additional advantage of being easily quantifiable. Were we to use another measure of inequality, e.g., wealth, the disjuncture between it and increases in educational attainment would be even larger. Although the distribution of wealth in U.S. society has remained fairly stable since the Depression, the gap between rich and poor increased in the 1980s and 1990s. Although accurate data are difficult to obtain, a 1992 study by the Federal Reserve found that in 1989 the top one-half of one percent of households held 29 percent of the wealth held by all households.

8. Jerry A. Jacobs, "Gender and Race Segregation Between and Within Colleges" (paper presented at the Eastern Sociological Society, Boston, MA, April 1996).

9. Randall Collins, *The Credential Society* (New York: Academic Press, 1979).

10. Jean Anyon, "Social Class and the Hidden Curriculum of Work," *Journal of Education* 162(1) (1980): 67–92; Jean Anyon, "Social Class and School Knowledge," *Curriculum Inquiry* 10 (1981): 3–42.

11. Samuel Bowles and Herbert Gintis, *Schooling in Capitalist America: Educational Reform and the Contradictions of Economic Life* (New York: Basic Books, 1976); Roslyn Arlin Mickelson, "The Case of the Missing Brackets: Teachers and Social Reproduction," *Journal of Education* 169(2) (1987): 78–88.

48

WELFARE REFORM, FAMILY HARDSHIP, AND WOMEN OF COLOR

Linda Burnham

Tens of thousands of women's and human rights activists gathered in September 1995 at the United Nations Fourth World Conference on Women, held in Beijing, China, to focus their attention on improving the condition and status of women worldwide. Working through cultural, religious, political, economic, and regional differences, women from the nations of the world produced a comprehensive document, the Beijing Platform for Action, that detailed actions to be taken by governments, nongovernmental

From Randy Albelda and Ann Withorn, eds., *Lost Ground: Welfare Reform, Poverty, and Beyond* (Cambridge, MA: South End Press, 2002), pp. 43–56. Reprinted by permission of the South End Press.

organizations, and multilateral financial and development institutions to improve women's conditions. The platform for action called on governments to take action to relieve "the persistent and increasing burden of poverty on women" and address gender "inequality in economic structures and policies, in all forms of productive activities and in access to resources" (United Nations 1995).

Yet . . . since Beijing, in a time of unparalleled national prosperity, policies contradictory to the spirit and intent of the platform for action were promulgated in the United States, targeting the most vulnerable citizens and, rather than assisting women onto the path of economic security, driving many deeper into poverty. While U.S. officials pledged in international forums to uphold women's human rights, those rights were substantially undermined by the 1996 passage of the Personal Responsibility and Work Opportunities Reconciliation Act (PRWORA).

INCREASING FAMILY HARDSHIP

There are many studies that document how much worse off women are due to welfare reform. Those who remain in the welfare system, those who leave for employment, and those who might have used Aid to Families with Dependent Children (AFDC) are in worse shape, with less support than the woefully inadequate earlier system provided. . . .

The stated intent of welfare reform was at least twofold: to reduce the welfare rolls and to move women toward economic self-sufficiency. The first objective has been achieved: welfare rolls have declined dramatically since 1996. Welfare reform has stripped single mothers of any sense that they are entitled to government support during the years when they are raising their children.

Despite the "success" of welfare reform, research has repeatedly found that many women who move from welfare to work do not achieve economic independence. Instead, most find only low-paid, insecure jobs that do not lift their families above the poverty line. They end up worse off economically than they were on welfare: they work hard and remain poor. Others are pushed off welfare and find no employment. They have no reported source of income.

Women in transition from welfare to work—or to no work—face particular difficulties and crises related to housing insecurity and homelessness and food insecurity and hunger.

Low-income people in the United States faced a housing crisis long before the passage of the PRWORA. In most states, the median fair-market cost of housing for a family of three is considerably higher than total income from a Temporary Aid to Needy Families (TANF) grant (Dolbeare 1999).

Further, as a consequence of two decades of declining federal support for public and subsidized housing, the great majority of both current and former TANF recipients are at the mercy of an unforgiving private housing market. . . .

Utility payment problems are another important indicator of housing insecurity because they reveal that many families, while they may have a roof over them, spend at least some time without heat and light. And utility problems are often a prelude to inability to pay the rent. A 1998 survey of social service clients who had left welfare within the previous six months found that 25 percent had had their heat cut off (Sherman et al. 1998, 13). A recent Illinois study found that 61 percent of TANF recipients who were not working could not pay their utility bills. But former recipients who were working were also struggling with their budgets, and 48 percent were unable to meet their utility payments (Work, Welfare and Families 2000, 25). . . .

Welfare reform has also put severe pressures on an already strained shelter system. The U.S. Conference of Mayors reported that requests for emergency shelter increased by 12 percent between 1998 and 1999 in the 26 cities surveyed and were at their highest levels since 1994 (U.S. Conference of Mayors 1999, 94). "When I started here three years ago, we had plenty of family space. Since welfare reform, I don't have a bed," said a social service worker in a Salvation Army Shelter in New Orleans (Cobb 1999, 1). . . .

Although the PRWORA was trumpeted as a step toward strengthening families, increased housing insecurity and homelessness have led to families being split apart. Most family shelters do not take men, so the fathers of two-parent families that become homeless must either go to a single men's shelter or make other housing arrangements. Many shelters also do not accommodate adolescent boys or older male teens. Family breakup may be required for a shelter stay.

The housing instability of poor women and their children has profound consequences, both for them and for society as a whole. Homelessness compromises the emotional and physical health of women and children, disrupts schooling, and creates a substantial barrier to employment. It widens the chasm between those who are prospering in a strong economy and those who fall ever farther behind. In the six years since the United States made its Beijing commitments to improving women's lives, welfare policy, rather than widening poor women's access to safe and affordable housing, has created higher levels of housing instability and homelessness.

Like homelessness, the problems of food insecurity predate welfare reform. Low-income workers and welfare recipients alike have struggled for years to provide adequate food for themselves and their families. The robust economy of the late 1990s did not fundamentally alter this reality. Of families headed by single women, one in three experiences food insecurity and one in ten experiences hunger (Work, Welfare and Families 2000, 25).

Welfare reform has made women's struggles to obtain food for themselves and their families more difficult. Several studies document that former recipients cannot pay for sufficient food and that their families skip meals, go hungry, and/or use food pantries or other emergency food assistance.

The figures are astoundingly high. In New Jersey, 50.3 percent of former recipients who were not working reported an inability to sufficiently feed themselves or their children. Former recipients who were working were no better off: Almost 50 percent reported the very same problem (Work, Poverty and Welfare Evaluation Project 1999, 58). . . . The higher costs associated with participating in the labor force, combined with reduction or elimination of the food stamp allotment, meant women's access to adequate food became more precarious rather than less so as they moved from welfare to work. Entering the workforce came at a very high price.

The Food Stamp Program is intended to ensure that no family goes hungry, but many families do not receive the food stamps to which they are entitled. Even before welfare reform, the rate of participation in the Food Stamp Program was declining more rapidly than the poverty rate. The number of people receiving food stamps dropped even more steeply later, from 25.5 million average monthly recipients in 1996 to 18.5 million in the first half of 1999 (U.S. General Accounting Office 1999, 46). The rate of participation is the lowest it has been in two decades, with a growing gap between the need for food assistance and families' use of food stamps.

Welfare reform has itself contributed to the underutilization of food stamps. Many families that leave the welfare system do not know that as long as their income remains below a certain level, they are still eligible for food stamps. Believing that termination of TANF benefits disqualifies them from receiving food stamps as well, they fail to apply or to reconfirm eligibility. Confusion and misinformation on the part of eligibility workers, or their withholding of information, are also factors in the low participation of former recipients. Additional contributing factors include the lack of bilingual staff and burdensome application and recertification processes (Venner, Sullivan, and Seavey 2000, 17). Among families who had left welfare, only 42 percent of those who were eligible for food stamps were receiving them (Zedlewski and Brauner 1999, 1–6). . . .

WOMEN OF COLOR AND IMMIGRANT WOMEN

Welfare reform is a nominally race-neutral policy suffused with racial bias, both in the politics surrounding its promulgation and in its impact. It may not have been the intent to racially target women of color for particular punishment, yet women of color and immigrant women have nonetheless been particularly hard hit in ways that were highly predictable.

Feminist theory has for some time recognized that the social and economic circumstances women of color must negotiate are shaped by the intersection of distinct axes of power—in this case primarily race, class, and gender. The relationships of subordination and privilege that define these axes generate multiple social dynamics that influence, shape, and transform each other, creating, for women of color, multiple vulnerabilities and intensified experiences of discrimination.

Welfare reform might legitimately be regarded as a class-based policy intended to radically transform the social contract with the poor. Poverty in the United States, however, is powerfully structured by racial and gender inequities. It is not possible, therefore, to institute poverty policy of any depth that does not also reconfigure other relations, either augmenting or diminishing race and gender inequalities. By weakening the social safety net for the poor, PRWORA necessarily has its greatest effect on those communities that are disproportionately represented among the poor. Communities of color and immigrant communities, already characterized by significantly higher levels of minimum-wage work, homelessness, hunger, and poor health, are further jeopardized by the discriminatory impact of welfare reform.

As a consequence of the historical legacy and current practices of, among other things, educational inequity and labor market disadvantage, patterns of income and wealth in the United States are strongly skewed along racial lines, for example, the disproportionate burden of poverty carried by people of color. While the white non-Hispanic population constituted 72.3 percent of the total population in 1998, it made up only 45.8 percent of the population living below the poverty line. In stark contrast, blacks made up just over 12 percent of the general population but 26.4 percent of the U.S. population in poverty. People of Hispanic origin, of all races, constitute 23.4 percent of the people below the poverty line, while making up 11.2 percent of the total population. While 8.2 percent of the white non-Hispanic population lives in poverty, 12.5 percent of Asian and Pacific Islanders do (U.S. Census Bureau 1999, 2000).[1]

Economic vulnerabilities due to race and ethnicity may be further compounded by disadvantages based on gender and immigration/citizenship status. Thus, for households headed by single women, the poverty rates are also stark. Over 21 percent of such white non-Hispanic households were below the poverty line in 1998, as compared to over 46 percent of black and 48 percent of Hispanic female-headed households (U.S. Census Bureau 1999). Immigrants, too, are disproportionately poor, with 18 percent below the poverty line as compared to 12 percent of the native born (U.S. Census Bureau 1999). Given the disproportionate share of poverty experienced by people of color, and the significant poverty of single-mother households, it is no surprise that the welfare rolls are racially unbalanced, with women of color substantially overrepresented (see Table 1).

Table 1
TANF Recipients by Race, 1998
(In percentages)

White	32.7
Black	39.0
Hispanic	22.2
Native	1.5
Asian	3.4
Other	0.6
Unknown	0.7

Source: U.S. Department of Health and
Human Services, 1999.

This racial imbalance has been cynically used for decades in the ideological campaign to undermine support for welfare—a crude but ultimately effective interweaving of race, class, gender, and anti-immigrant biases that prepared the consensus to "end welfare as we know it." Having been maligned as lazy welfare cheats and something-for-nothing immigrants, Latinas, African American women, and Asian women of particular nationality groups are now absorbing a punishing share of welfare reform's negative impacts.

Much of the data on welfare reform are not disaggregated by race. We will not know the full impact of welfare reform on women of color until we have county, statewide, and national studies of women transitioning from welfare to work that consistently include race as a variable. However, to the extent that communities of color experience some of the most devastating effects of poverty at exceptionally high rates, and to the extent that welfare reform has rendered these communities more, rather than less, vulnerable, we may expect that the policy will deepen already entrenched inequalities.

For example, African American women are massively overrepresented in the urban homeless population. Their particular vulnerability to homelessness has been shaped by, among many factors, high rates of reliance on welfare in a period in which the value of the welfare grant plummeted and housing costs climbed steeply; low marriage rates and, therefore, lack of access to a male wage; overconcentration on the bottom rungs of the wage ladder; and high unemployment rates, especially for young women with less than a high school education.

Beyond intensified impact due to disproportionate representation in the affected population, additional factors compound the disadvantages of women of color and immigrant women. One Virginia study found noteworthy differences in how caseworkers interact with black and white welfare recipients. A substantial 41 percent of white recipients were encouraged to go to school to earn their high school diplomas, while no black recipients were. A much higher proportion of whites than blacks found their caseworkers to be helpful in providing information about potential jobs (Gooden 1997). Other studies showed that blacks were removed from welfare for noncompliance with program rules at considerably higher rates than white recipients, while a higher proportion of the cases of white recipients were closed because they earned too much to qualify for welfare (Savner 2000). . . .

Some of the most punitive provisions of PRWORA are directed at immigrants. The 1996 legislation banned certain categories of legal immigrants from a wide array of federal assistance programs, including TANF, food stamps, Supplementary Security Income, and Medicaid. In the year following passage, 940,000 legal immigrants lost their food stamp eligibility. Strong advocacy reversed some of the cuts and removed some restrictions, but legal immigrants arriving in the United States after the passage of the legislation are ineligible for benefits for five years. States have the right to bar pre-enactment legal immigrants from TANF and nonemergency Medicaid as well (National Immigration Law Center 1999).

These restrictions have had profound effects on immigrant communities. First of all, many immigrant women who are on welfare face significant barriers to meeting TANF work requirements. Perhaps the most formidable obstacles are limited English proficiency and low educational levels. A study of immigrant recipients in California found that 87 percent of the Vietnamese women and 48 percent of the Mexican American women had limited or no proficiency in English. Many of these women were also not literate in their native languages, with the Mexican Americans averaging 6.5 years in school and the Vietnamese 8.7 years (Equal Rights Advocates 1999, 7). A study of Hmong women found 90 percent with little or no English proficiency, 70 percent with no literacy in the Hmong language, and 62 percent with no formal education whatsoever (Moore and Selkowe 1999).

Limited English, lack of education, and limited job skills severely restrict immigrant women's options in the job market, making it very difficult for them to comply with welfare-to-work requirements. Language problems also impede their ability to negotiate the welfare bureaucracy, which provides very limited or no translation services. These women lack information about programs to which they are entitled, and they worry about notices that come to them in English. When immigrant women recipients are able to find work, it is most often in minimum-wage or low-wage jobs without stability or benefits (Center for Urban Research and Learning 1999, 5; Equal Rights Advocates 1999, 31). . . .

Immigrant women recipients are also likely to experience severe overcrowding and to devote a huge portion of their income to housing. They share housing with relatives or with unrelated adults; live in garages or other makeshift, substandard dwellings; and worry constantly about paying the rent.

A more hidden, but still pernicious, impact of welfare reform has been the decline in applications for aid from immigrants who are eligible to receive it. One report documents PRWORA's "chilling effect on immigrants" who mistakenly believe they are no longer eligible for any benefits. Reporting on the numbers of TANF applications approved each month, this study showed a huge drop—71 percent—in the number of legal immigrant applicants approved for TANF and MediCal between January 1996 and January 1998. That number fell from 1,545 applicants in January 1996 to only 450 in January 1998 (Zimmerman and Fix 1998, 5). The intensive anti-immigrant propaganda that accompanied the passage of PRWORA and statewide anti-immigrant initiatives appears to have discouraged those who need and are entitled to aid from applying for it, surely undermining the health and welfare of immigrant women and their families.

WELFARE REFORM IS INCOMPATIBLE WITH WOMEN'S HUMAN RIGHTS

One of the chief accomplishments of the Beijing conference and the Platform for Action was to position women's issues squarely within the context of human rights. Building on the foundational work of activists worldwide, Beijing became the first U.N. women's conference in which "women's rights are human rights" was articulated not as a platitude but as a strategic assertion. Indeed, the phrase was taken up by former First Lady Hillary Rodham Clinton, who, in her September 5, 1995, speech to the conference, asserted that "women will never gain full dignity until their human rights are respected and protected."

PRWORA is wholly incompatible with the strategic objectives of the Beijing Platform for Action and profoundly compromises the exercise of women's human rights. Rather than improving the status of poor women, the legislation has deepened the misery of tens of thousands of women and their children. By undermining women's access to a stable livelihood, welfare reform constructs barriers to their exercise of political, civil, cultural, and social rights.

Undoing the damage of welfare reform—and bringing U.S. policy in line with its stated commitments to the world community—will require the promulgation and implementation of policies that restore and strengthen the social safety net for women and children while funding programs that support women along the path to economic self-sufficiency. In the absence of the political will for such a comprehensive reworking of U.S. social welfare policy, advocates for poor women and families face an extended, defensive battle to ameliorate the cruelest and most discriminatory effects of this radically regressive policy.

NOTE

1. In citing Census Bureau statistics, I use their terminology. Elsewhere, I use the term "Latino" to refer to immigrants from Mexico, Central and South America, and the Spanish-speaking Caribbean and their descendants in the United States.

References

Center for Urban Research and Learning. 1999. *Cracks in the System: Conversations with People Surviving Welfare Reform.* Chicago: Center for Urban Research and Learning, Loyola University, Howard Area Community Center, Organization of the NorthEast.

Clinton, Hillary. 1995. Remarks by First Lady Hillary Rodham Clinton for the United Nations Fourth World Conference on Women, 5 Sept.

Cobb, Kim. 1999. Homeless Kids Problem Worst in Louisiana; Welfare Reform, Housing Crunch Are Among Reasons. *Houston Chronicle*, 15 Aug.

Dolbeare, Cushing. 1999. *Out of Reach: The Gap Between Housing Costs and Income of Poor People in the United States.* Washington, DC: National Low-Income Housing Coalition.

Equal Rights Advocates. 1999. *From War on Poverty to War on Welfare: The Impact of Welfare Reform on the Lives of Immigrant Women.* San Francisco.

Gooden, Susan. 1997. Examining Racial Differences in Employment Status Among Welfare Recipients. In *Race and Welfare Report.* Oakland, CA: Grass Roots Innovative Policy Program.

Moore, Thomas and Vicky Selkowe. 1999. *The Impact of Welfare Reform on Wisconsin's Hmong Aid Recipients.* Milwaukee: Institute for Wisconsin's Future.

National Immigration Law Center. 1999. *Immigrant Eligibility for Public Benefits.* Washington, DC.

Savner, Steve. 2000. Welfare Reform and Racial/Ethnic Minorities: The Questions to Ask. *Poverty & Race* 9(4):3–5.

Sherman, Arloc, Cheryl Amey, Barbara Duffield, Nancy Ebb, and Deborah Weinstein. 1998. *Welfare to What: Early Findings on Family Hardship and Well-Being.* Washington, DC: Children's Defense Fund and National Coalition for the Homeless.

United Nations. 1995. *Fourth World Conference on Women Platform for Action.* Geneva, Switzerland.

U.S. Census Bureau. 1999. *Poverty Thresholds in 1998 by Size of Family and Number of Related Children Under 18 Years.* Washington, DC.

U.S. Conference of Mayors. 1999. *A Status Report on Hunger and Homelessness in America's Cities.* Washington, DC.

U.S. Department of Health and Human Services, Administration for Children and Families. 1999. *Characteristics and Financial Circumstances of TANF Recipients.* Washington, DC.

U.S. General Accounting Office. 1999. *Food Stamp Program: Various Factors Have Led to Declining Participation.* Washington, DC.

Venner, Sandra H., Ashley F. Sullivan, and Dorie Seavey. 2000. *Paradox of Our Times: Hunger in a Strong Economy.* Medford, MA: Tufts University, Center on Hunger and Poverty.

Work, Poverty and Welfare Evaluation Project. 1999. Assessing Work First: What Happens After Welfare? Report for the Study Group on Work, Poverty and Welfare. Legal Services of New Jersey, New Jersey Poverty Research Institute, Edison, NJ.

Work, Welfare and Families. 2000. *Living with Welfare Reform: A Survey of Low Income Families in Illinois.* Chicago: Chicago Urban League and UIC Center for Urban Economic Development.

Zedlewski, Sheila R. and Sarah Brauner. 1999. *Are the Steep Declines in Food Stamp Participation Linked to Falling Welfare Caseloads?* Washington, DC: Urban Institute.

Zimmerman, Wendy and Michael Fix. 1998. *Declining Immigrant Applications for Medi-Cal and Welfare Benefits in Los AnGeles County.* Washington, DC: Urban Institute.

49

AID TO DEPENDENT CORPORATIONS*
Exposing Federal Handouts to the Wealthy

Chuck Collins

In 1992 rancher J. R. Simplot of Grandview, Idaho, paid the U.S. government $87,000 for grazing rights on federal lands, about one-quarter the rate charged by private landowners. Simplot's implicit subsidy from U.S. taxpayers, $261,000, would have covered the welfare costs of about 60 poor families. With a net worth exceeding $500 million, it's hard to argue that Simplot needed the money.

Since 1987, American Barrick Resources Corporation has pocketed $8.75 billion by extracting gold from a Nevada mine owned by the U.S. government. But Barrick has paid only minimal rent to the Department of the Interior. In 1992 Barrick's founder was rewarded for his business acumen with a $32 million annual salary.

Such discounts are only one form of corporate welfare, dubbed "wealthfare" by some activists, that U.S. taxpayers fund. At a time when Congress is attempting to slash or eliminate the meager benefits received by the poor, we

---

*Editors' note: This is a play on words regarding Aid to Families with Dependent Children—the federal welfare program that was eliminated in 1996 by the Personal Responsibility and Work Opportunities Reconciliation Act.

From *Dollars & Sense* 1 (May/June 1995): 15–17, 40. Reprinted by permission.

are spending far more to subsidize wealthy corporations and individuals. Wealthfare comes in five main varieties: discounted user fees for public resources; direct grants; corporate tax reductions and loopholes; giveaways of publicly funded research and development (R&D) to private profit-making companies; and tax breaks for wealthy individuals. . . .

TAX AVOIDANCE

The largest, yet most invisible, part of wealthfare is tax breaks for corporations and wealthy individuals. The federal Office of Management and Budget (OMB) estimates that these credits, deductions, and exemptions, called "tax expenditures," will cost $440 billion in fiscal 1996. This compares, for example, to the $16 billion annual federal cost of child support programs.

Due both to lower basic tax rates and to myriad loopholes, corporate taxes fell from one-third of total federal revenues in 1953 to less than 10% today (see "Disappearing Corporate Taxes," *Dollars & Sense*, July 1994).* Were corporations paying as much tax now as they did in the 1950s, the government would take in another $250 billion a year—more than the entire budget deficit.

The tax code is riddled with tax breaks for the natural resource, construction, corporate agri-business, and financial industries. Some serve legitimate purposes, or did at one time. Others have been distorted to create tax shelters and perpetuate bad business practices. . . .

One particularly generous tax break is the foreign tax credit, which allows U.S.-based multinational corporations to deduct from their U.S. taxes the income taxes they pay to other nations. Donald Bartlett and James Steele, authors of *America: Who Really Pays the Taxes*, say that by 1990 this writeoff was worth $25 billion a year.

While in many cases this credit is a valid method of preventing double taxation on profits earned overseas, the oil companies have used it to avoid most of their U.S. tax obligations. Until 1950, Saudi Arabia had no income tax, but charged royalties on all oil taken from their wells. Such royalties are a payment for use of a natural resource. They are a standard business expense, payable *before* a corporation calculates the profits on which it will pay taxes.

These royalties were a major cost to ARAMCO, the oil consortium operating there (consisting of Exxon, Mobil, Chevron, and Texaco). But since royalties are not income taxes, they could not be used to reduce Exxon and friends' tax bills back home.

When King Saud decided to increase the royalty payments, ARAMCO convinced him to institute a corporate income tax and to substitute this for

---

*Editors' note: 9.9% in fiscal year 2000.

the royalties. The tax was a sham, since it applied only to ARAMCO, not to any other business in Saudi Arabia's relatively primitive economy. The result was that the oil companies avoided hundreds of millions of dollars in their American taxes. Eventually the other oil-producing nations, including Kuwait, Iraq, and Nigeria, followed suit, at huge cost to the U.S. Treasury.

In contrast to the ARAMCO problem, many corporate executive salaries should not be counted as deductible expenses. These salaries and bonuses are often so large today that they constitute disguised profits. Twenty years ago the average top executive made 34 times the wages of the firm's lowest paid workers. Today the ratio is 140 to 1.* . . .

OTHER VITAL MATTERS

Taxes are but one form of wealthfare. . . . Many corporations also receive direct payments from the federal government. The libertarian Cato Institute argues that every cabinet department "has become a conduit for government funding of private industry. Within some cabinet agencies, such as the U.S. Department of Agriculture and the Department of Commerce, almost every spending program underwrites private business."

Agriculture subsidies typically flow in greater quantities the larger is the recipient firm. Of the $1.4 billion in annual sugar price supports, for example, 40% of the money goes to the largest 1% of firms, with the largest ones receiving more than $1 million each. . . .

The Progressive Policy Institute estimates that taxpayers could save $114 billion over five years by eliminating or restricting such direct subsidies. Farm subsidies, for example, could be limited to only small farmers.

The government also pays for scientific research and development, then allows the benefits to be reaped by private firms. This occurs commonly in medical research. One product, the anti-cancer drug Taxol, cost the U.S. government $32 million to develop as part of a joint venture with private industry. But in the end the government gave its share to Bristol-Myers Squibb, which now charges cancer patients almost $1,000 for a three-week supply of the drug.

WHO IS ENTITLED?

Beyond corporate subsidies, the government also spends far more than necessary to help support the lifestyles of wealthy individuals. This largess pertains to several of the most expensive and popular "entitlements" in the federal

---

*Editors' note: The AFL-CIO reports that since 1980 the average pay of working people has increased 74 percent; CEO pay, 1,884 percent. The AFL-CIO maintains a Web site, "Executive Pay Watch." See www.afl-cio.org

budget, such as Social Security, Medicare, and the deductibility of interest on home mortgages. As the current budget-cutting moves in Congress demonstrate, such universal programs have much greater political strength than do programs targeted solely at low-income households.

While this broad appeal is essential to maintain, billions of dollars could be saved by restricting the degree to which the wealthy benefit from universal programs. If Social Security and Medicare payments were denied to just the richest 3% of households this would reduce federal spending by $30 to $40 billion a year—more than the total federal cost of food stamps.

Similarly, mortgage interest is currently deductible up to $1 million per home, justifying the term "mansion subsidy" for its use by the rich. The government could continue allowing everyone to use this deduction, but limit it to $250,000 per home. This would affect only the wealthiest 5% of Americans, but would save taxpayers $10 billion a year.

Progressive organizations have mounted a renewed focus on the myriad handouts to the corporate and individual rich. One effort is the Green Scissors coalition, an unusual alliance of environmental groups such as Friends of the Earth, and conservative taxcutters, such as the National Taxpayers Union. Last January Green Scissors proposed cutting $33 billion over the next ten years in subsidies that they contend are wasteful and environmentally damaging. These include boondoggle water projects, public land subsidies, highways, foreign aid projects, and agricultural programs.

Another new organization, Share the Wealth, is a coalition of labor, religious, and economic justice organizations. It recently launched the "Campaign for Wealth-Fare Reform," whose initial proposal targets over $35 billion in annual subsidies that benefit the wealthiest 3% of the population. The campaign rejects the term "corporate welfare" because it reinforces punitive anti-welfare sentiments. Welfare is something a humane society guarantees to people facing poverty, unemployment, low wages, and racism. "Wealthfare," in contrast, is the fees and subsidies extracted from the public by the wealthy and powerful—those who are least in need.

Today's Congress is not sympathetic to such arguments. But the blatant anti-poor, pro-corporate bias . . . has already begun to awaken a dormant public consciousness. This will leave more openings, not less, for progressives to engage in public education around the true nature of government waste.

References

Bartlett, Donald, and James Steele. 1994. *America: Who Really Pays the Taxes?* New York: Simon & Schuster.

Crittendon, Anne. 1993. *Killing the Sacred Cows.* New York: Penguin Books.

Friends of the Earth. 1995. *Green Scissors Report: Cutting Wasteful and Environmentally Harmful Spending and Subsidies.* Washington, DC: Green Scissors Campaign of Citizens United to Terminate Subsidies.

Shapiro, Robert. 1994. *Cut-and-Invest to Compete and Win: A Budget Strategy for American Growth*. Washington, DC: Progressive Policy Institute.

Shields, Janice C. 1994. *Aid to Dependent Corporations*. Washington, DC: Essential Information.

50

RACE, POVERTY AND DISABILITY: THREE STRIKES AND YOU'RE OUT! OR ARE YOU?

Pamela Block, Fabricio E. Balcazar, and Christopher B. Keys

INTRODUCTION

Throughout the twentieth century, theories of biology and culture presented images of race, class, and disability in terms of deficiency and dependence. Biological models represented certain ethnic and racial groups as genetically inferior. Cultural models represented these groups as trapped in an inescapable cycle of poverty. Both models represented people of color with disabilities as social victims and/or socially threatening. Policies and practices based on these theories projected pejorative images on low-income ethnic and racial groups, and on people with disabilities. Individuals belonging to more than one of these categories—or all three—were especially vulnerable to social stigma.

Such images of biological and cultural pathology have been rejected by many modern theorists who have adopted a minority group model for the analysis of groups disenfranchised on the basis of race, class, gender, sexual orientation, and/or disability. In these formulations, racism, classism, ableism and other forms of prejudice create barriers that result in social and economic marginalization for members of disenfranchised groups. African Americans and Latinos with disabilities face multiple challenges of

From Pamela Block, Balcazar, Fabricio E., Keys, Christopher B. "Race, Poverty, and Disability: Three Strikes and You're Out! Or Are You?" (*Social Policy*, Fall 2002.) Reprinted by permission of the authors.

discrimination and social barriers related to race and class, as well as to disability. However, insufficient attention has been given to the interaction of these variables.

RACE, POVERTY AND DISABILITY AS BIOLOGICAL PATHOLOGY

From the time of the early eugenics family studies until eugenics' recent revival in academic and popular discussion, biological theories have always intersected theories of race, class, and disability. In the early 1900s, eugenics was the primary ideological framework in which policies and practices were developed to manage marginalized populations. Eugenics, the science of the genetic improvement of the human race, was used to establish race and class distinctions as "natural" and incontrovertible. The dominance of the upper class was mandated by their superior genetic heritage; the poor remained in poverty because of their degenerate genes.

Many proponents of eugenics believed in a hierarchy of "lower" and "higher" races. These theorists sought a state-controlled program to improve the quality of the human gene pool by optimizing the breeding of elite white Anglo-Saxon Protestants (positive eugenics), and controlling the reproduction of "degenerates," "morons," and those of "inferior" racial or ethnic groupings (negative eugenics). Special attention was given to those of "mixed" heritage and to foreigners from places other than Western Europe. "Mongrel" families (mixed Caucasian, African-American and Native American racial heritage) were considered unstable and degenerate. The genetic inferiority of the new wave of immigrants was widely discussed. Alarmed at the supposed decrease in the birthrate of white Anglo-Saxon Protestants, eugenicists feared "race suicide." One psychologist advocated that "morons" be allowed to serve in the army in World War One, so that fewer "normal men" would be wasted.

Eugenicists believed that racial degeneration would change the national character, subsuming a primarily Nordic-European population under a "tide" of unwanted immigrants. Adherents of the biological-pathology model developed standardized tests that they believed proved the inferior intelligence of African Americans and immigrants. The biological model highlighted multiple stigma as justification for regressive social policy. Some case studies showed how racial character, poverty, and disability interacted with other factors such as illicit pregnancy, prostitution, gambling, alcoholism, drug addiction, tuberculosis, and syphilis. When several of these factors coexisted, it was considered an indication of degeneration due to pathological inheritance. Policymakers and high profile health professionals in the United States responded by establishing programs for the institutionalization and sterilization of supposedly pathological populations. Hundreds of thousands of individuals considered "feeble-minded" were institutionalized, sometimes for life, in facilities that still exist today.

The extreme example of both positive and negative eugenics was Nazi Germany. Those with Aryan characteristics were encouraged to have large families, while thousands of others were involuntarily sterilized and millions of others were annihilated under a policy of racial purification. Advances in the science of genetics and the example of Nazi Germany served to discredit the eugenics movement in the United States. However, eugenicists continued to take an active role in many professions, including population science and social service provision for marginalized groups (e.g., people on welfare, psychiatric patients, and people with cognitive disabilities).

The term "eugenics" disappeared from professional and popular discourse when it was discredited and thus no longer considered an effective means of program implementation. However, decades after eugenics disappeared from official public policy, eugenicists continued to influence the social service system by advocating institutionalization and sterilization of people with developmental disabilities and sterilization of women on welfare. The legacy of treatment models developed by eugenicists in the early 1900s (such as segregation from the opposite sex and sterilization) is still apparent in practices, such as genetic counseling, which encourage the abortion of fetuses with disabilities like Down Syndrome. It is also visible in the physical and organizational structures of mental institutions and in the psychological scars of people who have been institutionalized for long periods. Additionally, eugenics ideologies persisted through the subtle influence of cultural beliefs concerning marginalized groups, evidenced by contradictory representations of people with disabilities in literature, film, and television as social victims or social threats. People with disabilities are often portrayed as unable to control their sexuality and capable of erupting into random and unpredictable acts of violence. Society and those with disabilities are only considered safe when such people are locked behind the walls of an institution or when deceased.

RACE, POVERTY AND DISABILITY AS CULTURAL PATHOLOGY

In the 1930s, biological theories began to be replaced by the theories of culture promulgated by sociologists and anthropologists. Various views of poverty were presented: as cultural disintegration and deprivation; as inspiring pathological forms of cultural structure, i.e., the "culture of poverty"; or as a result of the loss or lack of culture.

Although recognizably distinct from earlier biological theories, the new cultural theories included regressive images of people living in poverty that were disturbingly close to earlier models. Whether the explanation was biological or cultural, these differences (e.g. to be poor, a racial minority, or to have a disability) were presented as a form of self-defeating and self-perpetuating pathology.

Whether defined as a pathological lack of culture, or a culture that was pathological, the people living in poverty were considered deficient by leading theorists and in public policy. For example, the concept of "culture of poverty" impacted Department of Labor and War On Poverty thinking in the 1960s.

The prevalence of the deficiency approach has also characterized societal perceptions of people with disabilities. For example, the 1994 reauthorization of the Developmental Disabilities Assistance and Bill of Rights Act (PL 103-230), defined developmental disabilities as a series of "substantial functional limitations" in "self care," "self-direction," "capacity for independent living," and "economic self sufficiency." These "substantial functional limitations" were also exhibited by the "white trash" in an earlier period, with biology thought to be the root cause. Like pathological genes, the culture of poverty was reproduced from generation to generation, all but impossible to escape. Although by the 1950s and 1960s eugenics had been largely discredited, its ideas unintentionally provided a model of cultural pathology to supplant eugenics notions of biological pathology. Thus the social problems exhibited by minorities, such as teen pregnancy, alcohol and drug abuse, welfare culture, serial monogamy or multiple partners, and destabilized families, could be explained through cultural, rather than biological deficiencies. Whether in biological or cultural terms, the contours of these pathology arguments were quite comparable, focusing on the identification of individual deficits and blaming the victim for having them.

FROM MINORITY GROUP MODEL TO AN EMPOWERMENT FRAMEWORK OF ANALYSIS

Immediately after their appearance, scholars and activists began challenging the concepts of the culture of poverty and cultural deprivation, protesting that the supposed traits of people living in poverty were contemptuous distortions based on middle-class biases. Urban anthropologists wrote ethnographic accounts of African-American communities highlighting and valorizing cultural differences. Community, social, and developmental psychologists suggested that so-called "deficits" in language and learning actually reflected cultural differences, not cultural deficiency. Activists protested an approach that blamed victims for their problems and ignored the strengths of their cultures.

Like the eugenics family studies, the culture of poverty thesis functioned to justify blaming the poor for their poverty and blaming social problems on innate deficiencies. Culture became an alternative to biological explanations for the inferiority, dependency and marginality of certain social groups.

Individuals from marginalized groups became categorized as mentally retarded, not because of their inherent "incompetence", but due to racial and class bias within school and social service systems.

The contrary view claimed that social problems should be addressed through the elimination of unequal power relations and re-distribution of wealth and income. This social perspective on disability is based on a minority group model that has also been adopted to explain systematic exclusion on the basis of sex, race, and sexual orientation. This model functions to liberate individuals with disabilities from long-held societal prejudices and mistaken assumptions.

Identity politics grew out of collective movements for equality on the basis of gender, race, and sexual orientation. People with disabilities are now applying this principle to their own situations. However, within the minority group model, a single issue (such as race, gender, or sexual orientation) is usually the focus for identity formation. Other issues are considered secondary or are not considered at all. Perhaps this is a response to earlier biological and cultural models that tended to use a multi-issue approach to "prove" the pathological nature (and culture) of marginalized groups. In the process of identity formation, attempts to stay as far away from the earlier pejorative images of race and poverty have resulted in the inadvertent exclusion of individuals facing the "triple jeopardy" of race, poverty, and disability. Perhaps to overcome the pressures of marginalization and to rally a critical mass of support, it is more effective, especially initially, to focus on one common characteristic. But inevitably to some degree this single-focus strategy excludes those facing triple jeopardy and their multiple concerns.

Disability rights activists reject earlier models of disability, adopting instead a model that emphasizes overcoming social barriers rather than focusing on individual pathology. In contrast to static biological and cultural models, the minority group model is a dynamic view of disability resulting from the interaction of the individual and the environment. Disability-rights activists argue that social and cultural values encouraging discrimination or the segregation of people with disabilities must be changed. In this model, the emphasis shifts from the individual to the society, and from victim-blaming to strategies for social change. Education, organizing, a sense of community, and pride in identity replace earlier experiences of isolation and shame. Individuals can band together with others who face similar challenges and learn how to challenge and navigate existing systems to their advantage. A good example is the national advocacy organization of people with physical disabilities known as ADAPT (www.adapt.org). This organization originally focused on efforts to make public transportation accessible in major cities in the country. Since the passage of the Americans with Disabilities Act, the group has focused more on efforts to promote state and national legislation regarding needs for personal care attendants. This group tends to approach social change one-issue-at-a-time.

Earlier biological and cultural models focused on individual pathology, thus obscuring the significant social barriers faced by people with the multiple stigmas of race, poverty, and disability. With multiple stigmas (such as gender, race, and disability), opportunities for employment become increasingly limited and people become trapped in poverty. Disability, poverty, and minority status are linked and intensify the already negative relationship between economic status and the existence of a disability. For example, the majority of Latinos with disabilities live below the poverty level, and African Americans with disabilities are particularly disadvantaged. Biological and cultural theories cannot sufficiently explain the discrepancies between the disabled and non-disabled, minority and non-minority populations. People living with multiple stigmas have limited opportunities and resources available to them and face societal barriers and oppression that result in poverty and exclusion.

An empowerment framework, one that refers to the increased degree of control people can have over relevant aspects of their environment, better accounts for systemic inequalities faced by minorities with disabilities and attempts to overcome these obstacles. People living with multiple stigmas have limited opportunities and resources available to them and face societal barriers and oppression that result in poverty and exclusion.

The minority group model of disability must encompass the complex and multilayered identities held by people with disabilities. For some individuals, disability is only one of many stigmas they face. A disability-rights model that does not recognize the multiple barriers resulting from the "triple jeopardy" of race, poverty, and disability may inadvertently exclude a large number of people who deserve representation, many of whom are most likely to be left behind. The one-issue-at-a-time approach is an effective but narrow strategy for social change. An empowerment framework of analysis that incorporates an understanding of multifaceted issues can serve as a catalyst for helping people to overcome multiple stigmas and support their efforts to seek positive social change.

This framework encourages people from multiple constituencies to develop a common agenda based on shared unmet needs. It also promotes self-reliance and an increased awareness and understanding of the social forces that maintain oppression and discrimination. Empowered individuals or groups are more likely to challenge the status quo and to pursue remedy to the social inequality that characterizes the existence of low-income people of color with disabilities.

CONCLUSION

Throughout the twentieth century, several models have evolved to address the problems of people from marginalized groups, such as those living in poverty or who have disabilities. In the early decades of the twentieth century, a model of biological pathology was used to explain persistent social problems, and pathological inheritance was believed to cause mental and physical deficiency. In the decades following World War II, biological explanations gave way to models of cultural pathology. Cultural deprivation was related to mental and physical deficiency, resulting in deficits in language and learning. Both biological and cultural pathology models have been criticized for over-looking the importance of social and political inequality. The minority group model was developed in the 80s and 90s to explain the persistence of the social barriers faced by people with disabilities and other marginalized groups. Currently, an empowerment framework reconceptualizes the problem and specifies action sequences by which individuals from marginalized groups with multiple stigmas may gain the social, political, and economic support needed to overcome barriers to their full participation in society.

Early perceptions of people with disabilities as victims and threats have been increasingly replaced by images of social actors empowered to and capable of overcoming functional limitations and social barriers. Attempts continue to be made to better understand the complex interaction of multiple variables, such as disability, gender, race, and economic status. Developing theories of social change support the promotion of empowerment. Minorities with disabilities living in poverty can have the strength, understanding, and motivation to learn about their own situation and act to change it. They can develop a critical consciousness about their oppressed status, and then plan and take action to address the impact of negative societal attitudes on them and others in similar circumstances.

The barriers faced by people of color with disabilities living in poverty should not be underestimated. Racism, ableism, and poverty severely limit opportunity. Established organizations are usually unprepared to serve minority populations with multiple needs. For example, there is a growing population of inner-city minorities who have become permanently disabled as a result of violence. Service providers have difficulty meeting their needs. In the past, such situations were addressed through single-issue movements, and service provision that divided and dealt with each issue in isolation.

What is needed now is greater implementation of empowerment approaches that address the nexus of race, poverty, and disability. With critical awareness, support and social change, individuals and groups facing multiple stigmata need not be relegated to the sidelines of society. Essential to this important mission are more indigenous leaders and grassroots groups who have experience working on these different levels to meet the needs, affirm the rights and enhance the choices of people of color with disabilities living in low-income neighborhoods. Three strikes need not mean you're out, but rather playing a game with a greater degree of difficulty.

51

JUST CHOICES
Women of Color, Reproductive Health, and Human Rights

Loretta J. Ross, Sarah L. Brownlee, Dazon Dixon Diallo, Luz Rodriquez, and SisterSong Women of Color Reproductive Health Project

Making just choices around reproductive health is difficult for women of color. Just choices are not simply a range of options, but of options that make sense in order to optimize our reproductive health. We don't expect perfect choices, but we want choices that don't violate our sense of dignity, fairness, and justice. Our ability to control what happens to our bodies is constantly challenged by poverty, racism, sexism, homophobia, and injustice in the United States.

We face political regimes that seek to restrict our migration, to punish us for poverty, and to incarcerate us for behaviors politicians have criminalized. We are subject to various population control schemes, carriers of our own internalized oppression, and objects of unprincipled medical research. The race, gender, and class discrimination faced by women of color interferes with our ability to acquire services or culturally appropriate reproductive health information, particularly information on reproductive tract infections (RTIs). Mental health issues—such as oppression, depression, substance abuse, physical and sexual violence, lack of education, the lack of availability of services, and poverty—are related to racial, gender, and economic inequalities that specifically limit the potential of women of color to live healthy lives.

Women of color have not been passive victims in the face of this onslaught. In the words of Francesca Miller, we are "repressed but not resigned."[1] Yet organizing around reproductive health issues for women of color has not been easy. As women of color, we have always sought to protect our reproductive freedom, but issues of power and subordination complicate our efforts to bring attention to the reproductive health issues that threaten our lives.

From Jael Silliman and Anannya Bhattacharjee, eds., *Policing the National Body: Race, Gender, and Criminalization* (Boston: South End Press, 2002), pp. 147–74. Reprinted by permission of the South End Press.

Sometimes we work with predominantly white organizations that marginalize issues of race and class, and privilege abortion rights over other issues of reproductive justice. . . .

Some of us work with people of color organizations that marginalize gender and class issues, and where women's reproductive health issues are tangential to struggles against racism. Occasionally, women's reproductive health issues reach the agenda of these organizations, particularly in the areas of sterilization abuse and population control, but they rarely sustain any long-term momentum.

A number of women of color work with anti-poverty organizations that sometimes neglect race and gender issues altogether, assuming that class issues subsume concerns about reproductive health. Women of color numerically dominate organizations that work on poverty, homelessness, and welfare reform, but rarely do these organizations address the reproductive health needs of women of color. Similarly, programs that address violence against women of color sometimes highlight the connection between violence and poor health, but again, reproductive health issues are not their primary concern.

Few women of color organizations have significant programs that focus on reproductive health issues. Most women of color organizations address gender and racial discrimination, but many of these organizations believe that reproductive rights, particularly abortion rights, are too controversial in their communities. . . .

White women's organizations increasingly attempt to mobilize women of color in order to advance their political agenda and broaden their funding options. Organizations such as Planned Parenthood and NARAL want to present a picture of a diverse, inclusive movement and, at the same time, convince funders that they are capable of organizing women of color. While these efforts may be well intentioned, they are inadequate for including significant numbers of women of color. Moreover, these efforts are prone to the same issues of racism, classism, and homophobia that beset previous attempts to engage women of color in white organizations. . . .

The funding issues are also problematic because of their racial implications. While many women of color organizations suffer from a lack of sufficient funding to achieve organizational stability, many white women's organizations are provided with generous funding for their "women of color" projects, without a visible track record. This trend has several implications for women of color: the funding we desperately need to organize in our own communities is diverted to outside groups and we are forced to compete for funding on the terms set by the agencies with access to more resources. If funders prefer public policy strategies, for example, we have to produce policy papers in order to secure support.

Another consequence of funding white organizations to work on reproductive rights in communities of color is that such efforts often poison the soil, because racism is synonymous with genocide in the minds of many people of color. If issues of white supremacy, racism, or classism are not addressed by the white organizations, these defects contaminate efforts by women of color, making it difficult to avoid the stigmas left in the wake of more visible and better funded organizations. For example, it is difficult to counter charges that abortion is genocide when a white pro-choice organization displays racist or insensitive behavior in a community of color. A clear example was during the debate over immigration reform in 1996. Several pro-choice organizations actually agreed with the white majority in limiting the rights of immigrants, making it harder for women of color to join with them in solidarity in efforts to stop the "partial birth abortion" bills in Congress.

Even more problematic than the efforts of white pro-choice organizations are the inroads made by the religious right in communities of color. Among the religious right organizations that have increased their appeal to women of color are the Christian Coalition, Operation Rescue, Blacks for Life, and other groups opposed to abortion. Many people of color are drawn into supporting the ambitions of the religious right because those groups do not use open racism to promote their agenda. Because religiously cloaked bigotry is well disguised, it is difficult for most people to identify and challenge.

The religious right opposes women's reproductive freedom by cloaking itself in the moral mantle of the civil rights movement, for example by comparing the rights of unborn fetuses to the rights of African-Americans. It is not uncommon for anti-abortionists like Operation Rescue to use imagery of Martin Luther King, Jr. in their opposition to abortion, even though King was pro-choice. Such appropriation of civil rights language and symbols mocks the integrity of the civil rights movement's struggle for equality and freedom.

Strategists of the religious right use money to appeal to many religious leaders, by providing the funding that progressives fail to supply. In the 1990s, many anti-poverty programs in communities of color were funded by the religious right, often with several caveats such as mandates for organizations to embrace "abstinence only" language for sex education, and calls for the termination of abortion and contraceptive support. Anti-poverty organizations applying for funds from Catholic Charities in the 1990s were forced to sign an agreement that they would not work with pro-choice organizations in their communities, as was reported by anti-poverty groups like the Georgia Citizens' Coalition on Hunger and the Up and Out of Poverty Network. This coercive strategy was lamentably successful as alternative funding from progressive organizations was not available.

This situation is guaranteed to worsen under President George W. Bush, who has already established several faith-based initiatives to provide government funds to religious institutions. Even if one disregards the blurring line between church and state, it is impossible to overlook the fact that such funding will effectively promulgate the president's anti-choice agenda. Not only are women's health issues jeopardized by the president's personal agenda, but increased spending on the military and anti-terrorist campaigns in the wake of the September 11, 2001 attack on the United States will most likely divert significant funds away from addressing all domestic health care concerns.

These attempts to organize women of color demonstrate that much work remains to be done in order to formulate a collaborative, global reproductive health movement that tackles the lack of just choices for women of color. In the twenty-first century, women of color need to examine their previous organizing efforts. For the past decade, women of color working on reproductive health issues have attempted a dual strategy: working within our own communities to advance issues of reproductive health, while also working with the mainstream women's health movement to advance issues for women of color. This dual focus is critical and necessary, but after ten years of making relatively little progress on either front, it is now time to question the splitting of our energies.

Thus, it is critical that women of color again mobilize to defend our reproductive freedom. We are fighting battles on many fronts, and the health of our communities is at stake. We have to use new organizing strategies that do not create an artificial division between public policy advocacy and grassroots mobilizing, and we have to resist the blandishments of the religious right and the mainstream pro-choice movement if they do not truly represent our own agendas. . . .

NATIVE AMERICAN/INDIGENOUS COMMUNITY

According to the Indian Health Service (IHS), Native American women account for 15 percent of AIDS cases in the United States, compared with 7 percent for non-minority women. Cervical cancer affects 20 percent of Native American women, a rate more than twice that of the US national average of 8.6 percent. The death rate for Native women from cervical cancer is also higher due to delayed diagnosis. Chlamydia rates are thirteen times higher among Native American women than for other American women.[2]

In part due to a cultural attitude of mistrust that Native people feel toward researchers, many Native Americans do not participate in research studies. Health professionals estimate that the prevalence of RTIs may be as high as 65 percent for Native Americans. The prevalence of myth, mystery, and misinformation about sexuality in Native communities presents another major challenge to the promotion of reproductive health. Alcoholism and drug abuse, as well as physical and emotional abuse, all increase the risk of RTIs. The migrant-worker status of many Native Americans also exacerbates their risk. . . .

Health care is controlled by the federal government for many Native Americans. Just thirty-four Indian Health Service (IHS) clinics serve over

1.3 million Indian people nationwide, leaving 75 percent virtually without any health care. Urban Indians, the majority of all American Indians, receive less than 1 percent of the IHS budget.[3] The government's ban on traditional reproductive health care, such as midwifery, has only exacerbated the RTI-related problems.[4] Native American women with high-risk pregnancies are left with inadequate federal health care and their option for more community-based care is eroded. . . .

Forced sterilization, with the use of Depo-Provera and Norplant, has been utilized as a form of population control. Physicians offer Norplant implants for free but charge more than $300 to have them removed. Women are pressured into a procedure that limits their reproductive capacity. Physicians take advantage of the low-income status of many women by limiting their options for reproductive health.

Oftentimes, women are not aware of the choices they have in health services. Physicians do not take the time to explain health care options, and there is little effort toward public education. Another factor that influences public awareness of health issues is education level. Because many Native American women are not high school graduates, some information that is available is not accessible due to the high reading levels required for the material.

Culturally appropriate health education material that is "tradition-inclusive" is necessary to increase public awareness of health options. Approaches that empower people in the community to take control of their health choices are also paramount. . . .

ASIAN/PACIFIC ISLANDER AMERICAN COMMUNITY

According to the US Census Bureau, Asian/Pacific Islanders (A/PIs) are the fastest growing minority group in the United States.[5] Consisting of immigrants from over twenty countries who speak more than 120 languages, this population numbered more than 10 million people in 1997.[6] The majority of this population live in urban areas, mostly in California, Hawaii, and Washington. . . .

Because much of the A/PI community is non-English speaking, mainstream health education and disease prevention efforts have had little impact on these communities, and over 11,500 new cases of sexually transmitted diseases were reported for Asian-Americans and Pacific Islanders in 1998.[7] Moreover, health care professionals have limited knowledge of the different cultures and endemic diseases from immigrants' countries of origin, and thus lack the expertise to serve immigrant clients. In addition, A/PI women often cannot afford the care that may be available.

Cultural and family influences also affect the rate of health care access. A/PI women have traditionally placed the health needs of their families at the forefront and put less emphasis on individual needs.[8] Cultural taboos surrounding the body, sexuality, and pregnancy also contribute to the low rates of health service access. Many A/PI women feel uncomfortable discussing health issues.

The misperception of Asian-Americans as a healthy and well-off "model minority" has limited the development of research studies to document any poor status in health of the A/PI community. Contrary to this stereotype, over two-thirds of Asian-American women are sexually active, but less than 40 percent always use protection against STDs. One-quarter have never visited a health care provider for reproductive health services, or received education on reproductive tract infections.[9]. . .

One way to facilitate the provision of adequate care is through more research on nontraditional methods. It is critical for A/PI women to control their bodies, and to have influence over the care provided them. A national effort is necessary to achieve this goal and more voices need to be heard within the policy and medical arenas. Collaborative efforts to make resources known are a crucial first step.

LATINA/HISPANIC COMMUNITY

The Latina population has many factors contributing to high risk for RTIs. Approximately 30 percent of Latinos live below the poverty line, and nearly half the poor Hispanic families are female-headed. In 1995, 30 percent of the Hispanic population was not covered by health insurance. Medicaid coverage for Latinos varies by state and in many states poor undocumented Latinos are ineligible for Medicaid and often cannot afford health insurance. Welfare reform has also increased the number of Latinos ineligible for publicly funded health insurance. Women who are left without care then turn to self-medication and share medicine.[10]

Latinas also underutilize available health care services. A lack of United States citizenship often deters undocumented immigrant Latinos from using public clinics and other health facilities for fear of detection and deportation. In addition, Hispanics traditionally seek family members' advice before getting professional health care, which contributes to Latinas' low or delayed utilization of health care services. In many families, women's low status impedes their ability to seek and negotiate for their own health care. Many Latinas also work in the agriculture industry which exposes workers to pesticides that place them at risk for a range of health problems, including RTIs. Hispanics are also more likely to have diabetes, placing them at risk for a range of health problems, including RTIs. Hispanics are also more likely to have diabetes, placing them at greater risk for endogenous RTIs, further complicating and prolonging the treatment regime.[11] . . .

High rates of cesareans and sterilization abuse cause distrust of the medical community among many Latinas. For example, according to a national fertility study conducted in 1970 by Princeton University's Office of Population Control, 20 percent of all Mexican-American women had been sterilized. The disproportionate number of Puerto Rican women who have been sterilized reflects United States government policy that dates back to 1939, when an experimental sterilization campaign was implemented. By the 1970s, more than 35 percent of all Puerto Rican women of child-bearing age had been surgically sterilized.[12]

Unfortunately, structural, cultural, and social influences often prevent Latinas from actively asserting their rights for adequate and appropriate health care services. In many cases, Latinas, particularly immigrants, do not feel they are in a position of power. Religion plays an integral role in inhibiting women from feeling confident about reproductive health needs due to the connection with sexuality. The health beliefs of many Latinas relate to their views about God as the omnipotent creator of the universe, with personal behavior subject to God's judgment. Fatalistic beliefs such as these make it difficult to establish the importance of preventive health behaviors. Cultural factors also influence the spread of HIV infection and AIDS because they often are unwilling to discuss intimate and emotional matters such as illness and sex unless they are able to speak to someone in Spanish.[13]

THE BLACK/AFRICAN-AMERICAN COMMUNITY

The Black population in America consists primarily of African-Americans, although significant numbers of African and African-Caribbean immigrants have become part of this group in the last fifteen years. . . .

Available data on the health status of African-American women indicate that they suffer higher rates of undetected diseases, higher incidences of diseases and illnesses, and more chronic conditions, as well as higher morbidity rates than non-minority American women. According to statistics, African-American women exhibit very high rates of cervical and breast cancer and reproductive track infections (RTIs).[14]

Yet, despite high rates of serious health problems within the community, far too many women have never had a Pap smear or gynecological exam. In 1995, one in four African-American women did not receive a Pap smear, and one-third failed to receive a clinical breast exam. More than half of African-American women age 50 to 64 did not receive mammography screening between 1994 and 1995. One in seven (14 percent) rely on emergency rooms for basic health services.[15] Obesity, a contributing factor for some cancers, is most prevalent among African-American women.[16]

Appropriate mental health services are even worse in many cases. The influence of racial and gender oppression as it relates to depression, substance abuse, physical abuse, access to quality education, and the availability of services is often overlooked. One of the most obvious factors affecting the rate of health care access is the availability of appropriate services. In rural areas of the United States, services geared toward African-American women are frequently non-existent.[17] The lack of health care access in both rural and urban areas has led to a gap in research regarding Black women's health, including in areas of birth control, HIV/AIDS transmission, and RTIs. . . .

The lack of appropriate services, information, and research requires holistic approaches to health care that include advocacy and education. In addition, powerful and positive women motivators from the African-American community need to guide and lead dialogue around reproductive health issues. . . .

RECONCEPTUALIZING THE HUMAN RIGHTS FRAMEWORK

Global structural adjustment policies imposed by the World Bank on developing countries have resulted in cuts in social services, fees for public services, privatization, and the removal of subsidies for food, medicines, clean water, and transportation. In the United States, welfare reform is, in effect, acting as a structural adjustment program. A high level of poverty forces thousands of girls and women to sell their bodies as a means of survival.[18] Sadly enough, even in monogamous relationships, women's sexuality becomes their only bargaining tool for survival. Violence against women also tends to increase poverty, risks of STDs, unintended pregnancies, drug and alcohol abuse, and mental illness. . . .

Organizations concerned with reproductive health issues in the United States are increasingly drawing inspiration and tools from the international human rights movement, and those working within a traditional human rights framework are gradually including issues related to reproductive health. Women, particularly women of color, have spearheaded this rearticulation of the human rights framework in the United States. . . .

Liberal human rights interpretations often do not recognize that equality of opportunity is an illusion in a society based on competitive individualism in which one ethnic group (whites) has social, political, and economic advantages in relationship to other ethnic groups (people of color). Thus, individualistic rights frameworks often neglect the importance of group rights of ethnicity and culture.[19] For example, while an individual African-American may have the legal freedom and the financial means to purchase a home in any community, that potential buyer must be protected from racial discrimination against African-Americans as a group, in order to enjoy that individual right.

Parental consent laws, for-profit health care, welfare reform policies, and immigration policies impact women's health choices and detrimentally affect the quality of care available. In order to ensure access to health care and treatment, and to address the intersection of class, race, and gender that affects women of color, a comprehensive human rights–based approach is necessary.

This new and comprehensive, human rights–based reproductive health agenda challenges the traditional American liberal human rights framework, by giving economic, social, and cultural rights the same consideration given to civil and political rights. The United States government has an obligation to provide an environment in which policies, laws, and practices enable women to realize their reproductive rights, and to refrain from creating conditions that compromise or restrict such rights.

NOTES

1. Francesca Miller, *Latin American Women and the Search for Social Justice* (Hanover, NH: University Press of New England, 1991), 207.

2. National Institutes of Health, *Women of Color Health Data Book* (1998), 75.

3. Ibid., 2.

4. Ibid., 3.

5. United States Department of Commerce, Bureau of the Census CB97–FS.04, 1997.

6. Ibid.

7. National Asian American Women's Health Organization, "Community Solutions: Meeting the Challenge of STDs in Asian Americans and Pacific Islanders" (2000), 7.

8. Ibid., 13.

9. Ibid.

10. National Institutes of Health, *Women of Color Health Data Book* (1998), 9.

11. Ibid., 11.

12. Angela Davis, *Women, Race and Class* (New York: Knopf, 1981), 219.

13. National Institutes of Health, *Women of Color Health Data Book* (1998), 11.

14. Deborah R. Grayson, "Necessity Was the Midwife to Our Politics: Black Women's Health Activism in the "Post-" Civil Rights Era (1980–1996)," in *Still Lifting, Still Climbing: African American Women's Contemporary Activism*, ed. Kimberly Springer (New York: New York University Press, 1999), 133.

15. Ibid., 70.

16. "Women's Health: Choices and Challenges," *The Commonwealth Fund Quarterly*, Special issue (1996).

17. Susan F. Feiner, *Race and Gender in the American Economy: Views Across the Spectrum* (Englewood Cliffs, NJ: Prentice-Hall, 1994), 315.

18. Kamala Kempadoo and Jo Doezema, *Global Sex Workers: Rights, Resistance and Redefinition* (New York: Routledge Press, 1998), 17.

19. William Felice, *Taking Suffering Seriously: The Importance of Collective Human Rights* (Albany, NY: SUNY Press, 1996), 35.

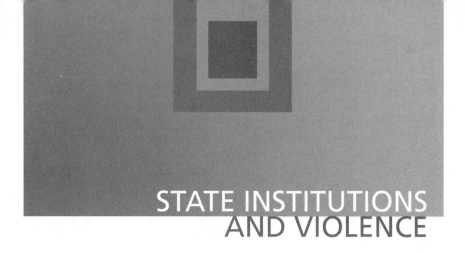

STATE INSTITUTIONS AND VIOLENCE

52

THE FIRST AMERICANS
American Indians

C. Matthew Snipp

By the end of the nineteenth century, many observers predicted that American Indians were destined for extinction. Within a few generations, disease, warfare, famine, and outright genocide had reduced their numbers from millions to less than 250,000 in 1890. Once a self-governing, self-sufficient people, American Indians were forced to give up their homes and their land, and to subordinate themselves to an alien culture. The forced resettlement to reservation lands or the Indian Territory (now Oklahoma) frequently meant a life of destitution, hunger, and complete dependency on the federal government for material needs.

Today, American Indians are more numerous than they have been for several centuries. While still one of the most destitute groups in American society, tribes have more autonomy and are now more self-sufficient than at any time since the last century. In cities, modern pan-Indian organizations have been successful in making the presence of American Indians known to the larger community, and have mobilized to meet the needs of their people

From Silvia Pedraza and Rubén G. Rumbaut, eds., *Origins and Destinies: Immigration, Race, and Ethnicity in America.* (Belmont, CA: Wadsworth, 1996), pp. 390–403. Reprinted by permission.

(Cornell 1988; Nagel 1986; Weibel-Orlando 1991). In many rural areas, American Indians and especially tribal governments have become increasingly more important and increasingly more visible by virtue of their growing political and economic power. The balance of this [reading] is devoted to explaining their unique place in American society.

THE INCORPORATION OF AMERICAN INDIANS

The current political and economic status of American Indians is the result of the process by which they were incorporated into Euro-American society (Hall 1989). This amounts to a long history of efforts aimed at subordinating an otherwise self-governing and self-sufficient people that eventually culminated in widespread economic dependency. The role of the U.S. government in this process can be seen in the five major historical periods of federal Indian relations: removal, assimilation, the Indian New Deal, termination and relocation, and self-determination.

Removal

In the early nineteenth century, the population of the United States expanded rapidly at the same time that the federal government increased its political and military capabilities. The character of Indian-American relations changed after the War of 1812. The federal government increasingly pressured tribes settled east of the Appalachian Mountains to move west to the territory acquired in the Louisiana Purchase. Numerous treaties were negotiated by which the tribes relinquished most of their land and eventually were forced to move west.

Initially the federal government used bargaining and negotiation to accomplish removal, but many tribes resisted (Prucha 1984). However, the election of Andrew Jackson by a frontier constituency signaled the beginning of more forceful measures to accomplish removal. In 1830 Congress passed the Indian Removal Act, which mandated the eventual removal of the eastern tribes to points west of the Mississippi River, in an area which was to become the Indian Territory and is now the state of Oklahoma. Dozens of tribes were forcibly removed from the eastern half of the United States to the Indian Territory and newly created reservations in the west, a long process ridden with conflict and bloodshed.

As the nation expanded beyond the Mississippi River, tribes of the plains, southwest, and west coast were forcibly settled and quarantined on isolated reservations. This was accompanied by the so-called Indian Wars—a bloody chapter in the history of Indian-White relations (Prucha 1984; Utley 1963). This period in American history is especially remarkable because the U.S.

government was responsible for what is unquestionably one of the largest forced migrations in history.

The actual process of removal spanned more than a half-century and affected nearly every tribe east of the Mississippi River. Removal often meant extreme hardships for American Indians, and in some cases this hardship reached legendary proportions. For example, the Cherokee removal has become known as the "Trail of Tears." In 1838, nearly 17,000 Cherokees were ordered to leave their homes and assemble in military stockades (Thornton 1987, p. 117). The march to the Indian Territory began in October and continued through the winter months. As many as 8,000 Cherokees died from cold weather and diseases such as influenza (Thornton 1987, p. 118).

According to William Hagan (1979), removal also caused the Creeks to suffer dearly as their society underwent a profound disintegration. The contractors who forcibly removed them from their homes refused to do anything for "the large number who had nothing but a cotton garment to protect them from the sleet storms and no shoes between them and the frozen ground of the last stages of their hegira. About half of the Creek nation did not survive the migration and the difficult early years in the West" (Hagan 1979, pp. 77–81). In the West, a band of Nez Perce men, women, and children, under the leadership of Chief Joseph, resisted resettlement in 1877. Heavily outnumbered, they were pursued by cavalry troops from the Wallowa valley in eastern Oregon and finally captured in Montana near the Canadian border. Although the Nez Perce were eventually captured and moved to the Indian Territory, and later to Idaho, their resistance to resettlement has been described by one historian as "one of the great military movements in history" (Prucha 1984, p. 541).

Assimilation

Near the end of the nineteenth century, the goal of isolating American Indians on reservations and the Indian Territory was finally achieved. The Indian population also was near extinction. Their numbers had declined steadily throughout the nineteenth century, leading most observers to predict their disappearance (Hoxie 1984). Reformers urged the federal government to adopt measures that would humanely ease American Indians into extinction. The federal government responded by creating boarding schools and the allotment acts—both were intended to "civilize" and assimilate American Indians into American society by Christianizing them, educating them, introducing them to private property, and making them into farmers. American Indian boarding schools sought to accomplish this task by indoctrinating Indian children with the belief that tribal culture was an inferior relic of the past and that Euro-American culture was vastly superior and preferable. Indian children were forbidden to wear their native attire, to eat their native foods, to speak their native language, or to practice their traditional religion. Instead, they were issued Euro-American clothes, and expected to speak English and become Christians. Indian children who did not relinquish their culture were punished by school authorities. The curriculum of these schools taught vocational arts along with "civilization" courses.

The impact of allotment policies is still evident today. The 1887 General Allotment Act (the Dawes Severalty Act) and subsequent legislation mandated that tribal lands were to be allotted to individual American Indians, . . . and the surplus lands left over from allotment were to be sold on the open market. Indians who received allotted tribal lands also received citizenship, farm implements, and encouragement from Indian agents to adopt farming as a livelihood (Hoxie 1984, Prucha 1984).

For a variety of reasons, Indian lands were not completely liquidated by allotment, many Indians did not receive allotments, and relatively few changed their lifestyles to become farmers. Nonetheless, the allotment era was a disaster because a significant number of allottees eventually lost their land. Through tax foreclosures, real estate fraud, and their own need for cash, many American Indians lost what for most of them was their last remaining asset (Hoxie 1984).

Allotment took a heavy toll on Indian lands. It caused about 90 million acres of Indian land to be lost, approximately two-thirds of the land that had belonged to tribes in 1887 (O'Brien 1990). This created another problem that continues to vex many reservations: "checkerboarding." Reservations that were subjected to allotment are typically a crazy quilt composed of tribal lands, privately owned "fee" land, and trust land belonging to individual Indian families. Checkerboarding presents reservation officials with enormous administrative problems when trying to develop land use management plans, zoning ordinances, or economic development projects that require the construction of physical infrastructure such as roads or bridges.

The Indian New Deal

The Indian New Deal was short-lived but profoundly important. Implemented in the early 1930s along with the other New Deal programs of the Roosevelt administration, the Indian New Deal was important for at least three reasons. First, signaling the end of the disastrous allotment era as well as a new respect for American Indian tribal culture, the Indian New Deal repudiated allotment as a policy. Instead of continuing its futile efforts to detribalize American Indians, the federal government acknowledged that tribal culture was worthy of respect. Much of this change was due to John Collier, a long-time Indian rights advocate appointed by Franklin Roosevelt to serve as Commissioner of Indian Affairs (Prucha 1984).

Like other New Deal policies, the Indian New Deal also offered some relief from the Great Depression and brought essential infrastructure development to many reservations, such as projects to control soil erosion and to build hydroelectric dams, roads, and other public facilities. These projects created jobs in New Deal programs such as the Civilian Conservation Corps and the Works Progress Administration.

An especially important and enduring legacy of the Indian New Deal was the passage of the Indian Reorganization Act (IRA) of 1934. Until then, Indian self-government had been forbidden by law. This act allowed tribal governments, for the first time in decades, to reconstitute themselves for the purpose of overseeing their own affairs on the reservation. Critics charge that this law imposed an alien form of government, representative democracy, on traditional tribal authority. On some reservations, this has been an ongoing source of conflict (O'Brien 1990). Some reservations rejected the IRA for this reason, but now have tribal governments authorized under different legislation.

Termination and Relocation

After World War II, the federal government moved to terminate its long-standing relationship with Indian tribes by settling the tribes' outstanding legal claims, by terminating the special status of reservations, and by helping reservation Indians relocate to urban areas (Fixico 1986). The Indian Claims Commission was a special tribunal created in 1946 to hasten the settlement of legal claims that tribes had brought against the federal government. In fact, the Indian Claims Commission became bogged down with prolonged cases, and in 1978 the commission was dissolved by Congress. At that time, there were 133 claims still unresolved out of an original 617 that were first heard by the commission three decades earlier (Fixico 1986, p. 186). The unresolved claims that were still pending were transferred to the Federal Court of Claims.

Congress also moved to terminate the federal government's relationship with Indian tribes. House Concurrent Resolution (HCR) 108, passed in 1953, called for steps that eventually would abolish all reservations and abolish all special programs serving American Indians. It also established a priority list of reservations slated for immediate termination. However, this bill and subsequent attempts to abolish reservations were vigorously opposed by Indian advocacy groups such as the National Congress of American Indians. Only two reservations were actually terminated, the Klamath in Oregon and the Menominee in Wisconsin. The Menominee reservation regained its trust status in 1975 and the Klamath reservation was restored in 1986.

The Bureau of Indian Affairs (BIA) also encouraged reservation Indians to relocate and seek work in urban job markets. This was prompted partly by the desperate economic prospects on most reservations, and partly because of the federal government's desire to "get out of the Indian business." The BIA's relocation programs aided reservation Indians in moving to designated cities, such as Los Angeles and Chicago, where they also assisted them in finding housing and employment. Between 1952 and 1972, the BIA relocated more than 100,000 American Indians (Sorkin 1978). However, many Indians returned to their reservations (Fixico 1986). For some American Indians, the return to the reservation was only temporary; for example, during periods when seasonal employment such as construction work was hard to find.

Self-Determination

Many of the policies enacted during the termination and relocation era were steadfastly opposed by American Indian leaders and their supporters. As these programs became stalled, critics attacked them for being harmful, ineffective, or both. By the mid-1960s, these policies had very little serious support. Perhaps inspired by the gains of the Civil Rights movement, American Indian leaders and their supporters made "self-determination" the first priority on their political agendas. For these activists, self-determination meant that Indian people would have the autonomy to control their own affairs, free from the paternalism of the federal government.

The idea of self-determination was well received by members of Congress sympathetic to American Indians. It also was consistent with the "New Federalism" of the Nixon administration. Thus, the policies of termination and relocation were repudiated in a process that culminated in 1975 with the passage of the American Indian Self-Determination and Education Assistance Act, a profound shift in federal Indian policy. For the first time since this nation's founding, American Indians were authorized to oversee the affairs of their own communities, free of federal intervention. In practice, the Self-Determination Act established measures that would allow tribal governments to assume a larger role in reservation administration of programs for welfare assistance, housing, job training, education, natural resource conservation, and the maintenance of reservation roads and bridges (Snipp and Summers 1991). Some reservations also have their own police forces and game wardens, and can issue licenses and levy taxes. The Onondaga tribe in upstate New York have taken their sovereignty one step further by issuing passports that are internationally recognized. Yet there is a great deal of variability in terms of how much autonomy tribes have over reservation affairs. Some tribes, especially those on large and well-organized reservations have nearly complete control over their reservations, while smaller reservations with limited resources often depend heavily on BIA services. . . .

CONCLUSION

Though small in number, American Indians have an enduring place in American society. Growing numbers of American Indians occupy reservation and other trust lands, and equally important has been the revitalization of tribal governments. Tribal governments now have a larger role in reservation affairs than ever in the past. Another significant development has been the urbanization of American Indians. Since 1950, the proportion of American Indians in cities has grown rapidly. These American Indians have in common with reservation Indians many of the same problems and disadvantages, but they also face other challenges unique to city life.

The challenges facing tribal governments are daunting. American Indians are among the poorest groups in the nation. Reservation Indians have substantial needs for improved housing, adequate health care, educational opportunities, and employment, as well as developing and maintaining reservation infrastructure. In the face of declining federal assistance, tribal governments are assuming an ever-larger burden. On a handful of reservations, tribal governments have assumed completely the tasks once performed by the BIA.

As tribes have taken greater responsibility for their communities, they also have struggled with the problems of raising revenues and providing economic opportunities for their people. Reservation land bases provide many reservations with resources for development. However, these resources are not always abundant, much less unlimited, and they have not always been well managed. It will be yet another challenge for tribes to explore ways of efficiently managing their existing resources. Legal challenges also face tribes seeking to exploit unconventional resources such as gambling revenues. Their success depends on many complicated legal and political contingencies.

Urban American Indians have few of the resources found on reservations, and they face other difficult problems. Preserving their culture and identity is an especially pressing concern. However, urban Indians have successfully adapted to city environments in ways that preserve valued customs and activities—powwows, for example, are an important event in all cities where there is a large Indian community. In addition, pan-Indianism has helped urban Indians set aside tribal differences and forge alliances for the betterment of urban Indian communities.

These alliances are essential, because unlike reservation Indians, urban American Indians do not have their own form of self-government. Tribal governments do not have jurisdiction over urban Indians. For this reason, urban Indians must depend on other strategies for ensuring that the needs of their community are met, especially for those new to city life. Coping with the transition to urban life poses a multitude of difficult challenges for many

American Indians. Some succumb to these problems, especially the hardships of unemployment, economic deprivation, and related maladies such as substance abuse, crime, and violence. But most successfully overcome these difficulties, often with help from other members of the urban Indian community.

Perhaps the greatest strength of American Indians has been their ability to find creative ways for dealing with adversity, whether in cities or on reservations. In the past, this quality enabled them to survive centuries of oppression and persecution. Today this is reflected in the practice of cultural traditions that Indian people are proud to embrace. The resilience of American Indians is an abiding quality that will no doubt ensure that they will remain part of the ethnic mosaic of American society throughout the twenty-first century and beyond.

References

Cornell, Stephen. 1988. *The Return of the Native: American Indian Political Resurgence*. New York: Oxford University Press.

Fixico, Donald L. 1986. *Termination and Relocation: Federal Indian Policy, 1945–1960*. Albuquerque, NM: University of New Mexico Press.

Hagan, William T. 1979. *American Indians*. Chicago, IL: University of Chicago Press.

Hall, Thomas D. 1989. *Social Change in the Southwest, 1350–1880*. Lawrence, KS: University Press of Kansas.

Hoxie, Frederick E. 1984. *A Final Promise: The Campaign to Assimilate the Indians, 1880–1920*. Lincoln, NE: University of Nebraska Press.

Nagel, Joanne. 1986. "American Indian Repertoires of Contention." Paper presented at the annual meeting of the American Sociological Association, San Francisco, CA.

O'Brien, Sharon. 1990. *American Indian Tribal Governments*. Norman, OK: University of Oklahoma Press.

Prucha, Francis Paul. 1984. *The Great Father*. Lincoln, NE: University of Nebraska Press.

Snipp, C. Matthew and Gene F. Summers. 1991. "American Indian Development Policies," pp. 166–180 in *Rural Policies for the 1990s*, edited by Cornelia Flora and James A. Christenson. Boulder, CO: Westview Press.

Sorkin, Alan L. 1978. *The Urban American Indian*. Lexington, MA: Lexington Books.

Thornton, Russell. 1987. *American Indian Holocaust and Survival: A Population History since 1942*. Norman, OK: University of Oklahoma Press.

Utley, Robert M. 1963. *The Last Days of the Sioux Nation*. New Haven: Yale University Press.

Weibel-Orlando, Joan. 1991. *Indian Country, L.A.* Urbana, IL: University of Illinois Press.

53

POLICING THE NATIONAL BODY
Sex, Race, and Criminalization

Jael Silliman

American politicians, eager to garner support from the large middle-class, promote "family values," endlessly debate issues of abortion, and outdo each other as champions of "working families" (read "middle-class" families). . . .

Essentially, what we have is an America deeply divided across class and race lines. This makes it possible for mainstream America—its politicians and media—to ignore or rarely address issues of poverty, criminalization, and race that are pressing for communities of color. Incarceration rates for people of color are disproportionately high and assaults and searches by police, the Immigration and Naturalization Service (INS), and border patrol forces are daily occurrences in communities of color. This aggressive law enforcement regime is increasingly accepted by the mainstream as the price to be paid for law and order. A lead article in the February 2001 edition of the *New York Times Magazine* marks this decisive shift in public attitude in New York City from a more libertarian, turbulent, and nonconformist city towards a greater acceptance of aggressive law enforcement.

. . . The new wisdom in New York City—one of the bastions of liberalism in the country—is "We no longer believe that to solve crime we have to deal with the root causes of poverty and racism; we now believe that we can reduce crime through good policing."[1]

Aggressive law enforcement policies and actions are devastating women of color and their communities. Though there is a strong and growing law enforcement accountability movement,[2] the women's movement in general has not seen state violence as a critical concern.[3] The mainstream reproductive rights movement, consumed with protecting the right to abortion, has failed to respond adequately to the policing, criminalization, and incarceration of large numbers of poor people and people of color. It has not sufficiently addressed cuts in welfare and immigrant services that have made one of the most fundamental reproductive rights—the right to have a child and to rear a family—most tenuous for a large number of people.

From Jael Silliman and Anannya Bhattacharjee, eds., *Policing the National Body: Race, Gender, and Criminalization* (Boston: South End Press, 2002), pp. x–xxvi. Reprinted by permission of the South End Press.

The mainstream reproductive rights movement, largely dominated by white women, is framed around choice: the choice to determine whether or not to have children, the choice to terminate a pregnancy, and the ability to make informed choices about contraceptive and reproductive technologies. This conception of choice is rooted in the neoliberal tradition that locates individual rights at its core, and treats the individual's control over her body as central to liberty and freedom. This emphasis on individual choice, however, obscures the social context in which individuals make choices, and discounts the ways in which the state regulates populations, disciplines individual bodies, and exercises control over sexuality, gender, and reproduction.[4]

The state regulates and criminalizes reproduction for many poor women through mandatory or discriminatory promotion of long-acting contraceptives and sterilization, and by charging pregnant women on drugs with negligence or child abuse. An examination of the body politics, the state's power of "regulation, surveillance and control of bodies (individual and collective)," elucidates the scope and venues through which the state regulates its populations "in reproduction and sexuality, in work and in leisure, in sickness and other forms of deviance and human difference."[5] . . .

Women of color have independently articulated a broad reproductive rights agenda embedded in issues of equality and social justice, while keenly tuned to the state's role in the reproduction and regulation of women's bodies. In an effort to protect their reproductive rights, they have challenged coercive population policies, demanded access to safe and accessible birth control, and asserted their right to economic and political resources to maintain healthy children. Through these demands, they move from an emphasis on individual rights to rights that are at once politicized and collectivized. African-American women leaders articulate the barriers to exercising their reproductive rights:

> Hunger and homelessness. Inadequate housing and income to provide for themselves and their children. Family instability. Rape. Incest. Abuse. Too young, too old, too sick, too tired. Emotional, physical, mental, economic, social—the reasons for not carrying a pregnancy to term are endless and varied.[6]

These leaders remind us that a range of individual and social concerns must be engaged to realize reproductive rights for all women. . . . A key concern among women of color and poor communities today is: the difficulty of maintaining families and sustaining community in the face of increasing surveillance and criminalization. . . . Particular communities and women within them are conceived and reproduced as threats to the national body, imagined as white and middle-class. . . .

. . . Poor women and women of color are criminalized. Bhattacharjee elaborates upon the prison system, police, INS, and border patrol forces to illustrate how they routinely undermine and endanger women's caretaking, caregiving, and reproductive functions. She shows how systemic and frequent abuses of reproductive rights and threats to bodily integrity are often over-looked by narrow definitions of reproductive rights and single-issue move-ments. . . . Greater coalition-building efforts between the women's move-ment, the reproductive rights movement, the immigrant rights movement, the violence against women movement, and the enforcement account-ability movement are needed to break down barriers and to ensure the safety and self-determination of women of color. . . .

CRIME AND PUNISHMENT IN THE UNITED STATES

The criminal justice system has become a massive machine for arrest, deten-tion, and incarceration. The events of September 11, 2001 have intensified this trend. Citing "national security" and the "war against terrorism," President Bush has furthered the power of the criminal justice system to ar-rest noncitizens and to circumvent the court system. Immigrants and com-munities of color will bear the brunt of the intensified assault on civil liber-ties. In 1998, on any given day, there were approximately six million people under some form of correctional authority. The number of people in Ameri-can prisons is expected to surpass two million by late 2001. Federal Judge U. W. Clemon, after a visit to the Morgan County Jail in Alabama, wrote in a blistering ruling, "To say the Morgan County Jail is overcrowded is an understatement. The sardine-can appearance of its cell units more nearly resemble the holding units of slave ships during the Middle Passage of the eighteenth century than anything in the twenty-first century."[7] Imprison-ment is the solution currently proffered for drug offenses in minority com-munities and for the other social problems spawned by poverty. As welfare and service programs are gutted, the only social service available to many of America's poor is jail![8]

Despite this surge in incarceration rates, it is widely accepted that prisons encourage recidivism, transform the occasional offender into a habitual delin-quent,[9] fail to eliminate crime, and ignore the social problems that drive indi-viduals to engage in illegal actions. French historian and social critic Michel Foucault explains the political rationale behind what the terms the "produc-tion of delinquency," and its usefulness for those in power:

> [T]he existence of a legal prohibition creates around it a field of illegal practices, which one manages to supervise, while extracting from it an illicit profit through elements, themselves illegal, but rendered manipulable by their organization in delinquency. . . . Delinquency represents a diversion of illegality for the illicit circuits of profit and power of the dominant class.[10]

The building and maintenance of policing and prison systems is politically expedient and highly profitable. Prisons boost local economies. Fremont County, Colorado, home to thirteen prisons, promotes itself as the Corrections Capital of the World. In *Going Up the River*, Joseph Hallinan explains how prisons have become public works projects that require a steady flow of inmates to sustain them.[11] Corporations engage in bidding wars to run prisons, and the federal government boasts about saving money by contracting out prison management to the private sector.

People of color are disproportionately represented in the prison industrial complex. Bureau of Justice statistics indicate that in 1999, 46 percent of prison inmates were Black and 18 percent were Hispanic. In "Killing the Black Community," Judith Scully argues that the war on drugs is used to justify and exercise control over the Black community. She contends that the United States government has historically maintained control over the Black community by selectively enforcing the law, arbitrarily defining criminal behavior and incarceration, and failing to punish white people engaged in lawless acts against the Black community, as exemplified in the infamous Rodney King and Amadou Diallo verdicts. The war on drugs demonstrates how government officials employ legal tools as well as racial rhetoric and criminal theory to criminalize and destroy Black communities. Scully explores how the creation of drug-related crimes such as the "crack baby" demonizes Black motherhood and undermines Black childbearing. Her essay exposes the institutional links between Blackness, suspicion, and criminality.

As strongly as class and race biases determine the criminal justice system, so does gender bias. Since 1980, the number of women in state and federal correctional facilities has tripled.[12] Amnesty International figures indicate that the majority of the over 140,000 women in the American penitentiary system are Black, Latina, and poor women, incarcerated largely for petty crimes.[13] For the same offense, Black and Latina women are respectively eight and four times more likely to be incarcerated than white women. The United Nations special report on violence against women in US state and federal prisons noted the trend in prison management that emphasizes punishment rather than rehabilitation and a widespread reduction in welfare and support services within the criminal justice system. . . .

The criminal justice system works collaboratively with government, corporate, and professional institutions to perform and carry out disciplinary functions deemed necessary to uphold the system of injustice. The recent exposés on racial profiling, discriminatory sentencing, and the compliance of hospitals, medical professionals, and private citizens in administering drug tests or reporting substance abuse among pregnant women are a few examples of the ways in which a range of actors are drawn in (sometimes reluctantly) to the surveillance and disciplinary system. For example, feminist lawyer Lynn Paltrow, executive director of National Advocates for Pregnant Women, describes how the Medical University Hospital in Charleston instituted a policy of reporting and facilitating the arrest of pregnant patients, overwhelmingly African-Americans, who tested positive for cocaine. African-American women were dragged out of the hospital in chains and shackles where the medical staff worked in collaboration with the prosecutor and police to see if the threat of arrest would deter drug use among pregnant women.[14]

Such violations are not going unchallenged. In *Ferguson vs. City of Charleston* (March 2001), a lawsuit engineered by Lynn Paltrow, the US Supreme Court agreed that Americans have the right, when they seek medical help, to expect that their doctor will examine them to provide diagnosis and treatment, and not search them to facilitate their arrest.[15] . . .

It is essential that we do not separate the more blatant forms of policing—videocameras within prisons that track every move of a prisoner, racial profiling, drug tests disproportionately administered in poor communities, and the raids on illegal immigrants crossing over to the United States—from the disciplinary apparatus being deployed across society. The wide use of differential forms of control and discipline is apparent in the ways in which the public has acquiesced to the policing and surveillance increasingly employed in everyday lives.

As a society we are no longer outraged when we hear that public schools in poor neighborhoods are routinely policed and equipped with metal detectors, and that students are hauled away in handcuffs for petty misdemeanors. The bodies being patrolled, segregated by race, determine the form of discipline applied. Perhaps this differential treatment explains why, in response to the spate of shootings in public schools across the country, parents in affluent neighborhoods have rallied and called for greater policing to ensure their children's safety. Middle-class parents invite policing to "protect their children." This contrasts sharply with the policing imposed in schools in poor communities and communities of color that criminalizes rather than protects. Though surveillance and policing differ according to whether they are there to protect or to criminalize, both kinds of interventions further extend state control over individual and collective bodies. The overt and insidious intrusions consolidate power in state and corporate entities.

BIOLOGICAL CONTROL

Women of color have been the target of biological control ideologies since the founding of America. In her book *Killing the Black Body*, Dorothy Roberts traces the history of reproductive rights abuses perpetrated on the Black community from slavery to the present. Roberts shows how control over reproduction is systematically deployed as a form of racial oppression and argues that the denial of Black reproductive autonomy serves the interests of white supremacy.[16] Others have documented the history of sterilization abuse in the

Latina and Native American communities, indicating that population control has a long history in the United States. A Native American reproductive activist reports that on the Pine Ridge reservation today, pregnant women with drinking problems are put in jail, as it is the only holding place for them.[17] . . .

The potential to extend biological control has expanded exponentially. Advances in data collection and storage through the computer, Internet, and genetic revolutions have made surveillance systems more efficient and invasive. The nineteenth-century "panoptical gaze" made it possible for a prisoner to be seen at all times, and through that process the prisoner internalized surveillance.[18] The new technologies radically expand the ability to collect, process, and encode large amounts of information on ever smaller surfaces. This makes it possible for the human body to be manipulated and controlled in radically new ways—from within the body itself. This intensification takes control from a mental to a physiological realm.

Like policing, corporate intrusion into the private sphere is increasingly naturalized. A great deal of data on individuals is bought, sold, and traded. In this instance, it is information on the rich and middle-class that is particularly coveted. The Internet revolution has made it possible for corporate and security interests to track every move made by an individual on the web to determine a person's consumer preferences, interests, and purchases, in addition to getting credit card information. Such intrusive data collecting techniques regarding an individual's tastes and preferences for corporate niche marketing is rarely framed as a surveillance problem. Critics have discussed it sometimes as a privacy concern, but by and large these incursions are accepted as a market-driven intrusion into our life.

Emerging reproductive technologies, such as cloning, have the potential to blur the distinctions between genetically distinct and genetically determined individuals. This raises ethical questions regarding who would count as fully human with the attendant civil rights and liberties. Valerie Hartouni points to how standards of humanity get "partialized" (making some less human than others) in this process.[19] She fears that, in the current social context, such technologies will be used to manage and contain diversity and the proliferation of difference.[20] Other critics are concerned with the eugenic possibilities of cloning and similar practices that work on humans from the inside out. The commodification of human life and the disruption that such technologies could have on kinship structures and human relations are a source of grave concern.

SURVEILLANCE AND NATIONAL (IN)SECURITY

Whereas the prison and policing systems are supposed to protect the nation from dangers within, the military, Border Patrols, and INS are ostensibly designed to protect the public from danger and threats that emanate from outside the national body. The discretionary authority and budgets of these institutions have expanded exponentially since September 11, 2001. . . . An influx of immigrants, the rhetoric of explosive population growth in the Third World, and angry young men inside and outside the United States are manufactured as a threat to national security.[21]

Immigrants in the United States are constructed as a source of danger. This threat has been used to justify the allocation of billions of dollars to the enforcement programs of the INS that patrol the nation. At present, the INS has more armed agents with arrest power than any other federal law enforcement agency.[22] Mandatory detention provisions have made immigrants the fastest growing incarcerated population in the United States. Stringent controls and border security forces are positioned at strategic places along the United States-Mexico border. Military-style tactics and equipment result in immigrants undertaking more dangerous, isolated routes to cross over where the risks of death, dehydration, and assault are exponentially higher.

Immigrant rights organizations and the press record detailed accounts of immigrants risking their lives to make their way through tortuous terrain to find work in the United States. The Mojave Desert in Southern California with its inhospitable terrain has become one such death trap for immigrants.[23] This dangerous crossing is a dramatic example of the extreme risks that immigrants take to escape INS agents and provide adequately for their families.

Vigilante groups and private citizens in Arizona have taken it upon themselves to "help" patrol ranchers "hunt" Mexican undocumented immigrants. Jose Palafox reports on the roundup of over 3,000 undocumented immigrants on Roger and Don Barnett's 22,000-acre property in Douglas, Arizona, near the United States-Mexico border. Ranchers circulated a leaflet asking for volunteers to help patrol their land while having "Fun in the Sun." Immigrants were considered "fair game."[24]

While border patrol forces and private citizens tighten their grip on illegal immigration and regulate the mobility of poor workers, social services are being slashed for legal immigrants. The latter are often portrayed as a drain on national resources and a direct threat to low-wage workers in the United States, and female immigrants of color are particularly targeted for their family settlement and community building roles. . . .

Even though many studies have shown that immigrant labor contributes to the economy, there is a widely held perception that they represent a financial drain. Despite the proverbial anti-immigrant sentiment, the United States economy depends on cheap immigrant labor. Very often undocumented workers perform jobs or are made to engage in activities usually considered too low-paying or too risky for citizens and residents. It has been estimated that 45,000 to 50,000 women and children are trafficked annually into and across the United States for the sex industry, sweatshops, domestic labor, and agricultural work. The INS compares the trafficking in women and children with the drug and weapons smuggling industry. . . .

BEYOND ANALYSIS: BUILDING A MOVEMENT

The . . . Committee on Women, Population, and the Environment (CWPE) [is] a multiracial alliance of feminist activists, health practitioners, and scholars committed to promoting the social and economic empowerment of women in a context of global peace and justice. We work toward eliminating poverty, inequality, racism, and environmental degradation. A crucial feature of our work . . . is our identification and cultivation of a political common ground, given our widely ranging ethnic and national identities. . . .

CWPE asserts that the oppression of women, not their reproductive capacities, needs to be eliminated and calls for drug treatment for women with substance abuse problems, decent jobs, educational opportunities, and mental health and child-care services. It is the lack of these services that deny human dignity and exacerbate conditions of poverty, social status, and gender discrimination. . .

This [essay] is directed at activists, students, policy-makers, and scholars who seek to understand the connections between the criminalization of people of color and the poor, and social and population control. We seek to [foster] a dialogue that builds collaborations between social movements to move beyond single-issue and identity-based politics towards an inclusive political agenda across progressive movements.

NOTES

1. Quoting Myron Magnet, editor of *City Journal*.

2. The law enforcement agencies referred to include local and state police agencies; prison systems at the local, state and federal levels; the United States Border Patrol and Interior Enforcement Operations of the Immigration and Naturalization Service (INS); and the rapidly expanding INS detention system.

3. This is not true in other parts of the world. For example, state violence has been a critical issue for the contemporary women's movement in India. Radha Kumar in *The History of Doing* writes: "The issue of rape has been one that most contemporary feminist movements internationally have focused on, firstly because sexual assault is one of the ugliest and most brutal expressions of masculine violence towards women, because rape and the historical discourse around it reveal a great deal about the social relations of reproduction, and thirdly because of what it shows about the way in which the woman's body is seen as representing the community. In India, it has been the latter reason which has been the most dominant in the taking up of campaigns against rape." (Delhi: Kali for Women, 1993), 128.

4. Foucault, in *The History of Sexuality*, refers to this form of state control as "bio-power."

5. Nancy Scheper-Hughes and Margaret Lock, "The Mindful Body: A Prolegomenon to Future Work in Medical Anthropology," *Medical Anthropology Quarterly*, Vol. 1 (1987), 6–41.

6. "We Remember: African American Women are for Reproductive Freedom" (1998); statement signed and distributed by leaders in the African-American community

including Byllye Avery, Reverend Willie Barro, Donna Brazil, Shirley Chisholm, and Dorothy Heights in support of keeping abortion safe and legal.

7. David Firestone, "Alabama's Packed Jails Draw Ire of Courts, Again," *New York Times*, May 1, 2001, A1.

8. Eve Goldberg and Linda Evans, "The Prison Industrial Complex and the Global Economy," *Political Environments* (Fall 1999/Winter 2000), 47.

9. Dr. James Gilligan, a Harvard psychotherapist who has worked on prisons and recidivism, argues that punishing violence with imprisonment does not stop violence because it continues to replicate the patriarchal code. See *Violence: Reflections on a National Epidemic* (New York: Vintage, 1997).

10. Michel Foucault, *Discipline and Punish* (New York: Vintage, 1995), 280.

11. Joseph Hallinan, *Going Up The River: Travels in a Prison Nation* (New York: Random House, 2001).

12. Jennifer Yanco, "Breaking the Silence: Women and the Criminal Justice System," *Political Environments*, No. 7 (Fall 1999/Winter 2000), 20.

13. This document, "The UN Special Report on Violence Against Women" by Special Rapporteur Radhika Coomaraswamy, is available from United Nations Publications at www.un.org.

14. Lynn Paltrow, "Pregnant Drug Users, Fetal Persons, and the Threat to *Roe v. Wade*," *Albany Law Review*, Vol. 62, No. 3 (1999), 1024.

15. This decision affirms the Fourth Amendment to the US Constitution that protects every American, including those who are pregnant and those with substance abuse problems, from warrantless, unreasonable searches.

16. Dorothy Roberts, *Killing the Black Body* (New York: Vintage, 1998).

17. Native American Health Education Resource Center, SisterSong Native Women's Reproductive Health and Rights Roundtable Report (Lake Andes, SD: January 2001), 17.

18. Foucault, *Discipline and Punish*, 195–228.

19. For a rich discussion of this set of issues, see Valerie Hartouni, "Replicating the Singular Self," in *Cultural Conceptions: On Reproduction Technologies and the Remaking of Life* (Minneapolis, MN: University of Minnesota Press, 1997), 110–132.

20. Ibid., 119.

21. For more on the subject see Betsy Hartmann, "Population, Environment, and Security: A New Trinity" in Jael Silliman and Ynestra King, eds., *Dangerous Intersections* (Cambridge, MA: South End Press, 1999), 1–23.

22. Maria Jimenez, "Legalization Then and Now: An Eighty Year History," *Network News* (Oakland, CA: National Network for Immigrant and Refugee Rights, Summer 2000), 6.

23. Ginger Thompson, "The Desperate Risk of Death in a Desert," *New York Times*, October 31, 2000, A12.

24. Jose Palafox, "Welcome to America: Arizona Ranchers Hunt Mexicans," *Network News* (Summer 2000), 4.

54

MILITARY MIRRORS A WORKING-CLASS AMERICA

David M. Halbfinger and Steven A. Holmes

They left small towns and inner cities, looking for a way out and up, or fled the anonymity of the suburbs, hoping to find themselves. They joined the all-volunteer military, gaining a free education or a marketable skill or just the discipline they knew they would need to get through life.

As the United States engages in its first major land war in a decade, the soldiers, sailors, pilots and others who are risking, and now giving, their lives in Iraq represent a slice of a broad swath of American society—but by no means all of it.

Of the 28 servicemen killed who have been identified so far, 20 were white, 5 black, 3 Hispanic—proportions that neatly mirror those of the military as a whole. But just one was from a well-to-do family, and with the exception of a Naval Academy alumnus, just one had graduated from an elite college or university.

A survey of the American military's endlessly compiled and analyzed demographics paints a picture of a fighting force that is anything but a cross section of America. With minorities overrepresented and the wealthy and the underclass essentially absent, with political conservatism ascendant in the officer corps and Northeasterners fading from the ranks, America's 1.4 million-strong military seems to resemble the makeup of a two-year commuter or trade school outside Birmingham or Biloxi far more than that of a ghetto or barrio or four-year university in Boston.

Today's servicemen and women may not be Ivy Leaguers, but in fact they are better educated than the population at large: reading scores are a full grade higher for enlisted personnel than for their civilian counterparts of the same age. While whites account for three of five soldiers, the military has become a powerful magnet for blacks, and black women in particular, who now outnumber white women in the Army.

But if the military has become the most successfully integrated institution in society, there is also a kind of voluntary segregation: while whites and blacks seek out careers in communications, intelligence, the medical corps and other specialties in roughly equal numbers; blacks are two and a half times as likely to fill support or administrative roles, while whites are 50 percent more likely to serve in the infantry, gun crews or their naval equivalent.

David A. Halbfinger, Holmes, Steven A., "Military Mirrors a Working Class America." *The New York Times*, March 30, 2003 pA1.
Editor's note: As of March 2006, 2,292 U.S. servicemen and women had been killed in Iraq.

Sgt. Annette Acevedo, 22, a radio operator from Atlanta, could have gone to college but chose the Army because of all the benefits it offered: travel, health coverage, work experience and independence from her parents. The Army seemed a better opportunity to get started with her life and be a more independent person, she said.

Specialist Markita Scott, 27, a reservist from Columbus, Ga., called up as a personnel clerk in an Army deployment center, says she is now planning to make a career of the Army. "Oh, yes, I am learning a skill," said Specialist Scott, who is black. "I get a lot of papers that are not correct, and so I know I'm helping the person. It could be making sure the right person is notified in case of an emergency, or maybe I tell them, 'You know, if you do your insurance this way, the money will not go directly to the child, but the child's guardian,' and they say, 'Oh, I don't want it going to my ex.'"

Lt. James Baker, 27, of Shelbyville, Tenn., who is white, enlisted in the National Guard. The Tennessee Guard had no infantry units, so he chose artillery instead. "Artillery is exciting," he said. "I get to blow a lot of stuff up and play in the woods. The Army is the biggest team sport in the world."

Confronted by images of the hardships of overseas deployment and by the stark reality of casualties in Iraq, some have raised questions about the composition of the fighting force and about requiring what is, in essence, a working-class military to fight and die for an affluent America.

"It's just not fair that the people that we ask to fight our wars are people who join the military because of economic conditions, because they have fewer options," said Representative Charles B. Rangel, a Democrat from Manhattan and a Korean War veteran who is calling for restoring the draft.

Some scholars have noted that since the draft was abolished in 1973, the country has begun developing what could be called a warrior class or caste, often perpetuating itself from father or uncle to son or niece, whose political and cultural attitudes do not reflect the diversity found in civilian society— potentially foreshadowing a social schism between those who fight and those who ask them to.

It is an issue that today's soldiers grapple with increasingly as they watch their comrades, even their spouses, deploy to the combat zone. "As it stands right now, the country is riding on the soldiers who volunteer," said Sgt. Barry Perkins, 39, a career military policeman at Fort Benning, Ga. "Everybody else is taking a free ride."

THE WAY IT WAS: THE VIETNAM WAR AND THE DRAFT'S END

The Vietnam War looms large as the defining epoch in the creation of what has become today's professional, blue-collar military.

It led to the creation of an all-volunteer force, when the Nixon administration, in an attempt to reduce opposition to the war, abolished the draft in 1973.

Because the draft provided deferment to college students, the burden of being sent to Vietnam fell heavily on the less well educated and less affluent. And because of the unpopularity of the war, military service was disdained by many members of the nation's elite, leading their children to lose the propensity to serve that had characterized earlier generations of America's privileged.

As a result, the Americans who fought in the Vietnam War looked very different from the professional corps now fighting in Iraq and stationed around the globe.

The 2,594,000 troops who served in Vietnam between 1965 and 1972 were younger, much less likely to be married and almost entirely male, according to a study of Defense Department data by Richard K. Kolb, the editor and publisher of VFW magazine.

The average soldier in a combat unit in Vietnam was 19 or 20 years old and unmarried, Mr. Kolb said. Of the 58,000 Americans killed in Vietnam, 61 percent were 21 or younger; of the enlisted men killed, only about 25 percent were married.

"I can only recall one guy I served with who was married, and he was about 30 and a lifer," said Mr. Kolb, who was a 19-year-old radio operator in Vietnam in 1970.

By contrast, the average age of the 28 men killed in the war with Iraq so far is 26, and 8 of the 22 enlisted men who died, or 36 percent, were married.

In the Army, about 25 percent of enlisted men were married in 1973. Today that figure has almost doubled.

Another major difference, of course, is that few women served in Vietnam, and women were not allowed in combat units. Only 7,494 women served in Vietnam, of whom 6,250 were nurses, according to the Defense Department. Of the 58,000 Americans who died in Vietnam, only eight were women, all of them nurses, and only one is officially listed as killed in action.

There were no female prisoners of war in Vietnam. By contrast, one female soldier has already been captured in Iraq and two others are listed as missing in action. Women are enlisting in far greater numbers today, especially since the Pentagon lifted many of the restrictions on women serving in combat. Fifteen percent of all officers and enlisted personnel are women.

The existence of the draft during the Vietnam War, and the war's growing unpopularity as the years passed without victory, also created fundamental differences in the makeup of the armed forces. Soldiers tended to enlist for single tours of duty and then go back quickly to civilian life, making for a higher turnover rate and less professionalism than the Pentagon boasts of now. Today, the average enlistee stays about seven years, up from less than two years in 1973.

But Mr. Kolb and other experts say the widespread idea that the Army in Vietnam was made up mostly of draftees is incorrect. In fact, only 25 percent of all American forces in Vietnam were draftees, compared with 66 percent in World War II.

"With me, it was not a question of whether I would enlist, but when," Mr. Kolb said. "I grew up in a small town, and my father and uncles had all served in World War II. Enlisting was what we did in my family."

Among the many myths of Vietnam that persist today, experts say, is that it was a war fought by poor and black Americans, who died in greater proportions than whites.

Although that was true in the early stages of the American ground war, in 1965 and 1966, when there were large numbers of blacks in front-line combat units, Army and Marine Corps commanders later took steps to reassign black servicemen to other jobs to equalize deaths, according to Col. Harry G. Summers Jr. in "Vietnam War Almanac."

By the end of the war, African-Americans had suffered 12.5 percent of the total deaths in Vietnam, 1 percentage point less than their proportion in the overall population, Colonel Summers wrote.

Servicemen from states in the South had the highest rate of battlefield deaths, 31 per 100,000 of the region's population, Mr. Kolb found. Soldiers from states in the Northeast had the lowest rates, 23.5 deaths per 100,000.

Since the end of the draft, that geographic skew on the battlefield has extended to the services as a whole. The percentages of people from the Northeast and Midwest have dropped, while the proportion from the West has climbed and from the South has skyrocketed—even after accounting for southward and westward population shifts in society at large. For the year ending Sept. 30, 2000, 42 percent of all recruits came from the South.

Over all, Mr. Kolb said, 76 percent of the soldiers in Vietnam were from working-class or lower-income families, while only 23 percent had fathers in professional, managerial or technical occupations.

The disparity created by the Vietnam draft can be seen on the walls of Memorial Hall and Memorial Church at Harvard University, where the names of Harvard students and alumni who died for their country are inscribed. There were 200 Harvard students killed in the Civil War and 697 in World War II, but only 22 in Vietnam.

For Stanley Karnow, the journalist and author of "Vietnam: A History," who began reporting from Vietnam in 1959, the contrast with World War II was personal. When he turned 18 in 1943, he dropped out of Harvard and enlisted in the Army. In 1970, when his son turned 18 and became eligible for the draft, he was also a Harvard student. "We did everything we could to keep him out of the draft," Mr. Karnow said.

SIGNING UP: RECRUITING OFFICE AS MELTING POT

If the nation's wealthy and more well-educated youth have shunned the military, others less privileged have gravitated toward it.

Compared to their contemporaries in civilian life, the armed forces have a greater percentage of minorities, a higher proportion of high school graduates and better reading levels. As a group, about 60 percent of enlisted men and women are white; they tend to be married and upwardly mobile, but to come from families without the resources to send them to college.

While blacks make up about 12.7 per cent of the same-age civilian population, they constitute about 22 per cent of enlisted personnel. Perhaps most striking is the number of enlisted women who are black: more than 35 percent, according to Pentagon figures, indicating not only that black women enlist at higher rates, but that they stay in the military longer. In the Army, in fact, half of all enlisted women are black, outnumbering whites, who account for 38 percent.

In Chicago Heights, Ill., the Marine Corps recruiting office was filled on Wednesday with the huffs and puffs of more than a dozen fresh young recruits, mostly wearing buzz cuts, doing crunches and chin-ups.

The afternoon workout is a ritual for these newest marines, a gregarious group made up mainly of 17- and 18-year-olds who still have to get fitted for prom tuxes and graduate from high school before shipping out in just a few months. They resemble the American melting pot: Hispanics, blacks, whites, young men and one young woman.

Patriotism and the prospect of getting a chance to go to Iraq, where the action is, played a role in their decisions to enlist, the recruits said. But Lori Luckey, 24, a single mother of three girls, said the main reasons she signed up for the Marines were to get a chance at a career and the opportunity for advancement, to see the world, and to obtain a dental plan and other benefits.

Others, like Myles Tweedy, 18, a high school senior whose baby face is adorned with a goatee, said joining the military was a family tradition. Mr. Tweedy's father was an infantryman in Vietnam, and his grandfather was in the Army as well. "Now it's my turn," Mr. Tweedy said. "It's something I knew I was always going to do."

Jonathan Lewis, 18, who said he enlisted for the benefits, and out of a sense of patriotism, said he figured he had less to fear as a marine in Baghdad than in the streets of Chicago, where he lived for 12 years until his family moved to the south suburbs.

"Being over in Baghdad, you've got a thousand people 100 percent behind you," he said. "Around here, who says you can't be going to McDonald's and that's it? Over there, you're part of everybody, you're with your friends and family, you're still safe."

Ms. Luckey has already made plans for her two oldest daughters, 6 and 4, to stay with their paternal grandmother when she leaves in May for 16 weeks of basic training. Her youngest daughter, not yet 2, will stay with Ms. Luckey's mother.

A corrections officer for six years, she says her job "was just so dead-end." She decided to resign in November and enlisted in the Marines, eyeing not just the benefits but also a fairer chance of advancement.

THE RACE ISSUE: EQUAL OPPORTUNITY ON THE BATTLEFIELD

Though Hispanics are underrepresented in the military, their numbers are growing rapidly. Even as the total number of military personnel dropped 23 percent over the last decade, the number of Hispanics in uniform grew to 118,000 from 90,600, a jump of about 30 percent.

While blacks tend to be more heavily represented in administrative and support functions, a new study shows that Hispanics, like whites, are much more likely to serve in combat operations. But those Hispanics in combat jobs tend to be infantry grunts, particularly in the Marine Corps, rather than fighter or bomber pilots.

"The Air Force is substantially more white, and the officer corps is substantially more white than Latino," said Roberto Suro, director of the Pew Hispanic Center, which issued a report last week on Hispanics in the military. "So you won't see Latinos flying airplanes over Iraq."

There are as many explanations for why Hispanics are flocking to the armed forces as there are individuals—but the explanations are not that different.

Specialist Joel Flores joined the Army five years ago on an impulse. Already in his late 20's, married and the father of two daughters, he was fed up with his sales clerk job at a crafts store in San Antonio, where he had worked for nine years. "They kept passing me up for management," Specialist Flores, 34, said. "I got tired of it."

So one Friday after work he walked into a recruitment office to ask about his options in the military. Two hours later he was signing papers to enlist. "When I saw that first paycheck, it was 'Oh my God,'" said Specialist Flores, now an Army cook. His take-home pay was half what he had made at the store.

But he says he does not regret his decision even now, when he is among more than 12,000 troops waiting to depart Fort Hood, Tex., for the war in the Persian Gulf.

Specialist Flores, who was born in Texas to Mexican-American parents and was the first person in his family to join the military, has since re-enlisted. He says he has found a more level playing field in the Army than in the outside world.

He has moved up a few notches, from private to a specialist supervising other cooks, and says he wants to retire after reaching sergeant major. In the Army, he said, "It doesn't matter who you are if you can do the job."

For many soldiers like Specialist Flores, the military has not disappointed. Some complain about the low pay compared to what they could be making in the private sector, as well as the long hours and the time they spend away from their families.

But they say they have found a more egalitarian and racially harmonious society, one in which prejudice is trumped by meritocracy, discipline and the need to get along to survive.

Sgt. Nathalie Williams, 29, said that in her hometown, Tuskegee, Ala., her closest friends would probably be black, like her. At Fort Hood, they are black, Puerto Rican and white. "You can't judge somebody by their skin color," she said. "That one person who you don't like could be the person who saves your life."

Sergeant Williams's father served in the military, and an older sister is also in the Army. She said she joined the Army in 1992, after graduating from high school, to seek exposure to different kinds of people and travel. A dream came true when she was posted in Hawaii for three years.

But Sergeant Williams, the wife of a nursing assistant and the mother of three children, now faces going to war. Her sister, a staff sergeant, is already in Kuwait.

WHAT LIES AHEAD: A NEW DRAFT OR A WARRIOR CASTE?

For those who support a return to the military draft, the question is whether the wealthy and elite of America—the sons and daughters of members of Congress, among others—were meant to serve as well.

Charles C. Moskos, a professor of sociology at Northwestern University who has written extensively in support of a national draft for the armed services, domestic security and civilian service, argues that the military must represent every stratum of society.

"In World Wars I and II, the British nobility had a higher killed-in-action rate than the working class," he said. "Our enlisted ranks resemble the British: they're lower- to middle-class, working-class, intelligent people, who are joining for both the adventure and economic opportunity. But the officer corps today does not represent American nobility. These are not people who are going to be future congressmen or senators. The number of veterans in the Senate and the House is dropping every year. It shows you that our upper class no longer serves."

Dr. Moskos said the pitfalls of having leaders who do not share in the casualties of war were common knowledge in Homeric times: "Agamemnon was willing to sacrifice his daughter Iphigenia," he said. Today's military recruiters, he said, grasp what the ancient Greeks understood—"that nobody'll accept casualties unless the elite are willing to put their own children's lives on the line."

"I once addressed a group of recruiters and asked them, would you prefer to have your advertising budget tripled or see Chelsea Clinton joining the Army—and they all said Chelsea Clinton joining the Army," he said. "That would be the signal that America was serious about joining the military. Imagine Jenna Bush joining the military—that would be the signal thing saying, this is a cause worth dying for."

Dr. Moskos says support for the Vietnam War ended when it became possible for the elite to win draft deferments. Other experts on military demographics dispute this.

James Burk, a professor of sociology at Texas A&M University, acknowledged that few wealthy citizens today choose military service. "But if you say, is the all-volunteer force not representative of the country as a whole, I'd say it's more representative than the upper class," he said.

Dr. Moskos and others also suggest that the citizen soldier who serves out his term and then returns to civilian life is being replaced by a class, or caste, of career soldiers—even in frontline combat positions that do not require the expertise and experience of years of service. On top of that, experts say, members of the military are far more likely to have parents who served in the armed forces, suggesting that such a caste is self-perpetuating.

"To carry the logic further, why don't you hire a foreign legion and be done with it?" Dr. Moskos said. "Go out, hire foreigners, say they can join the American military and get a decent salary. Oh, no—maybe Americans should fight for America?"

Those who warn of a warrior class cite a study by the Triangle Institute for Security Studies in North Carolina showing that between 1976 and 1996 the percentage of military officers who saw themselves as nonpartisan or politically independent fell from more than 50 percent to less than 20 percent. The main beneficiary of this shift has been the Republican Party.

"The officer corps has always been more conservative," said Richard H. Kohn, a professor of military history at the University of North Carolina. "But even so, the change there is dramatic."

Dr. Kohn and other scholars worry that with fewer families having sons or daughters in the military, especially among the affluent, and with a high percentage of enlistees coming from military families, a potential cultural and political gap could open up between civilian and martial societies.

"One of my concerns is effective civilian control of the military," he said. "The decline in the number of members of Congress who are veterans is dramatic. Up until 1995 Congress had a larger percentage of veterans than there was in the general population. After 1995 it was less—and that's after the Republican takeover. That means there is potentially a less knowledgeable, less effective oversight from Congress."

Even among academics, to be sure, those concerns are narrowly felt. "When the troops come back, many of them will get out; they'll have some memories," said John Allen Williams, a retired Navy captain who is a political science professor at Loyola University Chicago. "A military that self-identified as different from, and possibly superior to, the civilian society it served, with a distinct set of values, and that might be willing to act on them opposed to civilian leaders? The thought that we could have that in this country is just inconceivable."

Both Mr. Burk and Mr. Williams say they support the idea of a draft, though they suggest it could never be enacted in today's political environment.

Ask a squad of today's volunteer soldiers whether they like the idea of a draft, and you'll get a platoon's worth of answers.

Pfc. Michael Philbert, 18, had just finished basic training on Thursday and was browsing at Ranger Joe's, a uniform and equipment store outside Fort Benning, with his father and 13-year-old brother. He said a draft was a bad idea.

"It sounds kind of fair," Private Philbert said. "It's not fair that some poor kids don't have much of a choice but to join if they want to be productive because they didn't go to a good school, or they had family problems that kept them from doing well, so they join up and they're the ones that die for our country while the rich kids can avoid it.

"From the other side, it's not someone's fault that they're born rich or poor. Just because someone is rich doesn't mean you have to yank them out of the comfort of their life just to get even. And most poor people are glad they had this kind of opportunity. They're glad they got in."

But Sgt. Barry Perkins, the military policeman at Fort Benning, who has been around the block a few more times than a buck private, said America's military—and its youth—would benefit from a draft that included both men and women. "If you look at today's society, teenagers are staying at home, not doing a thing," he said. "They need a productive life. It should be straight across the board. As long as you don't allow power, money and wealth to influence it, it will be straight across the board—it will be fairer."

Specialist Markita Scott, the reservist from Columbus, Ga., said she thought a draft was unnecessary. "Already with callbacks you can see the morale is down lower," she said. "They're like, 'I had a job.' Just think if you had a whole draft of people who didn't want to be there. I think of that guy who threw the grenade—you wonder if there would be a lot more like that."

55

RAPE, RACISM, AND THE LAW

Jennifer Wriggins

The history of rape in this country has focused on the rape of white women by Black men. From a feminist perspective, two of the most damaging consequences of this selective blindness are the denials that Black women are raped and that all women are subject to pervasive and harmful sexual coercion of all kinds. . . .

THE NARROW FOCUS ON BLACK OFFENDER/WHITE VICTIM RAPE

There are many different kinds of rape. Its victims are of all races, and its perpetrators are of all races. Yet the kind of rape that has been treated most seriously throughout this nation's history has been the illegal forcible rape of a white woman by a Black man. The selective acknowledgement of Black accused/white victim rape was especially pronounced during slavery and through the first half of the twentieth century. Today a powerful legacy remains that permeates thought about rape and race.

During the slavery period, statutes in many jurisdictions provided the death penalty or castration for rape when the convicted man was Black or mulatto and the victim white. These extremely harsh penalties were frequently imposed. In addition, mobs occasionally broke into jails and courtrooms and lynched slaves alleged to have raped white women, prefiguring Reconstruction mob behavior.

In contrast to the harsh penalties imposed on Black offenders, courts occasionally released a defendant accused of raping a white woman when the evidence was inconclusive as to whether he was Black or mulatto. The rape of Black women by white or Black men, on the other hand, was legal; indictments were sometimes dismissed for failing to allege that the victim was white. In those states where it was illegal for white men to rape white women, statutes provided less severe penalties for the convicted white rapist than for the convicted Black one. In addition, common-law rules both defined rape narrowly and made it a difficult crime to prove. . . .

From Jennifer Wriggins, "Rape, Racism and the Law" *Harvard Women's Law Journal 6* (Spring 1983):103–141.

After the Civil War, state legislatures made their rape statutes race-neutral, but the legal system treated rape in much the same way as it had before the war. Black women raped by white or Black men had no hope of recourse through the legal system. White women raped by white men faced traditional common-law barriers that protected most rapists from prosecution.

Allegations of rape involving Black offenders and white victims were treated with heightened virulence. This was manifested in two ways. The first response was lynching, which peaked near the end of the nineteenth century. The second, from the early twentieth century on, was the use of the legal system as a functional equivalent of lynching, as illustrated by mob coercion of judicial proceedings, special doctrinal rules, the language of opinions, and the markedly disparate numbers of executions for rape between white and Black defendants.

Between 1882 and 1946 at least 4715 persons were lynched, about three-quarters of whom were Black. Although lynching tapered off after the early 1950s, occasional lynch-like killings persist to this day. The influence of lynching extended far beyond the numbers of Black people murdered because accounts of massive white crowds torturing, burning alive, and dismembering their victims created a widespread sense of terror in the Black community.

The most common justification for lynching was the claim that a Black man had raped a white woman. The thought of this particular crime aroused in many white people an extremely high level of mania and panic. One white woman, the wife of an ex-Congressman, stated in 1898, "If it needs lynching to protect woman's dearest possession from human beasts, then I say lynch a thousand times a week if necessary." The quote resonates with common stereotypes that Black male sexuality is wanton and bestial, and that Black men are wild, criminal rapists of white women.

Many whites accepted lynching as an appropriate punishment for a Black man accused of raping a white woman. The following argument made to the jury by defense counsel in a 1907 Louisiana case illustrates this acceptance:

> Gentlemen of the jury, this man, a nigger, is charged with breaking into the house of a white man in the nighttime and assaulting his wife, with the intent to rape her. Now, don't you know that, if this nigger had committed such a crime, he never would have been brought here and tried; that he would have been lynched, and if I were there I would help pull on the rope.[1]

It is doubtful whether the legal system better protected the rights of a Black man accused of raping a white woman than did the mob. Contemporary legal literature used the term "legal lynching" to describe the legal system's treatment of Black men. Well past the first third of the twentieth century, courts were often coerced by violent mobs, which threatened to execute the defendant themselves unless the court convicted him. Such mobs often did lynch the defendant if the judicial proceedings were not acceptable to them. A contemporary authority on lynching commented in 1934 that "the local sentiment which would make a lynching possible would insure a conviction in the courts." Even if the mob was not overtly pressuring for execution, a Black defendant accused of raping a white woman faced a hostile, racist legal system. State court submission to mob pressure is well illustrated by the most famous series of cases about interracial rape, the Scottsboro cases of the 1930s. Eight young Black men were convicted of what the Alabama Supreme Court called "a most foul and revolting crime," which was the rape of "two defenseless white girls." The defendants were summarily sentenced to death based on minimal and dubious evidence, having been denied effective assistance of counsel. The Alabama Supreme Court upheld the convictions in opinions demonstrating relentless determination to hold the defendants guilty regardless of strong evidence that mob pressure had influenced the verdicts and the weak evidence presented against the defendants. In one decision, that court affirmed the trial court's denial of a change of venue on the grounds that the mobs' threats of harm were not imminent enough although the National Guard had been called out to protect the defendants from mob executions. The U.S. Supreme Court later recognized that the proceedings had in fact taken place in an atmosphere of "tense, hostile, and excited public sentiment." After a lengthy appellate process, including three favorable Supreme Court rulings, all of the Scottsboro defendants were released, having spent a total of 104 years in prison.

In addition, courts applied special doctrinal rules to Black defendants accused of the rape or attempted rape of white women. One such rule allowed juries to consider the race of the defendant and victim in drawing factual conclusions as to the defendant's intent in attempted rape cases. If the accused was Black and the victim white, the jury was entitled to draw the inference, based on race alone, that he intended to rape her. One court wrote, "In determining the question of intention, the jury may consider social conditions and customs founded upon racial differences, such as that the prosecutrix was a white woman and defendant was a Negro man."[2] The "social conditions and customs founded upon racial differences" which the jury was to consider included the assumption that Black men always and only want to rape white women, and that a white woman would never consent to sex with a Black man.

The Georgia Supreme Court of 1899 was even more explicit about the significance of race in the context of attempted rape, and particularly about the motivations of Black men. It held that race may properly be considered "to rebut any presumption that might otherwise arise in favor of the accused that his intention was to obtain the consent of the female, upon failure of which he would abandon his purpose to have sexual intercourse with her."[3] Such a rebuttal denied to Black defendants procedural protection that was accorded white defendants. . . .

The outcome of this disparate treatment of Black men by the legal system was often the same as lynching—death. Between 1930 and 1967, thirty-six percent of the Black men who were convicted of raping a white woman were executed. In stark contrast, only two percent of all defendants convicted of rape involving other racial combinations were executed. As a result of such disparate treatment, eighty-nine percent of the men executed for rape in this country were Black. While execution rates for all crimes were much higher for Black men than for white men, the differential was most dramatic when the crime was the rape of a white woman.

The patterns that began in slavery and continued long afterwards have left a powerful legacy that manifests itself today in several ways. Although the death penalty for rape has been declared unconstitutional, the severe statutory penalties for rape continue to be applied in a discriminatory manner. A recent study concluded that Black men convicted of raping white women receive more serious sanctions than all other sexual assault defendants. A recent attitudinal study found that white potential jurors treated Black and white defendants similarly when the victim was Black. However, Black defendants received more severe punishment than white defendants when the victim was white.

The rape of white women by Black men is also used to justify harsh rape penalties. One of the few law review articles written before 1970 that takes a firm position in favor of strong rape laws to secure convictions begins with a long quote from a newspaper article describing rapes by three Black men, who at 3 a.m. on Palm Sunday "broke into a West Philadelphia home occupied by an eighty-year-old widow, her forty-four-year-old daughter and fourteen-year-old granddaughter," brutally beat and raped the white women, and left the grandmother unconscious "lying in a pool of blood." This introduction presents rape as a crime committed by violent Black men against helpless white women. It is an image of a highly atypical rape—the defendants are Black and the victims white, the defendants and victims are strangers to each other, extreme violence is used, and it is a group rape. Contemporaneous statistical data on forcible rapes reported to the Philadelphia police department reveals that this rape case was virtually unique.[4] Use of this highly unrepresentative image of rape to justify strict rape laws is consistent with recent research showing that it is a prevalent, although false, belief about rape that the most common racial combination is Black offender and white victim.[5]

Charges of rapes committed by Black men against white women are still surrounded by sensationalism and public pressure for prosecution. Black men seem to face a special threat of being unjustly prosecuted or convicted. One example is Willie Sanders.[6] Sanders is a Black Boston man who was arrested and charged with the rapes of four young white women after a sensational media campaign and intense pressure on the police to apprehend the rapist. Although the rapes continued after Sanders was incarcerated, and the evidence against him was extremely weak, the state subjected him to a vigorous twenty-month prosecution. After a lengthy and expensive trial, and an active public defense, he was eventually acquitted. Although Sanders was clearly innocent, he could have been convicted; he and his family suffered incalculable damage despite his acquittal. . . .

From slavery to the present day, the legal system has consistently treated the rape of white women by Black men with more harshness than any other kind of rape. . . .

This selective focus is significant in several ways. First, since tolerance of coerced sex has been the rule rather than the exception, it is clear that the rape of white women by Black men has been treated seriously not because it is coerced sex and thus damaging to women, but because it is threatening to white men's power over both "their" women and Black men. Second, in treating Black offender/white victim illegal rape much more harshly than all coerced sex experienced by Black women and most coerced sex experienced by white women, the legal system has implicitly condoned the latter forms of rape. Third, this treatment has contributed to a paradigmatic but false concept of rape as being primarily a violent crime between strangers where the perpetrator is Black and the victim white. Finally, this pattern is perverse and discriminatory because rape is painful and degrading to both Black and white victims regardless of the attacker's race.

THE DENIAL OF THE RAPE OF BLACK WOMEN

The selective acknowledgement of the existence and seriousness of the rape of white women by Black men has been accompanied by a denial of the rape of Black women that began in slavery and continues today. Because of racism and sexism, very little has been written about this denial. Mainstream American history has ignored the role of Black people to a large extent; systematic research into Black history has been published only recently. The experiences of Black women have yet to be fully recognized in those histories, although this is beginning to change. Indeed, very little has been written about rape from the perspective of the victim, Black or white, until quite recently. Research about Black women rape victims encounters all these obstacles.

The rape of Black women by white men during slavery was commonplace and was used as a crucial weapon of white supremacy. White men had what one commentator called "institutionalized access" to Black women. The rape of Black women by white men cannot be attributed to unique Southern pathology, however, for numerous accounts exist of northern armies raping Black women while they were "liberating" the South.

The legal system rendered the rape of Black women by any man, white or Black, invisible. The rape of a Black woman was not a crime. In 1859 the

Mississippi Supreme Court dismissed the indictment of a male slave for the rape of a female slave less than 10 years old, saying:

> [T]his indictment can not be sustained, either at common law or under our statutes. It charges no offense known to either system. [Slavery] was unknown to the common law . . . and hence its provisions are inapplicable. . . . There is no act (of our legislature on this subject) which embraces either the attempted or actual commission of a rape by a slave on a female slave. . . . Masters and slaves can not be governed by the same system or laws; so different are their positions, rights and duties.[7]

This decision is illuminating in several respects. First, Black men are held to lesser standards of sexual restraint with Black women than are white men with white women. Second, white men are held to lesser standards of restraint with Black women than are Black men with white women. Neither white nor Black men were expected to show sexual restraint with Black women.

After the Civil War, the widespread rape of Black women by white men persisted. Black women were vulnerable to rape in several ways that white women were not. First, the rape of Black women was used as a weapon of group terror by white mobs and by the Ku Klux Klan during Reconstruction. Second, because Black women worked outside the home, they were exposed to employers' sexual aggression as white women who worked inside the home were not.

The legal system's denial that Black women experienced sexual abuse by both white and Black men also persisted, although statutes had been made race-neutral. Even if a Black victim's case went to trial—in itself highly un-likely—procedural barriers and prejudice against Black women protected any man accused of rape or attempted rape. The racist rule which facilitated pros-ecutions of Black offender/white victim attempted rapes by allowing the jury to consider the defendant's race as evidence of his intent, for instance, was not applied where both persons were "of color and there was no evidence of their social standing.[8] That is, the fact that a defendant was Black was considered relevant only to prove intent to rape a white woman; it was not relevant to prove intent to rape a Black woman. By using disparate procedures, the court implicitly makes two assertions. First, Black men do not want to rape Black women with the same intensity or regularity that Black men want to rape white women. Second, Black women do not experience coerced sex in the sense that white women experience it.

These attitudes reflect a set of myths about Black women's supposed promiscuity which were used to excuse white men's sexual abuse of Black women. An example of early twentieth century assumptions about Black women's purported promiscuity was provided by the Florida Supreme Court in 1918. In discussing whether the prior chastity of the victim in a statutory rape case should be presumed subject to defendant's rebuttal or should be an element of the crime which the state must prove, the court explained that:

> What has been said by some of our courts about an unchaste female being a comparatively rare exception is no doubt true where the population is composed largely of the Caucasian race, but we would blind ourselves to actual conditions if we adopted this rule where another race that is largely immoral constitutes an appreciable part of the population.[9]

Cloaking itself in the mantle of legal reasoning, the court states that most young white women are virgins, that most young Black women are not, and that unchaste women are immoral. The traditional law of statutory rape at issue in the above-quoted case provides that women who are not "chaste" cannot be raped. Because of the way the legal system considered chastity, the association of Black women with unchastity meant not only that Black women could not be victims of statutory rape, but also that they would not be recognized as victims of forcible rape.

The criminal justice system continues to take the rape of Black women less seriously than the rape of white women. Studies show that judges generally impose harsher sentences for rape when the victim is white than when the victim is Black. The behavior of white jurors shows a similar bias. A recent study found that sample white jurors imposed significantly lighter sentences on defendants whose victims were Black than on defendants whose victims were white. Black jurors exhibited no such bias.

Evidence concerning police behavior also documents the fact that the claims of Black rape victims are taken less seriously than those of whites. A . . . study of Philadelphia police processing decisions concluded that the differential in police decisions to charge for rape "resulted primarily from a lack of confidence in the veracity of Black complainants and a belief in the myth of Black promiscuity."

The thorough denial of Black women's experiences of rape by the legal system is especially shocking in light of the fact that Black women are much more likely to be victims of rape than are white women.[10] Based on data from national surveys of rape victims, "the profile of the most frequent rape victim is a young woman, divorced or separated, Black and poverty stricken." . . .

CONCLUSION

The legal system's treatment of rape both has furthered racism and has denied the reality of women's sexual subordination. It has disproportionately targeted Black men for punishment and made Black women both particularly vulnerable and particularly without redress. It has denied the reality of women's sexual subordination by creating a social meaning of rape which implies that the only type of sexual abuse is illegal rape and the only form of illegal rape is Black offender/white victim. Because of the interconnectedness of rape and racism, successful work against rape and other sexual coercion must deal with racism. Struggles against rape must acknowledge the differences among women and the different ways that groups other than women are disempowered. In addition, work against rape must go beyond the focus on illegal rape to include all forms of coerced sex, in order to avoid the racist historical legacy surrounding rape and to combat effectively the subordination of women.

NOTES

1. *State v. Petit*, 119 La., 44 So. (1907).

2. *McQuirter v. State*, 36 Ala., 63 So. 2d (1953).

3. *Dorsey v. State*, 108 Ga., 34 S.E. (1899).

4. Out of 343 rapes reported to the Philadelphia police, 3.3% involved Black defendants accused of raping white women; 42% involved complaints of stranger rape; 20.5% involved brutal beatings; 43% involved group rapes.

5. In answer to the question, "Among which racial combination do most rapes occur?" 48% of respondents stated Black males and white females, 3% stated white males and Black females, 16% stated Black males and Black females, 33% stated white males and white females. Recent victim survey data contradict this prevalent belief; more than four-fifths of illegal rapes reported to researchers were between members of the same race, and white/Black rapes roughly equaled Black/white rapes.

6. Suffolk Superior Court indictment (1980).

7. *George v. State*, 37 Miss. (1859).

8. *Washington v. State*, 38 Ga., 75 S.E. (1912).

9. *Dallas v. State*, 76 Fla., 79 So. (1918).

10. Recent data from random citizen interviews suggest that Black women are much more likely to be victims of illegal rape than are white women.

56

HOW SAFE IS AMERICA?

Desiree Taylor

I saw a picture in a magazine in which a woman is walking away from the collapsed World Trade Center towers covered in orange dust from head to toe. Her face is twisted into a shocked and horrifying expression and she is turned

From Desiree Taylor, "How Safe Is America?" *Sojourner: The Women's Forum* (November 2001). Copyright © 2001 by the Sojourner Feminist Institute.

around slightly looking back at the photographer as she walks away from the scene. What strikes me about this picture is that I have never seen another like it, such an elegant and stylish depiction of war. The woman is so immaculately dressed, her hair so stylishly cut, that the whole scene looks like a clever fashion spread from an upscale magazine. This just couldn't be real, but it is. Looking at this picture, I try to really see the woman in it. I try to feel the horror of her experience, but as I do I can also see that she is not from my America. She is from an America that before September 11 was in many ways safer and freer than mine before or after that day.

On September 12, the day after the attack on the United States, I watched the media coverage and a very middle-class looking woman interviewed on the street said she "no longer felt safe in America." I was born and have grown up in this country. As a mixed race, half Black, half white woman born into poverty, I have never felt safe here.

In America, life within one class is nothing at all like it is in another. On September 11 thousands of people died in the collapsed World Trade towers. They were not alone. Every day in this country people die from exploitation that originates right here at home. Some who toil and slave in service to a system of wealth and prestige, who don't even earn a living for their trouble, slit their wrists out of desperation and pain. Some die used up and exhausted, in hospital beds with two dollars and eighty-five cents in their purse, like my own mother. Some people work two or more jobs and try to fit some kind of life in between, maybe an education, which gets harder and harder as they lose out on more and more sleep. The amount of safety one can truly feel in America is directly related to how much money you have.

SAFETY DEPENDS ON MONEY

I think about these people who were and are anything but safe here. I think about those who sweat out unappreciated labor to make the American Dream seem so real, to make the consumer culture function. I wonder if the woman in the picture ever looked as closely at the people who are dying in the class war here at home as I do at her.

It enrages me to hear people saying they no longer feel safe here. The United States that is being attacked is the one the woman in the picture belongs to. It is the prosperous, comfortable United States. It is not my United States. But all of a sudden we are all in it together. The flags are brought out and everybody sings, "I'm proud to be an American."

But it's impossible for me to suddenly forget that the United States empire was built upon and is still maintained by abuses against the poor and minorities. I think about those who will fight and die in this war. I think about all the poor, and often Black, students from my high school who enlisted in the armed services to earn money for college. I think about all the students who wouldn't have been caught dead joining the armed forces, kids for whom the military was not one of their few options to move out of poverty. I think about how many low-income families are worrying right now about the lives of their enlisted children. I wonder what proportion of persons who will fight in this war will be those who are not sharing in the "American Dream." I believe that it will be disproportionally high.

POOR INVISIBLE TO MAINSTREAM

The plight of low-income people in this country is invisible to mainstream America. This invisible other America, the poor, enters through side and back doors of hotels, through the servants' entrances. They live in segregated neighborhoods, and work jobs in which they are unseen even though they are in plain view.

For example, I went to Walgreens the other day and was handed a receipt that read at the top: "I'm Laqueeta [name changed]. I'm here to serve you." The message continued on the next line: "with our seven service basics." A middle-class person in this corporation decided that Laqueeta should hand this message out on every one of her receipts. What made someone earning a good salary think that this was a good idea? We're not even told what those seven service basics are, and they don't really matter. What matters is that the plantation-type American Dream is being acted out here. I, as a consumer, am for a moment in the seat of power with someone to serve me. This is meant to register with me, but the server is not. She doesn't matter. If she did, she would be able to survive doing this kind of work.

I decided to inquire about a cashier's job at Walgreens. The pay rate, I was told, is $6.75 an hour in Boston. When I worked hourly wage jobs in retail stores I learned that employers would keep employees just under 40 hours a week, so that officially they were not full-time and therefore not entitled by law to benefits. I do not know if Walgreens does this, but the practice is widespread. For 39 hours of work at $6.75 an hour, that is $263.25 a week before taxes and $758.16 per month after taxes. After subtracting $35 for a subway pass and at least $460 a month for rent and bills (and for rent this low that means living in a hovel with probably four other people she doesn't know), that leaves Laqueeta just $65.79 a week for food, clothing, savings, entertainment, household expenses, healthcare, and any other expense that might come up, including saving for college and a computer. I hope she doesn't have a child. How safe is Laqueeta in America? Does anybody care? The appearance of America's bounty is maintained by the exploitation of people right here at home who are in positions to be easily misused.

The United States feels very much to me like several countries made up of separate social/economic classes, who don't and perhaps won't take the time to really look at each other; they can't feel each other's pains, cannot relate, and largely live in separate worlds. Now that we're at war with outside forces, we are supposed to come together within the United States. We are all supposed to feel the same hurts and the same threats. We are all supposed to feel each other's pain. We are all supposed to defend justice and freedom.

During the past few weeks we have heard over and over again that these acts of terrorism are not only attacks on the United States, but on everything the country stands for. They tell us these are attacks on freedom and justice itself. But how is this possible when here at home justice, freedom, and the American Dream are denied to so many?

Suggested Readings for Part III

Collins, Patricia Hill. 1998. *Fighting Words: Black Women and the Search for Social Justice.* Minneapolis: University of Minnesota Press.

Ferber, Abby. 1998. *White Man Falling: Race, Gender, and White Supremacy.* Lanham, MD: Rowman & Littlefield.

Ragone, Helene, and France Winddance Twine. 2000. *Ideologies and Technologies of Motherhood: Race, Class, Sexuality, Nationalism.* New York: Routledge.

Roberts, Dorothy. 1997. *Killing the Black Body: Race, Reproduction, and the Meaning of Liberty.* New York: Vintage.

Russell, Diana E. H., and Roberta A. Harmes. 2001. *Femicide in Global Perspective.* New York: Teachers College Press.

Ruzek, Sheryl Burt, Virginia L. Olsen, and Adele Clark. 1997. *Women's Health: Complexities and Differences.* Columbus: Ohio State University Press.

 ## InfoTrac College Edition: Search Terms

Use your access to the online library, InfoTrac College Edition, to learn more about subjects covered in this section. The following are some suggested terms for searches:

genocide	racial profiling
hate crimes	rape and warfare
migration/immigration	sexual terrorism

 ## InfoTrac College Edition: Bonus Reading

You can use the InfoTrac College Edition feature to find an additional reading pertinent to this section and can also search on the author's name or keywords to locate the following reading:

Narayan, Uma. 1995. "Mail-Order Brides: Immigrant Women, Domestic Violence and Immigration Law." *Hypatia* 10 (Winter): 104–19.

Uma Narayan documents the heightened vulnerability of immigrant women to isolation, domestic violence, and threats of deportation. Her discussion of "mail-order brides" also reveals that race, gender, and class intermingle to create this phenomenon. Were she writing this article today, given the increased restrictions on immigrants since 9/11, what might she say about how race, class, and gender are now affecting the experiences of immigrant women?

Companion Website

For additional links, quizzes, and learning tools related to this part, see the book's companion website, at **http://sociology.wadsworth.com/andersen _hill_collins6e.**

IV

SOCIAL CHANGE AND SITES OF CHANGE

Margaret L. Andersen
and Patricia Hill Collins

Often at the end of this book, people want to know, "What can I do?" Once they know about the social injustices brought about by power relations of race, class, and gender, our readers want to go immediately to the site of individual activism. But the question is larger than what individuals can do. Individuals matter, but structural changes may be needed to foster social justice.

Other readers have a different reaction. Holding fast to the belief that social inequalities of race, class, gender, ethnicity, and sexuality are things that happen to other people, not to them, they tune out. Because they believe that they are not directly harmed by social inequalities, they think that an inclusive race, class, and gender framework does not apply to them. But thinking inclusively about race, class, and gender shows that no one can ever step outside of the current system. We all occupy positions of disadvantage and privilege within intersecting systems of race, class, and gender. Because of this, we encourage all of our readers to start an analysis of social action and sites of change by looking at your everyday life.

What in your life do you care about so much that it would spur you to work for social justice? Is it your family, your children, your faith, your neighborhood, a concern for a social issue, or an ethical framework that requires not just talk but action? Most people think that people who work for social justice must be somehow extraordinary like Martin Luther King Jr., or other heroic figures. But most people who engage in social activism are ordinary, everyday people who decide to take action about something that touches their lives.

Why don't we know more about these people? Remember that this book examines how entrenched power relations of race, class, and gender affect us all. In this context, dominant social institutions use ideologies to obscure the individual and collective political activism of everyday individuals who oppose social injustices. For example, by making the political activism of everyday people from historically marginalized groups invisible, social institutions suppress the strength of these groups and render them more easily exploited. Investigating forms of power used by historically marginalized groups offers one way of rethinking social injustices of race, class, and gender as well as how people work for social change. African Americans, Native Americans, new immigrant groups, women, Latinos, gays and lesbians, and members of the poor and working class have never been powerless. The question is how to identify and use forms of power that often go unrecognized.

The political activism of individuals from historically privileged groups is hidden as well. Many people who currently benefit within existing race, class, and gender arrangements have little interest in studying—much less showcasing—the ideas and actions of those who not only see the unfairness of race, class, and gender relations in the United States and globally, but who try to change them. The expected political protest from those harmed by existing race, class, and gender relations is routinely discredited. Stereotyping people of color, women, working-class and poor people, and gays, lesbians, and bisexuals as angry minorities, strident feminists, disgruntled trade unionists, or hypersensitive homosexuals effectively recasts political protest in negative terms and works to strip their protest of meaning. These tactics remain less effective against those who benefit from existing structures of race, class, gender, and sexuality but who decide to use their privilege in new ways. When individuals who are White, middle class, male, straight, Christian and/or American citizens reject current social arrangements that privilege them, they may be more threatening than other groups because they often have the power to make change. Consider how different things would be if employers provided health care benefits for all of their workers, if White middle-class parents taught their children new ways to be "White," or if straight men learned models of masculinity that do not demean women or ridicule gay men. Relegating political protest of this sort to the margins remains vitally important to dominant interests.

The essays in Part IV explore how thinking inclusively and using a race, class, and gender framework helps us understand where, why, and how social change occurs (both progressive and conservative). We have divided the readings into two sections, one that focuses on sites of change or specific social locations where people work for more just and fair social arrangements. If you are working for social justice, what are some potential institutional sites (pressure points) for such work? What are some of the challenges that confront people who work for change in financial organizations, churches, and grassroots organizations, for example? In the second section, we examine the processes of change, primarily by showing how a race, class, and gender framework has been used in organizing for change. There we take up issues of the very definition of activism, what it means to be an ally, and strategies used by everyday people who work for social justice.

SITES OF CHANGE

All social institutions demonstrate a persisting dilemma—they are simultaneously sites that reproduce social inequalities of race, class, gender, ethnicity, and sexuality as well as potential sites for changing these same injustices. Workplaces, families, schools, the media, the military, and the criminal justice system—some of the social institutions we examined in Part III—all represent important institutional locations. All potential sites of change contain contradictions. There is no pure site outside of power relations of race, class, and gender where you can escape social injustices. At the same time, when it comes to establishing a fair system, there is no site within current social institutions that gets everything right. Because power relations of race, class, and gender are global, the places where social injustices can be challenged are also broad.

In "The Starbucks Paradox," Kim Fellner illustrates how these contradictory relations shape one local workplace that is part of the new global economy. On the one hand, Starbucks constitutes a large and growing corporation that routinely runs its competitors out of business. It represents one face of globalization where global corporations expand, often at the cost of dismantling local cultures and ways of life. Anti-globalization initiatives typically criticize Wal-Mart, Nike, McDonald's, Starbucks, and similar icons of American culture as examples of the worst of globalization. Yet, on the other hand, as Fellner points out, as she went around the country, she noticed that Starbucks employees and customers seemed far more diverse by race and class than participants in the American anti-globalization movement. The race, class, and gender politics of Starbucks illustrate the contradictions associated with any one site of change.

Whether social actors are located inside the institutions that they wish to change or whether they stand outside its boundaries, the strategies that they select reflect the opportunities and constraints of each specific site. For insiders, working from within can mean trying to change the institutional policies and practices that either overtly discriminate based on race, class, and gender or that have unjust outcomes. In "Interrupting Historical Patterns," Nancie Zane studies how diversity training in a financial institution helped White men see how race and gender functioned in their work setting. Zane describes how difficult doing diversity workshops can be, yet her article is important in pointing out that changing current race, class and gender inequalities requires motivated insiders.

Whether by choice or by necessity, other individuals and groups work outside workplaces, schools, and other formal social institutions. The familiar boycotts, picketing, public demonstrations, leafleting, and other direct-action strategies long associated with social movements of all types typically constitute actions taken outside an institution designed to pressure it to change. Although activities such as these can be trivialized in the media, it is important to remember that direct action from outsider locations represents one important way to work for social justice.

Celene Krauss's article, "Women of Color on the Front Line," describes the challenges of working in a grassroots movement dedicated to changing environmental policy. Krauss tells how the majority of participants in the environmental justice movement are mothers who became involved out of concern for their children's health. They were neither employees of bureaucracies nor government officials. Her article highlights how women often become politically involved—through concerns over family, children, and quality of life in their neighborhoods. Still, women's activism often is overlooked. Although academic credentials, positions of authority, and economic resources can do much to help individuals challenge hierarchies of race, class, and gender, Krauss suggests that the individual and collective actions of ordinary people who are not policymakers or diversity trainers form the bedrock for many social movements. Krauss's article shows how the importance of applying a race, class, and gender framework to all efforts for social change is especially important for grassroots movements and organizations that are marginalized by dominant institutions. Yet these very same organizations themselves can fall victim to the same type of thinking as the institutions they oppose.

The selection "'Whosoever' Is Welcome Here: An Interview with Reverend Edwin C. Sanders II" describes how African American minister Sanders challenged the exclusionary practices of Southern African American churches by building a new church that included everyone. Reverend Sanders explains how a small group of people came together in Nashville, Tennessee, in search of a community of worship that did not exclude anyone and that was welcoming of everyone. From its small beginnings, the Metropolitan Interdenominational Church grew and is welcoming of people of different races, genders, classes, sexualities, and religious traditions. Possessing a vision of equality and an ethical framework that helps people see how inequalities of race, class, gender, and sexuality dehumanize us all helps make a social institution more just. Reverend Sanders reminds us that churches, even ostensibly conservative ones, can be important sites of change.

When it comes to changing the social institutions that reproduce social inequalities, it is important to remember that ordinary citizens cannot solve social problems by themselves. The state constitutes a vitally important site of change. Despite the cynicism that many people express regarding the proper role of government, many social issues cannot be addressed without government intervention of some sort. Thus, actions of the federal government were required to desegregate the American South in the 1950s and 1960s. While government cannot solve social issues created through current race, class, and gender arrangements, social issues such as homelessness, environmental concerns, violence against children, poverty, racial discrimination, and gender discrimination often require government partnership of some sort to support the actions of everyday citizens who care about these problems. At other times, actions of the government may be part of the problem, and people must find other means of challenging oppressive institutional arrangements.

There are, however, limits to this type of change. Because the state itself is structured around social inequalities of race, class, gender, ethnicity, and sexuality, there are limits to the kinds of change that can be achieved solely by it. Furthermore, even when African Americans, Native Americans, women, Asian Americans, the poor, gays and lesbians, Latinos, and other historically marginalized groups gain power within the state itself, change does not automatically follow. Replacing one type of dominant group with another of a different color or gender may improve the lives of some people without addressing the fundamental inequalities that pervade existing social institutions. Derrick Bell's (2002) analysis of how the Supreme Court's decision in *Brown v. Board of Education* did not produce the educational equality for African American children envisioned by its creators provides a sobering account of relying too heavily on the state as the primary site of change. In "Silent Covenants," Bell recounts how the presence of this momentous court decision convinced many Americans that racism had been legislated away. Social movements that advocated for the *Brown* decision could not anticipate the emergence of mass media that depicted an American society that had already achieved a colorblind, racial equality. In this context, the vivid images of the Black poor revealed through media coverage of Hurricane Katrina's devastation of New Orleans in 2005 came as a shock to many Americans. Many honestly thought that social injustices had been eliminated by decisions such as *Brown*. In this context, Bell wonders about the future of the federal government and its courts as sites of change.

PROCESSES OF CHANGE

Re-envisioning and exercising power within sites of change requires a sense of purpose that encourages us to look beyond what already exists. We must learn to see beyond what is in order to imagine what is possible. For example, what type of environmental policies would result if working-class

White women and women of color were central in the environmental movement's decision-making processes? If all religious institutions welcomed all people, how might families and communities be changed? How might immigrant communities be changed if all service workers were paid an adequate wage? If working-class people's need for affordable, reliable transportation were central to public policy, would more money be devoted to mass transit and less to highway repair? How might health care be organized if Native American women's ideas were central to planning? If men and women truly learned to work together, how might economic security be better provided for all? Thinking inclusively about race, class, and gender stimulates this type of vision. All sites of change contain emancipatory possibilities, if only we can learn to imagine them.

Vision, however, is not enough. We also need a framework for thinking about the range of strategies that individuals and groups use in working for social change within power relations of race, class, and gender. Thinking inclusively enables us to see processes of change that were invisible to us. Some people engage in individual strategies, yet if we cannot see a working-class Latina as a change agent, we miss the strategies that she deploys to bring about change. As the memoirs of political activists tell us, one well-placed individual with a clear sense of what is possible and why it is important to try can accomplish amazing things. Others engage in collective actions where a small group of like-minded individuals organize around some concern that is important to them. Groups that have been disadvantaged within power relations of race, class, and gender typically engage in this process of change. They realize that by engaging in strategic resistance, a few people can make a big difference if they use their resources wisely. They also realize that making their strategies known might lessen their effectiveness. Still other people may start small, for example, trying to organize the people in their workplace or the mothers in their neighborhood, but then find themselves involved in important regional, national, and global social movements. Global social movements rest on the bedrock of local initiatives.

It is important to remember that, despite their invisibility on both sides of privilege, most of the people who work for social justice are people just like you. Often some sort of catalyst spurs them to action. The needless death of a friend or relative, the placement of a toxic dump site in their neighborhood, losing a job when an employer closes shop, a police beating, or hearing a sermon about Christian brotherhood one Sunday morning in the familiarity of a racially segregated church have all been catalysts for activism. Because people who work for social justice come from all walks of life, their visions for change differ, their paths into social activism can be quite unexpected, and the strategies they select are richly diverse.

The readings in the second section of Part IV, Processes of Change, explore the various ways that people across race, class, and gender groups envision and participate in social activism. They also provide new visions about what is possible. Collectively, these authors apply the framework of race, class, and gender intersectionality to their social activism. In doing so, they show us the kinds of questions we might ask and actions that we might consider in working for social justice.

Regardless of how we are differentially positioned within power relations of race, class, and gender, one important issue surfaces repeatedly—the importance of building coalitions with people who are in different structural locations from ourselves. Bringing ordinary people together who have long been separated by race, class, gender, ethnicity, and sexuality identifies the necessity of building coalitions across differences and the difficulty of doing so. African American activist Bernice Johnson Reagon (1983) points out how individuals who have been harmed by the damaging effects of race, class, and gender oppression may need to create nurturing spaces and communities where they can try and recover. On some college campuses, for example, African American, Latino, women's, gay/lesbian/bisexual/transgendered, Asian, and similar identity-based organizations, aim to create such communities. Their expressed goal often is to offer space where students from historically marginalized groups can retreat from the difficulties many encounter on hostile campuses, learn ways of supporting one another, and develop strategies to enhance their success. These spaces can be valuable, but as Reagon also points out, they can become "barred rooms" that confine and constrict. Identity-based communities and the celebration of group difference that may accompany them can become self-defeating if groups fail to look beyond their own "rooms" and learn to appreciate similar struggles of other groups.

Groups of all sorts, whether identity based or founded around social issues, that fail to build coalitions with other groups may find themselves increasingly isolated and ineffective. Coalition building operates best when

individuals and groups share a concern for a common social issue while recognizing the diversity of ways that people experience, think about, and want
to deal with that issue. The women on the front line of the environmental
justice movement shared the gender of being women, yet they also had varying histories of race and class. They recognized that they needed to find ways
to work together. The members of Metropolitan Interdenominational
Church in Nashville realized that the tenets of their faith-based community
were tested by their ability to form coalitions with one another that tran-
scended the divisive issues of race, class, and sexuality. These examples
illustrate how thinking inclusively and applying a race-, class-, and gender-
inclusive framework to social activism is essential to working for social
justice.

In "How the New Working Class Can Transform Urban America,"
Robin D. G. Kelley sketches out a framework for working-class, coalition
politics that transcends the barriers of race, class, and gender. Kelley argues that a revitalized social movement that addresses the needs of working people is already underway and shows how coalition building is a core
principle of its success. He describes two organizations, the national Justice for Janitors unionization movement and the Bus Riders Union in Los
Angeles. Kelley points out that multiracial, working-class organizations are
not simply possible, but rather, as the stories of these two social movements illustrate, they already exist. Kelley's article points to the multiple
strategies used by these grassroots movements that draw upon traditional
organizing principles but that also respond to the new challenges of
urbanization.

Kelley paints a broad picture of the processes of grassroots activism from
the outside in. In contrast, Charon Asetoyer describes the process of working
for change from the inside out. In "From the Ground Up," Asetoyer points to
how much women and men can accomplish through building their own
organizations and social institutions. Community building constitutes an important process for change. When Asetoyer found herself moving to the
Yankton Sioux reservation in South Dakota, she did not explicitly search out
activist activities. Instead, they found her. Through conversations with her
neighbors, she learned of problems that women and children were having in
her new community. Health issues came up first, and these were the issues
that she and others initially addressed. Over time, the informal discussions
about women's health issues on the reservation grew to the point where her
group was able to purchase a building and organize the Native Women's

Reproductive Rights Coalition, involving women from eight states. Asetoyer's article provides a historical overview of how one individual decided to respond in the context of her everyday life instead of throwing up her hands in defeat.

Asetoyer's activism raises the question of how people imagine activism as a process of social change. They typically do not think of a Native American woman as the archetypal activist. When we ask students in our classes to describe an "activist," they often think of a "radical-looking" young person, typically with strange hair and unusual clothing, who gives fiery speeches and engages in losing causes. People who work for social change rarely fit this stereotype and actually reflect a much broader spectrum of folks. In "Manifesta," Jennifer Baumgardner and Amy Richards (2000) take on these myths of activism and help explain people such as Asetoyer are not typically seen as activists. By asking the simple question, "What is activism?", they sketch out the reasons that many people do not see themselves as activist material. There is no "typical" activist. Almost anyone can work for social justice in the context of her or his everyday life.

Baumgardner and Richards point out that working for social change takes time. One can take the long view or focus on the here and now. These are not either/or choices but two ways of looking at the same thing. Many people become cynical because they expect change to be immediate and dramatic rather than long-term and continual. How people deal with this disappointment is revealing. The White working-class women who became concerned about the effects of environmental dumping on their children initially trusted the government to provide solutions. When it did not, they could easily have become cynical and thrown in the towel. Instead, they tried to find another way, because too much was at stake. Their initial idealism became tempered by pragmatism. In contrast, the Justice for Janitors, the Bus Riders Union, and the women of the Yankton Sioux reservation had few illusions that the government would help them. Their struggle lay in trusting their own capacity to bring about change. These examples illustrate how taking a long view, seeing the connectedness among all sorts of people, and involving people across race, class, and gender—and beyond—will be necessary to bringing lasting change. Clearly this will not happen tomorrow. But if the mothers, janitors, bus riders, and reservation dwellers did not engage processes of change, change would not have occurred.

It seems obvious that people who are disadvantaged within power relations of race, class, and gender might use distinctive strategies to bring about change. Yet how might people who are privileged within these same systems work as change agents? By taking up the difficult question of how people can work for change across differences in power, in "What Does an Ally Do?", Paul Kivel points us back to the processes of coalition building, this time from the site of privilege. Kivel's seemingly simple question examines the challenges that privileged people face in trying to be allies to historically marginalized groups. Being an ally across differences of race, class, gender, ethnicity, sexuality, and age is not easy. Coalition building requires hard work, and Kivel offers some important hands-on strategies for doing it.

Youth are vitally important for any efforts to transform social institutions and generate new processes of change (Bynoe 2004). Ironically, many young adults think that all the important social activism happened before their time. Like Shani Jamila in her article "Can I Get a Witness? Testimony from a Hip Hop Feminist," they think that they have "missed" the real social activism. Because they were too young to attend the marches of the Civil Rights Movement, or to participate in the picket lines of major union activism, or have only seen activism on film and DVD, many feel that social activism is a thing of the past. Because so many young adults now benefit from the struggles of their parents, teachers, and ordinary citizens—they attend integrated schools, possess formal reproductive rights, are assured legal equal opportunity in jobs, and have helped create an exciting, global multicultural youth culture— some question the need for social activism. But as Shani Jamila also reminds us, each generation inherits the task of forging a new path of social activism for themselves and for those who will follow. For Jamila, the task lies in synthesizing the received wisdom of feminism with the new challenges raised within some segments of hip-hop culture. In this quest, Jamila found that liberating her definitions of activism from the "constraints and constructs of the sixties" opened up her mind to new possibilities. As she points out, "The most important thing we can do as a generation is to see our new positions as power and weapons to be used strategically in the struggle rather than as spoils of war."

References

Baumgardner, Jennifer and Amy Richards. 2000. *Manifesta: Young Women, Feminism, and the Future*. New York: Farar, Straus and Giroux.

Bell, Derrick. 2002. *Ethical Ambition: Living a Life of Meaning and Worth*. New York: Bloomsbury.

Bynoe, Yvonne. 2004. *Stand and Deliver: Political Activism, Leadership, and Hip Hop Culture*. Brooklyn: Soft Skull Press.

Reagon, Bernice Johnson. 1983. "Coalition Politics: Turning the Century." Pp. 356–68 in *Home Girls: A Black Feminist Anthology*, ed. Barbara Smith. New York: Kitchen Table Press.

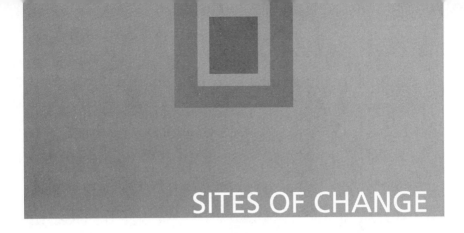

SITES OF CHANGE

57

THE STARBUCKS PARADOX

Kim Fellner

It was November 1999 in Seattle and the U.S. global justice movement had taken to the streets. Suddenly, there was a crash not 20 feet from where I stood, and the Starbucks window collapsed in a hail of glass. "Zowie," I said to my husband Alec, "I sure hate the WTO and capitalism, but that's our coffee store."

I've been pondering the contradictions ever since, watching my progressive colleagues devour the latest episode of *Friends*, gleefully shop for real estate, and sip their lattes. Political ideology notwithstanding, we were avid participants in popular culture and petty capital. How could we so glibly demonize that which we so cheerfully consumed?

And as I went around the country, I couldn't help notice that both the employees and habitués of Starbucks seemed far more diverse by race and class than the American anti-globalization movement. I wanted to know, was big, by definition, bad? Was Starbucks' touted commitment to "values" just a cynical ploy to complement its branding and market share?

Few people argued that coffee was inherently evil like bombs or SUVs. Rather, Starbucks stood accused of: buying coffee at prices that couldn't sustain the farmers; purchasing from farms that degraded the environment;

Kim Fellner, "The Starbucks Paradox" (*Colorlines* Spring 2004 v.7,i1). Reprinted by permission.

causing neighborhoods to gentrify and small cafes to wither; and representing the mega-branding that's killing small businesses and homogenizing the world.

I frankly like having Starbucks at the airport, and at strip malls in strange cities. I wouldn't mind independently-owned coffee shops instead, but Starbucks is usually what's there. Moreover, progressives have tended to romanticize small businesses; yet many sweatshops in this country have been small, family-owned enterprises, and that didn't benefit those who worked there. As a rule, racial minorities have fared better in larger institutions. Was Starbucks doing right by race? What about class and politics?

What, specifically, is wrong with this emblematic corporation? And is anything right? It seems to me that the movement is old enough to make some distinctions.

THE VIEW FROM HEADQUARTERS

The mermaid from the Starbucks logo peers coyly from the top of the refurbished Sears warehouse in Seattle that serves as company headquarters. Although one union official claims this is cultishness gone amok, I can't help seeing it as a humorous and engaging design feature.

The people I meet are also humorous and engaging. They include Paula Boggs, executive vice president, general counsel and secretary; Wanda Herndon, senior VP, Worldwide Public Affairs; David Pace, executive VP, Partner Resources; and Sandra Taylor, senior VP, Corporate Social Responsibility. While they are polished spokespeople for the Starbucks mission and policies, they don't really strike me as cult material. What does strike me is that three of the four are African American women. Women comprise barely 13 percent of Fortune 500 general counsel and women of color merely 1.6 percent of all corporate officer positions. At Starbucks, more than 34 percent of the top officers (vice president or higher) are women and/or people of color. And although Starbucks is cagey about its statistics, they're clearly far ahead of the miserable norm. "Certainly, at the top of this company, diversity in the form of race rings loud," says Boggs, the general counsel. "I would think, fairly, we have some work to do when it comes to middle management, but we're on the right path."

"You will see diversity by age, sex, race, sexual orientation, family status throughout the organization," David Pace asserts. "It holds an equal place in our guiding principles, just like respect and dignity, just like customer satisfaction."

Those principles are spelled out in the company's six-point mission statement, which is central to the way the company defines itself and acculturates its employees. Yet Pace is aware that, "Our guiding statement is probably not that different from people who are involved in scandals. The difference is the commitment to it."

MAKING GOOD ON EIGHTH STREET

Tawana Green, a lively 28-year-old African American, Washington, DC native with unruly dreads, believes in the Starbucks mission. She started with the company the same year as the Seattle protests and now, four years later, is the manager of the new Starbucks on SE Eighth Street, two blocks from my home on Capitol Hill.

It's the opportunity Green was looking for. "I've been on my own since I was 17," she relates, "and started work right out of high school. I did the office thing, but found myself sleeping at the computer. So I went into retail where I could work with people."

She was impressed by the full benefits for anyone working 20 hours or more, almost unheard of in the world of retail. In addition to a generous health, life, and disability insurance package, the company offers: a 401K with a match; Starbucks "bean stock," which reflects the annual success of the company and is allocated among employees based on hours worked; discounts on Starbucks public stock; and to top it off, a free pound of coffee every week.

She's hired a total of 15 workers, and all but one survived the first month. Visiting on different shifts, it's clear that she's assembled mostly people of color from the community; they start at $7.50 an hour plus tips, and most of them work enough hours to qualify for the health benefits. Although some Starbucks workers claim they have a difficult time getting those hours, the company says that more than two-thirds of all employees qualify.

As I listen to Green and take in the familiar décor, the comfortable chairs and small merchandise displays, I find myself thinking about what journalist/activist Naomi Klein describes as the branding phenomenon, where what's on sale is not just a product but an image and a lifestyle: not just coffee, but "The Starbucks Experience." Klein hates the clone-like nature of the stores and what she sees as the cynical manipulation of the consumer. And I honestly know what she means. Starbucks is putting in a bid to be a Pleasantville version of the village square.

Then I look at Green, her co-workers, and the customers, and it doesn't look like such a terrible thing. "My goal is to provide a great place to hang out and also give back to the community," Tawana Green tells me. "I'm not saying it's easy. But here I am, 28, with a high school education, and I'm a store manager with a piece of the company. Where else could I get this opportunity? It doesn't get much better than this!"

UNIFORM MISERY

However, for Sandra Evans, an employee at Cintas—the mega-company producing uniforms, laundry, and cleaning supply products with which Starbucks contracts—it doesn't get much worse. Evans, a 57-year-old African American, works 40 hours a week sorting shirts at the Cintas plant in Aspen, Pennsylvania. She also works 20 hours at the local K-Mart. "I've got two jobs, and I'm still struggling," she wryly notes. "This company is making millions, and people can't even pay their electric bills." She loves to walk, entertain, and cook, but "I'm just too busy working." And while she drinks a cup of coffee a day, she's never had a Starbucks, "although I hear they're excellent."

Driven by grievances of unpaid and forced overtime, discrimination and unsafe working conditions, she and her fellow workers are engaged in a campaign to join UNITE, the Union of Needletrades, Industrial and Textile Employees. Evans is also among a group of workers who recently filed an EEOC class action complaint against Cintas for gender and race discrimination. "When I got hired two years ago, they told me $8.50 was the starting rate. Then they hired an 18-year-old white girl, right out of high school, and started her at $9.50. Recently a Hispanic woman started, and they're paying her $8.25." Evans reports there's only one black supervisor at her plant; at another plant, they do not hire any blacks as drivers, even if they are well-qualified, and some plants are stratified by gender as well.

"It's a sad situation," Evans sighs. "I just hope they can be a fair company, hire people at the same rate, and a decent rate, and give people of color a chance to move up. It's not just about me, and it's not just about money. It's about finally treating people with respect."

VOICE VS. VOTE

"I've met Howard twice," Tawana Green tells me, easily referring to Starbucks board chair Howard Schultz. At a company leadership conference, "he told us, 'we take care of the partners, the partners take care of the customers, and the customers take care of the business.'"

Green avoids the word "employees" in favor of the company lexicon, "partners," and quickly corrects herself the one time the e-word slips in. However, a number of Starbucks workers in Canada and the U.S. have begged to differ on the partner/employee question.

Jef Keighley, a national representative for the Canadian Automobile Workers, is bitter when he describes his experiences organizing Starbucks in British Columbia, where the union is in a drawn-out contract negotiation covering 10 Vancouver stores. "We used to have 12 stores," he says, "but the company has had a hand in organizing decertifications at two of those stores, even selecting and paying for the lawyer. We've been at the Labor Board for a year and a half."

Keighley admires Starbucks' tactical and PR sophistication, but dismisses any sincerity around the mission statement as "an absolute crock." He's particularly exercised about the bean stock benefit. "Most would be better off with the money in their paychecks," he asserts. "Our committee knows they're only getting the sizzle while Starbucks keeps the steak."

In his own book, Howard Schultz—a Brooklyn boy made good—clearly expresses a belief that benevolent management should make unions superfluous. It's almost as though the desire to have outside representation is seen as a personal affront that hurts Schultz's feelings more than his profit margins.

UNITE says it has yet to hear from Starbucks about Cintas. But Starbucks General Counsel Paula Boggs insists that, "We take any allegation regarding our suppliers very seriously. We have instituted a supplier code of conduct, and we do look for partners that share our values. Is it perfect, always? No. But it's certainly worked in the main for us."

BRINGING IT ALL BACK HOME

So, what about the most common grievances against Starbucks?

A crucial concern on the global level has been the survival of coffee farmers and the environmental sustainability of production. Coffee is second only to petroleum on the world commodities market, and the price is at catastrophic lows of 40 to 50 cents per pound, threatening roughly 250 million small farmers. There seems little question that pressure from human rights and environmental groups in the mid-'90s spurred Starbucks' commitments in Third World coffee-growing countries. They instituted coffee-sourcing guidelines, and have negotiated long-term contracts and created direct relationships with suppliers to stabilize the income of the farmers. In 2002, they paid an average of $1.20 per pound up to a high of about $1.41. Steve Coats of the US/Labor and Education in the Americas Project (US/LEAP) suggests that, "They don't move any faster than you push them. They may purchase only 1 percent of the coffee, but they can set the standards and tone." However, both US/LEAP and Global Exchange acknowledge that Starbucks has made significant changes in its policies and practices.

There is also a pervasive belief that Starbucks is driving out the independents, but evidence is slim. As I recall, in the distant past of 15 years ago, most coffeehouses were near universities and in Italian neighborhoods. Cheap coffee was found at the local diner, and good coffee was an oxymoron. Are we really saying that there should be no coffee-houses in urban communities of color? Are we arguing against a decent latte at the airport? It may be an unnecessary luxury. But a sign of evil conspiracy? I'm not convinced.

Nor is Starbucks equivalent to Wal-Mart; it has not forced a downward spiral in either prices or wages, it is arguably the best employer in its sector, and it has not turned old main streets into ghost towns. However, Starbucks *has* joined McDonalds and Wal-Mart in hyper-aggressive expansion, especially abroad, thus setting itself up as a symbol of the Americanization of the world.

At the community level, though, it's often hard for people to understand why the store where they shop and work has been targeted. "I remember being in a demonstration where a McDonalds or Starbucks window, I forget which, was shattered," says Colin Rajah, a long-time global justice organizer, currently a program associate at the National Network of Immigrant and Refugee Rights. "We could see the staff, people of color, running toward the back of the store and cowering behind the counter, really scared. I was in a group of young global justice activists of color, and we immediately found ourselves identifying with the people inside the store. And we realized that tactic was a mistake.

"Sure we have to look at the larger picture and how the capitalist system works, but if these entities provide a service to the community, and are not abusing their workers, there's something to be said for that as well. What we should be looking for is the democratization of the process."

I couldn't really get an answer at Starbucks headquarters on how big was too big. "I guess too big is all relative," says Starbucks VP Wanda Herndon, "but big is not necessarily bad if you're doing good things." Mostly, she feels misunderstood by the protesters, who have continued to sporadically damage stores around the country. "The way I felt was that the people who were protesting didn't understand who Starbucks really is, the company, the culture, the people," she explains. "But because our siren makes good news, we became a symbol of all that went wrong with WTO.

"We've always tried to balance profitability with benevolence, and I think that's a concept that's hard for people to grasp. You want to be profitable, but you realize you need to give back if you want to be a part of the communities in which you do business."

As it turns out, Starbucks appears improved on trade, good on race, and a model on health care for part-timers. Amazingly, they have only recently acquired their first government relations staffer, and it remains to be seen whether they will parlay their position into fighting nationally for civil rights, the environment, or national health care.

"People who go into corporate management didn't sign up to be civil servants," notes global justice organizer Liz Butler. "But increasingly, the crucial decisions are being made in board rooms, and we need them to take on that role."

And, at Starbucks, there's some hope of getting through; after all, some of the top management were the anti-war activists of the '70s. Meanwhile, I'm certain that Tawana Green would care about the fate of Sandra Evans, though I wonder whether the company VP's will feel the same. I'm not holding my breath that they'll ever prefer union representation to benevolence. But I'd like to think that they will not be down with the race and gender discrimination of a Cintas.

As Liz Butler puts it, "McDonald's never says it's a good neighbor, but Starbucks does. It's our job to hold them to it." Perhaps then Starbucks won't be doing business with Sandra Evans' oppressor, and activists won't be throwing bricks through Tawana Green's window.

58

INTERRUPTING HISTORICAL PATTERNS: BRIDGING RACE AND GENDER GAPS BETWEEN SENIOR WHITE MEN AND OTHER ORGANIZATIONAL GROUPS

Nancie Zane

. . . Disparities in perceptions and experience raise important questions about the potential for successful cross-race, cross-gender communication and understanding. It also carries important implications about the obstacles to creating more just, equitable, and resourceful organizations. As a white female organizational researcher and consultant, I have become particularly interested in finding ways for whites to work more effectively and respectfully in heterogeneous settings. Most recently, I had the opportunity to do research in a predominantly white financial institution that I've called Eastern,[1] which was engaged in an organization-wide culture change process that included a commitment to becoming more diverse by race and gender. After documenting the senior managements' attempts to design and implement the first stages of a "Diversity Initiative,"[2] I have become convinced that change in the quality of race and gender relations and the development of aceptable notions of equity can only occur after people recognize the multiple, and often competing, social realities that exist among members of different race and gender groups. For whites in general, this means engaging in conversations

From Michelle Fine, Lois Weis, Linda C. Powell, and L. Mun Wong, eds., *Off-White: Readings on Race, Power, and Society*. (New York: Routledge, 1997). Reprinted by permission.

about race in which we listen as members of a racial group as well as from our individual perspectives. It also requires hearing others' experiences about the race and gender biases which permeate meritocratic policies and practices as well as identifying (and ultimately changing) the organizational norms which maintain the dominant power relations. Being open to such systemic concerns is particularly critical for white men who tend to face less obstacles in accessing the rewards bureaucracies have to offer. As a consequence, they are over (and often exclusively) represented at the senior most levels.

What might enable whites—and particularly senior white men—to be open to others' experiences that appear contradictory to their own? What might be the impact at the individual, group, and organizational levels if the senior white men positioned themselves to temporarily suspend their perceptual frames in order to hear the perception of others? *This chapter argues that there is a significant shift in senior level white men's conversations about race and gender when they have opportunities to have well-facilitated intra- and intergroup conversations about their organizational experiences in the context of a larger organizational change process.* Through the use of ethnographic and clinic research methods, I have found that as white men began to perceive themselves not only as *individual players* within the organization but also as *members of specific identity groups* which acknowledge race, gender, and organizational status, their understanding of themselves, race relations, and the distribution of organizational power changes. Not only do they change their beliefs about how white women and people of color are being treated within an organization, *they shift their analytic lenses* from blaming "flawed individuals" to understanding more about complex intergroup relationships and structural barriers. In addition, *they gain a perspective on the nature of white male privilege and their relationship to it.* In other words, as senior white men engage in "public talk" with other race and gender groups, they are able to construct new analyses about the problems and potential supports for and between themselves as white men and other race/gender groups. In addition, while I discuss how conversations (and even behaviors) among the senior white men and between the senior white men and other groups change as a consequence of structured race and gender/diversity workshops in which they have participated, I also attempt to contextualize white males' perspective by exploring the hidden *constructions of white masculinity within the postindustrial workplace* in the twentieth century.

THE SENIOR WHITE MALE DISCOURSES PRIOR TO THE DIVERSITY WORKSHOPS

In the six months preceding the Diversity Workshops, it was clear through various individual interviews and group observations that the majority of the senior white male managers had little interest in engaging cross-race or gender dialogues.[3] While aware that the CEO was supportive of the Diversity Initiative and that their attendance at the workshops was mandatory, there were two primary forms of talk that were most prevalent at the time which reflected their antipathy toward engaging such issues: the *Bottom Line* related to the financial problems associated with a Diversity Initiative and talk of the *Meritocracy* was a defense of the meritocracy against complaints of discrimination.

Undergirding the Bottom Line was the concern that engaging in a diversity initiative would mean that Eastern would either be ferrying race and gender tensions from the outside world into the organization or "stirring up" issues that would create intergroup problems within the organization. In either case, the white senior managers saw it as a distraction to the "real work" of making money and felt worried that the bank would lose control over the range of issues contained within its walls. As one senior Vice President, who flet that the organization already did too much to accommodate women and people of color, said, "If I had the authority, I'd change how the bank was doing things . . . not cow-towing to all these different groups . . . this isn't how the company used to run our business."

Other senior managers were less anxious about a diminution of organizational authority and thought that the changing demographics in the workforce required Eastern to acknowledge and consider the implications of race and gender for the workplace.

. . . While there were differences of opinion about whether diversity was an appropriate issue for the organization to engage, there was consensus that allocating considerable resources into a diversity program was a mistake—that the energy involved in highlighting race and gender issues and "becoming more diverse" would drain too much of the organization's resources and divert them from their primary task.

Perhaps the real bottom line was expressed by one of the Executive VP's when he said, "We have no evidence that diversity is actually economically valuable."

In addition to being concerned about the financial return on diversity, many white senior male managers believed that diversity or as they framed it—the concern for those who might be disadvantaged because of race or gender—was a false issue. Instead they believed in Meritocracy, which professed that anyone who worked hard and sought to self-improve could get ahead at Eastern. As one VP said,

> I feel that anyone can make it to the top here if they're willing to put in the effort. I don't know if I was promoted because I was a white male but I sincerely believe that people are not judged here on the basis of race and gender.

Of course, there was some acknowledgment that "talent" and "best qualifications" were not necessarily just a matter of personality differences, that different groups had access to different academic opportunities which influenced employers' perceptions of "the best qualified." In one example, a white manager explained how a black student from a local university was perceived as lower quality when compared to a white student from Stanford, because of the status of the institution:

> We need the best talent. If I'm choosing between a white from Stanford and a Black from [the local college] there's really no choice. The white student is more savvy. I feel that this is unfortunate, but who's responsibility is it to give Blacks the opportunity?

Even granting the possibility of differential opportunity, however, many of these senior managers were outraged about the oft-made accusation that employees at Eastern were being discriminated against by race or gender.

> Some people of color hide behind diversity issues when they are really performance issues. I don't have time to listen to people complain about racism if they're not performing. The [company] shouldn't prop you up just because you haven't had some opportunities in life.

For these white men, diversity was an issue based on false assumptions that belied the "reality" of fairness and equal opportunity.

THE WORKSHOP EXPERIENCE

For many of the senior managers with whom I spoke during and after the workshops, these workshops seemed to have a profound impact on its participants, leading to attitudinal and discursive changes. What happened across these five days that so many of the members of the Management Committee believed "their eyes had been opened" around issues of race and gender?

While different individuals felt they had learned a variety of lessons from the structured exercises the Diversity Consultants took them through during the workshops, the overwhelming majority attributed their sense of opening up, taking in new information, and changing their perspectives . . . to hearing the personal stories of white women and people of color. Although in the midst of one workshop, many white men reported that they could not relate to the kinds of experiences that members of different race/gender groups' shared, in retrospect, confronting the realities of these participants' painful work lives while sitting with the contrast of their own experiences was transformative. As Marv, an Executive VP who had little patience for the notion of discrimination in the organization, said:

> To me the biggest impact came from the personal stories that we heard in our two-day session . . . intellectually, I thought I was aware of some of these issues, but when you actually hear the depth of emotion and general

consistency in the stories, it made an impression on me that there is a problem here, and it is not just a couple of malcontents whining and complaining. . . .

In addition, the Diversity Consultants provided managers with new and broader frameworks for processing the data by distinguishing between individual, group, and institutional levels of analysis, a framework which for Evan, another Executive VP, meant he, like Marv, could "no longer dismiss individual concerns as idiosyncratic stories." Indeed, Marv and Evan's vision and understanding of some aspect of the world had been permanently altered.

As a way to try and capture some of the experience that led to a number of the senior white men's new outlook on race and gender issues at Eastern, I've tried to highlight a number of significant moments across several workshops in which the white men seemed to gain some significant insight into the dynamics of race, gender, power, and privilege.

SCENE I

After talking in small homogeneous groups[4] about some of the organization-wide data that had been collected at the beginning of the culture change process and categorically analyzed by race, gender, and level,[5] participants came back together to discuss the highlights of their conversations. People of color talked movingly about their pain of trying to "make it" in the organization and the systematic erosion of the psyche that takes place after continuously being exposed to racism.

> **Elaine,** a Chinese midlevel manager said: "It makes me sad that I'm always having to change myself . . . to adapt myself to others' expectations so they'll accept me. **Carol Brown,** the lead African-American Diversity Consultant responded: "What happens if they don't understand your perspective?" **Elaine:** "You take it in internally and I end up feeling like there's something wrong with me." **Bob,** an African-American midlevel manager added, "I'm used to being a minority . . . having to work hard to educate others . . . to make them understand that I'm o.k." **Yvonne,** an African-American senior level officer joined in as well: "I go home questioning my sanity, my intellect, my judgement . . . we hurt ourselves, put a lot of energy into saying, "I'm somebody, you can't make me feel like a nobody."

After hearing their comments, a number of white men asked the people of color in the group "Why do you take it?" "Why are you so docile?" "How come there isn't more activism in the streets?" With some impatience, different people of color talked about their fear of white violence and their fear for their children in the outside world—one in which their children could easily be killed by a cop or a gang member who sees their kid as "another nigger." Flora, an African-American midlevel woman manager elaborated:

> My son has everything going against him. The only thing he has is two intelligent parents. . . . I pray for him. . . . I know that if he gets an attitude he'll end up with a bullet in his ass . . . he's always suspect . . . he's already been asked by a white cop in our own neighborhood, "where do you live?"

While her story was quite gut-wrenching, the white men did not seem to relate to empathize with the emotionality. Yvonne, who was clearly angry about whites' assumption that blacks have choices about venting their rage, said forcefully:

> We put up with it because we have not choice. . . . we never get a leg up, we're still at the bottom . . . native people were wiped out . . . so we've learned to swallow hard. But you know what racism does to us? It destroys us systematically. . . . even with college degrees we can't find work . . . there are bright black men on street corners because there's no place for them in the system . . . they wait to die. Black men are an endangered species . . . you swallow until you can't take it anymore.

The white men begin to talk about their feelings of guilt and responsibility as well as their sense of powerlessness about changing the situation. Carol, the Diversity Consultant, asked people to move back into their same race/ gender groups and identify their reactions to what they've heard. On newsprint the white men wrote:

We often feel powerless or unaware of what to do to make a difference.
We want and need feedback—we will make mistakes.
We have feelings of fear, guilt, anxiety.
We feel a lot of the burden is (appropriately) on us and we want/need to help.

During the next intergroup dialogue, a number of people of color responded with surprise, "I had no idea that white men had feelings of impotence or uncertainty."

SCENE II

The group began with two white men acknowledging that they had been operating *only* from an individual perspective and did not understand group-level phenomena: "When I thought I 'had it' on an individual level I was most dangerous since I didn't get it on a group level."

Rosa, an upper-level Puerto Rican woman manager, went into depth about how, when she meets whites in power, she's either assumed to be stupid or, once seen as intelligent, assumed to be different than the "others" of her kind. This puts her in the position, if she wants to fit in and succeed, of having to choose to identify with those in power (whites) or her family, who are seen as inferior. "Every time it's a death that I die to think . . . my cousins are less than me. . . . its painful putting people behind the doors and making them invisible." Several other people of color and white women then told connecting stories related to this experience.

The white men appeared distant—again not connecting to Rosa's level of emotionality or her story. Finally one senior white man, Bill, admitted that "it's tough to hear this, because I can't relate to it." Initially some of the senior men tried to see it as a "people" story, but Donna, a white woman Diversity Consultant teaming with Carol Brown, quickly dispelled the notion that it was a universal story, and explained how it was different because of race and gender. She described how white men do not walk into a room and have to dispel negative stereotypes about themselves nor do they have to choose between themselves and their people to get into "the club." Essie raised the underlying issue, "How does it feel, that with the luck of the draw, you have the advantage? . . . You feel like you've earned your spot, but haven't recognized the group advantage."

Slowly, some of the white men began to let in the possibility that they have been privileged in certain ways. Chaz, an executive V.P., says, "You're saying that we got where we are because of who we are . . . you're putting down a life that's been hard to come by . . . that hurts my self image." John, a black man on the Diversity Consultation team asked, "Why do you hear her negating your hard work?" Chaz replied, "Well, most of us think we did it through hard work . . . but hard work or not we had an advantage."

As the conversation continued a few white men then described some of their resistance to being race and gender conscious—that they felt uncomfortable and awkward about having to be so conscious of what they say and how they say it: "Wouldn't it be better if we could all be comfortable?" Donna framed it as, "How does change occur and who's responsible for change? . . . We're willing to tell you about our experience but, you do have to change your behavior . . . to be more sensitive . . . to realize you didn't get there just by merit . . . it's uncomfortable to see this stuff and acknowledge it . . . over time you will feel more integrated."

SCENE III

During a large group session, Bill began to discuss his newfound belief about race, gender, and self-esteem—i.e., that while it takes a lot of energy for individuals to maintain their self-esteem, it must take more energy for white women and people of color given the daily psychic assaults with which they are confronted. He said, "As a white man, I carry a one-pound weight; not the 100-pound weight that women and people of color do. Self-esteem is everyone's issue, but for women and people of color it's worse." Bob, another white man, built on that idea and made the connection between self-esteem and power. "Some of us use our positions of power to feel good. . . . If you don't have self-confidence, you don't want to give up the power . . . and lots of us don't have it."

The conversation then moved to the question of what would motivate white men to share the prize/power/privilege. "I think it would be decency," said Bob. Tim responded in a matter-of-fact tone, "We know that doesn't work . . . we've been able to wall off others from getting their hands in the cookie jar . . . the system isn't working."

The white men began to problem-solve about how they should address these issues. "The only way to get out of this is to correct inequities . . . and go the other way . . . that means we should be hiring blacks that are less qualified and training them." Brown quickly intervened and reframed the issue: "The issue is not about less qualified blacks, but less qualified whites. . . . What does it do to his self-image and your relationship to him?" A senior white man mused that unknowingly, white men have, in the name of objectivity, "built in a whole lot of prejudice into the judgment tools and check marks." A middle-level white woman and black man both responded, "We don't understand what the check marks are that signify qualifications . . . we think some are subjective and about seeing yourself in others." A white man then linked the nature of the organizational structure to its function. "Structures have become invisible to protect white men's self-image." Donna then connected his comment to the question of change and responsibility: "White men's responsibility is to get people to say that the invisible structures which maintain inequity have to change."

UNRAVELING THE WORKSHOP DISCOURSE

In reflecting on these scenes from the Diversity Workshops, I was deeply moved by the power of the workshop dialogue; of the generosity of the white women and people of color to share at such emotionally meaningful levels— revealing their pain, vulnerabilities, and strengths;[6] and of the willingness of the white men to reveal their anxieties about their own limitations and failures. In regard to the white men, I was also struck by the psychological and cognitive leaps many of them demonstrated, in which they not only took in others' experiences as a valid expression of reality, but chose to work with this "new" information in a way that yielded fresh insight into their own perspectives.

The significance of the white men's openness became more impressive as I began to unravel the embedded discourses about work, organizational structures, maleness, and white privilege that underlay their conversations. For example, one tension that was evident in the workshop dialogues related to the credibility of the meritocracy, and the relationship between achievement at work and self-esteem. The senior white men were clearly invested in the notion that their hard work, ingenuity, and skills had won them their senior-level positions. As others talked about the fact that there were obstacles to their getting ahead, white men heard it as a condemnation that they somehow didn't "deserve" their position. During the diversity workshops, the consultants tried to assure the senior men that the implications of discrimination did not reflect a diminution of their hard work, but rather a statement about the structural barriers which certain others faced, disabling them from demonstrating or being recognized for their equally meritorious efforts. As the consultants and a number of white men ultimately acknowledged, one consequence of these impermeable barriers was that the pool of competitors that white men were vying against was smaller than it might have been.

But rather than simply framing the senior white men's anxiety about the legitimacy of their organizational status or their uneasiness about the discriminatory nature of the system as merely self-serving or a desire to maintain double standards, it is important to contextualize their reactions by examining the historical discourses which have permeated white middle-class work-life during the last two centuries.

In *American Manhood*, E. Anthony Rotundo explained that only at the turn of the nineteenth century, as the market economy emerged and the interconnected web of relationships between home, community, religious affiliation, and work disappeared, did white men's work take on heightened meaning and "provide the chief substance of their social identity." With the shift from a more communal to individualistic social context, white men and women's lives became more distinctly divided into private versus public spheres, in which men dominated the more powerful public or work sphere. From Rotundo's perspective this separation had important political implications:

> From the hierarchy and assigned social status of colonial society to the doctrine of the spheres . . . [the latter] enshrined individualism as a male privilege, making men's sphere the locus of individualism and women's sphere the place where a woman submerged her social identity in that of her husband . . .
>
> [*American Manhood*, E. Anthony Rotundo]

However, while white men's power was heightened, so were their anxieties about their work lives as the association between male work and self worth as a "male human" became pivotal. On the one hand, "Work could serve to reassure a man about his manhood and about the freedom and power that manhood beckoned." On the other, the thought of failure plagued the psyches of many middle-class white men. After all, not only did a man's individual achievements serve as a reflection of his character, but it also served to mark the social status of his whole family. Supported by an ideology of denial, in which white men were taught to deny their fears and forge ahead regardless of their feelings, there was great social pressure for men to exhibit individual initiative to get ahead within their chosen professions. Over time, sports and relaxation became extensions of the work world as well, so socializing in all (white) male lodges, restaurants, and athletic clubs in which competition and fraternization were intermingled were critical components of male work life.

During the twentieth century three major shifts occurred which impacted white middle-class men's work world. The first two related to gender relations: (1) women demanded and won the right to vote as well as the right to work, invading the boundaries of the male workplace, and (2) Darwinian theory shifted the negative judgment on the "primitive passions of men" into a more positive one. So while white women had been the keepers of the domestic and more contained, civilized sphere, as they moved into the workforce, white men reclaimed their right to define the elements of civility—despite/in spite of the judgments of women. The notion now included self-expressions of male passion—combative strength, ambition, and boldness. These characteristics, which in the workplace were tempered by virtues of cooperation and connection as it related to accomplishing the aims of the larger organization, became the marks of an independent, successful man. So at the time white women were gaining access to the workplace, white men were changing the rules about the kinds of behavior that would gain individual acclaim and recognition. Ultimately, white men continued to define and dominate the workplace. As Rotundo explains it:

> As we have seen historically . . . the middle-class workplace was constructed by men according to shared male values and customs that are culturally alien to women. In recent years, women have made statistical inroads in the world of the team player, but as yet there is little change—culturally or statistically—at the level where most power is wielded.

The third trend that affected the interiors of white men's organizational life pertains to race relations and civil rights. Prior to the 1960s, race and ethnicity were rarely overt topics of conversation within organizational settings and concerns about systemic barriers that prevented access to primarily white institutions were trivialized and denied. Maintaining an advantage over people of color, particularly blacks, was a reflection of the natural order of social and organizational relations—individuals with less skills, education, and/or motivation remained at the bottom of the hierarchy. Their place in the pecking order was the very justification for their being positioned there. Since whites tended to see the world in individual rather than group terms, patterns of discrimination and dominance were made invisible. However, the emergence of the civil rights movement highlighted racial differences and the myths of social and organizational mobility. The passage of the Civil Rights Act and the development of the notion of affirmative action forced organizations to confront the issue of racial discrimination.

However, even with people of color and their white allies pressing the legal and moral issues, middle-class whites—and white men in particular—have maintained their aversion to thinking in group-level terms, invested instead in asserting the myth of the "color-blind" meritocracy—a stance that allows white men to resist marking themselves as white and as dominant. Taking such a stance, according to Ruth Frankenberg, "is itself an effect of its dominance. Among the effects on white people both of race privilege and of the dominance of whiteness are their seeming normativity, their structured invisibility" (Frankenberg 1993, p. 6).

With notions of masculinity, whiteness, and self being inextricably intertwined with the dominant ideologies of individualism and meritocracy, it is not surprising that the senior white men at Eastern would cling to the images of themselves and their white male colleagues as hard-working, deserving employees. However, when they were no longer insulated from the pain that the white male bureaucratic culture imposed on "others," these men acknowledged the ways their own vision had been obstructed by the very systems they relied on to help them know their world. They could no longer deny the flaws in the meritocracy and the resulting patterns of institutional discrimination. Further, the jarring experiences of the Diversity Workshops and the cross gender/race relationships that were established may have forced a wedge in the tightly constructed historical web of white male privilege.

DISCUSSION

In listening to the conversations that took place during the Diversity Workshops as well as the reflections of the senior white men after the event, the senior white men seemed to have undergone a rather striking metamorphosis. Rather than maintaining a stance towards diversity characterized by negativity, they began to move towards a position of openness and genuine interest. How did this evolve? By participating in dialogue in which white women, women of color, and men of color spoke candidly both from their personal as well as their group-level experiences within the organization, the senior white men were confronted with collective data which was categorically different from their own. This exchange, facilitated by well-seasoned Diversity Consultants, provided a window into certain systematic patterns which could no longer be comfortably labeled as the specific problems of whiny individuals or undeserving minorities. In acknowledging the gaps between their and others' realities, many of the white men were able to hold previous assumptions at bay and hear old information in new ways. This served as a basis for constructing new, more complex critiques about others, themselves as a group, and their relationships to the organization. It also provided the foundation for the emergence of a new set of organizational discourses in which there was an embracing, rather than negation of, race and gender differences, as well as an eschewing of discriminatory policies and practices.

NOTES

1. Both the name of the organization and the names of individuals quoted in the text have been altered to protect confidentiality.

2. In the beginning of Eastern's culture change process, diversity was defined as a desire to value individual differences and encourage a range of perspectives in an environment of respect. Two years later it was cast as eradicating oppression at the institutional level and harnessing the talents and contributions that all bring to the organization.

3. There were approximately twenty-four senior white managers who were most responsible for top-level decisions.

4. There were four small groups: white women, white men, women of color, and men of color. The women of color were not racially homogeneous in that there were Asian-American, Hispanic-American, and African-American women present. The "men of color" group consisted of African-American men.

5. As a way to create some benchmarks for the culture-change process, the ad hoc committee responsible for designing and overseeing the process hired a consulting group to construct an organization-wide employee satisfaction survey. The survey was used to get an initial pulse of the organization. The data indicated that there were significant differences in how various race and gender groups felt about organizational practices as it related to recruitment, retention, and promotion of employees. Tower and her associates had participants in the workshop discuss the survey findings as a way to begin the conversation about differential experiences among groups at Eastern.

6. The question that remains unexplored is the cost (and gain) to white women and people of color for their self- and group-disclosures. For example, some of the women of color at Eastern reported in interviews with me after the workshop that they had continued to feel emotionally drained and exposed because they had discussed situations in which not only was the content upsetting, but it was about things they usually repressed in order to function. Consequently, they felt "left hanging" and "used." For others, the experience was cathartic—they felt heard and responded to. Many also felt that they had learned things about white men's experience and perspectives which they hadn't known before and which provided new understanding about certain racial differences. In addition, several white women and people of color mentioned that the workshops had given them an opportunity to get to know and network with senior white men that they hadn't known before. One result was that they found themselves gaining access to situations from which they were previously excluded. The flip side,

of course, was that they found themselves being tokenized in a variety of situations as well because now they were the one "black person" or "white woman" that was known by the senior manager who was trying to be more inclusive. While it is beyond the scope of this paper to address this issue in depth, it is a critical one, particularly since many diversity workshops use this model of intergroup dialogue in which white women and people of color "spill their guts" as a way to do consciousness-raising with white men about discrimination and institutional oppression.

7. Ruth Frankenburg, *White Women, Race Matters: The Social Construction of Whiteness* (Minneapolis, MN: University of Minnesota Press, 1993).

59

WOMEN OF COLOR ON THE FRONT LINE

Celene Krauss

Toxic waste disposal is a central focus of women's grass-roots environmental activism. Toxic waste facilities are predominantly sited in working-class and low-income communities and communities of color, reflecting the dispro-portionate burden placed on these communities by a political economy of growth that distributes the costs of economic growth unequally. Spurred by the threat that toxic wastes pose to family health and community survival, female grass-roots activists have assumed the leadership of community envi-ronmental struggles. As part of a larger movement for environmental justice, they constitute a diverse constituency, including working-class housewives and secretaries, rural African American farmers, urban residents, Mexican American farm workers, and Native Americans.

These activists attempt to differentiate themselves from what they see as the white, male, middle-class leadership of many national environmental or-ganizations. Unlike the more abstract, issue-oriented focus of national groups, women's focus is on environmental issues that grow out of their con-crete, immediate experiences. Female blue-collar activists often share a loosely defined ideology of environmental justice and a critique of dominant social institutions and mainstream environmental organizations, which they

From Robert D. Bullard, ed., *Unequal Protection: Environmental Justice and Communities of Color* (San Francisco: Sierra Club Books, 1994), pp. 256–71. Reprinted by permission.

believe do not address the broader issues of inequality underlying environmental hazards. At the same time, these activists exhibit significant diversity in their conceptualization of toxic waste issues, reflecting different experiences of class, race, and ethnicity.

This [essay] looks at the ways in which different working-class women formulate ideologies of resistance around toxic waste issues and the process by which they arrive at a concept of environmental justice. Through an analysis of interviews, newsletters, and conference presentations, I show the voices of white, African American, and Native American female activists and the resources that inform and support their protests. What emerges is an environmental discourse that is mediated by subjective experiences and interpretations and rooted in the political truths women construct out of their identities as housewives, mothers, and members of communities and racial and ethnic groups.

THE SUBJECTIVE DIMENSION OF GRASS-ROOTS ACTIVISM

Grass-roots protest activities have often been trivialized, ignored, and viewed as self-interested actions that are particularistic and parochial, failing to go beyond a single-issue focus. This view of community grass-roots protests is held by most policymakers as well as by many analysts of movements for progressive social change.

In contrast, the voices of blue-collar women engaged in protests regarding toxic waste issues tell us that single-issue protests are about more than the single issue. They reveal a larger world of power and resistance, which in some measure ends up challenging the social relations of power. This challenge becomes visible when we shift the analysis of environmental activism to the experiences of working-class women and the subjective meanings they create around toxic waste issues.

In traditional sociological analysis, this subjective dimension of protest has often been ignored or viewed as private and individualistic. Feminist theory, however, helps us to see its importance. For feminists, the critical reflection on the everyday world of experience is an important subjective dimension of social change. Feminists show us that experience is not merely a personal, individualistic concept. It is social. People's experiences reflect where they fit in the social hierarchy. Thus, blue-collar women of differing backgrounds interpret their experiences of toxic waste problems within the context of their particular cultural histories, starting from different assumptions and arriving at concepts of environmental justice that reflect broader experiences of class and race.

Feminist theorists also challenge a dominant ideology that separates the "public" world of policy and power from the "private" and personal world of everyday experience. By definition, this ideology relegates the lives and concerns of women relating to home and family to the private, nonpolitical arena, leading to invisibility of their grass-roots protests about issues such as toxic wastes. As Ann Bookman has noted in her important study of working-class women's community struggles, women's political activism in general, and working-class political life at the community level in particular, remain "peripheral to the historical record . . . where there is a tendency to privilege male political activity and labor activism."[1] The women's movement took as its central task the reconceptualization of the political itself, critiquing this dominant ideology and constructing a new definition of the political located in the everyday world of ordinary women rather than in the world of public policy. Feminists provide a perspective for making visible the importance of particular, single-issue protests regarding toxic wastes by showing how ordinary women subjectively link the particulars of their private lives with a broader analysis of power in the public sphere.

Social historians such as George Rudé have pointed out that it is often difficult to understand the experience and ideologies of resistance because ordinary working people appropriate and reshape traditional beliefs embedded within working-class culture, such as family and community. This point is also relevant for understanding the environmental protests of working-class women. Their protests are framed in terms of the traditions of motherhood and family; as a result, they often appear parochial or even conservative. As we shall see, however, for working-class women, these traditions become the levers that set in motion a political process, shaping the language and oppositional meanings that emerge and providing resources for social change.

Shifting the analysis of toxic waste issues to the subjective experience of ordinary women makes visible a complex relationship between everyday life and the larger structures of public power. It reveals the potential for human agency that is hidden in a more traditional sociological approach and provides us with a means of seeing "the sources of power which subordinated groups have created."[2]

The analysis presented in this [essay] is based on the oral and written voices of women involved in toxic waste protests. Interviews were conducted at environmental conferences such as the First National People of Color Environmental Leadership Summit, Washington, D.C., 1991, and the World Women's Congress for a Healthy Planet, Miami, Florida, 1991, and by telephone. Additional sources include conference presentations, pamphlets, books, and other written materials that have emerged from this movement. This research is part of an ongoing comparative study that will examine the ways in which experiences of race, class, and ethnicity mediate women's environmental activism. Future research includes an analysis of the environmental activism of Mexican American women in addition to that of the women discussed here.

TOXIC WASTE PROTESTS
AND THE RESOURCE OF MOTHERHOOD

Blue-collar women do not use the language of the bureaucrat to talk about environmental issues. They do not spout data or marshal statistics in support of their positions. In fact, interviews with these women rarely generate a lot of discussion about the environmental problem per se. But in telling their stories about their protest against a landfill or incinerator, they ultimately tell larger stories about their discovery or analysis of oppression. Theirs is a political, not a technical, analysis.

Working-class women of diverse racial and ethnic backgrounds identify the toxic waste movement as a women's movement, composed primarily of mothers. Says one woman who fought against an incinerator in Arizona and subsequently worked on other anti-incinerator campaigns throughout the state, "Women are the backbone of the grass-roots groups; they are the ones who stick with it, the ones who won't back off." By and large, it is women, in their traditional role as mothers, who make the link between toxic wastes and their children's ill health. They discover the hazards of toxic contamination: multiple miscarriages, birth defects, cancer deaths, and so on. This is not surprising, as the gender-based division of labor in a capitalist society gives working-class women the responsibility for the health of their children.

These women define their environmental protests as part of the work that mothers do. Cora Tucker, an African American activist who fought against uranium mining in Virginia and who now organizes nationally, says:

> It's not that I don't think that women are smarter, [she laughs] but I think that we are with the kids all day long. . . . If Johnny gets a cough and Mary gets a cough, we try to discover the problem.

Another activist from California sums up this view: "If we don't oppose an incinerator, we're not doing our work as mothers."

For these women, family serves as a spur to action, contradicting popular notions of family as conservative and parochial. Family has a very different meaning for these women than it does for the middle-class nuclear family. Theirs is a less privatized, extended family that is open, permeable, and attached to community. This more extended family creates the networks and resources that enable working-class communities to survive materially given few economic resources. The destruction of working-class neighborhoods by economic growth deprives blue-collar communities of the basic resources of survival; hence the resistance engendered by toxic waste issues. Working-class women's struggles over toxic waste issues are, at root, issues about survival. Ideologies of motherhood, traditionally relegated to the private sphere, become political resources that working-class women use to initiate and justify their resistance. In the process of protest, working-class women come to reject the dominant ideology, which separates the public and private arenas.

Working-class women's extended network of family and community serves as the vehicle for spreading information and concern about toxic waste issues. Extended networks of kinship and friendship become political resources of opposition. For example, in one community in Detroit, women discovered patterns of health problems while attending Tupperware parties. Frequently, a mother may read about a hazard in a newspaper, make a tentative connection between her own child's ill health and the pollutant, and start telephoning friends and family, developing an informal health survey. Such a discovery process is rooted in what Sara Ruddick has called the everyday practice of mothering.[3] Through their informal networks, they compare notes and experiences and develop an oppositional knowledge used to resist the dominant knowledge of experts and the decisions of government and corporate officials.

These women separate themselves from "mainstream" environmental organizations, which are seen as dominated by white, middle-class men and concerned with remote issues. Says one woman from Rahway, New Jersey: "The mainstream groups deal with safe issues. They want to stop incinerators to save the eagle, or they protect trees for the owl. But we say, what about the people?"

Another activist implicitly criticizes the mainstream environmental groups when she says of the grass-roots Citizens' Clearinghouse for Hazardous Wastes:

> Rather than oceans and lakes, they're concerned about kids dying. Once you've had someone in your family who has been attacked by the environment—I mean who has had cancer or some other disease—you get a keen sense of what's going on.

It is the traditional, "private" women's concerns about home, children, and family that provide the initial impetus for blue-collar women's involvement in issues of toxic waste. The political analyses they develop break down the public-private distinction of dominant ideology and frame a particular toxic waste issue within broader contexts of power relationships.

THE ROLE OF RACE, ETHNICITY, AND CLASS

Interviews with white, African American, and Native American women show that the starting places for and subsequent development of their analyses of toxic waste protests are mediated by issues of class, race, and ethnicity.

White working-class women come from a culture in which traditional women's roles center on the private arena of family. They often marry young;

although they may work out of financial necessity, the primary roles from which they derive meaning and satisfaction are those of mothering and taking care of family. They are revered and supported for fulfilling the ideology of a patriarchal family. And these families often reflect a strong belief in the existing political system. The narratives of white working-class women involved in toxic waste issues are filled with the process by which they discover the injustice of their government, their own insecurity about entering the public sphere of politics, and the constraints of the patriarchal family, which, ironically prevent them from becoming fully active in the defense of their family, especially in their protest. Their narratives are marked by a strong initial faith in "their" government, as well as a remarkable transformation as they become disillusioned with the system. They discover "that they never knew what they were capable of doing in defense of their children."

For white working-class women, whose views on public issues are generally expressed only within family or among friends, entering a more public arena to confront toxic waste issues is often extremely stressful. "Even when I went to the PTA," says one activist, "I rarely spoke. I was so nervous." Says another: "My views have always been strong, but I expressed them only in the family. They were not for the public." A strong belief in the existing political system is characteristic of these women's initial response to toxic waste issues. Lois Gibbs, whose involvement in toxic waste issues started at Love Canal, tells us, "I believed if I had a problem I just had to go to the right person in government and he would take care of it."

Initially, white working-class women believe that all they have to do is give the government the facts and their problem will be taken care of. They become progressively disenchanted with what they view as the violation of their rights and the injustice of a system that allows their children and family to die. In the process, they develop a perspective of environmental justice rooted in issues of class, the attempt to make democracy real, and a critique of the corporate state. Says one activist who fought the siting of an incinerator in Sumter County, Alabama: "We need to stop letting economic development be the true God and religion of this country. We have to prevent big money from influencing our government."

A recurring theme in the narratives of these women is the transformation of their beliefs about government and power. Their politicization is rooted in the deep sense of violation, betrayal, and hurt they feel when they find that their government will not protect their families. Lois Gibbs sums up this feeling well:

> I grew up in a blue-collar community. We were very into democracy. There is something about discovering that democracy isn't democracy as we know it. When you lose faith in your government, it's like finding out your mother was fooling around on your father. I was very upset. It almost broke my heart

> because I really believed in the system. I still believe in the system, only now I
> believe that democracy is of the people and by the people, that people have
> to move it, it ain't gonna move by itself.

Echoes of this disillusionment are heard from white blue-collar women throughout the country. One activist relates:

> We decided to tell our elected officials about the problems of incineration
> because we didn't think they knew. Surely if they knew that there was a toxic
> waste dump in our county they would stop it. I was politically naive. I was really
> surprised because I live in an area that's like the Bible Belt of the South. Now I
> think the God of the United States is really economic development, and that
> has got to change.

Ultimately, these women become aware of the inequities of power as it is shaped by issues of class and gender. Highly traditional values of democracy and motherhood remain central to their lives. But in the process of politicization through their work on toxic waste issues, these values become transformed into resources of opposition that enable women to enter the public arena and challenge its legitimacy. They justify their resistance as a way to make democracy real and to protect their children.

White blue-collar women's stories are stories of transformations: transformations into more self-confident and assertive women; into political activists who challenge the existing system and feel powerful in that challenge; into wives and mothers who establish new relationships with their spouses (or get divorced) and new, empowering relationships with their children as they provide role models of women capable of fighting for what they believe in.

African American working-class women begin their involvement in toxic waste protests from a different place. They bring to their protests a political awareness that is grounded in race and that shares none of the white blue-collar women's initial trust in democratic institutions. These women view government with mistrust, having been victims of racist policies throughout their lives. Individual toxic waste issues are immediately framed within a broader political context and viewed as environmental racism. Says an African American activist from Rahway, New Jersey:

> When they sited the incinerator for Rahway, I wasn't surprised. All you have
> to do is look around my community to know that we are a dumping ground
> for all kinds of urban industrial projects that no one else wants. I knew this
> was about environmental racism the moment that they proposed the
> incinerator.

An African American woman who fought the siting of a landfill on the South Side of Chicago reiterates this view: "My community is an all-black community isolated from everyone. They don't care what happens to us." She describes her community as a "toxic doughnut":

> We have seven landfills. We have a sewer treatment plant. We have the Ford Motor Company. We have a paint factory. We have numerous chemical companies and steel mills. The river is just a few blocks away from us and is carrying water so highly contaminated that they say it would take seventy-five years or more before they can clean it up.

This activist sees her involvement in toxic waste issues as a challenge to traditional stereotypes of African American women. She says, "I'm here to tell the story that all people in the projects are not lazy and dumb!"

Some of these women share experiences of personal empowerment through their involvement in toxic waste issues. Says one African American activist:

> Twenty years ago I couldn't do this because I was so shy. . . . I had to really know you to talk with you. Now I talk. Sometimes I think I talk too much. I waited until my fifties to go to jail. But it was well worth it. I never went to no university or college, but I'm going in there and making speeches.

However, this is not a major theme in the narratives of female African American activists, as it is in those of white blue-collar women. African American women's private work as mothers has traditionally extended to a more public role in the local community as protectors of the race. As a decade of African American feminist history has shown, African American women have historically played a central role in community activism and in dealing with issues of race and economic injustice. They receive tremendous status and recognition from their community. Many women participating in toxic waste protests have come out of a history of civil rights activism, and their environmental protests, especially in the South, develop through community organizations born during the civil rights movement. And while the visible leaders are often male, the base of the organizing has been led by African American women, who, as Cheryl Townsend Gilkes has written, have often been called "race women," responsible for the "racial uplift" of their communities.[4]

African American women perceive that traditional environmental groups only peripherally relate to their concerns. As Cora Tucker relates:

> This white woman from an environmental group asked me to come down to save a park. She said that they had been trying to get black folks involved and that they won't come. I said, "Honey, it's not that they aren't concerned, but when their babies are dying in their arms they don't give a damn about a park." I said, "They want to save their babies. If you can help them save their babies, then in turn they can help you save your park." And she said, "But this is a real immediate problem." And I said, "Well, these people's kids dying is immediate."

Tucker says that white environmental groups often call her or the head of the NAACP at the last minute to participate in an environmental rally because they want to "include" African Americans. But they exclude African Americans from the process of defining the issues in the first place. What African American communities are doing is changing the agenda.

Because the concrete experience of African Americans' lives is the experience and analysis of racism, social issues are interpreted and struggled with within this context. Cora Tucker's story of attending a town board meeting shows that the issue she deals with is not merely the environment but also the disempowerment she experiences as an African American woman. At the meeting, white women were addressed as Mrs. So-and-So by the all-white, male board. When Mrs. Tucker stood up, however, she was addressed as "Cora":

> One morning I got up and I got pissed off and I said, "What did you call me?" He said, "Cora," and I said, "The name is Mrs. Tucker." And I had the floor until he said "Mrs. Tucker." He waited five minutes before he said "Mrs. Tucker." And I held the floor. I said, "I'm Mrs. Tucker," I said, "Mr. Chairman, I don't call you by your first name and I don't want you to call me by mine. My name is Mrs. Tucker. And when you want me, you call me Mrs. Tucker." It's not that—I mean it's not like you gotta call me Mrs. Tucker, but it was the respect.

In discussing this small act of resistance as an African American woman, Cora Tucker is showing how environmental issues may be about corporate and state power, but they are also about race. For female African American activists, environmental issues are seen as reflecting environmental racism and linked to other social justice issues, such as jobs, housing, and crime. They are viewed as part of a broader picture of social inequity based on race. Hence, the solution articulated in a vision of environmental justice is a civil rights vision—rooted in the everyday experience of racism. Environmental justice comes to mean the need to resolve the broad social inequities of race.

The narratives of Native American women are also filled with the theme of environmental racism. However, their analysis is laced with different images. It is a genocidal analysis rooted in the Native American cultural identification, the experience of colonialism, and the imminent endangerment of their culture. A Native American woman from North Dakota, who opposed a landfill, says:

> Ever since the white man came here, they keep pushing us back, taking our lands, pushing us onto reservations. We are down to 3 percent now, and I see this as just another way for them to take our lands, to completely annihilate our races. We see that as racism.

Like that of the African American women, these women's involvement in toxic waste protests is grounded from the start in race and shares none of the white blue-collar women's initial belief in the state. A Native American woman from southern California who opposed a landfill on the Rosebud Reservation in South Dakota tells us:

> Government did pretty much what we expected them to do. They supported the dump. People here fear the government. They control so many aspects of our life. When I became involved in opposing the garbage landfill, my people told me to be careful. They said they annihilate people like me.

Another woman involved in the protest in South Dakota describes a government official's derision of the tribe's resistance to the siting of a landfill:

> If we wanted to live the life of Mother Earth, we should get a tepee and live on the Great Plains and hunt buffalo.

Native American women come from a culture in which women have had more empowered and public roles than is the case in white working-class culture. Within the Native American community, women are revered as nurturers. From childhood, boys and girls learn that men depend on women for their survival. Women also play a central role in the decision-making process within the tribe. Tribal council membership is often equally divided between men and women; many women are tribal leaders and medicine women. Native American religions embody a respect for women as well as an ecological ethic based on values such as reciprocity and sustainable development: Native Americans pray to Mother Earth, as opposed to the dominant culture's belief in a white, male, Anglicized representation of divinity.

In describing the ways in which their culture integrates notions of environmentalism and womanhood, one woman from New Mexico says:

> We deal with the whole of life and community; we're not separated, we're born into it—you are it. Our connection as women is to the Mother Earth, from the time of our consciousness. We're not environmentalists. We're born into the struggle of protecting and preserving our communities. We don't separate ourselves. Our lifeblood automatically makes us responsible; we are born with it. Our teaching comes from a spiritual base. This is foreign to our culture. There isn't even a word for dioxin in Navajo.

In recent years, Native American lands have become common sites for commercial garbage dumping. Garbage and waste companies have exploited the poverty and lack of jobs in Native American communities and the fact that Native American lands, as sovereign nation territories, are often exempt from local environmental regulations. In discussing their opposition to dumping, Native American women ground their narratives in values about land that are inherent in the Native American community. They see these projects as violating tribal sovereignty and the deep meaning of land, the last resource they have. The issue, says a Native American woman from California, is

> protection of the land for future generations, not really as a mother, but for the health of the people, for survival. Our tribe bases its sovereignty on our land base, and if we lose our land base, then we will be a lost people. We can't afford to take this trash and jeopardize our tribe.
>
> If you don't take care of the land, then the land isn't going to take care of you. Because everything we have around us involves Mother Earth. If we don't take care of the land, what's going to happen to us?

In the process of protest, these women tell us, they are forced to articulate more clearly their cultural values, which become resources of resistance in helping the tribe organize against a landfill. While many tribal members may not articulate an "environmental" critique, they well understand the meaning of land and their religion of Mother Earth, on which their society is built.

CONCLUSION

The narratives of white, African American, and Native American women involved in toxic waste protests reveal the ways in which their subjective, particular experiences lead them to analyses of toxic waste issues that extend beyond the particularistic issue to wider worlds of power. Traditional beliefs about home, family, and community provide the impetus for women's involvement in these issues and become a rich source of empowerment as women reshape traditional language and meanings into an ideology of resistance. These stories challenge traditional views of toxic waste protests as parochial, self-interested, and failing to go beyond a single-issue focus. They show that single-issue protests are ultimately about far more and reveal the experiences of daily life and resources that different groups use to resist. Through environmental protests, these women challenge, in some measure, the social relations of race, class, and gender.

These women's protests have different beginning places, and their analyses of environmental justice are mediated by issues of class and race. For white blue-collar women, the critique of the corporate state and the realization of a more genuine democracy are central to a vision of environmental justice. The definition of environmental justice that they develop becomes rooted in the issue of class. For women of color, it is the link between race and environment, rather than between class and environment, that characterizes definitions of environmental justice. African American women's narratives strongly link environment justice to other social justice concerns, such as jobs, housing, and crime. Environmental justice comes to mean the need to resolve the broad social inequities of race. For Native American

women, environmental justice is bound up with the sovereignty of the indigenous peoples.

In these women's stories, their responses to particular toxic waste issues
are inextricably tied to the injustice they feel as mothers, as working-class
women, as African Americans, and as Native Americans. They do not talk
about their protests in terms of single issues. Thus, their political activism has
implications far beyond the visible, particularistic concern of a toxic waste
dump site or the siting of a hazardous waste incinerator.

NOTES

1. Sandra Morgen, "'It's the Whole Power of the City Against Us!': The Development of Political Consciousness in a Women's Health Care Coalition," in *Women and
the Politics of Empowerment*, eds. Ann Bookman and Sandra Morgen (Philadelphia:
Temple University Press, 1988), p. 97.

2. Sheila Rowbotham, *Women's Consciousness, Man's World* (New York: Penguin, 1973).

3. See Sara Ruddick, *Maternal Thinking: Towards a Politics of Peace* (New York: Ballantine, 1989).

4. Cheryl Townsend Gilkes, "Building in Many Places: Multiple Commitments and
Ideologies in Black Women's Community Work," in *Women and the Politics of
Empowerment*, op. cit.

60

"WHOSOEVER" IS WELCOME HERE
An Interview with Reverend Edwin C. Sanders II

Gary David Comstock

Reverend Edwin C. Sanders II is the founding pastor of Metropolitan Interdenominational Church, which is located in a working class neighborhood of
small houses in Nashville, Tennessee. Reverend Sanders is African American
and the congregation is predominantly African American. Lesbian/bisexual/

From Eric Brandt, ed., *Dangerous Liaisons: Blacks, Gays, and the Struggle for Equality* (New York:
The New Press, 1999), pp. 142–57. Reprinted by permission of the New Press.

gay/transgendered people are welcome and encouraged to participate in the life of the church. I attended a packed Sunday morning service in June 1998 and interviewed Rev. Sanders in the afternoon.

GARY COMSTOCK: How did the church get started?

REVEREND SANDERS: I had been the Dean of the Chapel at Fisk University. I left in 1980 in a moment of controversy. A new president had come, and we weren't able to mesh. I left and had no where to go. I didn't have a plan. And instantly there were folks who were part of the chapel experience there at Fisk who wanted to organize a new church. I felt no spiritual interest whatsoever in organizing a new church, but about seven months later I felt like I clearly heard the voice saying, "This is something to do." I'm glad it worked out that way, because I think if I had done it directly after Fisk it would have been born out of a reaction and we probably wouldn't have developed the kind of identity, sense of mission, and direction the way we did. There were twelve people who came together and said they wanted to do this.

One of my good friends, Bill Turner, is a sociologist, and we were at Fisk together. Bill has a theory he advanced that institutions—and he built his theory around black institutions—cannot break out of the mold from which they were born. There was something about the way an institution is framed in its beginning, and no matter what you do you don't escape it. I thought that was absurd, but in time I came to think that he had something. The congregation was a mix of white and black men and women from all kinds of denominational backgrounds, and that mix turned out to be significant because from the beginning people identified us as being inclusive at least across racial terms and definitely inclusive and equal in gender terms. . . .

In that original group we had also a young man—one of my very dear friends—who was gay. Don was living a bisexual lifestyle at that point, but mainly to keep up appearances for professional purposes. Another one of my dearest friends went through a major mental breakdown at the time we were starting the church. I felt it very important not to abandon him and to include him. So we had a guy going through major psychological problems, somebody who was gay, and we had the racial mix.

We did not have the class mix at the beginning. Most of the folks were associated in some way with the academic community. Nothing like we have now. Today we have an unbelievable mix of people. I mean there are people who are doctors, lawyers, dentists and business people, and we also have a lot of folks who are right off the street, blue collar workers, in treatment for drugs and alcohol, going through a lot of transition. And that mix has evolved. Although we said in the beginning that's what we wanted to be, in actuality the current mix goes beyond that of the original twelve members.

The presence of Don, the one gay black male in the original congregation, had a lot to do with our current mix of people, and it had a lot to do with how we got so involved with HIV/AIDS ministry. The church began in '81 and he died in '84. It's almost hilarious when I think about it because I'm so involved in HIV/AIDS work now, but when he died I remember he was real sick, we didn't know what was going on, and they told us he died of toxicosis. I remember saying what in the world is that? I researched it and found out that it had something to do with cat and bird droppings, but Don didn't have cats. It was AIDS. You'd hear people talking about this strange disease because then it was 1984, but what that meant for us was that we got involved before it became a publicly recognized and discussed issue. Don's presence and death immediately pushed us in ministering to and being responsive to folks with AIDS and in dealing with the issue of homosexuality.

The other thing I was going to tell you which is kind of funny is the name. I will never forget when I told one of my friends we were going to name the church Metropolitan Interdenominational. He said are you sure you want to do that. I said what do you mean, you know, I was pretty naive. He said all the gay churches across the country are called Metropolitan churches. I said that's where I feel the Lord leads me, I feel Metropolitan. In my mind what that meant was that Nashville happens to have been the first metropolitan government in the United States. It's the first place where the county and city combined, so everything in and around Nashville is referred to as metropolitan government. But my friend said to me that everybody is going to instantly say you're the gay church. I said so be it and we went on with it. Like I said, there was a hand bigger than mine at work. . . .

COMSTOCK: What was the turnaround point for the class mix? How and when did it happen?

REV. SANDERS: It was real clear. Early on what happened was we got involved in prison ministry—actually directed a ministry called the Southern Prison Ministry for a while. Going in and out of the prisons we started to develop relationships that translated to folks coming out of prison and getting involved in the church. After I had done the prison ministry for a while it became crystal clear to me that 80 percent of the people I was dealing with in prison were there for alcohol and drug related issues. I started reassessing this whole issue of drugs and alcohol and decided that's an area we had to begin to focus our ministries. So, I got involved, did the training, and became certified as a counselor. I would venture to say that 25 percent of the people in this church are folks that I first met in treatment. Thirty to 35 plus percent of this congregation are folks who are in treatment from alcohol and drug use. This is a place where a lot of folks know they can come.

We've got all these names, you know, the drug church, the AIDS church, we get those labels. But it's all right because that's what we do. We hit those themes a lot.

I've learned some things over the years that I pretty much hold to and this is one of them. . . . We don't say we are a black church, we don't say that we are a gay church or a straight church, we don't say that we are anything other than a church that celebrates our oneness in Christ. I'm convinced that has turned out to be the real key to being able to hold this diverse group of folks together. I must admit I'm a person that has a negative thing about the word diversities. I don't use it much. We don't celebrate our differences, we celebrate our oneness. That ends up being an avenue for a lot of folks being attracted and feeling comfortable here. New folks say I got here and I just felt like no one was looking at me strange, no one was treating me different, I was just able to be here. . . .

COMSTOCK: I was impressed by the informality of the service today. People seem to relax and fit in. The choir is not so focused on performance that they're not interacting with the congregation. And your own manner is informal. It's a style that lets people in. You aren't just saying all people are welcomed here, you actually do something that let's them feel at home. I was also struck by the openness of the windows—the plants inside and the view into the park. . . .

REV. SANDERS: . . . We have the sense of informality. People are arriving from the time we welcome the guests at the beginning until just after the sermon when there's maximum presence in the audience. People come in slow, and we give folks an opportunity to leave early. We even say it in the bulletin, we just say if you need to leave just leave quietly. And we know folks do. There's a lot of folks who want to hear the choir or they want to hear the sermon, but they don't want all the rest of it. So we do it that way. It works out. One of the real hooks for just about everyone at Metropolitan is the fellowship circle at the end. We actually have a few Jews and a couple of Muslims who worship here regularly. The Muslim family does a very interesting thing which helped me to appreciate the significance of the fellowship circle at the end. We offer communion—the Eucharist, the Lord's supper—every Sunday, and they stay until we get to that part of the service. Then they go outside or into the vestibule, but they come back in. I remember when Omar first started attending, I said to him it's interesting to me that you don't leave at that point. He said, "No, no, no, I wouldn't miss the fellowship circle." And it made me realize that the communion of the fellowship circle is more important than the bread and the wine. Probably the real communion is what we do when we stand there at the end and sing "We've Come Too Far to Turn Back Now." We do that every week. It's our theme. That's a very significant moment. I've heard people tell me when they have to be late that they rush to get here just to catch the end of it. One woman said to me it was enough for her if she just got here for the fellowship circle.

A lot of the informality is very intentional. For instance, the only thing at Metropolitan that's elevated is the altar. Nothing else is above ground level. None of the seating is differentiated. In most churches the ministers have different, higher, bigger chairs than everyone else. We don't do that. We sit in the same seats the other folks do. My choir director is always telling me we'd get better sound if we could elevate the back rows. I say no, everybody's got to be on the same level and got to sit in the same seats. We do a lot of symbolic things like that.

COMSTOCK: Do other clergy give you much flack for working with needle exchange, welcoming gay folks, and working on issues that they may see as too progressive?

REV. SANDERS: They do. But let me tell you something. I have been able to have a level of involvement with ministers in this community that probably has brought credibility to what we do. I would like to think that we have maintained our sense of integrity especially as it relates to our consistency in ministry. Folks tend to respect that, so even when they disagree, they also look more seriously and harder at what it is they're questioning. . . .

COMSTOCK: "Whosoever" is from John 3:16–17: "For God so loved the world that he gave his only Son, that whosoever believes in him should not perish but have eternal life." Has it been an expressed theme from the beginning?

REV. SANDERS: It's been our theme for the last seven or eight years. . . . I think we're growing in this inclusivity all the time. The language issue was big for us. We try to use inclusive language. If somebody else comes into the church that is not into that, it sticks out like a sore thumb. Does our inclusivity also mean that there is a real tolerance for folks who are perhaps not where we think folks should be in terms of issues like inclusive language, issues that relate to sexuality, gay and lesbian issues? I think the answer to that question is yes, you have to make room for those folks too. That's a real struggle. Another one of our little clichés, and we don't have a lot of them, is we say we try to be inclusive of all and alienating to none. Not being alienating is a real trick. It's amazing how easy you can alienate folks without realizing it, in ways that you're just not aware of. . . .

COMSTOCK: What would you do if some new people had trouble with cross dressing, transgendered, lesbian or gay people? How do you get them to stay and deal with it rather than leave?

REV. SANDERS: We tracked that issue a couple of times. Let me tell you what's happened. Most folk are here for a while before some of it settles in, before they start to notice everything. It's amazing to me how people get caught up in Metropolitan. They'll join and get involved and then they'll go through membership class, that's usually when it starts to hit them, that they say to themselves, "Oh oh, I'm seeing some stuff that I'm not sure about here." But what we've discovered is that what seems to help us more than anything else is that folks end up remembering what their initial experience had been when they first came here. We even have one couple, this is my favorite story to tell, who has talked about coming here on one of those Sundays when we were hitting the theme of inclusive hard. And they left here and said what kind of church is that? But then a couple of weeks later they said let's go back over there again. They came back and then they didn't come again for about two or three months. They were visiting other churches. They said when they got down to thinking about all the churches, they had felt warmth and connection here. They said you know that church really did kind of work; and they ended up coming back. When folks are here there's a warmth they feel, there is a connection they feel, there's a comfort zone in which they'll eventually deal with the issues that might be their point of difference. We've seen folks move in their thinking and there's some folks that have not been able to do it. I've got one young man—I really do think he just loves being here—who says, "I just can't fathom this gay thing. Why do you insist on it." I said, "You know, you're the one who's lifting this up."

As I said, we try to make sure that when any issue is brought up, it's in the course of things. It's not like we stop and have gay liberation day, just like we don't celebrate Black History month. We don't focus on or celebrate these identities or difference, but yet if you're around here you can't help but pick up on the church's support for these issues and differences. Today, for instance, we sang "Lift Up Your Voice and Sing," which is known as the black national anthem. But we call it "Our Song of Liberation," and I've tried to help people to understand that. . . .

I have a lot of divinity students who serve as my pastoral assistants, and most of them are women. This place has become a real refuge for black women in the ministry. There are not a lot of clergy opportunities for them, so I've tried to figure out how to incorporate them into the life and ministry of the church. They actually run a lot of our ministries. And most of them are extremely well prepared academically. They're more prepared than I am to do the work and they do it well. When they started coming we suddenly became a magnet, a place where there was this rush of folks out of divinity school to come and be a part of ministry here. At one level I probably seem like I'm extremely freewheeling and loose, but I'm probably a lot more intentional about how things are going than folks realize, especially as they relate to the focus of ministry here at the church. One of my real concerns was not having the time to orient the young ministers, to bring them into a full awareness of what makes this place click. What I have discovered is that if I get the inclusive piece established in the beginning with them, I don't have to worry about the rest of it as much. If they buy into understanding that inclusivity is at the heart of this church, I don't have to worry about keeping my eye on them all the time. . . .

COMSTOCK: You know that the example here of accepting and welcoming lesbians and gay men is an anomaly in the Church. You provide inspiration and hope, an example of something positive that is actually happening. Most gay people feel alienated from their churches, but I've found that African-American more often than white gay people emphasize the importance of religion in their family, community, and history and say that most of the pain and sadness in their lives centers around the Church. They claim that being rejected by the black church is especially devastating because this institution has been, and continues to be, the only place where they can take real refuge from the racism they experience in the society. Clearly that's not happening here at Metropolitan.

REV. SANDERS: We realized when we started doing our HIV/AIDS ministry that there are organizations that were established by gay white men who had done a good job of developing services, but we kept seeing there was something that was not happening for gay and lesbian African Americans. And we realized it was community. No matter how much they tried to get that in other communities, there is the whole thing of cultural comfort. They were looking for the context where there were people who looked like them, who were extensions of their family supporting them. It became clear to me that what we needed to do was to establish a place where people could literally come and where people had a sense of community. Consequently, what we call the Wellness Center here is more than anything else just a place where you can come and feel at home. It has sofas and tables and chairs. Folks sit around. It's a place where there is a community that is an insulating, supporting place to come to. And although we provide some direct services for those folks, more than anything else I think the greatest service we provide is a safe place, a comfort zone, a community, a way to be connected to community. So I know real clearly what you're talking about, and I've heard it spoken too. It's one of the real issues for African Americans who are gay and lesbian. So our simple response has been to try to create a space where folks will have a certain level of comfort.

The problem I often run into, which speaks to what you were asking about, is that I think the greatest trouble we have sometimes is folks in the gay and lesbian community want to celebrate their sense of life and lifestyle more than Metropolitan lends itself to. In the same way, I have folks who don't understand why we don't do more things that are clearly more defined as being Afrocentric. There's a strong Afrocentric movement now within religious circles, and I end up dealing with them the same way I do with the folks who want to have ways in which they celebrate being gay and lesbian. My greatest struggle ends up being with folks who want to lift that up more, and I say the only thing we lift up is the basis of our oneness. I think the Church has been a place where folks have not been able to find community, when they have been rejected. The African American church is a pretty conservative entity, always has been. It's probably be even better at holding up the conventions of American Christianity than other institutions. Consequently folks can draw some pretty hard lines, and that's what we've been dealing with at Metropolitan. But the other side of the Black church is that it is known as being an institution of compassion. So at the same time you have folks giving voice to some conservative ideas and practices, you can also appeal to a tradition and practice of compassion. That's why in our HIV/AIDS ministry we've been able to bring other churches into the loop. We're trying to get thirty churches to be involved in doing education and intervention on HIV/AIDS. We've been able to engage them on the level of compassion. Once we get them involved at that level then, we see folks open their eyes to other issues. African American churches have been very effective in compassion ministry for years around issues of sickness, death and dying. What we're trying to do is get folks to put as much emphasis on living and not just being there to minister to sickness and dying.

Another thing is the contradictions in the Church. The unspoken message that says it's all right for you to be here, just don't say anything, just play your little role. You can be in the choir, you can sit on the piano bench, but don't say you're gay. We had an experience here in Nashville which I'm sure could be evidenced in other places in the world. You know how a few years ago in the community of male figure skaters there was a series of deaths related to HIV/AIDS. The same thing happened a few years ago with musicians in the black churches. At one point here in Nashville there were six musicians who died of AIDS. In every instance it was treated with a hush. Nobody wanted to deal with the fact that all of these men were gay black men, and yet they'd been there leading the music for them. It's that contradiction where folks say yeah you're here but don't say anything about who you really are, don't be honest and open about yourself. I believe that the way in which you get the Church to respond is to continue to force the issue in terms of the teachings of Christ, to be forthright in seeing how the issue is understood in relationship to Jesus Christ. One thing I've learned about dealing with inner city African Americans is that you have to bring it home for them in a way that has some biblical basis. I'm always challenged by this, but I'm always challenging them to find a place where Jesus ever rejected anyone. I don't think anyone can find it. I don't think there's anybody that Jesus did not embrace.

61

SILENT COVENANTS

Derrick Bell

Graduation day at Yale University in late May 2002 was blessed with warm, clear weather. It is the hope for such a beautiful morning that enables outdoor commencements to survive the rain-soaked disappointment of those hopes on far too many better-forgotten occasions. Yale's Old Campus was filled with faculty, administrators, soon-to-be graduates, and their well-dressed families and friends. Under the canopy-covered stage, there were ten individuals designated to receive honorary degrees because of their significant achievements.

I was there at the invitation of one of those honorees, Robert L. Carter, my mentor and friend for more than forty years. Then eighty-five, a senior judge on the federal district court with thirty years of service, Carter had previously enjoyed a long and distinguished career as an NAACP civil rights attorney and, for a few years, a partner in a large law firm. All of these accomplishments would be worthy of the praise and warm applause that other candidates received. When, though, Yale University president Richard Levin announced that Judge Carter was an important member of the legal team that planned the strategies and argued the landmark case of *Brown v. Board of Education*, noting that the decision was only two years short of its fiftieth anniversary, the audience leaped to its feet and, with great enthusiasm, applauded and cheered.

On that happy day, Judge Carter was the recipient of the audience's appreciation for his work in helping litigate a case in which the Supreme Court had held racial segregation in the public schools unconstitutional. The mainly white audience that had assembled for the commencement exercises at one of the nation's premier universities was not unsophisticated. For them, and so many others regardless or status or race, *Brown v. Board of Education* evoked awe and respect. If asked, most would have agreed that the decision was the finest hour of American law. In their view, this long-awaited and now much-appreciated decision had erased the contradiction between the freedom and justice for all that America proclaimed, and the subordination by race permitted by our highest law.

Even as I stood and joined in the applause, I wondered. How could a decision that promised so much and, by its terms, accomplished so little, have

From Derrick Bell, *Silent Covenants: Brown v. Board of Education and the Unfulfilled Hopes for Racial Reform.* (New York: Oxford, 2004).

gained so hallowed a place among some of the nation's better-educated and most-successful individuals that its mere mention in connection with one of its lawyer advocates sparked a contained but very real demonstration?

I had every reason to be leading the applause rather than musing about the causes of the crowd's enthusiasm. After all, on May 17, 1954, the day on which the Supreme Court handed down a decision we hoped would remove the protective cloak of law from policies of racial discrimination that for generations had burdened the lives of black people, I was on a ship heading home from a year's military duty in Korea. While there, I had applied to law school, planning to enroll when I completed the two years of active duty required when I signed up for ROTC in college.

I entered law school that fall. The only black in a class of about 140 white males, I was determined not to be among the two-thirds of first-year law students who, routinely in those days, failed to graduate. My hard work paid off and, after the first year, my grades led to an invitation to join the law review. Quite soon, I began submitting so much writing on racial issues that the law review's faculty advisor asked me—only half in jest—whether it was my intention to change the name of the publication to the University of Pittsburgh Civil Rights Journal.

Nothing in my legal education altered my assumption that the *Brown* decision marked the beginning of the end of Jim Crow oppression in all its myriad forms. For black Americans long burdened by our subordinate status, there was, to paraphrase the spiritual, "a great day a-coming.". . .

Over the decades, the *Brown* decision, like other landmark cases, has gained a life quite apart from the legal questions it was intended to settle. The passage of time has calmed both the ardor of its admirers and the ire of its detractors. Today, of little use as legal precedent, it has gained in reputation as a measure of what law and society might be. That noble image, dulled by resistance to any but minimal steps toward compliance, has transformed *Brown* into a magnificent mirage, the legal equivalent of that city on a hill to which all aspire without any serious thought that it will ever be attained.

Considered within the context of American political, economic, and cultural life, the *Brown* decision is a long-running racial melodrama. As with a film or play, the decision stimulated varying feeling. It energized the law, encouraged most black people, enraged a great many white people, and, like so many other racial policies, served the nation's short-term but not its long-term interests. Generating an emotionally charged concoction of commendations and condemnations, the *Brown* decision recreated the nineteenth century's post–Civil War Reconstruction/Redemption pattern of progress followed by retrogression. It stirred confusion and conflict into the always-vexing question of race in a society that, despite denials and a frustratingly flexible amnesia, owes much of its growth, development, and success to the ability of those dominant members of society who use race to both control and exploit most people, whatever their race.

As had happened in the past, the law employing the vehicle of a major judicial decision offered symbolic encouragement to the black dispossessed. The substantive losses so feared by its white adversaries evolved almost unnoticed into advances greater for whites than for blacks. And a half-century later, as must now be apparent to all, the nation's racial dilemma—modernized and, one might say, "colorized,"—has become more complex rather than simplified. The ever-widening racial disparities in all aspects of life overshadow the gains in status achieved by those black Americans who, by varying combinations of hard work and good fortune, are viewed as having "made it." Indeed, although it did not achieve what its supporters hoped for, historians and other social scientists, safely removed from the fray, may come to view *Brown* as the perfect precedent. As a dictionary would define perfect, it was: "pure, total; lacking in no essential detail; complete, sane, absolute, unequivocal, unmitigated, an act of perfection.". . .

The question is whether another approach than the one embraced by the *Brown* decision might have been more effective and less disruptive in the always-contentious racial arena. . . .

Brown . . . served to reinforce the fiction that, by the decision's rejection of racial barriers posed by segregation, the path of progress would be clear. Everyone can and should make it through individual ability and effort. One would have thought that this reinforcement of the status quo would placate if not please even the strongest supporters of segregation. To the contrary, the *Brown* decision provided politicians with a racial issue through which to enrage and upset large groups of white people, initially in the South, but far more generally as efforts to implement the decision moved across the country. . . .

An understandable but, in retrospect, serious misjudgment was our over-reliance on court orders to achieve racial equality. In our school desegregation campaigns, equality would be realized when schools were no longer identifiable by race. This equality by "definitional fiat" limitation is circumscribed, as Brandon Lofton, a student in my constitutional law class points out, because we designated the U.S. government as maker and guarantor of the promise of equality. Lofton cites the speeches of Martin Luther King, Jr., and other black leaders who insisted that the government must honor its commitment to racial equality.

By so doing, Lofton argues, "the civil rights leadership limited its conception of African-American identity and freedom to the American legal and social context." This tactic helped the movement dismantle segregation at the point when the blatant "Jim Crow" system threatened the nation's policy-makers' designs for world leadership after World War II. Thus when, with persistent pleading from the State and Justice Departments, the Supreme

Court proclaimed that separate facilities were now to be inherently unequal, as Michael Seidman noted:

> The demand for equality had been satisfied and blacks no longer had just cause for complaint. The mere existence of *Brown* thus served [to] legitimate current arrangements. True, many blacks remained poor and disempowered. But their status was no longer a result of the denial of equality. Instead, it marked a personal failure to take advantage of one's definitionally equal status.[1]

Equality by proclamation not only failed to truly reflect the complexity of racial subordination, it also vested the government and the courts with the ultimate moral authority to define African-American freedom. When the *Brown* decision was followed by civil rights laws, mostly motivated by black activism that highlighted the continuing racism that undermined our Cold War battles with the Soviet Union, policymakers and much of white society easily reached the premature conclusion that America was now fair and neutral. With implementation of the moderate civil rights laws, the trumpets of "reverse discrimination" began sounding the alarm. In quick response, the government and the courts began giving priority to the rights of "innocent whites" caught in the remedial web of civil rights laws that, to be effective, had to recognize and correct the priorities of race that some whites had deemed vested and permanent.

Soon the cocophony settled into a virtual orchestra playing a melody that in this century resembles the song that begins: "The party's over." I am not sure what that policy-activated orchestra was playing in the nineteenth century when the nation abandoned Reconstruction policies. In both eras, though, there is the readiness to mute any sound of the racial remedies earlier and solemnly promised to blacks in order to maintain stability and solidarity among whites whose own social and economic status varies widely.

Today, black people and many Hispanics are trapped in a racial time warp. We are buffeted by the painful blows of continuing bias as the law upon which we relied for remedies is reinterpreted with unsupported assurances that the disadvantages we suffer must be caused by our deficiencies because, we are told without even a trace of irony, racism is a thing of the past. The hypocrisy so apparent in the claims of a color-blind society illustrate the harsh and disconcerting truth about racial progress. We prefer to ignore or rationalize rather than confront these truths because they disrupt our long-settled expectations of eventual racial equality.

Given the setbacks in civil rights suffered in recent decades, and the decline in the relative well-being of so many people of color, civil rights adherents need to reconsider our racial goals. We need to examine what it was about our reliance on racial remedies that may have prevented us from recognizing that these legal rights could do little more than bring about the cessation of one form of discriminatory conduct that soon appeared in a more subtle though no less discriminatory form. I hope that this examination leads us to redefine goals of racial equality and opportunity to which blacks have adhered for more than a century.

NOTE

1. Michael Seidman, *Brown and Meranda*, 80 Calif. L. Rev. 672, 717 (1992).

PROCESSES OF CHANGE

62

HOW THE NEW WORKING CLASS CAN TRANSFORM URBAN AMERICA

Robin D. G. Kelley

. . . Corporate downsizing, deindustrialization, racist and sexist social policy, and the erosion of the welfare state do not respect the boundaries between work and community, the household and public space. The battle for livable wages and fulfilling jobs is inseparable from the fight for decent housing and safe neighborhoods; the struggle to defuse cultural stereotypes of inner city residents cannot be easily removed from the intense fights for environmental justice. Moreover, the struggle to remake culture itself, to develop new ideas, new relationships, and new values that place mutuality over materialism and collective responsibility over "personal responsibility," and place greater emphasis on ending all forms of oppression rather than striving to become an oppressor, cannot be limited to either home or work.

Standing in the eye of the storm are the new multiracial, urban working classes. It is they, not the Democratic Party, not a bunch of smart policy analysts, not corporate benevolence, who hold the key to transforming the city and the nation. . . . But my point is very, very simple.

Robin D. G. Kelley. 1997. *Yo' Mama's Disfunktional: Fighting the Culture Wars in Urban America.* (Boston: Beacon, 1997)

MAKING OF THE NEW URBAN WORKING CLASS

. . . The pervasive imagery of the "underclass" makes the very idea of a contemporary urban working class seem obsolete. Instead of hardworking urban residents, many of whom are Latino, Asian-Pacific Islanders, West Indian immigrants, and U.S.-born African Americans, the dominant image of the "ghetto" is of idle black men drinking forty-ounce bottles of malt liquor and young black women "with distended bellies, their youthful faces belying the fact that they are often close to delivering their second or third child." White leftists nostalgic for the days before identity politics allegedly undermined the "class struggle" often have trouble seeing beyond the ruddy-faced hard hats or European immigrant factory workers who populate social history's images of the American working class. The ghetto is the last place to find American workers.

If you are looking for the American working class today, however, you will do just as well to look in hospitals and universities as in the sooty industrial suburbs and smokestack districts of days past. In Bethlehem, Pennsylvania, for example, once a stronghold of the steel industry, nursing homes have become the fastest growing source of employment, and the unions that set out to organize these workers have outgrown the steelworkers' union by leaps and bounds. The new working class is also concentrated in food processing, food services, and various retail establishments. In the world of manufacturing, sweatshops are making a huge comeback, particularly in the garment industry and electronics assembling plants, and homework (telephone sales, for example) is growing. These workers are more likely to be brown and female than the old blue-collar white boys we are so accustomed to seeing in popular culture. . . .

Organizing the new immigrant labor force is perhaps the fundamental challenge facing the labor movement. For one, a substantial proportion of immigrant workers is employed by small ethnic firms with little tolerance for labor unions. Besides obvious language and cultural barriers, union leaders are trying to tackle the herculean task of organizing thousands of tiny, independent, sometimes transient firms. Immigrants are also less represented in public sector jobs, which tend to have a much higher percentage of unionized employees. (Indeed, the heavy concentration of native-born black people in public sector jobs partly explains why African Americans have such a high unionization rate.) The most obvious barrier to organizing immigrant workers, however, has been discriminatory immigration policy. . . . The 1986 Immigration Reform and Control Act imposed legal sanctions against employers of "aliens" without proper documents. Thus, even when unions were willing to organize undocumented workers, fear of deportation kept many workers from joining the labor movement.

Unions are also partly to blame for the state of labor organizing among immigrant workers. Until recently, union leaders too often assumed that

Latino and Asian workers were unorganizable or difficult to organize—arguments that have been made about women and African American workers in the past. . . . Even when union organizers were willing to approach undocumented workers, they often operated on the assumption that immigrants were easily manipulated by employers, willing to undercut prevailing wages, or were "target workers" whose goal was to make enough money to return to their place of origin. . . .

Several decades of grassroots, rank-and-file efforts on the part of workers of color [have tried to] re-orient unions toward issues of social justice, racism, sexism, and cultural difference within their ranks. Indeed, one of the most significant labor-based social justice movements emerged out of the Service Employees International Union (SEIU). . . . Launched in 1985, Justice for Janitors sought to build a mass movement to win union recognition and to address the needs of a workforce made up primarily of people of color, mainly immigrants. As Sweeney explained, "The strategy of Justice for Janitors was to build a mass movement, with workers making clear that they wanted union representation and winning 'voluntary recognition' from employers. The campaigns addressed the special needs of an immigrant workforce, largely from Latin America. In many cities, the janitors' cause became a civil rights movement—and a cultural crusade." Throughout the mid- to late 1980s, Justice for Janitors waged several successful "crusades" in Pittsburgh, Denver, San Diego, Los Angeles, and Washington, D.C. With support from Latino leaders and local church officials, for example, their Denver campaign yielded a sudden growth in unionization among janitors and wage increases of about ninety cents an hour.

From its inception, Justice for Janitors has been deeply committed to antiracism and mass mobilization through community-based organizing and civil disobedience. Heirs of the sit-down strikers of the 1930s and the Civil Rights movement of the 1950s and 1960s, they have waged militant, highly visible campaigns in major cities throughout the country. In Los Angeles, for example, Justice for Janitors is largely responsible for the dramatic increase in unionized custodial employees, particularly among workers contracted out by big firms to clean high-rise buildings. The percentage of janitors belonging to unions rose from 10 percent of the workforce in 1987 to 90 percent in 1995. Their success certainly did not come easily. Indeed, the turning point in their campaign began around 1990, when two hundred janitors struck International Service Systems (ISS), a Danish-owned company. A mass march in Century City, California, in support of the strikers generated enormous publicity after police viciously attacked the demonstrators. Overall, more than sixty people were hospitalized, including a pregnant woman who was beaten so severely she miscarried. An outpouring of sympathy for the strikers turned the tables, enabling them to win a contract with ISS covering some 2,500 janitors in Southern California. . . .

In Washington, D.C., Justice for Janitors led the struggle of Local 82 of the SEIU in its fight against U.S. Service Industries (USSI)—a private

janitorial company that used nonunion labor to clean downtown office buildings. But because they conceived of themselves as a social movement, they did
not stop with the protection of union jobs. In March 1995, Justice for Janitors
organized several demonstrations in the district that led to over 200 arrests.
Blocking traffic and engaging in other forms of civil disobedience, the protesters demanded an end to tax breaks to real estate developers as well as cutbacks
in social programs for the poor. As union spokesperson Manny Pastreich put
it, "This isn't just about 5,000 janitors; it's about issues that concern all D.C.
residents—what's happening to their schools, their streets, their neighborhoods." Many people who participated in the March demonstrations came
from all over the country, and not all were janitors. Greg Ceci, a longshore-
man from Baltimore, saw the struggle as a general revitalization of the labor
movement and a recognition, finally, that the unions need to lead a larger fight
for social justice. "We need to reach out to the workers who have been ignored
by mainstream unions. We need to fight back, and I want to be a part of it."

Indeed, D.C.'s Justice for Janitors is made up precisely of workers who
have been ignored—poor women of color. Black and Latino women make up
the majority of its membership, hold key leadership positions, and have put
their bodies on the line for the SEIU as well as the larger cause of social
justice. Twenty-four-year-old Dania Herring is an example of Justice for
Janitors' new leadership cadre. A mother of four and resident of one of the
poorest neighborhoods in the southeast section of the District, whose
husband (at the time of the demonstrations) was an unemployed bricklayer,
Herring had quit her job to become a full-time organizer for Local 82 and
Justice for Janitors. Yet, these women were so militant that members of Washington's District Council dismissed them as "hooligans." "Essentially, they
use anarchy as a means of organizing workers," stated African American
councilman Harold Brazil. "And they do that under the mantle of justice—
for janitors—or whoever else they want to organize."

In the end, their challenge to the city and to USSI paid off. In December
1995, the National Labor Relations Board (NLRB) concluded that USSI had
"a history of pervasive illegal conduct" by threatening, interrogating, and
firing employees they deemed unacceptable, especially those committed to
union organizing. African American workers, in particular, had suffered most
from the wave of firings, in part because USSI, like other employers, believed
immigrant workers were more malleable and less committed to unionization
because of their tenuous status as residents. The pattern was clear to Amy
Parker, a janitor who had worked under USSI for three years. "Before USSI
got the contract to clean my building, there were 18 African-Americans.
Now, I am the only one." After three steady years cleaning the same building,
she earned only $5.50 an hour. The NLRB's decision against USSI, there-
fore, was a substantial victory for Local 82 of the SEIU. It meant that USSI
could no longer discriminate against the union and it generated at least a
modicum of recognition for Justice for Janitors.

Such stories have been duplicated across the country. Justice for Janitors, in short, is more than a union. It is a dynamic social movement made up primarily of women and people of color, and it has the potential to redirect the entire labor movement. . . .

LABOR/COMMUNITY STRATEGIES AGAINST CLASS-BASED RACISM

. . . Urban working people spend much if not most of their lives in their neighborhoods, in their homes, in transit, in the public spaces of the city, in houses of worship, in bars, clubs, barber-shops, hair and nail salons, in various retail outlets, in medical clinics, welfare offices, courtrooms, even jail cells. They create and maintain families, build communities, engage in local politics, and construct a sense of fellowship that is sometimes life sustaining. These community ties are crucial to the success of any labor movement. . . .

Working people live in communities that are as embattled as the workplace itself. Black and Latino workers, for example, must contend with issues of police brutality and a racist criminal justice system, housing discrimination, lack of city services, toxic waste, inadequate health care facilities, sexual assault and domestic violence, and crime and neighborhood safety. And at the forefront of these community-based movements have been women, usually struggling mothers of all ages dedicated to making life better for themselves and their children—mothers who, as we have seen, have become the scapegoats for virtually everything wrong with the "inner city." In cities across the United States, working-class black and Latina women built and sustained community organizations that registered voters, patrolled the streets, challenged neighborhood drug dealers, defended the rights of prisoners, and fought vigorously for improvements in housing, city services, health care, and public assistance. . . .

Whereas most community- and labor-based organizations limit their focus to an issue or set of issues, even when they are able to see the bigger picture, once in a while there are movements that attempt to fight on all fronts. Such organizations, where they do exist, are often products of the best elements of Third World, feminist, and Black Liberation movements. Rather than see race, gender, and sexuality as "problems," they are, instead, pushing working-class politics in new directions. . . .

One of the most visible and successful examples of such a broad-based radical movement is the Labor/Community Strategy Center based in Los Angeles. The leaders of the Strategy Center have deep roots in social movements that go back to Black Liberation and student activism of the 1960s, urban antipoverty programs, farmworkers' movements, organized labor, and popular left movements in El Salvador and Mexico. They have been at the forefront of the struggle for clean air in the Harbor area of Los Angeles—a region with a high concentration of poor communities of color. They have worked closely with Justice for Janitors, providing crucial support to Local 660 of the SEIU. . . .

The Strategy Center's most important campaign during the last few years has been the Bus Riders Union (BRU), a multiracial organization of transit-dependent working people who have declared war on race and class inequality in public transportation. . . . Public transportation is one of the few issues that touches the lives of many urban working people across race, ethnic, and gender lines. And ultimately, equal access to affordable transportation is tied to equal access to employment opportunities, especially now that manufacturing and other medium- to high-wage jobs have migrated to suburban rings or industrial parks. The combination of rising fares and limits on services has sharply curtailed the ability of workers to get to work. The cost of transportation for many families is a major part of their monthly budget. The average working-class commuter in Los Angeles rides the bus between sixty and eighty times a month, including for work, family visits, medical care, and shopping. For transit-dependent wage earners, bus fare could potentially comprise up to one-fourth or more of their total income! For many poor people even a small increase makes riding prohibitive. They might visit family less often, skip grocery shopping, or even miss work if they do not have bus fare. Forcing low-income riders off the buses with higher fares moves the Los Angeles County Metropolitan Transit Authority (MTA) out of the business of transporting the urban poor.

After three years of conducting research and riding the buses to recruit members, in 1994 the Strategy Center and the Bus Riders Union, along with the Southern Christian Leadership Conference and the Korean Immigrant Workers' Advocates as coplaintiffs, filed a class action suit against the MTA on behalf of 350,000 bus riders, the vast majority of whom are poor people of color. Represented by the National Association for the Advancement of Colored People's Legal Defense and Educational Fund, the plaintiffs challenged proposals to raise bus fares from $1.10 to $1.35; eliminate monthly bus passes, which cost $42 for unlimited use; and introduce a zone system on the blue line commuter rail that would increase fares by more than 100 percent for half of the passengers. . . . The plaintiffs argued that the MTA's policies violate Title VI of the Civil Rights Act of 1964, which provides that no person "shall on the ground of race, color, or national origin, be excluded from participation in, be denied the benefits of, or be subjected to discrimination under any program or activity receiving Federal financial assistance."

The evidence that the MTA *has* created a separate and unequal transit system is overwhelming. On one side is the underfunded, overcrowded bus system which carries 94 percent of the MTA's passengers (80 percent of whom are African American, Latino, Asian-Pacific Islander, and Native

American) yet receives less than one-third of the MTA's total expenditures. As a result, riders of color experience greater peak-hour overcrowding and tend to wait at neighborhood bus stops that are benchless and unsheltered. On the other side is the lavish commuter rail system connecting (or planning to connect) the predominantly white suburbs to the L.A. downtown business district. Although commuter line passengers make up 6 percent of the ridership, the system receives 70.9 percent of the MTA's resources. To make matters worse, the fare hike and proposed elimination of the monthly bus passes were to be accompanied by massive cutbacks in bus service.

. . . The proposed rail system has already created a two-tiered riding public—luxury trains for the white middle class, buses for the colored poor. Furthermore, the MTA paid for its Metrolink (train) lines with revenues earned from poor and working-class bus riders. Monies that should have been earmarked to improve bus service instead went to a partially finished, impractical rail system that will cost approximately $183 billion and only serve 11 percent of the population. It doesn't take a high IQ to realize that poor black and brown riders who have to crowd onto South Central, Inglewood, and East Los Angeles buses have been subsidizing the commuter rail. The average commuter rail rider is a white male professional with a household income of $64,450, who receives a $58 transportation subsidy from his employer and owns a car. By contrast, a typical bus rider is a person of color with no car and whose household income falls below $15,000. Put another way, the MTA's subsidy for bus #204, which runs through predominantly black and Latino neighborhoods along Vermont Avenue, will remain 34 cents per passenger, while the projected subsidy for the proposed Azusa and Torrance rail lines will be $55.64 and $52.87, respectively. Of course, the MTA will use revenues from sales tax and fare-box receipts to pay for this, but it is also dependent on federal funding: hence the violation of Title VI of the Civil Rights Act.

Like the Student Non-Violent Coordinating Committee in the 1960s, Strategy Center and BRU organizers take litigation *and* mass organizing seriously, but they are very clear which component drives the process. They have held legal workshops for members, conducted hours and hours of background research, prepared the initial strategy document on which the case is based, and carefully examined and re-examined all legal documentation pertaining to the suit. At the same time, they have worked hard to ensure that "the class" has a voice in the class action suit. In addition to collecting detailed declarations from riders, their main core of organizers are also plaintiffs—that is, bus riders. . . .

The Bus Riders Union has been incredibly successful. Besides building a truly multicultural, multiracial mass movement, the BRU . . . wrested a settlement from the MTA that imposed a two-year freeze on bus fares, a substantial reduction in the price of monthly and biweekly bus passes, a 5-percent increase in the number of buses in the MTA fleet in order to reduce over-crowding, the creation of new bus lines with the intention of eradicating "transportation segregation," and the creation of a joint working group in which the BRU would play a major role in drafting a five-year plan to improve bus service for all. Hence a solidly antiracist movement resulted in a victory for all riders, including transit-dependent white workers, the disabled, the elderly, and students.

While the settlement marks a critical landmark in the history of civil rights struggle, Strategy Center organizers understand that the specific legal challenge is less important than the social movement that grows out of it. . . . Through their own struggles, in the courts and city council chambers, on the streets and buses of Los Angeles, the Bus Riders Union has advanced a radical vision of social justice. . . . Lacking such a vision, many of us have not been able to see why the struggle over public transportation is so important for working people, or how antiracism benefits the entire working class. . . . The bus campaigns powerfully demonstrate that the issues facing the vast majority of people of color, for the most part, are working-class issues. Thus, unless we understand the significance of the "billions for buses" campaign or the historic class action suit against the MTA, we will never understand the deeper connections between welfare, workfare, warfare, and bus fare . . . or bus riders and unions, for that matter.

In this tragic era of pessimism and defeat, these grassroots, working-class radical movements go forward as if they might win. . . . The women and men who have built and sustained these organizations do not have the luxury *not* to fight back. In most cases, they are battling over issues basic to their own survival—decent wages, healthy environment, essential public services. At the heart of these movements are folks like my mother and the many other working-class women of color . . . who have borne the brunt of the material and ideological war against the poor. They understand, better than anyone, the necessity of fighting back. And they also understand that change does not come on its own. As Dr. Martin Luther King, Jr., so eloquently explained:

> A solution of the present crisis will not take place unless men and women work for it. Human progress is neither automatic nor inevitable. Even a superficial look at history reveals that no social advance rolls in on the wheels of inevitability. Every step toward the goal of justice requires sacrifice, suffering, and struggle; the tireless exertions and passionate concern of dedicated individuals. Without persistent effort, time itself becomes an ally of the insurgent and primitive forces of irrational emotionalism and social destruction. This is no time for apathy or complacency. This is the time for vigorous and positive action.

The time is now.

63

FROM THE GROUND UP

Charon Asetoyer

My husband is Dakota Sioux from the Yankton Sioux reservation, located in the South Central part of South Dakota. His father passed away in 1983, and in 1985 we moved to his reservation in order to fulfill our traditional commitment. It is a tradition to hold a memorial on the anniversary of a loved one's death for the following four years. It was to be a temporary stay, until our commitment was over. We had planned to move to Oklahoma so I could work for my tribe.

After we had moved to South Dakota, I applied for a job with the Yankton Sioux Tribe. The tribe is small and jobs were held by members of the tribe; it was not likely that I would be hired. I was turned down. But word got around that Clarence Rockboy had married a Comanche woman and had returned home with her, and people were curious to meet me.

Women in particular started to drop by, and I took that opportunity to invite others to come and talk. Before long a group of women were meeting regularly in my home to talk about "women's things." We moved the meetings to an empty bedroom in our basement. Out conversations centered around problems that women and children were having in the community and what we might do to address them.

By 1986 we were incorporated as a nonprofit organization. My small basement bedroom turned into an office. Women would stop in to have coffee and talk about their problems at home. Early one morning a woman came by to ask me what I knew about Fetal Alcohol Syndrome (FAS). She told me that she had gone on drinking during her pregnancy and that her child, now a teenager, was having many learning problems. She wanted to know where she could get the child tested for FAS. She was frustrated and had nowhere to turn for support or help. Before long we were meeting on a regular basis; she began bringing other mothers to join in. Soon we had a community task force on FAS, the beginning of our first project, "Women and Children in Alcohol."

It was natural that health issues should come up first: in reservation communities across the U.S., health problems are devastating, and some of the worst are on the Yankton Sioux Reservation. The infant mortality rate has

From *Women's Review of Books* 11 (July 1994): 22.

been as high as 23.8 per thousand. Diabetes affects 70 percent of the people over the age of 40, and the rates of secondary health conditions caused by diabetes, such as kidney failure, heart attacks, stroke, amputations and blindness, are alarmingly high. Alcoholism is out of control and contributes to many of these health problems, including domestic abuse and fetal alcohol births—one out of four children has FAS. Many health problems are related to poor nutrition, caused by years and even generations of eating government commodity foods that are high in salt, sugars and fat and low in fiber.

Native activists have brought the Indian Health Service under fire for years for their neglect and mistreatment of Native women. In the 1960s sterilization abuses surfaced, as they did again in the eighties when it was revealed that the Indian Health Service had used Depo-Provera on Native women who were developmentally disabled before it was FDA approved. Today the Indian Health Service is still abusing Native women's reproductive rights by limiting our contraception choices. They are promoting contraceptives like Depo Provera and Norplant, as well as sterilization. When the Hyde Amendment took away federal funding for abortion, Native women lost their access to abortion altogether: the Indian Health Service, our primary health care provider, is a division of the U.S. Public Service—that is, the Federal government.

The direction our programs have taken has been determined by the women who have come through our doors. I was sitting at my desk one afternoon working on an article for our newsletter when the phone rang. "Is it true that a tubal ligation can be temporary and that I can have it reversed when I want to have a child?" the caller asked. When I asked her why she wanted the information, she said an Indian Health Service doctor had recommended that she have her tubes tied. The procedure, he hold her, could be reversed later if she wanted. Incidents like this spurred us to create a reproductive health program.

Other issues evolved after we started doing workshops in the community. One Saturday morning a young woman came to my front door, banging for someone to let her in. I opened the door and she ran in. I recognized the look of fright and helplessness on her face, and locked the door behind her. During my first marriage I too had been a victim of domestic violence. There I was, standing in the hallway of my home faced with something that I had wanted to leave behind. Only this time I was not the one in need of someone to take me in.

In the course of time we created a program to assist women like this one and their children. We started out with a safe house program, sheltering women in local motels. In 1991, after a long court battle over zoning, the Native American Community Board opened a shelter for women and children fleeing from domestic violence and sexual assault. It now houses eighteen women and children and has provided services for over 900 women and children over the past two and a half years.

As more concerns were brought forward, we needed additional programming and additional staff. The office had grown too small for the organization. Several months earlier I had visited the National Black Women's Health Project in Atlanta, Georgia. The Project was located in a large house which seemed ideal: there was room to grow in, space for program work, a kitchen, a yard, and a strong sense of pride among the staff in their unique working environment. It all seemed so right: why not for us too? We wanted to do nutrition work to address diabetics, so we needed a place to prepare food; we wanted to work with children, so we needed space for them as well as for office work. And if we could buy a house we would no longer have to pay rent to a landlord.

Owning our own place seemed like a good idea but no more than a dream at that point, so I put it in the back of my mind. Who would fund a group of women to buy a house anyway, especially a group of Native American women living on a reservation in South Dakota? I had no idea what the cost of real estate might be in Lake Andes, South Dakota. But I kept thinking about the idea. A friend mentioned a small house she knew of, a fixer-upper, around $5,000 to $7,000. I went to look at it: it did seem to suit our needs.

Shortly after, I was invited to a conference sponsored by the National Women's Health Network, a health advocacy organization based in Washington, D.C. At a networking reception the first evening, I met another woman of color, Luz Alveolus Martinets, the director of the National Latina Health Organization. We talked about the work we were doing, and I eventually told her about our dream of buying a house for our project. When I told her what it would cost, she thought I meant the down payment. But $6,000 was the price for the entire house.

Luz told me that most of the women attending the conference were working women and could afford to make a contribution toward the house. All I had to do was to get up during lunch the next day, when we all had to introduce ourselves, and make an appeal for donations. At lunch I tried to avoid Luz: it seemed too hard to stand up in a crowded room of women I really did not know and ask for money. But Luz found me. Still, when it was my turn to introduce myself, I started to sit down without making my request for donations. Luz kept encouraging me to go ahead and make my request. Before long, all the women in the room wanted to know what we were arguing about. So I went ahead and asked for their help. Then I saw Byllye Avery of the National Black Women's Health Project, across the room, reach into her pocketbook and pull out her checkbook. Byllye held up the first check and announced to the room, "I donate $100." The pocketbooks opened and the checks piled up. It was like a dream: the house was soon to become a reality. I left the conference with about half of the money we needed.

Soon after we purchased the house, people from the community came to help clean, paint and panel the walls. A few weeks of hard work transformed the little brick house across from my home into a warm environment where women and children could come together to share in health education activities and to organize around issues confronting our community. In February 1988, the doors opened on the first Native American Women's Health Education Resource Center based on a reservation, located in Lake Andes, South Dakota, on the Yankton Sioux Reservation.

Not long after the Resource Center opened a young Yankton Sioux woman walked in, introduced herself and asked if she could do her college internship with us. She was interested in working with children. It was time, we decided, for us to examine how we could provide services for children with special needs. The Child Development Program was our answer.

The Program brought children with special needs together to work, play and learn in an after-school program. Fetal alcohol-affected children, latchkey children, gifted children, and children from highly stressed families participate in the program. Today the program has evolved into a Dakota Cultural program in which elders of the Yankton Sioux tribe work with children, teaching them Dakota language, values and spirituality.

An Adult Education Program was not something we had even thought about developing—until one day a call came in from one of the local high school counselors, asking if a sixteen-year-old pregnant student could continue her schooling at the Resource Center with tutoring from our staff. "She's getting too big to sit in class all day long," he said. We said "Sure," and the next week we had a student. Soon after that a mother of one of the children in our Child Development Program asked if we could show her how to use a computer. She said that she already knew how to type, and she could get a job if she knew how to use a computer. This was the beginning of a program that offered job readiness skills and GED completion.

As more women heard about the work and the services that the Resource Center was providing, a feeling of trust was established. Women turned to us for help concerning sterilization abuse, and for information about sexually transmitted diseases, AIDS, family planning and abortion. A high school student came into the Resource Center one afternoon wanting information about pregnancy, AIDS and condoms. She asked if we could get her a home pregnancy test kit, since she thought that she might be pregnant, but if she went down to the local drugstore for it, the clerk would recognize her and call her mother.

It was not long before we were going into the schools with AIDS and contraception information, and conducting AIDS workshops in the community. We hired four high school students, two girls and two boys, and trained them to be AIDS peer counselors, so they could go back into the community and schools to give out accurate information to other young people.

It became obvious to us that no one else in our community, and no other Native women's groups on other reservations, were doing this kind of work. As women turned to us for information about abortion and issues of reproductive health, we knew that we needed to organize our reproductive health work more formally. Our next move was to bring Native women together in a project that would address our unmet health care needs and the reproductive abuses committed by the Indian Health Service. In 1990, 36 Native women met in Pierre, South Dakota, to form the first Native Women's Reproductive Rights Coalition. The Coalition has developed a reproductive rights agenda that defines the issues of reproductive rights and health as Native women ourselves understand them.

Over the past three years the Native Women's Reproductive Rights Coalition has grown to involve over 150 women from eight states, and it continues to grow each year. It organizes Native women to address such concerns as Norplant and Depo-Provera abuse, environmental issues, abortion, and the oppressive effects of organized religion in reservation communities.

Another central part of the Coalition's work has been to include the teachings of our elders. The passing down of traditional methods of birthing, child spacing, abortion, parenting and "becoming a woman" ceremonies is an important issue for Native women and has become a major mission of the Coalition. Through its work, combined with the direct services of our Resource Center, we can bring into the national and international arena practices and policies that we ourselves have shaped and that truly represent the issues confronting us.

64

MANIFESTA

Jennifer Baumgardner and Amy Richards

. . . Knowing there is feminist work to be done, and that the second most frequently asked question at Ask Amy is "What is activism?," it seemed necessary to lay out the nuts and bolts of personal activism—from radical-feminist Yom Kippur cards to general advice, incentive, and myth-busting.

From Jennifer Baumgardner and Amy Richards, *Manifesta: Young Women, Feminism, and the Future* (New York: Farrar, Straus and Giroux, 2000).

The first myth is that activism will bring an immediate and decisive victory. In reality, the journey to justice is usually damn long. So while the click of consciousness brings immediate gratification in itself, social change, even on a small scale, is slow and arduous work.

One example of this (on the large scale) is the active call for birth control, begun by Margaret Sanger around 1916 in response to American women's overwhelming need and desire to control fertility. A nurse in New York City, Sanger witnessed firsthand the hideous conditions experienced by poor women on the Lower East Side. After a stream of pregnancies, these women were so exhausted by bearing and rearing children that they often met an early death. Sanger made and distributed pamphlets telling women how to avoid pregnancy, and also conducted teach-ins. For both, she was jailed, yet she eventually founded both the first birth-control clinic and the American Birth Control Association (the precursor to Planned Parenthood). She converted many eminent doctors and literally millions of citizens to her cause.

Despite this popular support and demonstrated need, birth control was not legalized in all states until 1964, when the Supreme Court decided in *Griswold v. Connecticut* that married couples had the right to seek contraception. Fifty years of agitating for birth control had to happen before that legal barrier fell. Even with that hard-earned triumph, it took the radical feminists of the seventies to extend the right of privacy won by *Griswold* to protect the rights of single men and women to seek birth control.

Another famous example: before Rosa Parks refused to give up her seat to a white man on December 1, 1955, the act that initiated the Montgomery Bus Boycott, she and others had spent years as activists. They had been trained at the Highlander Folk School, a progressive political training ground founded in 1932 in Tennessee. This one act, a black woman's refusal to stand up for a white man, symbolizes the civil-rights movement to modern audiences. Parks herself is often depicted as a spontaneous actor, almost an accidental activist. In actuality, her act was a conscious part of a campaign, and nearly ten more years of nonstop activism by Parks and thousands of others were necessary before the Civil Rights Act was passed in 1964.

Change doesn't occur overnight, and the expectation that it will is often what breaks the spirit and heart of many an impassioned idealist. *The Feminist Memoir Project*, an anthology by Rachel Blau du Plessis and Ann Snitow, chronicles the voices of some activists struggling with Second Wave letdown. Carol Hanisch, who is credited with coining the phrase "the personal is political," her life because she gave so much of her heart and time to the movement, and feels unsure of what was accomplished. Many suffragists died without seeing women enfranchised nationally. When Margaret Sanger died, birth control had been legal for only two years. If the push for the ERA picks up steam and passes sometime in the next decade or so, Alice Paul, who wrote it, and Bella Abzug, who lobbied for it tenaciously, will not have lived to see this triumph; nor will thousands of less famous women across the country who feverishly organized their state legislatures. Reproductive freedom, which most Second Wavers consider to be their major goal, is a campaign that we who call ourselves Third Wavers will probably be working on in this country and internationally all our lives.

The second myth about activism is that it has to be huge—*A Million March on Washington!* Thousands of men and women marched on Washington in August 1968 to hear Martin Luther King, Jr.'s "I Have a Dream" speech. However, that glistening moment of victory and grandeur was only one event in years of unexciting, tedious, utterly essential organizing—much of it, again, women's work. Splashy events get attention, but the work behind them doesn't. Activists might not even recognize themselves as part of this process.

The third myth is the importance of the superleader. *Gandhi organizes India! Gloria Steinem organizes American women! Martin Luther King, Jr. organizes black Americans! Cesar Chavez organizes farmworkers! Ralph Nader figures out what to boycott! Or, in our own generation, Rebecca Walker is the Third Wave! Katie Roiphe is the anti–Third Wave! Kathleen Hanna IS Riot Grrrl!* It is a myth that effective activism is the result of one person, or even a few. Using the example of the civil-rights movement, while you've heard of Rosa Parks and Martin Luther King, Jr., it is less likely that you know about the Women's Political Caucus, Jo Ann Gibson Robinson, Ella Baker (who trained the young Martin Luther King, Jr.), and all the other women whose organizing was responsible for the Montgemery Bus Boycott. Similarly, you know Mahatma Gandhi and Jawaharlal Nehru, but it's unlikely that you have heard about the Indian women's movement of the late nineteenth and early twentieth centuries, which pioneered nonviolent resistance and the strategy of going from community to community to organize the grass roots. Seeking independence from male colonization of their bodies and lives, they campaigned against child marriages and *sati* (widow burning). Gandhi not only borrowed their techniques but tapped into their already existing movement, which then became part of the drive toward independence from British rule. (Speaking of men creating historic events off the backs of women's organizing, the Boston Tea Party was precipitated by women who refused to buy tea that was taxed by England.)

The leader of a movement has an important but misunderstood role. Because of charisma and oratorical skills, leaders attract media and mass. They usually have a gift for inspiring hope by stating a possibility that could become real, thus raising consciousness and righteous anger. But they are just the tip of the iceberg, and would have no impact without the activists who form the foundation of the movement. They are the ones who fold and mail the flyers, answer the phones, and translate the agenda to and from the grass roots—whether there is any media attention at all.

At the beginning of a new century and a new millennium, Third Wave feminists shouldn't be discouraged that we don't have the equivalent of a

Betty Friedan or a Rosa Parks—an icon that the whole movement can be reduced to at our rallies. And, even when we do, nothing will be accomplished without a truly aggressive Third Wave movement to push that iceberg's tip above sea level.

Although we may not yet have a critical mass of Third Wave activists, we need to dispel the fourth and final myth: that our generation is politically, um, impotent. Our purported lack of activism is usually chalked up to vague notions of apathy. We were reared by the boob tube, and made cynical by the cold-war politics and consumerism of the Reagan-Bush era. For a while, ad executives and media pundits conjectured that Generation X was simply lazy and irresponsible—fullfilling the slacker persona of the early nineties. The apathy rap has some truth when it comes to feminism. Some people do believe that everything is fine now, and that there is no need for feminism, either because they have low expectations or because they haven't been in the outside world long enough to experience the limitations brought on by sexism. Many younger women in general haven't yet smacked up against job discrimination by sex and race—though they have certainly, however subtly, faced it socially and culturally. But history tells us that for each big leap, for each crystal-clear moment in which people refused to give up their seats on the bus or at the lunch counter, there is a time of collecting energy and stating new visions—a time of pre-emergence. Understanding that change takes time will lead us to a redefinition of our generation politically.

65

WHAT DOES AN ALLY DO?

Paul Kivel

Being allies to people of color in the struggle to end racism is one of the most important things that white people can do. There is no one correct way to be an ally. Each of us is different. We have different relationships to social organizations, political processes, and economic structures. We are more or less powerful because of such factors as our gender, class, work situation, family,

---

From Paul Kivel, *Uprooting Racism: How White People Can Work for Racial Justice* (Gabriola Island, BC: New Society Publishers, 2002). Reprinted by permission.

and community participation. Being an ally to people of color is an ongoing strategic process in which we look at our personal and social resources, evaluate the environment we have helped to create, and decide what needs to be done.

. . . Times change and circumstances vary. What is a priority today may not be tomorrow. What is effective or strategic right now may not be next year. We need to be thinking with others and noticing what is going on around us so we will know how to put our attention, energy, time, and money toward strategic priorities in the struggle to end racism and other injustices.

This includes listening to people of color so that we can support the actions they take, the risks they bear in defending their lives and challenging white hegemony. It includes watching the struggle of white people to maintain dominance and the struggle of people of color to gain equal opportunity, justice, safety, and respect.

We don't need to believe or accept as true everything people of color say. There is no one voice in any community, much less in the complex and diverse communities of color spanning our country. We do need to listen carefully to the voices of people of color so that we understand and give credence to their experience. We can then evaluate the content of what they are saying by what we know about how racism works and by our own critical thinking and progressive political analysis.

It is important to emphasize this point because often we become paralyzed when people of color talk about racism. We are afraid to challenge what they say. We will be ineffective as allies if we give up our ability to analyze and think critically, if we simply accept everything that a person of color states as truth.

Listening to people of color and giving critical credence to their experience is not easy for us because of the training we have received. Nevertheless, it is an important first step. When we hear statements that make us want to react defensively, we can instead keep the following points in mind as we try to understand what is happening and determine how best to be allies.

We have seen how racism is a pervasive part of our culture. Therefore we should always assume that racism is at least part of the picture. In light of this assumption, we should look for the patterns involved rather than treating most events as isolated occurrences.

Since we know that racism is involved, we know our whiteness is also a factor. We should look for ways we are acting from assumptions of white power or privilege. This will help us acknowledge any fear or confusion we may feel. It will allow us to see our tendencies to defend ourselves or our tendencies to assume we should be in control. Then we may want to talk with other white people both to express our feelings and to get support so our tendencies towards defensiveness or controlling behavior don't get in the way of our being effective allies.

We have many opportunities to practice these critical listening and thinking skills because we are all involved in a complex web of interpersonal and institutional relationships. Every day we are presented with opportunities to analyze what is going on around us and to practice taking direct action as allies to people of color.

People of color will always be on the front lines fighting racism because their lives are at stake. How do we act and support them effectively, both when they are in the room with us and when they are not?

BASIC TACTICS

Every situation is different and calls for critical thinking about how to make a difference. Taking the statements above into account, I have compiled some general guidelines.

1. **Assume racism is everywhere, every day.** Just as economics influences everything we do, just as our gender and gender politics influence everything we do, assume that racism is affecting whatever is going on. We assume this because it's true and because one of the privileges of being white is not having to see or deal with racism all the time. We have to learn to see the effect the racism has. Notice who speaks, what is said, how things are done and described. Notice who isn't present. Notice code words for race, and the implications of the policies, patterns, and comments that are being expressed. You already notice the skin color of everyone you meet and interact with—now notice what difference it makes.
2. **Notice who is the center of attention and who is the center of power.** Racism works by directing violence and blame toward people of color and consolidating power and privilege for white people.
3. **Notice how racism is denied, minimized, and justified.**
4. **Understand and learn from the history of whiteness and racism.** Notice how racism has changed over time and how it has subverted or resisted challenges. Study the tactics that have worked effectively against it.
5. **Understand the connections between racism, economic issues, sexism, and other forms of injustice.**
6. **Take a stand against injustice.** Take risks. It is scary, difficult, and may bring up feelings of inadequacy, lack of self-confidence, indecision, or fear of making mistakes, but ultimately it is the only healthy and moral human thing to do. Intervene in situations where racism is being passed on.
7. **Be strategic.** Decide what is important to challenge and what's not. Think about strategy in particular situations. Attack the source of power.
8. **Don't confuse a battle with the war.** Behind particular incidents and interactions are large patterns. Racism is flexible and adaptable. There will be gains and losses in the struggle for justice and equality.

9. **Don't call names or be personally abusive.** Since power is often defined as power over others—the ability to abuse or control people—it is easy to become abusive ourselves. However, we usually end up abusing people who have less power than we do because it is less dangerous. Attacking people doesn't address the systemic nature of racism and inequality.

10. **Support the leadership of people of color.** Do this consistently, but not uncritically.

11. **Learn something about the history of white people who have worked for racial justice.** There is a long history of white people who have fought for racial justice. Their stones can inspire and sustain you.

12. **Don't do it alone.** You will not end racism by yourself. We can do it if we work together. Build support, establish networks, and work with already established groups.

13. **Talk with your children and other young people about racism.**

GETTING INVOLVED

It can be difficult for those of us who are white to know how to be strong allies for people of color when discrimination occurs. In the following interaction, imagine that Roberto is a young Latino just coming out of a job interview with a white recruiter from a computer company. Let's see how one white person might respond.

Roberto is angry, not sure what to do next. He walks down the hall and meets a white teacher who wants to help.

Teacher: *Hey, Roberto, how's it going?*

Roberto: *That son of a bitch! He wasn't going to give me no job. That was really messed up.*

Teacher: *Hold on there, don't be so angry. It was probably a mistake or something.*

Roberto: *There was no mistake. The racist bastard. He wants to keep me from getting a good job. Rather have us all on welfare or doing maintenance work.*

Teacher: *Calm down now or you'll get yourself in more trouble. Don't go digging a hole for yourself. Maybe I could help you if you weren't so angry.*

Roberto: *That's easy for you to say. This man was discriminating against me. White folks are all the same. They talk about equal opportunity, but it's the same old shit.*

Teacher: *Wait a minute. I didn't have anything to do with this. Don't blame me. I'm not responsible. If you wouldn't be so angry maybe I could help you. You probably took what he said the wrong way. Maybe you were too sensitive.*

Roberto: *I could tell. He was racist. That's all. (He storms off.)*

What did you notice about this scene? The teacher is concerned and is trying to help, but his intervention is not very effective. He immediately downplays the incident, discounting Roberto's feelings and underestimating the possibility of racism. He seems to think that racism is unlikely—that it was just a misunderstanding, or that Roberto was being too sensitive.

The teacher is clearly uncomfortable with Roberto's anger. He begins to defend himself, the job recruiter, and white people. He ends up feeling attacked for being white. Rather than talking about what happened, he focuses on Roberto's anger and his generalizations about white people. He threatens to get Roberto in trouble himself if Roberto doesn't calm down. As he walks away, he may be thinking it's no wonder Roberto didn't get hired for the job.

You probably recognize some of the tactics described. . . . The teacher denies or minimizes the likelihood or racism, blames Roberto, and eventually counterattacks, claiming to be a victim of Roberto's anger and racial generalizations.

This interaction illustrates some of the common feelings that can get in the way of intervening effectively where discrimination is occurring. First is the feeling that we are being personally attacked. It is difficult to hear the phrases "all white people" or "you white people." We want to defend ourselves and other whites. We don't want to believe that white people could intentionally hurt others. Or we may want to say, "Not me, I'm different."

There are some things we should remember when we feel attacked. First, this is a question of injustice. We need to focus on what happened and what we can do about it, not on our feelings of being attacked.

Second, someone who has been the victim of injustice is legitimately angry and may or may not express that anger in ways we like. Criticizing the way people express their anger deflects attention and action away from the injustice that was committed. After the injustice has been dealt with, if you still think it's worthwhile and not an attempt to control the situation yourself, you can go back and discuss ways of expressing anger.

Often, because we are frequently complacent about injustice that doesn't affect us directly, it takes a lot of anger and aggressive action to bring attention to a problem. If we were more proactive about identifying and intervening in situations of injustice, people would not have to be so "loud" to get our attention in the first place.

Finally, part of the harm that racism does is that it forces people of color to be wary and mistrustful of all white people, just as sexism forces women to mistrust all men. People of color face racism every day, often from unexpected quarters. They never know when a white friend, co-worker, teacher, police officer, doctor, or passerby may discriminate, act hostile, or say something offensive. They have to be wary of all white people, even though they know that not all white people will mistreat them. They have likely been hurt in the past by white people they thought they could trust, and therefore they may make statements about all white people. We must remember that although we want to be trustworthy, trust is not the issue. We are not fighting racism so that people of color will trust us. Trust builds over time through our visible efforts to be allies and fight racism. Rather than trying to be safe and trustworthy, we need to be more active, less defensive, and put issues of trust aside.

When people are discriminated against they may feel unseen, stereotyped, attacked, or as if a door has been slammed in their face. They may feel confused, frustrated, helpless, or angry. They are probably reminded of other similar experiences. They may want to hurt someone in return, or hide their pain, or simply forget about the whole experience. Whatever the response, the experience is deeply wounding and painful. It is an act of emotional violence.

It's also an act of economic violence to be denied access to a job, housing, educational program, pay raise, or promotion that one deserves. It is a practice that keeps economic resources in the hands of one group and denies them to another.

When a person is discriminated against it is a serious event and we need to treat it seriously. It is also a common event. For instance, the government estimates that there are over 2 million acts of race-based housing discrimination every year—20 million every decade. We know that during their lifetime, every person of color will probably have to face such discriminatory experiences in school, work, housing, and community settings.

People of color do not protest discrimination lightly. They know that when they do, white people routinely deny or minimize it, blame them for causing trouble, and then counterattack. This is the "happy family" syndrome [described earlier].

People of color are experts in discrimination resulting from racism. Most experience it regularly and see its effects on their communities. Not every complaint of discrimination is valid, but most have some truth in them. It would be a tremendous step forward if we assumed that there was some truth in every complaint of racial discrimination, even when other factors may also be involved. At least then we would take it seriously enough to investigate fully.

How could the teacher in the above scenario be a better ally to Roberto? We can go back to the guidelines suggested earlier for help. First, he needs to listen much more carefully to what Roberto is saying. He should assume that Roberto is intelligent, and if he says there was racism involved then there probably was. The teacher should be aware of his own power and position, his tendency to be defensive, and his desire to defend other white people or presume their innocence. It would also be worthwhile to look for similar occurrences because racism is usually not an isolated instance but a pattern within an organization or institution.

Let's see how these suggestions might operate in a replay of this scene.

Teacher: *Hey, Roberto, what's happening?*

Roberto: *That son of a bitch! He wasn't going to give me no job. He was messin' with me.*

Teacher: *You're really upset. Tell me what happened.*

Roberto: *He was discriminating against me. Wasn't going to hire me cause I'm Latino. White folks are all alike. Always playing games.*

Teacher: *This is serious. Why don't you come into my office and tell me exactly what happened.*

Roberto: *Okay. This company is advertising for computer programmers and I'm qualified for the job. But this man tells me there aren't any computer jobs, and then he tries to steer me toward a janitor job. He was a racist bastard.*

Teacher: *That's tough. I know you would be good in that job. This sounds like a case of job discrimination. Let's write down exactly what happened, and then you can decide what you want to do about it.*

Roberto: *I want to get that job.*

Teacher: *If you want to challenge it, I'll help you. Maybe there's something we can do.*

This time the teacher was being a strong, supportive ally to Roberto.

AN ALLY MAKES A COMMITMENT

Nobody needs fly-by-night allies, those who are here today and gone tomorrow. Being an ally takes commitment and perseverance. It is a lifelong struggle to end racism and other forms of social injustice. People of color know this well because they have been struggling for generations for recognition of their rights and the opportunity to participate fully in our society. The struggle to abolish slavery took over 80 years. Women organized for over 60 years to win the right to vote. I was reminded about the long haul recently when my sister sent me a news clipping about my old high school in Los Angeles, Birmingham High.

The clipping was about the 17-year struggle to change the "Birmingham Braves" name and caricatured image of an "Indian" used by the school teams to something that did not insult Native Americans. I was encouraged to hear that the name and mascot were now being changed, but was upset to read that there was an alumni group resisting the change and filing a lawsuit to preserve the old name.

Soon after receiving the article I had the good fortune to talk with a white woman who had been involved with the struggle over the mascot. The challenge had originated with a group of Native Americans in the San Fernando Valley. This woman decided to join the group—the only white person to do so. She started attending meetings. For the first two or three years all she did was listen, and the group hardly spoke to her. After a time, members of the group began to acknowledge her presence, talk with her, and include her in their activities. This woman learned a tremendous amount about herself, the local Native cultures, and the nature of white resistance during the 15 years she was involved with this group. They tried many different strategies and eventually, because they met with so much intransigence at the high school, they went to the Los Angeles school board.

When the school board made its decision to eliminate Native-American names and logos in school programs, it affected every school in the Los Angeles area. Subsequently the decision became a model for the Dallas school district's policy and is being considered for adoption in other school districts across the country.

This was a long struggle, but much public education was accomplished in the process. This work is part of a national effort by Native Americans and their allies to get sports teams and clubs to relinquish offensive names and mascots.

If the woman I talked with had been discouraged or offended because nobody welcomed her or paid her special attention during those first meetings, or if she felt that after a year or two nothing was going to be accomplished, or if she had not listened and learned enough to be able to work with and take leadership from the Native American community involved in this struggle, she would not have been transformed by the struggle the way she had been able to celebrate the success of this struggle for Native-American dignity and respect. Her work as an ally reminded me of what commitment as an ally really means.

66

CAN I GET A WITNESS?
Testimony from a Hip Hop Feminist

Shani Jamila

I used to think I had missed my time. Thought I was meant to have come of age in the sixties when I could've been a Panther freedom fighter, challenging the pigs alongside Assata, Angela and Kathleen. Oh, but I went deeper than

---

From Daisy Hernandez and Bushra Rehman eds., *Colonize This! Young Women of Color on Today's Feminism* (New York: Seal Press, 2002), pp. 382–99. © 2002 Daisy Hernandez and Bushra Rehman. Reprinted by permission.

that. I saw myself reading my poetry with Sonia, Ntozake, Nikki and June . . . being a peer of Audre, Alice and Paula Giddings . . . kickin' it with revolutionary brothers like Huey, Haki, and Rap . . . all while rocking the shit out of my black beret. When she needed advice, I would've *been* there for Patricia Hill Collins as she bounced her preliminary ideas about *Black Feminist Thought* off me. Now can't you see the beauty in this? I would have been building and bonding with a community of artists and activists that had this whole vibrancy radiating from its core, and so many of my role models would've just been crew.

I know right now some of y'all are probably like, "OK, this child's on crack . . . that decade was not all that!" But don't front. When you heard the stories of your parents, aunts, uncles and family friends—or even if you just watched some TV special talking about the mystique of the sixties—didn't it ever make you wonder what happened with our generation? Who were our revolutionaries? What sparked our passions so high that we were willing to risk our lives to fight for it? Where was our national Black Arts Movement?

It seemed natural that we should have one—after all, we had flavor for days . . . high-tops and Hammer pants, jellies and Jheri Curls bear witness to that! And as an African-American child coming of age in the first generation to endure the United States post-integration, I can *definitely* testify that we had our own struggles: AIDS, apartheid, affirmative action, the prison industrial complex and underdeveloped inner cities are only a few examples. Growing up, these were the things that would run through my mind as I'd cut out collages from *Right On!*, and wonder what happened to us. Seemed like coping with issues like these would've hyped us up enough to create our own culture of resistance. The glossy pages trying to stick to the walls of my room competed futilely with the vibrations emanating from my spastic MTV imitations as Power 99FM's bass blasted. I danced around the images of Public Enemy and Queen Latifah that now decorated my floor, rapping all the lyrics to "Fight the Power" as I mourned our inactivity.

As I got older, I realized what I'd missed in my youth. Largely due to globalization and growing technology, in addition to some banging beats and off-the-chain lyrics, we'd had an *international* Black Arts Movement shaping our generation. As a kid, I didn't recognize hip hop as a vibrant and valuable sociocultural force—I just thought the culture was cool. I loved the music but never conceived of it as a revolutionary outcry. After all, I'd learned in school that activism was a concept confined to the sixties . . . so even though I felt empowered by the Afrocentric vibes and in-your-face lyrics, it seemed like the culture came a few decades too late for a critical context. In fact, individuals and organizations whose work challenged me to think critically about Black people rarely even entered the public school curriculum. In my high school's halls we were taught a very narrow and revisionist view of world history that boiled down to this: white was right, Africa was an afterthought.

In addition to the massive amounts of potentially empowering information that was erased by those messages, a holistic history just was not taught.

Not only were my people not reflected in the syllabi, but I didn't see a proportionate reflection in the faces of my classmates either. As one of only three Black faces in the honors program, all of whom were middle-class females, I often questioned why our representation was so disproportionate. The subtext shouted that the reason wasn't a deficiency in the newly integrated school system but rather the failings of people of color. We were tacitly taught that our token presence proved racism and sexism were over, so the problem must have been our peers' inability to achieve. I knew this wasn't true but as a child I was often frustrated because I didn't know how to prove it, as it was often demanded that I do.

See, my generation came of age with the expectancy that we could live, eat and attend school among whites. Race and gender were no longer inscribed in the law as automatic barriers to achievement, making the injustices we encountered less obvious than those our predecessors had faced. But the issues didn't go away. Instead, we found that an adverse consequence of integration and the "gains" of the sixties was even more heavily convoluted notions of race and gender oppression. Economic class stratification has also continued to evolve as a serious complication.

The paradox of the Black middle class as I experienced it is that we are simultaneously affirmed and erased: tokenized and celebrated as one of the few "achievers" of our race but set apart from other Black folks by our economic success. It is the classic divide-and-conquer technique regularly employed in oppressive structures; in this case saying that Black people are pathological—but you somehow escaped the genetic curse, so you must be "different." These lessons were regularly reinforced with camouflaged compliments such as, "Wow, you're so pretty/smart . . . are *both* of your parents Black?" Other times the insults would blaze brazenly, like the comments made by the white girls in my Girl Scouts carpool when we drove by a group of Black children playing in their yard: "Ooooh, Mom! Look at the little niglets playing on the street!" Their snickers echoed in a familiar way that suggested they'd shared this joke before. As the pain and rage began to well up within me, their dismissive comments also gathered force: "God, like, don't be so sensitive, Shani. We're not talking about *you*. You're different." I waited expectantly for the adult in the car to tell her children they were out of line and to apologize. She said nothing. I began to wonder if I was overreacting. Maybe it wasn't such a big deal. Maybe I *was* different. Maybe I thought too much.

Over the years I learned how to censor myself and adapt to different surroundings, automatically tailoring my tongue to fit the ear of whatever crew I was with. Depending on the composition of the crowd, the way I'd speak and even the things I'd talk about were subject to change. White people automatically got a very precise speech, because I knew every word out of my mouth was being measured and quantified as an example of the capabilities of the entire Black race. Around Black people I slipped into the vocabulary I felt more comfortable with but remained aware that I was still being judged. This time it was to see how capably I could fall back into "our talk" without sounding like a foreigner, if I could prove my suburban upbringing and elitist education had not robbed me of my authenticity as a Black woman.

Passing this litmus test meant the most to me. Because if the daily trials weren't enough, when the flood of college acceptance and rejection letters began pouring in and I got into schools my white "friends" weren't admitted to, all of a sudden the color they didn't see before came back fierce. My GPA, test scores, extracurricular activities, and recommendations were rendered irrelevant when they viciously told me the only conceivable reason I was getting in over them had to be affirmative action. I realized the racial logic being used against me was something that pervaded all class spheres. Whether you were a beneficiary of affirmative action or you were seen in the imagery of welfare queens (whose depiction as poor Black women defies actual numerical stats), we were all categorized as niggers trying to get over on the system.

While most of my memories from childhood are happy ones, I also remember a constant struggle to find a sense of balance. For every "reward" token status bestowed, it simultaneously increased the isolation I felt. I didn't think there were many people who could understand how and why I was struggling when by societal standards I was succeeding. I worried that I was being ungrateful because I knew so many who had come before me had given their lives in the hopes that one day their children could have the opportunities I'd grown up with. Despite the public accolades I received for my accomplishments, until I went to college I felt shunned by whites and suspected by Blacks. I was looking for a place to belong.

In 1993 I took my first steps on the campus of Spelman College, a Black woman's space in the middle of the largest conglomeration of historically Black colleges and universities in the world. This is not your typical institution. One of only two colleges of its kind surviving in the States—at Spelman Black women walk proud. Our first address from "Sista Prez" Johnnetta B. Cole told us so. As is characteristic of speeches to incoming first-year students, she instructed us to look to our right and look to our left. We dutifully gazed upon each other's brown faces. She spoke: "Other schools will tell you one of these students will not be here in four years when you are graduating. At Spelman we say we will all see to it: your sister *better* be at your side when you *all* graduate in four years!" Loud cheers erupted—we were our sisters' keepers.

At Spelman I learned new ways of learning, thinking and challenging. It was in this place that I was first introduced to a way of teaching that was unapologetically rooted in Black women's perspectives, that addressed the reality of what it means to be at the center of intersecting discriminations like race, class and gender. My formal education about my people began to expand beyond Malcolm and Martin. I learned about activists like Sojourner Truth and Maria W. Stewart, journalists and crusaders like Ida B. Wells, preachers like Jarena Lee, freedom fighters and abolitionists like Harriet Tubman, scholars like Anna Julia Cooper, poets like Frances Ellen Watkins Harper and community leaders like Mary Church Terrell. Here our core courses were entitled "African Diaspora and the World" and "Images of Women in the Media." The required reading on the syllabi included books like Paulo Freire's *Pedagogy of the Oppressed*, Frantz Fanon's *The Wretched of the Earth*, and Patricia Hill Collins's *Black Feminist Thought*. In these books and classes I found the answers to questions I didn't even have the language to ask with the education I'd received in high school.

This is what made attending a historically Black college such a turning point in my life. I don't want to romanticize my collegiate experience to the point where it was like I opened up a book and suddenly became some sort of guru, but what being exposed to this community of scholars and activists did do was give me a framework for my feelings. The value of having my thoughts nurtured, legitimized and placed into a historical context, in addition to the power of being surrounded by sisters and brothers who were walking refutations to the stereotypes I'd grown up with, gave me a space to blossom in ways I couldn't have imagined. I felt validated and affirmed by the idea that I no longer had to explain why Black folks were different from the purported standard. Instead of being made to justify what mainstream society perceived as deviance, I was supported in the effort to critically challenge how societal norms even came to be. I loved that when we would discuss slavery, an integral part of the conversation was slave revolts—Black resistance had finally entered the curriculum. It was the first time I saw people reflective of myself and my experiences both inside and outside of the classroom. Living and learning like this was revolutionary for me. It changed my life.

Of course, being on an all women's campus, gender was also a regular topic of conversation. I was part of some beautiful dialogues where brothers would share the struggles they endured excelling academically that they didn't face when they'd shine in the more "acceptable" realms of sports or music. Sisters would relate back with testimonies of feeling forced to choose between our Blackness and our womanhood—a choice as impossible, a professor pointed out, as choosing between our left and right sides. In stark contrast to the race debates, however, these moments of raw honesty took place on a slippery slope. Gendered analyses were not granted the same sense of universal urgency attributed to race. Rather, they were received with suspicion. Many people perceived the debate over gender dynamics as a way to pit Black folks against each other. In heated conversations my peers would choose camps, placing race, gender and class in a hierarchy and declaring loyalty to one over the other. Protests would be peppered with frequent warnings that Spelman was notorious for inculcating crazy mentalities in its students. We were told we better watch our backs before we turned into one of those (gasp!) feminists too.

Yup, the dreaded F-word continues to be so weighed down by negative connotations that few people are willing to voluntarily associate with it. Hurled out like an accusation, it is enough to make many sistas start backpedaling faster than the rising stats on violence against women. The reluctance to be identified with something perceived as an internally divisive force inside historically oppressed communities is understandable. Many feminists of color felt it too, which is largely why Black feminist theory and womanism emerged. Unfortunately, much of what Black feminism really stands for has been stereotyped or obscured by school systems that don't devote time to Black women's intellectual traditions. A sad consequence has been that in addition to having something designed to advance our people become a tool of division, millions of people have been kept in the dark (so to speak) from a wealth of really important information and support networks.

Because of all the drama surrounding the word "feminism," there are mad heads who identify with feminist principles but feel conflicted about embracing the term. But let's examine what it really means. At root, Black feminism is a struggle against the pervasive oppression that defines Western culture. Whether taking aim at gender equity, homophobia or images of women, it functions to resist disempowering ideologies and devaluing institutions. It merges theory and action to reaffirm Black women's legitimacy as producers of intellectual work and reject assertions that attack our ability to contribute to these traditions. In stark contrast to the popular misconception that Black feminism is a divisive force that pits sisters against brothers, or even feminists against feminists, I view it as an essential part of a larger struggle for all of our liberation. Our fight for freedom has to be inclusive.

Of course, my understanding of Black feminism is rooted in the theoretical texts written decades before I was first introduced to them in college. Many of these theories remain relevant, at the very least as an essential historical base. However, for any movement to maximize its effectiveness, it has to be applicable to the times. It is incumbent upon us as hip hop feminists not to become complacent in the work that has come before us. We have to write our own stories that address the issues that are specific to our time. For example, some people think it's an oxymoron when I juxtapose a term like feminism alongside a genre of music that has been assailed for its misogyny. It seems obvious to me, however, that just as the shape of what we're fighting has changed, we need to examine how we as a community of activists have changed as well. Hip hop is the dominant influence on our generation.

Since my birth in 1975 four years before the first rap single achieved mainstream success, I have watched the hip hop movement, culture and music evolve. I mark important events in my life by the hip hop songs that were popular at the time, linking my high-school graduation with the Souls of

Mischief's album *'93 til Infinity* and my first school dance with the song "It Takes Two" by Rob Bass. My ideas of fashion have often been misled by hip hop artists like Kwamé, whose signature style resulted in the proliferation of polka dots in American schools around 1989. My taste in men has also been molded by hip hop aesthetics. I entered my love life interested in brothers who were rocking gumbies like my first boyfriend. As I got older, I discovered my own poetic voice, and I cannot begin to place a value on the amount of inspiration I got from this musical movement and the culture it birthed. I am a child of the hip hop generation, grounded in the understanding that we enter the world from a hip hop paradigm.

Those of us who embrace feminism can't act like hip hop hasn't been an influence on our lives, or vice versa, simply because claiming them both might seem to pose a contradiction. They are two of the basic things that mold us. However, we must not confuse having love for either one with blind defense. We have to love them enough to critique both of them and challenge them to grow—beyond the materialism and misogyny that has come to characterize too much of hip hop, beyond the extremism that feminism sometimes engages in. As women of the hip hop generation we need a feminist consciousness that allows us to examine how representations and images can be simultaneously empowering and problematic.

We have to engage with the rap lyrics about women and the accompanying images found in video scenes. A friend, Adziko Simba, once told me, "It seems bizarre to me that we African women have reached such an 'enlightened' point that we are defending our right to portray ourselves in ways that contribute to our degradation. . . . Did Sojourner Truth walk all those miles and bear her breast in the name of equality so that her heirs could have the right to jiggle their breasts on BET?" I completely feel her, though I don't think the role of feminism is to construct "proper" femininity, or to place limits on how women are able to define and present themselves. I think doing so is actually antithetical to the movement. Teaching women not to be sensual and erotic beings, or not to show that we are, is diminishing and subverts the locus of our own uniqueness as females. Why shouldn't we be able to celebrate our beauty, sensuality, sexuality, creative ability or our eroticism? They are all unique sites of women's power that we should not be taught to hide, or only display when someone else says it's appropriate. On the flip side we shouldn't support each other to the point of stupidity. We have to demand accountability from each other, no doubt. We need to be cognizant of the power in this music and of how we are representing ourselves on a global scale and on the historical record. These examples demonstrate how wide open the field is for sisters of the hip hop generation to address the constantly shifting space women occupy. But these areas of concern should not be solely relegated to the Black feminist body of work. Hip hop activists, intellectuals and artists all need to take a leading role in confronting the fragmenting issues our generation deals with.

So, yeah, I used to think I had missed my time. I thought the flame lighting the hearts of activists had been snuffed, *Survivor*-style. But liberating my definitions of activism from the constraints and constructs of the sixties opened up my mind to a whole new world of work and progressive thought. Now I draw strength from the knowledge that people have been actively combating sexism, racism and other intersecting discriminations for a long time. Many of those icons I respect are still on the scene actively doing their thing for us. That knowledge is my ammunition as I join with them and my peers to continue fighting those battles and the other fronts unique to our time. We can't get complacent. The most important thing we can do as a generation is to see our new positions as power and weapons to be used strategically in the struggle rather than as spoils of war. Because this shit is far from finished.

Suggested Readings for Part IV

Brandt, Eric, ed. 1999. *Dangerous Liaisons: Blacks, Gays, and the Struggle for Equality.* New York: The New Press.

Bullard, Robert D. 1994. *Unequal Protection: Environmental Justice and Communities of Color.* San Francisco: Sierra Club Books.

Espiritu, Yen Le. 1992. *Asian-American Pan-Ethnicity: Bridging Institutions and Identities.* Philadelphia: Temple University Press.

Freeman, Jo, and Victoria Johnson. 1999. *Waves of Protest: Social Movements Since the Sixties.* Totowa, NJ: Rowman & Littlefield.

Hernández, Daisy, and Bushra Rehman, eds. 2002. *Colonize This! Young Women of Color on Today's Feminism.* New York: Seal Press.

Torres, Andrés, and José E. Velázquez, eds. 1998. *The Puerto Rican Movement: Voices from the Diaspora.* Philadelphia: Temple University Press.

 ### *InfoTrac College Edition: Search Terms*

Use your access to the online library, InfoTrac College Edition, to learn more about some of the subjects covered in this section. The following are some suggested terms for searches:

Black power movement
Civil Rights Movement
environmental racism
feminist movement
grassroots organizations
La Raza
liberation theology
National Welfare Rights Organization (NWRO)

 ### *InfoTrac College Edition: Bonus Reading*

You can use the InfoTrac College Edition feature to find an additional reading pertinent to this section and can also search on the author's name or keywords to locate the following reading:

Featherstone, Liza. 2000. "The Student Movement Comes of Age." *The Nation* (October 16): 23.

Liza Featherstone reports that contemporary student movements have managed to achieve an impressive measure of power on college campuses. Students have organized to protest the sweatshop labor conditions that are used to produce their college sweatshirts, t-shirts, and other college insignia. More attuned to issues of social justice, student movements have generated changes on many college campuses. Featherstone also raises the important question of how students might use this newfound power. How will students connect multiple movements, such as those against unfair labor practices, those for women's rights, and those for economic and racial justice? How might a race, class, and gender framework inform the work of contemporary student movements?

Companion Website

For additional links, quizzes, and learning tools related to this part, see the book's companion website, at **http://sociology.wadsworth.com/andersen _hill_collins6e.**

INDEX

Page references followed by "n" refer to notes.

Abortion, 435–36, 451, 544
Abuse, disabilities and, 187.
    See also domestic
    violence
Activism
    basic tactics, 552–53
    community organizations,
        539–42
    gay liberation, 234–37
    health services in
        reservation
        communities, 543–47
    hip hop feminists, 557–64
    history of, 547–50
    organizing the new urban
        working class, 536–39
    subjective dimension of,
        512–513
    Whites as allies to people
        of color, 550–57
    See also social change
ADAPT, 430
Additive model, 8–9
Advertising, sexuality and,
    228–33. *See also* media
Affirmative action, 93, 113,
    131, 374
African Americans
    Civil Rights Movement, 36
    definition of, 114
    as domestic workers,
        314, 315
    families in slavery, 324–27
    homelessness among, 78
    home ownership and,
        127–29
    homosexuality and,
        235, 251
    Hurricane Katrina
        and, 2–3
    interracial marriages of,
        249, 335–43
    at Jamestown, 33, 35

Koreans and, 196
Latinos and, 196
men
    lynching of, 280, 468–70
    rape by, 468–72
    sexuality of, 250–51
    soft skills in
        employment, 296–302
    sports and, 178–81
    stereotypes of, 81
    middle-class, 75, 132–33,
        136–43, 559
    in military service, 462–65
    passive tense and, 369–70
    poverty and, 75–76, 107,
        304, 417
    race relations at colleges,
        202–5
    in the racial hierarchy,
        215–17
    rape and, 468–72
    reproductive health,
        439–40
    residential segregation, 93,
        107, 137, 139
    school desegregation, 69,
        406–7, 530–34
    sexuality, 87, 247–52
    slavery of. *See* slavery
    sports and, 63–66, 172
    stereotypes of, 81, 247
    wealth gap and, 128–29,
        131–33
    women
        feminism and, 562–63
        imprisonment of, 453–54
        power and, 55–57
        rape of, 472–74
        sexuality of, 251–52
        sports and, 180
        at Starbucks, 191
        stereotypes of, 81
        violence against, 57–58

working-class activists,
    517–19
Africans, "loaded" words and,
    372–74
Agassiz, Louis, 284
Age, poverty and, 308–9
"Age, Race, Class, and Sex"
    (Lorde), 52–59
Ageism, unacknowledged, 54
Aggregate data, limitations
    of, 75
AIDS (acquired immune
    deficiency syndrome)
    church ministries and,
        524, 529
    education programs, 546
    globalization of sex work
        and, 244–45
    in Native Americans,
        436, 546
"Aid to Dependent Corpora-
    tions" (Collins),
    422–26
Aid to Families with Depen-
    dent Children, 311
Alba, Richard, 200
Álvarez, Julia, 80–81, 166–71
AMAS (Association for
    Women in
    Solidarity), 245
AMBAR (Venezuelan Associ-
    ation of Women for
    Welfare and Mutual
    Support), 245
AMEPU, 245
An American Dilemma
    (Myrdal), 131, 406
American Indians. *See* Native
    Americans
American Indian Self-
    Determination and
    Education Assistance
    Act of 1975, 447

American Manhood (Rotundo), 507–8
Americanness
  English language and, 18–19
  national identity, 84–85
  race and, 33, 85, 190–98
Amott, Teresa, 283–92
Andersen, Margaret L., 1–16, 61–90, 267–82, 481–92
Angela Lina (APRODEM), 245
Arab Americans, group identity of, 82
ARAMCO, tax breaks to, 423–24
Asch, A., 187–88
Asetoyer, Charon, 489, 543–47
Asian Americans
  as domestic workers, 314
  language stereotypes, 374–75
  as model minority, 110
  oppression of, 36
  panethnic identity of, 82–83
  poverty in, 75–76
  reproductive health, 437–38
  stereotypes of, 81, 156–57, 159–64
  as White, 109
  Yellow Peril and, 157–58
  See also under names of countries of origin
Asian/Pacific Islanders (A/PIs), 437–38. *See also* Asian Americans
Association for the Rights of Women, 245
Association for Women in Solidarity (AMAS), 245
Association of Women (Cormujer), 245
Athletic careers, 172–84
  gender identities and, 82
  men from higher-status backgrounds, 175–78
  men from lower-status backgrounds, 178–81
  race and, 63–66, 172–73
  See also sports
Attitude, employment and, 295
Audit studies, 69
Avery, Robert, 131

Baca Zinn, Maxine, 80, 147–56, 180
Balcazar, Fabricio E., 426–32
Bank loans, 103–5

Barkley, Charles, 400
Bartlett, Donald, 423
Basketball, 398–403
Baumgardner, Jennifer, 490, 547–50
Beauvoir, Simone De, 149
Beijing Platform for Action, 413–14, 420
Bell, Derrick, 486, 530–34
Bhagat families, 207–8, 210–11, 213–14
BIA (Bureau of Indian Affairs), 447
Bingham, Hiram, 48
Birdcage analogy, 31–32
Birth control, 548
"Black Picket Fences" (Pattillo-McCoy), 136–43
Blacks. *See* African Americans
"Black Sexuality" (West), 247–52
Black-White framework, 106–11
Blassingame, John, 326
Blauner, Robert, 203
Block, Pamela, 426–32
Blue-collar workers. *See* workers; working class
Blumenbach, Johann, 70
Body image
  media and, 228–33
  racism and, 248–49, 251
Bonilla-Silva, Eduardo, 68, 91–97
Bookman, Ann, 513
Bradley, Bill, 399
"Broken Levees, Unbroken Barriers" (De Parle), 143–46
Brown, Kenneth W., 292–93
Brownlee, Sarah L., 433–41
Brown v. Board of Education, 486, 530–34
BRU (Bus Riders Union), 540–42
Bureau of Indian Affairs (BIA), 447
Burgest, David R., 368
Burnham, Linda, 278, 413–22
Bus Riders Union (BRU), 540–42

Camarillo, Albert, 36, 330
Canada, immigrant domestic workers in, 318
"Can Education Eliminate Race, Class, and Gender Inequality?" (Mickelson and Smith), 404–13
"Can I Get a Witness?" (Jamila), 557–64

Capitalism
  class relations in, 6–7, 268–69, 289–91
  gays and lesbians and, 234–35
  income equality and, 409–10
  race and, 6–7
Captain Scarlet, 367–68
Carter, Robert L., 530
Caucasian, origin of term, 70. *See also* White Americans
Cervical cancer, 436
Change. *See* social change
"Chappals and Gym Shorts" (Sayeed), 358–64
Charitable giving, by income, 386n
Checkerboarding, 445
Cherokee removal, 444
Chicanos/Chicanas
  discrimination against, 69
  families of, 329–22
  immigration of, 36–37
  oppression of, 22–29
  reproductive labor, 329–32
  See also Hispanics; Latinos/Latinas; Mexican Americans
Children
  class and care of, 286, 348–58
  concerted cultivation *vs.* accomplishment of natural growth, 349–50, 356
  godparents of, 331-32
  homelessness among, 78
  individualism and, 353–54
  middle-class, 348–49
  Native American, 381
  in poverty, 76, 78
  in slavery, 324–27
  working-class, 310–12, 349–50
Childs, Erica Chito, 273, 335–43
Chin, Frank, 159–60
Chinese Americans
  discrimination against, 69
  immigration of, 36, 37, 39, 328–29
  sojourners, 328–29
  in the Yellow Peril, 157–58
  See also Asian Americans
Chinese Exclusion Act of 1882, 36
Churchill, Ward, 275, 376–83
Cintas, 496
Cisneros, Sandra, 41

Citizens' Clearinghouse
for Hazardous
Wastes, 515
Civil Rights Act of 1964, 315
Civil Rights Movement,
36, 277
Class, 71–79
capitalism and, 6–7,
268–69, 289–91
as culture, 119–21
gender and, 66–67,
286–87
as generational, 121
governing, 391–92
Hurricane Katrina and,
143–46
importance of, 354–55
inclusive thinking on,
12–16
income and, 72–73, 79
increasing divisions in, 78,
116–18
influence on experiences of
all, 4
job types and, 123, 124–25
limits of, 355
mass media on, 384–92
in matrix of domination,
5–7, 62
military service and,
459–67
myth of classless society,
78, 119
parenting methods and,
286, 348–58
power and, 77–78
race and, 75, 288–89
safety and, 476–77
stereotypes of, 81–82,
385–87
toxic waste disposal and,
514–22
unacknowledged
differences in, 54
warrior, 460
wealth and, 74–75, 128–31
Classism, ways to challenge,
125–27
Cloning, 455
Coalition building, 491
Cofer, Judith Ortiz, 393–97
Colleges
affirmative action and, 93
Black women's, 560–61
hiring in, 21
race relations in, 202–5
sports in, 63–66
Title IX and, 408
Collier, John, 445–46
Collins, Chuck, 278,
422–26
Collins, Patricia Hill, 1–6,
61–90, 267–82,
481–92

Colonialism, 107
Color-blind racism, 92–97
Color symbolism, 366–68
Combahee River Collective
Statement of 1977, 102
Committee on Women,
Population, and the
Environment
(CWPE), 457
Community organizations,
539–42
Compadrazgo system, 331–32
Comparative thinking,
limitations of, 8–9
Comstock, Gary David,
522–29
Connell, R. W., 151, 173,
178, 182–83
Contraception, 548
Cook, Blanche Wiesen, 344
"Cool pose," 180–81, 182
Corporations, government
aid to, 422–26
Correspondence
principle, 411
Credential inflation, 410–11
Creek nation, removal of, 444
"Crimes Against Humanity"
(Churchill), 376–83
Criminal justice system,
452–54
"Culturally deprived," 370
Cultural pluralism, 11
Culture
assimilation of Native
Americans, 444–45
bridging the gap, 358–64
class as, 119–21
iconography of, 232
language and, 365–66
media and, 275–77
parenting methods and,
351–53
of poverty, 428–30
CWPE (Committee
on Women,
Population, and the
Environment), 457

Davis, Angela, 325
Daws, Gavan, 48
Dear Abby letters, 201, 205
*The Declining Significance of
Race* (Wilson),
140–41
Dell, Floyd, 258
Deloria, Vine, 38
D'Emilio, John, 261
DeMott, Benjamin, 387–88
De Parle, Jason, 143–46
Diallo, Dazon Dixon,
433–41
Dibble, Sheldon, 48
Difference model, 7–12

"A Different Mirror"
(Takaki), 32–44
Dill, Bonnie Thornton,
272–73, 321–35
Disability
gender and, 82, 185–89
minority group model *vs.*
empowerment
framework, 429–31
race, poverty and, 426–32
statistics on, 185
Discrimination
of job applicants, 69
residential segregation, 93,
107, 137, 139
school segregation, 69,
406–7, 530–34
See also racism
Diversity
in difference model, 8–12
inclusive thinking on,
12–16
mythical norm and, 54
as voice, 9–10
Diversity workshops,
499–511
costs of disclosure
in, 510n
discussions after, 509–10
senior White male
discourses prior to,
500–502
workshop experiences,
502–6
"Doméstica" (Hondagneu-
Sotelo), 312–20
Domestic violence, 274,
280, 544
Domestic work, 312–20
global trends in, 317–19
immigration and, 316–17
poverty and, 305
recruiting for, 318–19
regional racialization of,
313–16
undocumented, 313
Domhoff, William, 391
Dominance bonding, 177
Dominicans
immigration of, 209–14
poverty among, 307–9
Double jeopardy, 8–9
Douglass, Frederick, 39
Draft, military, 460–62,
465–67
Dragon Lady stereotype, 156,
161–62
Drug treatment, imprison-
ment and, 454, 455
Dual citizenship, 212–14
Dualism, 111
Du Bois, W. E. B.,
131, 216
Dunkle, M., 180

Economy
  gays and lesbians and, 235
  global transformations in,
    271–72
  immigration and,
    191–92, 194
  as social institution, 268
  See also globalization
Education
  academic positions, 21
  class and, 120, 122–23
  credential inflation,
    410–11
  educational attainment of
    groups, 269, 408–10
  equalizing role of, 404–13
  fast food employment and,
    309–10
  gender inequalities in,
    408, 410
  hidden curriculum, 411–12
  inequalities in, 277–78
  of Native Americans,
    444–45
  otherness in, 18, 25–26
  parent-teacher
    conferences, 358
  persistence of inequality in,
    410–12
  policing schools, 454
  school desegregation, 69,
    406–7, 530–34
  Title IX and, 407–8
Ehrenreich, Barbara, 129–30
Ellison, Ralph, 19
Emotional labor, 294
Employees. *See* workers
Engelhardt, Tom, 161
English language, American-
  ness and, 18–19
Environmental activism, 485,
  511–22
Espiritu, Yen Le, 81, 156–65
Essentialism, 149
Ethnicity, 82–86
  immigration and, 83–86
  panethnic identities, 82–83
  as social phenomenon, 199
  symbolic, 85, 199–207
  See also race
Eugenics, 278, 427–28
European-Americans, 197.
  See also White
  Americans

Fair Housing Act, 103–5
Families
  of Chicanos, 329–22
  diversity among, 272–73
  of early Chinese
    immigrants, 328–29
  of gays and lesbians, 273,
    343–48
  godparents, 331–32

  headed by single mothers,
    305–6, 417
  housing shelters and, 415
  increasing hardship on,
    414–16
  interracial marriages and,
    338–39
  kinship networks,
    222–27, 327
  of low-wage earners,
    310–12
  "modern American," 322
  reproductive labor, 321–35
  sexual division of labor and
    class in, 290
  in slavery, 324–27
  as social institution, 272
  See also children
Fanon, Frantz, 46
Farmer, Paul, 244
Farnham, Marynia, 259
Farr, K. A., 177
FAS (Fetal Alcohol Syn-
  drome), 543–44
Fast food industry jobs, 307
Feagin, Joe, 68
Fellner, Kim, 484, 493–99
Female circumcision, 57
Female gender identity,
  disability and, 185–89
The Feminist Memoir Project
  (Blau du Plessis and
  Snitow), 548
Feminist movement
  activism and, 547–50
  African-American women,
    562–63
  middle-class White
    women, 124
  Muslim women, 358–64
  on subjective dimension,
    512–13
Ferber, Abby L., 70, 111–15
Fetal Alcohol Syndrome
  (FAS), 543–44
Film. *See* media
Financial risk, race and,
  103–5
Fine, M., 187–88
"The First Americans"
  (Snipp), 442–49
Fitzgerald, Frances, 344
Food insecurity, 415–16
Food Stamp Program, 416, 419
Foucault, Michel, 452
Franklin, Benjamin, 108
Franklin, C. W., II, 180
Freedman, Estelle, 261
Freire, Paulo, 59
Fried, Morton, 372
"From a Native Daughter"
  (Trask), 45–52
"From the Ground Up"
  (Asetoyer), 543–47

Frye, Marilyn, 15–16,
  29–32
Fuentes, Carlos, 41–42

Galarza, Ernesto, 36
Gandhi, Mohandas, 549
Gangs, Mexican, 218
Gans, Herbert, 199, 304
Garza, Jesus, 36
Gays
  class and, 234–35
  families and, 273, 343–48
  gay liberation movement,
    234–37
  race and, 235–37, 251
  sports and, 182
  See also homosexuality
Gender, 80–82
  abuse and, 187
  basketball and, 399–403
  capitalism and, 6–7
  class and, 66–67, 286–87
  diversity workshops,
    499–511
  homophobia and, 87
  immigration and, 86,
    221–27
  in inclusive thinking,
    12–16
  income and, 72–73, 269
  influence on experiences of
    all, 4
  in international contexts,
    151–52
  labor market class
    hierarchy and, 291–92
  low-wage work and, 310
  in matrix of domination,
    5–7, 62
  oppression and, 29–32
  poverty and, 76, 305
  "prism of difference,"
    147–48, 153–54
  racism and, 26–28
  relational character of,
    153–54
  sexual division of labor,
    285–86
  as social construction,
    80–81, 150–51, 285
  sports and, 65, 82, 407–8
  Title IX, 407–8
  in Vietnamese families,
    221–27
Gender anxiety, 257
Gendered institution, 80
Gender identity
  disability and, 185–89
  sports and, 174–81
Gender order, 173, 182
Gender passing, 286
General Allotment Act of
  1887, 445
Genocide, 379–83, 435

Gerschick, Thomas, 82, 185–89
Gibbs, Lois, 516–17
GI Bill of Rights of 1944, 113
Gide, André, 258
"Gladiators, Gazelles, and Groupies" (Malveaux), 398–403
Glazer, Nathan, 38
Globalization
 gender relations and, 151–52
 increased immigration and, 316
 migrant labor and, 83–84
 Starbucks and, 498
 transnational sex work, 243–45
"Globalizing Sex Workers' Rights" (Kempadoo), 238–46
Gluckman, Amy, 234–37
Gobineau, Arthur de, 284
Godparents, 331–32
Governing class, 391–92
Government
 aid to corporations, 422–26
 criminal justice system, 452–54
 as guarantor of equality, 532–33
 policing policies, 279, 450–58
 response to Hurricane Katrina, 2–4, 76, 143–46
 social change and, 485–86
 social policies of, 277–78
 violence and, 279–81
Greenfield, Thomas, 369–70
Green Scissors coalition, 425
Griswold del Castillo, Richard, 330–31
Griswold v. Connecticut, 548
"Growing Gulf Between Rich and Rest of Us" (Sklar), 116–18
Gruneau, R., 173
La Güera (Moraga), 14, 22–29
Guinier, Lani, 337
Gujarati immigrants, 207–8, 210–11, 213–14
Gutman, Herbert, 325

Hagan, William, 444
Halbfinger, David, 281, 459–67
Hallinan, Joseph, 453
Hanisch, Carol, 548
Hannaford, Susan, 187
Hare, J., 173

Hare, N., 173
Harlem, working poor in, 306–12
Hartouni, Valerie, 455
Hass, Robert, 232
Hawaiian Americans, 45–52
Health care
 abortion, 435–36, 451, 544
 Native American, 543–47
 reproductive health, 433–41
Hearst, William Randolph, 158
Hegemonic masculinity, 151, 163, 173
Herring, Dania, 538
Heterosexism, 87, 229
Heterosexuality, 252–64
 early definitions of, 255–57
 early Victorian True Love, 253–54
 Heterosexual Mystique, 257–58
 history of, 260–62
 impact of homophobia on, 86–87
 late Victorian Sex-Love, 254–55
 postwar hegemony of, 259–60
 use of heterosexuality/ homosexuality duo, 258
"The Hidden Cost of Being African American" (Shapiro), 127–35
Hijab, 360
Hip hop movement, 558, 562–63
Hirata, Lucie Cheng, 328
Hispanics
 in Los Angeles, 34
 in military service, 464
 in New Mexico, 19–20
 poverty in, 75–76
 reproductive health, 438–39
 See also Chicanos/Chicanas; Latinos/Latinas
The History of Doing (Kumar), 457n
Hochschild, Jennifer, 405
Holmes, Steven, 281, 459–67
Homelessness, 415, 418
Homeownership, 127–29
Homophobia, 86–87, 234–37
Homosexuality
 in Asian American stereotypes, 160
 beginning of use of term, 256
 Kinsey and, 259–60

 as negation of masculinity, 154
 See also gays; lesbians
Hondagneu-Sotelo, Pierrette, 80, 147–56, 271–72, 312–20
Hong Kong, immigrant domestic workers in, 318
Household work. *See* domestic work
Housing needs, 414–15
Housing segregation, 93, 107, 137, 139
"How Safe Is America?" (Taylor), 475–78
"How the New Working Class Can Transform Urban America" (Kelley), 535–42

Identity politics, 430
"Ideological Racism and Cultural Resistance" (Espiritu), 156–65
Ideology, application of, 96
IHS (Indian Health Service), 436–37, 544
Immigrant analogy, 215–17
Immigration, 36–40
 of Chinese, 36, 37, 39, 328–29
 of Dominicans, 209–14
 ethnicity and, 83–86
 gender and, 152, 220–27
 for global domestic work, 317–19
 of Gujaratis, 207–14
 of Hispanics, 36–37, 168–71
 imprisonment and, 456
 of Irish, 37, 38–39
 literacy and, 419
 of Mexicans, 85, 214–20
 poverty and, 75, 417
 remittances and, 209–10
 sojourning pattern, 328–29
 transnational migration, 211–14
 undocumented workers, 313, 316–17, 536–37
 of Vietnamese, 220–27
 vigilante groups to patrol borders, 456
 welfare system and, 417–20
 White America and, 190–98
 xenophobia and, 316
Immigration Reform Act and Individual Responsibility Act of 1996 (IRAIRA), 316
Immigration Reform and Control Act of 1986, 536

Inclusive thinking, 12–16
Income, 71–79
    capitalism and, 409–10
    changes in distribution of,
        116–18, 413n
    definition of, 72
    by educational attainment,
        269, 409–10
    by gender, 73, 76–77, 269
    by household type, 76–77
    median, 72, 117
    minimum wage jobs,
        305, 477
    people with disabilities
        and, 188
    by race, 72–79, 269
    safety and, 476–77
    wealth compared with,
        74–75, 132–33
    See also poverty
Indian Americans
    Gujarati immigrants,
        207–8, 210–11,
        213–14
    Muslim women, 358–64
Indian Claims Commis-
    sion, 446
Indian Health Service (IHS),
    436–37, 544
Indian New Deal, 445–46
Indian Removal Act of
    1830, 443
Indian Reorganization Act of
    1934, 446
Indians. See Native Americans
"The Indignities of Unem-
    ployment" (Brown),
    292–93
Individualism, children and,
    353–54
Inherited wealth, 128–31
Interaction skills, 294–98
Interracial marriage, 335–43
    of African Americans and
        Whites, 249, 335–43
    of Asian Americans and
        Whites, 157–58, 163
    family responses to,
        338–43
    of Jews with others, 115
    as a miner's canary, 336–37
"Interrupting Historical
    Patterns" (Zane),
    499–511
"The Invention of Heterosex-
    uality" (Katz), 252–64
"The Invisible Poor"
    (Newman), 303–12
IRAIRA (Immigration
    Reform Act and Indi-
    vidual Responsibility
    Act of 1996), 316
Irish Americans, 37, 38–39,
    191, 216

"Is This a White Country, or
    What?" (Rubin),
    190–98

Jackson, Andrew, 38
Jackson, Robert, 380
Jacobs, Harriet, 41
Jamestown colony, African
    Americans at, 33, 35
Jamila, Shani, 491, 557–64
Jamison, Kay Redfield, 187
Japanese Americans
    farm laborers, 39
    immigration of, 39–40
    internment of, 36, 158
    in the Yellow Peril, 158
    See also Asian Americans
JAPs (Jewish American
    princesses), 81
Jencks, Christopher, 144
Jews
    interracial marriage, 115
    labor strikes, 39
    as race, 70
    stereotypes of, 81
    in U.S. history, 37–38, 40
    White Supremacists on,
        111–15
Jhally, Sut, 232
Johnson, Magic, 400
Jones, Jacqueline, 327
Jordan, Michael, 400
"Just Choices" (Ross et al.),
    433–41
Justice for Janitors, 537–39

Karnow, Stanley, 462
Katrina, Hurricane, 2–4, 76,
    143–46
Katz, Jonathan Ned, 87,
    252–64
Katzman, David M., 313
Kelley, Robin D. G., 489,
    535–42
Kempadoo, Kamala, 88,
    238–46
Kepelino, 45
Kessler-Harris, Alice, 322
Keys, Christopher B., 426–32
Kibria, Nazli, 86, 220–27
Kilbourne, Jean, 86, 228–33
Killing the Black Body
    (Roberts), 454
Kim, Elaine, 162
Kinder, Donald, 95
King, Martin Luther, Jr., 36,
    237, 542
King, Rodney, 34
Kingston, Maxine Hong, 26
Kinsey, Alfred, 259–60
Kinship networks
    among African-American
        slaves, 327

    among Chicano families,
        331–32
    among gays and lesbians,
        347–48
    among Vietnamese
        immigrants, 222–27
    See also families
Kivel, Paul, 491, 550–57
Knowledge, importance of
    reconstructing, 4–5
Kochifos, Vic, 345
Korean Americans
    African Americans and, 196
    at college, 203–4
    in Rodney King riot, 34–35
    See also Asian Americans
Korkowski, Bob, 345
Krafft-Ebing, R. von, 256
Krauss, Celene, 484–85,
    511–22
Kristol, Irving, 38
Kumar, Radha, 457n
Kuykendall, Ralph, 48

Labor/Community Strategy
    Center, 539–42
Laborers. See workers
LaFeber, Walter, 400
Laissez-faire racism, 95–96
Land ownership, in Hawai'i,
    46–48
Langston, Donna, 118–27
Language
    Americanness and, 18–19
    "black" and "white," 366
    in churches, 526
    immigrants and, 419
    passive tense, 369–70
    politics and, 370–71
    racist stereotyping in,
        365–76
    Spanish, 331
Lareau, Annette, 273–74,
    348–58
Latinos/Latinas
    African Americans and, 196
    domestic work by, 316–17
    immigration of, 168–71
    invisibility of, 110
    reproductive health, 438–39
    school segregation of, 407
    stereotypes of, 81, 393–97
    See also Chicanos/Chicanas;
        Hispanics
Law enforcement policies,
    450–58
    criminal justice system,
        452–54
    against pregnant women,
        454, 455, 458n
    reproductive rights,
        451–52
    surveillance systems,
        455–56

Lemlich, Clara, 39
Lesbians
    class and, 234–35
    families and, 273, 343–48
    oppression of, 24
    race and, 57–58,
        235–37, 251
    working class, 123
    See also homosexuality
Levinson, D. J., 173, 175
Levitt, Peggy, 85–86,
    207–14
Life expectancy, 382
Literacy, 419
Lorde, Audre, 16, 27, 52–59
Los Angeles County
    Metropolitan Transit
    Authority (MTA),
    540–42
Lotus Blossom stereotype,
    161–62
Lower-status classes. *See*
    working class
Lundberg, Ferdinand, 259
Lynchings, 280, 468–70

Madrid, Arturo, 13, 17–22
Mahila Samanwaya
    Committee, 245
Majors, R., 180–81, 182
Male identity. *See* masculinity
Malveaux, Julianne, 276,
    398–403
"Manifesta" (Baumgardner
    and Richards),
    547–50
Mantsios, Gregory, 276,
    384–92
Margolis, Bernie, 345
Marriages, of Indian immi-
    grants, 358–64.
    See also interracial
    marriage
Martinets, Luz Alveolus, 545
Martinez, Elizabeth, 71,
    105–11
"Masculinities and Athletic
    Careers" (Messner),
    172–84
Masculinity, 172–84
    Asian American men,
        159–61, 163–64
    disability and, 185–89
    domination of women
        and, 178
    hegemonic, 151, 163, 173
    higher-status backgrounds
        and, 175–78
    homosexuality as negation
        of, 154
    lower-status backgrounds
        and, 178–81
    social construction of,
        150–51, 154

sports and, 172–84
wives as homemakers
    and, 322
Mass media. *See* media
Matrix of domination
    model, 5–12
Matsui, Robert, 36
Matthaei, Julie, 283–92,
    322–23, 325
Maxi Linder Association, 245
McCaffrey, Lawrence J., 37
McIntosh, Peggy, 68,
    98–102
Means, Russell, 377
Media
    Asian American stereotypes
        in, 160–63
    body image and, 228–33
    on class, 384–92
    color symbolism in,
        367–68
    culture and, 275–77
    newscasters, 163
    westerns, 383
"Media Magic" (Mantsios),
    384–92
Median income, 72, 117. *See
    also* income
Medicare payments, 425
Men
    African American. *See*
        African Americans,
        men
    Asian American, 159–61,
        163–64
    loss of power with
        immigration, 221–22
    as sex workers, 240
    social construction of
        masculinity, 150–51
    stereotypes of, 81
    unemployment responses
        by, 292–93
    See also masculinity
Meritocracy, 501–2, 507, 509
Messner, Michael, 80, 82,
    147–56, 172–84
Metropolitan Interdenomina-
    tional Church,
    Nashville, 489,
    522–29
Mexican Americans
    discrimination against, 69
    as domestic workers, 314–15
    as farm laborers, 39
    gangs, 218
    immigration of, 36–37,
        40, 85
    in military service, 464–65
    in New York, 214–20
    numbers of, 215
    in racial hierarchy, 216–17
    reproductive health,
        438–39

treaty of Guadalupe
    Hidalgo and, 329
as White, 109
See also Chicanos/Chicanas;
    Hispanics;
    Latinos/Latinas
"'Mexicanness' in New York"
    (Smith), 214–20
Mickelson, Roslyn Arlin,
    404–13
Middle class
    Black, 75, 132–33,
        136–43, 559
    children, 348–58
    declining, 66
    feminism, 124
    mass media and, 389–90
    race and, 66
"Migration and Vietnamese
    American Women"
    (Kibria), 220–27
"Military Mirrors a Working-
    Class America"
    (Halbfinger and
    Holmes), 459–67
Military service
    class and, 280–81, 459–67
    draft *vs.* warrior caste,
        465–67
    by members of Congress,
        466–67
    race and, 464–65
    recruiting offices, 463–64
Miller, Minnie, 41
Minnich, Elizabeth, 99
Miraflores, Dominican Re-
    public, 209–10
"Missing People and Others"
    (Madrid), 13, 17–22
Missing persons phenome-
    non, 19–20
Mixed marriage. *See* interra-
    cial marriage
MODEMU (Movement of
    United Women), 245
Mohanty, Chandra, 152
Moore, Robert B., 275,
    365–76
Moraga, Cherríe, 14, 22–29
Morrison, Toni, 33
Moss, Philip, 294–303
Motherhood, environmental
    activism and, 514–16
Motivation, in employment,
    294–95, 298–99
Movement of United Women
    (MODEMU), 245
MTA (Los Angeles Country
    Metropolitan Transit
    Authority), 540–42
Multiculturalism, in differ-
    ence model, 8, 11
Murphy, Robert, 186
Myrdal, Gunnar, 131, 406

Mythical norm, 54
"The Myth of the Latin
    Woman" (Cofer),
    393–97

NARAL, 434
National identity, 84–85
National Network of
    Prostitutes, 245
National Women's Health
    Network, 545
Native Americans
    assimilation of, 444–45
    discrimination against, 69
    gender roles of, 286
    genocide of, 379–83
    government policies and,
        279, 380–83, 442–49
    health care, 436–37,
        543–47, 544
    Indian New Deal, 445–46
    "loaded" words and,
        371–72
    negative symbolism of,
        275–76
    removal of, 443–44
    reproductive health,
        436–37
    self-determination, 447
    sports team names,
        376–79, 556–57
    termination and relocation
        of, 446–47
    "tribes" concept, 372
    urban, 448–49
    in U.S. history, 38, 380,
        442–49
    women activists, 519–21
Native Women's Reproduc-
    tive Rights Coalition,
    489–90, 546–47
Naturalization Law of
    1790, 37
"Navigating Interracial
    Borders" (Childs),
    335–43
Network of Sex Work
    Projects, 245
Newman, Katherine, 272,
    303–12
Newscasters, Asian
    American, 163
Nez Perce, 444
Nickel and Dimed
    (Ehrenreich), 129–30
Nuremberg proceedings,
    Native Americans and,
    379–83
Nurturant social skills, 294

Objectivity, 15–16
"Of Race and Risk"
    (Williams), 103–5
Ogbu, John, 204

"Okay," origin of, 40
Oklahoma bombing, 236
Oliver, Melvin, 74
Omi, Michael, 70, 288
Oppositional identities, 204
Oppression
    of Asian Americans, 36,
        157–58
    birdcage analogy of,
        31–32
    of Chicanos/Chicanas,
        22–29
    of Chinese Americans, 36,
        37, 39, 328–29
    of gays and lesbians, 24,
        235–37
    gender and, 29–32
    meaning of, 29–30
    of Native Americans, 279,
        380–83, 442–49
    otherness and, 25
    sexuality and, 86
    slavery. *See* slavery
    of workers, 108, 280
    See also discrimination;
        racism
"Oppression" (Frye), 29–32
"Optional Ethnicities"
    (Waters), 198–207
Otherness, 18–22, 390
"Our Mother's Grief" (Dill),
    321–35

Pacific Islander Americans,
    45–52, 437–38
"Pagan" religions, 373
Paltrow, Lynn, 453–54
Panethnic identity, 82–83
Paper sons, 328
Parenti, Michael, 389
Parent-teacher confer-
    ences, 358
Parkhurst, Charles, 257
Parks, Rosa, 548
Passing
    gender, 286
    racial, 171, 199
Pattillo-McCoy, Mary, 75,
    136–43
Personal appearances and
    customs, 204–5
Personal narrative, 15–16
Personal Responsibility and
    Work Opportunities
    Reconciliation Act
    (PRWORA), 414–20
Phillips, Kevin, 130
Planned Parenthood, 434
Pleck, J. H., 177
Poetry, class and, 54
Policing. *See* law enforce-
    ment policies
"Policing the National Body"
    (Silliman), 450–58

Politics, language and,
    370–71
Portes, Alejandro, 211
Poverty
    age and, 308–9
    disability and, 426–32
    federal poverty line, 76–77
    gender and, 76
    in Harlem, 306–12
    immigration and, 75, 417
    increases in, 2, 6, 67,
        116–18
    individual merit
        explanation for,
        118–19
    as lack of culture, 428–29
    media on, 385–87
    minority group model *vs.*
        empowerment
        framework, 429–31
    race and, 75–76, 107,
        304, 417
    redistribution of wealth,
        66, 116–18
    safety and, 477–78
    in single-parent families,
        305–6
    of transnationals, 213
    working poor, 76–77, 272,
        304–5
    in the young, 305
Poverty line, 76–77
Power
    class system and, 77–78
    definition of, 77
    ethnicity and, 82
    in matrix of domination
        model, 10–11
    unearned, 101
    women and race and,
        55–56
Prejudice, definition of, 67.
    See also racism
"Prism of difference,"
    147–48, 153–54
Prisons
    immigrants in, 456
    overcrowding in, 452
    pregnant women in, 454,
        455, 458n
    profit from, 453
    rate of imprisonment, 67
    recidivism and, 452
Pronger, B., 182
Proposition 187
    (California), 316
Prostitutes. *See* sex work
PRWORA (Personal Respon-
    sibility and Work
    Opportunities
    Reconciliation Act),
    414–20
Puerto Ricans
    poverty among, 307–8

in the racial hierarchy,
215–17
stereotypes of women,
393–97
Putative dominant ideology,
412n

Race, 67–71
Americanness and, 33,
190–98
capitalism and, 6–7
class and, 75, 288–89
classifications of, 70–71,
109, 114, 284
disability and, 426–32
diversity workshops,
499–511
domestic work and,
312–17
educational attainment by,
269, 408–10
eugenics, 427–28
within families, 273
gay and lesbian oppression
and, 235–37
hegemonic masculinity
and, 151
home ownership and,
127–29
housing loans and, 103–5
Hurricane Katrina and,
2–4, 76, 143–46
inclusive thinking, 12–16
income and, 72–73, 269
influence on experiences
of all, 4
inherited wealth and,
131–33
of Irish, 37, 191, 216
of Jews, 112
labor market hierarchy and,
291–92
lack of biological basis for,
69–70
military service and,
462–65
personal appearances and
customs and, 204–5
poverty and, 75–76, 107,
304, 307–8, 417
prisons and, 453
rape and, 468–72
reproductive health issues
and, 433–41
reproductive labor and,
324–27
as socially constructed
category, 62–63
souls and, 288
sports orientation and, 172
stereotypes of.
See stereotypes
symbolic ethnicity and,
199–207

toxic waste disposal areas
and, 511–22
"Race, Class, Gender, and
Women's Works"
(Amott and Matthaei),
283–92
"Race, Poverty and
Disability" (Block,
Balcazar, and Keys),
426–32
Racial formation, 70
Racial hierarchies,
215–17, 288
Racial identity
of Jews, 111–15
of Mexican immigrants, 85
oppositional identities, 204
of Whites, 192–93, 197
Racialization, 85
Racialized masculinity, 151
Racial optimists, 94
Racial passing, 171, 199
Racial pesoptimists, 94–95
Racial profiling, 84, 92
Racial purity, Jews and, 112
Racism
Asian Americans and,
159–64
Black-White framework,
106–11
color-blind, 68, 91–97
definition of, 53, 67–68
dualism and, 111
gender and, 26–28, 55
ideological, 156–65
increasing tension from,
34–35
labor unions and, 539–42
laissez-faire, 95–96
language stereotyping and,
365–76
as matrix of domination,
5–7, 62
racial hierarchies, 215–17
rape of Black women
and, 473
sexuality and, 156–57
sex work and, 242–43
symbolic, 95
systemic, 68
White privilege and,
98–102
Whites as allies to people
of color, 550–57
Whites' racial attitudes,
94–97, 190–98
without racists, 68, 91–97
Yellow Peril, 157–58
See also White Supremacy
"Racism without 'Racists'"
(Bonilla-Silva), 91–97
"Racist Stereotyping in the
English Language"
(Moore), 365–76

Rape, 468–75
denial of rape of Black
women, 472–74
feminist movements
against, 457n
focus on Black
offender/White
victim, 468–72
legal treatment of, 280
male domination and, 57
of unchaste women,
31, 474
"Rape, Racism, and the Law"
(Wriggins), 468–75
Reagon, Bernice
Johnson, 488
Redlining, 103
Reed, Betsy, 234–37
Reed, Ishmael, 42
Religion
African American
churches, 528–29
of immigrants, 210–11
inclusive churches, 485,
522–29
"pagan," 373
Religious right
organizations, 435
Remittances, 209–10
Rendall, Michael, 131
Representational realm, 66
Reproductive health, 433–41
Reproductive labor
of African-American slaves,
324–27
of Chicanas, 329–32
of Chinese sojourners,
328–29
meaning of term, 333n
of racial-ethnics in early
America, 324
of White women in early
America, 321–23
Reproductive rights
abortion, 435–36, 451, 544
imprisonment of pregnant
women, 454, 455, 458n
race and, 454–55
social justice and, 451–54
sterilization programs. *See*
sterilization programs
Residential segregation, 93,
107, 137, 139
Respect, athletic careers
and, 180
Rich, Adrienne, 42
Rich, Evelyn Jones, 372
Richards, Amy, 490, 547–50
Roberts, Dorothy, 454
Rodriquez, Luz, 433–41
Roediger, David, 216
Ross, Loretta J., 433–41
Rotundo, E. Anthony,
507–8

Rubin, Lillian, 85, 175, 190–98
Ruddick, Sarah, 515
Rudé, George, 513
Rudman, W. J., 172
Ryan, William, 387

Salaam, Kalamu ya, 57
"Salsa and Ketchup" (Levitt), 207–14
Sanders, Rev. Edwin C., II, 485, 522–29
Sanders, Willie, 471–72
Sanger, Margaret, 548
Sayeed, Almas, 274, 358–64
Schools. See colleges; education
School segregation, 69, 406–7, 530–34
Schultz, Robert, 229
Scully, Judith, 453
Sears, David, 95
"Seeing More Than Black and White" (Martinez), 105–11
Segregation
    residential, 93, 107, 137, 139
    school, 69, 406–7, 530–34
Seidman, Michael, 533
SEIU (Service Employees International Union), 537
September 11, 2001 terrorist attacks
    class and, 476
    ethnicity and, 84
    power of the criminal enforcement system and, 452
Service Employees International Union (SEIU), 537
Service workers, 535–42. See also domestic work
"Sex and Gender Through the Prism of Difference" (Zinn, Hondagneu-Sotelo, and Messner), 147–56
Sexism, 5–7, 53, 62
Sexual activity
    advertising and, 232–33
    balancing level for women, 30–31
    rape and, 31, 474
Sexual harassment, 280
Sexuality
    advertising and, 228–33
    African American stereotypes, 87, 247–52
    Asian American stereotypes, 156–65

heterosexism, 86–87
heterosexual hegemony, 259–60
    oppression and, 86
    racism and, 156–57
    social construction of, 87–88
    uncertain, 362
    Victorian, 253–55
Sex work, 238–46
    Chinese American, 328
    concept of, 238–41
    organization of, 88
    racism and, 242–43
    transnational, 243–46
Sex Worker Education and Advocacy Taskforce (SWEAT), 245
Sex Workers! Encourage, Empower, Trust and Love Yourselves! (SWEETLY), 245
Shakespeare, William, 33
Shapiro, Thomas, 74, 75, 127–35
Share the Wealth, 425
Shoji, Tomo, 41
"Silent Covenants" (Bell), 530–34
Silko, Leslie Marmon, 41
Silliman, Jael, 279, 450–58
Silverstein, Charles, 346
Sioux Indians, 543–47
SisterSong Women of Color Reproductive Health Project, 433–41
Skin color, importance of, 23, 166–71
Sklar, Holly, 116–18
Slavery
    as both class and racial oppression, 284–85
    families in, 287
    in Hawai'i, 48
    Jamestown colony and, 33, 35
    master-slave phrases, 368–69
    rape and, 468, 472
    reproductive labor in, 324–27
    U.S. history and, 35–36
Smith, Barbara, 87–88, 234–37, 346
Smith, Robert, 85, 214–20
Smith, Stephen Samuel, 404–13
Snipp, Matthew, 279, 442–49
Snitow, Ann, 232
Social change
    diversity workshops, 499–511

environmental activism, 511–22
    history of activism, 547–50
    by Native Americans, 543–47
    processes of, 486–91
    sites of, 483–86
    Whites as allies to people of color, 550–57
    See also activism
"Social Change and Sites of Change" (Andersen and Collins), 481
Social institutions, 267–82
    definition of, 267–68
    race, class, and gender in, 268–71
    work and economic transformation and, 271–72
Social interaction realm, 66
Social policies, 277–78
Social Security payments, 425
Social skills. See soft skills
Social structural realm, 66
Soft skills, 294–303
    employer perceptions of, 299–302
    growing importance of, 294–96
    interaction skills, 294–98
    motivation, 294–95, 298–99
"'Soft' Skills and Race" (Moss and Tilly), 294–303
Sojourners, Chinese, 328–29
Southern Prison Ministry, 524
Sowell, Thomas, 38
Spelman, Elizabeth, 285
Spelman College, 560–61
Sports
    gays and, 182
    immigrant women and, 361
    male identity and, 174–83
    men's basketball, 398–403
    Native American team names, 376–79, 556–57
    Title IX, 407–8
    Whites' and Blacks' orientation to, 172–73
    women's basketball, 401
    See also athletic careers
Standing Bear, Luther, 38
Staples, Robert, 173
"The Starbucks Paradox" (Fellner), 484, 493–99
State, as gendered institution, 270
Steele, James, 423
Stereotypes
    African American sexuality, 81, 247

Asian American sexuality, 156, 159–64
English language and, 365–76
Jews, 81
Latinas, 81, 393–97
of the poor, 385–87
White women, 81
Yellow Peril, 157–58
Sterilization programs
of Latinas, 439, 454–55
of Native Americans, 287, 381, 437, 454–55, 544
of people with developmental disabilities, 428
of Puerto Ricans, 287
of women on welfare, 428
Stigmatization, disability and, 186
"Straight Is to Gay as Family Is to No Family" (Weston), 343–48
Streicher, Julius, 379–80
"The Structure of Social Institutions" (Andersen and Collins), 267–82
Surveillance systems, 455–56
SWEAT (Sex Worker Education and Advocacy Taskforce), 245
SWEETLY (Sex Workers! Encourage, Empower, Trust and Love Yourselves!), 245
Symbolic ethnicity, 85, 199–207
Symbolic racism, 95
Systemic racism, 68. *See also* racism
"Systems of Power and Inequality" (Andersen and Collins), 61–90

Takaki, Ronald, 4, 16, 32–44
Tax breaks, 423–24
Taylor, Desiree, 281, 475–78
Temporary Aid to Needy Families (TANF), 414–15, 418–20
Thomas, Clarence, 249
Thurmond, Strom, 248
Tilly, Chris, 294–303
"Tired of Playing Monopoly?" (Langston), 118–27
Title IX of the 1972 Higher Education Act, 407–8
Torres, Gerald, 337
"Toward a Theory of Disability and Gender" (Gerschick), 185–89
Toxic waste, 511–22

Trade unions. *See* unions
Trafficking, 244. *See also* sex work
Trail of Tears, 444
Transnational families, 84
Transnational migration, 211–14
Transnational sex work, 243–45
Trask, Haunani-Kay, 15, 45–52
Treaty of Guadalupe Hidalgo of 1848, 329
"Tribes" concept, 372, 373
Triple jeopardy, 8–9
Truong, Than-Dam, 239
Tuchman, Barbara W., 42
Tucker, Cora, 514, 518–19
Turner, Frederick Jackson, 38

Udah Bhagat families, 207–8, 210–11, 213–14
Undocumented workers, 313, 316–17, 536–37
Unemployment, responses to, 292–93
"Unequal Childhoods" (Lareau), 348–58
Unions
Bus Riders Union, 540–42
of immigrant labor, 536–37
Justice for Janitors, 537–39
Starbucks and, 496–97
UNITE, 496
Unión Única, 245
UNITE (Union of Needletrades, Industrial and Textile Employees), 496–97
United States, as a White country, 190–98
Unknown, fear of, 26–27
Upper class
athletic careers and, 175–78
as governing class, 391–92
mass media and, 387–91
wealth and, 74–75, 127–33
U.S. Service Industries (USSI), 537–38
Utility payments, 415

Venezuelan Association of Women for Welfare and Mutual Support (AMBAR), 245
Victorian sexuality, 253–55
Vidal, Gore, 260
Vietnamese Americans
changes in gender relations, 220–27
immigration of, 86

kinship networks of, 222–27
stereotypes of, 161
See also Asian Americans
Vietnam War, 460–62
Violence
against Black women, 56–58
within families, 274, 280, 544
military and, 280–81
in prisons, 453
rape. *See* rape
state institutions and, 279–81
Vocational counselors, 124–25

WAR (White Aryan Resistance), 112
The War Against the Poor (Gans), 304
Warrior class, 460, 465–67
Waters, Mary, 85, 198–207
Watney, Simon, 343
Wealth
cumulative advantage of, 74–75
definition of, 73
growing disparities in, 116–18
inheritance and, 128–33
mass media and, 387–91
opportunities and, 127–28
patterns of, 73–74, 116–18
Wealth and Democracy (Phillips), 130
Wealthfare, 422–26
"Welfare Reform, Family Hardship, and Women of Color" (Burnham), 413–22
Welfare system
aid to corporations, 422–26
dual, 121, 278
Harlem households and, 311
immigrants and, 417–20
increasing family hardship, 414–16
race and, 417–19
reproductive health and, 436–40
welfare reform, 67, 414–15, 420
women of color and immigrant women and, 416–20
Wellman, D., 172
West, Cornel, 87, 186, 247–52
Weston, Kath, 273, 343–48

"What Does an Ally Do?"
    (Kivel), 550–57
"What White Supremacists
    Taught a Jewish
    Scholar about Iden-
    tity" (Ferber), 111–15
"Where Has Gay Liberation
    Gone?" (Gluckman
    and Reed), 234–37
White Americans
    as allies to people of color,
        550–57
    changing definitions of,
        109, 216, 334n
    diversity workshops and,
        499–511
    as European-Americans, 197
    immigration and, 190–98
    income of, 72–79, 269
    on interracial marriages,
        339–41
    Irish as, 37, 191, 216
    men's work world, 507–9
    as minority group, 33–34
    poverty in, 6, 75–76
    racial attitudes of, 94–97
    racial identity of, 102, 114,
        192–93
    reproductive labor of,
        321–23
    sports orientation of, 172
    stereotypes of women, 81
    symbolic ethnicity for,
        198–207
    unhyphenated, 199
    white privilege, 98–102
    working-class women
        activists, 515–17
White Aryan Resistance
    (WAR), 112
"White Privilege" (McIntosh),
    68, 98–102
White Supremacy
    on Jewish identity, 70,
        111–15
    need for unity against, 107
    Oklahoma bombing
        and, 236
"A White Woman of Color"
    (Álvarez), 166–71
Whores. See sex work
"'Whosoever' is Welcome
    Here" (Comstock),
    522–29
"Why Race, Class, and
    Gender Still Matter"
    (Andersen and
    Collins), 1–16
Williams, Patricia J., 68,
    103–5

Wilson, William Julius,
    140–41, 301
Winant, Howard, 70, 288
Women
    abortion and, 435–36,
        451, 544
    African American. See
        African Americans,
        women
    Asian American, 161–64
    of Color, as other, 55, 67
    with disabilities, 185–89
    domestic violence, 274,
        280, 544
    environmental activism by,
        514–22
    feminism and cultural
        differences, 358–64
    globalization and, 152
    income of, 72–73
    kinship networks and,
        222–26
    Latina, 329–32, 393–97
    in military service, 461
    in prisons, 453
    rape of, 468–75
    reproductive health of,
        433–41
    reproductive labor of,
        321–35
    sexual activity balancing
        level for, 30–31
    as sex workers, 238–46
    sports and domination of,
        178, 182
    stereotypes of, 81, 161–64,
        393–97
    Vietnamese American,
        220–27
    See also gender
"Women of Color on the
    Front Line" (Krauss),
    511–22
Women's studies
    challenges to gender
        stereotypes, 149–50
    early views in, 148–49
    hip hop feminists, 557–64
Womyn Take Back the Night
    march, 363
Wong, Eugene Franklin,
    160–61
Wong, Sau-Ling Cynthia,
    157, 317
Workers
    African American men,
        296–98
    changes in economy and,
        77–78
    class hierarchy of, 291–92

dual labor market, 269
    employees vs., 390–92
    environmental activism
        of, 514–15
    global economy and, 152,
        271–72
    migrant, 83–84
    oppressive treatment
        of, 108
    poverty of, 76–77, 304–12
    racial mixes of, 297–98
    sexual division of labor,
        285–86, 290
    sexual harassment, 280
    sex workers, 88, 238–46
    soft skills and, 294–98
    stereotypes of, 291
    undocumented, 313,
        316–17, 536–37
    unemployment response,
        292–93
    unions and, 122, 536–42
    young, 305, 308–9
Working class
    athletic careers and,
        178–81
    attitudes toward
        immigration, 193–94
    children, 349–58
    heterogeneity of, 121
    individualism and, 123–24
    lesbians, 123
    middle-class feminism
        and, 124
    military service and, 281
    new urban, 536–39
    types of jobs for, 123,
        124–25
Working poor, 76–77, 272,
    304–12
World cities, 83
Wriggins, Jennifer, 280,
    468–75
Wright, Gwendolyn, 326
Wu, William F., 160, 162

Yankton Sioux reservation
    (South Dakota),
    543–47
Yellow Peril, 157–58
"You Talkin' to Me?"
    (Kilbourne), 228–33
Youth
    activists, 491
    young workers, 305,
        308–9

Zane, Nancie, 484, 499–511
Zimmerman, D. H., 186